DATE DUE

GAYLORD   PRINTED IN U.S.A.

WOMEN, CULTURE, AND
DEVELOPMENT

WIDER

Studies in Development Economics embody the output of the research programmes of the World Institute for Development Economics Research (WIDER), which was established by the United Nations University as its first research and training centre in 1984 and started work in Helsinki in 1985. The principal purpose of the Institute is to help identify and meet the need for policy-oriented socio-economic research on pressing global and development problems, as well as common domestic problems and their interrelationships.

WOMEN, CULTURE, AND DEVELOPMENT

A Study of Human Capabilities

Edited by

MARTHA C. NUSSBAUM
AND
JONATHAN GLOVER

*A study prepared for the World Institute for Development Economics
Research (WIDER) of the United Nations University*

CLARENDON PRESS · OXFORD
1995

Oxford New York
Athens Auckland Bangkok Bombay
Calcutta Cape Town Dar es Salaam Delhi
Florence Hong Kong Istanbul Karachi
Kuala Lumpur Madras Madrid Melbourne
Mexico City Nairobi Paris Singapore
Taipei Tokyo Toronto
and associated companies in
Berlin Ibadan

Oxford is a trade mark of Oxford University Press

Published in the United States
by Oxford University Press Inc., New York

World Institute for Development Economics Research (WIDER)
Katajanokanlaituri 6B, FIN-00160 Helsinki, FINLAND

British Library Cataloguing in Publication Data
Data available

Library of Congress Cataloging-in-Publication Data
Women, culture, and development : a study of human capabilities /
edited by Martha C. Nussbaum and Jonathan Glover.
p.   cm. — (Wider studies in development economics)
"Prepared for the World Institute for Development Economics
Research (WIDER) of the United Nations University."
Includes bibliographical references.
1. Women's rights. 2. Sex role. 3. Women in development.
I. Nussbaum, Martha Craven, 1947- . II. Glover, Jonathan.
III. World Institute for Development Economics Research.
IV. Series: Studies in development economics.
HQ1236.W6377 1994 94-42602 305.42—dc20
ISBN 0-19-828917-0
ISBN 0-19-828964-2 (Pbk)

Typeset by Best-set Typesetter Ltd., Hong Kong

Printed in Great Britain
on acid-free paper by
Bookcraft Ltd., Midsomer Norton, Avon

FOREWORD

This volume is a worthy successor to the UNU/WIDER volume *The Quality of Life*, edited by Martha Nussbaum and Amartya Sen (1993). It continues the path-breaking project of bringing philosophy and economic thought together in a way that prompts searching foundational criticism of some current approaches to development policy. Whereas *The Quality of Life* focused on mapping out debates on a variety of foundational issues, the present volume has a more concrete emphasis and arrives at a practical consensus. Starting from a variety of different philosophical positions, the contributors assess and in most respects strongly support the contributions of the 'capabilities' approach pioneered by Amartya Sen. They argue that it is superior to utilitarian-economic and cultural-relativist approaches in analysing the problems of women in developing countries and in generating creative proposals for change. They show the practical importance of this sort of basic philosophical work by relating their arguments to Martha Chen's field study of women's rights to work in India and Bangladesh, which is a centrepiece of this volume.

The problems of women in developing countries call urgently for new forms of analysis and for an approach that moves beyond utilitarian economics to identify a number of distinct components of a human being's quality of life, including life-expectancy, maternal mortality, access to education, access to employment, and the meaningful exercise of political rights. Even when a nation seems to be doing well in terms of GNP per capita, its people may be doing poorly in one or more of these areas. This is especially likely to be the case for women, who have been treated unequally in many traditional societies, and who nowhere enjoy, on average, a 'quality of life' equal to that of men, when this is measured by the complex standard recommended by the 'capabilities' approach.

The influence and value of this approach to development in general and to sex inequality in particular can already be seen in the 1993 and 1994 volumes of the UNDP *Human Development Report*. The present volume presents and examines the arguments that supply the basis for that influence. Under the leadership of Martha Nussbaum and Jonathan Glover, the quality of life project has continued to generate new modes of analysis while grappling very concretely with the urgent practical concerns of women in developing nations. The volume is noteworthy for its emphasis on the direct practical value of theoretical inquiry, and for the dialogue it represents among thinkers from many different nations and traditions. It is entirely appropriate, therefore, that it appears before the forthcoming United

Nations Summit on Women, in Beijing as UNU/WIDER's contribution to that conference.

Lal Jayawardena
Economic Adviser to the
President of Sri Lanka

Former Director, UNU/WIDER
(1985–1993)

CONTENTS

PART IV WOMEN'S EQUALITY: REGIONAL PERSPECTIVES

LIST OF CONTRIBUTORS

LINDA ALCOFF, Professor of Philosophy
Syracuse University
Syracuse, NY
USA

SEYLA BENHABIB, Professor of Government
Harvard University
Cambridge, Mass.
USA

MARTHA CHEN
Harvard Institute for International Development (HIID)
Harvard University
Cambridge, Mass.
USA

DAVID A. CROCKER, Senior Research Professor
Center for Philosophy and Public Policy
University of Maryland
College Park, Md.
USA

JONATHAN GLOVER, Fellow and University Lecturer
New College
Oxford
England

CHRISTINE KORSGAARD, Professor of Philosophy
Harvard University
Cambridge, Mass.
USA

XIAORONG LI, Research Professor
Center for Philosophy and Public Policy
University of Maryland
College Park, Md.
USA

CATHERINE LUTZ, Professor of Anthropology
University of North Carolina at Chapel Hill
Chapel Hill
USA

MARTHA C. NUSSBAUM, University Professor and Professor of Philosophy,
    Classics, and Comparative Literature
Brown University
Providence, RI
USA

NKIRU NZEGWU, Professor of Philosophy
State University of New York at Binghamton
Binghamton
USA

SUSAN MOLLER OKIN, Professor of Political Science and Director of Program
in Ethics and Society
Stanford University
Stanford
USA

ONORA O'NEILL, Principal
Newnham College
Cambridge
England

HILARY PUTNAM, Walter Beverley Pearson Professor of Modern Math-
ematics and Mathematical Logic
Department of Philosophy
Harvard University
Cambridge, Mass.
USA

RUTH ANNA PUTNAM, Professor of Philosophy
Wellesley College
Wellesley, Mass.
USA

AMARTYA SEN, Lamont University Professor and Professor of Economics
and of Philosophy
Harvard University
Cambridge, Mass.
USA

CASS R. SUNSTEIN, Karl Llewellyn Professor of Jurisprudence
The Law School
University of Chicago
Chicago
USA

MARGARITA VALDÉS, Professor of Philosophy
Instituto de Investigaciones Filosoficas
Universidad Nacional Autonoma de México
Mexico

ROOP REKHA VERMA, Professor of Philosophy
University of Lucknow
Lucknow
India

SUSAN WOLF, Professor of Philosophy
Johns Hopkins University
Baltimore
USA

Other Conference Participants

NANCY CHODOROW, Professor of Sociology
University of California at Berkeley
Berkeley, Calif.
USA

MARJA-LIISA KAKKURI-KNUUTTILA, Lecturer in Philosophy and Women's
Studies
Helsinki School of Economics
Finland

SABINA LOVIBOND, Fellow and University Lecturer
Worcester College
Oxford
England

PÄIVI SETÄLÄ, Professor of Women's Studies
Helsinki University
Finland

LAWRENCE THOMAS, Professor of Philosophy
Syracuse University
Syracuse
USA

Introduction

Martha C. Nussbaum

'I may die, but still I cannot go out. If there's something in the house, we eat. Otherwise, we go to sleep.' So Metha Bai, a young widow with two young children in Rajasthan, India, described her plight as a member of a caste whose women are traditionally prohibited from working outside the home—even when, as here, survival itself is at issue. If she stays at home, she and her children may die shortly. If she attempts to go out, her in-laws will beat her and abuse her children.[1]

In this case, as in very many others throughout the world, cultural traditions pose obstacles to women's health and flourishing. Depressingly many traditions have portrayed women as less important than men, less deserving of basic life support, or of fundamental rights that are strongly correlated with quality of life, such as the right to work and the right to political participation. Sometimes, as in the case of Metha Bai, these traditions are resisted by the women themselves. Sometimes, on the other hand, they have become so deeply internalized that they seem to record what is 'right' and 'natural', and women themselves frequently come to endorse their own second-class status.

What should people concerned with justice say about this? And should they say anything at all? On the one hand, it seems impossible to deny that traditions perpetrate injustice against women in many fundamental ways, touching on some of the most central elements of a human being's quality of life—health, education, political liberty and participation, employment, self-respect, and life itself. On the other hand, hasty judgements that a tradition in some distant part of the world is morally retrograde are familiar legacies of colonialism and imperialism, and are correctly regarded with suspicion by sensitive thinkers in the contemporary world. To say that a practice endorsed by tradition is bad is to risk erring by imposing one's own way on others who surely have their own ideas of what is right and good. To say that a practice is all right wherever local tradition endorses it as right and good is to risk erring by withholding critical judgement where real evil and real oppression are surely present. To avoid the whole issue because the matter of proper judgement is so fiendishly difficult is tempting, but perhaps the worst option of all. It suggests all too clearly the sort of moral collapse depicted by Dante, when he describes the crowd of souls who mill around in the vestibule of hell, dragging their banner now one way now another, never willing to set it down and take a definite stand on any moral

---

[1] For this case and others like it, see Marty Chen, 'A Matter of Survival: Women's Right to Employment in India and Bangladesh', in this volume.

or political question. Such people, Dante implies, are the most despicable of all: they can't even get into hell because they have not been willing to stand for anything in life, one way or another. To put our position extremely briefly, we would rather risk charges of imperialism (however unjustified, as we think, such charges would be) than to stand around in the vestibule waiting for a time when everyone will like what we are going to say.

The situation of women in the contemporary world calls urgently for moral stand-taking. Women, a majority of the world's population, receive only a small proportion of its opportunities and benefits. According to the 1993 UN *Human Development Report*, there is no country in the world in which women's quality of life is equal to that of men, according to a complex measure that includes longevity, health status, educational opportunities, employment, and political rights.[2] Some countries have much larger gender disparities than others. (Among the industrial countries, for example, Japan and Canada perform relatively poorly in these areas, Sweden, Denmark, and New Zealand relatively well.) If we turn our attention to the developing countries—this volume's central topic—we find, once again, uneven achievements but, in the aggregate, a distressing situation. On average, the employment participation rates of women are only 50% of those of men (in South Asia 29%, in the Arab states only 16%). Even when women are employed, their situation is undercut by pervasive wage discrimination and by long hours of unpaid household labour. (If women's unpaid housework were counted as productive output in national income accounts, global output would increase by 20–30%.) Outside the home, women are generally employed in a restricted range of jobs offering low pay and low respect. Their situation in the workplace is frequently undermined by sexual discrimination and sexual harassment.

Women are much less likely than men to be literate. In South Asia, female literacy rates average around 50% of those of males. In some countries the rate is still lower: e.g. in Nepal 35%, Sierra Leone 37%, Sudan 27%, Afghanistan 32%. Two-thirds of the world's illiterate people are women. In higher education, women lag even further behind men, in both developing and industrial nations.

Although some countries allowed women the vote early in this century, some still have not done so. And there are many informal obstacles to women's effective participation in political life. Almost everywhere, they are underrepresented in government: in 1980, they made up only around 10% of the world's parliamentary representatives and less than 4% of its cabinet officials.

---

[2] See the end of this Introduction for the relevant figures and tables from the report. All the data in this and the following paragraphs are drawn from the report: *Human Development Report* (New York: United Nations Development Program, 1993).

As Metha Bai's story indicates, employment outside the home has a close relationship to health and nutrition. So too, frequently, does political voice. And if we now turn, in fact, to the very basic issue of health and survival, we find compelling evidence of discrimination against females in many nations of the world. It appears that when equal nutrition and health care are present, women live on average slightly longer than men, even allowing for a modest level of maternal mortality. Thus in Europe the female:male ratio in 1986 was 105:100, in North America 104.7:100.[3] But it may be objected that it is for several reasons inappropriate to compare these developed countries with countries in the developing world, so let us, with Jean Drèze and Amartya Sen, take as our 'base' the ratio in sub-Saharan Africa, where there is great poverty but little evidence of gender discrimination in basic health matters. The female:male ratio is 102.2:100. If we examine the sex ratio in various other countries and ask the question, 'How many more women than are now in country C would be there if its sex ratio were the same as that of sub-Saharan Africa?', we get a number that Sen has graphically called the number of 'missing women'. The number of missing women in south-east Asia is 2.4 million, in Latin America 4.4, in North Africa 2.4, in Iran 1.4, in China 44.0, in Bangladesh 3.7, in India 36.7, in Pakistan 5.2, in West Asia 4.3. If we now consider the ratio of the number of missing women to the number of actual women in a country, for Pakistan we get 12.9%, for India 9.5%, for Bangladesh 8.7%, for China 8.6%, for Iran 8.5%, for West Asia 7.8%, for North Africa 3.9%, for Latin America 2.2%, for south-east Asia 1.2%. In India, not only is the mortality differential especially sharp among children (girls dying in far greater numbers than boys), the higher mortality rate of women compared to men applies to all age groups until the late thirties.[4]

Poverty alone does not cause women to die in greater numbers than men. When there is a scarcity, custom frequently decrees who gets to eat the little there is, and who gets taken to the doctor. And custom is always crucial in determining who gets to perform wage labour outside the home, an important determinant of general status in the family and community. (Indeed, the situation of sub-Saharan Africa, where women perform a great part of productive agricultural labour, suggests a strong correlation between access to employment and basic health and nutritional status.) Custom decrees who gets access to the education that would open job opportunities and make political rights meaningful. Custom decrees who can go where in what clothing and with whom. Custom decrees who gets to make what sorts of protests against ill-treatment both inside and outside the family, and whose voice of protest is likely to be heard.

Customs, in short, are important causes of women's misery and death. It seems incumbent on anyone interested in justice, and aware of the infor-

---

[3] The statistics in this paragraph are taken from Drèze, J. and Sen, A. (1989) *Hunger and Public Action*. Oxford: Clarendon Press.   [4] See Drèze and Sen (1989: p. 52).

mation about women's status that studies such as the *Human Development Report* present, to ask about the relationship between culture and justice. It then seems incumbent on her to try to work out an account of the rational assessment of tradition that is neither do-gooder colonialism nor an uncritical validation of the *status quo*. The urgent need for such an account is the motivation for the present volume.

Our work grew out of the work, linking philosophy with economics, that had produced the 1993 volume *The Quality of Life*, edited by Martha Nussbaum and Amartya Sen. This volume asked various foundational questions about how policy-makers should measure the 'quality of life' in a country. One of the questions that turned out to be most urgent was that of women's life quality and its relation to that of men. Another was the question of cultural relativism and universalism: whether, that is, we should seek a universal measure or measures of quality of life for all men and women, or defer, instead, to the many different norms that traditional cultures have selected. These questions were clearly connected. The choice between the voice of tradition and a critical universalism had especially large consequences for the assessment of women's status, given that many traditional norms do not make full equality in the many functions of life a goal for females.

These questions were broached in *The Quality of Life*, but we saw that they were too large and too complex to be dealt with well in a volume covering so many different aspects of the quality of life issue. We therefore decided at that time to pursue our interest in women's equality in a second volume, connected to a second conference. Whereas the aim of *The Quality of Life* was in general to canvass various different positions on the issues it confronted, laying the debate out in a clear and mostly even-handed way, the aim of the second volume would be, instead, to advance a more or less unified position on the question of women's functioning, a critical universalism that would nonetheless not be blankly insensitive to history and to tradition, and that would attempt to answer some of the objections most commonly made against universalist accounts.

We were aware that this inquiry would take us at times away from ethics and politics and economics narrowly construed, into the debate about relativism in other areas of philosophy. Indeed it was our aim to present the whole question of relativism in a more sophisticated way philosophically than is frequently done in economic writings, where a simple and unexamined distinction between 'fact' and 'value' still prevails in many circles, and in which it is therefore assumed that ethical judgements are hopelessly soft and arbitrary by contrast to another domain of judgement, the domain of science. Hilary Putnam had already offered a subtle critique of this division in his paper in *The Quality of Life*; we asked him to develop his views further in the context of feminism. And we invited a wide-ranging group of philosophers and social scientists to address the relationship between tradition and life quality, focusing on Martha Chen's case study of women's right to work, which we commissioned for the project.

Throughout the project, our focus was on an approach pioneered within economics by Amartya Sen, now widely known as the 'capabilities approach'. This approach to the measurement of quality of life, and to defining the goals of public policy, holds that we should focus on the question, 'What are the people of the country in question actually able to do and to be?' This focus on capabilities for functioning, unlike a focus on opulence (say, GNP per capita), asks about the distribution of resources and opportunities—for (in the manner of the *Human Development Report*, and in a way that fundamentally influenced the structure of those reports) Sen's approach asks how all the groups in the population are doing, and insists on comparing the functioning of one group to that of another. Unlike an approach that focuses on utility, where utility is construed as the satisfaction of subjective preferences, the capability approach maintains that preferences are not always reliable indicators of life quality, since they may be deformed in various ways by oppression and deprivation. Unlike an approach that focuses on the equal distribution of resources, the capability approach maintains that resources have no value in themselves, apart from their role in promoting human functioning. It therefore directs the planner to inquire into the varying needs individuals have for resources, if they are to become capable of an equal level of functioning.[5]

The capability view is in principle compatible with cultural relativism—with, that is, the view that the proper criteria of ethical and political choice are those given in each culture's traditions. It would always be possible to construct culturally varying lists of the most important functions and the associated capabilities, and to measure the life quality of individuals against such standards in each society. That, however, is not the direction in which the capability view has been developed by Sen and others, as it has been put to work in, for example, the construction of the measures used in the *Human Development Report*. Instead, the view has taken a stand, indeed an increasingly specific stand, on what functions of human beings are most worth the care and attention of public planning, the world over. And it has also taken a clear stand on gender equality, pointing to the unequal level of functioning of the world's women as a bad state of affairs to be altered. This universalist non-relative aspect of the view needs further development, however, if it is to prove possible to answer the legitimate worries of those who have seen all too much paternalistic imposition of some people's ways upon others.

---

[5] All these points have been made in a series of fundamental studies by Sen: for a recent summary, see 'Capabilities and Well Being' in *The Quality of Life*, with references to earlier studies. In the present volume, see especially the papers by Sen, Nussbaum ('Human Capabilities'), and Crocker, which defend the approach further and comment on its relationship to other approaches.

One part of our strategy in grappling with this problem has been, as we said, to ask the help of philosophers who work on the issue of relativism in a general overarching way, not confined to issues of public policy. Another part of our strategy has been to draw into our project, as it has progressed, an increasingly international group of thinkers, whose responses and criticisms would give us some confidence that we were not simply imposing a parochial view that happened to be our own. Martha Chen's field study brings into our work a large number of voices of non-philosophers, of women simply commenting on their situation as women in a traditional society. The work done in our project by Xiaorong Li from China, by Margarita Valdés from Mexico, by Roop Rekha Verma from India, and by Nkiru Nzegwu from Nigeria has added not only their own sophisticated critical perceptions but also the voices of the many women of their own societies with whom they have lived and spoken in the course of their work.

There are fewer papers by professional economists in this volume than in *The Quality of Life*: and yet its bearing on the central issues of development economics should be evident. Like its predecessor, this volume asks the reader to think critically about the central foundational concepts used in development economics, and suggests major criticisms of current economic approaches from that foundational viewpoint. Its territory used to lie at one time within 'political economy'—in the days of Adam Smith, when economists understood that they needed to think philosophically in order to do their own job completely and well—but has now too frequently been redefined as that of 'another field', especially by those who are unwilling to ask questions that might lead to changes in the way important economic matters are modelled and understood. We argue that economics as now very often practised cannot deal adequately with the central issues at stake in the lives of women, and with their urgent claims. The conclusion we draw from this is not that economics should be scoffed at or bypassed, but that it should seek conceptual and mathematical tools better suited to grappling with these issues. That conclusion, and the reasoning that leads to it, ought to be of interest to economists, indeed ought to be seen as a conclusion with the science of economics.

The capabilities approach as a whole is critical of dominant approaches in mainstream economics, with their single-minded focus on utility, construed as satisfaction of preference or desire. But one concrete example will perhaps make the critical contribution of the work presented here more vivid. Sen's paper argues that if we focus on the functioning of females, as that is influenced by the traditional distribution of resources within the family in many parts of the world, we will be led to notice pervasive 'co-operative conflicts', that is, situations in which the interests of members of a co-operative body (such as the family is supposed to be) split apart, with some individuals doing well at the expense of the deprivation and misery of others. This observation entails a fundamental criticism of the dominant approach to the economic analysis of the family, that of Gary Becker,[6] who holds that the head of a household may be regarded as an altruistic agent of the interests of all the family's members. Sen's conclusion and ours, looking at the evidence, is that this assumption is false: males are quite often neglectful of the interests of females, whether wives or children, and make decisions inimical to those interests. Becker deserves much credit for putting these issues on the agenda of the profession in the first place; but models are only as valuable as the truth of their premises. And the truth is that Becker's picture of male motivation does not fit the evidence— especially if one looks not simply at women's satisfactions and preferences, which may often be deformed by tradition and lack of information, but at their actual functioning. Here as elsewhere, looking at how people are or are not able to live provides economic thought with new directions.

A MATTER OF SURVIVAL

The volume begins with Martha Chen's vivid field study. Out of the many issues affecting women's quality of life in the developing world, we chose to focus on the right to work because it plays such a pivotal role in relation to other 'capabilities' of women: in relation to health care and nutrition, to self-respect and autonomy, to full political functioning. Chen's earlier study of female literacy in rural Bangladesh was also before all of us as we worked, providing many of us with further, related, examples.[7] Although we might have worked from the data supplied by the *Human Development Report* and related sources alone, actually hearing the voices of women, as Chen's methodology amply encourages us to do, seemed especially important as we confronted the delicate issues of relativism and universalism.

WOMEN'S EQUALITY: METHODOLOGY, FOUNDATIONS

The second section of the volume contains papers exploring questions of methodology and basic normative approach where universalism of the sort we wish to defend is concerned. Philosophers are far from being herd animals, and we did not attain, nor did we seek, utter unity of perspective in our approaches to the grounding of a universalist ethics. Indeed, it is reason for optimism that the group of philosophers represented in this section, who exemplify a range of different approaches to the problems—

    [6] Gary Becker, *A Treatise on the Family* (Cambridge, Mass.: Harvard University Press, 1981).
    [7] Chen, *The Quiet Revolution: Women in Transition in Rural Bangladesh* (Cambridge, Mass.: Schenkman, 1983).

Nussbaum's liberal/Aristotelian approach, Glover's modified utilitarianism, O'Neill's liberal Kantianism, Putnam's pragmatism, Benhabib's dialogical approach derived from Habermas—should converge as substantially as they do on our central normative questions about the tenability of a historically sensitive universalism.

All the papers focus in some way on the capabilities approach, relating their own contributions to it. The section therefore begins with a paper by Nussbaum that sets out a version of that approach, showing its relation to other approaches to women's life quality and arguing that it can answer the most serious charges commonly made by relativists against ethical universalism. Susan Wolf comments on the prospects of the approach.

Jonathan Glover then proposes a 'research programme' for development ethics that makes questions of universalism and objectivity central, and considers them in close conjunction with questions of justice and equality. Focusing on women's issues, he argues that there is a 'central core' to the concept of justice on which we can agree, while differing about more subtle points around the periphery, and that the inequities caused by traditional forms of oppression in lives such as Metha Bai's are clear inequities in the terms of this central core, despite the appeal of views that stress the need to respect traditional cultures. He sorts out various strands in the argument against universalism of the sort defended by Nussbaum, and offers a carefully qualified response.

Onora O'Neill then argues vigorously against taking the satisfaction of preferences as a normative criterion in political economy. Defending the capabilities approach, she connects it closely to a form of Kantianism. She aruges that Kant's proposed test for principles—that we not act on principles that cannot be acted on by all—is still a valuable test in social policy, and one that yields powerful arguments against victimization, 'by violence, by coercion, by intimidation, or by deception'. This implies that it is of central importance to feminism.

David Crocker presents a meticulous exposition of the thinking underlying the capabilities approach, as both Sen and Nussbaum have developed it. His paper will serve as a comprehensive introduction to the approach for those who are unfamiliar with it, and a nuanced assessment and critique for those who are. He takes particular interest in the ways in which the approach has handled questions of freedom, justice, and rights.

Hilary Putnam now turns to the central issues of ethical objectivity and ethical truth that have been on our agenda from the start. How, he asks, can one justify an ethical claim, such as a claim of justice on behalf of Metha Bai, without tyrannizing over our opponents, while respecting the values of openness and mutual respect proper to a democratic society? He gives an answer built on the thought of the American pragmatists, especially John Dewey, arguing that there can be a rational basis for adopting ethical positions, and that democratic processes are necessary constituents of social rationality. In her response, Linda Alcoff urges Putnam to devote more thought to the criticisms some feminists have advanced against traditional conceptions of inquiry, and to follow philosophers such as Nietzsche and Foucault in recognizing the many ways in which power and desire may affect even the most apparently disinterested and democratic procedure.

Our methodological exploration concludes with Seyla Benhabib's vivid defence of cross-cultural standards of justice. Benhabib argues that many relativist views have neglected the existence of debate and opposition within traditional cultures, and that in that sense these views are simply bad sociology. She argues that cultural views are not radically incommensurable with one another, and that there is sufficient common ground among cultures to create a 'global dialogical community' that transcends ethnocentric particularism. Like Putnam, she calls on a certain understanding of democratic procedure to articulate this idea.

Among the issues on which consensus was not found in the present volume, this one appears the most urgent: should we give priority, in development ethics, to a procedural account, in particular an account of democratic debate, and allow that procedure to generate our substantive moral conclusions? Or should we focus on the normative theory of human functioning and its defence, and leave it an open question whether, in each particular situation, the form of government that will best promote human functioning is a democratic one? The gulf between partisans of these two approaches—between Nussbaum on the one hand, for example, and Benhabib on the other—is less wide than this formulation suggests, and is growing narrower all the time. Nussbaum incorporates political participation and an increasingly substantial list of social and political rights into her account of the basic human capabilities; if this does not evidently entail democratic government in all situations, it certainly makes it difficult for a non-democratic government to show that it has sufficiently promoted human functioning. Benhabib, meanwhile, with Habermas, defines democracy in a manner that is not merely procedural but includes substantive ethical elements—non-coercion, non-violence, and so forth—that have been well argued by O'Neill and others to yield specific conclusions in many of the areas of women's lives that are of concern to Nussbaum, Sen, and Crocker. A society in which women were deprived of equal health care, equal nutrition, or employment rights, for example, could not pass Benhabib's and Putnam's tests of democracy, no matter what it called its form of government. Differences remain: for example, it is hard to see how Nussbaum's concern with emotional development, with humour and play, with our relationship to animals and nature, are addressed at all in a procedural democratic approach. (Dewey is friendly to emotions as forms of insight, Habermas, following Kant, actively hostile to them as sources of delusion. Neither takes them as having an especially intimate relationship to democracy.) On the other hand, these are the parts of Nussbaum's list that have generated the most critical comment, and the parts that Sen is least disposed to endorse. It is evident that all these questions should remain on our agenda for future debate.

WOMEN'S EQUALITY: JUSTICE, LAW, AND REASON

Part III of the volume turns to more concrete issues of justice for women. Sen's paper introduces the issue of 'co-operative conflicts', and argues that these conflicts are frequently rooted in traditional conceptions of women's role, often internalized as 'natural' by the women themselves. He argues that the capabilities approach can handle these issues better than its major alternatives in the policy domain, Rawlsian liberalism and economic utilitarianism.

Okin pursues this theme further, arguing that what is unjust in the situation of women in developing countries is not different in kind from the injustices that unequal family structures produce in developed countries. In both cases, we find that an institution (the family) that claims to be a source of love and a school for ethical virtue frequently manifests and perpetuates injustice; these inequities, far from being 'natural', are supported by traditions, laws, and institutions that may be altered. Arguing against feminists who are opposed to generalizing about the situation of women, Okin argues that generalizing, with proper caution and sensitivity, can be a valuable and even a crucial part of good feminist argument, bringing to light what is salient, and deplorably widespread, in unjust laws and practices.

Ruth Anna Putnam examines feminist criticisms of liberalism that charge liberal theories of justice with illicit generalizing, in which the voice of one person is 'substituted' for the many different voices that ought to be heard from different positions and backgrounds. Like Okin, she believes that it is possible to develop a conception of moral argument, and the moral point of view, that effectively meets this challenge, generating a single set of conclusions valid for all, at least at a high level of generality. Thus she supports the approaches developed elsewhere in the volume by Sen, Nussbaum, Benhabib, and O'Neill, from within a framework that lies closest to O'Neill's in its focus on Kantian liberalism.

Cass Sunstein's paper turns directly to the issue of law and its impact on women's quality of life, asking how law has sustained and supported discrimination against women and how, on the other hand, it might embody a commitment to sex equality. He proposes what he calls an 'anticaste principle,' which forbids law from turning a morally irrelevant characteristic such as sex into a systematic source of social disadvantage. As a pervasive feature of 'caste systems' based on gender, he focuses on the situation in which women's sexual and reproductive capacities are turned into objects for the use and control of others. On this basis he offers a critique of current

American law in the area of sex discrimination, makes proposals for national and international legal change, and comments on the limitations of market mechanisms in ending discrimination.

Since a constant refrain in the traditions of argument against female equality through the ages (both Western and non-Western) has been that women are too emotional to be fully rational, Nussbaum now confronts this question, a central topic in 'political economy' since Adam Smith. She argues that when we have an adequate conception of what an emotion is, the opposition between emotion and reason will be seen to be incoherent, and emotions will be seen as Adam Smith saw them, as essential ingredients in rational ethical judgement. Nussbaum argues that emotions are best understood as forms of recognition of neediness and dependency with respect to the most important things in life, and are thus as appropriate and rational as are those recognitions and the beliefs that support them. Catherine Lutz comments on this argument from the point of view of anthropology.

In several of the papers a question about gender identification was raised: how important is it, why do societies need to have gender divisions of any kind, and how reasonable would it be to work toward a gender-free society? This question really raises a number of distinct issues; Christine Korsgaard disentangles and comments incisively on them.

WOMEN'S EQUALITY: REGIONAL PERSPECTIVES

Martha Chen's study was central to all our work in preparation for the conference. But we wanted, as well, to incorporate responses from other regions of the world, and from philosophers whose work has been deeply informed by membership in non-Western traditions. The volume's concluding section contains four examples of such responses, each commenting on the capabilities approach and its prospects in connection with her sense of her own traditions and their problems of sex inequality.

Xiaorong Li offers a trenchant account of women's inequality in China and its relation to traditional norms. Arguing against cultural relativist approaches to China and in favour of a more internationalist and critical approach, she concludes that the capabilities approach as developed by Sen and Nussbaum can diagnose what is wrong in the situation and promote women's equality, without patriarchal imposition or historical insensitivity.

Margarita Valdés offers an analysis of the situation in Mexico, identifying traditional obstacles to women's full access to constitutionally guaranteed equality of opportunity. She makes a number of subtle comparisons between the Mexican situation and the situation in India, as described in Martha Chen's paper, arguing, among other things, that traditional Mexican conceptions of the family offer more advantages than Indian conceptions do to women who seek equal participation in the labour force.

With Roop Rekha Verma's paper we return to India, and to a philosophical analysis based on ideas of rights and autonomy that complements Chen's empirical study. Verma argues that the Hindu traditions of India have been unremittingly hostile to women's demands for equality, and that a critical position should be sought from the Western Enlightenment and its ideas of rights and personhood, rather than from within those traditions. Verma thus takes up, along with Li, an anti-traditionalist and pro-Enlightenment stance that is considerably 'harder' and less conciliatory than the positions of most of the writers in this volume, who have tended to stress that traditions contain an internal plurality of voices, and that the voices of critical and rationalist traditions can frequently be deployed against the dominant tradition, where that is oppressive of women.[8]

The volume ends with a vigorous defence of one traditional conception of women's role. Nkiru Nzegwu argues that traditional Ibo values gave women a place of considerable power both in familial and personal relations and also in the management of the economy. This power was actually eroded by the influence of British norms of proper women's behaviour, insofar as these were imitated by the upwardly mobile classes. And assumptions based on European conceptions of the distinction between the 'private' and the 'public' spheres have proven pernicious in development work, where women's managerial knowledge has been neglected to the detriment of the interests of all. Meanwhile, Westernized family structures gave women vastly-reduced social power and legal autonomy, by comparison to their traditional familial and legal role.

Nzegwu's paper is a vivid case study of a situation that is familiar from the data on sub-Saharan Africa in the *Human Development Report*: the situation of an 'underdeveloped' country in which the productivity and autonomy of women are relatively well respected, and in which women's participation in the labour force, encouraged rather than stifled by tradition, gives them social entitlements that Metha Bai sorely lacks. Because it is not her theme, Nzegwu does not place emphasis on the obstacles to women's full equality that surely exist in the Nigerian context. (Women comprise only 20% of the labour force, considerably lower than in many nations of sub-Saharan Africa; female literacy is still only 63% of that of males, thought it has risen sharply; the population ratio of 102:100 is slightly below the average for sub-Saharan Africa, and maternal mortality, at 750 per 100,000 live births, is comparably high, more than triple that in Cape Verde, for example, and 2.5 times that of Botswana.) Nor does her

[8] See Nussbaum and Sen, 'Internal Criticism and Indian Rationalist Traditions', in M. Krausz (ed.), *Relativism* (Notre Dame, Ind.: Notre Dame University Press, 1989); also Sen, 'India and the West', *The New Republic*, June 1993, 27–34. In this volume, see especially the papers by Chen, Sen, and Benhabib.

negative account of current developments mention certain positive indications. (For example, during the past thirty years women's enrolment in primary education has risen from 59% of that of males to 93%, and the rate of post-secondary enrolment is now up to 38% of that of males.) It must also be said that it is not at all surprising that it should be our participant from sub-Saharan Africa who finds her tradition on the whole an ally and a source of illumination, rather than an impediment to be transcended. For the data do bear out Nzegwu's claim that the status of women in this region of the world is relatively good, and inequalities—in health, in nutrition, in labour, in access to education—far less profound than in many other parts of the developing world.

It is appropriate that we should end on this note, for we would not wish to be read as saying that all good ideas about women's equality come from the Western Enlightenment. The cultures of the Enlightenment have frequently been unjustly contemptuous of the traditions of the people they have colonized, and obtuse about discovering that those traditions are. Nzegwu is surely right that the Victorian wife (or even the contemporary American professional woman) might profit from acquaintance with the remarkable tradition of 'sitting on a man'. She might also study with profit its associated patterns of women's group affiliation and self-definition, strikingly at variance with Western customs in which women's social identity derives primarily from that of a male head of household. These recognitions are in no way incompatible with the sort of universalism we wish to defend, as we have emphasized throughout. We want to take good ideas where we find them, and then think how they might be implemented in a variety of concrete contexts. Having been on the whole highly critical of traditions, both non-Western and Western, we end with a non-Western female voice that speaks with pride of its own traditions, viewing these as valuable resources in the critical social thought and action of women the world over.

Postscript June 1994

In April 1994, Martha Chen and Jean Drèze held a conference at the Indian Institute of Management in Bangalore on the living conditions of Indian widows. The conference, the culmination of Chen and Drèze's study of 562 widows in fourteen villages spread over seven states, was the first in India to spotlight the conditions of widows, especially in rural areas. The problem is an enormous one, since the 33 million widows in India comprise about 8% of the country's female population, about the same as the proportion of agricultural labourers to the total male population. The conference brought together academics from various fields who have studied widowhood, social activists and feminists who have worked on widows' problems, and thirty-five widows from different parts of the country. One goal of the conference was to bring these widows out of their isolation, to foster self-confidence, and to encourage them to communicate their experiences to one another.

For these women, coming together with many other widows for the first time, and talking about who they are (as opposed to who society says they are) appeared to generate striking transformations. As *The Hindu Magazine* reports (24 April 1994):

Throughout the week they came to realise many things about themselves and their lives—especially how much they had internalised society's perceptions of them as daughters, wives, mothers and widows (their identity invariably defined in terms of their relationship to men). The workshop aimed to change their self-perception as objects of pity, unfortunate women who had lost their husbands and now had to beg for help from their families or sops from the state. They were encouraged to see themselves as persons who had a right to exist even if their husbands were dead, and as citizens who had a right to resources—such as land, housing, employment, credit and ration cards—which would enable them to live and bring up their children (if any) with dignity and self-respect.

That the process they went through in that week was a transforming one was evident on the last day, when they got together one more time in a symbolic and moving ceremony which reinforced their newly acquired sense of unity and strength. Before they bid each other farewell, they shared their individual decisions about what they would do to carry the message of the workshop back to their villages. While their promises to each other—most of them related to wearing forbidden things like bindi, sindoor, bangles or coloured clothes—may seem trivial to many of us, they represent huge strides in their march towards self-confidence and an identity that is all their own.

One of the widows who attended the Bangalore conference was Metha Bai. Her photograph appears in the *Hindu* story—a beautiful, reflective face, with enormous eyes. During the past few years her situation had degenerated, since she could not keep up mortgage payments on even the small plot of land she still retained, and was on the verge of losing it. According to Martha Chen, the conference was a transforming experience for her. Martha saw her smile broadly for the first time since she has known her. Metha Bai bought clothes in the forbidden colour of blue, and put on bangles. She laughed freely with the other widows. She also came up with a plan of action to raise the money to save her land. A loan she managed to get through her own initiative, acting on contacts made at the conference, has in fact enabled her to meet her mortgage payments securely for some time to come.

This is, at least for the time being, a happy ending. But in concluding we should set it in the context of the larger framework of Chen's research. I quote again from the *Hindu* story reporting the conference:

The impotence of many laws meant to secure gender justice is, once again, established by the study. For example, although widows in virtually all communities are legally entitled to inherit at least part of their deceased husband's property (if any),

Chen found that less than half exercise even use rights over what ought to be their land. Disputes over property often lead to violence against widows—sometimes in the form of fatal witch-hunts, which provide a convenient cover for the physical elimination of women who attempt to claim their rights.

. . . As women who have experienced the worst that the patriarchal order has to offer their gender, widows could well become the vanguard of the women's movement once they are enabled to break out of their isolation and fragmentation, scattered as they are in separate households across the country. Once they are empowered to become an organised political force, they will surely be potent agents of change who simply cannot be ignored by society or the state.

Meanwhile, public awareness of the condition of widows and public action both to prod the state into positive action and to encourage the full participation of widows in public life can pave the way towards gender justice for women with and without men.

The struggle for human capabilities is not just a theoretical construct. For women all over the world, and for everyone who cares about women's well-being, it is a way of life.

Martha Nussbaum, June 1994

Table 1 Status of women: developing countries

HDI rank	Life expectancy at birth (years) 1990	Maternal mortality rate (per 100,000 live births) 1988	Average age at first marriage (years) 1980–1985	Literacy rate (age 15–24 only) 1980–1989	Enrolment ratio Primary (net) 1988–1990	Secondary (gross) 1988–1990	Tertiary (gross) 1988–1990	Tertiary science and engineering enrolment (% female) 1987–1988	Administrative and managerial staff (% female) 1980–1989	Women in labour force (% of total) 1990	Women Parliament (% of seats occupied by women) 1991
High human development	73.8	120	22.0	93	..	65	23	..	13	29	8
20 Barbados	77.4	35	..	..	96	83	21	..	31	48	4
24 Hong Kong	80.1	6	25.3	..	..	75	9	..	12	36	..
27 Cyprus	78.6	10	24.4	..	..	91	16	24	7	37	5
30 Uruguay	75.5	50	22.4	99	..	..	54	32	25	31	6
31 Trinidad and Tobago	74.1	120	22.3	99	90	82	5	28	..	27	17
32 Bahamas	..	..	..	..	100	..	..	..	..	47	4
33 Korea, Rep. of	73.1	80	24.1	..	..	86	28	13	3	34	2
36 Chile	75.3	67	23.6	97	..	77	16	25	18	31	6
42 Costa Rica	77.3	36	22.7	98	87	43	..	..	22	29	12
43 Singapore	76.9	14	26.2	96	100	71	..	..	22	39	5
44 Brunei Darussalam	..	..	..	93	..	..	..	..	6	..	..
46 Argentina	74.4	140	22.9	97	..	78	44	35	..	21	5
50 Venezuela	73.2	130	21.2	94	62	41	27	..	15	22	10
51 Dominica	..	..	..	..	..	..	..	(.)	24	42	17
52 Kuwait	76.0	30	22.9	76	84	..	20	43	4	14	..
53 Mexico	73.0	150	20.6	91	..	53	12	..	15	31	12
55 Qatar	72.6	140	..	..	..	94	43	34	..	7	..

Medium human development	69.8	170	22.0	82	98	44	4	..	11	39	16
Excluding China	67.5	220	21.0	81	..	50	10	23	13	33	8
56 Mauritius	72.2	130	21.7	..	94	53	1	24	15	35	7
57 Malaysia	72.3	120	23.5	83	..	58	7	29	8	31	5
58 Bahrain	73.5	80	..	82	92	..	21	32	4	10	..
59 Grenada	..	..	..	..	..	..	..	..	..	49	..
60 Antigua and Barbuda	..	..	..	..	..	..	..	(.)	..	..	..
61 Colombia	71.7	150	20.4	..	..	57	14	28	21	41	..
63 Seychelles	..	..	..	..	..	..	..	(.)	12	42	16
65 Suriname	72.1	120	..	..	100	57	10	16	1	..	..
67 United Arab Emirates	73.5	130	18.0	56	100	72	21	54	22	6	(.)
68 Panama	74.5	60	21.2	93	92	62	26	39	..	27	8
69 Jamaica	75.3	120	25.2	..	96	63	4	48	..	31	5
70 Brazil	68.4	230	22.6	85	..	..	12	..	9	35	6
71 Fiji	67.1	150	21.6	91	98	53	3	27	19	19	..
72 Saint Lucia	..	..	..	..	..	..	..	6	3	..	(.)
73 Turkey	67.0	200	20.6	75	..	42	10	26	..	33	1
74 Thailand	68.1	180	22.7	96	..	32	..	..	21	47	4
75 Cuba	77.3	54	19.9	99	95	94	25	39	..	32	34
76 Saint Vincent	..	..	..	..	..	..	..	17	20	..	..
79 Saint Kitts and Nevis	..	..	..	..	..	..	..	1	14	..	7
81 Syrian Arab Rep.	68.1	200	22.1	..	93	43	17	24	33	15	8
82 Belize	..	..	..	..	..	..	..	(.)	12	33	(.)
84 Saudi Arabia	66.5	220	..	..	56	41	11	31	..	7	..
85 South Africa	64.7	250	..	..	..	..	..	..	17	33	..
86 Sri Lanka	73.1	180	24.4	90	..	77	4	20	7	37	5
87 Libyan Arab Jamahiriya	63.7	200	..	..	..	..	..	..	..	9	..

Table 1 *Continued*

| HDI rank | Life expectancy at birth (years) 1990 | Maternal mortality rate (per 100,000 live births) 1988 | Average age at first marriage (years) 1980–1985 | Literacy rate (age 15–24 only) 1980–1989 | Enrolment ratio | | | Tertiary science and engineering enrolment (% female) 1987–1988 | Administrative and managerial staff (% female) 1980–1989 | Women in labour force (% of total) 1990 | Women Parliament (% of seats occupied by women) 1991 |
					Primary (net) 1988–1990	Secondary (gross) 1988–1990	Tertiary (gross) 1988–1990				
89 Ecuador	68.2	200	22.1	93	:	57	23	15	15	30	6
90 Paraguay	69.3	200	22.1	94	94	31	8	39	:	41	6
91 Korea, Dem. Rep. of	73.3	130	:	:	:	:	:	:	:	46	20
92 Philippines	66.2	250	22.4	92	98	75	:	:	:	37	9
93 Tunisia	67.5	200	24.3	63	91	40	7	24	25	13	4
94 Oman	67.8	220	:	:	82	48	5	:	:	8	:
95 Peru	65.0	300	22.7	90	:	:	:	:	8	33	6
96 Iraq	66.1	250	20.8	:	78	37	11	28	:	6	11
97 Dominican Rep.	68.9	200	20.5	:	73	:	:	:	21	15	:
98 Samoa	:	:	:	:	:	:	:	:	19	:	:
99 Jordan	68.8	200	22.6	77	:	:	:	31	14	10	(.)
100 Mongolia	63.8	250	:	:	:	96	26	45	:	45	2
101 China	71.8	130	22.4	82	:	41	1	:	11	43	21
102 Lebanon	68.0	200	:	:	:	:	:	:	:	27	(.)
103 Iran, Islamic Rep. of	66.6	250	19.7	42	90	45	4	10	:	18	2
104 Botswana	62.8	300	26.4	:	93	47	3	:	36	35	5
105 Guyana	67.1	200	20.7	:	:	58	4	15	13	21	37
106 Vanuatu	:	:	:	68	:	:	:	:	:	46	4
107 Algeria	66.1	210	21.0	60	83	53	6	16	:	4	2
108 Indonesia	63.3	300	20.0	82	96	41	:	21	7	40	12

109	Gabon	54.2	600	..	..	..	..	3	..	..	38	..
110	El Salvador	67.7	200	..	71	71	26	14	12	16	45	8
111	Nicaragua	66.2	200	..	..	77	44	9	48	..	34	16
	Low human development	57.3	590	19.0	41	..	26	4	20	3	26	7
	Excluding India	55.6	610	19.0	42	..	20	3	16	..	27	7
112	Maldives	65.9	..	..	87	..	..	..	..	10	20	4
113	Guatemala	67.9	250	20.5	..	93	..	..	..	16	26	..
114	Cape Verde	64.8	200	..	..	..	20	(.)	..	..	29	6
115	Viet Nam	67.0	400	..	94	94	40	..	..	..	47	18
116	Honduras	..	220	..	..	..	..	7	..	..	18	12
117	Swaziland	58.6	400	..	75	84	49	3	..	..	40	..
118	Solomon Islands	..	..	..	..	..	..	..	..	..	..	(.)
119	Morocco	63.7	270	21.3	..	45	30	8	25	..	20	(.)
120	Lesotho	61.8	350	19.6	..	76	31	6	20	..	44	..
121	Zimbabwe	61.4	330	20.4	..	..	46	2	..	15	35	12
122	Bolivia	56.9	600	22.1	76	75	31	..	..	..	24	7
123	Myanmar	63.0	600	22.4	81	..	23	..	..	..	37	..
124	Egypt	61.5	300	21.3	38	..	69	13	26	14	11	2
125	São Tomé and Príncipe	..	..	..	74	..	..	..	..	9	..	11
126	Congo	56.3	900	..	..	..	..	2	8	..	39	..
127	Kenya	61.7	400	20.4	..	..	19	1	14	..	40	1
128	Madagascar	56.0	600	20.3	..	63	18	3	30	..	40	7
129	Papua New Guinea	55.7	700	..	..	67	10	..	8	..	39	(.)
130	Zambia	55.5	600	19.4	..	79	14	1	5	11	29	5
131	Ghana	56.8	700	19.3	..	..	31	1	9	9	40	..

Table 1 *Continued*

HDI rank		Life expectancy at birth (years) 1990	Maternal mortality rate (per 100,000 live births) 1988	Average age at first marriage (years) 1980–1985	Literacy rate (age 15–24 only) 1980–1989	Enrolment ratio Primary (net) 1988–1990	Enrolment ratio Secondary (gross) 1988–1990	Enrolment ratio Tertiary (gross) 1988–1990	Tertiary science and engineering enrolment (% female) 1987–1988	Administrative and managerial staff 1980–1989	Women in labour force (% of total) 1990	Women Parliament (% of seats occupied by women) 1991
132	Pakistan	57.8	600	19.8	25	:	13	2	:	:	11	1
133	Cameroon	55.3	550	17.5	59	69	21	:	:	6	30	14
134	India	59.3	550	18.7	40	:	33	4	22	2	26	7
135	Namibia	58.8	400	:	:	:	38	:	:	:	24	7
136	Côte d'Ivoire	55.2	680	17.8	:	:	12	:	:	:	34	5
137	Haiti	57.4	600	23.8	51	44	19	1	12	33	40	:
138	Tanzania, U. Rep. of	55.7	600	:	54	48	4	:	8	:	48	11
139	Comoros	55.5	500	19.5	55	50	15	(.)	10	:	41	(.)
140	Zaire	54.7	700	20.1	:	53	16	:	:	:	36	5
141	Lao People's Dem. Rep.	51.3	750	:	:	:	21	1	17	:	45	9
142	Nigeria	53.3	750	18.7	:	:	17	2	:	:	20	:
143	Yemen	52.0	800	17.8	:	:	10	:	:	:	13	3
144	Liberia	55.5	600	:	:	:	:	1	10	:	31	:
145	Togo	55.8	600	:	36	58	10	1	3	8	37	4
146	Uganda	53.7	700	:	:	50	:	1	11	:	41	12
147	Bangladesh	51.5	650	16.7	27	61	11	1	16	2	7	10
148	Cambodia	51.2	800	:	:	:	:	(.)	4	:	39	:
149	Rwanda	51.2	700	21.2	45	65	6	:	10	:	48	17
150	Senegal	49.3	750	17.7	:	41	11	1	11	:	26	13
151	Ethiopia	47.1	900	:	:	24	12	(.)	11	:	42	:

152	Nepal	51.6	850	17.9	15	43	17	:	:	:	34	3
153	Malawi	48.7	500	17.8	:	52	3	(.)	16	:	42	10
154	Burundi	50.2	800	20.8	:	46	4	(.)	13	:	:	:
155	Equatorial Guinea	48.6	800	:	:	:	6	1	8	:	36	:
156	Central African Rep.	52.0	650	:	18	43				:	46	4
157	Mozambique	49.2	800	17.6	25	37	4	(.)	17	:	48	16
158	Sudan	52.0	700	21.3	:	:	17	2	27	:	29	:
159	Bhutan	48.2	800	:	:	:	2	:	:	:	32	(.)
160	Angola	47.1	900	:	:	:	:	0	:	:	39	15
161	Mauritania	48.7	800	19.2	:	:	10	1	15	:	22	:
162	Benin	48.7	800	18.2	18	36	6	1	10	:	24	6
163	Djibouti	49.7	740	:	:	33	12	(.)	:	:	:	(.)
164	Guinea-Bissau	44.1	1,000	:	18	32	4	(.)	8	:	42	:
165	Chad	48.1	800	:	:	23	3	:	:	:	17	:
166	Somalia	47.6	900	20.1	:	8	7	1	10	:	39	:
167	Gambia	45.6	1,000	:	:	45	10	(.)	:	15	41	8
168	Mali	46.6	850	18.1	14	14	4	(.)	9	:	16	:
169	Niger	47.1	850	:	7	19	4	(.)	6	:	47	5
170	Burkina Faso	49.9	750	17.4	7	23	5	1	10	:	49	:
171	Afghanistan	43.0	1,000	17.8	11	13	5	1	:	:	8	3
172	Sierra Leone	43.6	1,000	:	:	:	12	(.)	:	:	33	:
173	Guinea	44.0	1,000	:	:	17	5	(.)	10	:	30	:
	All developing countries	64.2	420	20.7	65	86	36	5	20	8	33	12
	Least developed countries	52.0	740	18.9	36	45	12	1	14	:	29	9
	Sub-Saharan Africa	53.6	690	19.1	37	42	14	2	12	:	34	:
	Industrial countries	77.9	26	23.5	99	:	:	:	22	24	42	9
	World	67.3	370	21.2	69	:	:	:	21	12	34	11

Source: United Nations Development Program, UNDP, 1993.

MARTHA C. NUSSBAUM

Table 2 Female-male gaps: developing countries

HDI rank	Females as a percentage of males (see note)									
	Life expectancy 1990	Population 1990	Literacy 1970	Literacy 1990	Mean years of schooling 1990	Primary enrolment 1960	Primary enrolment 1988–1990	Secondary enrolment 1988–1990	Tertiary enrolment 1988–1990	Labour force 1990
High human development	110	100	90	98	86	95	100	99	80	42
20 Barbados	107	109	..	..	93	..	98	92	..	92
24 Hong Kong	107	94	71	..	63	85	99	106	56	57
27 Cyprus	107	101	..	..	86	..	100	102	114	60
30 Uruguay	109	103	100	99	110	100	98	..	114	45
31 Trinidad and Tobago	107	101	94	..	101	98	100	104	68	38
32 Bahamas	..	106	..	..	94	..	..	..	..	90
33 Korea, Rep. of	109	100	86	94	61	90	100	97	53	51
36 Chile	110	102	98	100	92	96	92	108	82	45
42 Costa Rica	106	98	99	101	97	98	100	105	68	40
43 Singapore	108	97	60	..	66	93	100	104	..	64
44 Brunei Darussalam	..	94	..	..	83	..	..	..	..	..
46 Argentina	110	102	98	100	105	101	107	113	117	27
50 Venezuela	109	98	90	103	97	100	103	..	91	27
51 Dominica	..	..	..	..	91	..	..	..	..	72
52 Kuwait	106	76	65	87	79	78	98	94	129	16
53 Mexico	110	100	88	94	96	94	97	102	76	46
55 Qatar	107	60	..	..	93	..	98	112	..	8

Medium human development	105	96	..	80	65	83	99	82	57	66
Excluding China	105	99	..	87	75	..	95	88	75	54
56 Mauritius	108	102	77	..	68	90	102	100	52	54
57 Malaysia	106	98	68	81	91	77	100	105	95	45
58 Bahrain	106	73	..	84	67	..	98	101	..	11
59 Grenada	..	..	..	..	93	..	..	..	..	94
60 Antigua and Barbuda	..	..	..	..	80	..	..	..	..	..
61 Colombia	109	99	96	98	106	100	103	119	108	69
63 Seychelles	..	101	..	..	92	..	99	100	..	74
65 Suriname	107	102	..	100	92	..	100	119	113	41
67 United Arab Emirates	106	48	29	..	101	..	100	114	..	7
68 Panama	106	97	100	100	106	96	106	109	..	37
69 Jamaica	106	101	101	100	97	101	98	111	75	45
70 Brazil	109	101	91	97	94	96	..	90	100	54
71 Fiji	107	99	..	..	83	..	101	104	57	23
72 Saint Lucia	..	106	..	..	96	..	..	..	..	..
73 Turkey	105	95	49	79	50	64	93	64	55	49
74 Thailand	106	99	84	96	76	90	..	97	..	88
75 Cuba	105	97	101	98	103	100	99	112	..	46
76 Saint Vincent	..	..	..	..	95	..	..	..	..	..
79 Saint Kitts and Nevis	..	..	..	..	97	..	..	..	..	..
81 Syrian Arab Rep.	106	98	33	..	60	44	93	72	72	18

Table 2 *Continued*

HDI rank	Females as a percentage of males (see note)									
	Life expectancy 1990	Population 1990	Literacy 1970	Literacy 1990	Mean years of schooling 1990	Primary enrolment 1960	Primary enrolment 1988–1990	Secondary enrolment 1988–1990	Tertiary enrolment 1988–1990	Labour force 1990
82 Belize	..	..	..	..	93	..	98	..	..	49
84 Saudi Arabia	106	84	13	66	26	..	81	75	73	8
85 South Africa	110	101	..	..	90	90	..	..	..	50
86 Sri Lanka	106	99	81	89	80	90	100	107	71	59
87 Libyan Arab Jamahiriya	106	91	22	67	23	26	90	..	..	10
89 Ecuador	107	99	91	95	92	91	98	104	68	43
90 Paraguay	107	97	88	96	88	86	99	107	88	70
91 Korea, Dem. Rep. of	110	101	..	..	63	..	..	100	..	85
92 Philippines	106	99	96	99	89	95	98	104	..	59
93 Tunisia	103	98	39	76	41	49	91	80	67	15
94 Oman	106	91	..	..	22	..	94	81	80	9
95 Peru	106	99	74	86	80	75	96	..	24	49
96 Iraq	103	96	36	71	69	38	87	64	64	6
97 Dominican Rep.	107	97	94	96	87	99	100	..	..	17
98 Samoa	..	..	..	..	78	..	..	..	..	..

99 Jordan	106	95	45	79	66	63	..	..	..	11
100 Mongolia	104	99	85	..	95	99	103	110	..	83
101 China	105	94	..	73	60	..	100	77	50	76
102 Lebanon	106	106	73	83	66	94	92	71	44	37
103 Iran, Islamic Rep. of	101	97	43	67	68	48	91	73	45	21
104 Botswana	111	109	..	78	97	..	106	..	76	55
105 Guyana	109	99	..	98	91	..	100	105	76	27
106 Vanuatu	..	92	..	..	71	..	..	..	..	86
107 Algeria	103	100	28	65	18	67	88	80	44	5
108 Indonesia	106	101	64	85	58	67	96	84	..	66
109 Gabon	107	103	51	66	33	..	..	..	41	61
110 El Salvador	111	104	87	92	98	..	103	100	73	81
111 Nicaragua	104	100	98	..	110	102	104	..	121	51
Low human development	103	97	44	59	39	50	99	62	41	39
Excluding India	105	100	45	65	43	50	81	63	35	42
112 Maldives	..	..	..	..	77	..	..	..	..	25
113 Guatemala	108	98	73	75	86	78	85	68	..	34
114 Cape Verde	103	112	..	..	39	..	95	100	..	41
115 Viet Nam	107	104	..	91	59	..	94	93	28	88
116 Honduras	107	98	91	94	93	99	106	..	65	22
117 Swaziland	107	103	..	..	82	..	105	96	68	67
118 Solomon Islands	..	..	..	..	70	..	..	..	..	..
119 Morocco	106	100	29	62	36	40	68	70	59	26
120 Lesotho	117	108	..	..	..	..	119	..	..	78
121 Zimbabwe	106	102	75	82	40	..	100	85	36	54

Table 2 *Continued*

HDI rank	Females as a percentage of males (see note)									
	Life expectancy 1990	Population 1990	Literacy 1970	Literacy 1990	Mean years of schooling 1990	Primary enrolment 1960	Primary enrolment 1988–1990	Secondary enrolment 1988–1990	Tertiary enrolment 1988–1990	Labour force 1990
122 Bolivia	109	103	68	83	60	64	90	84	..	31
123 Myanmar	106	101	67	81	72	85	98	92	..	60
124 Egypt	104	97	40	54	42	65	79	75	53	12
125 São Tomé and Principe	..	..	..	..	39	..	..	..	..	..
126 Congo	110	103	38	63	35	51	..	..	20	64
127 Kenya	107	100	43	..	42	47	96	70	45	67
128 Madagascar	106	102	77	83	65	78	98	90	82	66
129 Papua New Guinea	103	93	62	58	50	12	85	63	38	64
130 Zambia	104	103	56	81	45	67	98	56	37	40
131 Ghana	107	101	42	73	46	48	81	65	26	67
132 Pakistan	100	92	37	45	25	28	55	45	41	13
133 Cameroon	106	103	40	64	33	49	86	68	..	42
134 India	101	93	43	55	34	50	97	61	47	34
135 Namibia	104	101	..	..	..	..	..	..	..	31
136 Côte d'Ivoire	107	97	38	60	31	35	..	44	27	52
137 Haiti	106	104	65	80	63	84	100	95	35	67
138 Tanzania, U. Rep. of	107	102	38	..	45	55	104	80	33	93
139 Comoros	102	102	..	..	65	..	83	75	..	69
140 Zaire	107	102	36	73	33	36	79	50	..	56
141 Lao People's Dem. Rep.	106	99	76	..	59	47	80	68	50	81

142	Nigeria	107	102	40	63	26	59	93	77	38	25
143	Yemen	101	108	15	50	18	..	..	20	..	15
144	Liberia	105	98	30	58	26	40	..	55	31	44
145	Togo	107	102	26	54	31	38	68	30	15	58
146	Uganda	107	102	58	56	41	..	88	44	36	71
147	Bangladesh	99	94	33	47	30	39	88	50	22	7
148	Cambodia	106	101	..	46	71	..	..	..	..	64
149	Rwanda	107	102	49	58	31	..	100	67	20	92
150	Senegal	104	102	28	48	29	..	75	52	26	35
151	Ethiopia	107	102	..	..	43	27	75	71	23	71
152	Nepal	98	95	13	35	32	5	51	40	..	51
153	Malawi	103	103	43	..	46	..	95	50	27	72
154	Burundi	107	104	34	65	33	33	84	67	33	..
155	Equatorial Guinea	107	103	..	..	20	..	..	..	..	56
156	Central African Rep.	111	106	23	48	32	23	65	35	20	86
157	Mozambique	107	103	48	47	54	60	82	44	33	92
158	Sudan	105	99	21	27	45	40	71	74	68	41
159	Bhutan	97	93	..	..	32	..	65	29	..	48
160	Angola	107	103	44	51	52	..	82	..	15	64
161	Mauritania	107	102	..	45	29	23	70	45	14	28
162	Benin	107	103	35	49	29	39	52	38	15	31
163	Djibouti	107	98	..	..	33	..	73	67	..	..
164	Guinea-Bissau	108	105	..	48	27	..	55	44	..	72
165	Chad	107	103	10	42	31	14	44	25	11	21
166	Somalia	107	110	20	39	31	..	57	58	22	64

Table 2 *Continued*

HDI rank	Females as a percentage of males (see note)									
	Life expectancy 1990	Population 1990	Literacy 1970	Literacy 1990	Mean years of schooling 1990	Primary enrolment 1960	Primary enrolment 1988–1990	Secondary enrolment 1988–1990	Tertiary enrolment 1988–1990	Labour force 1990
167 Gambia	108	103	..	41	23	..	73	45	..	69
168 Mali	107	106	36	59	27	43	58	44	14	20
169 Niger	107	102	33	82	40	43	61	44	17	89
170 Burkina Faso	107	102	23	32	54	42	64	56	27	96
171 Afghanistan	102	94	15	32	12	13	52	45	18	9
172 Sierra Leone	108	104	44	37	26	..	75	57	20	49
173 Guinea	102	102	33	38	20	36	50	36	12	43
All developing countries	104	96	54	72	58	61	94	74	51	52
Least developed countries	104	100	38	58	43	44	81	58	28	48
Sub-Saharan Africa	107	102	42	64	46	52	85	64	32	55
Industrial countries	110	106	..	..	99	..	..	..	..	77
World	106	99	..	..	72	..	..	..	..	56

Note: All figures are expressed in relation to the male average, which is indexed to equal 100. The smaller the figure the bigger the gap, the closer the figure to 100 the smaller the gap, and a figure above 100 indicates that the female average is higher than the male.
Source: United Nations Development Program New York, UNDP, 1993.

Table 3 Female-male gaps: industrial countries

Females as a percentage of males (see note)

HDI rank	Life expectancy 1990	Population 1990	Mean years of schooling 1990	Upper secondary education		Tertiary education		Labour force		Unemployment 1990–1991	Wages 1990–1991
				Enrolment 1988	Graduates 1988	Full-time equivalent enrolment ratio 1988	Engineering and related science enrolment 1988	1970	1985–1991		
1 Japan	108	103	98	104	108	..	16	64	68	110	51
2 Canada	109	102	97	102	105	114	29	..	..	90	63
3 Norway	109	102	98	112	113	118	27	38	81	85	85
4 Switzerland	109	105	93	85	90	48	42	52	60	125	68
5 Sweden	108	103	100	109	102	130	25	61	92	77	89
6 USA	110	105	102	105	113	116	29	59	83	91	59
7 Australia	109	100	99	71	..	115	40	42	71	93	..
8 France	111	105	102	105	109	119	..	54	75	168	88
9 Netherlands	109	102	104	84	106	81	25	..	..	179	78
10 United Kingdom	108	105	102	106	105	93	..	55	74	..	67
11 Iceland	108	99	103	..	..	..	..	..	..	131	80
12 Germany	109	108	90	91	96	86	24	..	..	120	74
13 Denmark	108	103	98	100	115	120	24	58	85	130	82
14 Finland	111	106	98	130	139	119	35	73	89	62	77
15 Austria	110	109	90	85	110	89	25	..	..	112	78

Table 3 *Continued*

Females as a percentage of males (see note)

HDI rank	Life expectancy 1990	Population 1990	Mean years of schooling 1990	Upper secondary education Enrolment 1988	Upper secondary education Graduates 1988	Tertiary education Full-time equivalent enrolment ratio 1988	Tertiary education Engineering and related science enrolment 1988	Labour force 1970	Labour force 1985–1991	Unemployment 1990–1991	Wages 1990–1991
16 Belgium	109	105	100	:	:	120	34	42	70	201	64
17 New Zealand	108	102	104	106	:	103	48	38	77	87	81
18 Luxembourg	109	105	95	96	117	:	:	35	53	236	65
19 Israel	105	100	82	:	:	:	:	:	:	156	:
21 Ireland	108	99	102	125	112	84	48	36	44	64	62
22 Italy	109	106	99	104	113	95	53	:	:	234	80
23 Spain	108	103	92	115	113	105	28	24	54	194	:
25 Greece	106	103	89	:	:	:	:	:	:	255	68
26 Czechoslovakia	111	105	88	:	:	:	:	80	87	124	71
28 Hungary	111	107	102	:	:	:	:	70	85	83	:
39 Malta	105	103	92	:	:	:	:	27	34	56	:
40 Bulgaria	108	102	84	:	:	:	:	79	86	:	:
41 Portugal	110	107	76	129	:	:	37	34	76	206	76
48 Poland	112	105	92	:	:	:	:	85	83	:	:
77 Romania	108	103	89	:	:	:	:	83	86	:	:
78 Albania	107	94	93	:	:	:	:	:	:	:	:
Aggregates											
Industrial	110	106	99	:	:	:	:	59	77	:	:
Developing	104	96	58	:	:	:	:	:	52	:	:
World	106	99	72	:	:	:	:	:	56	:	:

OECD	109	105	99	103	109	106	29	55	75	128	66
Eastern Europe incl. former USSR	112	109	..	..	..	..	..	..	..	..	..
European Community	109	105	96	103	106	98	34	46	70	168	75
Nordic	109	103	99	112	115	123	27	59	88	89	84
Southern Europe	108	104	90	110	113	99	43	26	58	220	80
Non-Europe	109	104	101	103	110	115	26	60	76	98	59
North America	110	105	101	105	112	116	29	59	83	91	59
Other countries											
29 Lithuania	115	111	..	..	..	..	..	..	..	..	..
34 Estonia	115	114	..	..	..	..	..	..	..	..	..
35 Latvia	116	115	..	..	..	..	..	..	..	..	..
37 Russian Federation	116	114	..	..	..	..	..	..	..	..	..
38 Belarus	114	114	..	..	..	..	..	..	..	..	..
45 Ukraine	114	117	..	..	..	..	..	..	..	..	..
47 Armenia	110	104	..	..	..	..	..	..	..	..	..
49 Georgia	111	111	..	..	..	..	..	..	..	..	..
54 Kazakhstan	114	106	..	..	..	..	..	..	..	..	..
62 Azerbaijan	112	105	..	..	..	..	..	..	..	..	..
64 Moldova, Rep. of	110	110	..	..	..	..	..	..	..	..	..
66 Turkmenistan	111	103	..	..	..	..	..	..	..	..	..
80 Uzbekistan	110	102	..	..	..	..	..	..	..	..	..
83 Kyrgyzstan	113	105	..	..	..	..	..	..	..	..	..
88 Tajikistan	108	101	..	..	..	..	..	..	..	..	..

Note: All figures are expressed in relation to the male average, which is indexed to equal 100. The smaller the figure the bigger the gap, the closer the figure to 100 the smaller the gap, and a figure above 100 indicates that the female average is higher than the male.

Source: United Nations Development Program New York UNDP, 1993.

Table 4 Gender-disparity-adjusted HDI

Country	HDI value	Gender-disparity-adjusted HDI	Difference between HDI and gender-disparity-adjusted ranks
Sweden	0.977	0.921	4
Norway	0.978	0.881	1
France	0.971	0.864	5
Denmark	0.955	0.860	8
Finland	0.954	0.859	8
Australia	0.972	0.852	1
New Zealand	0.947	0.844	9
Netherlands	0.970	0.826	1
USA	0.976	0.824	−3
United Kingdom	0.964	0.818	0
Canada	0.982	0.816	−9
Belgium	0.952	0.808	3
Austria	0.952	0.782	1
Switzerland	0.978	0.768	−10
Germany	0.957	0.768	−4
Italy	0.924	0.764	3
Japan	0.983	0.763	−16
Czechoslovakia	0.892	0.754	4
Ireland	0.925	0.720	−1
Luxembourg	0.943	0.713	−3
Greece	0.902	0.691	0
Portugal	0.853	0.672	3
Cyprus	0.890	0.656	0
Costa Rica	0.852	0.632	2
Hong Kong	0.913	0.618	−5
Singapore	0.849	0.585	1
Korea, Rep. of	0.872	0.555	−3
Paraguay	0.641	0.546	1
Sri Lanka	0.663	0.499	−1
Philippines	0.603	0.451	0
Swaziland	0.458	0.344	0
Myanmar	0.390	0.297	0
Kenya	0.369	0.241	0

Note: A positive difference shows that the gender-disparity-adjusted HDI rank is higher than the unadjusted HDI rank, a negative the opposite.
Source: United Nations Development Program, UNDP, 1993.

The meaning: no country treats its women as well as it treats its men, a disappointing result after so many years of debate on gender equality, so many struggles by women and so many changes in national laws (Table 4 and Figures 1 and 2). But some countries do better than others, so adjusting for gender disparity makes a big difference to the rankings: Japan falls from number 1 to 17, Canada from number 2 to 11 and Switzerland from number 4 to 14. By contrast, Sweden improves its rank from number 5 to 1, Denmark from number 12 to 4 and New Zealand from number 16 to 7.

In industrial countries, gender discrimination (measured by the HDI) is mainly in employment and wages, with women often getting less than two-thirds of the employment opportunities and about half the earnings of men.

In developing countries, the great disparities, besides those in the job market, are in health care, nutritional support, and education. For instance, women make up two-thirds of the illiterate population. And South and East Asia, defying the normal biological result that women live longer than men, have more men than women. The reasons: high maternal mortality and infanticide and nutritional neglect of the girl-child. According to one estimate, some 100 million women are 'missing'.

Table 5 Female-male ratio (FMR) and 'missing women', 1986

Region	FMR	Missing women in relation to sub-Saharan African FMR	
		Number (millions)	Proportion (%)
Europe	1.050		
Northern America	1.047		
Sub-Saharan Africa	1.022		
South-east Asia	1.010	2.4	1.2
Latin America	1.000	4.4	2.2
North Africa	0.984	2.4	3.9
West Asia	0.948	4.3	7.8
Iran	0.942	1.4	8.5
China	0.941	44.0	8.6
Bangladesh	0.940	3.7	8.7
India	0.933	36.9	9.5
Pakistan	0.905	5.2	12.9

Source: Sen and Drèze.

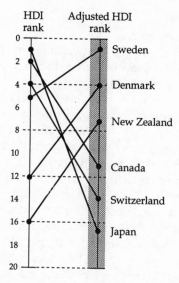

Figure 1 Changes in rank with a gender-disparity-adjusted HDI
Note: Ranks are for the 33 countries in Table 4.
Source: United Nations Development Program, UNDP, 1993.

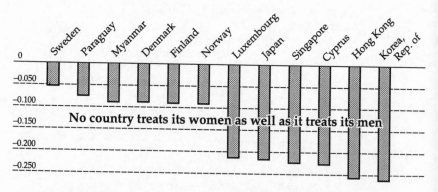

Figure 2 Difference between HDI and gender-disparity-adjusted HDI
Note: When the HDI is adjusted for gender disparity, no country improves its
HDI value.
Source: United Nations Development Program, UNDP, 1993.

PART I
WOMEN'S EQUALITY:
A CASE STUDY

A Matter of Survival: Women's Right to Employment in India and Bangladesh

Martha Chen

I worked in the fields at night, by moonlight, or at times when there was
the least likelihood of being seen. I did any kind of work I could find.

Saleha Begum, Bangladesh (1975)

I may die, but still I cannot go out. If there's something in the house,
we eat. Otherwise, we go to sleep.

Metha Bai, India (1991)

November 1975: a food-for-work site 40 kilometres west of Dhaka city,
Bangladesh. Bangladesh is still recovering from a famine in 1974. Saleha
Begum, the leader of a team of female labourers, tells the story of how she
first began to work outside her home after she and her husband became
landless. Despite family and community opposition, Saleha decided to
work and prove how hard she could work. Initially she was embarrassed to
be seen working, so she often worked at night or at other times when she
was not likely to be seen. As she grew accustomed to the work, the criticism
also died down. However, at the time when we found Saleha sitting in the
shade of a tree near a food-for-work site, she and the other women had just
been refused work at that site. The local officials turned them back, saying:
'Women in Bangladesh should not work outside their homes. We have
never hired women at food-for-work sites.'

February 1991: a village 40 kilometres north of Udaipur city, Rajasthan,
India. Metha Bai, an upper-caste widow with two minor sons, describes her
plight as a young widow from a caste which prohibits women from working
outside the homestead. Before her husband's death two years before,
Metha Bai had not been allowed to work outside their homestead, even to
fetch water or fuelwood (her husband performed all outside chores). Now,
she helps her father cultivate the land she inherited from her husband and
fetches water and fuelwood. However, her in-laws do not allow Metha Bai
to engage in any outside gainful employment. Her only source of support is
her father, who helps her till the land and brings regular gifts of food and
clothing.

This paper explores the predicament of poor women in poor economies,
like Saleha Begum and Metha Bai, who must break with tradition and act
independently because they lack the security the tradition is supposed to
offer. In communities where women are secluded, perhaps the most conspicuous and yet necessary way for women to break with tradition is to leave
their courtyards or homesteads in search of work.

The constitutions of Bangladesh and India guarantee women equal employment opportunities (as men) and equal pay for equal work. However, there is a remarkable degree of gender inequality in work opportunities and remuneration, and a remarkable range of variation in female labour force participation in both countries. Women who need or want to engage in gainful employment face one or more of the following constraints: norms of seclusion which confine women to their homes, segmentation of wage labour markets by gender, or exploitation within given trades or industries. This paper focuses primarily on the first type of constraint; the system of secluding women which denies them the right to gainful employment outside the home.

Most communities in the belt of South Asia which extends from Pakistan to Bangladesh across North India share a basic patriarchal kinship system, of which a sexual division of labour and status-based norms of female behaviour and seclusion are common elements. Admittedly, this system does not operate in exactly the same way for different religions, castes, or communities. Indeed, this paper will explore some differences across caste, class, and region within India and Bangladesh. However, the shared patriarchal ideology of the region has common implications for the status of women in general and for the occupational options of women in particular.

One of the prominent elements of this basic patriarchal system is a division of labour by gender. Under this sexual division, certain *types* of work are designated as male or female. In both India and Bangladesh, for example, ploughing is almost exclusively a male task whereas drying and storing grain are typically female tasks. Moreover, certain *spheres* of economic activity are designated as male or female. The homestead or private sphere is predominantly female; the public sphere of markets, roads, and towns is predominantly male. The intermediate sphere of fields and villages is both male and female in India but remains predominantly male in Bangladesh, where female seclusion is more widely enforced.

This shared patriarchal system is interwoven with a hierarchical social structure which, by ranking work appropriate to the status of each caste, further determines patterns of female work. An important symbol of a household's position in the social-status hierarchy is the type of work its women are allowed to do. Indeed, there is a sharp and systematic decline in the participation of women in work outside the home as wealth and status increase. So much so that, in both Bangladesh and North India, rural households can be divided into four main status groups according to the kind of work women are allowed to do.[1] In the top group of high-caste or

---

[1] In predominantly Muslim Bangladesh, where caste is not an explicit social category, households are most usefully ranked in terms of land-holding classes: surplus, middle, and small farm households plus landless labour households. In predominantly-Hindu North India, households are usefully ranked in terms of caste. See Boserup (1970: 69–70) for a summary of how caste influences women's work in India, and Chen (1983: 68) for a summary of how the land-holding class influences women's work in Bangladesh.

surplus farm households, in order to preserve household status, women take little or no part in any outdoor activities and often remain secluded in their homes. Below this group are the main local peasant caste or middle farmer group. Their women are occupied mainly with domestic duties but also work in their own fields. In the third group of middle castes or small farm households, women work mainly in their own fields but might work for a wage in the busy season. The fourth and lowest social group is composed of women belonging to the lowest castes or poorest households who regularly seek paid work in order to support their families (Boserup, 1970; Chen, 1983).

In the first part of this paper, I describe how women broke with tradition to join the work force in the aftermath of the 1974 famine of Bangladesh, and discuss the public response to their act of defiance. The story illustrates how local traditions and local policies can evolve and change in response to the contingencies of real life; in this case, the increasing demand for employment by large numbers of women in poor and female-headed households. It also illustrates a range of perspectives on women's right to employment both within the country and within the international donor community. In the second part of the paper, I describe the predicament of female heads of households from caste groups in India which, as a means of retaining social status or aspiring to 'higher' status, prohibits women from seeking gainful employment outside the home. The discussion illustrates how local tradition not only varies across castes and regions but also changes over time. In the final concluding section, I discuss the issue of women's right to gainful employment: first, as a matter of immediate survival for individual women and their families; secondly, as a matter, indirectly, of female mortality rates; thirdly, as a matter of women's status; and, finally, as a matter of human justice.

On a personal note, let me explain my background as a non-philosopher. I have worked for 20 years in India and Bangladesh. The focus of my concerns has been the economic status of poor women. I have sought through dialogue and action with poor women to identify the constraints to their full economic participation and productivity. In Bangladesh, I worked for the Bangladesh Rural Advancement Committee (BRAC), an indigenous private development agency. We developed a programme for women who, like Saleha Begum, needed to break out of enforced seclusion to enter the labour force. By providing training, credit, and extension services, we were able to enhance the productivity of women's traditional home-based work and to expand the range of women's activities outside their homes. My subsequent work with Oxfam America in India focused on women working as wage labourers, as home-based workers, and as vendors. In partnership with over 50 private development agencies, we developed a programme in support of women engaged in the urban informal sector and in several rural sectors. My current research on the economic status of widows in rural India has led me back full circle to the problems of secluded women, like Metha Bai, who must seek gainful employment outside their homes in order to provide for their children.

Martha Nussbaum (1993) characterized BRAC's style of operation as 'a combination of Aristotelian commitment to the human good with Aristotelian contextual sensitivity'. I would add that many of the indigenous private development agencies with which I have had the privilege to work share this style of operation. Committed to one or more human goods, such as women's right to gainful employment, they enter a participatory dialogue with local communities to seek appropriate and acceptable ways to promote these goods. Many are committed to women's right to employment because they have learned that most women from poor households need to earn in order, simply, to survive.

1 DEFYING TRADITION: WOMEN DEMAND EMPLOYMENT IN RURAL BANGLADESH

Until the recent past, when landlessness, poverty, and famine forced women to enter the labour markets, the sexual division of labour was more widely and uniformly enforced in Bangladesh than elsewhere in the region. Traditionally, most women in Bangladesh were physically confined to their homesteads or, if they needed to seek wage work, to the homesteads of others in their village. Most women did not work in the fields, even their own, or at construction sites; they did not go to markets, either to buy or sell. Women were effectively excluded from the public 'male' sphere of fields, markets, roads, and towns, and essentially confined to the private 'female' sphere of huts and homesteads. They were permitted to move about only at prescribed times and for prescribed purposes.

Purdah, which means, literally, 'curtain' or 'veil', is used figuratively to designate what is proper demeanour or behaviour for women, as opposed to what is improper (*bepurdah*). In its strictest form, *purdah* involves the seclusion of women within the boundaries of their homes and the veiling of women outside their homes. In a broader sense, *purdah* is used to designate what is 'appropriate' or 'respectable' work for women; what has been called 'occupational *purdah*' (Bardhan, 1985). The following story tells how women from poor and female-headed households in Bangladesh defied this occupational *purdah* to seek work.

From the end of June to early September 1974, Bangladesh suffered severe floods. Reports of starvation could be heard immediately following the flood, and grew in severity. The Government of Bangladesh officially declared famine in late September (Sen, 1981). From early October to late November, the government operated *langarkhanas* (gruel kitchens or free cooked-food distribution centres) to provide free food to destitute people

(Alamgir, 1980; Sen, 1981). Migrants from rural areas flooded the streets of Dhaka and other cities in search of food. Although by late November the famine was officially over, the effects of the famine dragged on.

One of the famine districts was Mymensingh in the north.[2] In late 1974, UNICEF staff visited the area and observed large numbers of women begging in Jamalpur town. In response, UNICEF decided to introduce an experimental food-for-work programme for women outside the town. They expected 100 women to participate: 840 joined the programme. The Jamalpur experience was symptomatic of a widespread problem: during and after the famine of 1974, large numbers of women had joined the ranks of those seeking wage labour opportunities. As late as November 1975, when the Government of Bangladesh (with international donor support) introduced food-for-work schemes throughout the country, women came forward in record numbers.

Bangladesh has a long history of food-for-work programmes in lean employment seasons and after floods or other crises, but the participation of women was a new phenomenon. The government was simply not prepared to accept women into its rural works programmes. Conditioned by tradition to believe women should not seek outside gainful employment, local officials regularly turned women back. Where they were recruited, women faced problems related to the work and payment norms.

In 1975, prompted by what we had seen and heard in Jamalpur, a group of women (of which I was one) began informally to meet and interview women at food-for-work sites in different parts of the country. That was when we met Saleha Begum. We found that the women faced two main problems: initially, many had been denied work; eventually, if they were employed, they were paid less than men. Because payments are tied to the amount of earth moved and because women in Bangladesh had no background in earth-work, women labourers consistently earned less than male labourers. We began to discuss these problems with responsible government and donor officials.

In March 1976 the Ministry of Relief and Rehabilitation requested advice on the integration of women into its food-for-work activities. The United Nation's World Food Programme formalized our 'ad hoc' group into an Advisory Committee on Women's Participation in Food-for-Work. The Committee's mandate was 'to advise an appropriate and effective means fully to integrate women into the food-for-work activities' (World Food Programme, 1977:1). After a number of field visits and numerous interviews with women labourers, the Committee, in a meeting with President Zia-ur-Rahman and his Cabinet, made two key recommendations:

---

[2] The 1974 famine was not due to a decline in food availability (indeed Mymensingh District enjoyed a substantial increase in output in 1974) but to a decline in wage employment and the rice-entitlement of wages (the floods came at the period of maximum wage employment in normal years). See Sen (1981).

that women be recruited in equal numbers as men and be paid the same as men (by adopting a separate work–payment norm for women). The President endorsed the recommendations and agreed to enforce them.

At a subsequent meeting with the donors involved in food-for-work programmes, there was a mixed reaction. Some donor representatives endorsed the recommendations and agreed to the specific policy measures required to promote women's equal participation and payment. Others were resistant to the recommendation of a separate work norm, arguing that women workers were generally supplementary, not primary, earners; that women should be able to lift and carry as much earth as men in a given time period; and that separate norms would encourage false entries in the work registers (i.e., that officials would list men workers as women workers in order to be allotted more wheat for specific schemes).

In response to these objections, the Advisory Committee asked two of us on the Committee to undertake a research study designed to determine the marital status, dependency ratio, work output, and energy requirements of women workers at food-for-work sites. With a team of investigators, we interviewed 303 women at 11 food-for-work sites in nine districts of Bangladesh. Fifty of this sample were selected for detailed life histories.

Our research revealed the following characteristics of women labourers (Chen and Ghuznavi, 1977). Women of all age groups worked at the sites. The vast majority were between 20 and 50 years of age. One-third were married. The husbands of most married women were either unable to earn or did not earn enough to meet family needs. Another third were widowed. The sons of most widows either could not be depended on as a source of support or did not earn enough to meet their own and their mother's needs. The remaining third were unmarried, deserted, or divorced. All came from households with insufficient male earnings to meet subsistence needs. Just under half (47%) were the principal income earners for their families. They averaged 3.7 dependants each. In brief, all the women, whether sole, primary, or supplementary earners in their families, worked because they had to.

One of the women we interviewed, a married woman with a disabled husband, evoked the frightening predicament of women forced to provide for their families when male support is withdrawn or proves insufficient:

One day, five years ago my husband returned home with a high fever, which continued unabated for six days, in spite of medication. After that he became bloated and doctors could not do anything to ease the condition. For the first time in my life, I knew what real fear was. I did all I could to get him the best medical care. I looked after him day and night but he did not get better. Today, he is still an invalid.

I was overwhelmed by my problem; I sold all our possessions to get my husband cured but it was not to be. We were faced with an impossible situation. My children were always hungry, there was never enough for them or for me and my husband.

I tried to get help from my brothers but by then no one's financial condition allowed them to offer any real help and I needed far too much.

So I decided that I would take the only recourse left to me. I would find work and support my family. And so I did. I accepted any kind of work I could find just so long as it helped us to survive. I have not been able to send my children to schools as before but there was nothing I could do about that. Today, I deeply regret not having learnt to weave from my husband.[3] I could have had a profession to see me through these difficult days—without always dreading whether I will have work tomorrow or whether my children will be crying in hunger?

When I first heard of earth-work I was hesitant about going for it. I was not sure I would be able to do those long hours or arduous work. Look at me today. I can not only do it but do it well. I earn enough wheat for my family's consumption. I even manage to save a little. It is not work that I am afraid of but the lack of work.   (Chen and Ghuznavi, 1980: 159–60)

The work output findings indicated that women, on average, moved 40 cubic feet of earth per day whereas men, on average, moved 70 cubic feet (Chen and Ghuznavi, 1977). To move these respective amounts of earth, taking average body weights into account, it was estimated that women would require 2,100 calories and men 3,000. A payment schedule for both sexes based only upon the male work norm would result in women receiving little more than half (57%) the wheat payment that men receive. Yet women's nutritional requirement would be over two-thirds (70%) that of men.

The research findings served to legitimize our earlier policy recommendations. Since 1976, the Government of Bangladesh and the responsible donors have promoted women's participation in food-for-work by recruiting female labourers more actively, by reserving separate areas or tasks at all sites for women, by operating all-women sites, and by adopting separate work–payment norms for women. In addition, special schemes for women, notably roadside tree-planting and road maintenance schemes, have been introduced.

Saleha's story has a happy ending. In early 1976, Saleha Begum and her co-workers were hired at a local food-for-work scheme. And, later that year, they were organized into a local women's group by BRAC. In every village where it works, BRAC organizes the poor into separate men's and women's groups. These groups not only are the beneficiaries of BRAC's programmes (in credit, enterprise development, health, and education) but also help shape the content and direction of these programmes and provide village-level cadre to help implement these programmes.

In 1977, Saleha's group, the Pachbarol Working Women's Group, collectively husked paddy for sale and cultivated potatoes and sugar cane on leased land. They leased four acres of land and purchased paddy seedlings

---

[3] Under the sexual division of labour in weaving communities in Bangladesh, men weave on the loom and women perform ancillary tasks, such as spinning and helping prepare the warp.

to transplant. They contracted two male relatives (including Saleha's husband) as their 'technical experts'. These men taught the women to broadcast and transplant paddy. When asked to describe the activities of her group, Saleha became animated: 'If we can handle livestock, surely we can transplant seedlings. Next year we will be able to perform all the agricultural tasks—including ploughing.'

Under her leadership, the women in Saleha's village took advantage of all that BRAC had to offer: they attended non-formal education classes; they negotiated loans; they received training in poultry rearing, fish culture, silkworm rearing, and agriculture; and they selected women from their group to be trained as paramedics, paraveterinarians, and paralegals. Eventually, Saleha Begum was elected to represent her women's group in the BRAC-organized local federation of women's and men's groups. A few years later, the federation nominated her as a candidate for local political office. Although she lost the local election, the fact that she did so by only a narrow margin was celebrated as a near-victory by the federation.

In retrospect, Saleha's victory at the food-for-work site was as significant as her near-victory in the local election. Saleha, her co-workers and the other women who demanded to be employed at food-for-work sites paved the way for countless other women to enter the labour force. They made 'visible' the plight of women in households where male incomes are insufficient to meet subsistence needs. They alerted national and international policy-makers to the economic contributions of women in such households and to the urgent need of such women for gainful employment.

Policy-makers in both the government and non-government sectors responded to this need. The government promoted large-scale wage employment of women through food-for-work programmes. By the late 1980s, over 95,000 women were being offered employment for more than 8.5 million womandays each year in two major food-for-work programmes. Two private development agencies, the Grameen Bank and BRAC, promoted the self-employment of women through rural credit. Between them, the Grameen Bank and BRAC have provided loans to over two million women. The women loanees have proved to be not only responsible loanees but also effective entrepreneurs, managing the day-to-day subsistence needs of their families.

Official estimates indicate that the female labour force rose threefold from 0.9 to 2.7 million between 1961 and 1985. A 1989 United Nation's study found that about 60% of landless and virtually 100% of female-headed households report female income earning activities either in wage work or self-employment (Safilios-Rothschild and Mahmud, 1989). Changes in the definition used to measure the size of the labour force and the participation of females account for some of this increase. However, the combined effect of increasing population, landlessness, and poverty and of expanded work opportunities for women account for most of this increase. Some credit for the increased work opportunities should go to the women, like Saleha, who first defied tradition and entered the wage labour market, thereby paving the way for others.

2 BOUND BY TRADITION: THE PLIGHT OF HIGH-CASTE WOMEN IN RURAL NORTH INDIA

As noted above, most communities in North India share a common patriarchal kinship system, which has direct implications for the condition of women in general and for the occupational options of women in particular. The major differences within this basic system are mediated by caste. These differences are particularly pronounced between the two poles of the caste hierarchy: at one end, the highly 'Sanskritized' upper castes; and, at the other, the so-called 'Untouchables' or lowest castes.

At the all-India level, the Hindu hierarchy of castes is traditionally divided into four groups or *varna*: Brahmin, Kshatriya, Vaishya, and Sudra. The first three *varna* are considered 'twice-born' or 'upper' castes; the fourth *varna* encompasses a large number of 'middle' castes. A fifth group of castes is regarded as 'untouchable' and outside the system. These untouchable or outcaste communities are commonly referred to as Harijans, the name given them by Mahatma Gandhi which means, literally, 'the children of God'.

At the local level, the reality is far more complex. Within any given area, there are innumerable, small, local caste groups called *jatis*. Mutual rank between these groups is vague, arguable, and alterable (Srinivas *et al.*, 1959: 138). For the purposes of this discussion, it is important to note that the caste system varies from region to region and that there is mobility within the system. That is, individual local castes can, and do, move up and down the social status hierarchy.

The social restrictions on the lifestyles of women tend to become more rigid as one moves *up* in the caste hierachy (Drèze, 1990: 52). Generally there is more seclusion of females in North India than in the South, and among upper castes and classes than among lower castes and classes (Miller, 1981: 780). Within upper caste communities in North India, women are often secluded and denied the right to gainful employment outside their homes. By contrast, lower caste women have greater freedom to take up gainful employment. Among the innumerable small local castes which constitute the vast 'middle' of the caste hierarchy, what is considered appropriate behaviour or work for women is closely linked with the family's position (ascribed or aspired) in the social-status hierarchy (Bardhan, 1985: 2207). As a means to acquiring status, those who can, follow upper caste norms in regard to women's lifestyles.

The striving for status differentiation is particularly strong in respect of the kind of work women are allowed to do.[4] So much so, that caste norms in regard to women's work can be taken as a symbol of caste rank. For instance, status-aspiring castes strive to have their women withdrawn from publicly visible manual labour, which is associated with low caste and tribal women (Bardhan, 1985: 2210). Given the preoccupation with status-appropriate work for women, villagers themselves often rank castes by whether they allow women to work:

only within their courtyards/homesteads,
only at their own farms,
only within the courtyards/homesteads of others,
only at the farms of others,
in other activities within their village,
in other activities outside their village.

Under this ranking scale, the more secluded the woman the higher her household's status or prestige.

In contemporary rural Bangladesh, as I noted above, the direction of change for women is dictated largely by the increasing rates of landlessness and poverty. So that, despite fairly uniform traditional norms against women's outside gainful employment, more and more women join the labour force each year. In contemporary rural North India, there is no single direction of change, especially among the innumerable small local caste groups in the middle regions of the caste hierarchy. In general, the highest status castes still confine women to their courtyards or homesteads; whereas the lowest status castes allow their women to engage in all types of wage work, including migrant wage work.[5] But among the middle caste groups, the norms regarding women's work are more fluid. In those households which suffer impoverishment or loss of male earnings, women often face *forced entry* into the labour markets. In those households which enjoy upward mobility, women often face *forced withdrawal* from the labour markets.

While the percentage of the population living in poverty has not decreased significantly, the numbers of households enjoying increased wealth has increased. As households acquire wealth or otherwise aspire to status, given rural India's preoccupation with caste and status, they often try to distance themselves from households perceived to be lower in social status and to imitate higher-status households. Different terms have been used to

[4] Other norms which are linked to the family's position in the social-status hierarchy include norms of marriage (and remarriage) and norms of female demeanour.
[5] This is not to say that upper caste and lower caste norms regarding women's work are immutable. In some upper caste households in rural India, especially those with an urbanized or 'Westernized' education, women are allowed to work at salaried jobs with status. And, a few lower castes in rural India have adopted upper caste norms and seclude their women (as will be discussed below).

denote this imitation of upper castes by lower castes. The most common term is 'Sanskritization', as certain Vedic or Sanskritic rites are confined to upper castes. The other common terms are 'Brahminization' (as Brahmins are most often imitated) and 'Rajputization' (as Rajput kings are also imitated).[6] The point here is not to argue for one or another term but to note the 'strength of the tendency to imitate and also the main direction of the tendency' (Dumont, 1980: 192).

Most social scientists have discussed this process in terms of how households imitate upper caste rituals and ceremonies in an attempt to achieve ritual distance from lower households. A few discuss the process in terms of how households imitate upper caste norms of marriage and norms regarding women: 'following the orthodox Brahmanical standards in child marriage, in the prohibition of widow remarriage, and in placing their women in seclusion' (Mandelbaum, 1948: 138). For women, this process of imitation has very specific implications: in particular, for the kind of work women are allowed to do. Generally, this process involves the *withdrawal* of women from the labour market.

But other processes are also at work in rural India. Not all households are able to imitate upper caste norms. Some are becoming poorer; others have remained poor. Current estimates vary, but as many as 42 per cent of households in rural India may have incomes below the poverty line (World Bank, 1989). And some households face the loss of male support. Again, current estimates vary. Census estimates using official definitions indicate that just under 10% of households in rural India are *de jure* headed by women (Visaria and Visaria, 1985). As Drèze points out, other studies, using more inclusive definitions, suggest that as many as 30 per cent of Indian households are *de facto* headed by women (Drèze, 1990).

A large number of women, especially female heads of households, are caught between the contradictory trends of Sanskritization, whereby caste norms confine them to their homesteads, and impoverishment or vulnerability, whereby they need to work in order to provide for their families. These include women from upper caste or status-aspiring but poor households. Particularly disadvantaged are women from upper caste or status-aspiring households with insufficient male support to meet subsistence needs, especially those who have suffered a recent sudden loss of male support. The plight of such women is acute because if they enter the labour

---

[6] The concept of 'Sanskritization' can be best presented in the words of M. N. Srinivas who popularized the concept: 'The caste system is far from a rigid system in which the position of each component caste is fixed for all time. Movement has always been possible, and especially so in the middle regions of the hierarchy. A low caste was able to rise to a higher position in the hierarchy by adopting vegetarianism and teetotalism, and by "Sanskritizing" its ritual and pantheon. In short, it took over as far as possible, the customs, rites and beliefs of the Brahmins, and the adoption of the Brahminical way of life by a low caste seems to have been frequent, though theoretically forbidden. This process has been called "Sanskritization" in this book, in preference to "Brahminization", as certain Vedic rites are confined to the Brahmins and the two other "twice-born" castes.' See Srinivas (1952: 30).

force they risk scorn, censure, and (sometimes) excommunication by their kin and caste groups, but if they do not enter the labour force they risk the welfare of their families.

The story of Metha Bai illustrates this predicament. Metha Bai was widowed two years before I met her, when she was 28. For three years prior to his death, her husband had been bed-ridden. Earlier, their two young daughters had died. Metha Bai was left with two young sons and a small parcel of land. Before his death, Metha Bai's husband and his brothers had separated their residences and partitioned their land. His mother lives with his younger brother. Metha Bai continues to live next to her in-laws but they offer no support or maintenance. Instead, they make her life miserable.

Metha Bai faces two major types of problems. First, caste norms which prohibit her from remarrying and from engaging in outside gainful employment. Before her husband's death, Metha Bai had not been allowed to work outside their homestead, not even to fetch water and fuel: her husband performed all outside chores. Now, she is forced to cultivate her share of land with the help of her father and to fetch water and fuel for herself and her sons. However, she is not allowed to engage in wage work or any gainful activities outside her home. As she expressed her predicament: 'I may die, but still I cannot go out. If there's something in the house, we eat. Otherwise, we go to sleep.'

Metha's second set of problems revolves around her relationship with her in-laws. Her mother-in-law, also widowed, has a fierce temper and reputation. After being widowed, she had several sexual partners and gave birth to a son out of wedlock. Metha Bai's husband used to quarrel regularly with his mother, as he was critical of her behaviour. Now, according to Metha Bai, her mother-in-law beats her and mistreats her sons. Both her mother-in-law and brothers-in-law have put pressure on Metha Bai to forego her claims on her husband's share of land and to leave the village. They will not let her contract a sharecropper to till her land. Allegedly, they forced Metha Bai to sell some of her jewellery to pay for the death ceremonies of her husband, and have taken some of her land and jewellery.

Metha Bai's only source of support is her father, now quite elderly. Her father helps her cultivate her share of land, using his own bullocks and plough which he must bring from his village as needed. He also brings regular gifts of food and clothing, whatever her parents can spare. Metha Bai is their eldest child; she has four younger brothers at home. Her constant refrain throughout my interview with her was: 'When my father dies, I will die.'

During the interview, Metha Bai was patching torn and used shorts and shirts for her two sons. Each item had been patched repeatedly. She used pulled threads from other used clothes and a large, twisted, rusty needle. Clearly, her situation is pathetic. She cannot afford the bus fare to visit her parents. When one of her sons fell ill and was taken to a hospital in Udaipur by her father, she could not afford the bus fare to visit him. And, clearly,

Metha Bai is deeply troubled and anxious. Throughout our interview, she kept looking over her shoulder to make sure her in-laws were not nearby. As she explained: 'My mind does not settle, I'm always upset. All day and night, for the last two years, I am always upset. I will just die.' When asked why she didn't return to her parental home to live, she had an immediate answer: 'My brothers will give me food and clothing, but will they give any rights to land or property to my sons? Here, my sons have some rights to land.'

Like other vulnerable upper caste women before her, Metha Bai will probably have to risk censure, abuse, and even disinheritance by her in-laws if she seeks work in order to feed her sons. She may begin by collecting and selling grass, fuelwood, cow dung cakes (trying to earn an income from the subsistence activities she has recently undertaken); she may move on to perform domestic services in other households; eventually she may work as an agricultural wage labourer. I have met other single upper caste women who have entered the wage labour market. They did so gradually, only after they recovered from the sudden loss of male support, took stock of their predicament, and then took the bold step of seeking gainful employment outside their homes.

It is important to note that the system of seclusion is being imitated not just by middle caste groups but also by lower castes and tribal groups. As part of their struggle to assert their ethnic identities, many tribal communities in which women have traditionally been free to engage in all types of work now pronounce the seclusion of women as part of their group heritage.[7] As part of their effort to raise their status, educated lower caste communities in some areas have begun to change their occupations and to seclude their women. For example, the Chandal caste in West Bengal encourages its men to become educated and seek salaried jobs, and, at least in one area, prohibits its women from working outside the home.[8]

Chobirani Prodhan is a young Chandal widow in Birbhum District, West Bengal. Jean Drèze interviewed her in 1988, three months after she was widowed:

When I met her in 1988, Chobi Prodhan had only been widowed for three months. She had four young daughters, and no sons. She and her children had subsisted since the death of her husband partly from the meagre produce of the half-acre of land they possess, and partly from a loan obtained from the local credit cooperative (they own no animals). But the future looked extremely bleak, and Chobi Prodhan was desperately anxious to find a means of surviving. Since her husband's death, she had not taken up wage labour, or any other kind of income-earning activity.

---

[7] Personal communication, Vina Mazumdar, Centre for Women's Development Studies (June 1991).

[8] Historically, the Chandals were depicted as 'outcast and helot people, performing menial duties for the Brahmans' (Risley, 1981: 183). As noted in a glossary of *The Tribes and Castes of West Bengal*, Census of 1951, among the Chandal community, 'a considerable number now follow the various so-called learned professions' (Government of India, 1951).

She laments, '*aami kicchu kam jaani na*', 'I don't know any work'. (Drèze, 1990: 82–3)

I interviewed Chobirani in early 1991, three years after she was widowed. In 1990, she sold her share of a local pond (*pukkur*) to marry one of her daughters. She is currently rearing a female calf on a sharecrop basis: in return for rearing the calf until its first delivery, she will be given one of its calves. Otherwise, her situation has not changed. For six months she and her remaining three daughters subsist off their share of harvest from their land; they have to take loans to meet their subsistence needs for the other six months of each year. When asked why she hasn't taken up any other economic activity, Chobirani explains that she was raised and educated in a nearby town, that she has few functional village skills, and that the Chandal caste elders discourage women from seeking outside work. Three years after her husband's death, she is still desperately anxious to find a means of survival.

In India, womens' employment has been a subject of growing interest both to social scientists and to policy-makers. However, the problems faced by a large female labour force have overshadowed the problems faced by secluded women. The public policy debate on women's work has centred on three broad sets of issues. First, the highly segmented labour markets in which women are typically relegated to low paying and insecure jobs. Secondly, exploitative relationships within given trades or industries which prevent women (and men) from realizing the full returns to their labour. And, thirdly, the failure of policy-makers to recognize women workers as legitimate clients of mainstream development programmes and policies. The patriarchal system of secluding women, which denies some women the right to gainful employment outside the home, has received comparatively less policy attention.

3   WOMEN'S RIGHT TO EMPLOYMENT

3.1. A Matter of Justice as well as Survival

As the preceding discussion has, I hope, illustrated, local traditions in regard to women's work and status are not uniform or unchanging in India and Bangladesh. Within the markedly hierarchical and patriarchal traditions of both countries, there has always been some room for mobility and manœuvring. As we have seen, change has often been initiated from below: by lower class or caste groups enabled by wealth or education to *imitate* upper caste-class norms or forced by impoverishment to *violate* upper caste-class norms.

It is important to note that change is also initiated and controlled from above: by upper classes and castes; by caste or village elders; by family patriarchs. The poor women with whom BRAC worked in Bangladesh often blamed the rich for dictating the norms that prohibited them from seeking work outside the village. Women at a BRAC-organized workshop described how the rich controlled their options:

Women work whole days in the homes of the rich: boiling paddy, drying paddy, cooking rice for them. In return, they are given only watery rice, boiled wheat or one quarter or half *seer* rice for a whole day's work.[9] They also have no fixed working hours which men have. The women start working early in the morning and until night . . . It is the village leaders' strategy to keep them working at low wages in their homes. If the women work outside, without *purdah*, then the rich people will not be able to advance credit to poor women at exhorbitant rates of interest. If the women work outside they might be economically better off . . . The rich in their own interest have made norms and laws. To suppress the poor, the rich, the *matbors* (village elders), and the *mullahs* (religious leaders) formulate religious policies and impose on them certain religious injunctions . . .   (Chen, 1983: 72–3)

In subsequent discussions with BRAC staff, I explored the women's line of analysis. I wanted to know how the rich managed to control the work options for women. What is at stake, the staff explained, is the definition of what is *purdah* (within the norms of *purdah*) and what is *bepurdah* (outside the norms of *purdah*). The rich and powerful in a village are able to adjust and change the norms of *purdah* to fit their convenience, as follows:

What is necessary for their wives to do is sanctioned as *purdah*. For example, if women from rich households need to go to the town to appear in court, even to remain in town for a few days, this is sanctioned as within the norms of *purdah*. When women from a BRAC-organized group want to go to town to attend a workshop or meeting, even for a single day, their action is condemned as *bepurdah*.   (Ibid.: 73)

In my recent interviews with widows in rural North India, many widows blamed caste elders and family patriarchs for limiting their options. When asked why they did not work outside their homes, many said they would either be 'excommunicated', 'disowned' or 'ostracized' by their husband's or their own family, kin, and caste. By excommunication, they meant they would be forced to leave the village in which they lived. By disowned, they meant they would be forced to give up their rightful shares to land or other property. By ostracized, they meant they would not be invited to attend any ceremonial, ritual, or social occasions. In contrast, some widows reported that their caste elders or in-laws, recognizing their need to work, had allowed them to seek work outside their home. Clearly, tradition is a human creation and the interpretation or enforcement of tradition is at some person's or some group's discretion: in many cases, at the discretion of the rich and powerful.

[9] A *seer* is a measure of weight equal approximately to two pounds.

3.2. A Matter of Immediate Survival

Women's right to gainful employment can be conceptualized and discussed from several perspectives: as a matter of immediate survival for individual women and their families; as a matter, indirectly, of female mortality rates; as a determinant of women's status; and as a matter of human justice. This paper has focused on individual women and the immediate needs of their families. As the paper suggests, women's right to gainful employment in India and Bangladesh is not a casual matter; it is a matter of immediate survival in many households.

There is growing evidence of the centrality of women's work and income in meeting the immediate day-to-day requirements of subsistence or survival. In poor households throughout the developing world, the welfare of individual women or their families is directly related to the ways women are allowed to earn an income. And current demographic and social trends suggest that increasing proportions of women throughout the developing world will bear the primary, if not sole, responsibility for the economic welfare of themselves and their children. Clearly, this feminization of poverty calls for policies which promote women's full economic participation and productivity.

3.3. A Matter of Female Mortality Rates

In recent years, some social scientists, notably Amartya Sen and Jean Drèze, have drawn attention to the importance of female participation in 'gainful' economic activity as a determinant of women's overall socio-economic status as well as their bargaining position within their families. In their book *Hunger and Public Action*, Drèze and Sen point out that 'there is considerable evidence that greater involvement with outside work and paid employment does tend to go with less anti-female bias in intra-family distribution'(Drèze and Sen, 1989: 58). They compare the ratios of 'economic activity rates' (roughly pertaining to outside work, including paid employment) of women *vis-à-vis* men, and the ratios of female life expectancy to male life expectancy (Ibid.: 59) (see Table 1). It turns out that the

Table 1 Activity-Rate Ratios and Life Expectancy Ratios, 1980

Regions	Activity-Rate Ratios (female–male)		Life Expectancy Ratios (female–male)	
	Values	Ranks	Values	Ranks
Non-Northern Africa Eastern and Southern	0.645	1	1.071	1
Eastern Asia	0.610	2	1.066	2
Western Asia	0.373	3	1.052	3
Southern Asia	0.336	4	0.989	5
Northern Africa	0.158	5	1.050	4

Source: Drèze and Sen (1989: 58).

ranking of the different regions in terms of life expectancy ratios is almost the same as that in terms of activity-rate ratios.

Within India, differentials in female and male workforce participation rates also seem to correlate with differential mortality rates of female and male infants and children. 'Across regions and communities in rural India, larger female participation in the generation of income or subsistence production is found to be associated with a more balanced sex-ratio in the population under age ten' (Bardhan, 1985: 2262). In her analysis of differences in sex ratios between North and South India, Barbara Miller reports a marked difference between North and South India in terms of women's involvement in 'outside' work and of juvenile sex ratios. Generally there is a lower female labour force participation rate and a less-balanced sex ratio in the North than in the South, and among upper castes and classes than among lower castes and classes.[10] As Miller concludes, where female labour force participation (FLP) is high 'there will *always* be high preservation of female life, but where FLP is low, female children may *or* may not be preserved' (Miller, 1981: 117).[11]

This correlation between the extent to which women work outside the home and the relative life expectancy of females requires further investigation and analysis. But, as Jonathan Glover has noted in his paper for this conference, 'it seems plausible that, in many communities in developing countries, the discouragement of women's paid work goes with favouring boys over girls in the provision of food and medical care, or with other kinds of female disadvantage' (Glover, 1991: 1). Given the plausibility of the correlation between women's gainful activity rates and women's life expectancy rates, the demand for women's right to work is not simply a demand for female autonomy or independence: it is, in all likelihood, a matter of female survival.

3.4. A Matter of Women's Status

It is important to recognize the broader value of gainful employment to women, outside the context of immediate survival. Engel's famous hypothesis that women's emancipation would come about with their full entry into

---

[10] According to the 1981 Census, about 27% of the women in four southern states were workers; the corresponding percentage in the Hindi-belt in the North was about 16%. See Nāgaraj (1991). According to the same Census, the sex ratio in the four southern states averaged 987 females to 1,000 males; the corresponding ratio in the Hindi-belt in the North was 923 females to 1,000 males (Government of India, 1991).

[11] For the region as a whole, the female-to-male sex ratios are some of the lowest in the world:

Pakistan	905 women to 1,000 males in 1986
India	929 women to 1,000 males in 1991
Bangladesh	940 women to 1,000 males in 1986

Sources: For Pakistan and Bangladesh, Drèze and Sen (1989). For India, Government of India (1991).

social production has been a subject of interest among feminists concerned with development issues, particularly in the Third World (Standing, 1985). Most feminists agree that women's right to gainful employment is a necessary, but not sufficient, precondition for women to achieve personal power and status in the public domain. This is particularly so if increased female labour force participation is accompanied by increased female earnings and by increased female control over income and the means of production.

Gainful employment outside the home, particularly as an independent wage or salaried worker, does, undeniably, affect the self-image and perceived value of women. It represents a means of escape from male control over female labour (particularly in peasant households). It represents a means of economic independence. It often leads to increased class, gender, and individual consciousness. It often serves to increase women's bargaining power and autonomy within the household. And it generally serves to increase the perceived value of women within the household and within society more broadly.

The right to gainful employment needs, therefore, in the context of this conference to be discussed as an important determinant of female *functioning*, as a basic female capability. But fundamental change for women cannot be based solely on increased labour force participation. The conditions under which women work must be *just*. Too many women, particularly in the Third World, work for low wages or under exploitative conditions. Some feminist theorists have identified collective action as a primary step for women in achieving *just employment* and justice more broadly (Sanday, 1974). Empirical support for this analysis is the impressive record of women's organizations in India which have organized women around economic concerns (Sebstad, 1982; Chen, 1989). Their achievements extend beyond increasing women's earnings and productivity, effecting changes in women's outlooks, or increasing their freedom within the family unit to enabling women to mobilize vital community resources, to gain a voice in local government, and to struggle for a just working environment (Bruce and Dwyer, 1988).

3.5. A Matter of Justice

Much has been written about the moral basis of subsistence relations in rural South Asia, particularly in terms of the reciprocal relations between castes in the caste hierarchy (Appadurai, 1984). Less has been written about the moral basis of gender relations within families. However, the literature on the joint family and on kinship relations reports that, under traditional patriarchy, women are to be maintained by their own families before marriage and by their husband's families after marriage.

And that widows are to be maintained by their husband's families or by grown sons.

Whether or to what degree South Asia's rural economy operated in a moral way in the past is open to question. But there is little question that, given the forces of modernization and the pressures of population growth, there has been an erosion of moral ties within (and between) caste and kin groups. As we have seen in the examples from India and Bangladesh, we can no longer assume that traditional family structures, which relegate women to domesticity and dependence, actually provide women with the supposed social security of that dependence. Indeed, the evidence suggests that increasing numbers of women receive little, if any, social security from traditional family structures and must act independently in order to provide for their families.

This reality poses a moral dilemma. Many women in rural South Asia appear to have been forced out of a situation in which they were maintained while remaining secluded into one in which they must remain at least partially secluded without being securely maintained. The demand that women be allowed to abandon seclusion and seek gainful employment outside the home should not be seen as an *outside challenge* to local culture and tradition but as a *local response* to changes in local culture and tradition.

As I hope this paper has shown, even within the shared patriarchal kinship system of Bangladesh and North India, tradition is not uniform or unchanging. There is significant variation across caste and class, even within individual villages, at any given point in time. And there is significant change across time. Tradition is a human creation subject to change. And it seems reasonable for insiders, but also outsiders, to demand change when local traditions put some members of local communities at risk. Given that women's need to earn is a matter of survival for many women and their households, especially in poor economies, it seems reasonable to propose that all women should have the right to gainful and just employment.

As Onora O'Neill (1993) argues, 'a serious account of justice cannot gloss over the predicaments of impoverished providers in marginalized and developing economies'. In this paper, I have discussed a predicament faced by many impoverished female providers in the Third World: that is, traditional cultural barriers to their equal participation in the workforce. Like Saleha Begum and Metha Bai, many women must break with tradition and act independently because they lack the security that tradition is supposed to offer. Under Martha Nussbaum's formulation of human capabilities (see 'Human Capabilities, Female Human Beings', in this volume), the opportunity for gainful employment would be seen as an essential human good, one of the basic human capabilities, without which a basic human life is often not possible. A serious account of justice should not, therefore, gloss over women's right to gainful and just employment.

BIBLIOGRAPHY

ALAMGIR, MOHIUDDIN (1980). *Famine in South Asia: Political Economy of Mass Starvation*. Cambridge, Mass.: Gunn and Hain.

APPADURAI, ARJUN (1984). 'How Moral is South Asia's Economy?—A Review Article', *Journal of Asian Studies*, XLII, 481–97.

BARDHAN, KALPANA (1985). 'Women's Work, Welfare and Status: Forces of Tradition and Change in India', *Economic and Political Weekly*, XX, Dec.

BOSERUP, ESTER (1970). *Woman's Role in Economic Development*. New York: St. Martin's Press.

BRUCE, JUDITH and DWYER, D. (1988). 'Introduction', in D. Dwyer and J. Bruce (eds.). *A Home Divided: Women and Income in the Third World*. Stanford: Stanford University Press.

CHEN, MARTHA (1983). *A Quiet Revolution: Women in Transition in Rural Bangladesh*. Cambridge, Mass.: Schenkman.

—— (1989). 'The Working Women's Forum: Organizing for Credit and Change in Madras, India', in Ann Leonard (ed.), *SEEDS: Supporting Women's Work in the Third World*. New York: Feminist Press.

CHEN, MARTHA and GHUZNAVI, R. (1977). *Women in Food for Work: The Bangladesh Experience*. Rome: World Food Programme.

—— (1980). 'Women in Bangladesh: Food-for-Work and Socio-Economic Change', in Alfred de Souza (ed.), *Women in Contemporary India and South Asia*. New Delhi: Manohar.

DRÈZE, JEAN (1990). *Widows in Rural India*. DEP Paper No. 26, Development Economics Research Programme. London: London School of Economics.

—— and SEN, A. K. (1989). *Hunger and Public Action*. Oxford: Clarendon Press.

DUMONT, LOUIS (1980). *Homo Hierarchicus: The Caste System and Its Implications*, trans. M. Sainsbury, L. Dumont, and B. Gulati. Chicago: University of Chicago Press.

GLOVER, JONATHAN (1991). 'Introduction to Conference on Human Capabilities: Women, Men, and Equality'. Paper prepared for the UNU/WIDER Conference on Human Capabilities: Women, Men and Equality. Helsinki: WIDER.

Government of India (1951). *Census Reports of India: West Bengal*. New Delhi: Government of India Publications.

—— (1991). *Census of India 1991: Provisional Population Tables*. New Delhi: Census Commission.

MANDELBAUM, DAVID G. (1948). 'The Family in India', *Southwestern Journal of Anthropology*, 4 (Summer).

MILLER, BARBARA D. (1981). *The Endangered Sex: Neglect of Female Children in Rural North India*. Ithaca: Cornell University Press.

NAGARAJ, K (1991). 'The "Missing" Women: The Declining Sex Ratio', *Frontline*, 25 May–7 June.

NUSSBAUM, MARTHA (1993). 'Non-Relative Virtues: An Aristotelian Approach', in *The Quality of Life*. Oxford: Clarendon Press.

O'NEILL, ONORA (1993). 'Justice, Gender and International Boundaries', in M. C. Nussbaum and A. Sen (eds.), *The Quality of Life*. Oxford: Clarendon Press.

RISLEY, H. H. (1981). *The Tribes and Castes of Bengal: Ethnographic Glossary*, vol. I. Calcutta: Firma Mukhopadhyay.

SAFILIOS-ROTHSCHILD, CONSTANTINA and MAHMUD, S. (1989). *Women's Roles in Agriculture—Present Trends and Potential for Growth*. Monograph for Agriculture Sector Review. Dhaka: UNDP and UNIFEM.

SANDAY, PEGGY R. (1974). 'Female Status in the Public Domain', in Michelle Rosaldo and Louise Lamphere (eds.), *Women, Culture, and Society*. Stanford: Stanford University Press.

SEBSTAD, JENNEFER (1982). *Struggle and Development Among Self-Employed Women: A Report on the Self-Employed Women's Association, Ahmedabad, India*. Office of Urban Development: Bureau for Development Support. Washington, DC: United States Agency for International Development.

SEN, AMARTYA K. (1981). *Poverty and Famines: An Essay on Entitlement and Deprivation*. Oxford: Clarendon Press.

—— (1990). 'Gender and Cooperative Conflicts', in Irene Tinker (ed.), *Persistent Inequalities: Women and World Development*. New York: Oxford University Press.

SRINIVAS, M. N. (1952). *Religion and Society Among the Coorgs of South India*. Oxford: Oxford University Press.

SRINIVAS, M. N., DAMLE, Y. B., SHAHANI, S., and BETEILLE, A. (1959). 'Caste: A Trend Report and Bibliography', *Current Sociology*, VIII.

STANDING, HILARY (1985). 'Resources, Wages, and Power: The Impact of Women's Employment on the Urban Bengali Household', in Haleh Afshar (ed.), *Women, Work, and Ideology in the Third World*. London: Tavistock Publications.

VISARIA, PRAVIN and VISARIA, L. (1985). 'Indian Households with Female Heads: Their Incidence, Characteristics and Level of Living', in D. Jain and N. Banerjee (eds.), *Tyranny of the Household: Investigative Essays on Women's Work*. New Delhi: Shakti Books, Vikas Publishing House.

World Bank (1989). *India: Poverty, Employment, and Social Services*. A World Bank Country Study. Washington, DC: The World Bank.

World Food Programme (1977). *Women in Food for Work: The Bangladesh Experience* (Note by the Executive Director). Interim Evaluation and Terminal Reports. Rome: World Food Programme.

PART II
WOMEN'S EQUALITY:
METHODOLOGY, FOUNDATIONS

Human Capabilities, Female Human Beings

Martha C. Nussbaum

Human beings are not by nature kings, or nobles, or courtiers, or rich. All are born naked and poor. All are subject to the miseries of life, to frustrations, to ills, to needs, to pains of every kind. Finally, all are condemned to death. That is what is really the human being; that is what no mortal can avoid. Begin, then, by studying what is the most inseparable from human nature, that which most constitutes humanness.

> Jean-Jacques Rousseau, *Emile*, Book IV

Women, a majority of the world's population, receive only a small share of developmental opportunities. They are often excluded from education or from the better jobs, from political systems or from adequate health care ... In the countries for which relevant data are available, the female human development index is only 60% that of males.

> *Human Development Report* 1993, United Nations Development Program

Were our state a pure democracy there would still be excluded from our deliberations women, who, to prevent depravation of morals and ambiguity of issue, should not mix promiscuously in gatherings of men.

> Thomas Jefferson

Being a woman is not yet a way of being a human being.

> Catharine MacKinnon

1 FEMINISM AND COMMON HUMANITY[1]

Begin with the human being: with the capacities and needs that join all humans, across barriers of gender and class and race and nation. To a person concerned with the equality and dignity of women, this advice should appear in one way promising. For it instructs us to focus on what all human beings share, rather than on the privileges and achievements of a

---

[1] The argument of this paper is closely related to that of several other papers of mine, to which I shall refer frequently in what follows: 'Nature, Function, and Capability', *Oxford Studies in Ancient Philosophy*, suppl. vol. 1 (1988), 145–84; 'Non-Relative Virtues: An Aristotelian Approach', *Midwest Studies in Philosophy* 13 (1988), 32–53, and, in an expanded version, in M. Nussbaum and A. Sen (eds.), *The Quality of Life* (Oxford: Clarendon Press, 1993), 242–76; 'Aristotelian Social Democracy', in R. B. Douglass, G. Mara, and H. Richardson (eds.), *Liberalism and the Good* (New York: Routledge, 1990), 203–52; 'Aristotle on Human Nature and the Foundations of Ethics', in *World, Mind, and Ethics: Essays on the Philosophy of Bernard Williams*, R. Harrison and J. Altham (eds.) (Cambridge: Cambridge University Press, 1995); 'Human Functioning and Social Justice: In Defense of Aristotelian Essentialism', *Political Theory* 20 (1992), 202–46.

dominant group, and on needs and basic functions, rather than power or status. Women have rarely been kings, or nobles, or courtiers, or rich. They have, on the other hand, frequently been poor and sick and dead.

But this starting point will be regarded with scepticism by many contemporary feminists. For it is all too obvious that throughout the history of political thought, both Western and non-Western, such allegedly-unbiased general concepts have served in various ways to bolster male privilege and to marginalize women. Human beings are not born kings, or nobles, or courtiers. They are, or so it seems,[2] born male and female. The nakedness on which Rousseau places such emphasis reveals a difference that is taken by Rousseau himself to imply profound differences in capability and social role. His remarks about human nature are the prelude to his account of Emile's education. Sophie, Emile's female companion, will be said to have a different 'nature' and a different education. Whether, as here, women are held to be bearers of a different 'nature' from unmarked 'human nature', or whether they are simply said to be degenerate and substandard exemplars of the same 'nature', the result is usually the same: a judgement of female inferiority, which can then be used to justify and stabilize oppression.[3]

I shall argue nonetheless that we should in fact begin with a conception of the human being and human functioning in thinking about women's equality in developing countries. This notion can be abused. It can be developed in a gender-biased way. It can be unjustly and prejudicially applied. It can be developed in ways that neglect relevant differences among women of different nationalities, classes, and races. But I shall argue that, articulated in a certain way (and I shall be emphatically distinguishing my approach from others that use an idea of 'human nature') it is our best starting point for reflection. It is our best route to stating correctly what is wrong with the situations that confronted Saleha Begum and Metha Bai,[4] the best basis for claims of justice on their behalf, and on behalf of the huge

[2] By this I mean that the difference in external genitalia figures in social life as it is interpreted by human cultures; thus we are never dealing simply with facts given at birth, but always with what has been made of them (see below, section 8 for discussion of the role of culture in biological claims about male/female differences). Thus, even the common distinction between 'gender', a cultural concept, and 'sex', the allegedly pure biological concept, is inadequate to capture the depth of cultural interpretation in presenting even the biological 'facts' to human beings, from the very start of a child's life. See Anne Fausto-Sterling, *Myths of Gender* (2nd edn., New York: Basic Books, 1992). I have discussed these issues further in 'Constructing Love, Desire, and Care', forthcoming in D. Estlund and M. Nussbaum (eds.), *Laws and Nature: Shaping Sex, Preference, and Family* (Oxford University Press).

[3] For a historical argument along these lines from the history of Western scientific thought, see Thomas Laqueur, *Making Sex* (Berkeley and Los Angeles: University of California Press, 1989). The papers in this volume by Amartya Sen, Xiaorong Li, and Roop Rekha Verma show that the use of ideas of nature to convey a false sense of appropriateness, 'justifying' unjust practices, is by no means confined to the Western tradition.

[4] See Martha Chen's paper in this volume.

numbers of women in the world who are currently being deprived of their full 'human development'.

I note that the concept of the human being has already been central to much of the best feminist and internationalist thinking. Consider, for example, J. S. Mill's remarks on 'human improvement' in *The Subjection of Women*; Amartya Sen's use of a notion of 'human capability' to confront gender-based inequalities; the Sen-inspired use of a notion of 'human development' in the UN Report to describe and criticize gender-based inequalities; Susan Moller Okin's proposal for a 'humanist justice' in her recent major work of feminist political theory; Catharine MacKinnon's graphic description of women's current situation, quoted as my epigraph; and, of course, the role that various accounts of 'human rights', or even 'The Rights of Man' have played in claiming justice for women.[5] Much the same can be said more generally, I think, about internationalist thought.[6] To cite just one example, I take my proposal to be the feminist analogue of the proposal recently made by Ghanaian philosopher Kwame Anthony Appiah when he wrote, 'We will only solve our problems if we see them as human problems arising out of a special situation, and we shall not solve them if we see them as African problems, generated by our being somehow unlike others.'[7]

My proposal is frankly universalist and 'essentialist'. That is, it asks us to focus on what is common to all, rather than on differences (although, as we shall see, it does not neglect these), and to see some capabilities and functions as more central, more at the core of human life, than others. Its primary opponents on the contemporary scene will be 'anti-essentialists' of various types, thinkers who urge us to begin not with sameness but with difference—both between women and men and across groups of women—and to seek norms defined relatively to a local context and locally held beliefs.[8] This opposition takes many forms, and I shall be responding to several distinct objections that opponents may bring against my universalist

[5] J. S. Mill, *The Subjection of Women* (Indianapolis: Bobbs Merrill, 1988); Amartya Sen, 'Gender and Cooperative Conflicts', in I. Tinker (ed.), *Persistent Inequalities* (New York: Oxford University Press, 1990); 'Gender Inequality and Theories of Justice' in this volume and 'More Than a Million Women are Missing', *New York Review of Books: Human Development Report 1993*, for the United Nations Development Programme (UNDP) (New York and Oxford: Oxford University Press, 1993); Susan Moller Okin, *Justice, Gender, and the Family* (New York: Basic Books, 1989), see my review of Okin, 'Justice for Women', *New York Review of Books* October 1992; Catharine MacKinnon, remark cited by Richard Rorty in 'Feminism and Pragmatism', *Michigan Quarterly Review* 30 (1989), 263. MacKinnon has since acknowledged the remark.

[6] For a compelling argument linking feminism and internationalism, see Onora O'Neill, 'Justice, Gender, and International Boundaries', in M. Nussbaum and A. Sen (eds.), *The Quality of Life*, 303–23.

[7] Kwame Anthony Appiah, *In My Father's House: Africa in the Philosophy of Culture* (New York and Oxford: Oxford University Press, 1992), 136.

[8] On the other hand, it is closely related to Kantian approaches using the universal notion of personhood. See, for example, Onora O'Neill, 'Justice, Gender, and International Bound-

proposal. But I can begin to motivate my enterprise by telling several true stories of conversations that have taken place at WIDER, in which the relativist position[9] seemed to have alarming implications for women's lives. I have in some cases conflated two separate conversations into one; otherwise things happened as I describe them.[10]

1. At a conference on 'Value and Technology', an American economist who has long been a left-wing critic of neoclassical economics delivers a paper urging the preservation of traditional ways of life in a rural area of India, now under threat of contamination from Western development projects. As evidence of the excellence of this rural way of life, he points to the fact that, whereas we Westerners experience a sharp split between the values that prevail in the workplace and the values that prevail in the home, here, by contrast, there exists what the economist calls 'the embedded way of life'; the same values obtaining in both places. His example: just as in the home a menstruating woman is thought to pollute the kitchen and therefore may not enter it, so too in the workplace a menstruating woman is taken to pollute the loom and may not enter the room where looms are kept. Amartya Sen objects that this example is repellant, rather than admirable: surely such practices both degrade the women in question and inhibit their freedom. The first economist's collaborator, an elegant French anthropologist (who would, I suspect, object violently to a purity check at the seminar room door), replies to Sen. Doesn't he realize that there is, in these matters, no privileged place to stand? This, after all, has been shown by both Derrida and Foucault. Doesn't he know that he is neglecting the

aries', with my commentary (324–35). In the present volume, see the papers of Onora O'Neill, Ruth Anna Putnam, and Roop Rekha Verma. Below I shall be making some criticisms of the concept of 'person' in feminist argument, and related criticisms of liberal Kantian approaches (on which see also ASD and my review of Okin). But these differences are subtle and take place against a background of substantial agreement. See also David Crocker, 'Functioning and Capability: The Foundation of Sen's and Nussbaum's Development Ethics', *Political Theory* 20 (1992), 584 ff.

[9] By relativism, I mean the view that the only available criterion of adjudication is some local group or individual. Thus relativism, as I understand it, is a genus of which the brand of reliance on individuals' subjective preferences frequently endorsed in neoclassical economics is one species. (Economists, of course, are relativist only about value, not about what they construe as the domain of scientific 'fact'.) This affinity will later be relevant to my comments on the Marglin project. My opponents also frequently employ the term 'postmodernist' to characterize their position: this is a vaguer term, associated in a very general way with the repudiation of both metaphysical realism (to be defined below) and universalism.

[10] Much of the material described in these examples is now published in *Dominating Knowledge: Development, Culture, and Resistance*, F. A. Marglin and S. A. Marglin (eds.) (Oxford: Clarendon Press, 1990). The issue of 'embeddedness' and menstruation taboos is discussed in S. A. Marglin, 'Losing Touch: The Cultural Conditions of Worker Accommodation and Resistance', 217–82, and related issues are discussed in S. A. Marglin, 'Toward the Decolonization of the Mind', 1–28. On Sittala Devi, see F. A. Marglin, 'Smallpox in Two Systems of Knowledge', 102–44; and for related arguments see Ashis Nandy and Shiv Visvanathan, 'Modern Medicine and Its Non-Modern Critics', 144–84.

otherness of Indian ideas by bringing his Western essentialist values into the picture?[11]

2. The same French anthropologist now delivers her paper. She expresses regret that the introduction of smallpox vaccination to India by the British eradicated the cult of Sittala Devi, the goddess to whom one used to pray in order to avert smallpox. Here, she says, is another example of Western neglect of difference. Someone (it might have been me) objects that it is surely better to be healthy rather than ill, to live rather than to die. The answer comes back: Western essentialist medicine conceives of things in terms of binary oppositions: life is opposed to death, health to disease.[12] But if we cast away this binary way of thinking, we will begin to comprehend the otherness of Indian traditions.

At this point Eric Hobsbawm, who has been listening to the proceedings in increasingly uneasy silence, rises to deliver a blistering indictment of the traditionalism and relativism that prevail in this group. He lists historical examples of ways in which appeals to tradition have been used to support oppression and violence.[13] His final example is that of National Socialism in Germany. In the confusion that ensues, most of the relativist social scientists—above all those from far away, who do not know who Hobsbawm is— demand that he be asked to leave the room. The radical American economist, disconcerted by this apparent tension between his relativism and his affiliation with the left, convinces them, with difficulty, to let Hobsbawm remain.

[11] For Sen's own account of the plurality and internal diversity of Indian values, one that strongly emphasizes the presence of a rationalist and critical strand in Indian traditions, see M. Nussbaum and A. Sen, 'Internal Criticism and Indian Relativist Traditions', in M. Krausz (ed.), *Relativism* (Notre Dame, Ind.: Notre Dame University Press, 1989)—a paper originally presented at the same WIDER conference and refused publication by the Marglins in its proceedings; and 'India and the West', *The New Republic*, 7 June 1993.

[12] S. A. Marglin, in 'Toward the Decolonization', 22–3, suggests that binary thinking is peculiarly Western. But such oppositions are pervasive in all traditions with which I have any acquaintance: in the *Upanishads*, for example (see the epigraph to 'Human Functioning'), in Confucian thought (see, again, the epigraph to 'Human Functioning'), in Ibo thought (see, for many examples, Chinua Achebe's *Things Fall Apart* (London: William Heinemann, 1958)). Critics of such oppositions have not explained how one can speak coherently without bouncing off one thing against another. I believe that Aristotle was right to hold that to say anything at all one must rule out something, at the very least the contradictory of what one puts forward. The arguments of Nietzsche, which are frequently put forward as if they undermine all binary oppositions, actually make far more subtle and concrete points about the origins of certain oppositions, and the interests served by them.

[13] See E. Hobsbawm and T. Ranger (eds.), *The Invention of Tradition* (Cambridge: Cambridge University Press, 1983). In his *New Republic* piece, Sen makes a similar argument about contemporary India: the Western construction of India as mystical and 'other' serves the purposes of the fundamentalist BJP, who are busy refashioning history to serve the ends of their own political power. An eloquent critique of the whole notion of the 'other', and of the associated 'nativism', where Africa is concerned, can be found in Appiah (above n. 7), especially in the essays 'The Postcolonial and the Postmodern', 137–57 and 'Topologies of Nativism', 47–72.

3. We shift now to another conference two years later, a philosophical conference organized by Amartya Sen and me.[14] Sen makes it clear that he holds the perhaps unsophisticated view that life is opposed to death in a very binary way, and that such binary oppositions can and should be used in development analysis. His paper[15] contains much universalist talk of human functioning and capability; he begins to speak of freedom of choice as a basic human good. At this point he is interrupted by the radical economist of my first story, who insists that contemporary anthropology has shown that non-Western people are not especially attached to freedom of choice. His example: a new book on Japan has shown that Japanese males, when they get home from work, do not wish to choose what to eat for dinner, what to wear, etc. They wish all these choices to be taken out of their hands by their wives. A heated exchange follows about what this example really shows. I leave it to your imaginations to reconstruct it. In the end, the confidence of the radical economist is unshaken: Sen and I are both victims of bad universalist thinking, who fail to respect 'difference'.[16]

Here we see the relativist position whose influence in development studies motivated the work that has led to the present volume. The phenomenon is an odd one. For we see here highly-intelligent people, people deeply committed to the good of women and men in developing countries, people who think of themselves as progressive and feminist and anti-racist, people who correctly argue that the concept of development is an evaluative concept requiring normative argument[17]—effectively eschewing normative argument and taking up positions that converge, as Hobsbawn correctly saw, with the positions of reaction, oppression, and sexism. Under the banner of their fashionable opposition to 'essentialism' march ancient religious taboos, the luxury of the pampered husband, educational deprivation, unequal health care, and premature death. (And in my own universalist Aristotelian way, I say it at the outset, I do hold that death is opposed to life in the most binary way imaginable, and freedom to slavery,

[14] The proceedings of this conference are now published as Nussbaum and Sen (eds.), *The Quality of Life* (n. 1 above).

[15] 'Capability and Well-Being,' in Nussbaum and Sen, 30–53.

[16] Marglin has since published this point in 'Toward the Decolonization', His reference is to Takeo Doi, *The Anatomy of Dependence* (Tokyo: Kedansho, 1971). On women and men in Japan, See *Human Development Report 1993*, 26: 'Japan, despite some of the world's highest levels of human development, still has marked inequalities in achievement between men and women. The 1993 human development index puts Japan first. But when the HDI is adjusted for gender disparity, Japan slips to number 17 ... Women's average earnings are only 51% those of men, and women are largely excluded from decision-making positions ... Their representation is even lower in the political sphere ... In legal rights in general, Japan's patrilineal society is only gradually changing to offer women greater recognition and independence. Japan now has political and non-governmental organizations pressing for change ...' The question of freedom of choice is thus on the agenda in Japan in a large way, precisely on account of the sort of unequal functioning vividly illustrated in Marglin's example, where menial functions are performed by women, in order that men may be free to perform their managerial and political functions.

[17] See S. A. Marglin, 'Toward the Decolonization'.

and hunger to adequate nutrition, and ignorance to knowledge. Nor do I believe that it is only, or even primarily, in Western thinking that such oppositions are, and should be, important.)

The relativist challenge to a universal notion of the human being and human functioning is not always accompanied by clear and explicit philosophical arguments. This is especially true in the material from development studies to which I have referred, where the philosophical debate concerning relativism in ethics and in science is not confronted, and universalism is simply denounced as the legacy of Western conceptions of *'episteme'*[18] that are alleged to be in league with imperialism and oppression.[19] The idea behind this volume as a whole was that to sort out various strands in the philosophical debate on these questions would be of the first importance in making further progress on women's issues; and the papers by Alcoff, Benhabib, Glover, and Hilary Putnam carry out various aspects of this anti-relativist project. Here, then, I shall simply set out rather schematically and briefly, for the purposes of my own argument, several objections to the use of a universal notion of human functioning in development analysis to which I shall later respond.

2 THE ASSAULT ON UNIVERSALISM

Many critics of universalism in ethics are really critics of metaphysical realism who assume that realism is a necessary basis for universalism. I shall

---

[18] See S. A. Marglin, 'Losing Touch'. I put the term in quotes to indicate that I am alluding to Marglin's use of the term, not to the concept as I understand it.

[19] See S. A. Marglin, 'Toward the Decolonization' and 'Losing Touch'. Similar claims are common in feminist argument. For example, in *The Feminist Theory of the State* (Cambridge, Mass.: Harvard University Press, 1989), Catharine MacKinnon argues that 'objectivity' as traditionally conceived in the Western epistemological tradition is causally linked to the objectification and abuse of women. This line of argument is effectively criticized in Louise M. Antony, 'Quine as Feminist: The Radical Import of Naturalized Epistemology', in L. M. Antony and C. Witt (eds.), *A Mind of One's Own: Feminist Essays on Reason and Objectivity* (Boulder, Colo.: Westview Press, 1992), 185–225. See also the detailed examination of MacKinnon's argument in the same volume by Sally Haslanger, in 'On Being Objective and Being Objectified', 85–125. MacKinnon's fundamental contributions in the areas of sexual harassment and pornography do not depend on this analysis, and are actually undermined by it. The core of her thought actually reveals a strong commitment to a type of ethical universalism, as my epigraph indicates. See, in the Antony volume, the persuasive analysis by Liz Rappaport, 'Generalizing Gender: Reason and Essence in the Legal Thought of Catharine MacKinnon', 127–43. Alcoff's contribution in the present volume continues the debate about feminism and reason; and see also L. Alcoff and E. Potter (eds.), *Feminist Epistemologies* (New York: Routledge 1993). For a healthy scepticism about the role of 'anti-essentialism' within feminism, see Seyla Benhabib, 'Feminism and the Question of Postmodernism', in *Situating the Self: Gender, Community, and Postmodernism in Contemporary Ethics* (New York: Routledge, 1992), 203–42; Sabina Lovibond, 'Feminism and Postmodernism', *New Left Review*, 178 (November–December 1989), 5–28; Val Moghadam, 'Against Eurocentrism and Nativism', *Socialism and Democracy*, fall/winter (1989: 81–104); Moghadam, *Gender, Development, and Policy: Toward Equity and Empowerment*, UNU/WIDER Research for Action series, November (1990).

argue that this assumption is false. By metaphysical realism I mean the view (commonly held in both Western and non-Western philosophical traditions) that there is some determinate way the world is, apart from the interpretive workings of the cognitive faculties of living beings. Far from requiring technical metaphysics for its articulation, this is a very natural way to view things, and is in fact a very common daily-life view, in both Western and non-Western traditions. We did not make the stars, the earth, the trees: they are what they are there outside of us, waiting to be known. And our activities of knowing do not change what they are.

On such a view, the way the human being essentially and universally is will be part of the independent furniture of the universe, something that can in principle be seen and studied independently of any experience of human life and human history. Frequently it is held that a god or gods have this sort of knowledge, and perhaps some wise humans also. This knowledge is usually understood to have normative force. The heavenly account of who we are constrains what we may legitimately seek to be.[20] It is this conception of inquiry into the nature of the human that the Marglins are attacking in their critique of what they call Western *episteme*. They clearly believe it to be a necessary prop to any ethical universalism.

The common objection to this sort of realism is that such extra-historical and extra-experiential metaphysical truths are not in fact available. Sometimes this is put sceptically: the independent structure may still be there, but we cannot reliably grasp it. More often, today, doubt is cast on the coherence of the whole realist idea that there is some one determinate structure to the way things are, independent of all human interpretation. This is the objection that non-philosophers tend to associate with Jacques Derrida's assault on the 'metaphysics of presence',[21] which he takes to have dominated the entirety of the Western philosophical tradition, and with Richard Rorty's closely related assault on the idea that the knowing mind is, at its best, a 'mirror of nature'.[22] But it actually has a far longer and more complicated history, even within Western philosophy, beginning at least as early as Kant's assault on transcendent metaphysics, and perhaps far earlier, in some of Aristotle's criticisms of Platonism.[23] A similar debate was long familiar in classical Indian philosophy, and no doubt it has figured in

[20] For an account of this sort of normative argument, see Alasdair MacIntyre, *After Virtue* (Notre Dame, Ind.: Notre Dame University Press, 1989).

[21] J. Derrida, *Of Grammatology*, trans. G. Spivak (Baltimore: The Johns Hopkins University Press, 1976). The term is meant to suggest the idea that reality is simply 'there' and that knowledge consists in being 'present' to it, without any interfering barrier or mediation.

[22] R. Rorty, *Philosophy and the Mirror of Nature* (Princeton, NJ: Princeton University Press, 1979).

[23] See, for example, G. E. L. Owen, '*Tithenai ta Phainomena*', in *Logic, Science, and Dialectic* (London: Duckworth, 1986), and M. Nussbaum, *The Fragility of Goodness: Luck and Ethics in Greek Tragedy and Philosophy* (Cambridge: Cambridge University Press, 1986). See also Hilary Putnam, *Aristotle After Wittgenstein*, Lindlay Lecture, University of Kansas, 1991.

other philosophical traditions as well.[24] Contemporary arguments about realism are many and complex, involving, frequently, technical issues in the philosophy of science and the philosophy of language.

The debate about realism appears to be far from over. The central issues continue to be debated with vigour and subtlety, and a wide range of views is currently on the table. On the other hand, the attack on realism has been sufficiently deep and sufficiently sustained that it would appear strategically wise for an ethical and political view that seeks broad support not to rely on the truth of metaphysical realism, if it can defend itself in some other way. If, then, all universalist and humanist conceptions in ethics are required to regard the universal conception of the human being as part of the independent furniture of the world, unmediated by human self-interpretation and human history, such conceptions do appear to be in some difficulty, and there may well be good reasons to try to do without them.

But universalism does not require such support.[25] For universal ideas of the human do arise within history and from human experience, and they can ground themselves in experience. Indeed, if, as the critics of realism allege, we are always dealing with our own interpretations anyhow, they must acknowledge that universal conceptions of the human are prominent and pervasive among such interpretations, hardly to be relegated to the dustbin of metaphysical history along with rare and recondite philosophical entities such as the Platonic forms. As Aristotle so simply puts it, 'One may observe in one's travels to distant countries the feelings of recognition and affiliation that link every human being to every other human being.'[26] Or, as Kwame Anthony Appiah eloquently tells the story of his bicultural childhood, a child who visits one set of grandparents in Ghana and another in rural England, who has a Lebanese uncle and who later, as an adult, has nieces and nephews from more than seven different nations, comes to notice not unbridgeable alien 'otherness', but a great deal of human

---

[24] See the illuminating discussion in B. K. Matilal, *Perception* (Oxford: Clarendon Press, 1985). It is worth noting that this fundamental work is not cited anywhere in Marglin and Marglin, although Matilal was present at the conference and delivered a paper critical of the Marglins' characterization of Indian traditions. This paper was dropped from the volume. Matilal also described the implications of the realism debate for Indian ethical thought: see 'Ethical Relativism and the Confrontation of Cultures', in Krausz (ed.), *Relativism* (Notre Dame, Ind.: Notre Dame University Press, 1989), 339–62.

[25] There is a longer version of my criticism of contemporary attacks on universalism in 'Human Functioning'. See also 'Skepticism About Practical Reason in Literature and the Law', *Harvard Law Review* 107 (1994), 714–44. In both of these papers I study the surprising convergence between 'left' and 'right' in the critique of normative argument, the 'postmodern' positions of many thinkers on the left proving, often, difficult to distinguish from claims about the arbitrariness of evaluation in neoclassical economics. In Barbara Herrnstein Smith's *Contingencies of Value* (Durham: Duke University Press, 1988), we even see a fusion of the two positions, a postmodernism concluding that, in the absence of transcendent standards, we should understand value judgements as attempts to maximize expected utility.

[26] Aristotle, *Nicomachean Ethics* VIII.I, 1155a 21–2. I discuss this passage in 'Aristotle on Human Nature' and 'Non-Relative Virtues'.

commonality, and comes to see the world as a 'network of points of affinity'.[27] Pursuing those affinities, one may accept the conclusions of the critics of realism, while still believing that a universal conception of the human being is both available to ethics and a valuable starting point. I shall be proposing a version of such an account, attempting to identify a group of especially central and basic human functions that ground these affinities.

But such an experiential and historical universalism[28] is still vulnerable to some, if not all, of the objections standardly brought against universalism. I therefore need to introduce those objections, and later to test my account against them.

2.1. Neglect of Historical and Cultural Differences

The opposition charges that any attempt to pick out some elements of human life as more fundamental than others, even without appeal to a transhistorical reality, is bound to be insufficiently respectful of actual historical and cultural differences. People, it is claimed, understand human life and humanness in widely different ways: and any attempt to produce a list of the most fundamental properties and functions of human beings is bound to enshrine certain understandings of the human and to demote others. Usually, the objector continues, this takes the form of enshrining the understanding of a dominant group at the expense of minority understandings. This type of objection is frequently made by feminists, and can claim support from many historical examples, in which the human has indeed been defined by focusing on the characteristics of males, as manifested in the definer's culture.

---

[27] K. A. Appiah, *In My Father's House*, pp. vii–viii: 'If my sisters and I were "children of two worlds", no one bothered to tell us this; we lived in one world, in two "extended" families divided by several thousand miles and an allegedly insuperable cultural distance that never, so far as I can recall, puzzled or perplexed us much.' Appiah's argument does not in any sense neglect distinctive features of concrete histories; indeed, one of its purposes is to demonstrate how varied, when concretely seen, histories really are. But his argument, like mine, seeks a subtle balance between perception of the particular and recognition of the common. In his essay 'The Postcolonial and the Postmodern' (137–57), Appiah shows that it is all too often the focus on 'otherness' that produces a lack of concrete engagement with individual lives. Speaking of the sculpture 'Yoruba Man with Bicycle' that appears on the cover of the book, Appiah comments: 'The *Man with a Bicycle* is produced by someone who does not care that the bicycle is the white man's invention—it is not there to be Other to the Yoruba Self; it is there because someone cared for its solidity; it is there because it will take us further than our feet will take us . . .' (157).

[28] In this category, as closely related to my own view, I would place the 'internal–realist' conception of Hilary Putnam articulated in *Reason, Truth, and History* (Cambridge: Cambridge University Press, 1981), *The Many Faces of Realism* (La Salle: Open Court Publishing, 1987), and *Realism With a Human Face* (Cambridge, Mass.: Harvard University Press, 1990); and also the views of Charles Taylor, for example in *Sources of the Self: The Making of Modern Identity* (Cambridge, Mass.: Harvard University Press, 1989), and 'Explanation and Practical Reason', in Nussbaum and Sen (eds.), *The Quality of Life*, 208–31.

It is far from clear what this objection shows. In particular it is far from clear that it supports the idea that we ought to base our ethical norms, instead, on the current preferences and the self-conceptions of people who are living what the objector herself claims to be lives of deprivation and oppression.[29] But it does show at least that the project of choosing one picture of the human over another is fraught with difficulty, political as well as philosophical.

2.2. Neglect of Autonomy

A different objection is presented by liberal opponents of universalism; my relativist opponents, the Marglins, endorse it as well. (Many such objectors, though not, I believe, the Marglins, are themselves willing to give a universal account of the human in at least some ways, holding freedom of choice to be everywhere of central importance.) The objection is that by determining in advance what elements of human life have most importance, the universalist project fails to respect the right of people to choose a plan of life according to their own lights, determining what is central and what is not.[30] This way of proceeding is 'imperialistic'. Such evaluative choices must be left to each citizen. For this reason, politics must refuse itself a determinate theory of the human being and the human good.

2.3. Prejudicial Application

If we operate with a determinate conception of the human being that is meant to have some normative moral and political force, we must also, in applying it, ask which beings we shall take to fall under the concept. And here the objector notes that, all too easily—even if the conception itself is equitably and comprehensively designed—the powerless can be excluded. Aristotle himself, it is pointed out, held that women and slaves were not full-fledged human beings; and since his politics were based on his view of human functioning, the failure of these beings (in his view) to exhibit the desired mode of functioning contributed to their political exclusion and oppression.

It is, once again, hard to know what this objection is supposed to show. In particular, it is hard to know how, if at all, it is supposed to show that we

---

[29] In this sense I am thoroughly in agreement with Susan Okin's reply to the charge of 'substitutionalism' that has been made against her book, and in agreement with both Okin and Ruth Anna Putnam that it is a mistake to conceive of the moral point of view as constituted by the actual voices of all disadvantaged parties, see Okin's and Putnam's papers in this volume. See my further comments below, Section 5.

[30] Can the Marglins consistently make this objection while holding that freedom of choice is just a parochial Western value? It would appear not; on the other hand, F. A. Marglin (here differing, I believe, from S. A. Marglin) also held in oral remarks delivered at the 1986 conference that logical consistency is simply a parochial Western value.

would be better off without such determinate universal concepts. For it could be plausibly argued that it would have been even easier to exclude women and slaves on a whim if one did not have such a concept to contend with. Indeed, this is what I shall be arguing.[31] On the other hand, it does show that we need to think not only about getting the concept right but also about getting the right beings admitted under the concept.

Each of these objections has some merit. Many universal conceptions of the human being have been insular in an arrogant way, and neglectful of differences among cultures and ways of life. Some have been neglectful of choice and autonomy. And many have been prejudicially applied. But none of this shows that all such conceptions must fail in one or more of these ways. But at this point I need to advance a definite example of such a conception, in order both to display its merits and to argue that it can in fact answer these charges.

3 A CONCEPTION OF THE HUMAN BEING: THE CENTRAL HUMAN CAPABILITIES

Here, then, is a sketch for an account of the most important functions and capabilities of the human being, in terms of which human life is defined. The basic idea is that we ask ourselves, 'What are the characteristic activities[32] of the human being? What does the human being do, characteristically, as such—and not, say, as a member of a particular group, or a particular local community?' To put it another way, what are the forms of activity, of doing and being, that constitute the human form of life and distinguish it from other actual or imaginable forms of life, such as the lives of animals and plants, or, on the other hand, of immortal gods as imagined in myths and legends (which frequently have precisely the function of delimiting the human)?[33]

We can get at this question better if we approach it via two somewhat more concrete questions that we often really ask ourselves. First is a question about personal continuity. We ask ourselves what changes or transitions are compatible with the continued existence of that being as a member of the human kind, and what are not. (Since continued species

---

[31] The politics of the history of Western philosophy have been interpreted this way, with much plausibility though perhaps insufficient historical argumentation, by Noam Chomsky, in *Cartesian Linguistics* (New York: Harper & Row, 1966). Chomsky argues that Cartesian rationalism, with its insistence on innate essences, was politically more progressive, more hostile to slavery and imperialism, than empiricism, with its insistence that people were just what experience had made of them. My analysis of Stoic feminist argument (below Section 7) bears this out.

[32] The use of this term does not imply that the functions all involve doing something especially 'active'. (See here Sen, 'Capability and Well-Being', in *The Quality of Life*, 30–53.) In Aristotelian terms, and in mine, being healthy, reflecting, being pleased, are all 'activities'.

[33] For further discussion of this point, and examples, see 'Aristotle on Human Nature'.

identity seems to be at least necessary for continued personal identity, this is also a question about the necessary conditions for continuing as one and the same individual.) Some functions can fail to be present without threatening our sense that we still have a human being on our hands; the absence of others seems to signal the end of a human life. This question is asked regularly, when we attempt to make medical definitions of death in a situation in which some of the functions of life persist, or to decide, for others or (thinking ahead) for ourselves, whether a certain level of illness or impairment means the end of the life of the being in question.[34]

The other question is a question about kind inclusion. We recognize other humans as human across many differences of time and place, of custom and appearance. Kwame Anthony Appiah writes about the experience of seeing his heterogenous nieces and nephews playing together, and the term 'the human future' naturally occurs to him.[35] Much though we may love our dogs and cats, we recognize such scenes as crucially different from scenes of a child playing with a dog or cat. On what do we base these recognitions? We often tell ourselves stories, on the other hand, about anthropomorphic creatures who do not get classified as human, on account of some feature of their form of life and functioning. On what do we base these exclusions? In short, what do we believe must be there, if we are going to acknowledge that a given life is human?[36]

This inquiry proceeds by examining a wide variety of self-interpretations of human beings in many times and places. Especially valuable are myths and stories that situate the human being in some way in the universe, between the 'beasts' on the one hand and the 'gods' on the other; stories that ask what it is to live as a being with certain abilities that set it apart from the rest of the world of nature and with, on the other hand, certain limits that derive from membership in the world of nature. The idea is that people in many different societies share a general outline of such a conception. This is not surprising, since they do recognize one another as members of the same species,[37] marry one another, have children together, and so forth—and indeed do tell one another such stories, without much difficulty

[34] Ibid. discusses the treatment of this point in contemporary medical ethics. Could one cease to be one's individual self without ceasing to be human? This is ruled out, I think, in Aristotle's conception, but is possible in some other metaphysical conceptions. But the sort of case that would most forcefully raise this possibility is not the sort involving illness or impairment, but instead the sort involving personality or memory change; and I shall not attempt to deal with such cases here.

[35] Appiah, *In My Father's House*, p. viii.

[36] In 'Aristotle on Human Nature', there is a more extended account of this procedure and how it justifies.

[37] This of course is not incompatible with calling certain groups non-human or subhuman for political purposes. But such denials are usually either transparent propaganda or forms of self-deception, which can be unmasked by critical argument. See below for a case involving women; and for an extensive analysis of the psychology of such self-deception, and its unmasking, see Raoul Hilberg, *The Destruction of the European Jews*, abridged edition (New York: Holmes & Meier, 1985), 274–93.

74 MARTHA C. NUSSBAUM

of translation. This convergence gives us some reason for optimism, that if we proceed in this way, using our imaginations, we will have in the end a theory that is not the mere projection of local preferences, but is fully international and a basis for cross-cultural attunement.

Several important methodological points must now be emphasized:

1. The procedure through which this account of the human is derived is neither ahistorical nor a priori. It is an attempt to set down a very general record of broadly shared experiences of human beings within history. A related point can be made about the results of the inquiry: they do not claim to be ahistorical or a priori truth, but, rather, an especially deep and continuous sort of experiential and historical truth.

2. On the other hand, the guiding questions of the inquiry direct it to cross national and temporal boundaries, looking for features that ground recognitions of humanness across these boundaries. Thus we can expect that its results will embody what is continuous rather than rapidly changing, international rather than local.

3. The account is neither a biological account nor a metaphysical account. (For these reasons I have avoided using the term 'human nature', which is usually associated with attempts to describe the human being either from the point of view of an allegedly value-free science or from the point of view of normative, often theological, metaphysics.) The inquiry pays attention to biology, but as it figures in and shapes human experience. It is an evaluative and, in a broad sense, ethical inquiry. It asks us to evaluate components of lives, asking which ones are so important that we would not call a life human without them. The result of this inquiry is, then, not a list of value-neutral facts, but a normative conception.[38]

4. The account is meant to be both tentative and open-ended. We allow explicitly for the possibility that we will learn from our encounters with other human societies to recognize things about ourselves that we had not seen before, or even to change in certain ways, according more importance to something we had thought more peripheral. (We may also shift to reach a political consensus.)

5. The account is not intended to deny that the items it enumerates are to some extent differently constructed by different societies. It claims only that in these areas there is considerable continuity and overlap, sufficient to ground a working political consensus.[39]

6. Although the account appeals to consensus in this way, it should be understood that the consensus is acceptable only if it is reached by

---

[38] In order to make this clear, I speak of it as a conception of the good, at a very minimal and general level. The phrase I have elsewhere used is 'the thick vague theory of the good'. The term 'thick' contrasts this account, in its comprehensiveness, with Rawls's 'thin' theory of the good, which is designed to avoid even partial comprehensiveness.

[39] On this see especially 'Non-Relative Virtues'.

reasonable procedures, where the notion of reasonableness has normative content.[40] In this way it is different from consensus as mere overlap.[41]

7. The list is heterogeneous: for it contains both limits against which we press and capabilities through which we aspire. This is not surprising, since we began from the intuitive idea of a creature who is both capable and needy.

8. The concept 'human being', as this view understands it, is in one way like the concept 'person' as used elsewhere in moral philosophy: that is, it is a normative ethical concept. On the other hand, because of its link with an empirical study of a species-specific form of life, and with what is most central in such a form of life, it may prove more difficult to withhold from certain beings in an arbitrary way (see Section 7 below). This may commend it to feminists: for the label 'person' has frequently been withheld from women, without substantial argument.[42]

Here then, as a first approximation, is a story about what seems to be part of any life we will count as a human life:

---

[40] I have discussed my own views about practical rationality elsewhere, particularly in 'The Discernment of Perception', in *Love's Knowledge* (New York: Oxford University Press, 1990). A related account, which I admire and to a large extent agree with, is given by Henry Richardson in *Practical Deliberation About Final Ends* (Cambridge University Press, 1994). Richardson's account is closely related, as well, to the pragmatist conception supported by Hilary Putnam in his paper in this volume.

Should the conception of reasonableness be defined with reference to *democratic* procedures, as Seyla Benhabib has recommended? I see the attractions of this proposal, but I have not followed it. First of all, it seems to me that democratic procedures as they actually are do not always embody reasonableness; so to describe what makes a democratic procedure reasonable we will have to have a notion of the reasonable that is to at least some extent independent of the notion of democracy. Secondly, to build democracy into the ground level of the conception of the human from the start prevents us from raising later on the question of what political arrangement will best secure to citizens the list of human capabilities, in a wide variety of circumstances. It may turn out that the answer will always be 'democracy'. But even then, I think it will rarely be *just* democracy (ancient Athenian or New England town-meeting style). No modern democratic state is a pure democracy, and it should at this point remain an open question as to what role should be played by relatively undemocratic institutions such as the US Supreme Court in promoting the capabilities of citizens.

[41] For Rawls's use of a notion of consensus, see Rawls, 'The Idea of an Overlapping Consensus', *Oxford Journal of Legal Studies*, 7 (1987), and now *Political Liberalism* (New York: Columbia University Press, 1993). Rawls's notion of consensus appears ambiguous between the two notions I identify here. See, on this, the exchange between Joshua Cohen and Jean Hampton in *The Idea of Democracy* (New York: Oxford University Press, 1992). Cohen argues that Rawls needs, and can consistently defend, the weaker 'overlap' reading; Hampton argues that, whatever Rawls intends, the plausibility of his argument rests on his opting for the normative reading. I concur with Hampton.

[42] To cite only a few recent examples with serious practical consequences: in the United Sates in the 1890s, the Supreme Court, denying a Virginia woman's appeal against a law forbidding women to practise law, judged that it was up to the state Supreme Court 'to determine whether the word "person"' in the statute on which the woman based her appeal 'is confined to males'. (*In re Lockwood*, 154 US 116, discussed in Okin, *Women*, 251 and n. 10, and see Sunstein's paper in this volume.) In Massachusetts in 1932, women were denied eligibility for jury service, although the law stated that 'every person qualified to vote' was eligible. The state Supreme Court wrote: 'No intention to include women can be deduced from the omission of the word "male"' (*Commonwealth v. Welosky*, 276 Mass. 398, cert.

3.1. Level One of the Conception of the Human Being:
The Shape of the Human Form of Life

3.1.1. Mortality All human beings face death and, after a certain age, know that they face it. This fact shapes more or less every other element of human life. Moreover, all human beings have an aversion to death. Although in many circumstances death will be preferred to the available alternatives, the death of a loved one, or the prospect of one's own death, is an occasion for grief and/or fear. If we encountered an immortal anthropomorphic being, or a mortal being who showed no aversion to death and no tendency at all to avoid death, we would judge, in both of these cases, that the form of life was so different from our own that the being could not be acknowledged as human.

3.1.2. The Human Body We live all our lives in bodies of a certain sort, whose possibilities and vulnerabilities do not as such belong to one human society rather than another. These bodies, similar far more than dissimilar (given the enormous range of possibilities) are our homes, so to speak, opening certain options and denying others, giving us certain needs and also certain possibilities for excellence. The fact that any given human being might have lived anywhere and belonged to any culture is a great part of what grounds our mutual recognitions; this fact, in turn, has a great deal to do with the general humanness of the body, its great distinctness from other bodies. The experience of the body is culturally shaped, to be sure; the importance we ascribe to its various functions is also culturally shaped. But the body itself, not culturally variant in its nutritional and other related requirements, sets limits on what can be experienced and valued, ensuring a great deal of overlap.

There is much disagreement, of course, about how much of human experience is rooted in the body. Here religion and metaphysics enter the picture in a non-trivial way. Therefore, in keeping with the non-metaphysical character of the list, I shall include at this point only those features that would be agreed to be bodily even by determined dualists. The more controversial features, such as thinking, perceiving, and emotion, I shall discuss separately, taking no stand on the question of dualism.

1. *Hunger and thirst: the need for food and drink.* All human beings need food and drink in order to live; all have comparable, though varying, nutritional requirements. Being in one culture rather than another does not

denied, 284 US 684 (1932)), discussed in Okin, *Women*, 251 and n. 11. Such readings no doubt reflect faithfully enough the views that the Founders had about the term 'person' when they used it in the Constitution: see my Jefferson epigraph. Although this construal of the term does not prevail today in American law, its legacy is with us in countless more informal ways.

make one metabolize food differently. Furthermore, all human beings have appetites that are indices of need. Appetitive experience is to some extent culturally shaped; but we are not surprised to discover much similarity and overlap. Moreover, human beings in general do not wish to be hungry or thirsty (though of course they might choose to fast for some reason). If we discovered someone who really did not experience hunger and thirst at all, or, experiencing them, really did not care about eating and drinking, we would judge that this creature was (in Aristotle's words) 'far from being a human being'.

2. *Need for shelter.* A recurrent theme in myths of humanness is the nakedness of the human being, its relative unprotectedness in the animal world, its susceptibility to heat, cold, and the ravages of the elements. Stories that explore the difference between our needs and those of furry or scaly or otherwise protected creatures remind us how far our life is constituted by the need to find protection through clothing and housing.

3. *Sexual Desire.* Though less urgent as a need than the needs for food, drink, and shelter (in the sense that one can live without its satisfaction) sexual need and desire are features of more or less every human life, at least beyond a certain age. It is, and has all along been, a most important basis for the recognition of others different from ourselves as human beings.

4. *Mobility.* Human beings are, as the old definition goes, featherless bipeds—that is, creatures whose form of life is in part constituted by the ability to move from place to place in a certain characteristic way, not only through the aid of tools that they have made, but with their very own bodies. Human beings like moving about, and dislike being deprived of mobility. An anthropomorphic being who, without disability, chose never to move from birth to death would be hard to view as human.

3.1.3. Capacity for Pleasure and Pain Experiences of pain and pleasure are common to all human life (though, once again, both their expression and, to some extent, the experience itself may be culturally shaped). Moreover, the aversion to pain as a fundamental evil is a primitive and, it appears, unlearned part of being a human animal. A society whose members altogether lacked that aversion would surely be judged to be beyond the bounds of humanness.

3.1.4. Cognitive Capability: Perceiving, Imagining, Thinking All human beings have sense-perception, the ability to imagine, and the ability to think, making distinctions and 'reaching out for understanding'.[43] And these abilities are regarded as of central importance. It is an open question what sorts of accidents or impediments to individuals in these

---

[43] Aristotle, *Metaphysics* I.I.

78 MARTHA C. NUSSBAUM

areas will be sufficient for us to judge that the life in question is not
really human any longer. But it is safe to say that if we imagine a group
of beings whose members totally lack sense-perception, or totally lack
imagination, or totally lack reasoning and thinking, we are not in any of
these cases imagining a group of human beings, no matter what they look
like.

3.1.5. Early Infant Development All human beings begin as hungry babies,
aware of their own helplessness, experiencing their alternating closeness
to and distance from that, and those, on whom they depend. This
common structure to early life[44]—which is clearly shaped in many different ways by different social arrangements—gives rise to a great deal of
overlapping experience that is central in the formation of desires, and
of complex emotions such as grief, love, and anger. This, in turn, is a
major source of our ability to recognize ourselves in the emotional
experiences of those whose lives are very different in other respects from
our own. If we encountered a group of apparent humans and then discovered that they never had been babies and had never, in consequence,
had those experiences of extreme dependency, need, and affection, we
would, I think, have to conclude that their form of life was sufficiently
different from our own that they could not be considered part of the same
kind.

3.1.6. Practical Reason All human beings participate (or try to) in the
planning and managing of their own lives, asking and answering questions
about what is good and how one should live. Moreover, they wish to enact
their thought in their lives—to be able to choose and evaluate, and to
function accordingly. This general capability has many concrete forms, and
is related in complex ways to the other capabilities, emotional, imaginative,
and intellectual. But a being who altogether lacks this would not be likely
to be regarded as fully human, in any society.

3.1.7. Affiliation With Other Human Beings All human beings recognize
and feel some sense of affiliation and concern for other human beings.
Moreover, we value the form of life that is constituted by these recognitions
and affiliations. We live with and in relation to others, and regard a life not
lived in affiliation with others to be a life not worth the living. (Here I would
really wish, with Aristotle, to spell things out further. We define ourselves
in terms of at least two types of affiliation: intimate family and/or personal
relations, and social or civic relations.)

---

[44] I discuss this issue in much more detail in Lecture 3 of my 1993 Gifford Lectures,
University of Edinburgh (forthcoming, Cambridge University Press).

3.1.8. Relatedness to Other Species and to Nature Human beings recognize that they are not the only living things in their world: that they are animals living alongside other animals, and also alongside plants, in a universe that, as a complex interlocking order, both supports and limits them. We are dependent upon that order in countless ways; and we also sense that we owe that order some respect and concern, however much we may differ about exactly what we owe, to whom, and on what basis. Again, a creature who treated animals exactly like stones and could not be brought to see any difference would probably be regarded as too strange to be human. So too would a creature who did not in any way respond to the natural world.

3.1.9. Humour and Play Human life, wherever it is lived, makes room for recreation and laughter. The forms play takes are enormously varied—and yet we recognize other humans, across cultural barriers, as the animals who laugh. Laughter and play are frequently among the deepest and also the first modes of our mutual recognition. Inability to play or laugh is taken, correctly, as a sign of deep disturbance in a child; if it proves permanent we will doubt whether the child is capable of leading a fully human life. An entire society that lacked this ability would seem to us both terribly strange and terribly frightening.

3.1.10. Separateness However much we live with and for others, we are, each of us, 'one in number',[45] proceeding on a separate path through the world from birth to death. Each person feels only his or her own pain and not anyone else's. Each person dies without entailing logically the death of anyone else. When one person walks across the room, no other person follows automatically. When we count the number of human beings in a room, we have no difficulty figuring out where one begins and the other ends. These obvious facts need stating, since they might have been otherwise. We should bear them in mind when we hear talk about the absence of individualism in certain societies. Even the most intense forms of human interaction, for example sexual experience, are experiences of responsiveness, not of fusion. If fusion is made the goal, the result is bound to be disappointment.

3.1.11. Strong Separateness Because of separateness, each human life has, so to speak, its own peculiar context and surroundings—objects, places, a history, particular friendships, locations, sexual ties—that are not exactly the same as those of anyone else, and in terms of which the person to some extent identifies herself. Though societies vary a great deal in the degree

---

[45] Aristotle, ubiquitously in the accounts of substance.

and type of strong separateness that they permit and foster, there is no life yet known that really does (as Plato wished) fail to use the words 'mine' and 'not mine' in some personal and non-shared way. What I use, live in, respond to, I use, live in, respond to from my own separate existence. And on the whole, human beings recognize one another as beings who wish to have at least some separateness of context, a little space to move around in, some special items to use or love.

This is a working list. It is put out to generate debate. It has done so and will continue to do so, and it will be revised accordingly.

As I have said, the list is composed ot two different sorts of items; limits and capabilities. As far as capabilities go, to call them parts of humanness is to make a very basic sort of evaluation. It is to say that a life without this item would be too lacking, too impoverished, to be human at all. Obviously, then, it could not be a good human life. So this list of capabilities is a ground-floor or minimal conception of the good. (In the sense that it does not fully determine the choice of a way of life, but simply regulates the parameters of what can be chosen, it plays, however, the role traditionally played in liberal political theory by a conception of the right.)[46]

With the limits, things are more complicated. In selecting the limits for attention, we have, once again, made a basic sort of evaluation, saying that these things are so important that life would not be human without them. But what we have said is that human life, in its general form, consists of the awareness of these limits plus a struggle against them. Humans do not wish to be hungry, to feel pain, to die. (Separateness is highly complex, both a limit and a capability. Much the same is true of many of the limits implied by the shape and the capacities of the body.) On the other hand, we cannot assume that the correct evaluative conclusion to draw is that we should try as hard as possible to get rid of the limit altogether. It is characteristic of human life to prefer recurrent hunger plus eating to a life with neither hunger nor eating; to prefer sexual desire and its satisfaction to a life with neither desire nor satisfaction. Even where death is concerned, the desire for immortality, which many human beings certainly have, is a peculiar desire: for it is not clear that the wish to lose one's finitude completely is a desire that one can coherently entertain for oneself or for someone one loves. It seems to be a wish for a transition to a way of life so wholly different, with such different values and ends, that it seems that the identity of the individual will not be preserved. So the evaluative conclusion, in mapping out a ground-floor conception of the good (saying what functioning is necessary for a life to be human) will have to be expressed with much caution, clearly, in terms of what would be a humanly good way of countering the limitation.

---

[46] On these issues, see further in 'Aristotelian Social Democracy'.

4 THE TWO THRESHOLDS

Things now get very complicated. For we want to describe two distinct thresholds: a threshold of capability to function beneath which a life will be so impoverished that it will not be human at all; and a somewhat higher threshold, beneath which those characteristic functions are available in such a reduced way that, though we may judge the form of life a human one, we will not think it a *good* human life. The latter threshold is the one that will eventually concern us when we turn to public policy: for we don't want societies to make their citizens capable of the bare minimum. My view holds, with Aristotle, that a good political arrangement is one 'in accordance with which anyone whatsoever might do well and live a flourishing life'.[47]

These are clearly, in many areas, two distinct thresholds, requiring distinct levels of resource and opportunity. One may be alive without being well nourished. As Marx observed, one may be able to use one's senses without being able to use them in a fully human way. And yet there is need for caution here. For in many cases the move from human life to good human life is supplied by the citizen's own powers of choice and self-definition, in such a way that once society places them above the first threshold, moving above the second is more or less up to them. This is especially likely to be so, I think, in areas such as affiliation and practical reasoning, where in many cases once social institutions permit a child to cross the first threshold its own choices will be central in raising it above the second. (This is not always so, however: for certain social conditions, for example certain mindless forms of labour or, we may add, traditional hierarchical gender relations, may impede the flourishing of affiliation and practical reason, while not stamping it out entirely.) On the other hand, it is clear that where bodily health and nutrition, for example, are concerned, there is a considerable difference between the two thresholds, and a difference that is standardly made by resources over which individuals do not have full control. It would then be the concern of quality-of-life assessment to ask whether all citizens are capable, not just of the bare minimum, but of *good life* in these areas. Clearly there is a continuum here. Nor will it in practise be at all easy to say where the upper threshold, especially, should be located.

I shall not say much about the first threshold, but shall illustrate it by a few examples. What is an existence that is so impoverished that it cannot properly be called a human life? Here we should count, I believe, many forms of existence that take place at the end of a human life—all those in which the being that survives has irretrievably lost sensation and consciousness (in what is called a 'permanent vegetative condition'); and also, I

---

[47] Aristotle, *Politics* VII.I: see 'Nature, Function, and Capability'.

would hold, some that fall short of this, but in which the capacity to recognize loved ones, to think and to reason, has irreversibly decayed beyond a certain point. I would include the extreme absence of ability to engage in practical reasoning that is often the outcome of the notorious frontal lobotomy. I would also include an absence of mobility so severe that it makes speech, as well as movement from place to place, impossible.

It follows from this that certain severely damaged infants are not human ever, even if born from two human parents: again, those with global and total sensory incapacity and/or no consciousness or thought; also, I think, those with no ability at all to recognize or relate to others. (This of course tells us nothing about what we owe them morally, it just separates that question from moral questions about human beings.)[48]

Again, we notice the evaluative character of these threshold judgements. The fact that a person who has lost her arms cannot play a piano does not make us judge that she no longer lives a human life; had she lost the capacity to think and remember, or to form affectionate relationships, it would have been a different matter.

Many such disasters are not to be blamed on social arrangements, and in those cases the first threshold has no political implications. But many are, where bad nutrition and health care enter in. The role of society is even more evident if we think of a more controversial group of first-threshold cases, in which the non-human outcome was environmentally caused: the rare cases of children who have grown up outside a human community, or in a severely dysfunctional home, and utterly lack language and reason, or lack social abilities in an extreme and irreversible way. We can focus the political question more productively, however, if we now turn from the question of mere human life to the question of good life, the level we would really like to see a human being attain.

Here, as the next level of the conception of the human being, I shall now specify certain basic functional capabilities at which societies should aim for their citizens, and which quality of life measurements should measure. In other words, this will be an account of the second threshold—although in some areas it may coincide, for the reasons I have given, with the first: once one is capable of human functioning in this area one is also capable, with some further effort and care, of good functioning. I introduce this list as a list of capabilities to function, rather than of actual functionings, since I

---

[48] It may support what James Rachels calls 'moral individualism' (*Created From Animals* (Oxford and New York: Oxford University Press, 1990)), in which our moral obligations flow from the endowments of the individual creature with whom we are dealing, rather than from its species, and our goal should be to promote—or at least not to impede—the form of flourishing of which the being is basically capable. On this view such an infant should get the same treatment that we would give to an animal of similar endowment. But we may also decide to give the fact that it is an offspring of humans some moral weight; nothing I have said here rules that out.

shall argue that capability, not actual functioning, should be the goal of public policy.

4.1. Level 2 of the Conception of the Human Being: Basic Human Functional Capabilities

1. Being able to live to the end of a human life of normal length,[49] not dying prematurely, or before one's life is so reduced as to be not worth living.

2. Being able to have good health; to be adequately nourished;[50] to have adequate shelter;[51] having opportunities for sexual satisfaction, and for choice in matters of reproduction;[52] being able to move from place to place.

3. Being able to avoid unnecessary and non-beneficial pain, so far as possible, and to have pleasurable experiences.

4. Being able to use the senses; being able to imagine, to think, and to reason—and to do these things in a way informed and cultivated by an

---

[49] Although 'normal length' is clearly relative to current human possibilities, and may need, for practical purposes, to be to some extent relativized to local conditions, it seems important to think of it—at least at a given time in history—in universal and comparative terms, as the Human Development Report does, to give rise to complaint in a country that has done well with some indicators of life quality, but badly on life expectancy. And although some degree of relativity may be put down to the differential genetic possibilities of different groups (the 'missing women' statistics, for example, allow that on the average women live somewhat longer than men), it is also important not to conclude prematurely that inequalities between groups—for example, the growing inequalities in life expectancy between blacks and whites in the USA—are simply genetic variation, not connected with social injustice.

[50] The precise specification of these health rights is not easy, but the work currently being done on them in drafting new constitutions in South Africa and Eastern Europe gives reason for hope that the combination of a general specification of such a right with a tradition of judicial interpretation will yield something practicable. It should be noticed that I speak of health, not just health care: and health itself interacts in complex ways with housing, with education, with dignity. Both health and nutrition are controversial as to whether the relevant level should be specified universally, or relatively to the local community and its traditions: for example, is low height associated with nutritional practices to be thought of as 'stunting', or as felicitous adaptation to circumstances of scarcity? For an excellent summary of this debate, see S. R. Osmani (ed.), Nutrition and Poverty, WIDER series (Oxford: Clarendon Press, 1990), especially the following papers: on the relativist side, T. N. Srinivasan, 'Undernutrition: Concepts, Measurements, and Policy Implications', 97–120; on the universalist side, C. Gopalan, 'Undernutrition: Measurement and Implications', 17–48; for a compelling adjudication of the debate, coming out on the universalist side, see Osmani, 'On Some Controversies in the Measurement of Undernutrition', 121–61.

[51] There is a growing literature on the importance of shelter for health: e.g. that the provision of adequate housing is the single largest determinant of health status for HIV infected persons. Housing rights are increasingly coming to be constitutionalized, at least in a negative form—giving squatters grounds for appeal, for example, against a landlord who would bulldoze their shanties. On this as a constitutional right, see proposed Articles 11, 12, and 17 of the South African Constitution, in a draft put forward by the ANC committee, advisor Albie Sachs, where this is given as an example of a justiciable housing right.

[52] I shall not elaborate here on what I think promoting this capability requires, since there is a future volume in the WIDER series devoted to this topic: J. Glover, M. Nussbaum, and C. Sunstein (eds.), Women, Equality, and Reproduction.

adequate education, including, but by no means limited to, literacy and basic mathematical and scientific training.[53] Being able to use imagination and thought in connection with experiencing and producing spiritually enriching materials and events of one's own choice; religious, literary, musical, and so forth. I believe that the protection of this capability requires not only the provision of education, but also legal guarantees of freedom of expression with respect to both political and artistic speech, and of freedom of religious exercise.

5. Being able to have attachments to things and persons outside ourselves; to love those who love and care for us, to grieve at their absence; in general, to love, to grieve, to experience longing and gratitude.[54] Supporting this capability means supporting forms of human association that can be shown to be crucial in their development.[55]

6. Being able to form a conception of the good and to engage in critical reflection about the planning of one's own life. This includes, today, being able to seek employment outside the home and to participate in political life.

7. Being able to live for and to others, to recognize and show concern for other human beings, to engage in various forms of social interaction; to be able to imagine the situation of another and to have compassion for that situation; to have the capability for both justice and friendship. Protecting this capability means, once again, protecting institutions that constitute such forms of affiliation, and also protecting the freedoms of assembly and political speech.

8. Being able to live with concern for and in relation to animals, plants, and the world of nature.

9. Being able to laugh, to play, to enjoy recreational activities.

[53] A good example of an education right that I would support is given in the ANC South African Constitution draft, Article 11: 'Education shall be free and compulsory up to the age of sixteen, and provision shall be made for facilitating access to secondary, vocational and tertiary education on an equal basis for all. Education shall be directed towards the development of the human personality and a sense of personal dignity, and shall aim at strengthening respect for human rights and fundamental freedoms and promoting understanding, tolerance and friendship amongst South Africans and between nations.' The public (or otherwise need-blind) provision of higher education will have to be relative to local possibilities, but it is at least clear that the USA lags far behind most other countries of comparable wealth in this area.

[54] On the emotions as basic human capabilities, see, in addition to my other chapter in this volume, my 1993 Gifford Lectures, *Upheavals of Thought: A Theory of the Emotions* (forthcoming, Cambridge University Press). My omission of anger from this list of basic emotional capabilities reveals an ambivalence about its role that I discuss at length, both in Gifford Lectures 3 and 10, and in *The Therapy of Desire: Theory and Practice in Hellenistic Ethics* (Princeton, NJ: Princeton University Press, 1994) chs. 7, 11, and 12. See also 'Equity and Mercy', *Philosophy and Public Affairs*, spring 1993.

[55] In my 1993 Gifford Lectures, I spell out what I think this entails where 'the family' is concerned. On the whole, I am in agreement with Susan Okin that some form of intimate family love is of crucial importance in child development, but that this need not be the traditional Western nuclear family. I also agree with Okin that the important educational role of the family makes it all the more crucial that the family should be an institution characterized by justice, as well as love. See Okin, *Justice, Gender, and the Family*.

10. Being able to live one's own life and nobody else's. This means having certain guarantees of non-interference with certain choices that are especially personal and definitive of selfhood, such as choices regarding marriage, childbearing, sexual expression, speech, and employment.

10a. Being able to live one's own life in one's own surroundings and context. This means guarantees of freedom of association and of freedom from unwarranted search and seizure; it also means a certain sort of guarantee of the integrity of personal property, though this guarantee may be limited in various ways by the demands of social equality, and is always up for negotiation in connection with the interpretation of the other capabilities, since personal property, unlike personal liberty, is a tool of human functioning rather than an end in itself.

My claim is that a life that lacks any one of these capabilities, no matter what else it has, will fall short of being a good human life. So it would be reasonable to take these things as a focus for concern, in assessing the quality of life in a country and asking about the role of public policy in meeting human needs. The list is certainly general—and this is deliberate, in order to leave room for plural specification and also for further negotiation. But I claim that it does, rather like a set of constitutional guarantees, offer real guidance in the ongoing historical process of further refinement and specification, and far more accurate guidance than that offered by the focus on utility, or even on resources.

A few comments are in order about the relationship of this version of the list to other versions I have published previously. First, taking some lessons from the *Human Development Report*, it is considerably more specific about matters such as education and work, so as to give the development theorist something concrete to measure. Secondly, it is far more explicitly concerned with guarantees of personal liberty of expression, reproductive choice, and religion.[56] This was not only called for in general, but called forth by the attempt to articulate the specific requisites of equal female capability.[57] Thirdly, in accordance with its commitment to the distinction between ends and means, it understands 'property rights' as instrumental to other human capabilities,[58] and therefore to a certain extent, as up for negotiation in general social planning.

The list is, emphatically, a list of separate components. We cannot satisfy the need for one of them by giving a larger amount of another. All are of central importance and all are distinct in quality. This limits the trade-offs

[56] 'Aristotelian Social Democracy' said that a list of such liberties needed to be added to the Aristotelian scheme, but it did not include them in the account of capabilities itself. These issues are further developed in a future WIDER volume on reproductive rights and women's capabilities, based on the papers given at our 1993 conference, and edited by Jonathan Glover and Martha Nussbaum.

[57] For reproductive choice as an equality issue, see Sunstein's paper in this volume, and also his 'Gender, Reproduction, and Law', forthcoming in Glover and Nussbaum.

[58] On this see also 'Aristotelian Social Democracy'.

that it will be reasonable to make, and thus limits the applicability of quantitative cost-benefit analysis. At the same time, the items on the list are related to one another in many complex ways. For example our characteristic mode of nutrition, unlike that of sponges, requires moving from here to there. And we do whatever we do as separate beings, tracing distinct paths through space and time. Notice that reproductive choices involve both sexual capability and issues of separateness, and bind the two together in a deep and complex way.

A further comment is in order, concerning the relationship of this threshold list to an account of human equality. A commitment to bringing all human beings across a certain threshold of capability to choose represents a certain sort of commitment to equality: for the view treats all persons as equal bearers of human claims, no matter where they are starting from in terms of circumstances, special talents, wealth, gender, or race. On the other hand, I have said nothing so far about how one should regard inequalities that persist once the threshold level has been attained for all persons. To some extent I feel this would be premature, since the threshold level has so rarely been attained for the complete capability set. On the other hand, one can imagine a situation—perhaps it could be that of the USA or Japan, given certain large changes in health support here, or educational distribution there, that would meet threshold conditions and still exhibit inequalities of attainment between the genders or the races. We have two choices here: either to argue that this situation actually contains capability failure after all; or to grant that the capability view needs to be supplemented by an independent theory of equality. I am not yet certain what I want to say about this, but I am inclined to the first alternative, since I think that gender inequality of the sort one sees in a prosperous nation does none the less push the subordinated racial or gender group beneath an acceptable threshold of autonomy, dignity, and emotional well being. Indeed, subordination is itself a kind of capability failure, a failure to attain complete personhood. So I am inclined to say that, properly fleshed out, the second threshold would be incompatible with systematic subordination of one group to another.

5 THE ROLE OF THE CONCEPTION IN DEVELOPMENT POLICY

My claim is that we urgently need a conception of the human being and human functioning in public policy. If we try to do without this sort of guidance when we ask how goods, resources, and opportunities should be distributed, we reject guidance that is, I think, superior to that offered by any of the other guides currently available.

I shall focus here on the area of most concern to our project: the assessment of the quality of life in a developing country, with special attention to the lives of women. For the time being, I shall take the nation state as my basic unit, and the question I shall ask is, 'How is the nation doing, with respect to the quality of life of its citizens?' In other words, I shall be asking the sort of question asked by the UN *Human Development Report*. I shall not propose a general theory about how the needs revealed by such an assessment should be met: whether by centralized government planning, for example, or through a system of incentives, and whether through direct subsidies or through the provision of opportunities for employment. Nor shall I ask what responsibilities richer nations have to poorer nations, in ensuring that the needs of all human beings are met the world over. That is an urgent question, and it must at a later date be confronted. For now, however, I shall focus on the correct understanding of the goal, where each separate nation is concerned.

The basic claim I wish to make—concurring with Amartya Sen—is that the central goal of public planning should be the *capabilities* of citizens to perform various important functions. The questions that should be asked when assessing quality of life in a country are (and of course this is a central part of assessing the quality of its political arrangements) 'How well have the people of the country been enabled to perform the central human functions?' and, 'Have they been put in a position of mere human subsistence with respect to the functions, or have they been enabled to live well?' In other words, we ask where the people are, with respect to the second list. And we focus on getting as many people as possible above the second threshold, with respect to the interlocking set of capabilities enumerated by that list.[59] Naturally, the determination of whether certain individuals and groups are across the threshold is only as precise a matter as the determination of the threshold; and I have left things deliberately somewhat open-ended at this point, in keeping with the procedures of the *Human Development Report*, believing that the best way to work toward a more precise determination is to allow the community of nations to hammer it out after an extended comparative inquiry, of the sort the report makes possible. Again, we will have to answer various questions about the costs we are willing to pay to get all citizens above the threshold, as opposed to leaving a small number below and allowing the rest a considerably above-threshold life quality. Here my claim is that capability-equality, in the sense of moving all above the threshold, should be taken as the central goal. As with Rawls's Difference Principle, so here: inequalities in distribution above the threshold should be

---

[59] With Sen, I hold that the capability set should be treated as an interlocking whole: for my comments on his arguments, see 'Nature, Function, and Capability'. Tensions will frequently arise among members of the list, and I shall comment on some of those below. But it should be clear by now that the architectonic role of practical reasoning imposes strict limits on the sort of curb on personal autonomy that will be tolerated for the sake of increased nutritional well-being, etc.

tolerated only if they move more people across it;[60] once all are across, societies are to a great extent free to choose the other goals that they wish to pursue.

The basic intuition from which the capability approach starts, in the political arena, is that human capabilities exert a moral claim that they should be developed. Human beings are creatures such that, provided with the right educational and material support, they can become fully capable of the major human functions, can cross the first and second thresholds. That is, they are creatures with certain lower-level capabilities (which I have elsewhere called 'basic capabilities')[61] to perform the functions in question. When these capabilities are deprived of the nourishment that would transform them into the high-level capabilities that figure on my list, they are fruitless, cut off, in some way but a shadow of themselves. They are like actors who never get to go on the stage, or a musical score that is never performed. Their very being makes forward reference to functioning. Thus if functioning never arrives on the scene they are hardly even what they are. This may sound like a metaphysical idea, and in a sense it is (in that it is an idea discussed in Aristotle's *Metaphysics*). But that does not mean that it is not a basic and pervasive empirical idea, an idea that underwrites many of our daily practises and judgements in many times and places. I claim that just as we hold that a child who dies before getting to maturity has died especially tragically—for her activities of growth and preparation for adult activity now have lost their point—so too with capability and functioning more generally: we believe that certain basic and central human endowments have a claim to be assisted in developing, and exert that claim on others, and especially, as Aristotle saw, on government. We shall see the work this consideration can do in arguments for women's equality. I think it is the underlying basis, in the Western philosophical tradition, for many notions of human rights. I suggest, then, that in thinking of political planning we begin from this notion, thinking of the basic capabilities of human beings as needs for functioning, which give rise to correlated political duties.

[60] Chris Bobonich 'Internal Realism, Human Nature, and Distributive Justice: A Response to Martha Nussbaum', *Modern Philology*, May 1993 supplement, 74–92, worries that this will impose enormous sacrifices. But I think that this is because he has not imagined things in detail, nor thought about my claim that once people have what they basically need, they can get all sorts of other good things through their own efforts. If I have enough food to be well-nourished, more food will just rot on the shelf or make me fat. If my basic health needs are met, it seems right that I should not be able to claim expensive unnecessary luxuries (say, cosmetic surgery) at the public expense so long as even one person in my country is without support for basic needs. And so forth. One must take seriously the Aristotelian idea, which is basic to both Sen's and my programmes, that resources are just tools for functioning and have a limit given by what is needed for that functioning. Above that limit, they are just a heap of stuff, of no value in themselves.

[61] See 'Nature, Function, and Capability', with reference to Aristotle; and below, Section 9.

There is, then, an empirical basis for the determination that a certain being is one of the ones to which our normative conception and its associated duties applies. It is the gap between potential humanness and its full realization that exerts a moral claim. If the worker described by Marx as not capable of a truly human use of his senses[62] had really been a non-human animal, the fact that he was given a form of life suited to such an animal would not be a tragedy. If women were really turtles, the fact that being a woman is not yet a way of being a human being would not be, as it is, an outrage. There is, of course, enormous potential for abuse in determining who has these basic capabilities. The history of IQ testing is just one chapter in an inglorious saga of prejudiced capability-testing that goes back at least to the Noble Lie of Plato's Republic. Therefore we should, I think, proceed as if every offspring of two human parents has the basic capabilities, unless and until long experience with the individual has convinced us that damage to that individual's condition is so great that it could never in any way arrive at the higher capability level.

The political and economic application of this approach is evident in a variety of areas. Amartya Sen has developed a number of its concrete implications in the areas of welfare and development economics, and has focused particularly on its application to the assessment of women's quality of life.[63] With his advice, the UN *Human Development Reports* have begun to gather information and to rank nations in accordance with the type of plural-valued capability-focused measuring the approach suggests. In a closely related study, Iftekhar Hossein has used the approach to give an account of poverty as capability failure.[64] Independently, a very similar approach has been developed by Finnish and Swedish social scientists, above all Erik Allardt and Robert Erikson.[65] Wishing to develop ways of gathering information about how their people are doing that would be more sensitive and informationally complete than polls based on ideas of utility, they worked out lists of the basic human capabilities for functioning, and then examined the performance of various groups in the population—above all women and minorities—in these terms, thus anticipating the procedures of the *Human Development Report*, which devotes a great deal of attention to gender differences, urban-rural differences, and so forth.

---

[62] Marx, *Economic and Philosophical Manuscripts of 1844*, discussed in 'Nature, Function, and Capability' and 'Aristotle on Human Nature'.

[63] See especially Sen's paper in this volume; also 'More than a Million Women are Missing', *New York Review of Books* 37 (1990) 61–6.

[64] Iftekhar Hossein, 'Poverty as Capability Failure', Ph.D. Dissertation in Economics, Helsinki University, 1990.

[65] See Allardt, 'Having, Loving, Being: An Alternative to the Swedish Model of Welfare Research', and Erikson, 'Descriptions of Inequality: The Swedish Approach to Welfare Research', in Nussbaum and Sen, *The Quality of Life*, 88–94 and 67–84.

The 'capabilities approach' has clear advantages over other current approaches to quality of life assessment. Assessment that uses GNP per capita as its sole measure fails to concern itself with the distribution of resources, and thus can give high marks to countries with enormous inequalities. Nor does this approach examine other human goods that are not reliably correlated with the presence of resources: infant mortality, for example, or access to education, or the quality of racial and gender relations, or the presence or absence of political freedoms. The *Human Development Report* for 1993 informs us, for example, that the United Arab Emirates has Real GNP per capita of $16,753—tenth highest in the world, higher, for example, than Norway or Australia—while overall, in the aggregation of all the indicators of life quality, it ranks only sixty-seventh in the world (out of 173 nations measured). Its adult literacy rate is 55%, far lower than any of the 66 countries generally ahead of it, and also than many generally below it. (Both Norway and Australia have adult literacy of 99%.) The maternal mortality rate of 130 per 100,000 live births is comparatively high. The proportion of women progressing beyond secondary education is very low, and only 6% of the labour force is female (as opposed, for example, to 42% in Seychelles, 35% in Brazil, 43% in China, 47% in Viet Nam, 26% in India, and 20% in Nigeria). In fact, in all the world only Algeria (4%) has a lower proportion of females in the labour force, only Iraq (6%) ties it, and only Qatar (7%), Saudi Arabia (7%), Libya (9%), Jordan (10%), Pakistan (11%), Bangladesh (7%) and Afghanistan (8%) come close. Evidence links female wage-earning outside the home strongly to female health care and life-expectancy.[66] And in fact, we find that the ratio of females to males in the United Arab Emirates is the amazing 48:100, lowest in all the world. If this is discounted as employment related, we may pursue the other countries in our low external employment comparison class. The ratio of females to males in nations in which there is no reason to suppose sexual discrimination in nourishment and health care is, Sen has shown, about 106:100 in Europe and North America—or, if we focus only on the developing world, taking sub-Saharan Africa as our 'norm', 102:100. In Qatar it is 60:100, in Saudi Arabia 84, in Libya 91, in Jordan 95, in Pakistan 92, in Bangladesh 94, in Afghanistan 94.

These are some of the numbers that we start noticing if we focus on capabilities and functioning, rather than simply on GNP. They are essential to the understanding of how women are doing. In fact, they are the numbers from which Sen's graphic statistics regarding 'missing women' emerge. (The number of 'missing women' is the number of extra women who would be in a given country if that country had the same sex ratio as sub-Saharan Africa.) They strongly support Martha Chen's argument that the right to work is a right basic to the lives of women not only in itself, but

---

[66] See Sen, 'More than a Million Women'.

for its impact on other basic capabilities and functionings. Saleha Begum's employment led to better nutritional and health status for herself and, indeed, her children and family. Metha Bai may soon become one of the statistics from which the number of missing women is made.

Would other available approaches have done the job as well? The common approach that measures quality of life in terms of utility—polling people concerning the satisfaction of their preferences—would have missed the obvious fact that desires and subjective preferences are not always reliable indicators of what a person really needs. Preferences, as Amartya Sen's work has repeatedly shown, are highly malleable.[67] The rich and pampered easily become accustomed to their luxury, and view with pain and frustration a life in which they are treated just like everyone else. Males are a special case of this: we do not need to go abroad to know that males frequently resent a situation in which they are asked to share child care and domestic responsibilities on an equal basis.[68] The poor and deprived frequently adjust their expectations and aspirations to the low level of life they have known. Thus they may not demand more education, better health care. Like the women described in Sen's account of health surveys in India, they may not even know what it is to feel healthy.[69] Like the rural Bangladeshi women so vividly described in Martha Chen's *A Quiet Revolution*,[70] they may not even know what it means to have the advantages of education. We may imagine that many women in the countries I have mentioned would not fight, as Seleha Begum did, for participation in the workforce; nor would they be aware of the high correlation between work outside the home and other advantages. As Sen argues, they may have fully internalized the ideas behind the traditional system of discrimination, and may view their deprivation as 'natural'. Thus if we rely on utility as our measure of life quality, we most often will get results that support the *status quo* and oppose radical change.[71]

[67] See also Jon Elster, *Sour Grapes* (Cambridge: Cambridge University Press, 1983); Cass R. Sunstein, 'Preferences and Politics', *Philosophy and Public Affairs*, 20 (1991), 3–34.
[68] Päivi Setälä, Professor of Women's Studies at the University of Helsinki, informs me that recent studies show that even in Finland, only 40% of the housework is done by males. This, in the second nation in the world (after New Zealand, in 1906) to give females the vote, a nation as committed to sex equality as any in the world. We can assume that the situation is causally related to male preferences.
[69] On the disparity between externally observed health status and self-reports of satisfaction about health, see Sen, *Commodities and Capabilities* (Amsterdam: North-Holland, 1985).
[70] Martha Chen, *A Quiet Revolution: Women in Transition in Rural Bangladesh* (Cambridge, Mass.: Schenkman, 1983). I describe this account of a rural women's literacy project, and its large-scale impact on women's quality of life, in 'Non-Relative Virtues', 'Aristotelian Social Democracy', and 'Human Functioning and Social Justice'.
[71] This is a criticism of economic utilitarianism, not of sophisticated philosophical forms of utilitarianism that build in means to filter or correct preferences. Nonetheless, the human-functioning approach would still object to the role played by the commensurability of values in utilitarianism, and to the related suggestion that for any two distinct ends we can, without loss of what is relevant for choice, imagine trade-offs in purely quantitative terms. Furthermore, most forms of utilitarianism are committed to aggregating utilities across lives, and thus

If these criticisms apply to approaches that focus on utility in general, they apply all the more pointedly to the sort of local-tradition relativism espoused by the Marglins, in which the measure of quality of life will be the satisfaction of a certain group of preferences, namely the traditional ones of a given culture. Indeed, it is illuminating to consider how close, in its renunciation of critical normative argument, the Marglin approach is to the prevailing economic approaches of which it presents itself as a radical critique. A preference-based approach that gives priority to the preferences of traditional culture is likely to be especially subversive of the quality of life of women who have been on the whole badly treated by prevailing traditional norms. And one can see this clearly in the Marglins' own examples. For menstruation taboos impose severe restrictions on women's power to form a plan of life and to execute the plan they have chosen. They are members of the same family of traditional attitudes about women and the workplace that made it difficult for Saleha Begum to support herself and her family, that make it impossible for Metha Bai to sustain the basic functions of life. And the Japanese husband who allegedly renounces freedom of choice actually enhances it, in the ways that matter, by asking the woman to look after the boring details of life. One can sympathize with many of the Marglins' goals—respect for diversity, desire to preserve aspects of traditional life that appear to be rich in spiritual and artistic value—without agreeing that extreme relativism of the sort they endorse is the best way to pursue these concerns.

As for liberal approaches that aim at equality in the distribution of certain basic resources, these have related problems, since these, too, refuse to take a stand on the ends to which the resources are means.[72] Wealth and income are not good in their own right; they are good only insofar as they promote human functioning. Secondly, human beings have widely varying needs for resources, and any adequate definition of who is 'better off' and 'worse off' must reflect that fact.[73] Women who have traditionally not been educated, for example, may well require more of the relevant resources to attain the same capability level: that is why, in the case

to neglecting separateness, which I have defended as fundamental. I have addressed some of these questions elsewhere, for example, in 'The Discernment of Perception' in *Love's Knowledge*, and in 'The Literary Imagination in Public Life', *New Literary History* (fall 1993). Sen's work has addressed them in greater detail. I therefore leave them to one side for the purposes of the present inquiry.

[72] For a detailed consideration of these approaches, see 'Aristotelian Social Democracy', 'Human Functioning', with references to related arguments of Sen. 'Aristotelian Social Democracy' contains a detailed account of the relationship between Rawls's resourcism and my project, which is a particularly subtle one. Rawls is willing to take a stand on certain items: thus liberty and the social conditions of self-respect figure on his list of 'primary goods', as well as wealth and income. On the other hand, he has repeatedly denied that his index of primary goods could, or should, be replaced by an index of functionings as in the *Human Development Report*.

[73] This is the central point repeatedly made by Sen against Rawls; for an overview, see 'Capability and Well-Being' in *The Quality of Life*, with references.

discussed by Martha Chen, the Bangladesh Rural Advancement Committee created a special female literacy programme, rather than a programme
that distributed equal resources to all. Thirdly, by defining being 'well-off'
in terms of possessions alone, the liberal fails to go deep enough in imagining the impediments to functioning that are actually present in many lives—
in their conditions of labour or exclusion from labour, for example, in
their frequently unequal family responsibilities, in the obstacles to self-
realization imposed by traditional norms and values.[74] The stories of Saleha
Begum and Metha Bai are vivid examples of such unequal obstacles. No
right-to-work effort, and no expenditure of resources in that connection,
were necessary in order to make men capable of working in the fields in
Bangladesh. No male of Metha Bai's caste would have to overcome threats
of physical violence in order to go out of the house to work for life-
sustaining food.

6 ANSWERING THE OBJECTIONS: HUMAN FUNCTIONING AND PLURALISM

I have commended the human-function view by contrast to its rivals on the
development scene. But I must now try to show how it can answer the
objections I described earlier.

Concerning *neglect of historical and cultural difference*, I can begin by
insisting that this normative conception of human capability and functioning is general, and in a sense vague, for precisely this reason. The list claims
to have identified in a very general way components that are fundamental
to any human life. But it allows in its very design for the possibility of
multiple specifications of each of the components. This is so in several
different ways. First, the constitutive circumstances of human life, while
broadly shared, are themselves realized in different forms in different societies. The fear of death, the love of play, relationships of friendship and
affiliation with others, even the experience of the bodily appetites never turn
up in simply the vague and general form in which we have introduced them
here, but always in some specific and historically rich cultural realization,
which can profoundly shape not only the conceptions used by the citizens
in these areas, but also their experiences themselves. Nonetheless, we do
have in these areas of our common humanity sufficient overlap to sustain a
general conversation, focusing on our common problems and prospects.

[74] In Rawls's liberalism the problem is even more acute, since the parties who are either well
or not well off are 'heads of households,' usually taken to be male, who are alleged to deliberate
on behalf of the interests of their family members. But women cannot in fact rely on the
altruism of males to guarantee their economic security, or even survival. In addition to Sen's
work on this issue, see Susan Moller Okin, *Justice, Gender, and the Family*. In my review of
Okin, I offer this as a reason for Okin to be more critical of resource-based liberalism than
she is.

And sometimes the common conversation will permit us to criticize some conceptions of the grounding experiences themselves, as at odds with other things human beings want to do and to be.

When we are choosing a conception of good functioning with respect to these circumstances, we can expect an even greater degree of plurality to become evident. Here the approach wants to retain plurality in two significantly different ways: what I may call the way of *plural specification*, and what I may call the way of *local specification*.

Plural specification means what its name implies. Public policy, while using a determinate conception of the good at a high level of generality, leaves a great deal of latitude for citizens to specify each of the components more concretely, and with much variety, in accordance with local traditions, or individual tastes. Many concrete forms of life, in many different places and circumstances, display functioning in accordance with all the major capabilities.

As for local specification: good public reasoning, I believe and have argued, is always done, when well done, with a rich sensitivity to the concrete context, to the characters of the agents and their social situation. This means that in addition to the pluralism I have just described, the Aristotelian needs to consider a different sort of plural specification of the good. For sometimes what is a good way of promoting education in one part of the world will be completely ineffectual in another. Forms of affiliation that flourish in one community may prove impossible to sustain in another. In such cases, the Aristotelian must aim at some concrete specification of the general list that suits, and develops out of, the local conditions. This will always most reasonably be done in a participatory dialogue[75] with those who are most deeply immersed in those conditions. For though Aristotelianism does not hesitate to criticize tradition where tradition perpetrates injustice or oppression, it also does not believe in saying anything at all without rich and full information, gathered not so much from detached study as from the voices of those who live the ways of life in question. Martha Chen's work, both here and in her book, gives an excellent example of how such sensitivity to the local may be combined with a conviction that the central values on the list are worth pursuing even when tradition has not endorsed them.

The liberal charges the capability approach with *neglect of autonomy*, arguing that any such determinate conception removes from the citizens the chance to make their own choices about the good life. This is a complicated issue: three points can be stressed. First, the list is a list of capabilities, not a list of actual functions, precisely because the conception is designed to leave room for choice. Government is not directed to push citizens into acting in certain valued ways; instead, it is directed to make sure that all

[75] Martha Chen and her fellow development workers, in the project described in *A Quiet Revolution*, were indebted in their practice to Paolo Freire's notion of 'participatory dialogue'.

human beings have the necessary resources and conditions for acting in those ways. It leaves the choice up to them. A person with plenty of food can always choose to fast. A person who has been given the capability for sexual expression can always choose celibacy. The person who has access to subsidized education can always decide to do something else instead. By making opportunities available, government enhances, and does not remove, choice.[76] It will not always be easy to say at what point someone is really capable of making a choice, especially in areas where there are severe traditional obstacles to functioning. Sometimes our best strategy may well be to look at actual functioning and infer negative capability (tentatively) from its absence.[77] But the conceptual distinction remains very important.

Secondly, this respect for choice is built deeply into the list itself, in the architectonic role it gives to practical reasoning. One of the most central capabilities promoted by the conception will be the capability of choice itself.[78] We should note that the major liberal view in this area (that of John Rawls) agrees with our approach in just this area. For Rawls insists that satisfactions that are not the outgrowth of one's very own choices have no moral worth; and he conceives of the two moral powers (analogous to our practical reasoning), and of sociability (corresponding to our affiliation) as built into the definition of the parties in the original position, and thus as necessary constraints on any outcome they will select.[79]

Finally, the capability view insists that choice is not pure spontaneity, flourishing independent of material and social conditions. If one cares about autonomy, then one must care about the rest of the form of life that supports it, and the material conditions that enable one to live that form of life. Thus the approach claims that its own comprehensive concern with flourishing across all areas of life is a better way of promoting choice than is the liberal's narrower concern with spontaneity alone, which sometimes tolerates situations in which individuals are in other ways cut off from the fully human use of their faculties.

I turn now to the objection about application; it raises especially delicate questions where women are concerned.

[76] Sen has stressed this throughout his writing on the topic. For an overview, see 'Capability and Well-Being'.

[77] This is the strategy used by Erikson's Swedish team, when studying inequalities in political participation: see 'Descriptions of Inequality'. The point was well made by Bernard Williams in his response to Sen's Tanner Lectures: see Williams, 'The Standard of Living: Interests and Capabilities', in G. Hawthorn (ed.), *The Standard of Living* (Cambridge: Cambridge University Press, 1987). To give just one example of the issue, we will need to ask to what extent laws regulating abortion, sodomy laws, the absence of civil rights laws, etc., restrict the capability for sexual expression of women and homosexuals in a given society. The gay American military officer who chooses celibacy for fear of losing his job has not, in the relevant sense, been given a capability of choosing.

[78] See also Sen, *Commodities and Capabilities*.

[79] The relevant textual references are gathered and discussed in 'Aristotelian Social Democracy'.

7 WHO GETS INCLUDED? WOMEN AS HUMAN BEINGS

In a now well-known remark, which I cite here as an epigraph, the feminist lawyer Catharine MacKinnon claimed that 'being a woman is not yet a way of being a human being.'[80] This means, I think, that most traditional ways of categorizing and valuing women have not accorded them full membership in the human species, as that species is generally defined. MacKinnon is no doubt thinking in particular of the frequent denials to women of the rational nature that is taken to be a central part of what it is to be human. It is sobering to remind oneself that quite a few leading philosophers, including Aristotle and Rousseau, the 'fathers' (certainly not mothers) of my idea, did deny women full membership in human functioning as they understood that notion. If this is so, one might well ask, of what use is it really to identify a set of central human capabilities? For the basic (lower-level) capacity to develop these can always be denied to women, even by those who grant their centrality. Does this problem show that the human function idea is either hopelessly in league with patriarchy or, at best, impotent as a tool for justice?

I believe that it does not. For if we examine the history of these denials we see, I believe, the great power of the conception of the human as a source of moral claims. Acknowledging the other person as a member of the very same kind would have generated a sense of affiliation and a set of moral and educational duties. That is why, to those bent on shoring up their own power, the stratagem of splitting the other off from one's own species seems so urgent and so seductive. But to deny humanness to beings with whom one lives in conversation and interaction is a fragile sort of self-deceptive stratagem, vulnerable to sustained and consistent reflection, and also to experiences that cut through self-deceptive rationalization.[81] Any moral conception can be withheld, out of ambition or hatred or shame. But the conception of the human being, spelled out, as here, in a roughly determinate way, in terms of circumstances of life and functions in these circumstances, seems much harder to withhold than other conceptions that have been made the basis for ethics—'rational being', for example, or (as I have suggested) 'person'.

To illustrate this point, I now turn to the earliest argument known to me in the Western philosophical tradition that uses a conception of the human being for feminist ends. It is not the first feminist argument in the Western tradition: for Plato's *Republic* precedes (and influences) it.[82] But Plato's

---

[80] The remark was cited by Richard Rorty in 'Feminist and Pragmatism', *Michigan Quarterly Review*, 30 (1989), 231; it has since been confirmed and repeated by MacKinnon herself.

[81] See n. 37 above on Raoul Hilberg's account, in *The Destruction of the European Jews*, of the Nazi device of categorizing Jews as animals or inanimate objects, and the vulnerability of that stratagem to 'breakthroughs', in which the mechanisms of denial were caught off guard.

[82] The most comprehensive and incisive account of Plato's arguments about women is now

argument in favour of equal education for women is heavily qualified by his élitism with respect to all functions for all human beings; thus it is able to generate only élitist conclusions for males and females alike. Platonic justice is not the 'humanist justice' of Susan Okin's powerful phrase. The argument I have in mind is, instead, the first argument of the Roman Stoic thinker Musonius Rufus in his brief treatise, 'That Women Too Should Do Philosophy', written in the first century AD.[83] This argument is all the more interesting in that it, in effect, uses Aristotelian concepts to correct Aristotle's mistake about women—showing, I think, that an Aristotelian who is both internally consistent and honest about the evidence cannot avoid the egalitarian normative conclusion that women, as much as men, should receive a higher education (for that is in effect what is meant by doing philosophy).[84]

The argument has a tacit premise. It is that—at least with respect to certain central functions of the human being—the presence in a creature of a basic (untrained, lower-level) capability to perform the functions in question, given suitable support and education, exerts a claim on society that those capabilities should be developed to the point at which the person is fully capable of choosing the functions in question. This premise needed no argument in the philosophical culture of Greco-Roman antiquity, since that moral claim is more or less taken to be implicit in the notion of capability itself. I have tried to give it intuitive support in the argument of this paper.

The argument itself now follows with a truly radical simplicity. Its second premise consists of an appeal to the experience of the imaginary recalcitrant male interlocutor. Women, he is asked to concede on the basis of experience, do in fact have the basic capabilities to perform a wide variety of the most important human functions. They have the five senses. They have the same number of bodily parts, implying similar functional possibilities in that sphere. They have the ability to think and reason, just as males do. And, finally, they have responsiveness to ethical distinctions, making (whether well or badly) distinctions between the good and the bad. Some time is then spent establishing a third premise: that 'higher education' of

in Stephen Halliwell, *Plato: Republic* Book V (Warminster: Aris and Phillips, 1992), Introduction and commentary to the relevant passages. See also Okin, *Women in Western Political Thought*.

[83] For Musonius' collected works see the edition by O. Hense (Leipzig: Teubner Library, 1905). Other works with radical conclusions for women's issues include 'Should Boys and Girls Have the Same Education?' (answering yes to that question); 'Should One Raise all the Children Who are Born?' (arguing against infanticide, a particular threat to female offspring); 'On the Goal of Marriage' (arguing against the sexual double standard and in favour of equal sexual fidelity for both sexes; arguing as well against the common view that female slaves were available for sexual use).

[84] Stoics are of course highly critical of much that passes for higher education, holding that the traditional 'liberal studies' are not 'liberal' in the right way, that is, do not truly 'free' the mind to take charge of its own reasoning. See Seneca, *Moral Epistle* 88.

the sort offered by the Stoic ideal of liberal education, is necessary for the full development of the perceptual, intellectual, and moral capabilities. Conclusion: women, like men, should have this education.

The puzzle, for us, is the second premise. Why does the interlocutor accept it? We see from the surrounding material that the interlocutor is a husband who interacts with his wife in a number of areas of life that are explicitly enumerated: planning and managing a household (where she is the one who manages most of the daily business); having and raising children (where he observes, or imagines, her in labour, enduring risk and pain for the sake of the family and, later, caring for and educating the child); having sexual relations with him, and refusing to have sex with others; having a real friendship with him, based on common contemporary ideas of 'sharing life together';[85] deciding how to treat the people around her; being fair, for example, to the household staff; and, finally, confronting all the dangers and the moral ambiguities of the politics of first century AD Rome—refusing to capitulate, he says, to the unjust demands of a tyrant. In all of these operations of life, the argument seems to be, he tacitly acknowledges, in fact strongly relies upon, his wife's capability to engage in practical reasoning and ethical distinction making. Indeed, he is depicted as someone who would like these things done *well*—for he wants his wife not to reason badly when political life gets tough, or to treat the servants with cruelty, or to botch the education of the children. So in his daily life he acknowledges her humanity, her possession of the basic (lower-level) capabilities for fully human functioning. How, then, Musonius reasonably asks him, can he consistently deny her what would be necessary in order to develop and fulfil that humanity?

This, I believe, is an impressively radical argument. And it led to (or reflected) a social situation that marked a high point for women in the Western tradition for thousands of years since and to come.[86] We do not need to show that the views of Musonius on women were perfect in all respects; in many ways they were not. But his argument shows, I believe, the power of a universal conception of the human being in claims of justice for women. For the interlocutor might have refused to acknowledge that his wife was a 'person': it was to some extent up to him to define that rather refined and elusive concept. He could not fail to acknowledge that she was a human being, with the basic capability for the functions in question. For he had acknowledged that already, in his daily life.

---

[85] See Musonius, 'On the Goal of Marriage'. Similar conceptions are defended by Seneca and Plutarch. On this shift in thinking about the marital relationship, see the useful discussion in Foucault, *History of Sexuality*, vol. III, trans. R. Hurley (New York: Pantheon, 1985).

[86] On the way in which Christianity disrupted the emerging feminist consensus, see G. E. M. de Ste. Croix, *The Class Struggle in the Ancient Greek World* (London: Duckworth, 1987).

8 WOMEN AND MEN: TWO NORMS OR ONE?

But should there *be* a single norm of human functioning? It has often been argued, in both non-Western and Western traditions, that there should be two different standards of human functioning and capability, corresponding to the different 'natures' of the male and the female. Usually these overlap in the areas of bodily health, mobility, and perception, but differ sharply in the areas of practical reason and affiliation. Most commonly, citizenship, public activity, and full practical autonomy are assigned to males, care for home and family to females. We must now confront the claims of this position.

Those who recognize separate spheres of functioning for males and females have taken up two importantly-different positions, which we need to be careful to distinguish. The first, which I shall call Position A, assigns to both males and females the same general normative list of functions, but suggests that males and females should exercise these functions in different spheres of life. The second, which I shall call Position B, insists that the list of functions, even at a high level of generality, should be different. (It is B rather than A that is usually associated with the claim that males and females have different 'natures'.)

Position A is compatible with a serious interest in equality and in gender justice. For what it says, after all, is that males and females have the same basic needs for capability development and should get what they need. It is determined to ensure that both get to the higher (developed) level of capability with respect to all the central functions. It simply holds that this can (and perhaps should) be done in separate spheres. It is a kind of gender-based local specification. A is, after all, the position of Musonius, who holds that the major functions of affiliation and practical reason may be exercised by the woman in the management of the home and by the man in the public sphere.[87] It evidently seems to him convenient, given women's childbearing role, that the customary divisions of duties should not be overturned, and he believes that all the major capabilities can flourish in either sphere. Is this any more problematic than to say that human functioning in India can, and even should, take a different concrete form from functioning in England?

The difficulty is, however, that once we have recognized the extent to which gender divisions have been socially constructed in morally arbitrary

---

[87] See the last section of 'That Women Too', where he answers the male interlocutor's imaginary objection that educated women will spend too much time sitting around and talking, and neglect their practical duties, by telling him that the very same issue arises for him: he too has practical duties that may seem less interesting than talking about ideas, and he too should make sure that he doesn't neglect them. It is, I think, because Musonius has a pretty low view of the worth of male public life that he can easily view that sphere as equivalent and equal to the female sphere.

and injurious ways, and once we insist, instead, on using common humanity as our moral and political basis, it is difficult to see what good arguments there are for Position A, which just happens to maintain in place divisions that have often proven oppressive to women. What could such arguments be?

I have mentioned biological differences. But how much separation of function is really suggested by women's childbearing, especially today? Even in the fourth century BC, Plato was able to see that the situation of males and females is not very different from the situation of male and female hunting dogs: the female needs a period of rest for childbearing and nursing, but this in no way requires, or even suggests, a life-long differentiation of functions. Advances in the control of reproduction are making this less and less plausible. And it should be evident to all that the disability imposed by childbearing for the member of the labour force is to a large extent constructed, above all by the absence of support for child care, both from the public sphere and from employers. Other bodily differences that have standardly been mentioned—for example, differences in bodily strength that have often been held to imply a differentiation of functions— are increasingly being found to be based on bad scientific argument,[88] and are also less and less plausible as bases for functional differentiation. Military functions, for example, depend less and less upon bodily strength and more and more on education. The recognition of this by the US Congress in its recent equalization of military roles simply grants what should long ago have been obvious.

One might also point to contingent social facts. Societies are already divided along gender lines. So if we are going to move to a situation in which women will be capable of exercising all the major functions, it will be prudent to develop the resources of that gender-divided structure, seeking greater independence and fulfilment for women within it, rather than trying to break it up. This, I think, is what is really going on in Musonius. As a Greek-speaking philosopher in Nero's Rome, he hasn't the ghost of a chance of making institutional changes of the sort recommended in Stoic views of the ideal city, in which males and females were to be fully equal citizens with no distinction of spheres and even no distinction of clothing![89] He does have a hope of convincing individual husbands to allow their wives access to education, so he does what he can. Much the same is true in Martha Chen's *A Quiet Revolution*. Neither Chen nor her colleagues proposed to jettison all gender divisions within the village. Instead, they found 'female jobs' that were somewhat more dignified and important than the old jobs, jobs that looked continuous with traditional female work but were outside the home and brought in wages.

[88] See Anne Fausto-Sterling, *Myths of Gender*.
[89] For the evidence, see Malcolm Schofield, *The Stoic Idea of the City* (Cambridge: Cambridge University Press, 1992).

Frequently this is a prudent strategy in bringing about real social change. As Martha Chen shows, the 'revolution' in women's quality of life never would have taken place but for the caution of the women, who at each stage gave the men of the village reason to believe that the transformations were not overwhelmingly threatening and were good for the well-being of the entire group. On the other hand, such pragmatic decisions in the face of recalcitrant realities do not tell us how things ought to be. To hold that a gender-divided two-spheres result is an acceptable specification of the norm is deeply problematic. For very often the traditionally female norm is socially devalued, and the traditionally male functions powerfully connected with important advantages. In Musonius' Rome, a husband can be both a citizen and a household manager; a wife does not have the choice to be a citizen. In Metha Bai's contemporary India, the confinement of women to the domestic sphere cuts them off from the choice to earn a living, a powerful determinant of overall capability status. In short, 'separate but equal' assignments usually serve the ends of a dominant group and perpetuate the oppression of the powerless.[90]

This point needs particular attention in thinking about divisions of labour within the family. It seems perfectly reasonable that in any household there should be a division of labour, even a long-standing one, with some members gaining greater skills at one task, some at another. It would already be great progress, *vis-à-vis* the current state of things in all known countries, if domestic duties were equally divided by time and effort. But even in that utopian situation, assignment of tasks along traditional gender-divided lines may be suspect, on account of its possible association with lack of respect and self-respect. If all and only girls are taught to cook, for example, this does not seem to be a morally neutral case of functional specialization (like teaching one child the piano, another the clarinet); for it reinforces stereotypes that are associated, historically, with the denial to women of citizenship and autonomy.

I conclude that there are no good arguments for position A, and that even the prudent use of A in promoting gradual social change should be viewed

---

[90] Is the Nigerian situation depicted in Nzegwu's paper an exception? We can agree with her that the traditional system in which women controlled certain vital agricultural functions and men others, was somewhat better, in capability terms, than the system of confinement to the domestic sphere imposed by British colonialism, without being altogether sure that the traditional system was morally acceptable. This would depend on a closer scrutiny of the whole system of functionings and capabilities, as affected by gender divisions. I am no expert in Ibo culture, clearly; but the traditional Ibo families depicted in Chinua Achebe's novels, for example, do not seem to me to manifest full gender equality in capability. Okonkwo (in *Things Fall Apart*) can decide to beat his wife; she cannot choose to beat him in return, or even to stop him, in all but the most egregious of cases. Okonkwo can choose to take another wife; no wife of his can choose another husband. The reason why Okonkwo keeps wishing that Ezinma had been a boy rather than a girl is that he perceives that, being a girl, she is debarred from many functions for which she seems well suited. His fear of being seen as a 'woman' is, by contrast, a fear of capability failure.

with caution, and with a constant awareness of more genuinely equal norms.

I turn now to Position B, which has been influentially defended by many philosophers, including Rousseau and some of his contemporary followers.[91] This position may be criticized in a number of different ways. First, we should insist that, insofar as it rests on the claim that there are two different sets of basic capabilities, this claim has not been borne out by any responsible scientific evidence. As Anne Fausto Sterling's *Myths of Gender* repeatedly shows, experiments that allegedly show strong gender divisions in basic (untrained) abilities are full of scientific flaws; these flaws removed, the case for such differences is altogether inconclusive.

Secondly, we should note that even what is claimed without substantiation in this body of scientific material usually does not amount to a difference in what I have been calling the central basic capabilities. What is alleged is usually a differential statistical distribution of some specific capacity for a high level of excellence, not for crossing the threshold, and excellence in some very narrowly defined function (say, geometrical ability), rather than in one of our large-scale capabilities such as the capability to perform practical reasoning (which may, recall, be done in a number of different ways, in accordance with the particular tastes and abilities of the individual). So: even if the claim were true it would not be a claim about capabilities in our capacious sense; nor, since it is a statistical claim, would it have any implications for the ways in which individuals should be treated. So the political consequences of such gender differences in our scheme of things, even had they been established, would be nil.

Finally, we must also note that it is in principle next to impossible, right now, to do the sort of research that would be required if such differences were ever to be convincingly established. For it has been shown that right now, from birth on, babies of the two sexes are differently treated by parents and other adults, in accordance with the perception of their external genitalia. They are handled differently, spoken to differently, given different toys. Their emotions are labelled differently—thus a crying infant tends to be labelled 'angry' if the observer believes it to be a boy, and 'frightened' if the observer believes it to be a girl.[92] This means that in the present gender-divided state of things we cannot get beneath culture reliably enough to get the necessary evidence about basic capabilities. I think this supports the conclusion I defended earlier: the potential for error and abuse in capability testing is so great that we should proceed as if every individual has the basic capabilities.

[91] On Rousseau, see Okin, *Women*, and Jane Roland Martin, *Reclaiming a Conversation* (New Haven: Yale University Press, 1985). On some related contemporary arguments, for example those of Allan Bloom, see Okin, *Justice*, ch. 1.
[92] On all this, see Fausto-Sterling.

But we can also criticize Position B in a different way. For I believe that it can also be shown that the differentiated conceptions of male and female functioning characteristically put forward by B are internally inadequate, and fail to give us viable norms of human flourishing.[93]

What do we usually find, in the versions of B that our philosophical tradition bequeaths to us? (Rousseau's view is an instructive example.) We have, on the one hand, males who are 'autonomous', capable of practical reasoning, independent and self-sufficient, allegedly good at political deliberation. These males are brought up not to develop strong emotions of love and feelings of deep need that are associated with the awareness of one's own lack of self-sufficiency. For this reason they are not well equipped to care for the needs of their family members, or, perhaps, even to notice those needs. On the other hand, we have females such as Rousseau's Sophie, brought up to lack autonomy and self-respect, ill equipped to rely on her own practical reasoning, dependent on males, focused on pleasing others, good at caring for others. Is either of these viable as a complete life for a human being?

It would seem not. The internal tensions in Rousseau's account are a good place to begin seeing this; they have been well described by Susan Okin and Jane Roland Martin. Rousseau, in *Emile*, places tremendous emphasis on compassion as a basic social motivation. He understands compassion to require fellow feeling, and a keen responsiveness to the sufferings of others. And yet, in preparing Emile for autonomous citizenship, in the end he shortchanges these emotional functions, allocating caring and responsiveness to the female sphere alone. It appears likely that Emile will be not only an incomplete person but also a defective citizen, even by the standards of citizenship recognized by Rousseau himself.

With Sophie, things again go badly. Taught to care for others, but not taught that her life is her own to plan, she lives under the sway of external influences and lacks self-government. As Rousseau himself shows, in his fascinating narrative of the end of her life, she comes to a bad end through her lack of judgement. Moreover—as Musonius already argued to his Roman husband, defending equal functioning—she proves to be a bad partner and deficient in love. For love, as we come to see, requires judgement and constancy if it is to be truly deep and truly perceptive. So each of them fails to live a complete human life; and each fails, too, to exemplify fully and well the very functions for which they were being trained, since those functions require support from other functions for which they were not trained. The text leads its thoughtful reader to the conclusion that the

[93] Here I am in agreement with the general line of argument in Okin, *Women*, and Martin, *Reclaiming*, and with the related arguments in Nancy Chodorow's *The Reproduction of Mothering*, which I discuss in my other chapter.

capabilities that have traditionally marked the separate male and female spheres are not separable from one another without a grave functional loss. They support and educate one another. So society cannot strive for completeness by simply adding one sphere to the other. It must strive to develop in each and every person the full range of human capabilities.

This more inclusive notion of human functioning admits tragic conflict. For it insists on the separate value and the irreplaceable importance of a rich plurality of functions. And the world does not always guarantee that individuals will not be faced with painful choices among these functions, in which, in order to pursue one of them well they must neglect others (and thus, in many cases, subvert the one as well). But this shows once again, I believe, the tremendous importance of keeping some such list of the central functions before us as we assess the quality of life in the countries of the world and strive to raise it. For many such tragedies—like many cases of simple capability failure—result from unjust and unreflective social arrangements. One can imagine, and try to construct, a society in which the tragic choices that faced Emile and Sophie would not be necessary, in which both males and females could learn both to love and to reason.

Being a woman is indeed not yet a way of being a human being. Women in much of the world lack support for the most central human functions, and this denial of support is frequently caused by their being women. But women, unlike rocks and plants and even dogs and horses, are human beings, have the potential to become capable of these human functions, given sufficient nutrition, education, and other support. That is why their unequal failure in capability is a problem of justice. It is up to us to solve this problem. I claim that a conception of human functioning gives us valuable assistance as we undertake this task.[94]

[94] I am grateful to all the members of our meeting for valuable comments, and especially to Amartya Sen for valuable discussions and to David Crocker, Jonathan Glover, Cass Sunstein, and Susan Wolf for helpful written comments. I am also grateful to Chris Bobonich, David Estlund, and Henry Richardson for comments on related earlier work.

Martha C. Nussbaum: Human Capabilities, Female Human Beings

Commentary by Susan Wolf

In 'Human Capabilities, Female Human Beings', Martha Nussbaum takes up a position she has been developing in other works, filling out aspects of it and bringing out implications it has specifically for issues relating to development and to gender. At its centre is a self-consciously normative conception of humanness—of what it is to be human and to live a good human life—involving a specification of basic human limits and capabilities, which in turn form the basis for a list of ten basic functional capabilities, the possession of which are offered as necessary conditions of human flourishing. Practically, the position is proposed as a basis for a development ethic, as both a response to and defence against the deep relativism to be found in much of the academy and as a significant alternative to those who would see development in terms either of GNP or utility.

In what I take to be its most important claims and goals, both practical and theoretical, I am in complete agreement with Nussbaum's position. The existence of a common humanity that we can recognize across centuries and continents, and the existence of associated functions, the realizations of which constitute common marks of human good, are things I have no wish or reason to deny. With Nussbaum, I believe that the theoretical challenges relativists and subjectivists raise against the project of finding universals in human life can be met by a suitably cautious, nuanced, and open-ended approach to the project. And with Nussbaum, I see the specification of such functions and the account of human thriving to which it points to be a vastly better foundation for a development ethic than the alternatives—GNP or utility—especially, I might add, with respect to the prospect of promoting equality across races, castes, and economic classes, as well as gender.

My comments, then, critical as they are inevitably apt to sound, are offered in the spirit of one wanting to join in a common enterprise. Rather than challenges to the basic way of proceeding, they are meant to point to ambiguities and complications, areas that, in the continuing effort to spell out this very ambitious foundation for an international ethic, seem to me especially worthy of attention.

1 GENERAL MATTERS

Let me begin with some remarks about the enterprise as a whole, about the very idea of developing 'an account of the most important functions of the human being, in terms of which human life is defined'. As Nussbaum stresses, the choice to take as central the concept of humanness, rather than that of personhood, is a conscious one. I agree with that choice, but would emphasize different reasons for it (and dangers of it) than Nussbaum does in this essay.

Nussbaum herself suggests that the hopes for achieving gender equality are more likely to be met if we start with the notion of a human being rather than that of a person. Specifically, she thinks it harder for the enemies of equality to deny humanity to women than it is to deny them the status of being a person. Of this I am sceptical—hard as it is to deny women and members of other oppressed groups membership of the species, it seems to me equally hard to deny them personhood. And if American courts have managed despite all intellectual obstacles to do the latter, so, as Nussbaum mentions, Aristotle himself was able to do the former. (It is also my impression that some contemporary Klan members continue to regard black people as literally subhuman.) With respect to the question of how, intellectually, to combat exclusion from moral attention, the choice between appeal to a common humanity and a common personality seems a small one.

At the same time, focusing on the flourishing of human beings rather than persons does seem to me to have substantive implications of considerable importance. For the term 'human being', as opposed to 'person', at least as one tradition uses the latter expression, refers to a biological as well as a spiritual being, and indeed, to a being whose physical needs and potentialities are inextricably interwoven with her spiritual and intellectual ones. Human flourishing is, then, more naturally suggestive of a complex, organic ideal, in which the ability to exercise physical powers and realize physical capabilities is not artificially separated from or denigrated in comparison with intellectual and spiritual ideals. In the context of articulating a development ethic, this appreciation of the physical and psychophysical needs and capabilities of human beings is perhaps especially important.

The choice to take as central a concept that is partly biological does, however, bring with it certain dangers that one must be careful to avoid. The first is that of speciesism—that is, a neglect or disregard for the welfare of species other than our own. The second is that of sexism. For precisely because the idea of a human being is in part a biological one, and because sex is a biological fact, the possibility of different sorts of human beings, with different natures, needs, and potentialities, must be admitted and recognized. An ethic centred on persons is more likely to declare sex irrelevant than an ethic based on biological human beings. Whether this is ultimately an advantage or a disadvantage of a human-based ethic is a topic I shall return to in the final section of this paper. But advocates of gender equality must at least recognize that calling explicit attention to biology is a risky business.

Setting out to define human life, and to define a good human life, is also risky business, and my remaining general worries about Nussbaum's project have to do with this aim. Specifically, it seems to me that there is a difference between setting out, as it were, to *characterize* humanity, and attempting literally to define it. The first project, which I wholeheartedly endorse, operates on the premise that there exists a common humanity that we can recognize across centuries and continents, and aims to articulate a set of associated functions, the realizations of which constitute common marks of human good. It involves a commitment to the idea that empirical questioning, deep reflection, and open-minded dialogue yield an ever-revisable but 'determinate account of the human being, human functioning, and human flourishing'. This project seems to me to capture all that is most valuable in Nussbaum's proposal, specifically, as the foundation of a development ethic, in ways that strongly contrast her position to the relativism of the Marglins and the utilitarianism of others. By far the greatest portion of 'Human Capabilities, Female Human Beings' can be interpreted as a stage in the fulfilment of this project. But there are moments in the paper that suggest an even more ambitious, and, I think, unnecessarily controversial goal.

Nussbaum herself describes what she is doing as giving an account of functions 'in terms of which human life is defined', offering a description of two thresholds, 'a threshold of capability to function beneath which a life will be so impoverished that it will not be human at all; and a somewhat higher threshold, beneath which those characteristic functions are available in such a reduced way that, though we may judge the form of life a human one, we will not think it a *good* human life'. These self-descriptions of her enterprise echo earlier papers in which Nussbaum refers to her project as a defence of a form of essentialism.

Taken literally, these remarks require us to interpret Nussbaum's lists of human functionings as proposals for sets of functionings, the capabilities of which are *essential* to the living, respectively, of a human life or of a good human life. A being who lacked the capacity to function in one of the ways listed in connection with Nussbaum's first threshold would not count, according to this proposal, as living a human life; one who lacked the capacity to function in a way associated with her second threshold could not be considered to live a *good* human life.

Such claims are extremely strong. If candidates for Nussbaum's lists are tested according to their ability to meet the conditions of essentialism, at least a few of Nussbaum's own suggestions would have to be ruled out. Conceiving of sufficiently deprived circumstances in which a child might be brought up, one can imagine a person who has become incapable of a positive relation to the world of nature, or even one who lacks the capacity to laugh or play, without being tempted to deny that person the status of humanity. Indeed, one might even imagine such a person living a *good* human life, of a sort—for the incapacity to function in these ways is compatible with the development of talents, the acquisition of virtues, the experience of pleasures, and the achievement of a wide remaining variety of worthwhile ends. One need only think of Stephen Hawking—or Stevie Wonder—to remember that some of the most inspiring examples of good human lives involve the overcoming or accommodation of severe disabilities and impairments.

To respond to this point by shrinking the lists to even more basic, 'more essential', human functions would be to miss their point and their value. For the claim that these functions are of tremendous value to people of all races and sexes, across centuries and continents, is not disproved by noting that a given individual here or there has managed to live a rich and fulfilling life without one or the other of these functional capabilities. (Parents of children with Down's Syndrome often talk about the joy they have experienced raising their children, the absence of regret for their decisions to have and to keep their babies. It would be foolish to conclude from this, however, that it would be good for every parent to have such an experience, much less that it is no better for parents, or more importantly, for the children themselves, that the children be able to develop intellectually, physically, and emotionally into mature adults.) The fact that one can live a valuable life without sight or limbs, without beauty or humour, does not mean that these things are of no or little value.

To avoid these misdirected criticisms, we need some clarification of the use to which Nussbaum's lists are to be put, of the purposes they are intended to serve. Plainly, they are not to be applied as tests for the humanity or the quality of individual lives. (What could be the interest of such an enterprise, anyway?) Nussbaum's references to human *forms* of life suggest that we do better understanding these lists as a basis for assessing communities, or more importantly, as constituting a set of needs and goals to which we must widely and persistently attend in devising and directing social, political, and economic policy.

The point we want to make, presumably, is that public policy must take into account these basic human functions, and, moreover, take them into account in a way that precludes trading them off in any drastic way for the sake of other significant goals. The fact that Stevie Wonder can live a fulfilling life does not legitimate an employer's decision to make her employees work in conditions that will predictably lead to blindness. Policies that would have people live in ways totally cut off from nature, or work in ways that deprive them of opportunity for play are unacceptable no matter how they bear on the ability to satisfy other basic needs.

Even if we emphasize the application of Nussbaum's thresholds to forms of life, rather than to individual lives, we must be careful to avoid the dangers of cultural imperialism that are inevitable in a project like this one. How can anyone or any group be in a position to list threshold criteria for good forms of human life? Nussbaum is sensitive to this concern, noting that 'the account is meant to be both tentative and open-ended. We allow explicitly for the possibility that we will learn from our encounters with other human societies to recognize things about ourselves that we had not seen before, or even to change in certain ways, according more importance to something we had thought more peripheral.' This point should be emphasized.

The language of essentialism tends to suggest that in constructing an account of human good, we are engaged in a project that, at least in principle, will eventually be both universal and complete, in need of no further revisions or exceptions. But the value and purpose of Nussbaum's project does not rely on any such expectation, and there is no harm in admitting, with many antiessentialists, that our ability to recognize a common humanity is apt to outstrip any list of criteria that theorists are likely to come up with. We theorists can offer a list of basic human functions— compiled from the empirical investigation, deep reflection, and dialogue appropriate to such a project—without going out on the further and possibly presumptuous limb of suggesting that any life or form of life without some one or other of these functions is to be ruled nonhuman.

If one did find that a community or culture accorded no value to one of these functions and yet, after a truly egalitarian sampling of its members' perspectives, appeared to be thriving, this would be cause, in the first place, for scrutiny, reflection, and dialogue. A community that might, on first inspection, appear to be flourishing, might not appear so on further scrutiny—instabilities, inconsistencies, and tensions of various sorts may be discovered lurking below the surface. Furthermore, with adequate explanations of why the function in which this community lacks interest seem so valuable to others (how it complements and enhances other mutually valued functions, how it offers its own unique form of enrichment) it is possible that the community in question will come to appreciate the value of this formerly neglected function and be able to incorporate it into its existing values in some relatively nondisruptive way. On the other hand, the theorists may ultimately conclude they were wrong about the universality or significance about a function they had thought basic, removing it from the list, or replacing it with a somewhat different one. Engaging in the project of developing an account of human good in a way that is self-consciously open-ended and tentative is still a far cry from embracing deep relativism or radical subjectivism.

2 MORE SPECIFIC CONCERNS

My comments so far have addressed some very general issues about how best to interpret Nussbaum's project of developing an account of the capability of basic human functions which are to serve as criteria for human good. My hope has been mainly to steer responses to the project away from some paths and toward others, to avoid certain philosophical controversies to which contemporary academics seem especially attracted but which seem to me irrelevant to the point and value of the project.

If debate about essentialism seems irrelevant, however, other sorts of debate are to be actively welcomed. Issues internal to the project's basic theoretical and normative commitments need to be confronted and worked out. To make concrete suggestions of the sort that seem called for is beyond my competence. Here I wish only to point to some questions that need to be asked and answered, aspects of the ongoing programme of elaborating a development ethic along Nussbaum's line that supporters of the project will want to work out, ideally through dialogue and debate.

Most obviously, the lists of human functionings corresponding to Nussbaum's two thresholds should be thoroughly scrutinized. Do all the items on the lists really belong there? Are they adequately described? Are there human functionings that are missing from the list? Understanding the point of the lists in the way I have suggested in the previous section—namely, as a set of functions capability which any good *form* of human life should value and aim to foster universally in its members—I find no item on Nussbaum's list that I would want to eliminate. But Nussbaum's discussion of 'strong separateness' and her inclusion of items 10 and 11—the abilities, respectively, 'to live one's own life and nobody else's' and 'to live one's own life in one's own surroundings and context'—in her list of the essentials of a good human life require discussion and clarification. Though in practical terms the inclusion of these items may have immediate beneficial implications for women, and more generally for groups who have been deprived of freedom and autonomy in the name of a false common good, they appear to assume a superiority of individualism over communitarianism at a level of theory that is, at least, controversial. The capability to exercise practical reason, to use one's own deliberative powers in the planning, shaping, and managing of one's life need not itself necessarily be channelled into individualistic activities and goals. Practical reason can be exercised in participatory forms as well, aimed at the articulation and achievement of communal ends. So, the degree to which Nussbaum's references to separateness are or ought to be understood as a demand for individual autonomy needs to be clarified, scrutinized, and defended.

As we need to look carefully at each of the items Nussbaum has suggested for the lists, we need to look widely in the world to see whether there are items that ought to be added to those already proposed. I notice that there is no explicit mention of capabilities to develop any aesthetic sensibilities or to respond to forms of beauty. This may be significant and universal enough to deserve a separate place. This suggestion, and suggestions of this type very generally, are best conducted, however, in close conjunction with empirical observation and cross-cultural and anthropological knowledge. As these lists are to be used both in the formulation of policy goals and in the avoidance of regrettable side-effects from policy, so they should be continually reviewed and revised as the tasks of concrete policy-making call attention to new controversies and dangers, and raise new questions about human good.

As important as questions about the individual items on Nussbaum's lists of human functionings are questions about priorities and trade-offs among them. In Nussbaum's paper, she warns against too readily ranking these functions and trading them off against each other. 'All', she writes, 'are of central importance and all are distinct in quality. We cannot satisfy the need for one of them by giving a larger amount of another one.'

There are good reasons for resisting agglomeration of these separate goods. Part of what distinguishes the human functionings view from utilitarianism is its appreciation of the incommensurable, distinctive values of separate functions and of the need to deal with the tasks of preserving and promoting the variety of human goods in a suitably complex way. As a long-term goal, we want to insist that the aim is the provision of all these capabilities to as many people as possible. And in constructing policies that focus on some of these capabilities or goods, we want to be careful not to close off or impair our potential to develop other capabilities at other times.

Still, limited resources in the face of enormous need require that choices be made and that priorities be set. Where people are starving it seems absurd to occupy oneself with the quality of their relationship to nature. As Nussbaum notes, promoting the capability to function in one way may enhance rather than compete with the capability to function in another. Policies that will encourage such complementarity are obviously preferable to ones that do not. Again, however, if the human functionings view is to be a useful tool for development policy, it will be necessary for its advocates to address these issues and to face up to the fact that one cannot help all of the people in all ways all of the time. Priorities do need to be set about which functional capabilities should be attended to first. And though setting priorities among values is not the same as trading off one value for another (promoting one good before another is not the same as sacrificing the latter for the former), one cannot entirely avoid the need to make trade-offs either.

Priorities, and possibly also trade-offs, must be considered, not only among the various functioning capabilities, but also among the people or groups of people in whom they are to be fostered. As we cannot improve all aspects of a community's life at once, neither can we benefit all segments of the community equally, at least in the short term. We need to develop a way to answer questions about whom to benefit first as well as a way to answer questions about what benefits to provide. It is not clear to me that a theory of human good can or should by itself provide the basis for dealing with these questions. A theory of justice (not necessarily independent of the theory of human good, but also not wholly contained in it) needs to be supplemented and explicitly defended in order to formulate a way to make these decisions.

Questions about how to set priorities or make trade-offs among people or goods may not be usefully pursued at the level of abstraction at which these papers are set. There may be no simple formulae ranking the values of some functions, available to ever-higher degrees, over the values of others, no simple principles of justice that can tell us how to distribute our efforts within a community. My point here is only to acknowledge that, at some level of specificity, such questions will arise, and that further elaboration of a development ethic based on a theory of human functional capabilities will have to provide a way of meeting them.

3 GENDER

The advantages of basing development policy on a conception of human functioning capabilities, especially for the most oppressed groups in developing countries, have been well described by Nussbaum and Sen. Such an approach allows us to record facts about the distribution of goods among a community's members that tend to be masked by an approach that assesses a society's well-being in terms of GNP. Moreover, unlike a preference-utilitarian approach, a functional capabilities approach can reveal deprivations and inequalities that members of the community themselves fail to recognize or to admit due to deeply-ingrained social expectations and norms. Women in particular, whose specific deprivations have frequently been overlooked by these other approaches, stand to benefit considerably by adopting an approach that calls attention to the capabilities to function that society affords all its members.

But, as I mentioned in my introductory remarks, one cannot simply *assume* that capabilities to function which a just and good society should afford its members are everywhere exactly the same for men and for women. An approach such as this one, that takes the category of human being as central, a category that, while partly normative, is also partly biological, must allow that it is in part an empirical matter whether the basic constituents for a good life for men are the same as they are for women.

Nussbaum herself, in the conclusion of her essay, argues for one norm of human functioning rather than two. As she points out, no philosophical account advocating different norms for men and women has ever been fully intellectually successful, and the uses to which such accounts have been put historically have been very bad. We all recognize that, to a very large extent, gender differences are socially constructed. In light of this, Nussbaum finds no good arguments for claiming that basic functioning capabilities differ with sex, and so advocates one norm common to all humans.

Here, as elsewhere in Nussbaum's paper, I would prefer a less bold conclusion. Like Nussbaum, I see no good arguments to support the claim that basic functioning capabilities differ with sex. But neither do I see any good arguments for the claim that they do not differ. For in the abstract, that claim seems to imply that, unlike our species membership, our sex does not fundamentally affect or define what would constitute good lives for us. A good human life is a good human life, whether it belongs to a man or a woman. Or at least, Nussbaum's remarks would seem to suggest, this is how it should be.

I have no reason to take an opposite view from this. Perhaps in a relevantly different society, men's and women's needs and capabilities (with the exception of those that are quite strictly dictated by anatomy) would be exactly the same, and so the basic constituents of a good life for men would likewise be the same for women. And perhaps, in such a society, the good lives which the luckiest would be able to attain would be even better than the best lives achievable within more gendered societies. Perhaps, in other words, a genderless world would be wonderful. But I cannot really conceive such a world in any detail, and I haven't any idea of how speculations about the possibility and desirability of eradicating gender altogether could be defended responsibly. At present, our gender so deeply affects who we are, how we are treated by others and how we think of ourselves, that it is difficult to imagine what it would be like for one's sex not to be a deep part of one's identity. In light of this, it seems we should be reluctant to make larger or more general claims about these issues than we need.

Rather than commit ourselves to an overall view about how, if at all, sex or gender affect the criteria for good human lives, we should proceed, as Nussbaum herself does, in a more constructive fashion, proposing, reflecting on, and debating specific functional capabilities themselves, and asking whether each type of human function that occurs to us is significant for men as well as for women, and to the same degree?

In the past, theories that were offered as theories of human nature tended actually to be theories of male human nature—theories constructed by men, formed by thinking about men, and intended to apply to and describe men. Obviously, we must protect against the exclusion of women from the definition, the imagination and the concern of the theory-builders (as well as the concern of the policy-makers whom it is hoped the theory will aid). The way to do this, however, is not by insisting, before the fact, that there will be one norm for men and women alike, but rather, by ensuring that women as well as men participate in the task of theory construction, that both be sensitive to the history and the dangers of excluding women from consideration, and that both be careful in their reflections sometimes to focus specifically on the real and imagined lives of women and sometimes to focus specifically on the real and imagined lives of men.

Nussbaum's own proposed lists of basic human functional capabilities constitute much more than a start on this project. The functions she lists do seem basic to women and men alike, suggesting, at this level of abstraction, a single conception of the criteria for a good life that will apply to all humans, *qua* humans. But this is compatible with a variety of ways in which differentiation along lines of sex or gender may ultimately be relevant to human individual and social ideals.

Reflection and research might uncover some form of functioning capability that is basic for one sex but not for the other. Or perhaps one form of functioning, while relevant to the quality of life for both sexes, will turn out to be more important, and its lack more crippling, to one sex than to the other.

Even if, at the abstract level, the list of basic human needs and functions is held in common, more specific descriptions of how these needs can be met and how these functions can be realized may bring out differences between men and women. Thus, for example, while all humans need to be adequately nourished, men's nutritional needs differ somewhat from women's (and pregnant women's from non-pregnant women's). It is an open question whether the specification of any emotional, intellectual, or other psychological needs also vary in accordance with sex.

If there are no significant particular differences among basic functional capabilities for men and women, it may yet be relevant to the quality of life that there be some differentiation or other regarding gender. The tendency to take one's sex seriously as a significant feature of one's identity may run very deep, causing society to endow sex with more than anatomical meaning even if there is no particular meaning to which nature points. Thus, even if no basic properties or functions are naturally gendered, if, in other words, the content of gender is always a product of a historical and contingent culture, it may be the case that gender of some sort is an inevitable aspect of any culture. We may embrace the need to revise norms relating to gender, to change both the practices and the values which perpetuate injustice along gender lines, without necessarily committing ourselves to the larger and more radical project of eradicating gender altogether. The issue of whether gender as such should be fought to the limit, of whether gender has any place in a utopian ideal, will be debated within and without feminist theory for many years. But it seems to me that we need not enter this battle or invoke it in order to affirm the value of the human functional capabilities approach, both intellectually and practically.

As I said, Nussbaum's own list of basic functionings constitutes a substantive core for this approach, which can be of immediate use, not just in directing further philosophical reflection, but also in assessing social problems and guiding proposals for reform. For whatever views we hold about the value or non-value of gender as such, and about the possibility and desirability of fully adequate genderless norms for human life, we can agree that norms for women and men must appreciate their common needs, for example, to have opportunities to exercise practical reason and to develop deep and mature affiliations, not to mention shared needs for adequate nourishment, shelter, mobility, and freedom from unnecessary pain.

In developing countries in particular, gender-differentiation tends to be so strong that discussions about the value of a genderless society may seem beside the point. There is no hope (or danger) of eradicating gender in the foreseeable future, and the work that can and desperately needs to be done to improve the conditions of women in these countries must be justified to and carried out in co-operation with the women and men whose values have been formed within highly gendered cultures.

Nussbaum herself wants to encourage a certain amount of utopian speculation, so as to combat people's tendency to 'lower their sights for themselves', and 'generate more productive and more radical thinking'. Certainly, she is right to warn against setting one's sights too low. There is a danger, particularly, of directing one's efforts in ways that will achieve small gains while reinforcing aspects of the *status quo* that, in the long run, pose structural obstacles to larger improvements in justice and equality.

On the other hand, practical interests should make us wary of inviting more controversy than we need, and theoretical considerations should restrain us from drawing conclusions we cannot support. From the stand-point of ethical theory, the basic human functional capabilities approach must eventually ask and answer some very large questions about the roles of sex and gender in ideal human functioning. But this conference has been more specifically exploring the value and implications of this approach as a basis for defending and guiding development policy. If, in this context, our theoretical vision stays only a few steps ahead of our practical options, that may be good enough.

The Research Programme of Development Ethics

Jonathan Glover

Martha Chen's paper has discussed specific cases which raise central problems about culture and economic development.[1] The high caste women in rural Northern India can find themselves trapped by social norms which make it difficult even to survive when there is no longer a man able to support them. Metha Bai has to support herself and two children, but caste norms prevent her from remarrying or from doing paid work. To return to her parental home would be to deprive her sons of any rights to land. And in Bangladesh women in a similar predicament have started to defy the system of 'occupational purdah' by joining food-for-work schemes and setting up working women's groups. The occupational purdah system, now being challenged, is a threat to the very survival of those women and their dependants who are trapped by it. And it seems vulnerable to Martha Chen's criticism that it is also unjust.

It is worth raising the question of how far generalizations can be based on these women in Northern India and Bangladesh. Of course we need specific cases. Discussion of 'women in the Third World' too easily becomes vague or out of focus. But any specific case will have some features which are representative of many cultures and some which are peculiar to its own. The particular caste norms of Northern India will not be reproduced in Thailand, Ethiopia or Guatemala.

Yet some generalization does seem possible. Evidence from Africa and other parts of Asia suggests that where more women work outside the home they also have a longer relative life expectancy. In many communities in developing countries, the discouragement of women's paid work goes with favouring boys over girls in the provision of food and medical care.

If the case of occupational purdah can be taken as being, in important ways, representative of widespread social restrictions on women in developing countries, it raises our central problem. Martha Chen plausibly calls the system unjust. It is hard to see how to defend the justice of social rules which ban women from working even if this means that they and their children starve. But, on the other hand, there are grounds for unease about moral over-confidence, which here may look like imperialism. Is the criticism of injustice made from the standpoint of the local values of the Western world?

Here I shall discuss how far it is possible to develop a shared framework for analysing and assessing the kind of cultural restraints Martha Chen

[1] See 'A Matter of Survival' in this volume.

describes. I shall consider arguments for and against the view that removing these restraints would be a good thing. The aim is to bring out underlying philosophical issues and to suggest an approach to some of them.

1 THE CASE AGAINST THE CULTURAL RESTRAINTS

Suppose that, in a developed Western country, a government backed by an anti-feminist tide of feeling proposed a reversion to more traditional roles for men and women. What would they be likely to do? They would probably make abortion generally unavailable. They would remove state provided child-care, and take away support for working women through the tax or social security system. In education, girls could be encouraged to choose courses centred around cooking and household management.

It is hard to imagine such a programme having public support. But now suppose that an even more traditionalist government issued guidelines about the role of women. They should not be allowed to inherit money. A girl should be given less food than her brothers, and should not go to school. Her marriage should be arranged without her consent, but her husband's consent should be bought by a dowry. When married, she should eat only what is left when her husband has finished his meal. If the couple are infertile, the woman should be blamed or punished. She should be obedient to her husband. Women lose any independent freedom of movement. Men are given the freedom to take additional wives.

If the original programme seemed far-fetched, this set of guidelines seems so appalling as to be, in the context of Europe or North America, merely ludicrous. But each feature of the guidelines is taken from things women in Bangladesh have said about their lives.[2] It is against this background that occupational purdah has to be understood.

How should the shift of scene to Bangladesh affect our reactions? On one line of thought, it should make very little difference. If it is outrageously unjust for a western woman to be denied equality of respect, to be given a humiliatingly subordinate role, and to be denied the protection of the rights given to men, why should it stop being unjust in a different country with different victims?

To consider this question, it is necessary to say something about the content of the criticism that occupational purdah and related social practices are unjust. What does this claim come to?

1.1. Justice and Equality

Disputes over rival philosophical accounts of distributive justice can generate a twinge of pessimism at this point. Philosophical defences have been

[2] See M. Chen, *A Quiet Revolution, Women in Transition in Rural Bangladesh* (Cambridge, Mass.: Schenkman, 1983).

made of virtually all views from extreme egalitarianism to, at the other extreme, Robert Nozick's libertarian view that income tax is an unjust violation of rights, on a par with forced labour.[3] The more upbeat way of describing the position is to say that justice 'is a live philosophical issue', but this may still leave us with the twinge of pessimism about using what philosophers say about justice to convince people to change their society.

But the pessimism about philosophers may be overdone. And if this is right about philosophers, something similar may turn out to be true more generally.

As often in philosophy, where reputations are not made by agreeing with other people, there is a concealed overlap between many of the different positions. There are family resemblances between different accounts of justice.

One way of thinking of the different accounts is to start from a principle that is tacitly accepted by virtually all of them. This principle, which I will call 'the formal principle of justice', is that inequalities of distribution have to be justified by citing some relevant difference between the people concerned. In his paper, Amartya Sen says that 'theories of justice are important in bringing out the tension between perceptions of justice and what may be required by the demands of fairness or impartial rational assessment'.[4] The formal principle of justice is derivable from the idea of impartial rational assessment: you are not impartial if you distribute benefits unequally without having any relevant differences to cite.

The formal principle of justice is one of passionate concern to children with brothers and sisters. Such children often have strong intuitions about justice, and a parent with three pieces of cake to share among three children should be well prepared with relevant differences before daring to choose any distribution other than the obvious one. The parent who says, 'I just feel like giving her two and you none', will seem to the children (and to most of the rest of us) to be lacking a sense of justice.

To start with the formal principle of justice may seem to load the discussion in the direction of egalitarianism. But reflection on the wide variety of differences between people which have been thought relevant to justifying inequalities may dispel this impression. The more plausible criticism is that the principle is *merely* formal: that all the work of reaching a substantive position is left to arguments over which differences are relevant. I signal acceptance of this point by using the name 'the formal principle of justice'.

The interesting debate is over which differences are relevant, and can be used to justify inequalities of distribution. One kind of egalitarian says that none are. Other theorists think that inequalities can be justified,

---

[3] R. Nozick, *Anarchy, State and Utopia* (New York, 1974).
[4] See 'Gender Inequalities and Theories of Justice' in this volume.

ɔut cite very different grounds. For some, desert is relevant. If you work harder or longer than I do, a greater reward for you is just. Others cite differences of need. Others cite contribution to the community, saying that, even if you do not work harder than I do, the fact that your greater talents enable you to do something more useful justifies your greater income.

Then there are second order views, which do not start by claiming that some difference between people is relevant, but aim to provide an account of how we should decide which differences are relevant. The theory proposed by John Rawls is an example: a difference is relevant if it would be accepted as such by rational and self-interested contractors setting up the ground rules of a society, each in ignorance of the position they would occupy in it.[5] Or there is the view that justice is a matter of respecting people's rights.

Critics of these second order views sometimes say that they just transfer all the problems of selecting relevant differences to another location. The Rawlsian 'original position' seems vulnerable to being weighted towards different first order views. There is the feminist criticism that injustice to women that happens within families may be invisible in the Rawlsian scheme.[6] In the original position, the contractors are 'heads of households' rather than individual people. Or, again, it may be that a bias towards a desired outcome can be created by rigging the psychology of the rational contractors, making them either gamblers or else risk-averse.

Similarly, the other common second order view, that justice is equivalent to respecting people's rights, transfers the problems to rights theory. How should we choose between the libertarian view that rights are negative, protecting our liberty against the interference of others (so that taxation is unjust) and the view that there are positive rights, for instance to a minimum standard of health care?

These disagreements over which differences between people are relevant to the justice of inequalities of distribution sometimes reflect real differences of view about what society should be like. But often there is a concealed area of partial agreement.

Sometimes there is some agreement about the values which are relevant. But this may be obscured by prominent disagreements, either about the position occupied by these values in a theoretical account or about their relative importance. Theories of justice often have small print acknowledgement of values given a central role in their rivals.

Sometimes the disputes arise from the use of different conceptual schemes which can perhaps be mapped onto each other. One case is the cluster of disagreements traceable to the use by some theorists of a wide version of justice and the use by others of a narrow one.

[5] J. Rawls, *A Theory of Justice* (Cambridge: Mass., 1971).
[6] See S. M. Okin, *Justice, Gender and the Family* (New York, 1989).

When Glaucon in the Republic is arguing that it is more profitable to be unjust than to be just, he characterizes the just man as one of true simplicity of character, who wants to be and not to seem good. Discussions of justice in Plato often seem to take this rather broad view, equating just people and just actions with morally good people and their actions. Aristotle distinguishes between justice which is the whole of virtue (at least in relation to other people) and justice which is part of virtue. For Aristotle, cowardice, bad temper, and meanness are vices, but they are not examples of injustice in the narrower sense, which is centrally concerned with fairness and equality. Aristotle sees that people often think in terms of the broader conception of justice, 'and therefore justice is often thought to be the greatest of virtues', but he thinks it important to get clear about the narrower version as well.

Current political philosophy resembles the Greek discussion of the virtues in sliding between wide and narrow versions of justice. When Rawls at the start of his book says that 'justice is the first virtue of social institutions', this is sometimes taken to be question-begging. Why should justice trump liberty, or social utility? This claim is the political equivalent of the moral claim about justice being the greatest of virtues, which Aristotle ascribes to those using 'justice' in the broader sense. It is then unsurprising that, in the Rawlsian theory, liberty and considerations related to utility do play a part within justice. The first Rawlsian principle of justice gives priority to liberty, and the second leaves room for inequalities which enrich society (subject to a constraint about *everyone* sharing the benefits).

Those who take a more austere view of justice sometimes wonder if liberty and economic benefits are really as relevant as Rawls supposes. For them, justice may be centrally about equality or desert, while liberty and economic benefits are seen as other values, potentially in competition with it. For instance, if justice requires equality of opportunity, this may conflict with the liberty of parents to choose to spend more resources on their children's education. But to those operating with the wide concept of justice, the same debate can still take place, but as a conflict within justice rather than between it and other values. Despite a verbal disagreement about the nature of justice, positions using the wide and narrow versions can often be mapped on to each other.

None of this should be taken as denying that there are real, and sometimes substantial, disagreements about justice. It is merely to suggest that the disagreements are sometimes less great than they seem, and that they take place against a background of widely shared assumptions. Indeed, there has to be *some* agreement for the debate to be about the same concept. Someone who thought that the most just distribution was the most arbitrary one would not be taken to be a serious participant in the debate. (This is not a peculiarity of the concept of justice. It reflects a general point—made with different emphasis by Wittgenstein, Quine, and

Davidson—that the use of shared concepts is interwoven with the posses-sion of shared beliefs.)

Among the shared background assumptions are the formal principle of justice (that inequalities of distribution have to be justified by citing some relevant difference between the people concerned) and various restrictions on the kinds of difference that are legitimate candidates for consideration here. Pure egalitarians, and those who believe in rewarding effort or ability, and supporters of Rawls or of Nozick, all see each other as legitimate opponents. None of them would grant this standing to someone who believed in giving most to people with the longest names.

The debate between supporters of the different 'legitimate' positions is sometimes seen as one over who is giving the correct account of justice. But, where all the positions have a substantial and sustained following, it may be that there is no account which is exclusively correct. Perhaps Rawls and Nozick do not need to think of each other as mistaken. There may be a family of related conceptions of justice. On this view, different theorists are best seen as policy advocates, arguing that we should give priority to some aspects of justice over others.

Martha Chen says that the exclusion of women from work necessary for their survival is unjust. The case for agreeing with her appeals only to the shared central core of the concept of justice.

The presumption is that inequalities of distribution need to be defended by citing some relevant difference. Being male or female is not in itself a relevant difference, any more than height, race or length of name. And being female does not reflect other differences which are candidates for relevance. Women do not need food less than men do, nor are they in some way undeserving of it. Martha Nussbaum has a nice dissection of the view that women are more emotional, and therefore less rational, than men.[7] The view seems to combine great confidence about differences between men and women with a naïve picture *both* of emotions and of rationality. It is perhaps worth adding the footnote that, even if women *were* less rational than men, the supporters of occupational purdah would still have another justificatory mountain to climb: that of showing irrationality to be a relevant difference. The principle that it is just to let irrational people starve has limited plausibility.

The inequalities which exclude these women do not satisfy the more abstract requirements of the prominent philosophical theories. For in-stance, they do not meet the Rawlsian requirement that they ultimately benefit the worst-off people, in this case these women themselves. And there is no reason to suppose that there is any historical story of the kind that might satisfy Nozick: it is highly unlikely that women once had equal opportunities, but either made less use of them or else freely bargained

---

[7] See 'Emotions and Women's Capabilities' in this volume.

them away. (The links between general theories of justice and the position of women are well discussed in Susan Moller Okin's book.[8])

To say all this about the lack of relevant differences is to labour the obvious. The point is simple. No plausible general account of justice supports the inequality of opportunity which makes Metha Bai say that when her father dies she will die.

1.2. Equality of What?

The burden of justification is on those who claim that inequalities of distribution are just. This principle needs filling in, not only with respect to what kinds of differences between people are relevant to justifying inequalities. The relevance or otherwise of some difference may vary according to what is being distributed and in what context. It may be reasonable to discriminate in favour of farmers if fertilizer is being distributed or in favour of children if toys are. But for social policy we often want to stand back from particular items, and to consider how different groups are doing as a whole. For considering the justice or injustice of the position of different groups, we may ask how far global inequalities between them are justified by relevant differences. Should we be concerned with inequalities of welfare or utility, or with inequalities of resources, as Ronald Dworkin suggests?[9] Or should we focus on inequalities of what Rawls calls 'primary goods'?

One emphasis in this book stems from the great influence in development studies of Amartya Sen's proposal that it is often best to think in terms of 'capabilities'. (This proposal has been developed both by Sen and by Martha Nussbaum. It is applied to the position of women in Amartya Sen's paper in this volume and the basis of the account is defended against relativist criticisms in Martha Nussbaum's paper on *Human Capabilities, Female Human Beings.*)

Among the things people manage to do or to be, some are more important than others. To do satisfying work is for most people more important than to watch television. To be a good parent is more important for many than to be a good dancer. These more important or valuable things that people succeed in doing or being are central to evaluating their lives. But in thinking about the justice of a society, what matters is not what people actually do, but what they have the capability to do. If people have opportunities which they choose not to take up, society can hardly be called unjust as a result.

Sen suggests that the capability to do valuable things or to reach valuable states is often what should be looked at, rather than the goods or utility people have. One point he cites about capabilities as against goods is there

[8] See *Justice, Gender and the Family.*

[9] R. Dworkin, 'Equality of Welfare' and 'Equality of Resources', *Philosophy and Public Affairs* (1981).

is less cultural variation in what is aimed for. People in different societies often aim for the same capability. Among the examples Sen has used are 'being able to take part in the life of the community' and 'being able to appear in public without shame'.[10] But the goods needed for these aims vary greatly.

One of the arguments for looking at capabilities rather than at utility is of particular relevance to many Third World women. If utility is a matter of people getting what they want, people's desires may be so shaped by their situation that their satisfaction is a poor guide to justice. Long established deprivation may lead to a 'realistically' low level of desires. People with a truncated psychology of this kind may have nearly all their desires satisfied in a way that masks their fundamental deprivation.

The argument against the utility approach raises an important issue. It is an argument related to the Marxist conception of 'false consciousness': people's actual desires do not always reflect their real interests or needs. Clearly there are problems about how people's real interests are to be identified. (One approach to these problems is to invoke a less crude idea of utility, appealing to what people would choose when free from certain kinds of ignorance and bias, though there are further questions about the evidence for such claims. Another approach is to appeal in an Aristotelian way to some idea of common human needs, though again there are further questions about how to support these claims.) Clearly there are dangers (of a kind which Isaiah Berlin has written about extensively) in too ready a willingness to 'correct' people's actual desires in the light of some view about their 'real' interests.

But, equally clearly, the idea that people's desires can be cramped and distorted by deprivation has a great deal to it. The women who turn up at food-for-work programmes obviously see very clearly what their interests and needs are. But this is one of the points where they may not be in all ways representative of deprived women in developing countries. Some more traditionally minded women may be much more content with what is still relative deprivation. To discuss the position of what I will call 'traditionalist' women, we need to discuss issues about false consciousness. One is whether a modest and defensible account of false consciousness can be developed. Another is the relative priority of alleviating the plight of those who resent their deprivation and of helping those who do not. Does the relative contentment of the second group mean that it is more important to help the first group? Or are both kinds of deprivation equally urgent to remedy?

Because there is clearly something to the false consciousness argument, the capabilities approach looks very promising in assessing the justice of distributions. But there are also some questions about it.

[10] 'Capability and Well-Being' in M. C. Nussbaum and A. Sen (eds.), *The Quality of Life* (Oxford, 1993).

The first question arises out of the need to make comparisons between groups who have different capabilities. Take people who leave a traditional rural way of life and migrate to a big city. Suppose the first generation to grow up in the city lacks a range of agricultural skills possessed by their parents. They also lose the benefits of the extended family, who in the country create a safety net for mutual support in hard times. In the city they also lose the emotional support the extended family gives in time of trouble. There is more risk of being violently attacked, or of being arrested by the police and thrown into jail. But in the city they may have more opportunities to earn money. And they may learn how to drive, and may develop many commercial, negotiating and other skills needed to survive in the city.

To compare the lives of those who stay in the village with the lives of those who go to the city, it is not enough to assess them in terms of a particular set of capabilities, as the ones they have are so different. We may need some way of giving relative weight to the greater capability to travel conferred by driving as against the reduced capability of avoiding attack or imprisonment. Or we may need some more general description, such as 'capability to determine one's own life-style' under which both these lower-level capabilities can be subsumed. But the more general the description (as in this example or in Sen's 'being able to take part in the life of the community'), the more vague the standards of comparison are likely to be. The way the comparisons turn out seems likely to depend a lot on which descriptions of capabilities are chosen.

This may seem an academic point. We often can get a very good idea that some people are generally more deprived of important capabilities than others. Clearly, on any plausible comparison, the women who face starvation because they are denied work are likely to come out as having far more restricted capabilities than do most of the men in their society. But, in other less clear-cut cases, the comparisons may be harder. As a result they will be more vulnerable to variation according to the way the relevant capabilities are picked out and described.

A second question which suggests itself about the capabilities approach is about the grounds on which some capabilities are considered important. (Perhaps a clear account of this will give a set of criteria for deciding on the appropriate description of capabilities.)

Sen makes a good case for the view that not all questions of value have to be decided at once, and that the advantages of the capabilities approach can be argued for independently of any particular view of how the more important capabilities are identified. But, granting this, the next stage of thinking these problems through is to discuss the basis of these claims about importance.

As with people's 'real' interests in the context of thinking about false consciousness, there are two main plausible lines of thought, each with its own problems.

One approach is tied to a broadly utilitarian view, based on what the people concerned do themselves think important, or what they would think important under less distorting circumstances.

The other main approach is the Aristotelian belief in common features of what constitutes human flourishing and the good life. This approach has been taken by Martha Nussbaum in her development of philosophical foundations for the capabilities approach.

Each of these approaches raises questions. In the utilitarian approach, the appeal to what people do now think important is inadequate, given the fact that desires wither under conditions of sustained deprivation. The question is whether there is a satisfactory version of the more sophisticated account which appeals to views the people would have had under different conditions. The questions for the Aristotelian view are about how determinate its conclusions are, and how the Aristotelian claims are established.

There are then various loose ends in the theoretical account of the injustice of the social norms which deprive women of the chance to earn the food they and their children need. I suggested that the question of which differences between people are relevant to the justice of inequalities does not affect the case for social change. That case need only appeal to something relatively undisputed: the central core of the concept of justice. A similar point can be made about the loose ends of the discussion about whether what matters is equality of utility, equality of resources, or equality of capabilities. Because of the denial of the right to work, the women in question have, compared to the men, less utility, a smaller share of the resources, *and* diminished capabilities. On none of the plausible views can injustice be denied. The case for supporting a change in their position is strong.

2 THE CASE FOR RESPECTING THE TRADITIONAL CULTURE

2.1. *Cultural Variety and Cultural Imperialism*

There is another line of thought which pulls in the opposite direction. The developed countries and the Third World have a history of very unequal relationships. First through colonization and later through economic dominance, the developed countries have had enormous influence. Whether through rule by a European colonial power or through the kind of economic and military dominance the United States has in Latin America, this influence has often been exercised without regard for its destructive effect on local ways of life. The destruction is not just political and economic. In the colonial period, while administrators were creating a legal system on the European model, missionaries were often trying to impose some version of Christian religion and morality. And, in the post-colonial period, it would be naïve to think that economic dominance can be separated from the spread of a set of values linked to the market and to what it makes available. Factories change those who work in them. Contraceptives change attitudes to sex. Television exposes people to other worlds and their values.

As anthropologists often point out, external influences often have a crudely disruptive effect on the subtle network of customs and values which make up a traditional way of life. For outsiders to try to change some aspect of a society's values or practices can be like cutting up a tree, sticking its branches together in a different pattern, and hoping it will still grow. We have started to notice the fine structure of the ecological networks destroyed by our casual damage to the environment. We have started to care about whether we destroy the niche in which some species lives. This new ecological awareness could usefully be extended to the survival systems of different human cultures. Do we want to replace the varied pattern of these cultures with a single homogeneous way of life and a single system of values?

When we think about the occupational purdah of women in Bangladesh and Northern India, our response is to see it as a denial of basic human rights, as an injustice needing remedy. But thinking of the ecology of cultures may make us pause. Is not any attempt to impose our ideas of justice and rights just another destructive form of cultural imperialism? What reformers intend is usually something weaker than this: not the *imposition* of our values, but the effort to persuade. But there is still the disturbing thought that this might be the secular equivalent of the cultural surgery performed by the religious missionaries. If the effort to persuade is successful, our culture will again have defeated theirs. There can seem something unfair about the unequal contest, and something sad about the diminished human variety of its outcome.[11]

2.2. Communitarianism

Anyone with some anthropological sensitivity is likely to feel sympathy with this case for caution. But, on the other hand, many of us will still feel troubled by accepting the *status quo*. It is not readers of books on anthropology who pay the price for this cultural variety. It is paid in the Third World by women and their children who have too little to eat. The anthropological case pulls one way, but concern with misery and oppression pulls the other.

When the issue is presented in this way, it may seem that it is just a matter of deciding whether the preservation of cultural variety is more or less important than ending certain kinds of oppression and injustice.

But another argument in defence of traditional cultures comes from communitarians and other theorists, who would object to this way of posing

[11] See F. A. Marglin and S. A. Marglin, *Dominating Knowledge, Development, Culture and Resistance* (Oxford, 1990).

the issue. For them, the discussion of justice so far in this paper is based on a premise which should be challenged: the premise that it is possible to give some substantive universal account of justice which is independent of the norms, or 'shared understandings' of a particular society or political community. Michael Walzer has argued that 'justice is relative to social meanings', and that 'a given society is just if its substantive life is lived in a certain way—that is, in a way faithful to the shared understandings of the members'. He claims that, 'Justice is rooted in the distinct understandings of places, honours, jobs, things of all sorts, that constitute a shared way of life. To override those understandings is (always) to act unjustly.'[12]

Walzer is surely right to stress the ways in which sets of values and particular ways of life are interwoven with each other. But there is something worrying about the severe limits he places on external criticism of the norms of a society. He considers an Indian village where food is distributed unequally according to position in the caste system, and allows that a visitor might persuade the villagers to give up the beliefs on which the system is based. But, in the absence of such persuasion, justice 'does not rule out the inequality of the portions; it cannot require a radical redesign of the village against the shared understandings of its members.' If there were such a requirement, Walzer says, justice itself would be tyrannical.

In this claim an attractive opposition to moral imperialism is paired up with a more dubious moral relativism, and the linking word is 'require'. To say that justice 'requires' the redesign of the village against the shared understandings of its members might be taken to suggest that justice enjoins this on the reluctant villagers. That would constitute moral imperialism, and would indeed support the claim that justice is tyrannical. But, on a different interpretation, to say that justice 'requires' the redesign of the village is simply to say that, without the redesign, the village remains unjust. To say that this claim fails where it goes against the shared understandings of its members is to adopt a relativist view of justice.

The communitarian view seems to suggest that only very restricted kinds of external criticism can be made of the norms of a society. For those of us who care about misery and oppression this would be worrying at any time. But it seems even more disturbing now that, as the result of the work of Sen and others, we are starting to see that famines are less the work of natural disasters than of social norms which deny people entitlement to food.[13] It may be that an effective strategy for ending starvation requires a shift of emphasis from agricultural improvements to the criticism and reform of social norms. The practices which discriminate against women are one aspect of something more general. It will be sad if, just as we have come

[12] M. Walzer, *Spheres of Justice* (New York, 1983), 312–14.
[13] See A. Sen, *Poverty and Famines* (Oxford, 1981); J. Drèze and A. Sen, *Hunger and Public Action* (Oxford, 1989).

to understand this role of social norms, communitarians persuade us to restrict criticism of them.

The communitarian opposition to moral imperialism is admirable. But the case for the relativist view needs to be argued. It does not follow from the fact that goods to be distributed derive part of their value from social understandings that the principles of just distribution are also culturally relative. Some more general moral relativism seems needed for this claim.

2.3. Relativism

There is a good deal of plausibility in moral subjectivism. Many people are inclined to think of values not as things 'out there' to be discovered, but as being rooted in our subjective reactions. When there is a clash between the values of different cultures, it seems that, if a subjectivist view of this sort is correct, there is no neutral vantage point from which it can be seen that one set of values is right, or at least nearer to being right than the other. The claim is that, from the denial of objective values, cultural relativism about morality follows. Things are only good or bad, just or unjust, from the subjective point of view of this or that person, this or that culture.

Relativism can lead to a lack of confidence about giving justice priority over the preservation of cultural variety. If the ideas of justice and injustice are purely relative to a given society, we may lose confidence in our judgement that women in Bangladesh are treated unjustly. Perhaps the relevance to Bangladesh of this opinion of ours is as little as the relevance to modern money markets of the medieval belief that usury is a sin?

It has been rightly pointed out by Bernard Williams that it is inconsistent to hold that all moral beliefs are relative and then to base on this a supposedly non-relative moral prohibition on intervention in other societies.[14] But other relativist thoughts cannot so easily be disposed of. The appeal may not be to some inconsistently non-relative ban on intervention. Rather, it may be that in *our* system of values, our recognition of that system's own local and limited status weakens the case for propagating it outside its own context.

2.4. The Appeal of Objectivity

Many people would say that the relativist case went wrong from the start, with the denial that there are objective values. If we think of some important moral prohibition, for instance that it is wrong to inflict pointless suffering on someone, it is hard to see this as a matter where one opinion is as good as another.

---

[14] B. Williams, *Morality, an Introduction to Ethics* (London, 1979).

We feel a strong pull towards the idea that these moral prohibitions are part of a moral law which holds independently of any particular person's attitude to it, something we discover rather than invent. One analogy here is with the laws of a country: whether something is prohibited by law can be objectively established (with a bit of fuzziness at the margins over the borderline cases which keep lawyers from being unemployed). Whether I approve or disapprove of a law is irrelevant to whether my act is illegal.

Our thinking is also influenced here by another set of analogies which also gives rise to talk of 'the moral law': analogies either with scientific laws or with the laws of mathematics and logic. There are parallels between the debates about the objectivity of morality and about whether systems of mathematics and logic are invented or discovered. The view that laws of logic are objectively there waiting to be discovered has a strong intuitive pull. Many people have just this feeling about an independently existing moral order. Kant said that he was filled with awe when he reflected on 'the starry heavens above me and the moral law within me', and said that the latter 'exhibits me in a world which has true infinity but which is comprehensible only to the understanding'.

2.5. Challenges to Objectivity

But may other people are sceptical about such views, seeing objectively existing values or an objective moral law as pieces of metaphysical baggage which have no place in a modern scientific view of the world.

One argument for this stresses the variations in moral outlook between different societies, variations which compare unfavourably with science. There is no Chinese version of molecular biology, or special Islamic approach to physics, in the way there are Chinese moral attitudes to old people or Islamic moral views on alcohol. The suggestion is that the degree of convergence often found in science reflects the fact that there is an objective world out there which science is exploring, while the lack of convergence in ethics suggests that values are more likely rooted in the subjective feelings of particular individuals or groups.

There is another line of argument, strongly urged by J. L. Mackie, against the objectivist idea that beliefs about values can be true or false.[15] Again there is a contrast with science. When someone puts forward a hypothesis in chemistry, we can use observation and experiment to test whether it corresponds to the facts. But in morality, it is unclear what counts as checking a belief against the facts. The idea of a moral fact is very obscure. It does not seem that we can just use our senses to notice moral facts, in the way that looking tells me that there are apples on a tree. Mackie argues that, if moral facts cannot be observed in the ordinary way, we have to postulate

[15] J. L. Mackie, Ethics, Inventing Right and Wrong (Harmondsworth, 1977), ch. 1.

some other psychological source of this knowledge, such as a faculty of moral intuition. It starts to seem better to abandon the belief in objective values rather than clutter up our scientific world picture with these peculiar extra items.

These arguments express widely held reasons for scepticism about objective values. But neither argument is conclusive. The first argument appeals to lack of agreement on morality between different societies. Some would challenge the premise, saying that surface disagreements obscure a deeper underlying agreement: that the same values can be reflected in different moral rules because the circumstances of different societies are so different. But, with beliefs in general, even deep disagreement does not entail subjectivism. If one group of people thinks that masturbation makes you blind, while another group disagrees, we do not have to conclude that there is no objective truth about the matter. One group may just be wrong.

As Hilary Putnam suggests,[16] the other argument, about the mysterious nature of moral facts and how we can come to know them, is also inconclusive. The argument depends on the premise that objective values require the existence of moral facts. The idea of moral facts is indeed obscure, and it is unclear what would count as observing one. But perhaps not all objective truths have to be thought of in terms of correspondence to the facts. This 'correspondence' view has plausibility as an account of empirical truths, though even there it is not universally accepted. But the idea of correspondence to the facts seems unhelpful in the case of mathematical truths. As Putnam suggests, an argument like Mackie's could be used to support the unlikely conclusion that mathematics is all subjective opinion, by asking such questions as where mathematical facts are located, which sense we use to observe them, and by saying how implausible is a special faculty of mathematical intuition.

In the case of mathematics, if the alternative is to accept that there are no objective mathematical truths, it seems better to abandon the assumption that objectivity requires observable 'facts' to which true statements correspond. The same strategy seems open to the believer in objective values.

These two sceptical arguments fail to prove that there are no objective values. But they do present two real challenges to the objectivist.

From the way the debate has gone, it is clear that the idea of the objectivity of values is understood differently on the two sides of the debate. The sceptic is denying the existence of moral 'facts' of a rather metaphysical kind. But this seems not to be what the objectivist has in mind. So the first challenge to the objectivist is one of clarification. If the claim is not one about values being 'out there', or—in a phrase of Mackie's—part of the

---

[16] See 'Pragmatism and Moral Objectivity' in this volume.

'fabric of the universe', it needs to be made clear just what is to be understood by the claim that there are objective values.

The second challenge is related to the contrast between a quite high level of agreement in science and what at least looks like a large area of disagreement between different cultures over values. It is too simple to think that this proves that science has an objective subject matter and ethics does not. But there are often striking differences between what can be said about a disagreement in science and one in ethics.

In many cases of scientific disagreement, there is at least some shared view about the kinds of further evidence which would tend to support one side or the other. An underlying consensus about method often leads to convergence of belief when new evidence comes in. This contributes greatly to the plausibility of the view that science does deal with questions to which there are objectively true answers. But in ethics the opportunities for this kind of progress are less obvious. It is not clear that a feminist and an Islamic fundamentalist do possess a shared method by which their disagreement over the rights of women can be resolved. It is possible that there are objective values, but that we have not discovered (or perhaps that we never will discover, or perhaps even that we could not discover) the method for settling what they are. But the case for objective values certainly looks less strong if there is little to be said about the research programme for getting knowledge of them. To say something worthwhile about this is the second challenge to the objectivist.

The two challenges are clearly connected. Progress in explaining the content of the belief in objective values is likely to be interwoven with progress in saying something about how we can hope to acquire knowledge of them.

2.6. Taking Stock of the Case for Respecting the Traditional Culture

Those who urge that it is misguided to try to promote change in, for instance, the position of women in Bangladesh and Northern India, have a good case against any kind of coercive policies by outside countries or agencies. Sensitivity to the ecology of different human cultures combines with a belief in the autonomy of local communities and a rejection of moral imperialism.

The philosophically-deeper part of their case rests on scepticism about the values, such as justice, appealed to in criticism of the traditional role of women. It is not simply that we should not *impose* justice, but we should not judge their society by our values. This depends on scepticism about the existence of objective values. We have seen that some arguments in support of this scepticism are inconclusive.

But, if this part of the traditionalist case is to be resisted, those who wish to do so have to respond to the challenges it poses. One strategy would be to argue that the legitimacy of criticism that a traditional society is unjust does not depend on justice being an objective value. The alternative strategy, that of defending the objective status of justice, requires saying more about what objectivity is, and about the possibility of progress in ethics.

3 CONVERGENCE AND CONVERSATION

3.1. Systems of Belief

To explore the content of the claim that there are objective values, it is worth looking at the idea of objectivity in a wider context. We have seen that questions of value are often contrasted with scientific questions in this respect. Questions about what things are of value do indeed seem very different from many questions about what the world is like. But there is also some room for 'free play' in our interpretation of what the world is like.

Take a rather humdrum medical belief. Suppose that I have gone to the doctor, who has diagnosed some minor illness and prescribed some medicine. I hold the belief that the medicine will make me better. This is based on some assumptions, including ones about the doctor's competence and about the general effectiveness of modern medicine for illness of that sort.

But suppose the medicine does not work. I then have to revise one or more of the assumptions which led me to the mistaken expectation. I have some choice about which assumptions to give up. I may decide that the doctor is not as competent as I thought. Or I may give up the belief that I am a relevantly typical patient: I may have some chemical abnormality which prevents the medicine from working. Or I may decide that this particular medicine is not as effective as people have thought. Or I may decide that modern drugs, or even modern scientific medicine as a whole, should be abandoned as ineffective. Or, most drastically of all, I may give up belief in such things as the scientific method or the general uniformity of nature.

Some of these decisions are more reasonable than others. But my view of this will depend on other beliefs I hold and other evidence available to me. If I have a lot of evidence for the general effectiveness of modern drug treatments, I will probably prefer a local revision of a belief about this drug, or my own chemistry, or this doctor, to any more sweeping revision. But my choice depends in this way on my wider system of beliefs, and is not simply determined by the fact that the treatment has not worked.

Beliefs, then, hang together as a system, and other parts of the system influence how evidence relating to a particular belief is interpreted. If you tell me your tumour was removed by surgery, I will normally simply believe you. But if you tell me that it was removed by divine intervention, I will need a lot of evidence before I am convinced. And, of course the belief systems of different people cause them to respond differently. If you think that God is always intervening in medical matters, you are likely to be satisfied with less evidence in this case than I need.

Often (perhaps always) people have in their system certain central beliefs which they are very reluctant to give up. Most of us have this attachment to the outlines of the everyday view of the world, the kinds of belief philosophy courses challenge people to find reasons for: the belief that things exist outside my own mind, that many generalizations based on past experience will continue to hold in the future, that other people are conscious. These are the relatively rigid beliefs in the system, the ones we either will not give up at all, or will only give up under the pressure of quite exceptionally convincing evidence or argument. For some people, other kinds of belief come into this category: often those related to religious or political views to which there is a strong emotional commitment.

It is *always* possible to defend *any* belief provided you are prepared to make sufficient changes in the rest of the system. You can defend the flat earth provided you are prepared to bend the laws of physics, or to postulate mass hallucinations on the part of many travellers and to explain satellite photographs as the product of distortions of light in space. Some believers in the biblical account of creation did explain the fossil evidence in terms of God having planted evidence to make it look as if evolution had taken place in order to test our faith.

Part of our system of beliefs is a set of what may be called 'structural' beliefs: beliefs about how to adjudicate between beliefs, about how to assess evidence or arguments. Most of us cannot accept the creationist method of explaining away the fossil evidence because it seems too implausible. This view about plausibility is one of the structural beliefs. Such beliefs are of great importance. Their role is like that of the load-bearing walls of a house: when one of *them* collapses, a lot of others collapse too.

It is impossible to prove *anything* to a sufficiently determined sceptic. This follows from the fact that any argument needs premises, and the sceptic can always reject any premise. But it does not follow that anything goes. Sometimes people ascribe to Nietzsche a version of 'perspectivism' according to which no 'perspective' is better than any other. Philosophy and science can show that the rejection of some beliefs has very high intellectual costs. It is always open to someone to choose to persist in rejecting them. But it is not easy to claim at the same time that their position is equally reasonable.

3.2. Objectivity as a Matter of Degree

In the debate over the objectivity of values, it sometimes seems to be assumed that objectivity is all-or-none. Either values are objective or they are not. But doubt is cast on this by the way a fairly simple factual belief, such as my belief that the medicine will work, is embedded in a whole system. If an objective truth is one whose acceptance is utterly independent of any subjective element of interpretation, then there are no objective truths. Even my belief that there is a physical world independent of my mind is one I cannot prove to a sceptic who shares none of my structural beliefs about the interpretation of evidence. But this does not mean that disbelief in the physical world is somehow a more rational position. Hilary Putnam rightly praises the pragmatists for their being aware of the fallibility of all our beliefs yet without supposing that, where arguments are inconclusive, the sceptic should be deemed to have won.

The fact that all beliefs are only justifiable in the context of other assumptions does not mean that any belief is as good as any other. This response is much too simple, and arises out of the expectation that objectivity has to be all-or-none. No belief can be proved to someone who rejects all the relevant premises. But still some beliefs can be supported by far better reasons than others.

It can be asked of a belief (thought of as something independent of any particular person who holds it) whether its truth or falsity is an objective matter. It can also be asked of someone who holds a belief whether his or her attitude towards its truth is objective. We can sometimes attain a high *degree* of objectivity, by being alert for bias, by looking for arguments or evidence against our beliefs and assessing them in the same way we would if they tended to support our beliefs, and so on. The important thing here is that the objectivity of a person considering a belief is a matter of degree. It is not an unattainable absolute, but something we can improve on.

In the same way, the question of the objectivity of a belief itself often does not admit of an all-or-none answer. No belief can be proved true to someone who rejects all the assumptions on which it rests. All the same, some beliefs are supported by much more substantial reasons than others. And perhaps some truths of logic are unavoidably presupposed by anyone who makes any claims at all. But the objectivity of many beliefs is a matter of degree, in a similar way to that in which the objectivity of those who hold them is.

This way of thinking of objectivity makes a difference to the debate over the objectivity of values. It makes it seem naïve to join one of the two rival parties. It has always been fairly unclear what is at stake in the dispute over the claim that 'values are objective' and the rival claim that 'values are subjective'. But, if we are dealing with questions of degree, the debate starts to look like one between 'people are tall' and 'people are short'. The claims about objectivity, like those about height, hover between being oversimplified and being nebulous.

3.3. The Research Programme of Ethics

Scepticism about objectivity might be better expressed as scepticism as to how far ethics has a viable research programme. There is the familiar point that science has both progress and a research programme designed to generate it. The sceptical suggestion is that ethics has no firm claim to either. What *is* the research programme of ethics?

The first method used in ethics is the effort to give a fuller, more articulate, and more precise account of what a person values or of what principles he or she believes should guide action. This requires asking questions (asking either other people or oneself) for clarification: 'You say you believe in rewarding people for merit: By "merit" do you mean effort, or natural talents, or both?' Answering such questions requires not just reaching for whatever will be easiest to argue for, but some real reflection on what one cares about, usually drawing on responses to particular cases.

As the account starts to become articulate, the second method, testing for consistency, comes into play. Someone attracted by 'negative utilitarianism' (the view that we should put the elimination of misery before all else) may perhaps be moved by such a test. The only certain way of eliminating all misery is the painless extermination of all conscious life. Few of those initially attracted by negative utilitarianism are prepared to accept this consequence. If they care about consistency, something has to give, and it is usually negative utilitarianism.

For most of us, this is a particularly easy case. A harder case is where policies conducive to liberty are inconsistent with those conducive to equality of opportunity. In this harder case people divide more evenly. There is a degree of free play. The consistency test shows that something has to give, but people have a choice about which belief it is to be.

For people whose values rise above a very primitive level of simplicity, the business of articulating them and then testing them for consistency can be a complex and lengthy affair. (For some philosophers it takes a lifetime, but not everyone has so much time to spend on it.) It is not just a matter of seeing if certain statements are consistent, but of seeing whether expressed principles are consistent with intuitive responses to particular cases. If they are not, there is the question of whether the intuitive response can be dismissed as biased, or immoral, or irrational, or whether one's principles require modification because they are an inadequate expression of one's values.

In this way, ethics is a *critical* affair. It is not just a matter of giving a description of the values that guide us, but of homing in on conflicts, of judging and often modifying some beliefs and responses in the light of others and in the light of theoretical reflection on the reasons behind them.

We aim to have a coherent system: a set of principles and emotional responses (or 'moral intuitions') in harmony with each other. Perhaps this is a regulative ideal rather than something fully attainable. If we are open to new experiences, these may generate new responses which will upset the previous harmony. With philosophers, we tend to think that they are intellectually dead when they stop modifying their views, and it may be that this can be generalized. But, if the ideal is unreachable for those who are intellectually alive, progress towards it is still progress. It is better to have a more complex, articulate and coherent set of values than to have crude and confused ones.

So far this has been about the coherence of the beliefs of an individual person. There is the further question of the prospects for some more general consensus. Even if something close to individual coherence can be attained, it does not follow that a general consensus will emerge. We can conceive a state of affairs where we have each worked out a fully articulate and coherent set of values, but they are all radically different.

Although this is conceivable, it is perhaps less likely than some suppose. Consensus is more likely if we adopt Hilary Putnam's community discussion model rather than methodological solipsism.[17]

(Though I am worried about an incompleteness in Putnam's case for the—attractive—democratization of enquiry. It is surely right that hierarchy may stunt the intellectual growth of the oppressed, and may encourage the privileged to produce rationalizations defending their position. To say this is to give two intellectual (and instrumental) drawbacks of hierarchy. A complete case would require looking at possible intellectual advantages of a less democratic mode of discussion, for instance the kinds of appeal to greater experience and knowledge that would be made by a defender of Aristotle's view of the superiority of middle-aged over youthful opinion in ethics. Or there is the view that intellectual progress depends on the kind of privilege which allows college professors so much more freedom than other people have to sit around thinking and talking. I do not want to argue that the instrumental case for democratization of enquiry in general fails. But to sustain it requires a detailed spelling out of what it comes to in different contexts, together with a complex balancing of gains and losses.)

The hope of at least approaching social consensus depends partly on shared structural constraints of plausibility. These constraints operate in ethics as in beliefs about scientific matters. It is not an accident that most people give up negative utilitarianism rather than embrace the destruction of all conscious life. I do not want to suggest that a universal consensus about all ethical matters is particularly likely, but the structural constraints which exist in ethics may enable reasoned discussion to narrow the areas of disagreement more than people might at first suppose.

[17] See 'Pragmatism and Moral Objectivity' in this volume.

3.4. Values and Human Psychology

Many of the structural constraints in ethics are those of human psychology. Values have to fit our psychology in at least two ways.

First, the way of life they suggest has to be one to which we can at least partly approximate. Anything not satisfying this condition is rightly dismissed as unrealistic.

The second way a proposed set of values has to fit our nature is in reflecting things we actually do care about. Locusts, if they are conscious, may only value things that can be eaten. Martians may be negative utilitarians (though, if they are, let us hope they do not discover us). But human beings have a psychology fitted neither by locust values nor by Martian ones. Subjectivists are right that the sort of metaphysical values attacked by Mackie are unlikely to exist. And so thinking about values is a matter of working out what *we* value. And the psychology we have in common as human beings is likely to set some shared limits.

In this way the Aristotelian approach to these questions, as exemplified by Martha Nussbaum's contributions to this debate, is right. But there are questions about the Aristotelian approach which we may need to discuss. One is about how far we can expect an Aristotelian picture of human life and of good human functioning to generate consensus about values. How much moral variety is compatible with the same picture of human flourishing? Another is about the criteria for identifying elements of the 'shape of the human form of life'. How far can the picture of good human functioning be independent of what people want, or at least independent of what under other conditions they would want? If it is not so radically independent, there will be a closer convergence with complex forms of utilitarianism than most Aristotelians might wish.

We may want to consider whether the Aristotelian account can avoid arbitrariness. What is the Aristotelian research programme? Is it a biological investigation of our species, or does it proceed by the kind of discussion of our values which is appropriate to ethics? Martha Nussbaum's version of Aristotelianism explicitly rejects any 'metaphysical' basis, in the sense of something external to the way people think of themselves. It makes no appeal to religion or to any biological account of the nature of our species. The phrase 'human nature' does not figure in the account. Instead, the appeal is to a shared consensus among human beings about what our distinctive needs are. She stresses that the list is an intuitive approximation, deliberately vague, and intended to be open-ended.

I share the view, urged by Amartya Sen and by Martha Nussbaum, that it is better to be vaguely right than precisely wrong. The lack of precision need not be a vice in the account. But there is a question about the open-endedness which perhaps we should discuss. What is the relationship between the 'internal' account, based on how we humans think of ourselves, and an 'external' account, based for instance on sociobiology? Open-endedness does seem to be a feature of our self-understanding, but one of the most striking ways in which our thinking about ourselves changes is under the impact of science. If we are in this way open to science-driven conceptual change, a question arises as to whether the concept of human nature can be altogether excluded in this way. If a convincing scientific account of human nature is developed, it is likely to enter and change our self-understanding.

Is there a prospect of such an account? Claims about a common human nature clearly have something to them, but the boundaries of that shared nature are notoriously elusive. A lot of work, both conceptual and empirical, remains to be done. Perhaps biology and the social sciences need to come together for this investigation. I like something said by Frans B. T. M. de Waal, in his book *Peacemaking Among Primates* (Cambridge, Mass.: Harvard University Press, 1989): 'For a biologist, the idea of infinite cultural flexibility is unacceptable. When I visit a foreign culture, I am always struck by the familiarity of everything: the way people laugh, how they argue and about what, the way young men look at young women and vice versa, the change in a mother's voice when she talks to her baby, the strutting of important men, and so on. I am among my own kind. A cultural anthropologist making the same trip will focus instead on unique concepts in the language and on peculiar habits, clothing, and social institutions. He sees many striking differences and arrives at the opposite conclusion from mine: these people may yawn and cough like the rest of us, but that is where the similarities end. Slowly, amid great reluctance, the two points of view are now moving closer to each other; there is obviously truth in both.'

3.5. Women of the Third World and the Conversation of Mankind

It is not that communitarianism and relativism are utterly wrong. We *are* members of local communities whose values have shaped us, but at the same time we are members of the global human community. As individuals we shape each other by doing things together, sharing experiences, and talking about things together. With modern communications, there is for the first time the possibility of doing this on a large scale by means other than conquest and domination. Local traditions can change. Traditions in all our countries benefit from being seen with the sharp and critical perspective of someone from outside. Sometimes criticism is resented, and this leads to a polite convention where only bland things are said. But it is a sign of real friendship to get beyond this, and to be able to express and listen to disagreement without giving or taking offence.

There is a lot of variety in the things we human beings care about. But there are also similarities. I do not suppose that every person on earth cares about justice. Fairly obviously, there have been, and are, some people who do not. But I hope—and am cautiously inclined to believe—that certain moral values, including some recognizable version of justice, are to be found in the part of our common humanity that crosses cultural boundaries. This may not guarantee 'objectivity', but it is enough to get a dialogue going. And the fact that some women in Bangladesh are starting to break out of their traditional roles is a reminder that society is a human creation, and that we can change it when it does not fit our human needs and values.

Justice, Capabilities, and Vulnerabilities

Onora O'Neill

Thinking about justice for those who endure acute poverty and vulnerability in distant parts of the world raises numerous difficulties, and suggests various possibilities. Jonathan Glover has charted both some possibilities and some of their difficulties, and in many respects I agree with his map. Putting the problem simply, it seems that cosmopolitan accounts of morality and justice, including many liberal accounts of justice, are often fellow-travellers with old and ugly forms of imperialism, and sometimes rely on exaggerated, indeed false, assumptions about human rationality, independence, and self-sufficiency. On the other hand, anti-cosmopolitan (e.g. communitarian) accounts of morality and justice fail the distant poor and vulnerable in even sharper ways, because they have nothing much to say about action towards those who are distant or different, since they exclude 'outsiders' from the domain of justice.

Both approaches, it seems, underplay or discount the predicaments and vulnerabilities of many people in the Third World, and in particular pay little attention to the special vulnerability of poor women in poor societies.[1] Yet in the contemporary world, action at a social distance, indeed action whose effects are felt across the world, is ubiquitous, and we can hardly expect to act justly or to keep our hands clean just by opting out. In our world we need an account of cosmopolitan justice that neither fails to appreciate the vulnerabilities of the vulnerable nor connives with the powers of the powerful.

1 JUSTICE AND PREFERENCES

Many contemporary accounts of liberal justice have a cosmopolitan surface but are fundamentally statist:[2] they tend to depict justice as justice within a State. A more deeply cosmopolitan account of justice needs a wider view of the domain of justice. Questions about the scope of principles of justice are being worked on by numerous authors in several disciplines, and I shall

---

[1] For further discussion of the failure of contemporary work on justice to engage with the predicaments of women's lives, and above all of women's lives in the Third World, see Onora O'Neill, 'Justice, Gender, and International Boundaries', in M. Nussbaum and A. Sen (eds.), *The Quality Of Life* (Oxford: Clarendon Press, 1993).

[2] For discussions of the lack of genuinely cosmopolitan accounts of justice and some attempted remedies see for example the *Ethics* Symposium: 'Duties Beyond Borders' vol. 98, 1988; B. Barry and R. E. Goodin (eds.), *Free Movement of Money and Peoples* (Harvester and Pennsylvania State University, 1992); Chris Brown (ed.), *Political Restructuring in Europe: Ethical Perspectives* (Routledge, 1994).

leave them aside here. In my view, although I shall not argue for it in this paper, a genuinely cosmopolitan conception of the scope of justice is possible, and an irredeemably communitarian position is a non-starter for thinking seriously about justice to the most vulnerable.

However, even if questions of scope can be resolved, an adequate cosmopolitan account of justice is not easily provided, for several reasons. One reason is that the broadly empiricist starting-points relied on by most contemporay accounts of cosmopolitan justice (even if freed from statist thinking) are ill-adapted to take the vulnerabilities of the poor, and in particular of poor women with dependants in markedly patriarchal societies, seriously.

Jonathan Glover points out that the cosmopolitan positions advocated by contemporary theorists of justice often disagree about the relative weight to be given to liberties and to equalities. For example, this weighting is in dispute between 'social justice' liberals such as John Rawls and libertarian liberals such as Robert Nozick. However, the deeper difficulties with these would-be cosmopolitan accounts of justice may lie not in these areas of disagreement, but in the premisses by which conclusions such as these are reached. The supposedly strong contrast between Rawls and Nozick, and their respective followers, is much less evident in their starting-points. Like most contemporary work on justice, including Utilitarian approaches, both start from up-to-date versions of broadly empiricist views of action, so accord with economic theory in depicting action as motivated by preferences. Correspondingly, both see practical reasoning as used to choose means to satisfy preferences. As Hume put the point, reason by itself is 'inert'; it has no ends of its own, and cannot yield us an account of good or of justice, but can work out means to given ends.

Those who see human action in this way offer a rather convincing account of motivation (which does not concern us here) but have some difficulty in providing a convincing account of the good or of justice. Most settle for a subjective account of the good, and identify it with the satisfaction of preferences. Utilitarians generalize this strategy by offering a subjective account of the general good—maximal utility—which they use as the basis for their account of justice. Other contemporary work on justice is more cautious. It too takes a subjective view of individual good: individual preferences provide reasons for action for individuals, and satisfaction of those preferences is a good for individuals, but it asserts that there is no way to aggregate preferences or preference satisfactions to provide an account of the general good, on which an account of justice could be based. Justice must then be seen as a set of *constraints* on preference satisfaction, rather than as the optimum of preference satisfaction for all. This is how liberties and equalities come to be seen as the components of justice in contemporary non-utilitarian liberal writing. Both social justice and libertarian accounts of justice depict human beings as pursuing their individual 'good' in doing what they prefer, and doing so justly when their action stays within constraints defined by certain liberties and required for certain equalities.

No doubt liberties and equalities, or at least some liberties and equalities, are important for justice. But the disputes about the merits of trying to build an account of justice out of these very abstract elements seems to me to obscure what is most fundamental to most recent liberal approaches of justice, which is the thought that rational action is efficient pursuit of individuals' subjective goods—or preferences. This claim is often seen as uncontroversial background; I believe that it is controversial and moreover that it is a reason why cosmopolitan accounts of justice can be derailed and even become hostage to questionable ideals and attitudes, which undercut justice towards distant and vulnerable others. However, it can be hard to trace exactly how these underlying assumptions create problems.

In part this obscurity arises because contemporary work on justice takes varying views of preferences. Some hold *realist* views of preferences; others see preferences as *revealed* in action; yet others slide between these two incompatible views of preferences. On the realist view, preferences are real states of agents and cause their acts; agents are viewed as rational if they pursue what they most prefer, and it is an empirical truth that human beings are more or less rational, so aim to satisfy their preferences to the greatest extent possible. On the revealed view, preferences are not seen as real states of agents but are ascribed to them on the basis of what they do, and it is a conceptual truth that rational agents always pursue what they prefer (because what they pursue will be taken as revealing what they prefer).

One difficulty, which Jonathan Glover identifies, arises from the possibility of false consciousness. If preferences, understood realistically, can reflect false views of one's own advantage and good, preference satisfaction may not provide suitable materials for constructing a theory of justice. In effect, the very data for building an account of justice may be systematically corrupted. It is well established that the most deprived often acquiesce in their lot—this is the traditional problem of the 'happy slave'. More specifically, it is well known that preferences adapt to realities, even to grim realities. So too do beliefs. Poor women, for example, have been shown to underestimate their own health problems, and to acquiesce in harsh subordination. The fact that preferences and beliefs 'adapt' to deprivation seems to me to put great strain on any project of working out what is ethically important or just within an account of action as governed by preferences. Where people accept that small mercies are all they deserve, when they see their oppressors as benevolent father-figures, these distorted preferences will be given undeserved weight within any fundamentally subjectivist approach to ethics and justice. Absent preferences which would, we may think, reflect a more accurate view of the situation, will have no part in ethical reasoning. Moreover, it is hard to see how 'false preferences' could be discounted without a powerful theory of real needs or interests, which is not available to those who start with a preference-based conception of action.

But if one takes a revealed view of preferences, matters are probably worse: for action is then seen as the evidence for preferences, and so the compliant actions of the intimidated and vulnerable will be interpreted as showing that they prefer to comply, so suggesting that they are getting what they prefer. The problem in this case is not that 'false preferences' will be given weight they may not deserve, but that the very notion of a 'false preference' may lack sense.

This approach may fail to recognize major injustices. If preferences reflect action, and preference satisfaction is taken as the source of ethical legitimation, all sorts of oppression and domination may be made to seem legitimate. More specifically, once preferences are taken as the basis for action, and their satisfaction (subject to constraints) as just, it will be hard to criticize the range of social phenomena we call patriarchy. For the victims of patriarchy have preferences that are highly adapted to their circumstances: yet on ordinary, pre-theoretical views such adaptation seems to many to exacerbate rather than obliterate or mitigate injustice.

If we want a better account of justice to the most vulnerable, it will surely be important not to set out from a perspective that so readily legitimates or minimizes vulnerability and oppression. Those who view action as governed by preferences, and justice as a set of constraints on preference satisfaction, face double trouble here. If they take a realist view of preferences they must acknowledge that the vulnerable will adapt their preferences to the realities; if they take a revealed view of preferences they will see all compliance and subordination as chosen. Consideration of the realities of the vulnerable lives of poor women in the Third World destroys the plausibility of thinking that preferences provide a guide to each individual's good. At most they provide a guide to each individual's current subjective perception of good, but one that can often be deeply misleading. The search for an account of justice cannot be seen merely as a search for constraints on the pursuit of preferences, once preferences are seen in this light.

2 FROM PREFERENCES TO CAPABILITIES

For these and other reasons I believe, as many others now do, that there is great promise in Amartya Sen's project of taking capabilities rather than preference satisfaction as the basis for approaching questions of development and justice. Concentration on securing capabilities, and in the process eliminating vulnerabilities, leads to a view in which both empowerment and liberty can be taken seriously, and in which apathy, false consciousness and adapted preferences cannot be invoked to legitimate action that harms the vulnerable.

However, if capabilities are to be the concern of justice, we need to consider how they are to be individuated, counted, and compared. Which capabilities and sets of capabilities are important for justice? How are they to be compared and judged better and worse? It won't be enough to say that one bundle of capabilities is better than another when it includes all that the other does and more besides. Pareto optimality will provide too weak an ordering of bundles of capabilities to be useful. The mere fact that we cannot this evening have the cake—or the bread—that we ate this morning highlights the fact that the most elementary decisions require us to weigh alternatives of which neither is Pareto optimal. In the real world we constantly face real costs as well as real opportunities.

Individuating and ranking (sets of) capabilities is not easy. As Jonathan Glover points out, their individuation will depend on the descriptions that are chosen,[3] and these have no intrinsic metric. This suggests that the capability approach is going to need in the background some other considerations—a theory of basic needs, an Aristotelian account of human flourishing, or of course both in tandem, or some further possibility. This background theory will have to provide the considerations by which better and worse, more and less important, capabilities and sets of capabilities are distinguished. Of course, one need not assume that such a theory would be able to recapture the whole metric structure which preference-based conceptions of action and the accounts of justice that build on them purportedly provide. However, it may be that very much less metric structure would be enough to make many judgements about which capabilities are more and which less important for public policy and personal life.

A highly-sympathetic way of providing a background theory, which would enable us to distinguish better from worse (sets of) capabilities, is the Aristotelian route that Martha Nussbaum has explored.[4] It would provide an account of objectivity in ethics, and as Jonathan Glover points out, could still be less difficult to establish than a more theoretical, Platonist form of moral realism. I do not doubt that *if* we could establish a convincing Aristotelianism it would provide a way of comparing and ranking bundles of capabilities. However, I am less sure how or whether this can be done.

It is striking that Aristotelians today are one thing in the English-speaking world and another in the German-speaking world. All Aristotelians hope to discern what human flourishing entails, but whereas many recent

---

[3] Glover, above p. 121.
[4] See above all her 'Aristotelian Social Democracy' in G. Mara and H. Richardson (eds.), *Liberalism and the Good* (Routledge, 1991).

Anglophone Aristotelians emphasize that human flourishing is highly variable and sensitive to context, many German-speaking Aristotelians tend to think that human flourishing is far more socially determinate, indeed that it is not that different from the Thomist vision of flourishing accepted in Catholic social thought. At a guess, it is the latter, socially conservative Aristotelian thinking that has the deeper and wider political significance today, via its influence on Christain Democratic politics. This makes a lot of difference: Christian Democratic Aristotelianism tends to endorse very different social practices from those recommended by Social Democratic Aristotelianism. Patriarchal social relations seem to many Christian Democratic Aristotelians the proper structure for human flourishing. Not so to Social Democrats. Of course, a great thinker will have many readings, and I am not suggesting that either Aristotle is the right one—but it does point out that if an Aristotelian account of human flourishing is to enable us to choose between bundles of capabilities, we will need to go one way or the other. Like Jonathan Glover I therefore want to understand where the Aristotelian research programme will lead. Will it, for example, show that the capabilities women need for poverty and patriarchy are better or worse than the capabilities women need for poverty and isolation?[5]

Martha Nussbaum has suggested that Social Democratic Aristotelians look to a *thick vague conception of the good*.[6] I have no difficulty with the vagueness. Any moral reflection at this level is going to be relatively indeterminate. Nor indeed do I have trouble with the thickness, that is with the thought that there are a lot of different matters that must be taken into account. But I am not sure whether what we will be looking at when we get this far is best thought of as a conception of the good, or of the good life, or rather as a set of constraints within which many good lives, and perhaps also some less good, yet not unjust, lives may lie. The metaphors are perhaps revealing. Martha Nussbaum uses the traditional Aristotelian metaphor of the *target*. But if we speak in terms of this metaphor, we will also be tending to the thought that there is a centre to the target, an optimal way of achieving the human good, an ideal of life. This picture puts heavy demands on any account of human flourishing, that were ostensibly met by many traditional readings of Aristotle. If it can provide this account of flourishing, Aristotelian Social Democracy will have to be rich not only in its conclusions, but also in its premisses. Yet thinking about justice in a way that takes account of human vulnerability and powerlessness should perhaps consider starting from more modest assumptions.

---

[5] While subjective preferences cannot be decisive for reasons stated above, we should listen carefully to those Eastern European women who say that they long to resume traditional social roles in the newly expected affluence: they are putting capabilities for the dependence on husbands that patriarchy requires ahead of capabilities for economic independence.

[6] 'Aristotelian Social Democracy', *above* n. 4, 215.

3 POVERTY AND PRACTICAL REASONING

The poverty of philosophy is usually taken to be a criticism. It is taken to mean that philosophy leads to meagre conclusions. But there could be another way of taking the metaphor, which perhaps would be particularly appropriate in a discussion of capabilities, poverty, and development. This would stress the meagreness of the initial materials, but also the possibility of seeking conclusions which were rich in relation to those starting-points. Poverty is then seen as a matter of having rather little material to start out with, and dealing well with poverty as a matter of making good use of that little. This image of how to proceed might be useful for seeing how we might work out which capabilities are important without needing to show what constitutes a flourishing life, nor which are the most flourishing lives. We might simply concentrate on establishing constraints that must be observed for *any* flourishing life.

In terms of a metaphor that Martha Nussbaum also draws from Aristotle, we would then be thinking about the *outline* or *limits* rather than the target. The shift in metaphor may help, for it suggests that what is important is that acts and policies not lie beyond a certain limit, rather that they cluster as close as possible to some central ideal.

There thoughts lead me in roughly the same direction as Jonathan Glover. Like him I shall try to trace a route that starts out thinking directly about action, about functionings and capabilities, but uses minimal and general considerations in trying to see which capabilities are the most important for human lives. The considerations which Jonathan Glover proposes as providing a method for ethics are *clarification* and *consistency*, which, he suggests, will lead us close to Rawls's Reflective Equilibrium.[7] I share his view that we should avoid strong and controversial assumptions, even if it means that we have to forgo some strong conclusions that might be reached by a full-blown Aristotelian position or by certain preference-based approaches to justice.

However, if we do not insert considerations of clarification and consistency into an Aristotelian account of flourishing, or a preference-based account of action, where should they be deployed? An alternative would be to apply them to the principles and norms already established in our lives and institutions or proposed for their reform. This is a plausible way of proceeding, because formal standards of clarity and consistency can apply directly only to elements that have propositional structure and content. Considerations of consistency and clarity cannot apply directly to lives and

---

[7] This specific direction seems to me unpromising. Although Rawls's approach is often labelled 'Kantian', by him and by others, it in fact relies on a fairly standard view of action as guided by preferences; and while he does not regard preference satisfaction as defining the aim for justice, he does see justice as a set of constraints on the pursuit of preference. It seems to me unlikely this approach will either preserve the most interesting features of a Kantian approach or escape the criticisms of preference-based approaches to justice sketched above.

institutions, but they can be applied to the (system of) principles, norms or maxims by which we structure lives and institutions, and to the categories by which we describe, individuate, and enumerate both capabilities and vulnerabilities. This shift of starting-point brings us close to Kant's own account of practical reasoning, but distances us from contemporary 'Kantian' work on justice, which for the most part takes a broadly empiricist view of action, and see preferences and their satisfaction rather than principles of action and their embodiment in human lives as the locus of reasoning about justice.[8]

Yet when this conception of action is combined with the spare, formal considerations to which Jonathan Glover draws our attention, it has surprising implications. For the combination of a conception of action that is not preference-based and a conception of critical clarification and consistency leads in the direction not of contemporary Kantian theories of justice but of Kant's own account of ethics, as oriented by the requirement of acting only on principles that can be acted on by all. Principles that do not meet this standard cannot coherently be recommended as principles for all.

Attempts to domesticate versions of Kant's criterion within a preference-based theory of action have been numerous, but also have proved endlessly paradoxical and highly destructive of the point of the criterion. Instead of the thought that we should act only on principles on which we hold that others too can act, we are led in the direction of conceptions of justice which demand institutions and policies that receive either actual consent from all affected or the hypothetical consent of beings with enhanced, idealized rationality or knowledge. It is obscure why either criterion should be thought of as defining justice. Kantian considerations cannot easily be exported into an empiricist framework in which actions are determined by preferences.

Yet the simple thought that justice demands principles on which others too could act has powerful implications for the range of capabilities that might be compatible with justice. For example, norms or principles of injuring others plainly cannot be regarded as norms or principles for all, because those who are injured will have their capabilities damaged, so will be hindered from injuring in their turn. Of course, sporadic injury can be reciprocal—think of vendettas—but systematic injury by all is impossible. A commitment to injury—by violence, by coercion, by intimidation, by deception, by poverty or by patriarchy—will always be a commitment that is possible for perpetrators but not for victims. It cannot be enacted by all, so is unjust. The capabilities that all can have do not therefore include capa-

---

[8] A view of human action as informed by certain descriptions, principles, laws or policies should, moreover, be congenial not only to traditional Kantians but to many others, provided they do not imagine that principles, rules, etc., demand uniform enactment hence lead to rigorism in ethics. These others include communitarians and contemporary defenders of virtue ethics, as well as to those whose approach to social inquiry is basically legal or sociological rather than economic.

bilities for injury, oppression, manipulation, coercion, deceit and the like. If none of these capabilities can be justly enjoyed, then institutions which make some vulnerable to others will be unjust. In particular, extremes of poverty, dependence, social isolation, overwork, and patriarchy, which burden so many women in poor, and even in less poor, economies are thereby shown unjust.

More concretely, since poverty is an enormous source of vulnerability and dependence of many sorts, it cannot be right to leave in place the institutional structures which produce and perpetuate poverty. Equally, since patriarchal social forms consist of unsafe structures of dependence that institutionalize vulnerabilities, these social forms cannot justly be left in place. Of course, if somebody suggests that poverty and patriarchy need only be mitigated and not abolished for justice to be instituted, this will be a matter for discussion—but the burden of proof will always be on those who suggest that there are ways of securing everyone's capabilities to act on the same deep principles while retaining these ancient structures of deprivation and subordination.

In some ways this Kantian conception of just social relations and their institutionalization is not far from the one that Martha Nussbaum sketches in 'Aristotelian Social Democracy' and elsewhere under the (rather Kantian) heading 'Architectonic Functionings'. There she suggests that the two key human functionings, which shape all others, are those of reasoning practically and of affiliation. She characterizes practical reasoning as planning and organizing all other functionings and affiliation as acting with and to others. These two ideas are part and parcel of the Kantian conception of practical reason and of justice as requiring both consistency and connection to others, which is articulated in the thought that right action conforms to principles all can share.[9]

4 AUTONOMY AND INDEPENDENCE

These conclusions may meet a sceptical response because it is generally supposed that Kantian approaches to the predicaments of the poor and vulnerable are flawed, in that they assume an excessive, idealized conception of human beings and of human autonomy. Kantian thinking is said to be too concerned with autonomy, which it depicts as an ideal or virtue, indeed sometimes as the cardinal virtue of a liberal political order. Communitarians, virtue ethicists, and certain feminist writers have criti-

---

[9] Kant combines the notions of consistency and possible community into his very conception of practical reason, which is intrinsically dialogical. (This may surprise both his detractors and his alleged defenders—yet the textual basis for the claim is strong.) For Kant, to act or to think reasonably is to rely on basic principles held to be available to all. For textual evidence see Onora O'Neill, 'Vindicating Reason' in Paul Guyer (ed.), *A Companion to Kant* (Cambridge: Cambridge University Press, 1992).

cized the view that self-sufficiency and independence are ideals of human life, and accused those who see these and other elements of autonomy as ideals of neglecting the realities of human vulnerability and powerlessness, and the importance of intimacy, affiliation, and other forms of relationship.

However, this line of criticism confuses two distinct problems. Cosmopolitan thinking about justice can take a Kantian approach to the valuing of capabilities without falling into the trap of neglecting vulnerability and powerlessness. The basic feature of a genuinely Kantian approach to justice is a certain attitude to *justification*, which is not to be derived either from actual preferences or from determinate ideals of human flourishing. As Kant himself makes quite explicit, neither empiricist nor perfectionist strategies are part of or compatible with Kantian ethics. The basic Kantian strategy is rather minimal, and best put as a modal claim: ethical principles, including principles of justice, must be principles that all *can* act on. In this respect Kantian strategies of justification fit well with a capabilities approach. For to secure capabilities is to ensure that certain ways of acting *can* be chosen.

Kantian justifications pick out certain principles as basic to just institutions and lives. The embodiment of these principles in actual institutions and lives secures certain capabilities, but equally eliminates other capabilities. The capabilities which can justly be secured are capabilities that will reduce and tend to eliminate the possibility of violence, coercion, deception, oppression and the like, since these latter capabilities embody principles that *could not* be followed by all. For example, the injustice of a 'head' of family's capability to prevent his dependants from undertaking activity outside the home, is evident from the fact that this capability *cannot* be extended to all.

Any set of capabilities which eliminates injustice must both exclude capabilities that cannot be held by all and secure capabilities that buttress the vulnerable and empower them, so that others do not enjoy unjust capabilities. This will demand not merely that capabilities for injuring and oppressing be limited, but that capabilities for nourishing and supporting self and others and for resisting personal and institutional demands for subservience be strengthened. Limiting vulnerability is the other face of limiting capabilities whose 'ideal' development would damage or undercut others' capabilities.

One reason why the capabilities approach fits well with a Kantian strategy of justification is that both positions take liberty seriously. Capabilities are for the sake of functionings, i.e. for the sake of acting and responding; but the particular uses of capabilities on a given occasion are up to those whose capabilities they are. In this approach to justice, human beings are not seen just as bearers of preferences to be satisfied by receiving certain resources, but as having capabilities which they can, but need not, use in a variety of functionings. A concentration on action and empowerment for action insists that the poor are to be thought of and respected as agents, rather than as mere recipients of development, that liberties are important for the vulnerable. This emphasis fits well with a conception of practical reasoning that focuses directly on principles of action, rather than invoking an ideal of flourishing as the fulcrum by which principles of action and their just embodiments are to be identified.

However, the importance of a focus on action has, I believe, been much distorted in some recent so-called Kantian ethics in two ways. The first oddity—of which I'll say nothing, although it has deep implications for development ethics—is that much recent Kantian ethics has stressed rights rather than obligations, recipience rather than agency, vulnerabilities rather than capabilities. One defect of this approach, but not the only one, is that ethical concerns that cannot be claimed by recipients tend to fade from view.

The second oddity of recent so-called Kantian ethics is that, contrary to its critics' claims, it has made a poor job of giving an adequate account of human autonomy. It is true that proponents of liberal accounts of justice lay much stress on the value of autonomy, and assert that other positions fail to do so. But their reliance on preference-based conceptions of action and rationality makes it extraordinarily hard for them to offer any adequate account of autonomy. The best-known approach is Frankfort's attempt to explain what it is to be an (autonomous) person in terms of being guided by second-order preferences, and many others have tried to make this the basis of an account of autonomy. In my opinion all these attempts fail: since preferences are endlessly cross-referring, second-orderedness is just too commonplace to pick out anything of much importance.[10]

Failure to provide an adequate account of autonomy has not, however, saved liberal theories of justice from the accusation that they have hinged everything on an excessive emphasis on autonomy. Critics of liberalism insist that what the liberal theories of justice support, under the heading of autonomy, is a fictional conception of the solitary and unaffiliated self, which is both empirically false and morally offensive. There is no time to enter into these debates here.[11]

---

[10] Harry Frankfort, 'Freedom of the Will and the Concept of a Person', *Journal of Philosophy*, 1970. I believe Frankfort was misled by concentrating on the special case of addiction. Second-orderedness—endorsement of one preference by another—may be important in this case, but is far too common to provide evidence of ethically important characteristics. For criticisms of this and kindred approaches to autonomy see Onora O'Neill 'Autonomy, Coherence and Independence' in W. W. Miller and D. Milligan (eds.), *Liberalism, Citizenship and Autonomy* (Avebury, 1992), 202–29.

[11] For well-known examples of this criticism see Iris Murdoch's eloquent attack on 'Kantian man' in *The Sovereignty of the Good* (London: Routledge & Kegan Paul, 1970) and Michael Sandel, *Liberalism and the Limits of Justice*, who accuses Kantian work (in this case Rawls and contemporary liberalism rather than Kant) of relying on the fiction of the 'deontological self' which lacks affiliation, connection, and relationships. Variants of the same criticism abound in feminist writing, see e.g. Carol Gilligan, *In A Different Voice: Psychological Theory and Women's*

However, it is rather easy to show that much of the polemic against autonomy arises from widespread failure to distinguish two quite separate notions. The classical texts on autonomy in the modern period are Kant's, but Kant's view of autonomy is wholly different from the one targeted in all these criticisms. Kant reserved the term *autonomy* for the conception of principles as available (strictly: willable) for all. Autonomy in Kant's sense is applied to certain principles and not to others; it is to be contrasted with *heteronomy*, which applies to principles that are conditional on desires. Autonomy understood in this way is not a predicate of persons, and not to be contrasted with dependence or relationship or affiliation. Strictly speaking, autonomy in this traditional and technical Kantian sense cannot be fitted within a preference-based theory of action at all.[12]

Contemporary concern with autonomy focuses on quite other considerations, and in particular on forms of independence or self-sufficiency, and their absence. Whereas Kantian autonomy is a matter of our principles being willable for all, contemporary accounts of autonomy stress independence and thereby call into question relationships and dependence. As critics of contemporary Kantian work have pointed out, not every form of dependence and relationship is wrong or unjust, or a source of wrong or injustice. Some forms of dependence are essential and others commonplace or enjoyable; moreover total self-sufficiency is mythical. We are all of us dependent in many ways.

These considerations cast a lot of doubt on positions that try to make independence itself an ideal of life. Autonomy as Kant conceived it may indeed be fundamental to ethics and ultimately to justice. However, that conception of autonomy, while critical of some ways of being dependent or making others dependent, is not invariably critical of human relations that secure and sustain others. On the contrary, a Kantian approach to autonomy is likely to be critical of forms of day-to-day autonomy that jeopardize capabilities for action, and in particular of those that jeopardize the meagre capabilities of the most vulnerable.

In our day-to-day discussions, the term *autonomy* is used as a relational predicate of persons and their characters, who are said to be more or less autonomous, autonomous of this or that but not of another agent or power. This everyday, gradated, relational sort of autonomy, is more perspicuously characterized as *independence*, which is clearly understood as gradated and relational. The structure of independence reveals why it is both valuable and threatening for the vulnerable. Independence is valuable if it consists of capabilities that limit how others can push one around; it is threatening

Development (Cambridge Mass.: Harvard University Press, 1982), and in certain critical theorists, see S. Benhabib and D. Cornell (eds.), *Feminism as Critique* (Oxford: Polity Press, 1986).

[12] See Thomas E. Hill Jr., 'The Kantian Conception of Autonomy', *Dignity and Practical Reason in Kant's Moral Theory* (Ithaca, NY: Cornell University Press, 1992), 76–96.

when it consists of capabilities that enable others to push one around. Independence is no unconditional ideal. It may be important to achieve specific configurations of independence, and to avoid others; but total independence is mythical, while over-extended independence injures the most vulnerable.

The reasons why we are particularly interested in the acute forms of dependence and vulnerability described in Martha Chen's paper is that these are forms of dependence on others which can stifle, even threaten, lives. The reason why we have to set this interest in the context of an account of justice is that it is never simple to work out which capabilities should be strengthened to avert injustice. Many ways of strengthening one person's capabilities restrict another's. Although the distribution of capabilities is not a zero-sum game, there are real conflicts. It is never possible to achieve more than a quite specific and limited configuration of capabilities—and of vulnerabilities. When we then ask which capabilities could in principle be secured for all, we discover that some capabilities cannot be achieved for all. These are capabilities that need and create victims; they are unjust capabilities. Other capabilities can be enjoyed by all, and when they are, will reduce vulnerability. To secure just rather than unjust configurations of capabilities, some sorts of dependence will no doubt have to be eliminated, but others may have to be secured. If justice is a matter of living by principles which could be followed by all it cannot be uniformly hostile to all forms of dependence and interdependence; it will be selectively hostile to unjust forms of dependence, unjust relationships—and unjust forms of independence.

Functioning and Capability: The Foundations of Sen's and Nussbaum's Development Ethic, Part 2

David A. Crocker

1 THE CAPABILITY ETHIC: FOUNDATIONS

My task here is to consider in some detail the capability ethic's foundational concepts of functioning and capability, its structure, and its relevance for a reconstruction of the social ideals of freedom, rights, and justice.

1.1. Functioning

A truly developed society, maintains Amartya Sen, would enable humans to be and do, and to live and act, in certain valuable ways. He employs the general terms 'valuable functionings' and 'achievements' to cover these intrinsically good 'beings and doings'. Let us first clarify Sen's theory of the nature of functioning before proceeding to discuss his closely related concept of capability.

Sen frequently tries to explain his concept of human functioning by the example of riding a bicycle (see Sen, 1984: 334, Sen, 1985a: 10). Important difference exists between the bicycle, the riding, and any mental state or utility that accompanies the riding. The bicycle itself is a mere object, a commodity. I may own the bike, be near it, and be sitting on it (even when it is moving), and yet not be *riding* it. To be riding the bike is to be engaged in a purposive human activity with or by means of the bike. The bike is necessary but not sufficient for the cycling. The cycling, as both process and result, is an 'achievement' of the rider—as any parent knows when their

This essay is a substantial revision of the second part of a paper presented to the IDEA Montclair Conference, 'Ethical Principles for Development: Needs, Capacities, or Rights', Montclair State College, January, 1991. The complete paper appears in the Conference proceedings, K. Aman (ed.), *Ethical Principles for Development* (Upper Montclair, NJ: Institute for Critical Thinking, 1991). A revision of the first part was published in *Political Theory* 20 (1992), 584–612. For the opportunity to give the paper I am grateful to the Institute for Critical Thinking, its directors Wendy Oxman and Mark Weinstein and to Kenneth Aman, Department of Philosophy. Thanks also to my conference commentators, Joan Whitman Hoff and Jerome M. Segal. I benefited from suggestions on various drafts from Les Blomberg, Cynthia Botteron, Geri Crocker, Lawrence Crocker, Michael Losonsky, Peter Penz, William Slauson, Teresa Chandler, and students in my graduate seminar on ethics and international development. I am especially grateful to Amartya Sen, Martha Nussbaum, and Tracy Strong for their encouragement and their enormously helpful comments on the original conference paper. I also gratefully acknowledge support for this research from the National Endowment for the Humanities Collaborative Grant # RO-22709-94. The views expressed are those of the author only, not necessarily of the funding agency.

child first begins to peddle the new bike. While riding, the cyclist may or may not be enjoying herself, satisfying some desire, or getting something out of the activity.

The bicycle example is somewhat misleading if it suggests that intentionality and purposiveness are necessary conditions for human functionings. Sen extends the concept of functioning beyond intentional action to include any 'state of existence of a person' (Sen, 1985a: 10). Included would be not only the choosing that initiates the riding but also the mental state—whether one of joy, boredom, or fear—that happens to accompany the activity. Moreover, also included under the concept are states of a person such as their being physically or psychologically fit (caused by the riding). Or to switch examples, the following are all distinguishable *functionings* related to food: (i) the *choosing to eat* (ibid.: 69–70; 1987b: 37, 1988c: 282, 294), (ii) the *intentional activity* of actually eating, (iii) the *enjoyment* (or its lack) in eating, (iv) the *process* of digesting the food, (v) the *state* of being nourished or free from malnourishment, and (vi) the subsequent intentional *activities*, such as working or playing, causally made possible by being nourished.

In relation to Sen's list of the types of functioning, Martha Nussbaum's concept of functioning is somewhat narrower. First, although Sen conceives of choosing (category i) as a distinguishable (intentional, mental, inner) functioning, Nussbaum understands choosings as not more than the voluntary or chosen dimension of an intentional human functioning. For Nussbaum, choosings without functionings would be more transcendental than human: the acts of will or disembodied angels, godlings, or Cartesian egos. Likewise, processes without choosings (category iv) would be less than human; for example, 'the sleeper's life of non-guided digestive functioning' (Nussbaum, forthcoming a), the lives of pigs (Nussbaum, 1990b: 211), and presumably the movements of compleat robots. One reason for Nussbaum's view is that she seems uneasy about a model in which choosings are inner acts of will.[1] As we shall see, this difference between Sen and Nussbaum has implications for the way in which they individuate functionings and for their views on human well-being and its relation to agency.

Although Nussbaum is reluctant to endorse Sen's view that choosing is a separate functioning, she does assume that choosing, as a component of human functioning, is made possible by a distinguishable personal *capa-*

---

[1] An argument in favour of Nussbaum's refusal to view choosings as functionings would be the following. If choosings are functionings, they would have to be inner acts of will. And if they are inner acts of will, then they would themselves be chosen or not. If they are not chosen, then chosen functionings seem to originate in something non-voluntary. If acts of will are themselves chosen, then we seem to be caught in an infinite regress. Better at the outset to construe choosings as an aspect of (intentional) functionings than to be faced with either non-voluntary functionings or infinite regress. For a treatment of this 'infinite regress' argument, see David A. Crocker, 'A Whiteheadian Theory of Intentions and Actions', Ph.D. dissertation (Yale University, 1970), 321–6.

bility that can be more or less fully 'developed' and exercised: 'One of the capabilities Aristotelian government most centrally promotes is the capability of choosing: of doing all these [valuable] functions in accordance with one's own practical reasoning' (Nussbaum, 1990*a*: 214, note omitted). Moreover, the following statement indicates her willingness to view practical wisdom, of which choosing is a part, as a functioning: 'The exercise of practical wisdom is itself a human excellence, an activity of intrinsic value apart from its tendency to produce virtuous actions' (Nussbaum, 1990*b*: 92).

A second difference in their respective concepts of human functioning concerns the mental states (category iii, above) of happiness or pleasure (or their opposites). Sen conceives such mental states as distinguishable functionings that have intrinsic value and can be pursued as such. Nussbaum, on the other hand, takes what she believes to be a less utilitarian and more Aristotelian position. Although she counts 'being able to have pleasurable experiences' as one of the valuable human functional capabilities, she refuses to make pleasure a separable functioning. Pleasure or satisfaction, argues Nussbaum, is supervenient on functioning rather than itself a functioning:

According to EN X [Aristotle, *Nicomachean Ethics*, Bk X] pleasure supervenes upon the activity to which it attaches, like the bloom on the cheek of a healthy young person, completing or perfecting it. Here pleasure is not identical with the activity; but it cannot be identified without reference to the activity to which it attaches. It cannot be pursued on its own without conceptual incoherence, any more than blooming cheeks can be cultivated in isolation from the health and bodily fitness with which they belong. Still less could there be a single item, pleasure, that is separable from *all* the activities and yielded up by all of them in differing quantities. (Nussbaum, 1990*b*: 57; see Nussbaum 1986*a*: 294–5)

Regardless of the extension of the concept, both Sen and Nussbaum conceive of humans as functioning in a variety of ways. Sen defines a person's 'achieved living' (Sen, 1990*c*: 113) as the person's combined 'doings and beings' (ibid.: 113), 'the set of functions a person actually achieves' (Sen, 1985*d*: 198):

Given *n* different types of functionings, an *n*-tuple of functionings represents the focal features of a person's living, with each of its *n* components reflecting the extent of the achievements of a particular functioning. (Sen, 1990*c*: 114)[2]

What is the ethical significance of this notion of functioning? The concept of functioning coupled with the (about to be discussed) notion of capability for functioning, provides Sen with a complex interpretation of

[2] Sen explains that 'an *n*-tuple is made up by picking one element from each of *n* sets' (1990*c*: 114). An example of such sets, which need not be quantitative, would be the set of alternative nutritional functionings that would include such items as 'being well nourished', 'being calorie deficient but otherwise well nourished' (ibid.: 114), and being poorly nourished.

human well-being and deprivation: the 'primary feature of a person's well-being is the functioning vector that he or she achieves' (Sen, 1985d: 198).[3] Moreover, this interpretation 'builds on the straightforward fact that how well a person is must be a matter of what kind of life he or she is living, and what the person is succeeding in "doing" or "being"' (Sen, 1985a: 46).

In contrast, the rival approaches are restricted to other, less urgent sorts of information. What the commodity approach values is, at best, only a means to well-being. Given interpersonal variability, different amounts and kinds of goods can result in the same sort and level of functioning (and freedom to function). And the same kinds and amounts of goods can result in wildly different levels of achievement (and freedom to achieve). A focus on functioning enables us to keep very clear about the constant ends and the variable means of development. The welfarist perspective, concerned only with the goal of utilities, neglects or 'muffles' all other sorts of human functioning. Happiness may be coupled with malfunctioning, and discontent may accompany or spur the most important of activities. Even the discipline of *development* economics has been one-sided, for it has emphasized quantity of life (longevity) and neglected the quality of the lives that are led, for example, *being* healthy and *being* educated (Sen, 1985a: 46). At this point, we have not treated Sen's and Nussbaum's views concerning which achievements are genuine. We do know, however, that development is *for* people and the lives they lead rather than *merely* a matter of whether they possess certain goods or satisfy certain preferences.

Before analysing Sen's and Nussbaum's related notion of capability for functioning, it is important to stress the normative role of functioning. G. A. Cohen, although correctly seeing how important capabilities are in Sen's ethics, fails to recognize that Sen also gives independent and intrinsic value to certain functionings.[4] Sen does put more normative emphasis—with respect to responsible adults—on 'freedom to achieve valuable ways of functioning' (Sen, 1990a: 52) than he does on the valuable functionings themselves. He does recognize, however, that the more valued (Sen, 1985d: 20) and valuable are one's functionings, the greater is the extent of one's freedom to function. One reason that reducing someone's freedom is bad is that it decreases her opportunities for achieving valuable functionings.

Nussbaum is both more explicit about the intrinsic value of certain functionings and gives a more balanced account of the comparative value of capabilities and functionings. For Nussbaum, valuable functionings and valuable capabilities to function are interconnected and are distinguishable sources of value:

---

[3] Here Sen uses 'functioning vector' for a person's set of functioning achievements (see 1985b: 198). At least once, however, he uses 'vector' to indicate that the elements of each of a person's sets 'are measured in terms of real numbers' (1990c: 114, n. 7).

[4] See Cohen, 'On the Currency of Egalitarian Justice', *Ethics* 99 (1989), 941–4; and 'Equality of What? On Welfare, Resources, and Capabilities', in M. Nussbaum and A. Sen (eds.), *The Quality of Life* (Oxford: Clarendon Press, 1993), 9–29.

Capability-needs are important because of the value of the functionings in which they naturally terminate; functionings are valuable, in part, for the way in which they realize capabilities. We cannot and should not prise the two apart. (Nussbaum, 1988a: 169)

The capability for good health is valuable because *inter alia* healthy bodily functioning is valuable. The capability of concern for others derives part of its value from the value of compassion as an action or achievement. 'Freedom for what?', we might say, is a question that cannot be replaced by 'Is there freedom?'

Nussbaum also stresses actual functioning as a platform for free choice. Public action should be concerned that human beings *actually* function at certain minimal levels such that they are free to choose to advance beyond or retreat from that level. A very sick person may not even be in a position to decide whether to strive for some level or other of healthy functioning. Only if a young person can read at some level, is she sufficiently informed to be able to decide to improve or abandon her reading. Responsible government not only gets citizens to minimal levels of actual functioning and capability; it also non-coercively *encourages* people to choose to function in valuable rather than trivial or evil ways.

We shall see below that this dual source of value reveals a difference between Sen and Nussbaum. It also presents, I argue, a problem of the relative value of capabilities and functionings that neither Sen nor Nussbaum fully confront. That problem only emerges because these two thinkers are sensitive to the ways in which both actual achievements and the freedom to achieve are intrinsically valuable ingredients in a good human life.

1.2. Capability

It is not enough to single out certain functionings as the content of the good human life, as the ultimate end of development. As Aristotle says, a distinction should be made between actuality and possibility. An important difference exists, for example, between a stone and a sleeping human, with respect to some activity like cycling. Neither the stone nor the sleeping cyclist are engaged in riding. Only the cyclist, however, *can* ride or is *capable* of cycling.[5] For Sen and Nussbaum, development is the promotion and expansion of valuable capabilities. Accordingly, to grasp their development ethic we must be clear on their concept of the nature, importance, and varieties of human capabilities.

[5] As we shall see, Nussbaum takes the concept of capability one step further than Sen when she distinguishes between a person's 'developed' and 'undeveloped' capabilities. Like the stone, the cyclist's infant offspring is incapable of cycling but unlike the stone the infant has an undeveloped capability for riding that can become a developed capability. We might say that the infant—unlike the stone—has a capability for (acquiring) a (riding) capability.

We must ask several questions, not all of which have been answered by Sen or Nussbaum. What, precisely, is meant by 'capability?' How do capabilities relate to functionings, on the one hand, and to freedoms, on the other? Given the high evaluation, just analysed, of actual functionings, why posit capabilities and insist on their intrinsic importance? Is there a problem—in general or in specific cases—of the relative worth of actual and possible functionings? And, most importantly, for the construction of an action-guiding ethic, which functional capabilities are most valuable and why? Finally, we shall identify, in a provisional way, some strengths and weaknesses of this approach.

What sorts of things are the capabilities that Sen proposes? A person's combination of actual functionings, her 'functioning vector', is the particular life she actually leads. The person is leading *this* life of 'beings and doings' but *could* lead alternative lives. The person's 'capability set' (Sen, 1985*d*: 201; Sen, 1988*c*: 289) is the total set of functionings that are 'feasible', that are within her reach, that the person could choose:

> While the *entitlement* of a person is a set of alternative *commodity bundles*, the *capability* of a person is a set of alternative *functioning* bundles. (Sen and Drèze, 1989: 13, n. 21; emphasis in text)
>
> A person's *capability set* can be defined as the set of functioning vectors within his or her reach. In examining the well-being aspect of a person, attention can legitimately be paid to the capability set of the person and not just to the chosen functioning vector. This has the effect of taking note of the positive freedoms in a general sense (the freedom 'to do this', or 'to be that') that a person has. (Sen, 1985*d*: 200–1; emphasis in text)
>
> The notion of 'capability' was introduced . . . to refer to the extent of the freedom that people have in pursuing valuable activities or functionings. (Sen and Drèze, 1989: 42; see also Sen, 1990*c*: 114)

On this conception, two people could have the same capability set and choose different bundles of actual functionings. Conversely, they could have different capability sets and choose the same (sorts of) functionings (Sen, 1990*c*: 116). One of Sen's favourite examples of the latter also amounts to an argument for adding capabilities to the moral space of functionings. Both the person starving and the person fasting—for example, the Somali refugee, and the Irish hunger striker—exemplify the functioning of being severely undernourished. But, it is clear, the two do not enjoy 'the same level of well-being' (Sen, 1988*b*: 17). The difference lies in the absence of certain options for the one and the presence of these options for the other. The former is not free not to be severely undernourished nor to function in many other undesirable ways. The latter, in contrast, has the significant capability not to starve: 'B [the faster] *could have* in a straightforward sense, chosen an alternative life style which A [the non-faster] could not have chosen' (Sen, 1985*d*: 201; emphasis in text).

Sen entertains but does not decide between two alternative ways of describing this sort of contrast (Sen, 1985a: 17–18; Sen, 1988c: 290–1; Sen, 1985d: 201–2). On the one hand, we can say that the faster's 'freedom to choose' or ability to choose not to starve herself is part of the faster's enhanced well-being in comparison to the person involuntarily starving. Here the list of functionings does not include the act of choosing: the value of the choosing is reflected both in the actual functioning chosen (the starving) and in 'the nature and the range of the capability set itself' (Sen, 1988b: 17). Alternatively, we can view the act of 'choosing' as itself a functioning. Then, we can say that the faster's choosing to starve is one of her functionings. It can be called a 'refined functioning' (ibid.: 18) and her functioning of starving—but not the non-faster's—can then be redescribed as the functioning of 'fasting'. Only starving that is chosen in the context of other alternatives can be called fasting: 'Choosing to do x when one could have chosen any member of a set S, can be defined as a "refined functioning"' (ibid.: 18; see Sen, 1987b: 37).[6]

Regardless of how described, what is important about Sen's discussion is that it gives us several reasons, in interpreting human well-being or deprivation, to add the category of 'capability to function' to the category of (unrefined) functioning. One reason that valuable functionings are valuable is that they realize valuable capabilities. Moreover, valuable functionings gain some of their value from the fact that they are chosen, 'done in accordance with practical reason' (Nussbaum, 1990a: 214), rather than determined or necessitated. Further, even though I am not now functioning in a valuable way, it is good that I have an array of options and even better when this array includes valuable functionings. Capabilities add something intrinsically and not merely instrumentally valuable to a human life, namely, positive freedom in the sense of available and worthwhile options. Finally, capabilities as well as functionings are important in grasping the aim and limits of good government. Responsible law-makers and development policy-makers aim at getting people over a threshold—of minimal human and valuable functionings—so that they are able, if they so choose, to function in more fully human ways. The purpose is not, as Rawls fears, to impose a certain conception of the good life on human beings but to

---

[6] Nussbaum would seem to be committed to a version of the first option. Following Aristotle, she would individuate *intentional* functionings precisely by reference to the choosing that is a component in the functioning. Fasting is not the functioning of starving plus the functioning of choosing to starve. Rather fasting is individuated as fasting (rather than starving) by reference to the motivating intention to fast. For Nussbaum, starving, as one functioning, could become fasting, an altogether *different* functioning, when a person who was dying (against her will) of food deprivation chose to fast (for the sake of some cause). Is there anything at stake in Nussbaum's siding with the first option rather than leaving the matter open? She might argue that the tighter link, provided by option 1, between intention to fast and the fasting is a beneficial Aristotelian corrective to the Platonic/Cartesian/Kantian tendency to make intendings and decidings spooky occurrences only related contingently to human actions.

enable them to cross a threshold so that they have certain choices. Nussbaum puts it well:

The conception [Aristotelian social democracy] does not aim directly at producing people who function in certain ways. It aims, instead, at producing people who are *capable* of functioning in these ways; who have both the training and the resources to so function, should they choose. The choice itself is left to them. And one of the capabilities Aristotelian government most centrally promotes is the capability of choosing; of doing all these functions in accordance with one's own practical reason ... The government aims at capabilities, and leaves the rest to the citizens. (Nussbaum, 1990*a*: 214; emphasis in text)

We need, however, to probe further Sen's and Nussbaum's conceptions of capability. Not only is the notion of capability susceptible to different interpretations, but a close reading reveals an important difference between the two thinkers. Let us begin with Sen's conception. What *sorts* of things are the capabilities that Sen describes? At least five interpretations are possible. Capabilities might be construed as (i) inclinations or desires, (ii) needs, (iii) concrete skills, (iv) general character traits, or (v) possibilities or opportunities. Let us look at each candidate in turn.

(i) It is clear that Sen does not identify capabilities with either inclinations or desires. The faster, who is capable (in Sen's sense) of being well-nourished, is not, all things considered, favourably disposed to be well-nourished or desires to be so. (ii) Likewise, capabilities need not be needs. Someone could have the capability of fasting but no need to fast unless she had certain political commitments. Also someone might have a biological need to be well-nourished; but, if she had decided to fast, Sen would say she was capable of being well-nourished but had no such need.

(iii) The relation of capabilities and concrete abilities or skills is more complicated. We need to be cautious here, because one ordinary use of 'capability' is that of 'ability' or 'skill'. A good midfielder in soccer must be capable of accurate passing, playmaking, and dribbling. And, Sen sometimes explicitly defines capabilities as abilities: 'A functioning is an achievement, whereas a capability is the ability to achieve.' (Sen, 1987*b*: 36) This definition, however, does not help much because Sen is using 'ability' in this context in a way that is similar in breadth to his use of the term 'capability'. For Sen, to say that someone has the capability or ability to move about freely (Sen and Williams, 1982: 20) is to speak not of powers, skills, or other traits *possessed by* the person but rather of possibilities or options *facing* the person. Moreover, for Sen, many of the functionings of which humans are capable are not intentional actions at all. Rather, they are states of being, such as being healthy or being free of malaria, that are not identical with skills. (There are certain skills useful for becoming or staying healthy, but being healthy is functioning in a healthy way and not itself a skill.)

(iv) A fourth theory of capability and its relation to functioning would be to conceive capabilities not as concrete skills, such as a surgeon's ability to use a scalpel, but as more general personal traits such as the capacity or power of a person to move about, imagine, or reason. So understood, capabilities would exhibit what Nussbaum calls different 'levels': they would be formed from an 'undeveloped' or latent state (a capacity for a capacity), maintained and exercised in one's maturity, and diminished or lost in old age. In my judgement, it is this interpretation of capabilities, as general powers of the person, that best fits Nussbaum's concept of *internal* capability (Nussbaum, 1988a: 160–72). Notice, for instance, how Nussbaum (misleadingly, I later argue), distinguishes between what she calls 'internal' and 'external' capabilities:

Internal capabilities are conditions of the person (of body, mind, character) that make that person in a state of readiness to choose the various valued functions. External capabilities are internal capabilities plus the external material and social conditions that make available to the individual the option of that valued function. (Nussbaum, 1990a: 228)

Nussbaum's 'state of readiness to choose' an actual functioning would be based on or include general powers that can be nurtured, acquired, developed, maintained, exercised, impeded, diminished, lost and (sometimes) restored.[7] These personal powers are (or fail to be) realized, embodied or expressed concrete activities. Good actions, which for Nussbaum (following Aristotle) compose 'flourishing living' (*eudaimonia*) (Nussbaum, 1986a: 6), would embody the best of these internal potentials.

Having these internal powers is necessary but not sufficient for good functioning, for one must also have available certain 'external and social conditions'. Suppose that the skill of riding a bicycle were one of valuable general capabilities, as conceived by Nussbaum. To perform the function of riding requires that one has (or immediately acquires) the internal ability to ride, access to a bike, and no social conditions that hinder bike riding. Instead of saying that external capabilities include both internal capabilities and external conditions, it would be more perspicuous if Nussbaum said that functioning both realizes *internal* capabilities and requires *external*

---

[7] Mihailo Marković, the Yugoslav revisionist Marxist theorist, worked out a very similar view more than twenty years ago. For Marković, human nature has evolved in such a way that it now includes 'a whole range of universal human capacities': 'These are in each normal human individual in the form of *latent predispositions*. Under certain unfavorable technological, economic, political, and cultural conditions they remain blocked, arrested, and thwarted. They reappear and are actualized at a mass scale as soon as conditions improve. They flourish in the life of individuals under favorable conditions of relative abundance, security, freedom and social solidarity.' See M. Marković, *From Affluence to Praxis: Philosophy and Social Criticism* (Ann Arbor, Mich: University of Michigan Press, 1974), 12. For an analysis and assessment, see D. Crocker, *Praxis and Democratic Socialism: The Critical Social Theory of Marković and Stojanović* (Atlantic Highlands, NJ: Humanities Press; England: Harvester Press, 1983) chaps. 2–4.

opportunities. These external options would depend on access to resources, the presence of enabling conditions (such as legal rights), and the absence of preventing conditions (such as legal prohibitions or threatening bayonets). As we shall see, on this view the task of government is to help its citizens acquire the actual or developed capability (as internal power) and 'to make sure that all citizens have the necessary resources and conditions' for acting, if they so choose, in the valued ways (Nussbaum, forthcoming b). Nussbaum's account appropriately emphasizes that good societies and good development promote, through various institutions and practices, good human development. Responsible institutions promote the formation, exercise, maintenance, strengthening, and restoration of certain good human powers.[8]

(v) The best interpretation of what Sen means by 'capability' is that it connotes a certain sort of *possibility* or *opportunity* for functioning. My claim is that, in contrast to Nussbaum, Sen restricts capabilities to opportunities. For Sen, capabilities are options or choices open to the person, possible functionings from which a person may choose.

What sort of possibility? Obviously not logical possibility, for it is not a logical contradiction that precludes the starving person from eating. Here an interchange between Bernard Williams and Sen is instructive (Sen, 1987b: 99–100, 109). Sen would say that someone living in Los Angeles lacks the capability of breathing unpolluted air. Williams, on the other hand, thinks Sen should say that this inhabitant lacks the 'ability' (ibid.: 99) of breathing unpolluted air 'here and now' (ibid.: 99), but has the general capability to breathe unpolluted air and could realize the capability by migrating to another location.

Sen's response is brief but revealing. First he agrees with another point that Williams makes, namely, that we must not think of capabilities singly but rather about 'sets of co-realizable capabilities' (ibid.: 109). Sen's way of putting the point is that capabilities are members of sets of capabilities and that such sets are 'sets of n-tuple functionings from which the person can choose any one n-tuple' (Sen, 1990c: 114; see Sen, 1987b: 109).

Sen means that we cannot simply ask whether a Los Angeles inhabitant has the capability of breathing fresh air. For the question would have to address a particular Los Angeles resident's set of co-realizable possibilities. One of those n-tuples presumably would include staying, due to irremediable lack of means, in an area that remains permanently beset with pollution. Another set would include the resident's possibility, due to (present or potential) wealth or (reckless) desperation, of migrating to a locale with fresh air. About the resident so conceived, Sen says that we can say that prior to migration she had the requisite capability to breathe unpolluted air

[8] The *Human Development Report 1990*, which Sen helped write, does speak of the 'formation' and 'use' of human capabilities; see 18, 26. But these locutions do not fit well with the 'capability as possibility' approach that Sen takes in his own writings.

because 'that alternative must be seen in terms of the post-migration n-tuple of *all* functionings' (ibid.: 109)—obviously including the living in a place with fresh air. Depending on her external options, however, there will be some point at which we can say that the Los Angeles resident has no (or little) capability for breathing fresh air due to the fact that her lack of real options makes it impossible for her to leave Los Angeles (or possible only with extreme risk or cost). On Sen's view, the issue for this Los Angeles resident is not whether to migrate from Los Angeles or clean it up so that she can *exercise* some *internal* ability to breathe clean air. The issue is, given that *something* can be done, whether or not it is *worth* giving up other options and gaining the option of breathing clean air by, for example, reducing the pollution in Los Angeles or moving somewhere with clean air.[9]

Hence, for Sen, capabilities are not powers of the person that might or might not be realized in different situations. They are, rather, options (sets of compossible options) for actions. Sen's concept of capability as possibility focuses rather on options for actions. These options may refer to but are not identical with traits of a person.

Sen, of course, could take personal traits into consideration to specify a person's capabilities as opportunities. One's internal powers would be relevant as *means* that make us free to do or be in certain ways. This response, however, would indicate a misunderstanding of Nussbaum's view and weaken Sen's own view. For Nussbaum, it is important conceptually to characterize and institutionally to promote valuable internal features of human beings if these citizens are to be able to take advantage of valuable external opportunities (resources and options). Moreover, Nussbaum contends that valuable capabilities to function, including the power of choice, are internal constitutive conditions of valuable functionings rather than merely contingent means to do and be. In valuable functioning we realize, exercise, and celebrate in action our valuable capabilities rather than merely use them, like Rawlsian social primary goods, as means to other things. In riding the bike, the child, having acquired the capability to ride the bike, realizes the power in riding rather than merely using it as a means to ride. (Riding, of course, also may be a means to other ends.) Moreover, if our internal powers were construed as merely means to good ends, then Nussbaum would rightly argue that the view threatens to 'commodify the self' (Nussbaum, forthcoming *b*). Just as economic utilitarianism commodifies the self by putting monetary value on human functionings, so construing capabilities only as means to functionings would alienate our powers from our activities.

Sen, I think, makes a minor mistake in his interchange with Williams. Williams had raised the question of whether 'everything that Sen counts as

---

[9] Sen emphasizes that this example shows that capabilities have to be treated not as isolated from each other but as ranges and 'sets of co-realizable capacities' (Sen, 1987*b*: 100).

a capability is directly related, at least, to choice' (Sen, 1987b: 98). Sen responds by arguing that 'we sometimes have the ability to do things in a genuine sense without being able to do their opposite' (ibid.: 111). Sen's argument is that 'Ann has the ability not to marry Bill' (ibid.: 111) without her having the capability of marrying him. And Bill has the capability of ending his life without always being able to keep on living (ibid.: 111). To use the above Los Angeles pollution example, Sen would say that Magic Johnson has the capability of breathing polluted air in Los Angeles without implying that he can breathe unpolluted air in Los Angeles. Sen's mistake here is to confuse choice of the opposite or contrary capability with choice of a contradictory option.

Sen is correct that Ann's capability not to marry Bill does not entail her marriage to Bill. If, however, she has the capability of rejecting Bill's *proposal*, she also has the capability of not rejecting it: either by changing the subject, asking for more time, or accepting it. Likewise, Bill's capability to take his life does not ensure survival, for he may be dying rapidly of inoperable cancer. But if Bill is capable of suicide he must be capable of non-suicide. He must have *some* choice, even though it does not include being able to continue living for more than a short time. He can decide not to kill himself and instead postpone his decision or decide to 'let himself' die of natural causes. If the latter, he can still decide whether to follow Dylan Thomas and 'rage against the dying of the light', adopt Nussbaum's stance and moderate the rage but still be fearful (Nussbaum, 1990b: 379), look forward to eternal bliss, or postpone this decision. That Magic has no capability of breathing unpolluted air in Los Angeles does not eliminate his choice to breathe. The general conclusion is that although the capability to do X does not imply the ability to do the opposite; choice of some sort is essential to capabilities as Sen conceives them. That our team is able not to lose, because it can attempt a tying field goal, does not necessarily entail winning.

1.3. Types of Functionings and Capabilities

Sen and Nussbaum sketch several distinct types of functionings and types of capabilities. We have already seen one distinction on which Nussbaum insists but that Sen, neglecting the internal dimensions of capabilities, fails to make, namely, a distinction between 'levels' of capability (see Nussbaum, 1988a: 160–72). In Nussbaum's typology, a basic capability is an undeveloped or potential capacity. When this potential is actualized, through nurture and maturation, the result is an 'internal' capability, which can be exercised or realized in the correlative functioning. An agent's capability is also 'external' to the extent that there are no external circumstances that block or prevent the realization in action of the internal capability. Although Sen construes capabilities as opportunities rather than personal powers, he does make a distinction analogous to Nussbaum's levels. As we have seen, he distinguishes between those opportunities that are more or less feasible. Here feasibility concerns not only empirical likelihood but also normative costs and benefits.

Sen identifies several additional types of functionings and capabilities. First, functionings and capabilities may be referred to either positively or negatively. For instance, not being diseased would be part of the positive functioning of being healthy. Secondly, actual and possible functionings can be described more or less hierarchically. The general capability of being able to be free of avoidable morbidity is further specified by being capable of being free from malaria. Being able to ride a bicycle presupposes and specifies being able to move about. The most inclusive or general capability would be the 'capability to function well' (Sen, 1985d: 200) or, as Nussbaum expresses it, the 'capability to live a rich and fully human life, up to the limit permitted by natural possibilities' (Nussbaum, 1990a: 217). Thirdly, functionings and capabilities can differ with reference to the activities of others. We have seen that the capability to appear in public without shame has a reference to the *judgements* of others in a way that is not true of the capability to be able to move freely. Moreover, some functionings and capabilities are more or less universal, shared or shareable by (almost) all human beings. Some, like the capability to play wide receiver, and not just the culturally relative goods that contribute to them, are specific to particular times, places, and physical abilities.

Sen's fourth classification of capabilities and functionings is based on a distinction between the well-being and agency dimensions of human beings (see Sen, 1985d; 1987a). When applied to functionings and capabilities, this dichotomy issues in two distinctions, one between well-being and agency functionings, and the other between well-being and agency capabilities. The basis for the distinction is one of part and whole. Well-being freedom and well-being functioning involve choices concerning one's own advantage. Agency freedom and achievements include the agent's well-being but can also be concerned with people and purposes other than and maybe at odds with the agent's well-being.[10] Hence, Sen provides conceptual space for a Kantian component of agency and breaks decisively with any psychological (or ethical) egoism that claims that humans are no more than 'strict maximizers of a narrowly defined self-interest' (Sen, 1990a: 54).

---

[10] In some of his most recent papers Sen identifies well-being capability/functioning with *all* capability/functioning. He then interprets what he earlier called agency capability/functioning with the wider notion of freedom/activity (see Sen, 1990c: 114, n. 8; GI 14–15). It is not clear why Sen has changed his view in this way. One hypothesis, which connects with my discussion of the difference between Sen's and Nussbaum's critique of Rawls, is that Sen now wants to distinguish his space of 'freedom to achieve' not only from Rawls's focus on social primary goods but also from Nussbaum's more determinate ('thicker') focus on valuable capabilities and functionings. For Sen, prior to and more fundamental than the issue of which concept of the good life to pursue, is the issue of having 'actual freedom' to pursue different kinds of lives.

Insofar as humans can devote themselves to people and causes beyond and against their own welfare, Sen can answer a sceptical realist's concern about any normative theory that proposes a just treatment of conflicting interests or freedoms:

> If conflicts of interest are very sharp and extensive, the practical feasibility and actual emergence of just social arrangements may pose deep problems. There are reasons for skepticism here, but the extent and force of that skepticism must depend on the view we take of human beings as social persons. If individuals do, in fact, incessantly and uncompromisingly advance only their narrow self-interests, then the pursuit of justice will be hampered at every step by the opposition of everyone who has something to lose from any proposed change. If, on the other hand, individuals as social persons have broader values and objectives, including sympathy for others and commitment to ethical norms, then the promotion of social justice need not face unremitting opposition at every move. (Sen, 1990a: 54)

Sen goes on to provide empirical filling for this sort of altruistic conceptual space by referring to his own empirical work (Sen, 1982a) and that of many other social scientists, such as Albert Hirschman (Sen, 1990a: 54; Sen, 1987a: 16–28). He also marshals evidence from momentous events suggested by the names 'Prague or Paris or Warsaw or Beijing or Little Rock or Johannesburg' as evidence that 'among the things that seem to move people . . . are concern for others and regard for ideas' (Sen, 1990a: 54).

Nussbaum, who agrees with Sen about the complexities of human motivation, softens his sharp distinction between well-being (capabilities and achievements) and agency (capabilities and achievements). Human well-being, she argues, consists only of those functionings that are both chosen and valuable. Choosing, rather than a separate functioning, is integral to all valuable functioning. Hence, she finds that she has no need to distinguish two different types of human achievement. Secondly, she does not restrict human well-being to personal advantage and, hence, there is no need to open conceptual space for the human agent to be able to choose other-directed actions. Instead, she persuasively includes two sorts of social virtues—social attachments and social affiliation (acting 'with and toward others')—as two sorts of good functionings that compose well-being (Nussbaum, 1990b: 98; 1990a: 226). She even goes so far as to designate affiliation, along with practical reason (including choice), as one of the two 'architectonic functionings' (ibid.: 226) that pervade all other valuable functionings. Sen conceives well-being achievements as a (self-interested) sub-class within agency achievement. Nussbaum, more Aristotelian and less Kantian, understands practical reason (which includes agency) and affiliation as two supreme human functions that 'infuse' and 'arrange all of the others, giving them in the process a characteristically human shape' (ibid.: 226). Hence, although dualities exist in both Sen's and Nussbaum's perspectives, they are drawn along different lines and serve different purposes. Perhaps Sen, addressing economists, has to start with a conception of humans as motivated by self-interest and defend a more expansive view that makes room for altruism and sacrifice. Nussbaum, more at home with the world of Greek thought, finds it difficult to draw the sharp modern distinction between individual and communal good.

Finally, and most importantly, capabilities and functionings can be ranked from the trivial to the important (Sen, 1987b: 108). Good development achieves the expansion of (valuable) capabilities and the promotion of valuable functionings. In the next section, I review the procedure that Sen and Nussbaum advocate for determining value and what results from their use of that method. Before doing so, however, I pause to raise a general issue about the valuation of capabilities. Sen views capabilities as ranging from the very valuable to the trivial, but he does not construe any capabilities as morally bad or evil. Why?

So far, Sen has neglected this question in his writings. However, I believe he would want to argue against the existence of morally evil capabilities in the following way.[11] Capabilities, he might argue, exist only in the realm of possibility. We are capable of doing many terrible things such as strangling our new born babies, running over pedestrians, poisoning wells, and torturing people. The evil, however, should be ascribed to the functionings, the actions, and not to the capabilities. Possible evil acts are not evil. Evil comes into the picture only with actuality; and it is compounded in an evil act, such as torturing, when that act is freely chosen rather than coerced. The capability for torturing would not be bad in itself, even if one could not resist—say, because of psychological conditioning—realizing that capability. Only the *actual* torturing would be evil: it would reveal that the torturer lacked the valuable capability of being able to refrain from torturing people. Likewise, on the issue of gun control, Sen would construe the argument against gun control to be not that guns give people an intrinsically bad capability of shooting people, but that this neutral capability is likely to be realized in disastrous acts (because the ability to shoot people will not be inhibited by the valuable capability of not shooting).

I have two problems with this argument on the level of general capabilities (in contrast to specific abilities). First, if we accept Sen's premise that what is evil occurs only on the level of functioning and not the level of capability, then we will have to say the same thing about the good and the valuable. Good would occur only in actual functioning and never in capabilities for functioning. Being able to be healthy, being able to choose, and being able to be concerned about the environment would not be good (or bad) in themselves. What is good would only be the healthy functioning,

[11] Sen gives this argument in personal correspondence of 3 February 1991 and in his response to my comments on his paper 'Gender Inequality and Theories of Justice', a paper presented at the WIDER Conference on Human Capabilities: Women, Men and Equality, Helsinki, August 1991.

the actual choosing, the demonstrated concern. But Sen correctly emphasizes that it is good to have the capability or freedom for good health just as
it is beneficial to function in a healthy way. It is good both to be able to
choose and actually to choose. It is good to be able to be a friend as well as
have friendships.

A second problem is that Sen's argument hinges on his incomplete
assumption that capabilities are (no more than) possible functionings rather
than (also) actual powers of persons. The capability, say for healthy bodily
functioning, is in the realm of possibility rather than actuality. A capability
for bodily health is just the same as healthy bodily functioning, with the
subtraction of one feature, namely, actual existence. (One is reminded of
Kant's refutation of the ontological argument by appealing to the difference
between 100 conceived thalers and actual thalers in the pocket.) Why call
something bad if it is only possible—unless it is tied by probability relations
to bad actuality?

Sen's mistake here, I believe, is precisely his assumption that capabilities
are possibilities facing the agent rather than, with Nussbaum, powers
possessed by the agent. If capabilities are powers, then they are also, in a
sense, actualities that we can, do, and should evaluate on a scale from good
through trivial to bad. A difference exists between a latent or undeveloped
human power and an actual or developed one. Some powers are worth
developing and having and some are not. Among the latter, some are bad
to have and this defect is not due merely to what their outcomes might or
likely will be. We want our children to acquire good character and valuable
abilities even though they may never have the chance to display the former
or exercise the latter. (We certainly *hope* that they can and will display their
virtue and excellence.) We oppose the nurturing of abilities to torture, rape,
and degrade; even though they would never issue in their counterpart
actions. For we believe that it is bad to *be* of bad character and have bad
abilities even when the person cannot and even could not express them in
action. Nothing may be wrong with the gourmet's capability of enjoying
exotic foods unless his exercise of that capability actually cuts into the
capability of others to have enough to eat. The ability to shoot, even to
shoot other people, is not necessarily bad and may be justified for police
and the military. But there is something wrong with *having* the unexercised
capability for child molesting or, more generally, the capacity for injustice.
In between (i) possible functionings and (ii) actual functionings, are (iii)
actual abilities to function. Even if we accept that (i) can not be bad, we can
and must be able to say that some examples of both (ii) and (iii) are bad.[12]

[12] In one passage Nussbaum talks of one-way 'ethical capabilities' (Nussbaum, 1988*a*: 161)
and rational skill-like 'two-way' capabilities but not of 'unethical' or 'bad' capabilities. Yet I
see no reason to deny and good reason to affirm that people can have 'unethical capabilities'
or non-relative vices whether or not the 'vice' is realized in unjust activity. Marković clearly
views good capacities as paired with equally universal but bad potentials. Humans have
evolved the capacities of acting intentionally or purposelessly, freely or unfreely, creatively or

If this second criticism of Sen is sound, we have another reason for modifying Sen's 'capabilities as possibilities' in the direction of Nussbaum's view of 'capabilities as powers'. The latter does more justice to our intuitions that some powers are bad: not just to exercise, but also to have, acquire, or nurture.

1.4. Valuation of Functionings and Capabilities

It is not enough to carve out the space of functionings and capabilities; for, as we have seen, these actual and possible functionings differ in value. What international and national development should do is to expand capabilities, especially *valuable* ones, and promote valuable functionings.[13] What are Sen's and Nussbaum's lists of good functionings and capabilities? What is the basis for the list and the rankings?

Sen clearly recognizes the importance of the task of developing his capabilities approach to include 'different evaluation exercises' (Sen, 1987*b*: 107): 'It is valuation with which we are ultimately concerned in the functionings approach' (Sen, 1985*a*: 32). However, he also recognizes the difficulty of the project: it is hard to put the right questions let alone get the right answers, and in 1985 he confessed that he had 'no magic solution to offer in dealing with these complex questions' (ibid.: 48). Moreover, as discussed earlier in Sen's critique of Rawls, Sen emphasizes a social commitment to the freedom that individuals 'actually enjoy to choose between different ways of living that they can have reason to value' (Sen, 1990*c*: 115). Sen evaluates positive (and negative) freedom as more basic than the identification of the more determinate valuable capabilities and functionings because the former provides the framework or format for the latter. Unlike Rawls, Sen is not opposed to a thick conception of the good and a 'perfectionist' conception of good government. He believes, however, that the norms of valuable capabilities and functionings presuppose and require the prior defence of the 'moral space' of freedoms and capabilities.

These disclaimers notwithstanding, Sen accepts that a development ethic can and should go beyond 'actual freedom' and (i) assess the living standard or well-being of people; that is, evaluate or rank how well people in the same or different countries are in fact living; and (ii) identify a cut-off point

routinely, altruistically or egoistically, with or without practical rationality. For Marković, the first capacity in each of these pairs is optimal. Action that realizes these good potentials is, in turn, good; and a life composed of these actions is a good life or a life of *praxis*. It is also possible, however, for people to choose to realize their opposing capacities and thereby live morally bad or defective lives. See Marković, *From Affluence to Praxis*, 73–7; D. Crocker, *Praxis and Democratic Socialism*, 37–9.

[13] The development model that I advocate for Costa Rica includes the ideal of 'real opportunity for personal development', with the latter summarized by the ideal of *praxis*. See 'The Hope for Just, Participatory Ecodevelopment in Costa Rica', in J. Ronald Engel and J. Gibb Engel (eds.), *Ethics of Environment and Development: Global Challenge and International Response* (London: Belhaven Press; Tucson: University of Arizona Press, 1990), 160–2.

or threshold, beneath which people are in poverty or seriously deprived. These purposes are served by formulating a theory of 'basic functionings' and 'basic capabilities' or 'primary capabilities' (Sen, 1984: 320). A basic capability is defined as 'being able to do certain basic things' (Sen, 1980: 218); and such basic doings are precisely supremely valuable functionings.[14]

Although Sen so far has offered only scattered suggestions and examples of valuable capabilities and functionings, Nussbaum has emphasized this evaluative task and proposed the outline of a systematic conception. Her aim, often employing Sen's concepts and arguments, is to articulate what she calls an Aristotelian view of 'good human functioning' that precedes and is the basis for considering the responsibilities and structures of a just political arrangement. I pointed out earlier that in Rawls's liberal (and 'political') theory, the right, with certain qualifications, is prior to the good. Rawls proposes what he takes to be a fair framework—albeit informed by ideals of moral personality and social co-operation—in which people, within limits, are free to pursue their own conception of the ultimate good. For Nussbaum, the good is prior to the right in that the aim of government goes beyond fairly distributing Rawls's primary goods and Sen's positive freedoms, as important as both these tasks are. The more determinate and guiding aim of just legislators should be that of promoting 'the capability to live a rich and fully human life' (Nussbaum, 1990a: 217). Nussbaum, taking the space of capabilities and functioning as settled, invites us to join her in working out a general and systematic account of good human functioning in two levels or stages. Who is the 'we', what are her two levels, and what are her tentative results?

The 'we' is best conceived if and when it includes people who discover or create—through an international dialogue—a provisional, revisable consensus on what it means to be human and to live well. Participants consult their own experience, the stories and self-understandings of their respective groups, and the insights of other groups and dialogue partners. International interdependence and boundary crossings of various kinds make it particularly imperative to forge together a global ethic and a conception, as widespread as possible, of being human and human flourishing.[15]

The first step in constructing an account of good human functioning is to work out an 'outline sketch' (Nussbaum, 1988b: 38–9; 1990b: 70) of being human, a 'thick vague conception of the human being' (1990a: 205) or 'the shape of the human form of life' (ibid.: 219). The second step, the

---

[14] Notice that by 'basic' Sen means a minimal level of the most important capabilities and functionings whereas by 'basic' capability Nussbaum generally means an undeveloped or potential capability. The one time when her usage is similar to Sen's is when she calls her Level 2 list 'Basic Human Functional Capabilities' (Nussbaum, 1990a: 225). Below I show how Sen employs the concept of rights in relation to basic capabilities and the need for a threshold.

[15] Cf. my 'Insiders and Outsiders in International Development Ethics', *Ethics and International Affairs* 5 (1991), 149–73.

thick vague conception of good human functioning (ibid.: 205), goes further and provisionally identifies, in a more determinate but still general way, the most important or 'basic human functional capabilities' (ibid.: 225), 'the totality of functionings that constitute the good human life' (ibid.: 209).

Nussbaum offers her theory as non-metaphysical in two senses: (i) it is not 'externalist' in the sense that 'it is not a theory that is arrived at in detachment from the actual self-understandings and evaluations of human beings in society' (ibid.: 217), and (ii) it is not a 'theory peculiar to a single metaphysical or religious tradition' (ibid.: 217). Nussbaum describes her own theory as 'internalist', in the sense of drawing on 'searching participatory dialogue' in and for human history and experience, and 'essentialist', in the sense of offering a normative yet revisable conception of human life's 'defining features' (Nussbaum, forthcoming b; see also forthcoming a). It seems clear, however, that Rawls would call Nussbaum's theory a 'metaphysical' rather than merely a 'political' conception of justice. Nussbaum is explicitly striving for a 'general and comprehensive' (in Rawls's senses) conception of the human good—albeit one that aims to be an 'overlapping consensus' concerning 'our recognitions of members of very different traditions as human across religious and metaphysical gulfs' (ibid.: 217). Rawls uses 'overlapping political consensus' in a much narrower sense to refer to agreement about the *political* domain for an already democratic society. Nussbaum, in contrast, aims to forge an international consensus about good human functioning (ibid.: 205). The common vision is to be general and comprehensive. It is also to be fallible, 'historically sensitive', and shareable regardless of one's particular religious or metaphysical commitments.[16] If the project succeeds, we will have 'the basis for a global ethic and a fully international account of distributive justice' (forthcoming b).

Let us look in more detail at Nussbaum's argumentation and results at each level. At the first level she tries to identify the 'constitutive conditions' or 'shape of the human form of life' (ibid.: 219; forthcoming b). What, according to Nussbaum, does or should the cross-cultural consensus count as human? What follows is her 'first approximation' (1990a: 219) (see 1988b: 48–9; 1990a: 219–24; 1991: 17–22; forthcoming b):

Level 1 of the Thick, Vague Conception: The Constitutive Circumstances of the Human Being (or: The Shape of the Human Form of Life)
   1. Mortality (Fact and awareness of death and aversion to it)
   2. The Human body
      2.1. The need/appetite for food/drink
      2.2. The need/desire for shelter

---

[16] A suitably reconstructed concept of metaphysics, such as that formulated and implemented by Whitehead, James, and Dewey, might be compatible with this 'internalist', fallibilist essentialism.

   2.3. Sexual desire
   2.4. The need/desire for mobility
3. Capacity for Pleasure and Pain
4. Cognitive Capability: Perceiving, Imagining, Thinking
5. Early Childhood Development (Helplessness, need, and dependence)
6. Practical Reason (Each evaluates, chooses, plans, and executes a conception of the good life)
7. Affiliation and Concern for Other Humans (Each 'lives to and with others')
8. Dependence on and Respect for Other Species and Nature
9. Humour and Play
10a. Separateness (Each is 'one in number')
10b. Strong Separateness (Each has her own peculiar context)

The list is not a value-neutral report from a biologist or externalist
metaphysician; it is already evaluative in a most general way. Moreover,
'this list of capabilities is a kind of ground-floor, or minimal conception of
the good', (1990*a*: 224) for a creature that lacked any one (let alone all) of
these traits 'would be too lacking, too impoverished, to be human at all'
(ibid.: 224) let alone have a good human life:

It [the list] recognizes certain aspects of human life that have a special importance.
Without them, we would not recognize ourselves or others as the sort of beings we
are; and they provide the basis for our recognition of beings unlike ourselves in
place, time, and concrete ways of life as members of our very own kind.   (Ibid.:
218)

   We say that a life without these items is not recognizable as human; and, given
that any life we can coherently wish for ourselves or for others will have to be, at
least, human, it sets an outline around our aspirations.   (Ibid.: 224; see also 1990*b*:
379 ff; 1991: 15; forthcoming *b*)

One problem here is that it is unclear how to interpret Nussbaum's
language of essentialism.[17] Suppose we interpret it in a strong way. Then
each part of each of the above conditions are viewed as necessary or
essential (and together sufficient) for something being counted as human
being. A creature would be 'lacking in humanity' if it were blind. However,
this strong interpretation would entail that Stevie Wonder was not human.
We certainly do want to say that perceiving in general and sight in particular
enhances the quality of life and even that it is part of human flourishing, but
that seems to take us to Nussbaum's second level.
   We can stay on the first level and give a weaker and more plausible
interpretation of Nussbaum's argument (see 1990*a*: 221). Instead of saying
that an irremediably sightless person was not human, we should adopt a
more Wittgensteinian 'family resemblance' view of definition and say that

---

[17] Susan Wolf perceptively develops the following argument in her comments on
Nussbaum's 'Human Capabilities, Female Human Beings', a paper presented at the WIDER
Conference on Human Capabilities: Women, Men and Equality, Helsinki, August 1991.

the more these central properties are irremediably missing, the less confidence we have in calling a creature human. Permanent blindness should not by itself disqualify someone from humanness. Total lack of perception would come closer to a disqualifying condition, but even then we might want to count a non-perceiving being that could imagine and think as at least partially human. In at least early episodes of *Star Trek*, Spock, born of human mother and Vulcan father, is not viewed as *fully* human because of his inability to have emotions. He was, however, initially counted as partially human and, in the later episodes, as increasingly human when he gradually acquired or permitted himself emotional capabilities. Nussbaum should replace her sharp 'threshold' of necessary and sufficient conditions with a 'more or less' minimum for what counts as human.

Nussbaum's Level 1 list includes a heterogeneous mixture of human traits, 'both limits against which we press and capabilities through which we aspire' (forthcoming *b*). In effect, Nussbaum includes in this first threshold of human capacities elements that are entirely absent from Sen, namely, the context of certain limits, vulnerabilities, and needs that are also part of the human mode of existence. It might be argued that Nussbaum should cleanly separate these limits and so forth from the first level capabilities. Nussbaum, however, emphasizes that our human powers only make sense in intimate connection with our human limitations. As humans we exercise our powers and capacities as we struggle against certain vulnerabilities and seek to meet characteristic sorts of needs. We are beings who must die, and in order to live and/or live well must meet certain bodily, psychological, and social needs. Being human, then, includes not just having and exercising certain capacities but doing so in the context of 'countering [our] limitations' and meeting our related needs in 'a humanly good way' (1990*a*: 224). For example, we 'press against' our bodily needs for food by preferring 'recurrent hunger plus eating to a life with neither hunger nor eating' (ibid.: 224). We struggle against our mortality by weakening our desire for other-worldly transcendent permanence and affirming that there is intrinsic value precisely in those human functionings in which we struggle against the limits, vulnerabilities, and transitoriness of human life (1986*a*: 2; 1990*a*: 224; 1990*b*: 365–91).

In seeking to deepen a needs-based development ethic, Sen's gloss of needs by capabilities unfortunately loses something that only a concept of need can supply. Nussbaum improves on Sen's account of human capabilities not only by making them personal traits but also by locating them within the context of other human features: the limits, vulnerabilities, and needs of lives we count as human. Our good human functionings, however we conceive them, occur in peculiarly human circumstances in which we cope—humanly and humanely—with certain features peculiar to the sort of creatures we find ourselves to be.

Level 2 of Nussbaum's proposal for a 'thick vague conception of the good' is her list of those human functional capabilities that are supremely valuable. We can call each item a virtue or excellence, for Nussbaum explicitly draws inspiration from Aristotle's conception of human flourishing as virtuous dispositions and activities. This conception of good human capabilities (and functioning) is 'based on' the above normative conception of human existence in the sense that the first-level perspective provides the starting-point and frame within which the second-level ethical inquiry identifies more specific—but still general—valuable human functionings and a second threshold of capability with respect to each functioning. Although this second-level list could be either one of valuable functionings or valuable capabilities for these functionings, Nussbaum chooses the latter. As we have seen, the aim of good government and good development is to promote valuable capabilities, that is, ensure that people get to a second threshold so that they have the positive *freedom to choose* whether or not to advance further (1990*a*: 224; see Sen and Drèze, 1989: 42–3; Nussbaum, forthcoming *b*):

We want to describe two distinct thresholds: a threshold of capability to function beneath which a life will be so impoverished that it will not be human at all; and a somewhat higher threshold, beneath which those characteristic functions are available in such a reduced way that, though we may judge the form of life a human one, we will not think it a *good* human life. The latter threshold is the one that will eventually concern us, when we turn to public policy. (Nussbaum, 1991: 23; emphasis in text)

We are now ready to summarize Nussbaum's list of 'Basic Human Functional Capabilities' (1990*a*: 225; see Nussbaum, forthcoming *b*; Nussbaum, 1991: 24) and to map Sen's scattered remarks onto Nussbaum's list. I have labelled the items in Level 2 with names of virtues, both to make explicit the relationships to the parallel items in Level 1 and to make the items easier to refer to and remember. N and S stand for 'Nussbaum' and 'Sen', respectively. The quoted items come from Nussbaum 1990*a*: 225 unless otherwise noted.

Level 2 of the Thick, Vague Conception: Basic Human Functional Capabilities
  1. Virtues in Relation to Mortality
     1.1. N and S: 'Being able to live to the end of a complete human life, so far as is possible' (see Sen, 1988*b*: 13)
     1.2. N: Being able to be courageous (see Nussbaum, 1990*b*: 374, 378)
  2. Bodily Virtues
     2.1. N and S: 'Being able to have good health' (see Sen, 1985*b*: 197)
     2.2. N and S: 'Being able to be adequately nourished' (see ibid.: 197)
     2.3. N and S: 'Being able to have adequate shelter' (see Sen, 1980: 218)
     2.4. N: 'Being able to have opportunities for sexual satisfaction'[18]

[18] This is the one 'functional capability' which Nussbaum describes as an 'opportunity' rather than an internal power. She considers various restrictions on such opportunities and

2.5. N and S: 'Being able to move about from place to place' (see Sen, 1980: 218; Sen and Williams, 1982: 20; Sen, 1982c: 200; Sen, 1985b: 199; Sen, 1987a: 64)
3. Virtue of Pleasure
   3.1. N and S: 'Being able to avoid unnecessary and non-useful pain and to have pleasurable experiences' (see Sen, 1985b: 195–6, 1987a: 64)
4. Cognitive Virtues
   4.1. N: 'Being able to use the five senses'
   4.2. N: 'Being able to imagine'
   4.3. N: 'Being able to think and reason'
   4.4. N and S: Being 'acceptably well-informed' (Sen, 1985b: 199; see Nussbaum, 1995: 24)
5. Virtues of Affiliation I (Compassion)
   5.1. N: 'Being able to have attachments to things and persons outside ourselves'
   5.2. N: 'Being able to love, grieve, to feel longing and gratitude'
6. Virtue of Practical Reason (Agency)
   6.1. N: 'Being able to form a conception of the good' (see Sen and Williams, 1982: 13)
       S: 'Capability to choose' (ibid.: 13); 'ability to form goals, commitments, values' (Sen, 1985b: 218; Sen, 1987a: 41)
   6.2. N and S: 'Being able to engage in critical reflection about the planning of one's own life' (see Sen, 1985b: 218)
7. Virtues of Affiliation II (Friendship and Justice)
   7.1. N: 'Being able to live for and to others, to recognize and show concern for other human beings, to engage in various forms of familial and social interaction'
   7.1.1. N: Being capable of friendship (Nussbaum, 1995: 24)
       S: Being able to visit and entertain friends (Sen, 1985b: 199)
   7.1.2. S: Being able to participate in the community (ibid.: 199).
   7.1.3. N: Being able to participate politically (Nussbaum, 1990a: 233) and be capable of justice (Nussbaum, 1988a: 161)
8. Ecological Virtue
   8.1. N: 'Being able to live with concern for and in relation to animals, plants, and the world of nature'
9. Leisure Virtues
   9.1. N: 'Being able to laugh, to play, to enjoy recreational activities'
10. Virtues of Separateness
   10.1. N: 'Being able to live one's own life and nobody else's'
   10.2. N: 'Being able to live in one's very own surroundings and context'
11. Virtue of Self-respect
   11.1. S: 'Capability to have self-respect' (Sen and Williams, 1982: 20)
   11.2. S: 'Capability of appearing in public without shame' (Sen, 1985b: 199)
12. Virtue of Human Flourishing

their bearing on judicial reasoning in sexual privacy cases in 'The Literary Imagination in Public Life', Alexander Rosenthal Lectures, Northwestern University Law School, 1991. See also Nussbaum, 1990b: 100–1 and forthcoming b. Sen's lists do not include this capability or opportunity.

12.1. N: 'Capability to live a rich and fully human life, up to the limit permitted by natural possibilities' (Nussbaum, 1990*a*: 217)

12.2. S: 'Ability to achieve valuable functionings' (Sen, 1985*b*: 200)

Four comments are in order with respect to the list. First, the items on Level 2 nicely parallel the items on Level 1 with one notable exception: Level 2's item 5, the Virtues of Affiliation (Compassion), are not as specific as they might be. Given that we want to count as human only those kinds of creatures that develop from infancy to young adulthood, it would be appropriate to specify further, by adding as 5.1.1 or 5.1.2, the virtue of being able to grow and be nurtured by adults as well as the virtue of good parenting. These virtues would fit nicely in an Aristotelian account in which good habits are a matter of training and education.[19]

Secondly, in order to simplify and help remember Level 2's list, I propose the labels ('virtue of . . .') for the types of valuable capabilities. Are there any even more general categories by which the virtues might be organized? Neither Sen nor Nussbaum offers any, although we have seen that Nussbaum suggests that practical reason and affiliation (what I have called 'Virtues of Affiliation II') are 'architectonic' in that they 'infuse' and 'organize' the other excellences. 'Infuse' suggests that the other capabilities can be exercised humanely just in case humans reason practically in and for others. (I would suggest that Virtue 11, Sen's 'virtue of self-respect', also should play this role.) 'Organize' suggests that these two capabilities give some structure to the long list. Perhaps Nussbaum intends that all the other virtues be classified as varieties of either practical rationality or affiliation (but not both), but that would be at odds with her notion of 'infusion'. Worth considering would be an ordering with three general types of virtue (with sub-types in parenthesis): Physical Virtues (1, 2); Individuality (or Agency) Virtues (3, 4, 6, 10, 11); and Reciprocity (or Social) Virtues (5, 7, 8, 9).[20] This trichotomy may be more trouble than it is worth, for it might suggest dichotomies that Nussbaum wants to avoid, e.g., physical/mental or individual/community. On the other hand, the excessive length of the present list makes some additional organization desirable. To facilitate this ordering, it might be better for practical rationality and affiliation to 'infuse' but not 'organize' the other virtues.

Thirdly, Sen's and Nussbaum's lists differ at a few points. For Sen, the bodily capabilities and functionings (2) are intrinsically good and not, as they are in some dualistic theories of the good life, *merely* instrumental means to other (higher) goods. In interpreting Aristotle, Nussbaum distinguishes between bodily functionings that are chosen and intentional, for instance, 'chosen self-nutritive and reproductive activities that form part of

---

[19] An explanation for why Level 1's Early Childhood Development is not reflected in Level 2 is that this item is importantly related to *all* the other virtues on Level 2. For 'growing up' can be understood as a normative process of acquiring the Level 2 virtues.

[20] In proposing these labels I benefited from some suggestions made by Tracy Strong.

a reason-guided life' and those that are non-intentional, such as digestion and other 'functioning of the bodily system in sleep' (forthcoming *a*). She may want to say that intentional bodily actions that *lead to* being well-nourished and healthy are intrinsically good, but that being healthy or having good digestion are not functionings (because not intentional) and are valuable only because of what they enable us to *do*. Another option open to her would be to adopt Sen's view that bodily states and processes, whether intentional or not, both as intrinsically and instrumentally good but as less valuable than other inherently good capabilities/functionings.

Furthermore, Nussbaum has included items 5 and 8–10, for which Sen has no counterparts. These items are welcome features. Item 8, which I have called 'ecological virtue', is an especially important recent addition to Nussbaum's outlook. In a period when many are exploring ways of effecting a convergence between environmental ethics and development ethics, it is important that an essentially anthropocentric ethic 'make room' for respect for other species and for ecological systems. Worth considering is whether Nussbaum's 'ecological virtue' is strong enough. Perhaps it should be formulated to read: 'Being able to live with concern for and in relation to animals, plants, and nature as *intrinsically valuable.*' Item 9 injects some appealing playfulness in a list otherwise marked by the 'spirit of serious-ness'. What explains the presence of these items on Nussbaum's list, their absence on Sen's list, and, more generally, the more concrete texture often displayed in Nussbaum's descriptions? One hypothesis is that the differ-ences are due to Nussbaum's greater attention, in her Level 1, to the limits, vulnerabilities, and needs of human existence. Further, it may be that Nussbaum's richer conception of human beings derives from making use 'of the story-telling imagination far more than the scientific intellect' (Nussbaum, 1990*a*: 217; see 1986*a*: 69; 1990*b*). On the other hand, Sen helpfully includes the good of self-respect, a virtue that enables him to find common ground with Rawls and to establish links with the Kantian ethical tradition, in which moral agents have the obligation to respect all persons, including themselves, as ends-in-themselves.

Fourthly, both thinkers make it clear that these goods are not only many but each is 'distinct in quality' and of 'central importance' (Nussbaum, forthcoming *b*). Valuable capabilities are, then, 'incommensurable' in two senses. First, 'we cannot satisfy the need for one of them by giving a larger amount of another one' (ibid.). Hence there are strict limits on the 'trade-offs' common in quantitative cost-benefit analysis. Secondly, the plural goods are incommensurable in the sense that they are irreducible to some common and 'deeper' measure such as utility. Nussbaum emphasizes that a science of rules cannot replace a practical wisdom that improvises in unique contexts, exercises the 'ability to discern, acutely and responsively, the salient features of one's particular situation' (1990*b*: 37), and affirms the ethical value of the emotions and imagination (ibid.).

One objection to Sen and Nussbaum here might be the following. On the surface, this concept of the good human life is attractive, but is not such a pluralistic vision of the good life going to run into insoluble problems when two or more of the capabilities cannot be simultaneously chosen as actual functionings? Sen and Nussbaum agree on an instructive and convincing response. First, neither of them dodge the 'conflict of principles' problem. Nussbaum stresses that two or more of the items, such as the capabilities for mobility and nutrition, often support each other (1990a: 225); she recognizes, however, that the 'components may in principle conflict with one another' (ibid.: 225). Sen, whose early fame rested on his important work in social choice theory, makes the point that it is better to be 'vaguely right' than 'precisely wrong' (1987b: 34). It is better to be correct in identifying the diversity of good functionings and be beset with the problem of ordering them than in using one homogeneous quality like utility that, at best, does justice to only one intrinsic good and, at worst, is wildly inaccurate with respect to human well-being and other goods.

Moreover, Sen argues that a pluralist approach can yield various sorts of 'partial orderings'—short of a complete ordering that would lay down ahead of time adjudication rules for every disagreement among lists of valuable functionings, priority rules for conflicts within the best list, and application of the one list to two functioning bundles (Sen and Williams, 1982: 17; Sen, 1984: 288; Sen, 1985a: 16, 54; Sen, 1987b: 29, 108). A thick, vague conception of the good, although general, is not indeterminate; by critical reflection it rules out many lists, 'weightings', and functioning vectors as pretty obviously inadequate. Here the appeal is to persistent, widely shared, and consistent intuitions.

Nussbaum especially addresses the ordering problem in relation to clashes between two valuable capabilities or two valuable functionings. Two component functionings may not be (equally) co-possible: 'Concern for other species may or may not fit well with our efforts to feed ourselves, to be mobile, to be healthy' (Nussbaum, 1990a: 226). Nussbaum attacks the 'conflict of goods' problem in two ways. First, it may turn out that by acting and, thereby, changing the world, we can have our cake and eat it too (see ibid.: 212). What at first seem to be 'tragic choices' may in fact be caused by a social order that can be changed (at a cost that does not outweigh the benefit of having both initially conflicting functionings). Here Nussbaum is assuming, contrary to Rawls and the liberal tradition, that it is possible to forge a national and international agreement on good human functionings. She is also assuming, again in contrast to Rawls and other liberals, that it is at least sometimes possible to resolve conflicts between two (or more) components of a generally agreed-upon conception of the good life.[21] Once we discern such a tension, we can

---

[21] Tracy Strong called my attention to Isaiah Berlin's formulation of this central liberal

identify its source and determine whether or not it can be eliminated or at least mitigated. For example, more efficient use of present energy may make it unnecessary to build a hydroelectric plant that would destroy the valley home of an indigenous tribe and an endangered mammal species. We may find that the conflict between preserving rainforests and ensuring that everyone is well nourished is not a 'tragic choice' but can be eliminated by a structural change in a nation's land tenure system. We judge both fulfilling work and loving child care to be intrinsically valuable human functionings, but we find that current and remediable institutional arrangements force into unnecessary tragic conflicts those women who pursue both ends.

Secondly, Nussbaum urges that we respond to apparent conflicts of goods by eschewing a priori priority rules. Giving a particularist spin to her conception of reflective equilibrium, she urges us to try to resolve conflicts among incommensurable goods by 'penetrating into the particularity' of mutable, complex, unique situations (Nussbaum, 1990*b*: 66–75). In doing so sometimes it will be quite clear which goods, in the particular context, should take precedent. We can construct provisional, working rules from repeated concrete deliberations, and these rules can guide us when our intuitions are confused, hazy, or inconsistent. Antecedent priority rules even help correct bias in concrete deliberations. There is, however, no rule for when priority rules should win out. The final appeal, as in doctoring or navigation, is to discern or discriminate in specific situations (ibid.: 73, 97).

Nussbaum concedes and even insists that it may turn out that 'one strand in our common humanness may not be harmoniously related to another, given the circumstances of life' (1990*a*: 226). Then we may have to live, in that situation at least, with a tragic value-conflict. Neither Sen nor Nussbaum offer an algorithm for resolving conflicts within their conception of the plural and diverse good. Conflicts within our conception of the good, like disagreements among conceptions of the good, may be one

---

tenet: 'The world we encounter in ordinary experience is one in which we are faced with choices between ends equally ultimate, and claims equally absolute' in Isaiah Berlin, *Four Essays on Liberty* (London and Oxford: Oxford University Press, 1969). One sense in which Rawls is a liberal is that he shares Berlin's assumption, at least with respect to a democratic society: 'The first fact is that the diversity of comprehensive religious, philosophical and moral doctrines found in modern democratic societies is not a mere historical condition that may soon pass away; it is a permanent feature of the public culture of democracy. A second and related fact is that only the oppressive use of state power can maintain a continuing common affirmation of one comprehensive religious, philosophical, or moral doctrine. (Rawls, 'The Domain of the Political and Overlapping Consensus', *New York University Law Review* 64 (1989), 234–5)

The urgent issue here is whether or not it is reasonable to hope that a democratic consensus, let alone an international one, can achieve anything more substantive than some (Rawlsian) thin theory of the good. On the issue of a transnational consensus, see Peter Penz, 'The Priority of Basic Needs: Toward a Consensus in Development Ethics for Political Engagement', in *Ethical Principles for Development*.

of the limits on our collective humanness and a creative expression of our cultural and individual particularity. But before we resign ourselves to moral impasses and tragic choices, we should consider changing the world, so as to eliminate conflict, and penetrating more deeply into the world, so as to discern the most pressing good in that context.

There is one ordering or valuation problem that so far neither Sen nor Nussbaum have addressed, namely, the relative weight to be given to (valuable) capabilities and (valuable) functionings. Nussbaum, we have seen, makes two points about the relation of a valuable capability to function and the actual functioning. On the one hand, each is valuable in itself and as related to the other: a valuable functioning is valuable, in part, because it realizes a valuable capability; and a capability is valuable, in part, because it is realized in a functioning that is valuable (see Nussbaum, 1988a: 169; 1988b: 15–16). Moreover, from the perspective of the law-giver, capabilities have priority because good government has the task not of making people function in a certain way but of getting people to a second (capability) threshold where they are able to choose whether or not to function in those ways. Or to put the same point in the language of (positive) freedom, it is good both to be free to choose among options and to choose the best option.

This nice balancing of our 'perfectionist' and 'liberal' intuitions, however, ignores the issue of those cases where we have to decide on the relative importance of good capability and the correlative good functioning. Is it better to award the prize (praise or a scholarship) to X who has greater capability for good functioning but is unlikely to choose to so function (and most likely will function at a lower level) or to Y who has less capability but likely will realize the capability that she does have in a good functioning (that surpasses what X is likely to achieve). When we cannot do both, should we reward X's greater capability relative to Y or Y's greater past achievement relative to X? Is there a general priority rule, even a rule of thumb, for this case? Do we penetrate into particularity and consider more specific types of cases or individual cases? Perhaps there is a general difference between (i) a forward-looking selection of a 'promising prospect' and (ii) a backward-looking award for past achievement? Frequently, however, awards such as scholarships have both forward- and backward-looking aspects. When we have to choose between a relatively superior capability (of one person) and a relatively superior functioning (of another person), which should we choose? Are there any reasonable principles or should we just improvise? A liberal will go with capability. A perfectionist will go with achievement. What of the liberal Aristotelian? Is there a difference that makes a difference between Sen and Nussbaum? My hunch is that Sen, more of a liberal, will rank positive freedom and capability more highly than actual achievement and that Nussbaum, more of an Aristotelian, will put achievement first.

1.5. Functionings, Capabilities, and Needs

A final issue: at several points Sen says that he is providing the basic needs approach to development (BNA) with needed 'foundations', that the BNA and other 'quality of life' approaches 'can be more explicitly developed, conceptually defended, and empirically applied' (Sen, 1988*b*: 16) by his capabilities approach. Still to be investigated, however, is whether a concept of needs has a role to play that cannot be accomplished by either capabilities and functionings. Has Sen avoided 'commodity fetishism' only to fall into 'capabilities fetishism'?[22]

Nussbaum identifies two non-reducible roles that need play in the capability ethic. First, humans *need* to develop their nascent valuable capacities into mature ones. Their 'undeveloped', implicit, or embryonic capabilities are 'needs for functioning' (Nussbaum, 1995: 31): 'the very powers of this being exist as needs for fulfillment' (1990*a*: 243). A need is satisfied when these implicit or potential capabilities become explicit or actual capabilities:

On this account, B-capabilities [Nussbaum's term for undeveloped or potential internal capabilities] are *needs* for functioning: they give rise to a claim because they are there and in a state of incomplete realization. They are conditions that reach towards, demand fulfillment in, a certain mode of activity. If that activity never arrives, they are cut off, fruitless, incomplete. As Aristotle insists, their very being makes reference to functioning; so without the possibility of functioning, they are only in a shadowy way even themselves.   (Nussbaum, 1988*a*: 169; see 1995: 31; emphasis in text)

As she makes clear, Nussbaum's appeal to needs here is not to subjective desires or preferences (see 1988*a*: 169). She means more than that we *should* value and promote the development of our own and others' potential capabilities and then realize them in functioning. Talk of our human *need* for *actual* capabilities and *actual* functionings is a way of saying that actuality is prior to possibility in the ethical sense that (i) actual capabilities are more valuable than merely latent ones and 'have a claim to be developed' (1991: 31) and (ii) actual (internal) valuable capabilities essentially refer forward to functioning and, hence, make a claim to be realized in functioning. This is not to say that valuable capabilities are not also valuable in themselves, but 'if functioning never arrives on the scene they are hardly even what they are' (ibid.: 31). In any case Bernard Williams's following question is to be answered affirmatively: 'Do we come out of the terminology of capabilities again, when we turn to their natural basis?' (Sen, 1987*b*: 101). It is not that we have found some value-neutral fact about our being that metaphysically entails an ethical duty. Rather, our cross-cultural human self-interpretations are such that we deem ourselves obliged to promote the acquisition and realization of certain capabilities (in ourselves

---

[22] James W. Nickel made this criticism in a discussion of an earlier version of this paper.

and others). And we view it as especially tragic when a young person, full of promise, dies before having the chance to develop and realize her excellent powers (Nussbaum, 1995: 31).

Nussbaum gives the concept needs a second role; for, as we have seen, she argues that *human* excellence is acquired and displayed precisely in relation to certain human lacks and limits. A good athlete presses against and makes recede her human limitations. But to extinguish them altogether—for instance, by gaining infinite speed by divine steroids—would eliminate both competition and the competitor. The same is true of virtue. Without various vulnerabilities like death, we would not have the ability to be courageous.

Sen has not really taken up these questions, but it seems clear that his intent is to push freedoms and capabilities as opportunities as far as he can without resorting to other concepts. Sen's theory of actual freedom would be more comprehensive and humanly nuanced if he followed Nussbaum and added internal powers to external opportunities and viewed humans not only as capable but as in need of nurture in a context of neediness. The decisions of how to grow and function—of how to develop, do and be—are to be made not just in relation to resources and opportunities but in relation to certain human limits and vulnerabilities that we must struggle against in humanly appropriate ways. If Nussbaum is correct, as important as the concept of capabilities proves to be, there still would be a continuing role for the language of needs.

2 THE CAPABILITY ETHIC: SOME IMPLICATIONS

2.1. Freedom

Sen's concept of capability and his critique of Rawls led us to touch on Sen's conception of the nature and value of positive freedom. For 'the capability to function is the thing that comes closest to the notion of positive freedom, and if freedom is valued then capability itself can serve as an object of value and moral importance' (Sen, 1984: 316). For Sen, positive freedom (i) is defined as 'the "capability" to achieve various alternative combinations of functionings, that is, doings and beings' (Sen, 1990c: 116) and (ii) can add intrinsic value to the actual options and functionings chosen. The good human life is, among other things, a life of freedom (Sen, 1985a: 70). Valuable human functionings include the act of choosing from among valuable functionings. In some of his recent writings Sen tends to use the concept of freedom even more than the concept of capability. The reason, I think is twofold. Against right wing libertarians such as Hayek, Friedman, and Nozick, Sen is trying to (re)claim the concept of freedom for the democratic left—whether that of social democracy or democratic (self-managing) socialism. In distinction from

Nussbaum, Sen gives an account of positive freedom that is 'thicker' than Rawls's primary goods but 'thinner' than Nussbaum's (and his own) concept of the good life.

Sen offers two distinctions to grasp the full complexity of the concept of freedom: (i) negative freedom/positive freedom, and (ii) well-being freedom/agency freedom. Let us briefly consider each. Sen roughly accepts Isaiah Berlin's classic distinction between negative and positive freedom but rejects Berlin's critique of the latter. A person is negatively free when one is not being interfered with by others—whether persons, governments, or institutions. Such interference, whether restraint or coercion, is bad because the interferer prevents the agent from doing what he chooses or choosing what he does. But Sen correctly sees that someone can be free from such external interference and still be radically unfree due to the absence of options in general and valuable options in particular. No one may be interfering with the starving person and yet she is not free not to starve, for bad fate is her only option. Nussbaum puts it well: 'Some policies of non-interference actually extinguish human freedom to choose what is valuable' (Nussbaum, 1988a: 213). The concept of positive freedom is important because it marks out how a person is really able to act, live, function or achieve. Positive freedom is 'what a person is actually able to do or be' (Sen, 1989b: 770).

To be positively free is to be able to live as one chooses, to have the effective 'power to achieve chosen results' (Sen, 1985b: 208). It is this dimension of positive freedom that R. G. Peffer emphasizes in his recent and important interpretation of Marx. 'By "positive freedom",' Peffer says, 'I mean freedom in the sense of being able to determine or control one's life,' that is, 'have a significant impact or effect upon the direction of one's own life and the circumstances under which one must live.'[23] Sen, however, goes further. He correctly sees that positive freedom also includes the real availability of an array of options and that freedom is increased to the extent that the number and goodness of these options are increased: 'the extent of freedom must not be judged only by the number of alternatives; it depends also on the goodness of the alternatives' (Sen, 1987b: 36, n. 17). Though both persons A and B are starving, A is more free than B, if A (the faster) has the real option of being adequately nourished. A's freedom is enhanced not only because A has more options than B but because only A is capable of additional functioning that is *valuable*. Another step that Sen could and should but does not take is to see that positive freedom is also enhanced insofar as there is an increase in either the diversity or probability of options.[24]

---

[23] R. G. Peffer, *Marxism, Morality, and Social Justice* (Princeton, NJ: Princeton University Press, 1990), 127.

[24] This view of positive liberty and its implications for the democratic left is worked out in detail in Lawrence Crocker, *Positive Liberty* (The Hague: Martinus Nijhoff, 1980); and D. Crocker, *Praxis and Democratic Socialism*, 68–76, 229–46.

Sen, consistent with his dual (well-being/agency) perspective on human beings, also distinguishes between well-being freedom and agency freedom. If I have the former I have the real opportunity to choose and achieve well-being; if I have the latter, I additionally have the opportunity to choose against my well-being. A good society would provide the material and institutional conditions for both types of freedom. However, Sen's discussion of agency freedom as a capability illustrates the weakness we identified earlier. His view of agency (or autonomy) as capability speaks only of opportunities or possible functionings and fails to follow Nussbaum's view of capability as (also) a trait or power of the person. For Nussbaum, the capability of a person to choose depends not simply on external features but also on whether that person has a *developed* power of choice (Nussbaum, 1988a: 160–72). Neither stones nor human infants can choose right now. The baby, however, has a latent or undeveloped power and, if all goes well, eventually will acquire the actual or developed power as an adult. And, with ageing the power may decline and finally be extinguished altogether.[25]

One purpose of good development is to ensure that this human ability for choice is acquired by the young, maintained by the mature, and restored (when possible) to those who lose it. Good governments, especially through education, facilitate the formation of good capabilities, remove impediments to their exercise, and provide means for their use. If the present argument is correct, Sen should deepen his notion of freedom so that it faces in two directions: toward both the *power* of choice and the *options* open to choice. One virtue of doing so would be to justify the educational dimension of good development (see Nussbaum, 1990a: 233–4; 1988a: 213). We shall see that another advantage would be that 'capability rights' could be related to features of the kinds of beings that humans find themselves to be and value.

Given this conception of the complex nature of positive freedom, how does Sen understand its value? Here the crucial distinction is between freedom's intrinsic and its instrumental value. Negative as well as positive freedom have both sorts of value. As we have seen, capabilities always add some value to actual functionings:

> Freedom is valuable in itself, and not only because of what it permits us to achieve or do. The good life may be seen to be a life of freedom, and in that context freedom is not just a way of achieving a good life, it is *constitutive* of the good life itself.   (Sen, 1989b: 770; emphasis in text)

It is intrinsically good to *choose* a way of life and not to fall or be forced into it (Sen, 1985a: 70). Sen's argument, for this claim, is an appeal to our

---

[25] Frederick Ferré works out an extensive comparison of the human power of freedom as 'creative self-determination' with the human power of speech. See Frederick Ferré, 'Self-determinism', *American Philosophical Quarterly* 10 (July 1973), 172.

intuitions about the starving/fasting examples discussed above (Sen, 1987a: 60). To say freedom (or autonomy) is intrinsically good is not to say, with Kantians, that freedom is the only good; there are many intrinsically valuable functionings. Due to individual variations, Sen argues that Rawls's primary goods are at best means to positive freedom and that equal positive freedom requires different amount of goods for different sorts of people, if they are to be free to pursue a full range of objectives. More determinately, he can join Nussbaum in saying that it is precisely our actual freedom that enables us to choose, weigh, and pursue valuable goals. Choice is a sort of super or 'architectonic' capability in that its exercise enhances the value, and thereby 'humanizes' other valuable functionings such as eating, loving, and communal participation (Nussbaum, 1990a: 226–8).

We see here a key element in Sen's and Nussbaum's strategy in meeting Rawls's objection to 'perfectionism'. Recall that Rawls, in his thin theory of the good, objects to the use of state power to impose one (general, comprehensive) conception of the good. Within 'wide limits, "justice as fairness" does not prejudge the choice of the sort of persons that men want to be'.[26] In going beyond primary goods to actual freedom Sen responds to the liberal challenge. Nussbaum fills in this space by building freedom as a personal power right into her concept of those important capacities that a good political arrangement is to promote. Moreover, although a good polity certainly promotes a conception of the good life, the 'vagueness' (generality) of this 'outline sketch' permits ample room for each society ('local specification') and each individual in a society ('plural specification') to exercise the capability for freedom by particularizing, in terms of its traditions and tastes, the thick conception.[27] Finally, individuals exercise their (capability) for autonomy when they decide the sphere(s) of life in which they will seek to realize their humanity, for example, family, employment, recreation, religion, or politics. Although the concept of the good life is relevant for all these domains, citizens are free to choose which one(s) are of special importance to them. In all these spheres, but especially in politics, their capability for choice can be realized by forming the group's goals and plans.

Sen correctly insists that the intrinsic value of freedom does not imply that it also cannot be instrumentally valuable in achieving other good

---

[26] Rawls, *A Theory of Justice* (Cambridge, MA: Harvard University Press, 1971), 260.

[27] For a similar view that takes seriously Rawls's antiperfectionism and yet argues that a good society promotes a concept of human flourishing that includes positive freedom to be freely specified, see D. Crocker, *Praxis and Democratic Socialism*, 229–46, especially 229–34. Nussbaum needs to go further than she has so far (Nussbaum, 1990b: 220–9) with respect to just what a good government can do to promote citizen choice of the good life and deter choices of bad lives. The point I made with respect to Marković and Stojanović applies equally to Nussbaum: 'What is needed is a conception of a good society in which the social fostering of individual excellence (*praxis*) takes place in a framework in which civil liberties are secured, a wealth of real options are provided (permitted), and in which such excellence is neither required nor manipulated.' (*Praxis and Democratic Socialism*, 233).

functionings. As Aristotle and Dewey note, but many forget, something can be both a means and an end, an instrumental good and a good in itself. For example, some of Sen's important empirical work traces the causal link between India's press freedom and its lack of famines since Independence. Press freedom is both good in itself and promotes the good of avoiding starvation.

2.2. Rights

From the perspective of his capability approach, Sen has begun to sketch out a suggestive theory of moral rights as 'capability rights' (Sen, 1982c: 222). These rights have an important role to play but are defined in relation to 'basic' functionings and capabilities or freedoms. Such rights are viewed as consequentialist goals rather than Nozickian deontological side constraints on goal-seeking action. Finally, Sen argues for positive or welfare rights in addition to negative rights or rights not to be interfered with. Let us take each point in turn.

In commenting on one of Sen's essays (Sen, 1987b), Bernard Williams makes an important observation and asks a significant question:

> We actually believe that people have a basic right to breathe clean air without having to go somewhere else to do it, but we do not believe that they have a similar right to go to expensive winter holiday resorts. I am not very happy myself with taking rights as the starting point. The notion of a basic human right seems to me obscure enough, and I would rather come at it from the perspective of basic human capabilities. I would prefer capabilities to do the work, and if we are going to have a language or rhetoric of rights, to have it delivered from them, rather than the other way around. But I think that there remains an unsolved problem: how we should see the relations between these concepts.   (Sen, 1987b: 100)

In response, Sen defines a basic right as a right to a minimum amount of basic capabilities or freedoms (see Sen 1982c: 199–200; 1984: 297):

> Some of the relevant freedoms can also yield straightforward notions of rights. For example, minimal demands of well-being (in the form of basic functionings, e.g., not to be hungry) and of well-being freedom (in the form of minimal capabilities, e.g., having the means of avoiding hunger), can well be seen as rights that command attention and call for support.   (Sen, 1985b: 217)

Rights, then, are defined as basic not because they are indispensable to the fulfilment of any other right but because they are a way of formulating the urgency of minimal levels of eminently valuable human (actual and possible) functionings.[28] It is intrinsically good for humans to be and do in

---

[28] Henry Shue defines basic rights by their indispensability 'for the enjoyment of all other rights' in *Basic Rights: Subsistence, Affluence, and U.S. Foreign Policy* (Princeton, NJ: Princeton University Press, 1980), 19. In an early review of Shue's important book, James W. Nickel and Elizabeth Haase argue that the relational conception of basic rights needs to be supplemented by grounding such rights in some intrinsically good feature of human beings. Sen has tried to do just that. See *California Law Review*, 69 (1981), 1569–86.

certain ways and to have the freedom to so function, to be above the 'threshold' that enables them to so function. To justify something as a fundamental right is to identify a human functioning as basic, that is, as intrinsically and supremely good. Rights are grounded in the good in the sense that they are justified with reference to valuable human functionings. For instance, recall that Nussbaum proposes 'separateness' and 'strong separateness', our being able to live our own lives in our own surroundings, as two of our basic human capabilities. Then she goes on to identify a governmentally protected private sphere as indispensable for the functioning of this capability:

Separateness and strong separateness have been read here to require the protection, around each citizen, of a sphere of privacy and non-interference within which what goes on will not be the business of political planning at all, though politics will protect its boundaries.   (Nussbaum, 1990a: 239)

What this sphere consists of would be a matter of political argument that would result in a 'local specification' of the basic norm. Such specification, in contrast to the 'plural specification' referred to above, is done collectively by citizens in a particular community when, through 'participatory dialogue' they particularize—'with rich sensitivity to the concrete context, to the characters of the agents and their social situation'—the general conception of the good life. It is clear, however, that Nussbaum herself approves of the Athenian consensus that included 'almost all speech, above all political speech, most of family and sexual life, and most, though not all, one's dealing with personal friends' (ibid.: 239; see forthcoming b). She also approves of the protection of religious freedom enshrined in the American separation of church and state. One has the right to 'use' one's separateness to choose (or not) to practice (with others) a religion.[29] Rights come on the scene, so to speak, as we further define and institutionally protect our human good of (strong) separateness: 'a scheme of basic rights . . . will be justified with reference to the role they play in protecting a way of life that citizens have agreed to be good for them as human beings' (Nussbaum, 1990a: 239).

Since some valuable functionings are more valuable than others, some rights are more fundamental than others. For instance, 'the ability to retain bodily safety is quite a different type of right from the ability to keep one's financial accounts private' (Sen, 1982c: 203). And Nussbaum remarks that

---

[29] Nussbaum treats religion in this way rather than by adding the virtue of piety to her list of valuable capabilities: not so much because she believes 'external' or other-worldly transcendence is incoherent with our beliefs in *human* flourishing but more because she has serious doubts about the possibility of achieving a 'political' consensus in matters of religion. A future topic would be to investigate whether or not this view reflects ethnocentric bias against, for example, Islamic societies instead of a universally appropriate view of human flourishing. An alternative solution would be to put 'being able to be concerned with transcendence' on the Level 2 list and to leave it sufficiently vague so as to include Nussbaum's preferred this-worldly or 'internal' transcendence as well as 'external' transcendence (see Nussbaum, 1990b: 365–91).

in Aristotelian social democracy there is no absolute right to property: land, money, and possessions are not intrinsically valuable but are good only to the extent that they promote the good functioning of citizens and, especially, their moving across the threshold. Basic rights would be formulated in relation to minimally acceptable levels of the eminently valuable functionings. Rights formulate justified demands that people be above a certain threshold of valuable functioning and freedom.[30]

The demand for this 'moral minimum'[31] is relevant to the tasks of good governments and the duties of other people, for example, the duty to eliminate or reduce poverty as an absolute level of deprivation (Sen, 1987*b*: 109; 1984: Essay 14). However, for Sen, such a relation between duty-bearer and rights-bearer is based finally on the relation of the right to certain valuable capabilities (1982*c*: 200). Hence, Sen calls his view a 'capability rights system' rather than a 'two-person (or two-agent)' rights system (ibid.: 200).[32]

A second point about Sen's capability-based theory of rights is that he offers it as one type of what he calls a 'goal rights system' (ibid.: 199). Such an ethics or 'moral system' is defined as one 'in which fulfillment and non-realization of rights are included among the goals, incorporated in the evaluation of states of affairs, and then applied to the choice of actions through consequential links' (ibid.: 199). To decide on the moral rightness or wrongness of human actions (commissions or omissions), we must *inter alia* consider the states of affairs that result from the action. Rights fulfilments and violations are then to be counted as ingredients in the states of affairs. Respecting of rights will be part of the value of a state of affairs, and violating of rights will be part of the disvalue: 'a tortured body, an unfed belly, a bullied person, or unequal pay for equal work, is as much a part of the state [of] affairs as the utility and disutility occurring in that state' (Sen, 1979: 488). Goal rights systems, although differing among themselves according to their lists of rights, would be 'pure' if they proposed no goals other than rights. They would be impure if they also included other goals, such as utility.

Sen situates his theory of rights as goals within his larger ethical project. This perspective, as worked out thus far, remains open either to an 'impure' and broad consequentialism, on the one hand, or a broad deontology with 'consequence sensitivity', on the other. Goal rights systems would be forms of ethical consequentialism, broadly conceived, if the rights and the other goals were *all* that mattered morally: 'for the consequentialist, even a broad one, the *rightness* of actions has no real sense other than what reflects the

---

[30] Shue offers the following definition of a moral right: 'A moral right provides (1) the rational basis for a justified demand (2) that the actual enjoyment of a substance be (3) socially guaranteed against standard threats' (*Basic Rights*, 13).

[31] Ibid., p. ix.

[32] It is beyond the scope of this paper to consider Sen's arguments (Sen, 1982*c*: 200–4) for the advantages of a 'capability rights system' over a 'two person' rights system.

goodness of states of affairs' (Sen, 1983: 130). A goal rights system, however, also could be part of a 'broad deontology' if it were what Sen calls 'consequence sensitive' (Sen, 1987a: 76). In this sort of deontology, the consequences of rights fulfilments or violations would matter, but things other than good consequences also would be morally relevant.

However Sen finally decides to stand on this issue of broad consequentialism versus broad deontology, he argues that a broad consequentialism, a 'goal rights system with consequence-based reasoning', is superior to any narrow deontology such as Nozick's. On Nozick's view, people have (negative) rights, such as a right not to have one's person or property interfered with (without one's consent). These are consequence-independent 'side constraints' rather than goals. That is, Nozick claims, that rights are not part of end states to be achieved but rather 'constrain your goal-directed behavior':

> The side-constraint view forbids you to violate these moral constraints in the pursuit of your goals; whereas the view whose objective is to minimize the violation of these rights allows you to violate the rights (the constraints) in order to lessen their total violation in the society.[33]

Nozick means that rights as side constraints (almost) never can be violated justifiably or overridden even if the consequence would avert an even greater violation of rights (or promote an overwhelming fulfilment of rights).[34]

In arguing for the superiority of his own view, Sen puts his finger exactly on the place where Nozick's view seems morally reprehensible. Sen has three compelling arguments. First, perfect fulfilment of Nozickian (negative) rights is compatible with 'terrible hardships and miseries' (Sen, 1988c: 275) in the lives of those who lack economic power. For example, as Sen's work on famine shows, 'even terrible famines are entirely consistent with a fully operative and fully complied entitlement system of negative rights of the kind outlined and defended by Robert Nozick' (ibid.: 275).

Secondly, Sen presents some actual and hypothetical cases in which he effectively appeals to 'resilient moral intuitions' (Sen, 1982c: 198) that an agent is justified in violating one Nozickian right as a positive means of respecting some other negative right, more pressing in the context. For example, in his 'Ali case' Sen persuasively argues that Donna is justified in breaking into Charles' room and, against his will, inspecting Charles' papers if that is the only way for Donna to prevent the 'bashing up' of her friend Ali. Our social 'multilateral interdependences' (ibid.: 190) are such

---

[33] R. Nozick, *Anarchy, State, and Utopia* (New York: Basic Books, 1974) 29.

[34] Nozick argues against a 'utilitarianism of rights' (ibid.: 28) and wants to avoid such questions as 'whether these side constraints are absolute, or whether they may be violated in order to avoid catastrophic moral horror' (ibid.: 30). Yet his use of a 'Lockean proviso' (ibid.: 178–82) shows both that he cannot avoid these questions and that he opens the door to the very sort of 'consequence sensitive' analysis that Sen is advocating. Cf. Sen, 1988d: 62 n. 8.

that third parties should sometimes violate rights to promote other rights. Negative freedoms and negative rights sometimes require not only omissions but also commissions.

Thirdly, and more generally, Sen convincingly argues that by affirming rights as goals, he can explain a third party's guaranteeing a weightier right by means of violating a less important one:

It is not adequate for me to resist molesting you; it is necessary that I value the things I can *do* to stop others from molesting you. I would fail to *value negative freedom* if I were to refuse to consider what I could do in defence of negative freedom. (Sen, 1984: 314; see also 1982c: 222; 1985b: 217; 1987a: 88–9; 1988c: 274–5; emphasis in text)

Finally, Sen's capabilities perspective on rights provides a way of defending what have come to be called positive or welfare rights. The stress on basic capabilities, such as being able to be minimally well-nourished, enables us to 'blur the distinction between rights that relate to so-called positive freedom and those related to negative freedom and non-coercion'. We can say two things about one capability. Reflecting traditional negative rights, we can say people have a right not to have the capability eliminated or impeded. For example, a right not to be hungry reflects the crucial importance that there be no obstacles to having or realizing one's capability to be well-nourished (see Sen, 1982e). Reflecting traditional positive rights, we can say people have the right to be provisioned in such a way that they can *choose* to be adequately nourished. And if we follow Nussbaum in supplementing Sen, we additionally can say that government and other development institutions have a duty to develop people's latent or embryonic capability so they are able and ready to exercise it.

In this connection there remain two areas for future investigation. We saw above that Nussbaum views the right to property as justified instrumentally only to the extent that it promotes valuable human capabilities and functionings. Lacking so far in Nussbaum's account is her consideration of the full range of basic human rights that could and should be related to her ample list of valuable functional capabilities. Whereas Sen makes it clear that basic rights should include welfare or subsistence rights, Nussbaum so far has restricted her attention to the rights to privacy and political speech. I see no reason, however, that Nussbaum could not join Sen and affirm that people have a basic right to the minimal level of all the most valuable capabilities. More positively, her most recent work suggests that undeveloped or 'basic capabilities . . . give rise to correlated political duties' and that 'this idea . . . is the underlying basis, in the Western philosophical tradition, for many notions of human rights' (Nussbaum, 1995: 31). On this positive basis and her full list of valuable functionings, Nussbaum can and should go on to work out a theory of positive rights.

Secondly, both Sen and Nussbaum should consider in greater depth how duties to respect the various rights are to be distributed. How, for example, should obligations to promote the welfare or personal security rights of persons in a poor country be apportioned among private individuals, the nation's government, rich nations and (foreign) individuals, and international organizations?[35] Moreover, how much is required (duty) and how much is praiseworthy (supererogatory) but not required.

Finally, Sen's approach enables us to justify overriding some less important or non-basic negative right, like the right to have my caviar and eat it too, insofar as it will allow us to reduce the violation or increase the fulfilment of some more important or basic right, such as the right to be able to meet minimal nutritional requirements.

This multiplicity of rights is a part of Sen's more general ethical pluralism. In addition to the points made earlier about 'partial ordering' and weighing of conflicting elements, it must also be noted that Sen urges us to conceive capability rights not only as intrinsically good but also as instrumentally good (Sen, 1988d). Respecting rights can be justified instrumentally when such an act is causally linked to other goods. For instance, respecting the capability rights of small farmers and day-labourers is not only good in itself but in many circumstances will causally promote the good goal of environmental respect. At this point Sen's view seems superior to Nussbaum's. For Nussbaum conceives of rights as purely instrumental (and negative): 'they will be justified with reference to the role they play in protecting a way of life that citizens have agreed to be good for them as human beings' (Nussbaum, 1990a: 239). Some rights theorists, such as Nozick and Shue, view rights as 'neither means nor ends' but as 'constraints on both means and ends'.[36] Some view rights as means but not ends (or vice versa). Sen suggestively conceives rights as both means and ends.

2.3. Justice

A normative theory of distributive justice is concerned with such questions as what should be distributed, who or what should be the agent and recipient of the distributing, and what are the circumstances of and bases for just distributions. Such a theory is the least-elaborated aspect of Sen's

[35] Sen raises some of the urgent questions in Sen 1982e: 352–3. Moreover, he recognizes what he calls 'metarights' to have policies pursued in which rights, not immediately realizable, become realizable in the future (see ibid.: 345–7). Hence, for Sen the assignment of duties must take into consideration both realizable and (immediately) unrealizable rights. Important contributions to the topic of the distribution of duties have been made by Henry Shue, 'Mediating Duties', Ethics 98 (1988), 687–704; and James W. Nickel, 'Rights and Development', in Ethical Principles for Development.

[36] Henry Shue, 'In the American Tradition, Rights Remain Unalienable', Center Magazine (January/February 1984) 14. Cf. Sen, 1988d: 58–9.

and Nussbaum's capability perspective. This judgement is true with respect to distributional issues both within and between nation-states. So far Sen's major contribution has been to sort out some of the issues (Sen, 1984: Essay 12), criticize some leading theories (1980), argue for a conception of *what* is to be distributed (ibid.; 1990*c*), and consider some distributive or 'combining' principles (ibid.: 112).

Nussbaum recently has gone further with respect to 'domestic' justice by sketching out what she calls an Aristotelian conception of political distribution and social democracy (1988*a*; 1990*a*; 1990*b*). Although what they have done so far is suggestive and promising, they correctly recognize that there is much to accomplish before we have a comprehensive capability-based theory of national justice, relevant to the internal structure of all nations, and international justice, relevant to the relations between nations and to global institutions.

It should come as no surprise how Sen answers the question of the 'what' of distribution and, what he calls, the 'territory of justice' (1990*c*: 115). Individuals' claims to just treatment are to be assessed not (merely) in terms of utility, Rawlsian social primary goods, or Nozickian negative rights but in terms of their capabilities or 'the freedoms they actually enjoy to choose between different ways of living that they can have reason to value' (ibid.: 115). Justice concerns how people are free to choose and able to function in valuable ways. Hence, what is to be distributed are, ultimately, freedoms and functionings. Supposing that an adequate theory of justice will be in some sense egalitarian, Sen as early as 1980 asked, 'equality of what?' His answer was 'equality of "basic capabilities": a person being able to do certain basic things' (1980: 218). Nussbaum agrees with Aristotle that a government's allocation programmes and even its entire structure 'will be chosen with a view to good human functioning' (Nussbaum, 1990*a*: 230):

The aim of political planning is the distribution to the city's individual people of the conditions in which a good human life can be chosen and lived. This distributive task aims at producing capabilities. That is, it aims not simply at the allotment of commodities, but at making people able to function in certain human ways. A necessary basis for being a recipient of this distribution is that one should already possess some less developed capability to perform the functioning in question. The task of the city is, then, to effect the transition from one level of capability to another. This means that the task of the city cannot be understood apart from a rather substantial account of the human good and what it is to function humanly. (Nussbaum, 1988*a*: 145–6)

To elucidate Sen's and Nussbaum's position, consider a citizen who is crippled. If a government distributed on the basis of marginal utility, the cripple might be passed over altogether because restorative operations or special walkways probably would not be the most socially efficient use of public funds. Regardless of how utility is conceived, the combining principle of 'sum-ranking' instructs us to assess the consequences simply by adding up the individual utilities. Although each unit of utility counts, what is irrelevant is the personal, separate, or individual *locus* of the utility: 'Persons do not count as individuals in this any more than individual petrol tanks do in the analysis of the national consumption of petroleum' (Sen and Williams: 4; see Nussbaum, forthcoming *b*).

The cripple might fare no better if her total utility (e.g., happiness) were somehow given priority. For, as we saw earlier, the cripple might have 'a jolly disposition', 'a low aspiration level' or be content with a disability she believed was due to God's will. Deficient functioning and limited freedom would be 'muffled' by contentment. The cripple's total utility might be best served by ignoring and even increasing her disability.

Moreover, Rawls's social primary goods will not do the distributive job needed; because Rawls, even if he included the good of health care, has no concern with human variability and the *conversion* of goods into freedoms or functionings. To enable the cripple to be able to choose to enjoy the non-cripple's 'ability to get around' is going to take more or different commodities—whether wheelchairs, access ramps, or income supplements. Sen, then, helpfully shifts the discussions of justice 'from goods to what goods do to human beings' (Sen, 1980: 219), from income and wealth to freedom to function in desirable ways. Such a focus justifies Nussbaum calling such a theory 'deep', since it concerns the ways humans are living.

In what sense is this approach to justice egalitarian? What does it mean to advocate 'basic equality capability'? (Sen, 1980: 220) First, both Sen and Nussbaum argue that equality means that a just society recognizes each citizen's justified claim to at least a minimal level of freedom and well-being. Nussbaum argues that good government enables its citizens to cross the two thresholds of being human and being able to flourish. Secondly, Nussbaum adds that equality here concerns 'width'. It means that *all*—rather than just some—citizens are empowered to cross over the lines; at least insofar that each is (or can become) capable of functioning at these minimal levels, and adequate resources are available. This demand rules out sexism, racism and other prejudicial applications of the norms (Nussbaum, 1995: 42–51). Thirdly, equality means that the government should make resources and education available such that each citizen has the opportunity to function 'not just minimally, but well, insofar as natural circumstances permit (Nussbaum, 1990*a*: 228). Recall, further, that one of Sen's criticism of the BNA was that it left the impression of 'basic needs and no more'.

Fourthly, when resources are limited, such that everyone cannot reach the two thresholds and advance to full human flourishing, equality means that it is more important to empower everyone—who so chooses—to get over the line than promote or permit an elite to ascend higher (ibid.: 229). Why? Because once one has crossed the line, more is not necessarily better;

and, even if it were, further attainments can be left to the person's own resourcefulness.

What if an elite's attainment of (or monetary rewards for) higher levels of functioning is or can be causally linked to more people crossing the threshold? Then, as in Rawls's difference principle, such inequalities would be justified. But what if elite achievements (or rewards) prevent those barely above the (first? second?) threshold either from advancing further or from closing the gap between the top and the bottom? Should elite achievement (rewards) be governmentally promoted at the cost of limiting the further advance of those just over the threshold?

Nussbaum begins to take up these questions when she argues that since more is not always better, elite achievements are not likely to require more resources, at least those such as money and property, that the less well-off need to get above the thresholds. Rather, elites can achieve either by making better use of what they already have or by excelling in ways that do not (or should not?) depend so much on income and wealth, for instance, friendship, aesthetic experience, and political participation. Or if some accomplishments—we might think of film making—require large sums, then those interested can pursue the needed resources on their own rather than receive governmental transfers from those barely over the threshold. In a good and just society the most important use of governmental expenditures will be of getting everyone 'across the threshold into capability to choose well' (ibid.: 229).

This answer is certainly a good start. It hinges, however, on certain assumptions that may not hold, even in a good and just society, with sufficient frequency, namely, (i) that the elite will choose to define achievement apart from their monetary rewards, bank accounts, and sports cars, and (ii) that genuine achievements in politics, science, and the arts will not require government subsidies. We look forward to further consideration by Sen and Nussbaum on the proper balance between the egalitarian and 'meritocratic' components in just distribution. We also anticipate that Nussbaum will clarify in more detail the nature and relation of the two thresholds and their implications for government responsibility.

Finally, who or what should receive the just benefit of basic capability equality? 'Each and every citizen', is Nussbaum's answer. Nussbaum effectively criticizes sexist and racist applications of the capability ethic, especially Aristotle's prejudicial exclusion of slaves and women for his concept of citizenship (see Nussbaum 1988a and 1995: 42–51). Moreover, she correctly recognizes that citizens who are incapable of minimal functioning *right now* can acquire or develop—with the appropriate public arrangements—the requisite capability (see Nussbaum, 1990a: 243). But suppose such 'line crossings' were only possible with outlays that put others below the line? What does justice or mercy require, if anything, with respect to genetic humans and other animals completely incapable of reaching the threshold?[37] What does (retributive) justice require with respect to those actions in which an agent's intentional or foreseeable action puts someone else below the lines or deprives them in some other way of human functioning? When should such harm be a crime and what would be an appropriate punishment? What does (compensatory) justice demand with respect to rectification owed to victims of rights violations? Again these further questions must be put on the agenda of the capability theory of distributive, redistributive, and compensatory justice.

Sen treats questions of the 'ethics of international income distribution' even more sketchily than he does domestic justice; and Nussbaum, so far, has only stated that rich countries should help foreign poor as well as help their own poor get above the capability threshold (Nussbaum, 1991: 25; forthcoming b). Sen restricts himself to four suggestive points but has failed to take up other related questions. First, he argues that we should avoid discussing inter-state justice as if nations were human persons, for such an approach would both prevent consideration of the absolute and relative deprivations of human individuals and tend to have the bad consequences of strengthening unjust national elites in both recipient and donor countries (Sen, 1984: 292–3, 297–9). So far, however, Sen has not considered what less-than-personal moral standing states can be said to have and how this standing should be weighed against the moral claims of persons.

Secondly, Sen argues that we should not presume that a given nation-state is entitled to its wealth and that it is only alterations in the *status quo* that require justification. For a nation's wealth may be due to unjust past and present actions in relation to other states and peoples (Sen, 1984: 293). Yet so far Sen has not reflected on the principles we should use to identify such actions and what compensatory justice requires.

Thirdly, although Sen is open to giving some moral weight to national self-interest, he correctly sees that such a concern has to be balanced with 'positional-neutral' evaluations of deprivation and well-being (Sen, 1984: 295–6). Again, we look forward to his moral assessment of nationality and national self-interest in an interdependent world.

Fourthly, Sen and Nussbaum both assert that a moral case for international redistribution from rich nations to poor nations can be made. Sen maintains that such a case should not be based on the fact that persons in richer countries have higher incomes (per capita) than persons do in poor countries. The variation in conversions of commodities to capabilities may

[37] In a recent paper Nussbaum acknowledges the need for 'other moral arguments to determine our responsibilities to our own near relatives, and to animals generally' (Nussbaum 1991: 43). An important challenge will be to decide how far the anthropocentric, Aristotelian ethic should be extended or supplemented to give an account of direct human duties to various sorts of non-human entities. J. Baird Callicott offers an important analysis of some of the options and arguments in 'The Search for an Environmental Ethic', in T. Regan (ed.), *Matters of Life and Death: New Essays in Moral Philosophy* 2nd edn. (New York: Random House, 1986), 381–424.

mean that the (per capita) well-being of persons in some poorer countries, such as Sri Lanka, is higher than that in some richer countries, such as Saudi Arabia or Brazil (ibid.: 294). Even apart from the problem that intra-nation distributions are hidden by national averages, we need to recognize that life expectancy and literacy would be better indices of functionings and capabilities than would per capita GNP. This important point, made possible by the capability perspective, does not yet make, however, the positive moral case for international redistribution and inter-state promotion of just development. It will be important, for example, for Nussbaum to clarify and defend further what she recognizes to be the international implication of her 'fundamental commitment . . . to bring each and every person across the threshold into capability for good functioning':

This view also generates clear global imperatives: for the countries whose citizens have a material surplus are, by holding on to that surplus, doing injustice to citizens in countries that are too poor to move everyone across the threshold (Nussbaum, forthcoming b).

In the light of their powerful capability ethic, then, Sen and Nussbaum need to consider the bases, nature, and extent of the moral responsibilities of rich nations, multinationals, or international bodies to reduce the following unconscionable deprivations that continue to exist in the developing world:

There are still nearly 900 million adults in the developing world who cannot read or write, 1.5 billion people without access to primary health care, 1.75 billion people without safe water, around 100 million completely homeless, some 800 million people who still go hungry every day and more than a billion who survive in absolute poverty.[38]

3 CONCLUSION

The capability ethic that Sen and Nussbaum are forging has given international development ethicists a challenging, richly nuanced, and fertile resource. It forcefully identifies both strengths and weaknesses of commodity-based, utilitarian, and deontological rights-based ethics. Building on and deepening the basic needs perspective, it promisingly evaluates development theory and practice by the plural criteria of valuable human capabilities and achievements. Recasting the traditional social ideals of human freedom, rights, and justice, the capability perspective has in effect launched a new development paradigm. To contribute to the paradigm's further evolution has been a major aim of the present essay.

[38] *Human Development Report 1990*, 17.

BIBLIOGRAPHY

NUSSBAUM, MARTHA (1986a). *The Fragility of Goodness: Luck and Ethics in Greek Tragedy and Philosophy*. Cambridge: Cambridge University Press.

—— (1986b). 'Therapeutic Arguments: Epicurus and Aristotle', in M. Schofield and G. Striker (eds.), *The Norms of Nature: Studies in Hellenistic Ethics*. Cambridge: Cambridge University Press.

—— (1988a). 'Nature, Function, and Capability: Aristotle on Political Distribution', *Oxford Studies in Ancient Philosophy*, suppl. vol., 145–84.

—— (1988b). 'Non-Relative Virtues: An Aristotelian Approach', *Midwest Studies in Philosophy*, 13, 32–53.

—— (1990a). 'Aristotelian Social Democracy', in R. B. Douglass, G. R. Mara, and H. S. Richardson (eds.), *Liberalism and the Good*. New York and London: Routledge.

—— (1990b). *Love's Knowledge: Essays on Philosophy and Literature* (New York and Oxford: Oxford University Press), esp. Essays 2, 7, and 15.

—— (forthcoming a). 'Aristotle on Human Nature and the Foundations of Ethics', in J. Altham and R. Harrison (eds.), a volume in honour of Bernard Williams. Cambridge: Cambridge University Press.

—— (forthcoming b). 'Human Functioning and Social Justice: In Defense of Aristotelian Essentialism', *Political Theory*.

—— (1995). 'Human Capabilities, Female Human Beings', in M. C. Nussbaum and J. Glover (eds.), *Women, Culture, and Development*. Oxford: Clarendon Press.

—— and SEN, AMARTYA (1989). 'Internal Criticism and Indian Rationalist Traditions', in M. Krausz (ed.), *Relativism, Interpretation and Confrontation*. Notre Dame, Ind.: Notre Dame University Press.

—— —— (eds.) (1994). *The Quality of Life*. Oxford: Clarendon Press.

SEN, AMARTYA (1973). *On Economic Inequality*. Oxford: Clarendon Press.

—— (1979). 'Utilitarianism and Welfarism', *Journal of Philosophy*, 76, 463–89.

—— (1980). 'Equality of What?', in S. M. McMurrin (ed.), *Tanner Lectures on Human Values*, i. Salt Lake City: University of Utah Press.

—— (1981a). *Poverty and Famines: An Essay on Entitlement and Deprivation*. Oxford: Clarendon Press.

—— (1981b). 'Public Action and the Quality of Life in Developing Countries', *Oxford Bulletin of Economics and Statistics*, 43, 287–319.

—— (1982a). *Choice, Welfare and Measurement*. Oxford: Blackwell, and Cambridge, Mass.: MIT Press.

—— (1982b). 'How is India Doing?', *New York Review of Books*, 29 (Christmas).

—— (1982c). 'Rights and Agency', *Philosophy and Public Affairs*, 11, 3–39.

—— (1982d). 'The Food Problem: Theory and Policy', *Third World Quarterly*, 4, 447–59.

—— (1982e). 'The Right Not to be Hungry', in G. Floistad (ed.), *Contemporary Philosophy: A New Survey*, vol. II. The Hague: Martinus Nijhoff.

—— (1983). 'Evaluator Relativity and Consequential Evaluation', *Philosophy and Public Affairs*, 12, 113–32.

—— (1984). *Resources, Values and Development*. Oxford: Blackwell, and Cambridge, Mass.: Harvard University Press.

—— (1985*a*). *Commodities and Capabilities*. Amsterdam: North-Holland.

—— (1985*b*). 'The Moral Standing of Markets', *Social Philosophy and Policy*, 2, 1–19.

—— (1985*c*). 'Rights as Goals', in S. Guest and A. Milne (eds.), *Equality and Discrimination: Essays in Freedom and Justice*. Stuttgart: Franz Steiner.

—— (1985*d*). 'Well-being, Agency and Freedom: The Dewey Lectures 1984', *Journal of Philosophy*, 82, 169–221.

—— (1987*a*). *On Ethics and Economics*. Oxford: Basil Blackwell.

—— (1987*b*). In Geoffrey Hawthorn (ed.), *The Standard of Living*. Cambridge: Cambridge University Press.

—— (1987*c*). *Hunger and Entitlements: Research for Action*. Helsinki: WIDER.

—— (1988*a*). 'Africa and India: What Do We Have to Learn from Each Other?', in K. J. Arrow (ed.), *The Balance between Industry and Agriculture in Economic Development*, I: *Basic Issues*. London: Macmillan.

—— (1988*b*). 'The Concept of Development', in H. Chenery and T. N. Srinivasan (eds.), *Handbook of Development Economics*, vol. I. Amsterdam: North-Holland.

—— (1988*c*). 'Freedom of Choice: Concept and Content', *European Economic Review*, 32, 269–94.

—— (1988*d*). 'Property and Hunger', *Economics and Philosophy*, 4, 57–68.

—— (1988*e*). 'Sri Lanka's Achievements: How and When', in T. N. Srinivasan and P. K. Bardhan (eds.), *Rural Poverty in South Asia*. New York: Colombia University Press.

—— (1989*a*). 'Economic Methodology: Heterogeneity and Relevance', *Social Research*, 56, 299–329.

—— (1989*b*). 'Food and Freedom', *World Development*, 17, 769–81.

—— (1989*c*). 'Indian Development: Lessons and Non-lessons', *Daedalus*, 118, 369–92.

—— (1990*a*). 'Individual Freedom as a Social Commitment', *New York Review of Books*, 37, 49–54.

—— (1990*b*). 'Gender and Cooperative Conflicts', in I. Tinker (ed.), *Persistent Inequalities*. New York: Oxford University Press.

—— (1990*c*). 'Justice: Means versus Freedoms', *Philosophy and Public Affairs*, 19, 111-21.

—— (1990*d*). 'More than 100 Million Women are Missing', *New York Review of Books*, 37, 61–6.

—— (1991*a*). 'Welfare, Preference and Freedom', mimeographed, Harvard University.

—— (1991*b*). 'On Indexing Primary Goods and Capabilities', mimeographed, Harvard University.

—— (1991*c*). 'Gender Inequality and Theories of Justice', in M. C. Nussbaum and J. Glover (eds.), *Women, Culture and Development*. Oxford: Clarendon Press.

—— and WILLIAMS, BERNARD (1982). *Utilitarianism and Beyond*. Cambridge: Cambridge University Press.

—— and DRÈZE, JEAN (1989). *Hunger and Public Action*. Oxford: Clarendon Press.

Pragmatism and Moral Objectivity

Hilary Putnam

The papers in the present volume resulted from the happy idea of bringing together philosophers used to dealing with issues of justice, issues about what constitutes flourishing for an individual or for a society, feminist issues and development issues, and also some people who, like Martha Chen, have firsthand knowledge of what those issues mean in the lives of the women and men of developing countries. (Some of us, like Amartya Sen, fell into both of these categories.) This paper, like the others, was and is intended to contribute to the discussion of those issues. If it has ended up being more 'abstract' than most of the others, that is not because the author got 'carried away' by a particular line of abstract thought. Rather, it is because it was my conviction, as well as the conviction of the organizers of the conference, that positions on the 'abstract' question of moral objectivity have real world effects. In one of his major works,[1] Jürgen Habermas repeatedly expresses the conviction that Max Weber's conclusion, that modern scientific rationality requires us to accept it as a *fact* that there can be no such thing as a rational foundation for an ethical position, and that we are 'committed to a polytheism of ultimate values', is both wrong on intellectual grounds and disastrous in its effect on the 'lifeworlds' of ordinary women and men. Of course no one can tell just how much influence a wrong philosophy has in contributing to such real world effects as the instrumentalization of human beings and the manipulation of their cultures. Nevertheless, to show that the justifications which are offered for ethical scepticism at a philosophical level will not stand up to examination, that the foundations of the idea that there is no rationality beyond purely instrumental rationality are in trouble, *may* help to combat that instrumentalization and that manipulation. This was also the conviction of John Dewey—whose philosophy I discuss in the fourth section of this paper—throughout his long philosophical life. And it was in that spirit that I decided (and was in fact encouraged) to devote my paper to the 'abstract' issue of moral objectivity.[2]

But not every defence of moral objectivity is a good thing. We live in an 'open society', a society in which the freedom to think for oneself about

[1] See J. Habermas, *The Theory of Communicative Action* trans. T. McCarthy (Boston: Beacon Press, 1984).

[2] I have chosen to speak of 'moral objectivity' rather than to use the currently fashionable term 'moral realism' because 'realism' is entangled in so many metaphysical and language-philosophical disputes at this time. Of course, talk of 'objectivity' is also open to metaphysical construals of various kinds; when I speak of objectivity here and in what follows, what is at stake is 'objectivity humanly speaking', the objectivity of what is objective from the point of view of our best and most reflective practice.

values, goals, and mores is one that most of us have come to cherish. Arguments for 'moral realism' can, and sometimes unfortunately do, sound like arguments against the open society; and while I do wish to undermine moral scepticism, I have no intention of defending either authoritarianism or moral a priorism. It is precisely for this reason that in recent years I have found myself turning to the writings of the American pragmatists.

In my case, turning to American pragmatism does not mean turning to a metaphysical theory. Indeed, the pragmatists were probably wrong in thinking that anyone could provide what they called a 'theory of truth', and Peirce was certainly wrong in thinking that truth can be defined as what inquiry would converge to in the long run. What I find attractive in pragmatism is not a systematic theory in the usual sense at all. It is rather a certain group of theses, theses which can be and indeed were argued very differently by different philosophers with different concerns, and which became the basis of the philosophies of Peirce, and above all of James and Dewey. Cursorily summarized, those theses are (1) antiscepticism: pragmatists hold that doubt requires justification just as much as belief (recall Peirce's famous distinction between 'real' and 'philosophical' doubt); (2) fallibilism: pragmatists hold that there are no metaphysical guarantees to be had that any of our beliefs will never need revision (that one can be both fallibilistic and antisceptical is perhaps *the* unique insight of American pragmatism); (3) the thesis that there is no fundamental dichotomy between 'facts' and 'values'; and (4) the thesis that, in a certain sense, practice is primary in philosophy.

The pragmatists did not only have an interesting set of very general theses, however. Contrary to the way James and Dewey in particular are often painted, they all had intricate arguments: arguments which are still not well known among analytic philosophers, and in the present essay I wish both to describe and also to build upon some of those arguments.

If one sees the four theses I listed as the fundamental theses of pragmatism, then one will not be surprised to learn that the several pragmatist arguments for ethical objectivity were related from the beginning to the effort to preserve and perfect the open society, and to preserve what was right in the epistemological critiques of authoritarianism and a priorism that appeared on the scene together with modernity.

1 'INDISPENSABILITY ARGUMENTS' IN SCIENCE AND IN ETHICS

As I just remarked, pragmatists believe that, in 'a certain sense' practice is primary in philosophy. It is necessary to say a little more about what that means, and doing so will bring us to the first of the arguments I have in mind. In philosophy of science, the most celebrated example of an appeal to practise in the course of a metaphysical argument is due to Quine: I am referring to what I have elsewhere[3] called his 'indispensability argument' for the acceptance of the conceptual scheme of set theory. Quine ignores the problem which goes back, in part, to Plato, as to how we can know that abstract entities exist unless we can interact with them in some way. Instead of arguing that we *can* causally interact with abstract entities, as one or two philosophers have,[4] or contending that we have some sort of supercausal or noncausal interaction with abstract entities (perhaps with the aid of the faculty of 'reason'), Quine deliberately displaces the discussion to a more humanly accessible region. Quine replaces questions about the 'mystery' of interaction with abstract entities with the question 'Why do we need the conceptual scheme of sets?'[5] Quine's argument is that the the conceptual scheme of set theory is *indispensable* to mathematics, and indeed to physical science[6] as well, and what is indispensable our best paradigms of knowledge cannot, Quine argues, be criticized from some supposedly 'higher' philosophical viewpoint; for there is no 'first philosophy' above and outside of science.

To be sure, Quine is in many ways a most atypical pragmatist. Although Morton White has argued early and late[7] that given Quine's own doctrines, in particular Quine's rejection of the 'dualism' of analytic and synthetic, Quine *ought* to reject the fact/value dichotomy, Quine has stubbornly refused to 'go along' with his old friend White. Indeed, Quine seems to have rejected one dichotomy (the dualism of analytic and synthetic) only to replace it with another (the dualism of science, or rather science as formalized in the notation of symbolic logic, and everything that Quine regards as of only 'heuristic' value, including intentional idioms, and value idioms). Although these elements of Quine's philosophy are more reminiscent of Viennese positivism than of American pragmatism, within the sphere of science Quine does give an account which is strongly influenced by pragmatism. I am thinking not only of the 'indispensability argument', but also of Quine's insistence[8] that the scientific method is not an algorithm, but an informal matter of 'trade-offs' between such desiderata as preservation of

---

[3] Cf. my 'Philosophy of Logic', reprinted as the final chapter in the second edition of *Mathematics, Matter and Method* (Cambridge: Cambridge University Press, 1979).

[4] This view has been defended in a series of papers by Penelope Maddy.

[5] Quine identifies all the abstract entities needed in science, including numbers, with sets.

[6] This has been challenged by H. Field in his *Science Without Numbers* (Oxford: Oxford University Press, 1980) and elsewhere. Field's controversial arguments, even if we concede that they are correct as far as they go, do not apply at all to modern quantum mechanics (for reasons unconnected with the 'measurement problem', by the way), and thus do not really show that physics *can* dispense with quantification over numbers and sets, however.

[7] In *Towards Reunion in Philosophy* (Harvard: Harvard University Press, 1956) and in 'Normative Ethics, Normative Epistemology, and Quine's Holism' in L.E. Hahn and P. A. Schilpp (eds.), *The Philosophy of W. V. Quine* (LaSalle, IL: Open Court, 1986) 649–62.

[8] Cf. 'Two Dogmas of Empiricism' in Quine's *From A Logical Point of View* (Harvard: Harvard University Press, 1953).

past doctrine, predictive efficacy, and simplicity. This account is strikingly reminiscent of, for example, William James.[9]

In any case, the classical pragmatists—Peirce, James, and Dewey—whatever their disagreements, did not hesitate to apply to the topic of values exactly the kind of indispensability argument that Quine applies to the topic of scientific ontology. Just as Quine displaces the traditional worry as to the mystery of our 'interaction' (if any) with abstract entities such as sets and numbers, the classical pragmatists displaced the equally ancient worry as to the nature of our 'interaction' (if any) with ethical properties and with value properties and normative properties generally. Like Quine, they found it fruitful to replace metaphysical conundrums with the more humanly accessible question, 'What function does this discourse serve?' According to the pragmatists, normative discourse—talk of right and wrong, good and bad, better and worse—is indispensable in science and in social and personal life as well. Even relativists and subjectivists frequently concede this; we make and cannot escape making value judgements of all kinds in connection with activities of every kind. Nor do we treat these judgements as matters of mere *taste*; we argue about them seriously, we try to *get them right*, and, as philosophers have pointed out for centuries, we use the language of objectivity in our arguments and deliberations: for example, we use the same laws of logic when we reason about an ethical question that we use when we reason about a question in set theory, or in physics, or in history, or in any other area. And, like Quine, the classical pragmatists do not believe that there is a 'first philosophy' higher than the practice that we take most seriously when the chips are down. There is no Archimedean point from which we can argue that what is indispensable in life *gilt nicht in der Philosophie*. Here at least, pragmatism rejects *revisionary* metaphysics.[10]

Of course, there is an obvious difference between set theory and ethics: there is a wide body of accepted doctrine in set theory (even if nominalists and intuitionists reject it), and there is a vast amount of disagreement about values in the modern world. The fact that pragmatists offer indispensability arguments in both areas does not mean that pragmatism fails to take moral

---

[9] In *Pragmatism*, James repeatedly mentions usefulness for prediction and control of experience ('extraordinary fertility in consequences verifiable by sense', p. 91), conservation of past doctrine ('we keep unaltered as much of our old knowledge, as many of our old prejudices and beliefs, as we can.', p. 83; 'A new belief counts as "true" just in proportion as it gratifies the individual's desire to assimilate the novel in his experience to his beliefs in stock.', p. 36), and simplicity ('what fits every part of life best and combines with the collectivity of experience's demands, nothing being omitted', p. 44). That success in satisfying these desiderate simultaneously is a matter of trade-offs rather than formal rules is also a Jamesian idea: 'Success in solving this problem is eminently a matter of approximation. We say that this theory satisfies it on the whole more satisfactorily than that theory; but that means more satisfactorily to our selves, and individuals will emphasize their points of satisfaction differently. To a certain degree, therefore, everything here is plastic.', p. 35. (All quotations are from *Pragmatism and the Meaning of Truth* (Cambridge, Mass.: Harvard University Press, 1978)).

[10] For the distinction between 'revisionary metaphysics' and 'descriptive metaphysics' see Strawson's *Individuals* (London: Methuen, 1959).

disagreement seriously. For pragmatists like John Dewey, moral disagreement of the kind that we find in an open society is not a metaphysical problem but a political problem—a problem and a challenge. The problem is to keep moral disagreement within the bounds of community and productive co-operation, and the challenge is to make moral disagreement serve as a stimulus to the kind of criticism of institutions and values that is needed for progress towards justice and progress in enabling citizens to live in accordance with their various conceptions of the good life. Pragmatism anticipated an idea that has become a commonplace in contemporary moral philosophy,[11] the idea that disagreement in individual conceptions of the good need not make it impossible to approximate (even if we never finally arrive at) agreement on just procedures, and even agreement on such abstract and formal values as respect for one another's autonomy, non-instrumentalization of other persons,[12] and such regulative ideas as the idea that in all our institutions we should strive to replace relations of hierarchy and dependence by relations of 'symmetric reciprocity'.[13] Ruth Anna Putnam and I have written elsewhere[14] about the ways in which the classical pragmatists attempt to justify these ideas, and I shall also speak about this in what follows.

2 AN IMPORTANT OBJECTION

Before we proceed any further, however, it is necessary to face a very important objection to the whole idea of 'the primacy of practice in philosophy'. The objection is most easily presented in the form of a parody, a parody of the 'indispensability argument'. Here is the parody:

If we find the belief that p 'indispensable', for any reason, then that is all the justification we need for saying that p is true—never mind that in our more reflective moments we may realize that p cannot possibly *be* true.

The parody carries the accusation that pragmatism does not care about truth, but only about 'successful practice'. A well-known variant of that accusation is that pragmatism dodges the whole issue by simply identifying truth with successful practice. To see how this accusation can be rebutted it is useful to look again at Quine's indispensability argument.

[11] e.g. J. Rawls, A. Heller, J. Habermas.
[12] Although I describe this as a 'formal value', A. Heller, in *A Philosophy of Morals* (Basil Blackwell, 1990) derives a number of quite substantive 'rules of thumb' from the idea of non-instrumentalization.
[13] This is one of Heller's 'rules of thumb' that I referred to in n. 12.
[14] See my 'A Reconsideration of Deweyan Democracy' in *The Southern California Law Review*, 1991; 'Epistemology as Hypothesis' (with R. A. Putnam) in *Transactions of the C.S. Peirce Society*, Fall 1990, xxvi, 407–33, and 'William James' Ideas' (with Ruth Anna Putnam) reprinted in my *Realism with A Human Face* (Cambridge, Mass.: Harvard University Press, 1990).

The problem that Quine ignored—I said that he 'displaced' it—is that (one hears it said) even if there were such things as sets, we could not possibly know of their existence (in a variant of the argument,[15] one could not so much as refer to them) because (it is said) knowledge (and reference) require causal interaction. Since we do not interact with sets causally, we cannot know anything about them (and we cannot refer to them). While Quine does not explicitly discuss this argument, I think I can guess what he would say. He would say that the premise of the argument is, in fact, the whole argument. And the premise is a 'dogma'. The philosopher who advances such an argument claims that whatever does not fit a certain paradigm is not knowledge (or not reference) at all. But this claim is not supported by anything one might call evidence; it is simply a metaphysical dogma. If we do not let ourselves be trapped by an appeal to what is 'evident to reason', we shall see that we do have evidence of a kind for set theory. Pragmatists do not urge us to ignore sound arguments against what we believe, when such arguments are advanced; they do urge us not to confuse the 'intuitions' of metaphysicians with genuine arguments.

It is pretty easy to see, on reflection, that Quine is right about set theory.[16] Philosophical arguments against set theory do depend on some 'fishy' metaphysical premises. But can we say the same about the well-known materialist arguments[17] against the very possibility of ethical knowledge? As those arguments were set out by John Mackie, in particular, they are strikingly similar to the arguments against set theory alluded to above. According to Mackie, moral properties would be 'ontologically queer'. What he meant by this was that they would not fit in to the picture of the world provided by modern science; and Mackie assumes that the picture of the world provided by modern science is not only approximately correct (which the pragmatists would not challenge) but that it is approximately complete (an assumption that they would challenge). Moreover, even to show that the existence of ethical properties (or of value properties in general) *is* incompatible with the world view of physics, Mackie needs to employ some pretty substantial premises, not all of which are made explicit. Value properties are, according to Mackie (this is supposed to be a concep-

[15] This variant is due to Paul Benacerraf, cf. his 'What Numbers Could Not Be', reprinted in P. Benacerraf and H. Putnam (eds.), *Philosophy of Mathematics, Selected Readings*, 272–94 (Cambridge: Cambridge University, 1964).

[16] I ignore here a difference between Quine's position and my own; my own view is that we should not speak of evidence for the *truth* of set theory, but rather of evidence for the *applicability* of the concepts of set theory in practice. I argue in a forthcoming paper that the *falsity* of set theory or arithmetic (apart from the possibility of its turning out to be inconsistent, omega inconsistent, or something of that kind) is not something that has any clear present *content*. But discussing this difference between my position and Quine's would lead us away from the present topic.

[17] Cf. J. Mackie, *Ethics; Inventing Right and Wrong* (Harmondsworth: Penguin, 1977) and B. Williams, *Ethics and the Limits of Philosophy* (Cambridge, Mass.: Harvard University Press, 1985).

tual truth) such that if something has a positive value property, then anyone who fully recognizes that it does is thereby moved to approve of the thing or action in question. They are, in a very strong sense, action guiding. But it is part of the world view of physics (according to Mackie) that one can know that something has a property without feeling either approval or disapproval. (In effect, Mackie seems to read the world view of economics into modern physics.)

Mackie's argument, like the argument against the truth of set theory, rests on a number of metaphysical 'intuitions' which look more and more suspicious as one begins to probe them. For example, is it really a conceptual truth (that is, a conceptual truth viewed from within moral language) that if I know that an action is good, then I will approve of it? After all, a person may perform a good action, but I may disapprove, because I think the person could have done something much better. It is also no contradiction at all to think that somebody's action is good, and not to approve of a similar action in another case (in particular, not to be moved to perform a similar action myself). This is so both because different cases require different actions, and because, as Agnes Heller observes,[18] there are different ways of being good, and another person's way may simply not be my way. (And there is also the rare but unfortunately not non-existent case of the person who does evil *because* it is evil; such a person knows that he is an enemy of the good, but he does not approve of the good.) But these are not the grounds on which I wish to criticize Mackie's argument.

Let us reformulate Mackie's incautious claim by saying that positive moral properties, if any such really exist, are conceptually required to be such that when one knows that something possesses one of them, then *ceteris paribus* that very knowledge will produce in one feelings of approval, and negative moral properties are conceptually required to be such that when one knows that something possesses them, then *ceteris paribus* that very knowledge will produce in one feelings of disapproval. Mackie's argument (whether or not we modify the premise by inserting *ceteris paribus* clauses as I just have) is that these conceptual requirements show that moral properties (if there be such) are 'ontologically queer'. But do they really?

It is easy to see that some properties whose existence we do not find at all incompatible with the world view of physics are, in fact, 'action guiding' in the way Mackie claims moral properties (and value properties generally) are conceptually required to be action guiding. I am thinking in particular of pain. The knowledge that something is extremely painful may not keep me from wanting it, or wanting to do it, under special circumstances, but it is certainly true that 'other things being equal' the very knowledge that something is painful will lead me to disapprove of it, to recommend against

---

[18] Heller, *A Philosophy of Morals*, 28 ff.

it, etc. In some sense, this seems to be 'conceptually linked' to pain, even if there are no 'analytic truths' in the old metaphysical sense in this area. And we don't find this at all 'queer'. On the positive side—and this example brings us closer to moral properties—consider the property of being intelligent. People who are themselves intelligent value their intelligence, other things being equal. If an intelligent person were offered a million dollars provided he or she agreed to undergo a brain operation which reduces IQ by 60 points, then he or she would have to be seriously disturbed or depressed to even consider saying 'yes'. Again, we don't find this fact particularly remarkable.

Of course, an unintelligent person might not care about losing or gaining in intelligence; but an unintelligent person does not have a good idea of what intelligence *is*. What makes this example relevant to the moral domain is that an ancient tradition in ethics, the Greek tradition, did in fact think that virtue was in these respects like intelligence; it held, on the one hand, that only the virtuous have an adequate idea of what virtue is, and that those who have an adequate idea of what virtue is do not *ceteris paribus* wish to lose their virtue. Perhaps most people do not believe any longer that the Greek tradition was right; but it is not clear that this disbelief is based on some piece of 'scientific knowledge' that we have gained in the meantime.[19]

Mackie would have replied that even if it is true, as a matter of empirical fact, that those who are highly intelligent do not (unless they are disturbed or depressed) wish to lose their intelligence, still there is no logical contradiction in the idea of a highly intelligent (and not mentally disturbed or depressed) person who has an adequate idea of what intelligence is and simply values something more than keeping his intelligence. On the other hand, there is, according to Mackie, a logical contradiction in saying that one recognizes that something is good, but one does not approve of it and one would not under any circumstances recommend acting in that way (if the thing in question is an action). The problem with this argument is that it assumes the metaphysical notion of analytic truth. Mackie himself may have been a firm believer in a sharp distinction between conceptual truth and empirical truth (and may have further believed that these are the only sorts of truths there are); but pragmatism was in large part an attack on the analytic/synthetic dichotomy. Once again we see that what was supposed to be a rational argument against the objectivity or cognitivity of ethics turns out to depend on a lot of suspect metaphysical baggage.

Perhaps a better line for a defender of Mackie's position to take today would be to argue that the value of intelligence (to animals possessing it)

---

[19] The claim that the person who does not engage in the *practice* of virtue cannot have a fully adequate idea of what virtue is may seem queer to many contemporary sensibilities, but the similar sounding claim that the person who does not engage in musical practice cannot have a fully adequate idea of what great music is does not sound so queer. In fact, something like this view has been defended in a well-known series of papers by J. McDowell.

was originally a purely instrumental value. It may indeed be, that as a result of evolution, intelligence has acquired a quasi-instinctual value for members of our species, or for members who possess it to a high degree, but there is no corresponding story to be told about virtue, and that is why the claim that there are action-guiding virtue properties is, or should be, suspect from a naturalistic point of view. But this argument is extremely 'blurry'. The story about the process by which intelligence was transformed from an instrumental value to a terminal value[20] is itself speculative, and, moreover, there is no reason to think that a parallel story could not be told in the case of at least some of the basic virtues; indeed, some writers have suggested that one can. More important, the supposed fact that intelligence was originally an instrumental value, and that it became a terminal value as a result of evolution, says nothing about whether that process was a rationally laudable process or one that we should rationally criticize and, if possible, try to reverse. Of course, it could be a premise of the argument that I just suggested that the transformation of values from instrumental values into terminal values is merely a 'psychological' process, that is, a process which cannot be rationally criticized; if so, then the premise is as strong as the desired conclusion. If we assume a sharp fact/value dichotomy as one of our premises, it is not surprising that we can pull out a sharp fact/value dichotomy as our conclusion.

In summary, I have just replied to the charge that pragmatism was anti-intellectual by trying to show that pragmatists do not seek to suppress or play down genuine intellectual difficulties with any of our beliefs, or with the justifications of any of our actions. What pragmatism does argue is that criticisms of our beliefs and actions which are associated with various kinds of intellectualistic metaphysics,[21] and with equally intellectualistic scepticism, will not stand up to close scrutiny. This is not something the classical pragmatists asked us to take on faith; on the contrary, every one of them was concerned to carry out a detailed criticism of the better-known metaphysicians of his own time. Pragmatism goes with the criticism of a certain style in metaphysics; but the criticism does not consist in wielding some exclusionary principle to 'get rid of metaphysics once and for all'. Indeed, as Strawson[22] has reminded us (and as Dewey remarked many years earlier)[23] revisionary metaphysics is not always bad, and we owe many insights, in science and in morals and in politics, to various kinds of revisionary metaphysics. But if revisionary metaphysics is not always bad,

---

[20] The terminology of 'instrumental' and 'terminal' values, and the idea that the line between these two constantly shifts in the course of inquiry, are both J. Dewey's, of course.

[21] The pejorative notion of intellectualistic metaphysics is one I take from W. James, who employed it early and late.

[22] Strawson, *Individuals*.

[23] e.g., in *Reconstruction in Philosophy* (reprinted by Beacon Press, 1948) and in *Ethics* (with James Hayden Tufts), reprinted as vol. 5 of *John Dewey, the Middle Works 1899–1924*, J. A. Boydston, ed. (Carbondale: Southern Illinois University Press, 1978).

neither is it always good. It does spawn more than one intellectual bugaboo; and the criticism of these intellectual bugaboos is a permanent task of the pragmatist philosopher.

So far, then, I have rehearsed a *negative* argument for the objectivity of values. The negative argument is that the belief in the cognitive status of value judgements underlies an enormous amount of our practice—indirectly, perhaps, the whole of our practice. Metaphysical arguments that say that even though we adopt a 'realist' stance towards value disputes in practice, realism with respect to values cannot *possibly* be right, are themselves unsupported by anything more than a collection of metaphysical dogmas. It is time now to consider more positive arguments.

3 INSTRUMENTAL RATIONALITY AND TOPIC-NEUTRAL NORMS

I now want to present and discuss an argument to the effect that instrumental rationality would be impossible if there were not topic-neutral norms whose claim to rational acceptability is not derived *simply* from the fact that they help us to achieve particular goals a certain percentage of the time. This argument is an important part of the case for the view that objective values of a kind (though, so far, not *ethical* values) are presupposed by science itself.

First a word on my choice of terminology. I have chosen to speak of 'topic neutral norms' rather than to employ some traditional language, for example, the language of 'intrinsic values', for a number of reasons. For one thing, talk of 'intrinsic values' is associated in the history of philosophy with many doctrines that pragmatists have always viewed with suspicion. For example, the pragmatists have typically been hostile to the natural law tradition, and especially to the form of that tradition according to which there are norms somehow built into the very structure of reality, norms which 'the wise' (as opposed to 'the many') have always been able to discern. That tradition is riddled with appeals to 'what is agreeable to reason', and pragmatists have always distrusted such appeals unless they are tempered by a healthy dose of fallibilism and experimentalism. Dewey, in particular, loved to point out how the discourse of 'natural law', 'what is agreeable to reason', and so forth, has provided rationalizations for the interests of privileged groups. Again, talk of 'intrinsic values' has sometimes gone with ethical intuitionism, in the style of G. E. Moore, and that is also a tradition that pragmatists distrust. Since I am trying to argue in the spirit of American pragmatism, even if the arguments I am giving are *only* 'in the spirit' of American pragmatism (they are not arguments found in the pages of American pragmatists in the form in which I give them, in spite of their obvious debt to the arguments of Peirce, Dewey, and James), I do not wish to use a terminology which presupposes just the sort of metaphysics that pragmatism was instrumental in overthrowing. There are topic neutral truths, to be sure (the truths of deductive logic are a well-known example), but even topic neutral truths emerge from experience, or better from *practice* (including reflection on that practice) and belong to conceptual schemes which have to show their ability to function in practice (which does not mean that they are 'empirical').[24] In the same way, I shall argue, there are topic neutral norms; but they too emerge from practice and have to show their ability to function in practice, as do all norms and values. The topic neutral norm I wish to discuss applies to behaviour that is directed towards a concrete goal, and that applies in circumstances in which it makes sense to think of the alternative actions as having known or fairly well-estimated probabilities of reaching the goal. The norm is, moreover, one whose justification at first blush seems to be entirely instrumental. It is simply this: *Act so as to maximize the estimated utility.* This norm is, of course, a famous rule of decision theory; and while there is controversy as to whether it applies in every situation (of goal oriented behaviour with known probabilities), there is no question but that it applies to the great majority of such cases. In particular, it applies to cases of the kind that Peirce discussed in 'The Doctrine of Chances'.[25] These are cases in which I must, on one single occasion, perform one of two actions, and one of the actions has a high probability of giving me an enormous benefit and the other has a high probability of giving me an enormous loss. In these situations, the rule of course directs me to perform the action which is associated with a high probability of an enormous benefit. But why is the justification of this rule not entirely instrumental ('if you follow the rule, you will get an enormous benefit a high percentage of the time')? Note that I say that the justification of the rule is not *entirely* instrumental. Obviously, *part* of its justification is instrumental. Whenever I (or a group to which I owe loyalty) have to engage in a series of repeated wagers (with known probabilities) we can say (or it *looks* as if we can say—Peirce raises an important problem here too) that obeying this norm will yield a better 'payoff' in the long run, and in many cases payoff in the long run is exactly what we are interested in. But, as Peirce pointed out, there is a very special problem about the single case. If what I am interested in is *not* success in some long run, but success in one, unrepeatable, single case,[26] I cannot justify performing the action with the higher estimated utility by saying that

---

[24] For the reasons why it is a mistake to identify a scheme's showing its ability to function in practice with its being 'empirical' see 'It Ain't Necessarily So', in my *Mathematics, Matter and Method, Philosophical Papers*, vol. 1, and 'Language and Philosophy' in my *Mind Language and Reality, Philosophical Papers*, vol. 2. (both, Cambridge: Cambridge University Press, 1975).

[25] Reprinted in C. Hartshorne and P. Weiss (eds.), *Collected Papers of Charles Sanders Peirce*, vol. II, 389–414 (Harvard: Harvard University Press, 1931).

[26] I review Peirce's argument briefly in *The Many Faces of Realism* (La Salle, Ill. Open Court, 1987), 80–6.

I know that that action will succeed, because I do *not* know which action will succeed (if I knew which action would succeed, I wouldn't need to talk of probabilities). And if I justify it by saying that I know which action will probably succeed, then I am simply saying that I am justified in performing the action which has the higher estimated utility because it has the higher estimated utility; for 'will probably succeed' is just an imprecise way of saying 'has the higher estimated utility'. (Indeed, Peirce develops his argument directly in terms of the rule that, in cases where the benefits are as described, one should perform the action with the higher probability of gain, rather than in terms of the notion of estimated utility. Peirce's point is that, for a self-interested player who has no long run to look forward to, the justification of this rule cannot be 'if you follow it in the long run, you will succeed in a large percentage of the cases'.)

Nor is the problem restricted to the unrepeatable[27] single case. Peirce points out[28] that when we say that the practise of betting on the action with the higher estimated utility will succeed in a high percentage of the cases in the long run, we had better not mean any given *finite* long run. For if we do, then what we are doing is, again, betting on an unrepeatable single case. If, for example, the entire future experience of the human race is contained within a time period of, say, a million years, then the statement that 'the percentage of the time that the recommended strategy (of betting on actions with a high estimated utility, or of performing actions whose probability of success is high) will succeed will not, in this one single run of cases, be improbably far below its expected value' is itself a statement about a single case. And what was just said about the justification of betting that the action with the higher estimated utility will probably succeed in a single case applies here too. Knowing the probability with which a policy will succeed in one particular unrepeatable finite 'long run', is not the same as knowing the percentage of the time (that is, the frequency) with which the policy will succeed in that one finite period of time; it is only knowing the expected value of that percentage. Betting that the actual value of that percentage will be close to the expected value is precisely to rely on the norm whose justification we are considering.

In *The Many Faces of Realism*, I said[29] that I found Peirce's own solution to the problem he raised to be unbelievable. Peirce believed that there was no problem about the infinitely long run, because he accepted the frequency theory of probability, according to which the probability just *is* the limit of the relative frequency in the infinite long run; he dealt with the problem of the single case (which is also the problem of any given finite 'long run') by arguing that the purpose of a rational person, in any action,

---

[27] Peirce ensures unrepeatability by imagining a case in which the alternatives are 'eternal felicity' and 'everlasting woe'; in *The Many Faces of Realism*, I modify Peirce's argument by imagining a case in which the choice is between an easy death and a hard death.
[28] Peirce, 'The Doctrine of Chances', 396 ff.   [29] p. 84.

should not be to benefit himself, but to act in accordance with the policy that would benefit all rational beings in the infinitely long run. A person who is not interested in the welfare of all rational beings in the infinitely long run is, according to Peirce, 'illogical in all his inferences'.[30] Even if I am facing a situation in which the alternatives are 'eternal felicity' and 'everlasting woe', on Peirce's view my belief that I, in this one unrepeatable situation, am somehow more rational if I perform the action that will probably lead to felicity than if I perform the action that will probably lead to everlasting woe, is fundamentally just a fictitious transfer[31] of a property which has only to do with what happens in the infinitely long run to a single case. What is true, and not fiction or projection, however, is that my fellows, the members of the ongoing community of inquirers with which I identify myself, will have eternal felicity 24 times out of 25 (or whatever),[32] if they follow the recommended strategy; or more generally, that even if this one particular situation is never repeated, if in all the various uncorrelated cases of this kind or of any other kind that they find themselves in, they always perform the action with the higher estimated utility, then in the infinitely long run they will experience more gains and fewer losses. But, as I asked in *The Many Faces of Realism*, is it really true that the reason that I would make the choice that is likely to give me eternal felicity and not everlasting woe is that I am *altruistic*?

Peirce's argument is that I ought to choose the arrangement that will probably give me eternal felicity for what one might describe as 'rule utilitarian' reasons: in choosing this arrangement I am supporting and helping to maintain a norm which will benefit the community of rational investigators in the infinitely long run. But is this really what is in my mind when what I am facing is torture? Obviously, it isn't. What Peirce himself attempts is to give a completely instrumental justification for the norm. In order to push through his instrumental justification, he needs not only an incorrect theory of probability (very few students of the subject would today subscribe to the claim that probability can be defined as the limit of a relative frequency in the infinitely long run); but he also needs two further dubious assumptions: (1) the assumption that the motive for all of my actions, insofar as they are rational, is entirely altruistic; and (2) the assumption that there will be rational investigators in the indefinitely far future, that is, that the community of rational investigators is literally immortal. But even if Peirce failed to provide a satisfactory solution to his

---

[30] 'The community . . . must reach, however vaguely, beyond this geological epoch, beyond all bounds. He who would not sacrifice his own soul to save the whole world, is, as it seems to me, illogical in all his inferences, collectively. Logic is rooted in the social principle.' Peirce, 'The Doctrine of Chances'.

[31] The term 'fictitious transfer' comes from Reichenbach's discussion of single case probabilities. Cf. *The Theory of Probability* (Berkeley, Calif.: University of California Press, 1940), 372 ff.

[32] 24/25ths is the probability involved in Peirce's example.

own problem, it remains the case that he was the philosopher who called our attention to its importance and its *depth*.

It is just because the problem Peirce rajsed is so deep that I want to examine it again, and to go further than I did when I discussed it in the closing pages of *The Many Faces of Realism*. In those pages, I discussed only the part of Peirce's argument that refers to extreme choices in unrepeatable situations. I did not discuss Peirce's claim that the problem of relying on knowledge of probabilities to guide our actions in the finite long run poses the same problem; and, indeed, I think that there are objections to this claim of Peirce's. One possible objection is this: while we can easily imagine that in any ordinary 'single case' an improbable event happens, imagining that improbable events happen 'across the board' for a very long time (a million years) may, in fact, go beyond what is conceivable. Can we really make sense of the notion that almost all events might be improbable 'flukes' for the next million years?[33] I won't try to decide this question here, but even if we assume, for the sake of Peirce's argument, that the answer is 'yes', there is still a further objection. For one might plausibly claim that the fact is that we firmly believe that this will not happen; that is, we don't just think it is improbable that the whole statistical pattern of events in the next million years (or even in the next ten years) will be a 'fluke', perhaps we find it inconceivable that in a run that long, the frequency will not be near its expected value. (When the time period is large enough, it may be that the very notion of 'probability' crumbles if we assume that all or most of the statistics we encounter are 'flukes'.) But, if that is so, relying on the norm of expecting what is probable to happen, and on the norm of performing the action with the higher estimated utility, does have an instrumental justification when our interests really are very long run success, and not in success in some small number of unrepeatable cases, or even in one moderately long series of cases. On the other hand—and this speaks in Peirce's favour—even if this is true, the problem of the single case is still worse than it looks at first. The problem does not arise only in cases which are literally unrepeatable.

To see this, consider any case whatsoever—and such cases are familiar enough—in which I am tempted to perform an action whose success is 'against the odds'. Let us say that I have a strong hunch that I am going to be lucky, so strong that I am tempted to stake my life savings or my family's savings on this hunch. I may perfectly well agree that if everyone followed the policy of relying on such hunches, then in the long run this would cause an enormous amount of suffering; but I am not recommending that other people follow that policy in the future. I do not even intend to follow that policy myself in the future, I only intend to follow it in this single case, let us assume.

[33] The discussion of the limits of conceivability in Wittgenstein's *On Certainty*, G. E. M. Anscombe and G. H. von Wright, eds. (Oxford: Basil Blackwell, 1969) is on my mind here.

It may be true that if I follow this policy in this single case, then I am bound to follow the same policy in the future, and that even if my hunch is correct this time, sooner or later 'the odds will catch up with me'. But it could be that I know myself well enough to say truthfully, 'I am going to gamble just this once; win or lose, I am not going to risk going against the odds again.' If that is my fixed intention, then even if I know that I would lose money if I made this gamble many times in the future, or that other people would lose money if they made such gambles many times in the future, that knowledge is *relevant* to the question, 'Will this risky gamble achieve my goal?'—only on the assumption that probability is relevant to single actions, that is to say, only if the topic neutral norm is in place.

Some theorists would, no doubt, try to get around the whole problem in the following way: they would argue that deciding what to do can be broken into two steps, namely the fixation of belief and the choice of an action. With respect to the first, the fixation of belief, it might be said that the operative norm is simply a norm of rationality: a rational man, it is said, proportions his subjective degrees of belief (his 'subjective probabilities') to the relevant objective statistical probabilities when those are known or assumed, which is the case that Peirce is discussing. (Note that Peirce is not discussing 'the problem of induction', that is to say, the problem of whether we *can* know the objective statistical probabilities when those relate to future events.) In the Peirce thought experiment, the agent knows that the objective probability that he will achieve 'eternal felicity' and avoid 'everlasting woe' if he follows the recommended policy is 24/25ths. If he is rational, he will therefore proportion his subjective degree of belief in the proposition 'I shall obtain eternal felicity if I follow the recommended policy' to this objective probability; that is, he will almost believe that if he performs the recommended action (choosing a certain deck of cards) he will gain eternal felicity. He does not absolutely believe that he will obtain eternal felicity if he performs the action, but he believes it to the very high degree of 24/25ths. Given that he believes (almost) that if he performs the action he will be successful, he would be irrational *not* to perform the action. In this way, performing the action is instrumentally justified.

In fact, however, this justification is not a completely instrumental justification because it assumes a norm of rationality which is itself not instrumentally justified: the norm that one should 'proportion one's subjective degrees of belief to the objective statistical probabilities when they are known'. That norm, like the norm that one should perform the action with the higher estimated utility, has a partial instrumental justification; in situations in which what we are interested in really is long run success, then one can argue that conforming to the norm will achieve the goal. (However, to do so, as we observed above, we must assume that in that particular 'long run', frequencies will be close to their expected values, which—Peirce would say—presupposes the very norm we are 'justifying'.)

But in any case, to say that it is 'rational' to conform to the norm even when what we are interested in is not very long run success, is just another way of saying that one *ought* to conform to that norm in those situations, and this, for reasons we have just rehearsed, is a belief which cannot be instrumentally justified.

At this point, if I am not mistaken, two objections to what I have been maintaining will occur to various of my readers, though probably not to the same readers. The first objection, which I shall call 'the naturalism objection' runs as follows: 'The norms you describe, like all norms, have evolved because they have a high degree of long run utility, to communities if not always to individuals. [When I use the word "evolved" in stating the objection, philosophers who are prone to sociobiological speculation may even think that Darwinian evolution is involved here, but in any case, social evolution is certainly involved.] But if we can understand perfectly well what the origin of these norms is, and what the origin is of the compulsion that each of us feels to conform to them, even when we don't know that that conformity will in fact bring us success in any particular individual case, then what's the problem?'

The objection is serious because it rests on an assumption which is undeniably correct; to say, as I have, that the norms cannot be completely justified instrumentally is not to deny that they do have long run instrumental value to communities. And the pragmatists certainly believed that the metaphor of 'evolution' is an appropriate one, in cases like these. The pragmatists also believed—and here I am thinking more of James and Dewey than of Peirce, perhaps—that one must take the agent point of view seriously, and not look at everything from the third person descriptive point of view. It is quite true that from a third person descriptive point of view there is no difficulty in understanding the origin of topic neutral norms like the ones I have been describing; that is, there is no difficulty in understanding the existence of such norms as a mere psychological fact. But if I as an agent put to myself the question 'What should I do?' in a situation of the kind we have been discussing, then the knowledge that I feel some compulsion to act one way, as a psychological fact about myself, does not answer my question. Indeed, if I also have a strong compulsion to 'be irrational for once', to act on a hunch, I may also be able to find some naturalistic explanation of the existence of *that* compulsion. Each compulsion is a brute fact; that I have both compulsions doesn't tell me what to do. The factual descriptive questions are certainly legitimate questions. But so are the normative first person questions.

Here is the second of the objections that I mentioned: 'Your question is really just why it is rational to do certain things, to act in accordance with probabilities (or, more precisely, estimated utilities), or to proportion one's subjective degrees of belief to probabilities. But it is just a tautology that these are rational things to do. To be rational is just to obey certain rules, for example, the rules of deductive logic and the rules of rational betting. So what's your problem?'

One problem (a decisive one) with this objection is that saying that something is rational is not merely to describe it as in accordance with some algorithm or quasi-algorithm or other.[34] If I say that believing something or acting in a certain way is rational, then, other things being equal, I am recommending that belief or that course of action. To say that something is rational, say that it is rational to bet in accordance with the probabilities (more precisely, the estimated utilities) is to say that, other things being equal, one ought to bet in accordance with the probabilities (the estimated utilities). In short, the fact that something is rational is precisely the sort of fact that Mackie regarded as 'ontologically queer'; it is an ought-implying fact.

Instead of creating spurious philosophical problems for ourselves by insisting that the causal-descriptive world view *must* be 'complete', in a sense which is never satisfactorily defined,[35] the pragmatists urged that the agent point of view, the first person normative point of view, and the concepts indispensable to that point of view, should be taken just as seriously as the concepts indispensable to the third person descriptive point of view.

In closing this part of my argument, it may be useful to compare once more the conclusion I have reached with the conclusion Peirce reached. What our arguments have in common—and, of course, mine is built out of the very materials Peirce provided—is that we both agree that the norm of acting in accordance with the probabilities or estimated utilities cannot be justified instrumentally if the only goals considered are the goals of the agent himself. Peirce concludes that all rational goal directed activity must be altruistic and personally disinterested, a conclusion that fits well with his own moral outlook, which tended to stress the 'Buddhistic'[36] virtues of self-

---

[34] Although for Carnap it was! Carnap at one time held the view that to say that a hypothesis is *confirmed* to a certain degree r is *just* the same as saying that a certain algorithm yields the number 'r' when applied to the evidence. On this view, anyone who knows that a certain mathematical function has the value r on a certain argument *ipso facto* knows something about rational belief; but this is clearly wrong.

[35] I am reminded here of Wittgenstein's distrust of philosophical 'musts'. When I say that the metaphysical notion of a 'complete' description has never been satisfactorily defined, I am thinking, among other things, of Quine's claim that the description given by physics is complete because no change of any kind can take place without a *physical* change taking place. However, it is also true that no change of any kind can take place without a change in *the gravitational field* taking place; but not even Quine would maintain that I have 'completely' described the world if I have only described the gravitational field! The combination of a 'must' with a concept that only *looks* as if it has been defined is characteristic of the philosophical phenomenon Wittgenstein wanted us to attend to.

[36] In a letter to James dated 13 March 1897, Peirce wrote 'Undoubtedly, its [philosophy's] tendency is to make one value the spiritual more, but not an abstract spirituality. It makes one dizzy and seasick to think of those worthy people who try to do something for "the poor", or still more blindly, "the deserving poor". On the other hand, it increases the sense of awe with which one regards Gautama Booda.' This letter will be published as part of the preface to the

abnegation and freedom from personal interest. As I have said, I cannot 'go
along' with this conclusion; we are, after all, talking about goal oriented
activity, and in this case our aims are usually not disinterested. The conclusion I draw from Peirce's problem is, rather, that even when I seek to
attain a goal (in a situation in which risk is involved either way), the rational
decision as to what I must do to attain my practical goal depends upon my
acknowledging the binding force of norms which do not possess a satisfactory instrumental justification in terms of my own goals. This conclusion is
not incompatible with Peirce's; but it is not as metaphysically daring.

Finally, to the inevitable question, 'how would I justify norms like the
one we have been considering, if a complete instrumental justification
cannot be given?', I would reply that the alternative to instrumental justification here is not transcendent knowledge but *reflection*. Norms like the
estimated utility rule were not discovered by mere trial and error, but by
normative reflection on our practice. Kant was right in urging us to realize
that reflection on the possibility of gaining knowledge from experience is
itself a source of knowledge, even if he was wrong in considering it to be an
infallible source (when properly conducted). Kant was further right in
supposing that we must reflect not only on the presuppositions of learning
from experience, but also on the presuppositions of acting in the ways in
which we do act. Most puzzles about the very 'possibility' of normative
knowledge spring from a too narrowly empiricistic picture of how knowledge is gained and how actions are justified.

4 'OUGHTS' AND BELIEF FIXATION IN PURE SCIENCE

I have described the facts that certain actions and beliefs are rational as
'ought-implying facts': by including *beliefs* here I mean to indicate that this
allegedly 'ontologically queer' phenomenon is one that does not appear
only in the context of goal oriented activity, and the context of moral
activity, but also in the context of 'pure' scientific activity. In *Reason, Truth
and History*,[37] I described some of the terms we use in appraising scientific
theories, e.g., the terms 'simple', elegant', and 'well confirmed', as having
just this character; for to describe a theory as simple, elegant, or well
confirmed is to say that, other things being equal, we *ought* to accept the
theory or at least consider it seriously. Although these ought-implying
characteristics are not ethical characteristics, they share many of the properties of the so-called[38] 'thick' ethical characteristics. Just as no non-ethical

text of C.S. Peirce, *Reasoning and the Logic of Things, the 1898 Cambridge Conference
Lectures*, K. L. Ketner and H. Putnam, eds. (Cambridge, Mass.: Harvard University Press,
1992).

[37] *Reason, Truth and History* (New York: Cambridge University Press, 1981) 136.
[38] On the notion of a 'thick' ethical characteristic cf. B. Williams, *Ethics and the Limits* and

term seems to have exactly the same descriptive range as the term 'cruel', so no non-normative term applied to theories seems to have exactly the same descriptive range as the term 'confirmed'.

It might be claimed, however, that even though there are 'oughts' connected with rational belief and rational action, that (at least in the case of rational belief) these 'oughts' are of quite a different kind from the 'oughts' that we encounter in connection with justice and in connection with morality. As far as I know, only one reason is ever given for suggesting that the ontological status of pure cognitive values is completely different from the ontological status of normative values, and that is, once again, that it is thought that at least the sorts of cognitive values I just mentioned—elegance, simplicity, predictive power, the conservation of past doctrine, and so on—are justified purely instrumentally (relative to truth as the goal of inquiry), and that the 'oughts' connected with them are thus purely hypothetical 'oughts'. To say that one ought to consider seriously theories which have striking predictive power or simplicity is, on this view, just to say that if you follow the policy of taking theories with these virtues seriously, in the long run you will arrive at a higher percentage of true or approximately true theories. Roderick Firth devoted his Presidential Address to the Eastern Division of the American Philosophical Association[39] to pointing out a major difficulty with this argument. One way of putting Firth's difficulty is the following: if the fact that the practice of accepting theories with these virtues has led to the discovery of truths is supposed to be an empirical justification of that practice, then it is flagrantly circular. It is circular, because the way we recognize that we have discovered truths in the past by using that practice is by relying on that very practice. It is not, after all, as if we had some way of telling that we had discovered a true (or approximately true) theory in the past independent of relying on the fact that acceptance of the theory is justified (in terms of successful prediction, simplicity, conservation of past doctrine, etc.), that is, relying on the rule that one should posit that theories which are sufficiently superior in these respects deserve to be provisionally accepted as true or approximately true. Of course, Firth did not wish to deny that theories which are 'justified' (as determined by the norms mentioned and other norms like them) *are* more likely to be true or approximately true; the point is, rather, that we could not possibly first discover that this is the case, and only the come to adopt the policy of accepting the justified theories. We cannot test the claim that acceptance of justified theories leads to acceptance of true (or approximately true) theories empirically; the most we can check empirically is the

my discussion in 'Objectivity and the Science/Ethics Distinction', in M. Nussbaum and A. Sen (eds.), *The Quality of Life* (Oxford: Oxford University Press, 1992). This essay is also reprinted in my *Realism with a Human Face*.

[39] 'Epistemic Merit, Intrinsic and Instrumental', in *Proc. and Addresses of the American Philosophical Society*, Sept. 1981, 55, 5–23.

frequency with which justified theories tend to remain justified later. The 'hold' of justification on our thought, the 'oughtness' of positing that justified beliefs are (probably, approximately) true, cannot be assimilated to the discovery of a useful empirical correlation, such as the correlation between building a fire and getting warm.

We can also see that it is not the case that we believe we ought to accept justified theories in each single individual case *only* because we have some kind of a non-empirical belief that doing so leads to the acceptance of a higher percentage of truths 'in the long run'; for if that were the complete justification for our reliance on these cognitive norms, then we would run into exactly the 'problem of the single case' that we ran into in connection with choosing an action. For both of these reasons, then, the strategy of saying, 'Oh yes, there are "oughts" connected with the fixation of belief, but those are purely hypothetical imperatives' is a failure. There are 'ought-implying facts' in the realm of belief fixation; and that is an excellent reason not to accept the view that there cannot be 'ought-implying facts' anywhere. If their sole reason for believing that 'there cannot be "ought-implying facts" in ethics' is that 'such facts cannot exist anywhere', then the opponents of moral objectivity (or 'moral realism') had better rethink.

4.1. *But What Does Any of This Have to do With Ethics?*

Perhaps the most detailed case for the view just defended, the view that all inquiry, including inquiry in pure science, itself presupposes values, is made by Dewey, in his *Logic*. Ruth Anna Putnam and I have analyzed Dewey's argument[40] elsewhere; here, I only want to discuss one aspect of Dewey's view, the insistence on a very substantial overlap between our cognitive values and our ethical and moral values.

We have already examined the claim that there is a fundamental onto-logical difference between cognitive or 'scientific' values and ethical values, and found that the reasons offered for believing that claim fail. But even apart from the 'ontological' question, a view like Dewey's will not be intelligible if one starts with what I may call a 'Carnapian' view of the scientific method. For this reason, I need to say a few words about the differences between the way in which a philosopher like John Dewey sees the scientific method and the way in which a philosopher like Rudolf Carnap did. First of all, it is noteworthy that in Carnap's great work on inductive logic[41]—the work to which he devoted almost all of his energy in the last two decades of his life—there is virtually no reference to *experiment*:—the word does not even occur as an entry in the index to *The Logical*

---

[40] In 'Epistemology as Hypothesis', *supra* n. 14.
[41] R. Carnap, *The Logical Foundations of Probability* (Chicago: University of Chicago Press, 1950), and *The Continuum of Inductive Methods* (Chicago: University of Chicago Press, 1952).

Foundations of Probability. Scientific theories are confirmed by 'evidence' in Carnap's systems of inductive logic, but it is immaterial (that is to say, there is no way to represent the difference in the formalism) whether that evidence—those 'observation sentences'—is obtained as the result of intelligently directed experimentation, or it just happens to be available. Passive observation and active intervention are not distinguished, and the question as to whether one has actually tried to falsify the hypotheses that have been 'highly confirmed' is not a question which can be asked or answered *in* the languages Carnap constructed. Even more important, for our purposes, is that fact that the term that Carnap used to characterize his own stance in the *Aufbau*, the term 'methodological solipsism', could also be applied, though in a different sense, to this later philosophical work. For just as it makes no difference from the point of view of Carnapian inductive logic whether our observation is passive or active, whether we just look or whether we intervene, it also makes no difference whether observation is *co-operative* or not. Fundamentally, the standpoint is that of a single isolated spectator who makes observations through a 'one-way mirror' and writes down observation sentences. Appraising theories for their cognitive virtues is then simply a matter of using an algorithm to determine whether a sentence has a mathematical relation to another sentence (the conjunction of the observation sentences the observer has written down), on this picture. The scientific method is reconstructed as a method of *computation*, computation of a function like Carnap's famous 'c*'.[42]

Dewey's picture is totally different. For Dewey, inquiry is co-operative human interaction with an environment; and all aspects, the active intervention, the active manipulation of the environment, and the co-operation with other human beings, are vital. The first aspect, the aspect of intervention, is connected with pragmatist fallibilism. Of course, Carnap was also a fallibilist, in the sense of recognizing that future observation might disconfirm a theory which is today very well confirmed; but for the pragmatists this was not fallibilism enough. Before Karl Popper was even born, Peirce emphasized that[43] very often ideas will not be falsified unless we go out and actively *seek* falsifying experiences. Ideas must be put under strain, if they are to prove their worth; and Dewey and James both followed Peirce in this respect. In what follows, however, I want to focus on the other aspect of Dewey's thought, that is, the conception of scientific inquiry as a form of co-operation.

For the positivists—e.g., for both Carnap and Reichenbach—the most primitive form of scientific inquiry, and the form that they studied first when they constructed their (otherwise very different) theories of induction was induction by simple enumeration. The model is always a single scientist

[42] Cf. *The Logical Foundations of Probability*, 294 ff.
[43] Cf. 'Pragmatism and Pragmaticism' in *Collected Papers of Charles Sanders Peirce* (vol. V, ch. 6, pp. 399–430 esp. p. 419).

who determines the colours of the balls drawn successively from an urn, and tries to estimate the frequencies with which those colours occur among the balls remaining in the urn. For Dewey, the model is a *group* of inquirers trying to produce good ideas and trying to test them to see which ones have value.

One more point must be mentioned at the very outset of any discussion, however brief, of Dewey's conception of inquiry: the model of an *algorithm*, like a computer program, is rejected. According to the pragmatists, whether the subject be science or ethics, what we have are maxims and not algorithms; and maxims themselves require contextual interpretation. Not only that, the problem of subjectivity and intersubjectivity was in the minds of the pragmatists from the beginning. They insisted[44] that when one human being in isolation tries to interpret even the best maxims for himself or herself and does not allow others to criticize the way in which he or she interprets those maxims, or the way in which he or she applies them, then the kind of 'certainty' that results is always fatally tainted with subjectivity. Even the notion of 'truth' makes no sense in such a 'moral solitude' for 'truth presupposes a standard external to the thinker'.[45] Notions like 'simplicity', for example, have no clear meaning at all unless inquirers who have proven their competence in the practice of inquiry are able to agree, to some extent at least, on which theories do and which theories do not possess 'simplicity'. The introduction of new ideas for testing likewise depends on co-operation, for any human being who rejects inputs from other human beings runs out of ideas sooner rather than later, and begins to consider only ideas which in one way or another reflect the prejudices he has formed. Co-operation is necessary both for the formation of ideas and for their rational testing.

But—and this is the crucial point—that co-operation must be of a certain kind in order to be effective. It must, for example, obey the principles of 'discourse ethics'.[46] Where there is no opportunity to challenge accepted hypotheses by criticizing the evidence upon which their acceptance was based, or the application of the norms of scientific inquiry to that evidence, or by offering rival hypotheses, and where questions and suggestions are systematically ignored, then the scientific enterprise always suffers. When

[44] Cf. The omnipresence of this theme in Peirce's philosophy is the subject of K. O. Apel's *C. S. Peirce, from Pragmatism to Pragmaticism* (Amherst: University of Massachusetts Press, 1981). See also James in 'The Moral Philosopher and the Moral Life' in *The Will to Believe and other Essays in Popular Philosophy* (reprinted by Harvard University Press, 1979), and Dewey, 'Nature, Communication, and Meaning' in *Experience and Nature* (Mineola, NJ: Dover, 1958) ch. V (first published in 1925 by Open Court).

[45] James in 'The Moral Philosopher and the Moral Life'.

[46] This is the approach to ethics made famous by Habermas, and Apel. Cf. Habermas' *The Theory of Communicative Action* (in two volumes) (Boston: Beacon Press), and Apel's *Diskurs und Verantwortung; Das Problem des Übergangs zur Postkonventionellen Moral* (Frankfurt am Main: Suhrkamp, 1985). For a comparison of discourse ethics and pragmatism see 'A Reconsideration of Deweyan Democracy', *supra* n. 14.

relations among scientists become relations of hierarchy and dependence, or when scientists instrumentalize other scientists, again the scientific enterprise suffers.[47] Dewey was not naïve. He was aware that there are 'power plays' in the history of science as there are in the history of every human institution. He would not have been surprised by the findings of historians and sociologists of science; but he differs from them (or from some of our contemporary ones) in holding that it makes sense to have a *normative* notion of science.

Moreover, it is not just that, on Dewey's conception, good science requires respect for autonomy, symmetric reciprocity, and discourse ethics—that could be true even if scientific theories and hypotheses were, in the end, to be tested by the application of an algorithm, such as the inductive logic for which Carnap hoped—but, as we already observed, the very interpretation of the non-algorithmic standards by which scientific hypotheses are judged depends on co-operation and discussion structured by the same norms. Both for its full development and for its full application to human problems, science requires the democratization of inquiry.

What I have just offered is, in part, an instrumental justification of the democratization of inquiry. But Dewey opposes the philosophers' habit of dichotomization. In particular, he opposes both the dichotomy 'pure science/applied science' and the dichotomy 'instrumental value/terminal value'. Pure science and applied science are interdependent and interpenetrating activities, Dewey argues.[48] And similarly, instrumental values and terminal values are interdependent and interpenetrating. Science helps us to achieve many goals other than the attainment of knowledge for its own sake, and when we allow inquiry to be democratized simply because doing so helps us achieve those practical goals, we are engaged in goal oriented activity. At the same time, as we saw above, even when we are engaged in goal oriented activity we also are guided by norms of rationality which have become terminal values for us, and which cannot be separated from the modern conception of 'rationality' itself. Moreover, we are not—nor were we ever—interested in knowledge *only* for its practical benefits; curiosity is coeval with the species itself, and pure knowledge is always, to some extent, and in some areas, a terminal value even for the least curious among us. And just as the norm we discussed in connection with Peirce's problem has become inseparable from the modern conception of 'rationality', so the norms Dewey discusses have become inseparable from the modern conception of proceeding 'scientifically', inseparable that is, from our normative conception of what it is to be scientifically rational. It is not, for us, any longer just a sociological-descriptive fact that choosing theories for their predictive power and simplicity, and fostering democratic co-operation and

[47] I have used the vocabulary of A. Heller's *A Philosophy of Morals* in this sentence to bring out the 'ethical' tone of the norms governing scientific inquiry.
[48] This is discussed in R. A. Putnam's and my 'Epistemology as Hypothesis' *supra* n. 14.

openness to criticism in the generation and evaluation of theories, are part of the nature of scientific inquiry; these norms describe the way we *ought* to function when the aim is knowledge. Saying this is not the same as saying that inquiry which follows these norms produces knowledge in the way fire produces warmth; as Firth showed, we are not dealing with mere empirical correlation here. Nor is it saying that it is 'analytic' that inquiry which does not meet these standards does not produce justification and knowledge; 'knowledge' and 'justification' are not the sorts of words that can be analytically defined once and for all. Concepts of knowledge are essentially contested concepts; they are always open to reform. What we can say is that the applicability of our present conception to practice is constantly being tested (it is not a priori that, for example, the concept of 'probability' can be successfully used in practice) *and* that conception itself is partly constituted by norms which represent values which are now terminal but not immune to criticism. And this 'messy' state of affairs is one that, I would say, Dewey wanted us to see as typical.

4.2. *Was Dewey Trying to Derive Ethics from the Logic of Science?*

It would be a mistake to see Dewey's project in the *Logic* as 'deriving an ethic from science' (or from the theory of inquiry). What Dewey's argument does show is that there is a certain overlap between scientific values and ethical values; but even where they overlap, these values remain different. Scientific values are not simply instrumental (the relation between the 'means', scientific justification; and the 'goal', knowledge, is too 'internal' for that story to work), but they are relativized to a context—the context of knowledge acquisition—and knowledge acquisition itself is something that can be criticized ethically.[49] Yet there *was* a close connection between inquiry and ethics, in Dewey's view, for more than one reason.

First, all co-operative activity involves a moment of inquiry, if only in the ongoing perception that the activity is going smoothly/not going smoothly. What is essential to the rational, or, to use the word that Dewey preferred, the *intelligent* conduct of inquiry is thus, to some extent, essential to the intelligent conduct of all co-operative activity. Perceiving this can help us to understand why, as the modern conception of rationality gains the upper hand, one sees an insistence on extending democratization to more and more institutions and relationships.

Secondly, ethics itself requires inquiry. Experiencing ourselves as ethical fallibilists, as persons who do not inherit values which cannot be questioned, as persons who have, in fact, criticized many inherited values (even if we have not all criticized the same inherited values), we more and more see ethical disputes as disputes to be settled, if possible, by intelligent

[49] Cf. My 'Scientific Liberty and Scientific License', in *Realism with a Human Face* (Cambridge, Mass.: Harvard University Press, 1991).

argument and inquiry, and not by appeals to authority or to a priori principles. Now nothing Dewey wrote, and nothing James wrote, or Peirce wrote, can *prove* that there are objective ethical norms, ideals, rules of thumb, or even situation specific values; but—and here I state the argument in a more 'Kantian' way than Dewey himself would—*if* there are ethical facts to be discovered, *then* we ought to apply to ethical inquiry just the rules we have learned to apply to inquiry in general. For what applies to inquiry in general applies to ethical inquiry in particular.

If this is right, then an ethical community—a community which wants to know what is right and good—*should* organize itself in accordance with democratic standards and ideals, not only because they are good in themselves (and they are), but because they are the prerequisites for the application of intelligence to the inquiry. It is true that some inquiries can be conducted with only partial democratization; a tyrant, for example, may allow his physicists a freedom of discussion (in certain areas) that is generally forbidden in the society. But—and this is an empirical presupposition of Dewey's argument—any society that limits democracy, that organizes itself hierarchically, thereby limits the rationality of those at both ends of the hierarchy. Hierarchy stunts the intellectual growth of the oppressed, and forces the privileged to construct rationalizations to justify their position.[50] But this is to say that hierarchical societies do not, in these respects, produce solutions to value disputes that are rationally acceptable.

At this point it may look as if Dewey is 'pulling himself up by his bootstraps'. For even if we assume that inquiry into values should be democratized, that the participants should, *qua* seekers after the right and the good, respect free speech and the other norms of discourse ethics, not instrumentalize one another, etc., what *criteria* should they use to tell that their inquiry has succeeded?[51]

This objection overlooks another feature of the pragmatist position; we do not, in fact, start from the position of 'doubting everything'. As long as discussion is still possible, as long as one is not facing coercion or violence or total refusal to discuss, the participants to an actual discussion always share a large number of both factual assumptions and value assumptions that are not in question in the specific dispute. Very often, participants to a disagreement can agree that the disagreement has, in fact, been resolved, not by appeal to a universal set of 'criteria', but by appealing to values which are not in question in *that* dispute. (Recall again Peirce's distinction—which all the pragmatists accepted—between real and 'philosophic' doubt.) It may, of course, happen that the criteria accepted by even one of the participants are in conflict with themselves; but in that case, rational reconstruction is called for. Pragmatism is not against rational reconstruction; but it sees rational reconstruction as one among other tools to be used

---

[50] Cf. 'A Reconsideration of Deweyan Democracy'.
[51] This objection was suggested by Harry Frankfurt.

in resolving problems, not as a route to a set of universal principles applicable to all situations.

Moreover, Dewey stressed[52] that one does not always need a set of criteria to tell that a problem has been resolved. We have all had the experience of discovering that the satisfactory resolution to a problem in our own lives was one that would not have counted as satisfactory by any of the 'criteria' we had in mind at the beginning of our search for a solution. (A corollary to this is that when we have solved a collective or an individual problem we may not, at the end, know whether it was an 'ethical' problem or some other kind of problem that we solved; and is that a bad thing?) And finally, believing that ethical objectivity is possible is not the same thing as believing that there are no undecidable cases, or problems which, alas, cannot be solved. The point is that, once we give up the metaphysical claim that there cannot be such a thing as ethical objectivity, and once we observe that objectivity in other areas is strongly connected with values, we can begin to see not just that ethical objectivity might be possible, but, more importantly, that investigating ethical problems requires just the values that have come to be linked with the open society.

5 CONCLUSION

In closing, I want to say just a word about my reasons for writing this paper. Besides my long-standing interest in the problem of moral objectivity there was, as I indicated, another reason: to combat the idea that there is no intellectual structure worth taking seriously to the arguments of the American pragmatists. I have laid out some of that structure here in my own way, and without a lot of scholarly apparatus, because my interest was in the living relevance of what American pragmatism bequeathed to us, and that is something one can only explain in one's own words, because they are the only words one can take full responsibility for.

In particular, I hope to have shown that the appeal to the primacy of practice (e.g., the 'indispensability arguments') in pragmatism is always accompanied by critique of those metaphysical criticisms of practice that make it look 'irresponsible' to take practice as seriously as pragmatists do.[53] I have tried to give some sense of the range, the complexity, and the depth of the investigations of the pragmatists into such questions as the value presuppositions of goal oriented activity and pure science, and the overlap (though never the identity) between science and ethics. If this leads other students of these questions to take the pragmatists seriously, I shall feel this all too brief account of some of their thought was well worth the effort it took me to present it.

[52] This is gone into in 'Epistemology as Hypothesis'.
[53] This may be a part of what Dewey meant when he defined philosophy as 'the critical method of developing methods of criticism' in *Experience and Nature*, 437.

Democracy and Rationality: A Dialogue with Hilary Putnam

Linda Alcoff

Hilary Putnam's main project is to show that there can be a rational basis for adopting ethical positions and even ultimate values. His defence of this claim is based on an ingenious argument, via American pragmatism, to the conclusion that rationality and democratic values are intrinsically connected. The case he makes for the objectivity of morality is not airtight, as he himself recognizes; at certain junctures he merely demolishes one possible objection and on that basis moves forward. And there are places where one might wish to hear more, for example when he suggests that a concept of 'reflection' can serve as an alternative to an instrumental justification for the norms of rationality. These small problems, however, do not seem worth pursuing here. What I think will be more fruitful is to accept his argument in its broad outlines and to explore the implications of his claim that democratic processes are necessary for social rationality.

One of the most important conclusions to be drawn from the stories of Saleha Begum and Metha Bai, as reported in Martha Chen's paper, is that projects of emancipation can never be successful unless democracy is built into the process of reasoning that identifies goals and the means of their accomplishment. Only in this way can we negotiate between the problems of cultural imperialism and cultural relativism that must beset any transcultural project that seeks human freedom. I will return to these issues after exploring Putnam's argument.

1 POLITICS AND INQUIRY[1]

Hilary Putnam shows that there is a necessary connection between both the processes and the products of inquiry, on the one hand, and political relations on the other. Once we acknowledge that hierarchies of power and privilege, as well as institutions of exploitation and discrimination, have a significant effect on the participants in inquiry and their interrelationships (and therefore on the form that inquiry takes), it follows that these political phenomena have an effect on knowledge. It is therefore simply implausible to maintain that science or any area of study can be neutral with respect to politics, or can understand itself as above the fray of political struggle.

[1] Some of the arguments in this section are based on my essay, 'How is Epistemology Political?' in R. Gottlieb (ed.), *Radical Philosophy: Tradition, Counter-Tradition, Politics* (Philadelphia: Temple University Press, 1993).

Putnam describes one connection between politics and inquiry, but there are other connections as well, some of which follow directly from his argument. He describes the connection of politics to inquiry in terms of the conditions of the production of knowledge. Knowledge does not occur through an individual's passive observation of reality—a picture Adorno described as 'peephole metaphysics'. As Putnam says, it is the product of co-operative human interaction with an environment. The nature of that interaction—its inclusiveness, the degree and nature of its democracy and reciprocity, the quality of its co-operation—will have an impact on the knowledge produced. And as Putnam points out, political relations of hierarchy and privilege in any society will affect its possibilities for democratic interaction in inquiry.

In Western countries the group of people who have effective access to participation in inquiry is delimited through the distribution of access to higher education. But higher education is not distributed solely in accordance with merit (or aptitude) and interest: wealth, social class, gender, and race all play a role. Furthermore, even within the élite who participate in inquiry, political and economic hierarchies affect the dynamics of interrelationships—a fact to which Putnam alludes when he refers to the necessity of a 'discourse ethics'. Who is listened to, who is given credibility, and whose views are taken seriously: all this is determined in no small part by general processes of socialization connected to existing hierarchies of power, as well as by inequalities of power and privilege that obtain between the individual participants. To maintain this we do not need to allege conscious discriminatory intent.[2] It often happens quite unconsciously that there is a presumption in favour of the views and arguments advanced by certain kinds of people over those of others. And often these groups are demarcated by class, wealth, gender, race, and nationality.

It is true that the nature of the subject matter can also affect the distribution of authority in an inquiry. But in practice this legitimate consideration is frequently eclipsed by others that seem more suspect. Take the authority to make general and universal claims about human experience. One might suppose that anyone at all could in principle advance such claims. But in fact the authority to make universal claims is often restricted along lines of race, gender, class, and sexuality. Within US society, African–Americans may be generally acknowledged experts on the needs of their own communities, but rarely will an African–American political candidate be seen by whites as capable of understanding the situation of the whole community; whites more often assume that white candidates can achieve this universal point of view. Where literary descriptions of experience are

---

[2] Sometimes, however, such discrimination is both conscious and defended as justifiable. See M. Levin's apologia for the predominance of whites in philosophy in his letter to the *Proceedings and Addresses of the APA* (1990), 63, 62–3.

concerned, bell hooks has argued persuasively that black writers are too often read by whites as writing about 'Blackness', whereas white writers are assumed to write about 'life'.[3]

There are many more such instances, many quite irrational. Midwives with extensive experience of attending to women in labour, as well as personal experience of childbirth, are less likely to be believed than male obstetricians fresh out of medical school. Assembly line workers with decades of experience are routinely ignored in decisions about how to increase efficiency on the line, deference being given instead to college trained 'efficiency experts'. Impoverished women in developing countries are rarely given the chance to contribute their experience to the formation of development policy. Because such cases so sharply violate intuitive ideas about evidence, favouring less experience over more, indirect knowledge over direct, they reveal the distorting role that political forces can play in the formation of knowledge.

Feminist philosophers have argued, furthermore, that some traditional debates in the history of Western philosophy show the effects of these distortions, and that ideals of reason developed in the course of these debates may be closely connected to ideals of masculinity.[4] (They are talking here not about biological masculinity, but about socially constructed norms of maleness—for example, about the idea that a 'real man' should be detached, self-sufficient, and always in control.) Such ideals, when accepted as criterial in inquiry, may put both women and the truth at a disadvantage.

Hilary Putnam has long claimed that metaphysical and normative background assumptions are operative in (and indispensable to) all forms of inquiry. The feminist work I have just cited expands on this to say that the collection of assumptions and values with which any given individual works, can be connected in interesting ways to that person's social, cultural, and political identity. This is the meaning of the often misunderstood feminist claim that there exists a relationship of *partial* determination between theories and the social identity of theorists. And it is important to note that in its general form this claim places no necessary primacy on

---

[3] bell hooks, *Yearning: race, gender, and cultural politics* (Boston: South End Press, 1990).

[4] See, for example, Naomi Scheman, 'Othello's Doubt/Desdemona's Death: The Engendering of Skepticism', in J. Genova (ed.), *Power, Gender, Values* (Edmonton: Academic Printing and Publishing, 1987), 113–33; Susan Bordo, *The Flight to Objectivity: Essays on Cartesianism and Culture* (Albany, NY: SUNY Press, 1987); Elizabeth Potter, 'Making Gender/Making Science: Gender Ideology and Boyle's Experimental Philosophy', in *Gender Politics in Seventeenth Century Science* (forthcoming); Andrea Nye, *Words of Power: A Feminist Reading of the History of Logic* (New York: Routledge, 1990); Genevieve Lloyd, *The Man of Reason: 'Male' and 'Female' in Western Philosophy* (Minneapolis: University of Minnesota Press, 1984); Lorraine Code, *What Can She Know? Feminist Theory and the Construction of Knowledge* (Ithaca, NY: Cornell University Press, 1991), 8, 302, 310; see also Code's 'Taking Subjectivity Into Account', in Alcoff and Potter (eds.), *Feminist Epistemologies* (New York: Routledge, 1993).

gender over culture or race as the principal component of identity.[5] The
influence of these assumptions and values cannot be restricted to the so-
called 'context of discovery' because they have an important impact on the
formulation of hypotheses, on which hypotheses are taken to be plausible,
on the kinds of analogies and models that get seriously entertained, and on
the determination of the kinds of evidence considered necessary or sufficient to justify theories. When cultural and social facts affect inquiry in
such pervasive and central ways, they become *epistemically* relevant.

But this argument in and of itself does not establish that we ought to
increase the role of democracy in inquiry. Putnam seems to have two
arguments for this conclusion. First, because science has an effect on social
relations as well as being affected by them, there are ethical and political
reasons why we should want a democratization of inquiry. In other words,
if we want more democracy in the society at large, the increase of democracy within science can help us toward achieving that goal. But—and
this is Putnam's second argument—there are also epistemic reasons for
maximizing democracy within science. Putnam suggests that the full development of science and its full application to social problems will be advanced in proportion to the degree of democratic inclusiveness in the
enterprise. This claim is not based on a relativist position that everyone's
view has an equal claim to truth. It is based on the more plausible view that
truth is more likely to be obtained through a process that includes the
articulation and examination of all possible views. And this means that the
artificial exclusion of views, or their exclusion from the realm of debate for
epistemically irrelevant reasons such as sexism or racism, is a matter of
epistemic concern. Such practices have a deleterious effect on the strength
and comprehensiveness of the views that emerge from inquiry. A striking
implication of this argument is that it is not the influence of politics *per se*
that we need to eliminate from rational inquiry: it is the influence of
oppressive politics.

To such an argument for inclusiveness, one might object that no good
will come of including participants from so-called 'traditional' cultures on
a question such as the question of women's liberation. Since they are
opposed to this goal, their inclusion in the decision-making will impede us
from reaching it. But this, as Seyla Benhabib has argued, is to assume that
these cultures are monolithic, without a history of internal critique and the
contestation of their dominant ideas. If we reject this simplistic notion, and
instead recognize the variety of positions that exist within any culture, we
can continue to insist on the merits of the participatory approach to inquiry.
The question that we must always ask is: whose views are included? Whose
opinion is asked? Only those in positions of privilege, or also those who are

[5] For a feminist argument closely related to Putnam's, see Helen Longino, *Science as Social
Knowledge: Values and Objectivity in Scientific Inquiry* (Princeton, NJ: Princeton University
Press, 1990).

suffering most acutely? I am not suggesting that we should consult only the current preferences of the most oppressed, since, as Amartya Sen argues in this volume, their awareness of their oppression may be as yet incomplete. Nor do I suppose that achieving meaningful inclusion will be easy, or that it will always be clear how to achieve this goal. But in any culture there is a tradition of internal critique that should inform any project for improvement.[6] Our case studies by Martha Chen and Nkiru Nzegwu show two very different examples of such internal plurality and contestation.

Putnam argues, as I have said, that the limits of democracy in a society will also impose limits on its social rationality. Since we believe that social processes ought to be rational, it follows that we ought to promote democracy. But if all this is so, then we must face a further challenge: we must examine our philosophical theories themselves with this end in view. Philosophical theories may consolidate or buttress views about the possibilities of social equality, or they may affect the authority of certain participants in inquiry. Biological theories have had well-known effects on social views about women and the division of labour. Many theories in the social sciences have influenced the definition of supposed racial categories. Similarly, philosophical theories of knowledge are likely to have an effect on the possibilities for democratic inquiry.[7]

There is a wealth of work on such political effects. Marx, for example, argued that ahistorical positivist conceptions of knowledge—which he believed to be causally linked to capitalism—have the political effect of producing fatalism about the *status quo*. Adorno and Horkheimer argued that philosophy's conception of nature as an inert object, and its insistence that prediction and control are the goals of scientific inquiry, are more than coincidentally related to capitalism's wish to maximize the exploitation of resources and to pursue the domination of nature without constraint. Moreover, when the object of inquiry is not nature but other human beings, a conception of this type can support the wish to dominate and oppress large sectors of humanity. And, as I have already said, feminist philosophers have recently argued that dominant epistemological theories have (unjustifiably) excluded women's voices and undermined their claims to know.[8]

---

[6] In addition to Sen's paper in this volume, see M. Nussbaum and A. Sen, 'Internal Criticism and Indian Rationalist Traditions', in M. Krausz (ed.), *Relativism* (Notre Dame, Ind.: Notre Dame University Press, 1989).

[7] The special importance of philosophy derives from the fact that it sets out the criteria of legitimation for all other types of discourse. Like Marx, I would reject the view that philosophy, as a body of texts and ideas, actually provides the causal mechanism that makes possible the emergence of other modes of discourse. Like Hegel, I would hold, instead, that philosophy usually originates in the midst of other modes of discourse and provides the arguments and theories which then 'justify' them. Even without absolute causal power, however, philosophy and epistemology are crucial because of their influence in the crafting of criteria of justification for other knowledge claims.

[8] For example, Elizabeth Potter has argued that Locke's development of an empiricist epistemology had the political effect of silencing the emerging voices of lower-class sectarian

In these ways and still others,[9] our philosophical methods and theories themselves may be impeding the democratization of inquiry, and thus, according to Putnam's argument, impeding our progress toward fully adequate theories and toward full social rationality.

Given that we have—if we follow Putnam's two arguments—both political and epistemic reasons to maximize the democratization of inquiry, such an analysis of the effects of our theories should become standard in philosophy. I cannot develop here an account of the way in which such an analysis ought to proceed. But one might argue, following the pragmatist tradition, that where there are two theories with similar evidential support but divergent political effects, those effects might be used as a criterion of adjudication.

Thus the connection Putnam makes between politics and inquiry is a deep one, with radical implications. His argument does not show that the sociology of knowledge should replace normative epistemology; or that epistemic considerations must be replaced as a whole by political ones, or that inquiry is determined by the forces of unreason and power. Pragmatic reasoning, as he envisages it, is still a form of reasoning. And it seems likely that an exploration of the connections between politics and inquiry, rather than undermining knowledge, will increase the accuracy of its self-understanding and enhance its ability for self-critique. But for this to occur, I have argued, the methods of analysis and debate internal to philosophy need to be re-examined.

2 POWER AND DESIRE

Embedded in this issue is a further one, at which I have so far only hinted. Perhaps the sharpest difference between the analytical and the contemporary continental philosophical traditions lies in the preoccupation of the latter with questions of motivation and desire. Traditions of philosophy tracing their origins to Descartes have tended to deny or to set aside concerns about the ways in which desire is operative in every rational deliberation. Neo-Hegelian traditions have been more likely to place these

women: see 'Locke's Epistemology and Women's Struggles', in Bat-Ami Bar On (ed.), *Modern Engenderings: Critical Feminist Readings in Modern Western Philosophy* (Albany, NY: SUNY Press, 1994). Together with Vrinda Dalmiya, I have argued that the privileging of 'knowing that' over 'knowing how' in the history of Western epistemology since Descartes has had the political effect of demoting much of women's traditional knowledge, such as the knowledge of midwifery—as well as the traditional knowledge of men involved in manual work. See Alcoff and Dalmiya, 'Are Old Wives' Tales Justified?', in Alcoff and Potter (eds.), *Feminist Epistemologies* (New York: Routledge, 1993).

[9] One might also consider the tyranny of a subjectless, emotionless conception of objectivity, which marginalizes personalized voices that argue with emotion and open commitment. For a discussion of the role of emotions in rationality, see Martha Nussbaum's second paper in this volume.

issues at the heart of their analyses of knowledge; and post-structuralist theories have on some views effected a total replacement of the intellect by desire.

A wide variety of non-intellectual elements are held, by thinkers in the continental tradition, to have an influence on belief formation and theory choice. These include the unconscious effects of a culture-bound, gender-bound, or class-bound world view, the unexamined meanings given in a language or practice, libidinal desire, and the will to power. And these elements are in turn said to manifest their influence in a wide variety of ways. First, as I have already mentioned, knowledge and communication always require a background layer of unquestioned and unjustified beliefs. Secondly, a rhetorical examination of any argument will reveal the use of metaphor, imagery, and analogy; these can borrow their persuasiveness from associations, desires, and fears that exist at a semi-conscious or unconscious level. Thirdly, it has been argued that deliberation cannot completely transcend its embodiedness and its embeddedness in a specific cultural, racial, and gender context.

In his insistence that background assumptions and values are always entangled in the process of rational inquiry, Putnam links himself to this continental tradition of argument. And Putnam has been very forthright about this for a long time. But the point of his defence of moral objectivity is to insist that, despite the untenability of the fact/value distinction and the incursion of ethics into the domain of science, we need not succumb to the dictates of irrational forces. Ethical beliefs are always involved, but these are susceptible to deliberation and even to the constraints of objectivity.

I see a tension between these two tendencies in Putnam's work: the tendency to expand and complicate our understanding of what is involved in inquiry (to insist on what he calls its 'messiness') and the tendency to contain the forces of power and desire and to segregate these outside the domain of rational deliberation. The tension arises because the former tendency makes it exceedingly difficult to pursue the latter tendency with complete success. I want to suggest an alternative position that can offer a resolution to this tension.

Foucault has argued, borrowing from Nietzsche, that the development of the social or human sciences cannot be adequately understood as separate from the consolidations and contestations of institutional power in the social organizations that have been historically allied with these sciences, in particular in medicine, psychiatry, and the prison system. For example, the development of psychiatry, he argues, depended on a confessional model borrowed from Catholicism, in which the priest extracted and passed judgement on confessions by his practitioners, mainly concerning sexual practices. This suggests that an analysis of psychiatry should scrutinize the relationship between its methodology and grounding theory on the one hand and the power relations between confessor and confessee on the other. These latter relations, Foucault argues, are affected by the pleasure produced in and for the priest/therapist by the confession as well as by the expanded institutional role psychiatry has come to play in criminal determinations and social control. The point is that we cannot understand the development of psychiatric *theory* without taking into account this expansion and distribution of powers and desires. This does not mean that all of psychiatry is mere manipulation. Foucault rejects the view that power is simply a distorting influence on knowledge. Power, he holds, is necessary to the development and circulation of knowledge, in the same way that a stable layer of background assumptions or a reigning paradigm is necessary for 'normal' science. And conversely, power is manifested and extended through claims of knowledge; a claim to know is simultaneously an authorization of power.[10]

Foucault uses this model to explore other systems of knowledge as well, formulating the more general concept of what he calls power/knowledge. In this dyadic concept, neither power nor knowledge can be reduced to or subordinated to the other. The purpose of the dyadic structure is precisely to deny that knowledge is simply the play of power struggles, and rather to insist that power and knowledge cannot be separated. To analyze knowledge in its relationships to the strategies and effects of power and to insist that a fully adequate account of existing knowledge systems can never simply leave aside these relationships is not to reduce knowledge to the conspiratorial machinations of power: it is simply to complicate the analysis of knowledge (or to make it messy) and, in my view, to make it more plausible.

An analysis of this sort is in fact a natural continuation of the pragmatist tradition. For if we are truly determined to theorize knowledge as a practice, as an active process, in its actual rather than idealized context, we must be willing to explore the complications of its seemingly ever present connections to power and desire. Such a project does not entail that we dispense with the normative dimension of epistemological analysis, or surrender to the forces of irrationalism. It is a project fundamentally motivated by Enlightenment goals of liberation and of progress (both epistemic and ethical) through expanded self-awareness. A greater awareness of the roles of power and desire in our inquiries should increase our ability to maximize their democratic character and thus, on Putnam's argument, to improve social rationality itself.

Let me conclude by relating this issue to the problems of cultural imperialism and cultural relativism that many of the other papers in this volume have discussed. Cultural relativism often arises as a reaction to cultural imperialism, or the oppressive imposition of one culture's presup-

---

[10] For an excellent account of Foucault's analysis and an explanation of why it does not undermine the whole of the human sciences, see Gary Gutting, *Michel Foucault's Archaeology of Reason* (New York: Cambridge University Press, 1989).

positions on another culture through economic, military, or political pressures. But universalist theories of justice need not be imperialist or oppressive. They may in fact be motivated by the desire to extend compassion beyond one's national borders. We need to avoid a cultural imperialism that would reinforce the global hierarchy of nations, but to avoid also a relativism that would justify inaction in the face of oppression and suffering. Martha Nussbaum has argued that this relativist collapse can be avoided by understanding our universal theories as historically rooted and fallible. But in order to pursue this project further than she does, we need to develop Hilary Putnam's concept of pragmatist reasoning.

Putnam, following Dewey and Habermas, gives what might be called a procedural account of rationality. He holds, that is, that rationality consists in a practice that involves democratic, non-hierarchical inclusiveness and symmetrical relations of co-operation. The dilemma between cultural relativism and universalism, I believe, requires a similar procedural solution. It is unreasonable to assume that the élite, even the well-meaning portion of the élite, can accurately determine the needs of the oppressed in a process that is not characterized by democratic inclusiveness and symmetrical relations of co-operation. Moreover, the very structure of a political deliberation in which the privileged determine and then represent the needs, situation, or capabilities of the non-privileged, reinforces systems of hierarchy between nations, and groups within nations, about who is more likely to have the truth. This is both patronizing and disempowering.

In order to realize Putnam's aim of democratizing the process of inquiry, we must explore all the ways in which cultural imperialism can manifest itself in a deliberative process. How are the elements of power and desire operative in such a project? The motivation of the élite to participate in such projects may involve many ingredients, but will probably include a desire for mastery, a desire to attain the status of hero or saviour, a desire to be in control. (We can see the likelihood of this all the more clearly when we think of the ways in which desire is shaped in the social construction of our gender norms, especially our norms of maleness.) When élites are represented as having the best plan, they are automatically positioned as superior to the oppressed in epistemic, political, and even moral terms. The false consciousness of tradition is often seen to weigh down the oppressed, but not the well-intentioned élite. Once we acknowledge the accuracy of this description, it becomes easy to see how desire may play a strong, and sometimes a distorting, role in the pursuit of deliberative projects.

The solution to this problem will indeed be, as Putnam argues, a democratic, practice-oriented, process of inquiry. Only this will establish the mechanisms for real improvement in conditions of oppression. But those of us who are in the position of élites must become more aware of the ways in which our own practices and self-understandings may work against democracy. For this awareness to occur, an analysis of the operations of power and desire in our own reflection must become a standard feature of rational inquiry. Liberatory programmes work within a global context structured by past and present forms of imperialism, and these programmes cannot free themselves from the effects of this context any more than they can pretend that power and desire are not intrinsic to their own practices. They can, however, acknowledge their own social positioning and democratize their practices of rational deliberation.

Cultural Complexity, Moral Interdependence, and the Global Dialogical Community

Seyla Benhabib

1 INTRODUCTION

The formulation of a concept of justice which could be employed cross-culturally such as to illuminate the condition of men and women globally, but particularly in developing countries, has become a pressing issue of our times. In 'Aristotelian Social Democracy' Martha Nussbaum formulates this desideratum precisely. 'Especially in light of the increasing interaction among diverse societies and the frequency of communications,' she writes, 'cross-cultural debate about questions of justice is both possible and actual. It seems to me to be an advantage in a philosophical view if it can both explain this debate and provide a framework for its continuation and enhancement . . . And it is urgent that this discussion should develop further. Many of the most urgent problems of justice and distribution that face human beings who live within nation-states are problems that are now, in their very nature, international problems, requiring worldwide communication and common effort for their effective solution.'[1]

I join Martha Nussbaum in her sense of the significance and urgency of this task, yet I think it is very important to embark upon it with a precise awareness of the intellectual developments of the last two decades which seem at first to make the search for such a concept of justice both illusory and methodologically naïve. Indeed, among the most disheartening intellectual developments of the last two decades is the irony that as the world has grown together and the globe become unified to a hitherto unprecedented degree, our theoretical discourse has turned local, contextualist, parochial, and has shied away from thinking globally and reflecting about the principles of planetary interdependence. The worldwide decline of Marxism as a political ideology has brought in its wake, in Europe in particular, the 'post-modernist' turn away from 'grand theories and narratives'. Any theory which formulates its justification with reference to concepts like progress, the betterment of humanity, the class struggle,

An earlier version of this paper was read at the Conference on Human Capabilities: Women, Men and Equality, organized by UNU/WIDER and held at Helsinki, August 1991, and was formulated largely as a response to Marty Chen's contribution. I have expanded and substantially revised it for inclusion in this volume.

[1] Nussbaum, 'Aristotelian Social Democracy', in R. B. Douglass, G. Mara, and H. Richardson (eds.), *Liberalism and the Good* (New York: Routledge, 1990) 207.

and the march of freedom is to be rejected, argue postmodernists, since these categories are theoretically indefensible and perhaps politically sinister. European intellectuals have turned to the 'local narratives' of cultures, in the words of Jean-François Lyotard to those 'petits recits', whose only justification is that they certify themselves 'in the pragmatics of their own transmission without having recourse to argumentation and proof'.[2]

This withdrawal away from the grand narratives of progress, Enlightenment, and class struggle toward local knowledge on the part of disillusioned left European intellectuals has been met in recent years with enthusiasm by an impressive group of Anglo-American thinkers who have engaged in their own pilgrimage away from liberalism to communitarianism, from transcendental arguments to contextual ones, and from the seriousness of the democratic vistas of early American pragmatists to the irony and contingency of ethnocentric liberalism.[3]

If this depiction of our current intellectual mood is not mistaken, then the desideratum formulated so cogently and poignantly by Martha Nussbaum of articulating a concept of justice that can further cross-cultural co-operation and global communication, will fall today on less than receptive ears. Yet, as the fascinating study by Martha Chen entitled 'A Matter of Survival: Women's Right to Employment in India and Bangladesh' shows (in this volume), confronted with the plight of women and children in Bangladesh and rural North India, and indeed all over the world, the methodological sophistication of Western intellectuals, their contextualist scruples and postmodernist hesitations, might appear morally callous, humanely indifferent and politically pernicious. Nonetheless, philosophical positions cannot be refuted by moral intuitions and political goals. On the one hand we have to trust our intuitions that the 'Purdah' system, which does not allow women in Bangladesh to obtain gainful employment outside the home, and the criss-crossing of caste, gender, and class relations in Northern India which confines women's work and activity to rigidly defined locations and occupations, are unjust and even cruel to the individuals involved. On the other hand, we have to ask how we can articulate the principles behind these intuitions in a philosophically defensible way, from where we stand today, *après la lutte*—so to speak? How can we bring our principles and intuitions into some kind of 'reflective equilibrium' which we can defend as the most theoretically reasonable and morally fair position under the circumstances? What shall we say to the contextualist and Rortyian pragmatist who argue that these are just 'our' intuitions and 'our'

[2] Jean François Lyotard, *The Postmodern Condition: A Report on Knowledge*, trans. G. Bennington and B. Massouri, foreword by F. Jameson (Minneapolis, Minn.: University of Minnesota Press, 1984), 27.

[3] I develop the communitarian, postmodernist, and feminist challenges to contemporary universalist ethical theories from Rawls to Habermas more extensively in my collection of essays, *Situating the Self. Gender, Community and Postmodernism in Contemporary Ethics* (New York and Cambridge, UK: Polity Press and Routledge Press, 1992).

moral scruples but that they have no cross-cultural validity? We know such questions and the objections to them only too well.

In this essay, I would like to reconsider aspects of the cultural relativism/ universalism debate first in the light of certain sociological hypotheses about the reproduction and interdependence of cultures. Martha Chen's work will serve as my point of reference in outlining these theoretical premises. Building on these observations, in the second place I would like to take issue with the 'poor sociology' that is implicit in much of the cultural relativism debate. Through an examination of Rorty's version of 'ethnocentric liberalism', I would like to outline how Rortyian 'communities of conversation' must give way to 'communities of planetary interdependence' and to a 'global dialogical moral community'.

2 MATERIAL VERSUS SYMBOLIC REPRODUCTION OF A LIFE FORM: THE CASES OF BANGLADESH AND RURAL NORTH INDIA

Martha Chen makes an admirably lucid and compelling case of presenting the plight of the women of Bangladesh and rural North India, while also providing us with innumerable insights into the elaborate criss-crossing of gender, caste, and class relations in these patriarchal systems. Contained in her empirical account of the condition of women in these communities, are a set of methodological and theoretical insights which have implications for the relativism/universalism debate. To show how this is so, I need first to introduce several sets of distinctions.

In thinking about social practices and ways of life we can distinguish between 'material' and 'symbolic' levels of reproduction.[4] By material reproduction I mean those activities and processes which enable the continuity (over time) of the life of the members of a society and culture, the economic provision of means of subsistence, and the maintenance of the material goods of such a community—like its buildings, roads, systems of communication, and cultural and artistic artefacts. By symbolic reproduction I mean the continuity (over time) of the way of life of a community in three ways: (1) every human community socializes its individuals so as to function within a certain language and a certain set of reciprocal social expectations; (2) every human community that possesses a minimum level of culture seeks to reproduce the system of meanings and values through which it interprets and views the world; and (3) as a result of the complex

---

[4] This distinction has been clearly articulated by Jurgen Habermas first in *The Legitimation Crisis*, trans. T. McCarthy (Boston, Mass.: Beacon Press, 1975), 1–24. It is related to but not identical with the 'system' and 'life-world' distinction with which Habermas also operates. See also *The Theory of Communicative Action*, vol. 2. *Lifeworld and System. A Critique of Functionalist Reason*, trans. T. McCarthy (Boston, Mass.: Beacon Press, 1985).

processes of socialization and cultural reproduction, the members of a particular human community co-ordinate their activities in accordance with certain rules, sanctions, and reciprocal expectations. This is the dimension of social integration or social co-ordination.

Add to this distinction between 'material' and 'symbolic' reproduction a second one, namely the distinction between the standpoints of the 'participant' and the 'observer' in the study, research, and evaluation of social and cultural life. Martha Chen in producing this paper has to adopt both standpoints at once: on the one hand, she has to see the world as Metha Bai and Saleha Begum see it; on the other hand, she also sees things about their world and the limits of their world which they do not see. Note that the standpoints of the observer and the participant do not necessarily coincide with those of the outsider/insider, member of a social group/social scientist. Individuals themselves can also become observers of their own ways of life if they acquire a critical distance from it and begin to challenge its normative order. The increase of this kind of social reflexivity and the growth of criticism which allows members of a society and culture to challenge these practices in the name of some normative standards is one of the sociological constants of the transition from tradition to modernity. Modern societies allow their members to be at once observers of and participants in their normative orders.

In order to survive and to continue over time, societies and cultures must reproduce themselves materially and symbolically first and foremost from the standpoint of their participants. While to outside observers it may be obvious that a way of life is coming to an end and a social structure is dissolving, unless this way of life and this social structure also cease to make sense to the participants themselves and cease to motivate them, they cannot be transformed. They may perish, as cultures and civilizations without the capacity to change and to adopt to new circumstances have perished. The continuing identity of a society and culture is based upon its capacity to deal with outside challenges and contingencies while also retaining the belief of its members in its normative systems and value structures. Social transformation, more often than not, comes about as a result of social systems adopting to crises, that is changing without being destroyed.

The ways of life studied by Martha Chen, and particularly the one in Bangladesh, are in crisis. In the aftermath of the famine of 1974, and as a result of increasing landlessness and poverty, ever larger numbers of women are forced to seek work outside the home. In one of the food-for-work sites, it is reported that nearly 47% of the women interviewed are the principal earners of their families. Clearly, here is a situation where the imperatives of material reproduction (to sustain the lives of nearly half the women and the children in the community) clash with the structures of symbolic reproduction: the system of belief called 'purdah' which prohibits women's work, thus rendering some destitute and desperate. Caught in such conflicts, individuals might go under through their inability to negotiate a way out of the contradictions of their circumstances, they might escape their current circumstances through migration to the cities or to a different country, or they might seek methods of change from within. Saleha Begum was fortunate to have the aid of BRAC (Bangladesh Rural Advancement Committee) organizers. With their help she began to break down certain value systems and social expectations in her community; she became a social reformer and pioneer. In this process of social transformation, some of the women made the transition from the standpoint of 'participant' to that of 'observer' of their social systems. The processes whereby power relations were defined and sustained and values perpetrated became somewhat clearer to them. I quote Chen quoting one of the women. 'What is necessary for their wives to do is sanctioned as *purdah*. For example, if women from rich households need to go to the town to appear in court, even to remain in town for a few days, this is sanctioned as within the norms of *purdah*. When women from a BRAC-organized group want to go to town and attend a workshop or meeting, even for a single day, their action is condemned as *bepurdah*.' Martha Chen concludes that 'Clearly, tradition is a human creation and the interpretation and enforcement of tradition is at some person's or some group's discretion: in many cases, the discretion of the rich and the powerful.' I would add that under the weight of problems of material reproduction, the symbolic system of 'purdah' has come into question. We may be observing here a crisis in tradition, the one clear indicator of which is the sense that the rules of the social structure no longer serve everybody's interests equally well; quite to the contrary, they are considered partial toward the rich and not fair for all. Some of these women have left behind the status of acquiescent social participants: faced with life's necessity, they have become observers and reformers of their own ways of life. Whether or not what they have started will continue or be squashed will depend upon the behaviour of other social actors on the scene: their national government and its policies; the local officials and networks through which such policies get translated down; international lending and development agencies to whom the national government turns for relief, and the like. In each case, the outcome is far from certain: the move backwards from tradition to reaction is just as possible as the move forward toward the liberalization of 'purdah' and the transformation of the social and cultural norms governing women's work.

The case of the rural communities of North India is far more complex than the Bangladeshi one and the condition of women like Metha Bai far more desperate. Unlike the women organized by BRAC, she is unwilling to make the final break with her community, which would lead to the disinheritance of her sons; but in accepting the strictures which require her not to work she is risking starvation, once her father who is currently caring for her and her family, dies. Given also that as many as '42 per cent of households in rural India may have incomes below the poverty line' (Chen), the question is whether the caste system will prove symbolically resourceful enough to sustain itself over time while also allowing the material continuation of the life of the members of its communities. Precisely because the caste norms and hierarchies are complex and flexible, and because they allow mobility within the system, it seems that they might be able to keep adopting themselves to newer situations. None the less, here too the signs of crisis are apparent: the system of familial solidarity and interdependence has collapsed leaving widows like Metha Bai destitute and desperate.

What then follows from all this for the philosophical questions of universalism versus cultural relativism? Do these distinctions, as between material and symbolic reproduction, and the participant and observer perspectives, allow us to come any closer to an answer? The principal conclusion that I draw from the account presented above is that philosophical defences of 'cultural relativism', more often than not, suffer from a poor sociology. Very often, cultures are presented as hermetic and sealed wholes; the internal contradictions and debates within cultures are flattened out; the different conceptual and normative options which are available to the participants of a given culture and society are ignored. Neglecting the reality of cultures as systems of value, meaning, and intepretation which must also be reconciled with the imperatives of material reproduction of a way of life, most philosophers in debating these issues proceed from abstractions. They turn their eyes away from the dilemmas which most cultures and societies experience today. Since the fifteenth and sixteenth centuries, what was once the unique and peculiar experience of the West's confrontation with modernity, has today become globalized. The encounter between tradition and modernity, the imperatives of nation-states to survive in a world economic system, to maintain growth, to participate in international means of communication, production, commerce, and transport, not to mention armament, have all created the inevitability of modernity and modernization processes in the technical, economic, communication, and military organizational domains. In some cases, this technical modernization has been accompanied by modernization in the spheres of law and the organization of the state apparatus. Martha Chen remarks that 'The constitutions of Bangladesh and India guarantee women equal employment opportunities as men and equal pay for equal work.' In these societies there is a clash between the political and legal modernization adopted by the nation-states, with their democratic and egalitarian constitutions, and the rural communities whose value systems are clearly much less progressive and egalitarian than these national constitutions.

One way, then, of beginning to recast the terms of the cultural relativism debate is to redefine the sociological situation in which we find ourselves.

The situation today is that of a world-wide confrontation and interchange between the imperatives of tradition and modernity. This confrontation undermines the posture of bemused detachment which the cultural relativist would like to assume: for as the participants of other cultures and societies themselves begin to question their social order and assume the attitude of observer *vis-à-vis* their own value systems, they engage in a moral conversation with us and draw us into their circle of meaning and value. Martha Chen's activity and discourse as a development sociologist and activist shows this very well. The activities of organizations like BRAC cannot be said to be 'exporting' value transformations into the perfectly peaceful and tranquil islands of other cultures. There is a moral imperative behind all developmental aid, which is that, given the know-how (medical, agricultural, communications) in science and technology which we in the 'west' possess today, is it fair and just of us not to share these with others who could clearly benefit from the fruits of our knowledge and skill? In the process of world-wide communication and modernization, there are only participants who exert moral claims upon each other.

3 CULTURAL RELATIVISM AS POOR MAN'S SOCIOLOGY

Consider now the poor man's sociology of the cultural relativist position. The following quote from Jean-François Lyotard illustrates this issue well. You will note how Lyotard's characterization of narrative knowledge and the moral gesture of anti-imperialism are quickly brought together.

I have said that narrative knowledge does not give priority to the question of its own legitimation and that it certifies itself in the pragmatics of its own transmission without having recourse to argumentation and proof . . . The scientist questions the validity of narrative statements and concludes that they are never subject to argumentation and proof. He classifies them as belonging to a different mentality: savage, primitive, underdeveloped, backward, alienated, composed of opinions, customs, authority, prejudice, ignorance, ideology. Narratives are fables, myths, legends, fit only for women and children. At best, attempts are made to throw some rays of light into this obscurantism, to civilize, educate, develop.

This unequal relationship is an intrinsic effect of the rules specific to each game. We all know its symptoms. It is the entire history of cultural imperialism, from the dawn of Western civilization. It is important to recognize its special tenor, which sets it apart from all other forms of imperialism: it is governed by the demand for legitimation.[5]

Lyotard concludes that the epistemologically enlightened postmodernist as opposed to the imperialistically oriented Eurocentric scientist does not seek legitimation, but instead assumes the attitude of the curator of a conceptual museum and 'gaze(s) in wonderment at the variety of discursive species, just as we do at the diversity of plant or animal species.'[6] Need one

⁵ J.-F. Lyotard, *The Postmodern Condition*, 27.   ⁶ Ibid. 26.

add more? Here are all the weapons in the arsenal of the cultural relativist: the assumption that reflexivity of cultures and the drive toward legitimation are foreign, 'western' elements; that the western epistemologist must solidarize with the 'others' by assuming the attitude of a detached and bemused observer, etc.

Whereas for Lyotard the question of cultural relativism is but an aspect of the larger problem of the incommensurability of discourses and language games, Richard Rorty maintains that even the very terms of this debate as between 'universalism' and 'relativism' are outmoded today: 'they are remnants of a vocabulary which we should try to replace'.[7] Rorty sees his own commitment to the values of 'liberalism' and particularly his own endorsement of the crucial distinction between the public and the private in liberalism as reflecting the choice of a certain self-description, and not as defensible in terms of any foundational or essentialist arguments. At times Rorty, like Lyotard, argues that the narratives of our cultures do what they do without any need for further justification: 'we do not need to scratch where it does not itch',[8] at other points, he acknowledges that liberal culture institutionalizes the search for justification in science, ethics, aesthetics, jurisprudence, and politics but refuses to attribute to this fact any gain in rationality. For Rorty the attempt to question and to challenge the values and norms of one's own culture or that of any other in terms that transcend their self-understanding is illusory. 'The importance of this shift is that it makes it impossible to ask the question "Is ours a moral society?" It makes it impossible to think that there is something which stands to my community as my community stands to me, some larger community called "humanity" which has an intrinsic nature.'[9]

This latter claim is clearly false. Not every appeal to a concept of 'humanity' must presuppose an 'essentialist' ontology, a belief in some 'intrinsic nature'. The concept of 'humanity' in most ethical systems of modernity, from Kant to Jean-Paul Sartre, has functioned as a 'regulative' ideal, defining a vision of human solidarity and community and has not been understood as describing a given essence.[10] Perhaps more important though is that Rorty's claim is so empirically inadequate in the face of

---

[7] R. Rorty, *Contingency, Irony and Solidarity* (Cambridge: Cambridge University Press, 1986), 44.

[8] R. Rorty, 'Habermas and Lyotard on Postmodernity', *Praxis International*, 4, 34; see also *Contingency, Irony and Solidarity*, 54.

[9] Ibid., 59.

[10] It may be interesting to recall that Sartre, from his early writings onwards, adopted the Heideggerian concept of Dasein as a being for whom the question of existence is paramount. To think that human beings have an essence would be an act of 'bad faith', an act of abdicating the responsibility for the choices that only one can make for oneself to another being, entity, or principle. In this sense, for Sartre 'existentialism was a humanism', for one chose humanity as a principle of one's actions. See also Jean-Paul Sartre, *Being and Nothingness*, trans. H. E. Barnes (New York: Philosophical Library, 1956), 73 ff.

cultural and political history. Since the Enlightenment and the political articulation of the ideals of universal brotherhood and eventually sisterhood, cultures, movements, nations, and communities have debated, argued about, and clearly felt the imperatives both of allegiance to one's own context and the pull of the moral ideals of humanity and international solidarity. Think of the great debates in Europe about pacifism during the First World War which cut right across the political spectrum. Think of the ideals of international solidarity in the worker's movement. Think of the anti-war movements in the USA during Vietnam. It is the legacy of all modern political revolutions that the idea of a community larger than one's own can at times stand in a closer relation to one than one's homeland. What conceptual and empirical justification is there for forgetting this aspect of the political history of modernity and for claiming that it is impossible to think that 'there is something which stands to my community as my community stands to me'? Obviously, many individuals in different cultures have thought so, and have been moved by belief in a human community which stood at times closer to them than their own community. Rorty could maintain that they were epistemologically deluded in thinking so, but this would require a much more careful engagement with cultural and political history than the vague phrase 'standing to me' suggests. We would need to know much more precisely whether all those who evoked humanity as an ideal and felt greater solidarity with humankind than with their own parish walls, did so because they subscribed to some deluded foundationalist epistemology.

In his continuing references to the 'we' and 'us', to 'them' and 'our' group, Rorty seems to ignore that most of us today are members of more than 'one' community, one linguistic group, one ethnos. Millions of people the world over engage in migrations, whether economic, political, or artistic. Every western nation-state in Europe today is facing the challenge of multi-culturatism and multi-nationalism. In countries like the USA, Canada, New Zealand, and Australia, multi-nationalism, the presence of more than one 'we' community within the limits of the same political constitution is the norm. In fact, the belief that there may be one homeland, one language, and one culture which defines 'really' who we are may itself be part and parcel of the essentialism which Rorty otherwise so eloquently dispenses with. True nations, pure linguistic groups, and unsullied ethnic identities are 'imagined' communities.[11] They never existed historially, but were created through the imagination of nineteenth-century poets, novelists, historians, and, of course, statesmen and ideologues. What compelling reasons has Rorty provided us with to accept this particular 'self-definition'

---

[11] See Benedict Anderson, *Imagined Communities. Reflections on the Origin and Spread of Nationalism* (London: Verso Books, 1983). I am indebted to Lorenzo Simpson's trenchant critique of Rorty in his forthcoming book, *Technology and the Human Conversation: The Domination of Nature and the Domestication of Time*, ch. 7.

of the citizens of western democracies as being the methodologically privileged standpoint from which to pose our questions? Who are 'we'? And what is 'ours'?

Rorty concludes his reflections on cruelty and solidarity with the claim that 'We have to start from where we are . . . What takes the curse off this ethnocentrism is not that the largest such group is "humanity" or "all rational beings"—no one, I have been claiming, can make that identification, but, rather, that it is the ethnocentrism of a "we" ("we liberals") which is dedicated to enlarging itself, to creating an ever larger and more variegated ethnos.'[12] I think where 'we' are today globally is a situation in which every 'we' discovers that it is in part a 'they'; that the lines between 'us' and 'them' are continuously redefined through the global realities of immigration, travel, communication, the world economy, and ecological disasters. Neglecting these material imperatives of world civilization, Rorty continues to pose the problem in terms which would be most appropriate to nineteenth-century travellers like the German scholar Alexander von Humboldt. Indeed through his journeys to the Americas von Humboldt aided, in Rorty's words, 'in the inclusion among "us" of the family in the next cave, then of the tribe across the river, then of the tribal confederation beyond the mountains, then of the unbelievers beyond the seas . . .'[13] The gesture of the ethnographer whose travels expand the limits of our moral imagination such that we can see 'others' as falling under descriptions with which we can identify: this individualist and aestheticizing gesture, which Rorty finds so compelling, hardly yields an outlook which can do justice to the material and symbolic complexities of cross-cultural communication, multiple identities and planetary interdependence in today's global civilization.

In this respect, studies such as the one supplied by Martha Chen which analyse the dilemmas and contradictions of traditional belief structures in certain cultures, can be useful to us philosophically in helping us question certain methodological assumptions about culture and society, which philosophers have taken for granted in recent debates. The first of these is the tendency to treat cultures and value systems as self-consistent, pre-reflexive wholes; the second is a cultural hermeticism which seals off cultures from one another and minimizes the significance of cross-cultural dialogue; the third is a privileging of imaginary senses of unity and oneness—a certain monism of cultures if you wish; the final one is a certain idealism which refuses to consider the implications of the fact that cultures are systems of meaning, value, and interpretation which must also be reproduced over time by individuals under the constraints of a material way of life.

[12] See Benedict Anderson, 198. Note also Rorty's use of the term 'ethnos', when to characterize the identity of a democratic community, the term 'demos' would have been preferable. In a democracy citizens may be members of more than one ethnos or way of life.
[13] R. Rorty, *Contingency, Irony and Solidarity*, 196.

4 FROM THE ETHNOCENTRIC PREDICAMENT TO COMMUNITIES OF CONVERSATION

The charges of cultural hermeticism and monism which I have been expressing against Lyotard's views and some of Rorty's statements, are a sociological variation of arguments recently raised by D. Davidson and W. V. Quine against the radical incommensurability of conceptual frameworks and the radical untranslatability of languages.[14] Radical incommensurability and radical untranslatability are incoherent notions, for in order to be able to identify a form of thought, a language, and we may add a culture, as the complex meaningful human systems of action that they are, we must be in a position at least of recognizing that concepts, words, rituals, and symbols in these other systems have a meaning and reference which we can specify, select, and describe in a manner intelligible to us. But this implies that there cannot be radical incommensurability and untranslatability: if radical incommensurability were the case, we would not even be able to identify certain units of thought in other cultures as being concepts as opposed to (let us say) exclamations; if radical untranslatability were true we could not even recognize the other set of utterances as cohering together in something like a language, a practice that is more or less rule governed and shared in fairly predictable ways by a certain group of humans. Likewise if cultures were so radically divergent, then we would not be in a position to isolate a complex set of human activities with its myths, rituals, and symbols as a meaningful and intelligible whole, such as to describe for example a marriage ceremony, a feast, or a prayer. As Hilary Putnam has pointed out: 'It is a constitutive fact about human experience in a world of different cultures interacting in history while individually undergoing slower or more rapid change that we are, as a matter of universal human experience, able to *do* this; able to interpret one another's beliefs, desires, and utterances so that it all makes some kind of *sense*.' (Emphasis in the text.)[15]

Rorty agrees with this claim and likewise rejects radical incommensurability and untranslatability. In 'Solidarity or Objectivity' he writes: 'Part of the force of Quine's and Davidson's attack on the distinction between the conceptual and the empirical is that the distinction between different cultures does not differ in kind from the distinction between different theories held by members of a single culture. The Tasmanian aborigenes and the British colonists had trouble communicating, but this trouble was different only in extent from the difficulties in communication experienced by

[14] See Davidson, 'On the very idea of a conceptual scheme', in D. Davidson, *Inquiries into Truth and Interpretation* (Oxford: Clarendon Press, 1985), 183–99; W. V. Quine, 'Ontological Relativity', and 'Speaking of Objects', in W. V. Quine, *Ontological Relativity and Other Essays* (New York: Columbia University Press, 1966).

[15] H. Putnam, 'Two Conceptions of Rationality', *Reason, Truth and History* (Cambridge: Cambridge University Press, 1981), 117.

Gladstone and Disraeli . . . The same Quinean arguments which dispose of the positivists' distinction between analytic and synthetic truth dispose of the anthropologists' distinction between the intercultural and the intracultural.'[16] The consequences of this argument are much more radical for Rorty's position than he acknowledges.

If in effect there is no asymmetry between disputations among members of one culture and another; if this is a matter of the degree and extent of divergent belief systems subscribed to by different groups, then Rorty's talk about 'us' versus 'them', about 'our ehtnocentrism' versus 'theirs' is profoundly misleading as well as self-contradictory. The lines between us and them do not necessarily correspond to the lines between members of our culture and those of another. In the case of the Bengali women studied by Martha Chen for example, the relevant us as opposed to them are not the Bengalis versus the Westerners; rather those Bengali women questioning and challenging tradition, development workers and officials from Bangladesh as well as progressive social scientists are on one side of the divide, whereas traditionalists in the various communities, the local authorities and wealthy landowners supporting them are on the other side. The community with which one solidarizes is not ethnically or ethnocentrically defined; communities of solidarity may or may not be ethnically established. There is no necessary overlap between solidarity and ethnocentrism but only a contingent one. It is inconsistent of Rorty, after having admitted that there is no essential asymmetry between intercultural and intracultural disputes, to continue to assert that 'the pragmatist, dominated by the desire for solidarity, can only be criticized for taking his own community too seriously. He can only be criticized for ethnocentrism, not for relativism. To be ethnocentric is to divide the human race into the people to whom one must justify one's beliefs and others. The first group— one's ethnos—comprises those who share enough of one's beliefs to make conversation possible.'[17]

This manner of putting the issue is misleading. The word 'ethnos' since Aristotle refers to those who share a certain way of life and a certain set of values. In our days, this word has also come to designate a certain linguistic and cultural descent. Thus, in the United States today we speak of Italian–Americans, Jewish–Americans, Chinese–Americans, Afro-Americans and others as constituting 'ethnic' groups. Certainly, it would be a moral and political calamity if what Rorty meant was that Italian–Americans needed to justify their views and beliefs about other groups only to other Italian–Americans. This kind of justification of solidarity would only be a philosophical whitewash for all sorts of ethnic and cultural prejudice and racism to run rampant in society. Rorty does not mean this; his political statements

---

[16] R. Rorty, 'Solidarity or Objectivity', in J. Rajchman and C. West (eds.), *Post-Analytic Philosophy* (New York: Columbia University Press, 1985), 9.
[17] Ibid. 13.

make clear that this is not his intention. Why then does he continue to write and speak in ways which, on the one hand, echo older forms of hermetic, and pre-Davidsonian cultural relativism, while on the other hand, rejecting radical cultural relativism and incommensurability? Distinguishing between the general idea of a 'community of conversation' and a culturally specific ethnic community would help sort out some of Rorty's contradictions.

By Rorty's own philosophical admission, all that the pragmatist is warranted to say is that: 'Among human beings there are those who can be actual or potential participants with me in a community of conversation and those who are not and may never be.' This community of conversation has a shifting identity and no fixed boundaries. It is not necessarily coincident with an ethnos, though it may be. What determines who are and who are not members of this community is the topic of the conversation, the task at hand, and the problem being debated. For a true pragmatist, the formation and definition of identity would follow suit upon the identification of a set of shared interests, be these scientific, artistic, cultural, linguistic, economic, or national. We are all participants in different communities of conversation as constituted by the intersecting axes of our different interests, projects, and life situations. A consistent pragmatist could only say that all inquiry, whether scientific or moral, and all justification, whether in aesthetics or jurisprudence, and all demonstrations, whether in banking or in physics, are conversations that can only occur in the presence of others who share enough of my beliefs such as to enable us to communicate with one another. To refer to this community of conversation as an 'ethnos' though, is to revert to the kind of naïve cultural relativism which falsely privileges the homogeneity of cultures and identifies one axis of self-definition and identification, namely the ethnic one, as being philosophically privileged and relevant. This pre-Davidsonian form of cultural relativism is based on a poor man's sociology that flies in the face of the realities of global interdependence, the formation of multiple identities, and the universal interaction of cultures and ways of life.[18]

5 FROM COMMUNITIES OF CONVERSATION TO COMMUNITIES OF INTERDEPENDENCE

In *Ethics and the Limits of Philosophy*, Bernard Williams introduces a distinction between *real* and *notional* confrontations. 'A real confrontation be-

[18] See for example the extremely touching story about the 'Yuqui' Indians of the Amazon rain forest, one of the last groups to have lived in the jungle, and the efforts of Christian missionaries on the one hand and progressive development workers on the other to help this group to maintain some form of identity. The ethical and political implications of these divergent development strategies are spelled out very clearly in the article, 'Accidents of History', by Sandy Tolan and Nancy Postero, *The New York Times Magazine*, 23 February 1992, 38 ff.

tween two divergent outlooks occurs at a given time if there is a group of people for whom each of the outlooks is a real option. A notional confrontation, by contrast, occurs when some people know about two divergent outlooks, but at least one of these outlooks does not present a real option. The idea of a "real option" is largely, but not entirely, a social notion.'[19] Williams adds that: 'A relativist view of a given type of outlook can be understood that for such outlooks it is only in real confrontations that the language of appraisal—good, bad, right, wrong and so on—can be applied to them; in notional confrontations, this kind of appraisal is seen as inappropriate, and no judgments are made.'[20] Williams calls relativism seen in this way *the relativism of distance*. 'The distance that makes confrontation notional, and makes this relativism possible, can lie in various directions. Sometimes it is a matter of what is elsewhere, and the relativism is applied to the exotic. It is naturally applied to the more distant past. It can also be applied to the future . . .'[21]

What is helpful in Williams's distinction between 'real' and 'notional' confrontations is the attempt to modulate the stark terms of the opposition between relativism and universalism. I would like to put the point behind the idea of a 'relativism of distance' in terms of the philosophy of hermeneutics. All understanding, of the past, of a different culture, of a work of art, of another person, begins with a methodological and moral imperative to reconstruct meaning as it appears to them. There can be no such reconstruction of meaning without interpretation; but interpretation always proceeds from the standpoint of beliefs and presuppositions which make sense for us. In this sense all understanding is interpretation.[22] The relativism of distance then can be understood as the view that interpretation need not entail strong evaluation, be it of a moral, political, aesthetic, or religious sort. In notional confrontations we may 'suspend' judgement and seek to understand the world as it appears through the eyes of the other. There is an important and unresolved conceptual issue today as to whether all understanding of the meaning of another must entail strong evalution or whether one can also be in a position to suspend judgement without engaging in strong evaluations.[23] Williams thinks that in the case of notional

[19] Bernard Williams, *Ethics and the Limits of Philosophy* (Cambridge, Mass.: Harvard University Press, 1985) 160.
[20] Ibid. 161.   [21] Ibid. 162.
[22] See Hans-Georg Gadamer, *Truth and Method* (New York: The Seabury Press, 1975); Georgia Wranke, *Gadamer, Hermeneutics, Tradition and Reason* (Cambridge: Polity Press, 1987); David Hoy, *The Critical Circle. Literature, History and Philosophical Hermeneutics* (Berkeley, Calif.: University of California Press, 1978).
[23] Jürgen Habermas has been the defender of the strong view that all understanding involves assuming the participants' point of view, but that to assume this standpoint entails entering into a dialogue with members of another culture and assenting or dissenting from their claims. What is not possible, according to Habermas, is to understand from a standpoint of methodological detachment, from the observer's standpoint alone. Put differently, Habermas argues that questions of meaning and of validity cannot be detached. See J. Habermas, *The Theory of Communicative Action. Reason and the Rationalization of Society*, i. 106 ff.

confrontations as opposed to real ones such suspension of disbelief is appropriate. While I am not ready to argue that all interpretation and understanding need entail strong evaluation, I think it would be wrong to conclude, as Williams does, that even in the case of notional confrontations we must always suspend judgement and belief. To a large extent this will depend on the moral and conceptual distance between where we stand today and those whom we are studying and trying to understand. Some cultural practices may seem so morally abhorrent to us—take the case of widow burning in ancient and even today's modern India, of human sacrifice, of necrophilia, etc.—that we cannot help but take a strongly evaluative attitude toward them. Such strong evaluation need not culminate in the philistinism of cultural self-satisfaction; to understand precisely what is so abhorrent to us, we must engage in an even deeper hermeneutic, in an even more compelling act of interpretation to see the world as it appears to others. It may be impossible to refrain from strong evaluation, but this need not hamper good scholarship and interpretation; in fact it may even be a necessary precondition for it. In reflecting about how to write the history of totalitarianism and particularly of the Holocaust in this century, Hannah Arendt put this matter as follows: 'To describe the concentration camps *sine ira* (without indignation SB) is not to be "objective" but to condone them; and such condoning cannot be changed by a condemnation which the author may feel duty bound to add but which remains unrelated to the description itself.'[24]

One way of putting the disagreement between Lyotard and Rorty on the one hand and universalists like myself on the other is that whereas both Rorty and Lyotard would like to transform all cultural confrontations into notional ones and insist upon the suspension of strong evaluation, I see the suspension of strong evaluation entailing epistemic as well as moral problems which need to be carefully addressed. While many activities of historical, artistic, textual interpretation and understanding cannot but proceed without the suspension of strong evaluation, many more cannot proceed but with its rigorous exercise. Furthermore, the condition of global interdependence in which we find ourselves today has practically transformed all cross-cultural communication and exchange in the present into a real confrontation. Even the very act of attempting to document another way of life on the part of an anthropologist or a film maker, for the sake of a notional confrontation for example, involves a real confrontation between cultures and ways of life.

Williams's insight that the notion of real confrontation is to some extent a social notion is crucial. As a consequence of the world-wide development of means of transportation and communication, in the wake of the emergence of international markets of labour, capital, and finance, with the

---

[24] Hannah Arendt, 'A Reply', *Review of Politics*, 15, 79.

multiplying and increasing effects of local activities on a global scale—take
the case of ecological damage—today the real confrontation of different
cultures has produced not only a community of conversation but also a
community of interdependence. It is not only what we say and think but
also what we eat, burn, produce, and waste that have consequences for
others of whom we may not have the foggiest idea but whose lives may be
affected by our actions. While the relativism of distance expresses an
essential aspect of all understanding and interpretation, the conceptual,
moral, and political condition that we find ourselves in today is not one of
'distance' but one of 'coexistence' and 'interdependence'. Twentieth-cen-
tury developments have diminished the cultural distances of the present. It
is at the level of real confrontations that the most pressing moral issues on
a global scale today arise.

In this context, the articulation of a pluralistically enlightened ethical
universalism on a global scale emerges both as a possibility and as a
necessity. The preceding sections of this essay have clarified some of the
methodological assumptions for embarking upon such a project.

1. The discussion in Part 2 has established that the interpretation of
cultures as hermetic, sealed wholes that are isolated from one another as
well as being internally self-consistent is untenable and reflects what I have
called the 'poor man's sociology'.

2. The discussion in Parts 3 and 4 has shown that this view of cultures
is also refuted by philosophical arguments concerning the impossibility of
radical incommensurability and untranslatability.

3. If all understanding and interpretation of the other(s) must also make
sense to us from where we stand today, then the boundaries of the community of conversation extend as wide as those ever-widening attempts at
understanding, interpreting, and communicating with the other(s).

4. While some would like to claim that these ever-widening attempts can
also be exercised in notional confrontations, and that in such confrontations we can refrain from strong evaluations, I am claiming that
today, in the global situation that we are in, our interactions with others
are largely real and no longer notional. We have become moral contem-
poraries, caught in a net of interdependence, and our contemporaneous
actions will also have tremendous uncontemporaneous consequences. This
global situation creates a new community, a 'community of interdependence'. One of the moral imperatives of the present is to translate the
community of interdependence into a community of conversation across
cultures.

5. If in effect the contemporary global situation is creating real confrontations between cultures, languages, and nations, and if the unintended
results of such real confrontation is to impinge upon the lives of others, then
we have a pragmatic imperative to understand each other, and to enter into
a cross-cultural dialogue.

6. Such a pragmatic imperative bears moral consequences. A community of interdependence becomes a moral community if it resolves to settle those issues of common concern to all via dialogical procedures in which all are participants. This 'all' refers to all of humanity, not because one has to invoke some philosophically essentialist theory of human nature, as Rorty seems to assume, but because the condition of planetary interdependence has created a situation of world-wide reciprocal exchange, influence, and interaction. All dialogue in order to be distinguished from cajoling, propaganda, brain washing, strategic bargaining, and the like presupposes certain normative rules. Minimally formulated, these normative rules entail that we recognize the right to equal participation among conversation partners; the right to suggest topics of conversation, to introduce new points of view, questions, and criticism into the conversation; and the right to challenge the rules of the conversation insofar as these seem to exclude the voice of some and privilege those of others. These rules of conversation can be summed up with the norms of 'universal respect' and 'egalitarian reciprocity'.[25]

7. In the context of cross-cultural, international, and global exchanges, but not only in such cases, these rules are counterfactual guides to action. The limits of universal respect are always tested by differences between us and others; egalitarian reciprocity is likely never to be complete in a world community where states and peoples are at different levels of technological, economic, and military development; not to mention the fact that they are also subject to different social, historical, and cultural structures and constraints, and dispose over widely divergent reasons. What these norms of 'universal respect' and 'egalitarian reciprocity' articulate, however, is a limit for our intuitions: in some deep sense we know that the plight of women like Metha Bai and her condemnation practically to death by an outmoded and irrational *purdah* system is unjust. It is unjust because we recognize her common humanity with us. We recognize this common humanity not because we share some belief in some philosophical concept of essence; but because we can understand her language, her actions, her emotions, her needs, and because we can communicate with her and see the world, more or less, maybe never wholly but adequately enough, as she sees it. Our common humanity is established every day through our innumerable contacts and conversations. We also know that her choice is a tragic one: either to perish or to face the cultural disinheritance of her sons. If we recognize her need and our common humanity, and if we respect her neediness, the relevant moral question becomes: is there any way for us to help her preserve her way of life without forcing her to destroy herself and her

---

[25] For an elaboration of the justification and content of discourse or communicative ethics and for a discussion of where I differ from Jürgen Habermas and Karl-Otto Apel in their formulations, see my *Situating the Self. Gender, Community and Postmodernism in Contemporary Ethics*, esp. Introduction and ch. 1.

human dignity? How can we aid in the material continuity of those symbolic forms of life such that these ways of life can be made more compatible
with universal human respect and dignity?

This is a question that is faced every day in a situation of global interdependence and vast inequalities among peoples in the distribution of economic, technological, scientific, medical, and educational resources. What a
universalist ethics seeks to establish is that in face of the needs and suffering
of others, we have to engage in moral conversation and action; that we
cannot abdicate the responsibility of responsiveness to the other with facile
arguments about cultural relativism. As long as we can understand the
others' language more or less, as long as we can identify the meaning of
their cultures more or less, we need no further proof of their shared
humanity with us; they are partners with us in a communication community. We will discover what separates us as well as what unites us in the
course of this conversation; these differences cannot constitute reasons for
exclusion from the conversation. Ironically, in order to understand
how different the other really is from us, we must first respect that the other
is a human being in some sense like us; we must begin with the attempt
to understand and to converse. The recognition of cultural difference is
predicated upon the recognition of a common humanity.

6 TOWARD THE GLOBAL DIALOGICAL COMMUNITY

The preceding reflections have attempted to outline an argumentative
strategy which leads us from 'ethnocentric liberalism' to the idea of an
infinite community of conversation and to a community of global interdependence. The community of interdependence is a descriptive term which
may acquire normative force. Certainly, no moral imperatives can be derived from descriptive claims no matter how realistic and cogent these may
be. Whence does the moral imperative to treat others with universal respect
and according to egalitarian reciprocity derive? Would not the Rortyian
ironist smile at this point and say 'You see; you cannot overcome the
ethnocentric predicament after all; willy nilly you will have to admit that
these norms are the deep legacy of the Western culture of the Enlightenment.' I think the only honest and sensible response in the face of this
observation is that indeed these norms only make sense against the background of the hermeneutic horizon of modernity; but also to point out that
modernity, although the most significant elements constituting it were first
assembled in the West, is a world-wide process and phenomenon.[26] From

---

[26] Max Weber's reflections still remain indispensable for this task today. See the opening
statements of *The Protestant Ethic and the Spirit of Capitalism*. 'The son of the modern European cultural world (*Kulturwelt*) will examine the problems of universal history, unavoidably
and justifiably, from the perspective of the following question: which chain of circumstances

its very inception, the dynamic of modernity has set world-historical forces into motion which have in turn transformed it into a common human project, and not just a Western one. Once the ideas of universal equality, liberty, and brotherhood—and eventually sisterhood—were formulated through the political revolutions of modernity, there no longer was a historical option of going back to premodern conceptions. What ensued was a dialectic of equality and inequality, freedom and servitude, exclusivity versus solidarity on a global scale. The universalist message of modernity created its own exclusions and its own forms of domination and repression; but to tell this complex tale of how modernist universalism and Western imperialism, racism, sexism, and xenophobia fit together is and will remain an unfinished task. Just imagine how one-sided and inadequate it would be to tell the narrative of political and moral modernization today without including those non-Western struggles, beginning with the anti-imperialist resistances to British, French, and Spanish colonization and extending to Third World national liberation movements. Despite their 'anti-Western' rhetoric, many of these movements were carried out in the name of Western principles of political modernity, like self-determination of the people, nationalism, and some form of democratic rule. Moral philosophy can benefit a great deal from this complex tale. The brief answer to the ethno-centric liberal would be that fundamental aspects of the culture of the West have long become a global reality; the issue is less what 'our' norms are versus 'theirs' but rather the following: what will dominate on a global scale? The principles of instrumental and technological modernization or the universalist egalitarian, democratic moral, and political principles which are also part of the legacy of Western modernity?

The principle of a dialogical global community based on the norms of universal respect and egalitarian reciprocity is certainly not new; its honourable ancestor is Kant's idea of the 'republican constitution', which when conceptualized as a principle of interaction among nations, yields the cosmopolitan point of view.[27] Certainly, Amartya Sen's and Martha Nussbaum's pathbreaking work on developing international principles of

---

has led to the fact that exactly in the West, and in the West alone, cultural phenomena have appeared, which nonetheless—or at least as we like to think—lie in a line of development having universal significance (*Bedeutung*) and validity (*Gültigkeit*)?', in 'Die Protestantische Ethik und der Geist des Kapitalismus', in *Gesammelte Aufsätze zur Religionssozilogie* (Tübingen: Mohr, 1920), 1. I have compared this passage with the English translation rendering of Talcott Parsons, Max Weber, *The Protestant Ethic and the Spirit of Capitalism* (New York: Scribner, 1958), p. 13 but have corrected it. For a further discussion of the implications of this questioning and the legacy of modernity, see my *Critique, Norm and Utopia. A Study of the Foundations of Critical Theory* (New York: Columbia University Press, 1986), 254 ff.

[27] See Immanuel Kant, 'Idea for a Universal History from A Cosmopolitan Point of View', and 'Perpetual Peace', in Lewis White Beck (ed.), *On History*, trans. L. W. Beck, R. E. Anchor, and E. L. Fackenheim (New York: The Bobbs-Merrill Company, 1963), 11–26, 85–135.

distributive justice based on the 'capabilities' approach[28] shows that the Kantian tradition is not the only one on the basis of which one can successfully and cogently take a position on these issues today. Indeed, Martha Nussbaum's reinterpretation of an Aristotelian understanding of the good human life and of human flourishing has yielded a cosmopolitan and universalist perspective, which she calls 'Aristotelian Social Democracy'. This perspective will surely give rise to an increasing exchange and debate in contemporary moral philosophy with more deontological and rights-based approaches. It has not been my purpose in this essay to engage in this debate but rather to clear up some of the meta-ethical and the methodological ground in the exchange with relativism. In conclusion I would like to suggest wherein the main bone of contention between the kind of dialogical universalism of the discourse ethic and a neo-Aristotelian ethic of human capabilities would lie.

Much can be done to reconcile these two positions by showing that some, perhaps many, aspects of what Martha Nussbaum has outlined as the 'thick vague conception of a human being',[29] would be presupposed by conceptions of the autonomous personality, also essential to discourse ethics. They may even constitute the bodily, psychic, and material preconditions of the autonomous moral agent. Yet the difficulty lies elsewhere, in a domain which I would describe as the 'methodology of normative argumentation'. The 'thick vague conception of the human being', Nussbaum tells us, is not 'metaphysical'. Although she does not explicitly use this formulation, it appears to correspond to a Humean formulation of the 'circumstances of justice'.[30] I think though that the step that leads from a formulation of the 'thick vague conception of a human being' to 'the task of politics in relation to the thick, vague conception' is illicit. The thick vague conception of the human being, in Nussbaum's language, defines the boundaries for reasoning about normative matters. These correspond in Rawlsian terms to the preconditions of the 'original position'; in Habermasian terms of a 'discourse ethic', they would define the presuppositions of the 'dialogue situation', or of 'the ideal speech situation'. The norms to which we would like to ascribe moral validity and political legitimacy would have to be ones, however, which moral agents under such conditions would be likely to choose and accept as binding on themselves. Insight into validity is a precondition of validity. This may be another way of expressing Kant's

[28] Cf. Amartya Sen, *Poverty and Famines: An Essay on Entitlement and Deprivation* (Oxford: Clarendon Press, 1981); Amartya Sen, 'The Concept of Development', in H. Chenery and T. N. Srinivasan (eds.), *Handbook of Development Economics*, vol. 1 (Amsterdam: North-Holland, 1988), 9–26; Amartya Sen, 'Justice: Means vs. Freedoms', *Philosophy and Public Affairs* (1990), 11–21; Martha Nussbaum and Amartya Sen (eds.), *The Quality of Life* (Oxford: Clarendon Press, 1993).

[29] Martha Nussbaum, 'Aristotelian Social Democracy', 203–52.

[30] Cf. David Hume, 'Of the Origin of Justice and Property', in *Political Essays*, ed. and Intro. Charles Hendel (New York: The Bobbs-Merrill Company, 1953), 32 ff.

formula that the moral law cannot exist in nature; for it is only through their reasoning capacity that human beings can at all articulate and act according to the principle of treating other human beings as ends and never only as means. The moral law is self-legislated in the sense that only a being endowed with rational comprehension can even understand what it means to act according to such a principle. If rational insight is a fundamental precondition of validity, then one's moral methodology must express this principle through certain procedures. What I find lacking in the Aristotelian account of human capabilities is the space, both in theory and in practice, which allows one's understanding of the 'human condition' in Aristotelian terms to be translated into actively generated moral insight on the part of human actors. By contrast, discourse ethics claims that only those norms and normative institutional arrangements are valid which all those affected would agree to in a situation of practical discourse; likewise for the Rawlsian principles of justice, it is crucial that they would be chosen by the agents in the original position behind the 'veil of ignorance'.

This Kantian principle of *autonomous insight* leads both the Rawlsian theory of justice and the discourse theory of ethics to establish the centrality of the consensual generation of political legitimacy. Although Martha Nussbaum also stresses that 'a human life should be according to practical reason and affiliation',[31] this good for her is one among others and does not occupy either a methodological or institutional priority. Yet, without the articulation of such a condition of autonomy or moral consent generated through rational insight, and without the formulation of institutional provisions as to how this may be attained, what results from Aristotelian social democracy is, in fact, what a lot of Scandinavian societies have ended up with, namely a paternalistic welfare state which guarantees welfare but not necessarily the most extensive democratic freedoms for all.[32] Such welfarism ends up in a non-Aristotelian spot: a disjunction emerges between mere life and the good life, for Aristotle as well, the life of *praxis* in common association and deliberation with others was the humanly highest form of life. As he told us, the Gods need no politics for they are self-sufficient; the beasts do not need it for they do not enjoy language;[33] it is only needy, finite and dependent creatures like ourselves who need politics both to sustain life and also to enjoy the good life—the life primarily of acting and speech in the ethico-political community. When reflecting on a global scale as well; welfare and democracy, the sustenance of life and the pursuit of the good life should not be separated from each other. Aristotelian social democracy would have to be both *social* and *democratic*.

[31] Nussbaum, 'Aristotelian Social Democracy', 227.

[32] For a provocative analysis of this issue also from the standpoint of women and feminism, see Helga Maria Hernes, *Welfare State and Woman Power. Essays in State Feminism* (Oslo: Norwegian University Press, 1987).

[33] Aristotle, *Politics*, in *The Basic Works of Aristotle*, ed. and Intro. Richard McKeon (New York: Random House, 1966), 20th printing, 1253a ff., 1129.

PART III

WOMEN'S EQUALITY:
JUSTICE, LAW, AND REASON

Gender Inequality and Theories of Justice[1]

Amartya Sen

1 PRACTICE AND THEORY

Empirical research in recent years has brought out clearly the extent to which women occupy disadvantaged positions in traditional economic and social arrangements. While gender inequalities can be observed in Europe and North America (and in Japan), nevertheless in some fields women's relative deprivation is much more acute in many parts of the 'Third World'. Indeed, there are extensive inequalities even in morbidity and mortality in substantial parts of Asia and North Africa. Despite the biological advantages that women have in survival compared with men (the ratio of women to men averages around 1.05 or so in Europe and North America, partly due to biological differences in mortality rates), the number of women falls far *short* of men in Asia and North Africa, though not in sub-Saharan Africa. If we took the European and North American ratios as the standard, the total number of 'missing women' in Asia and North Africa would be astonishingly large (more than 50 million in China alone). Even if the sub-Saharan African ratio of females to males is taken as the standard, the number of 'missing women' would be more than 44 million in China, 37 million in India, and a total exceeding 100 million world-wide.[2] While looking at female:male ratios in the population is only one way of examining the relative position of women, this approach does give some insight into the acuteness of the problem of gender inequality in matters of life and death. It also throws some indirect light on the history of inequalities in morbidity and of unequal medical care. Direct observation of these other data confirm the intensity of gender inequality in vitally important fields.[3]

I have begun with a rather stark account of some features of gender inequality. What bearing does a theory of justice have on our understanding and analysis of these dreadfully practical matters? One bearing is obvious enough. In describing some arrangements as 'unjust' we invoke—explicitly or by implication—some conception of justice, and it is necessary at some stage to come to grips with the appropriateness of the respective theories of

[1] A revised version of a paper presented at the WIDER conference on Human Capabilities: Women, Men and Equality, in Helsinki, August 1991. In revising the paper. I have benefited from the comments of David Crocker, Jonathan Glover, Martha Nussbaum, and Ruth-Anna Putnam.
[2] See Sen (1989; 1992*b*). See also Coale (1991); Klasen (1994) for other bases of estimates, and Harriss and Watson (1987) for a general discussion of the underlying issues.
[3] I have tried to discuss the available evidence in Sen (1990*c*); and also in my joint work with Jean Drèze; Drèze and Sen (1989), ch. 4. See also Boserup (1970); Lincoln Chen *et al.* (1981); Kynch and Sen (1983); Sen (1985*b*).

justice to pronounce judgement on these matters. An observation of *inequality* can yield a diagnosis of *injustice* only through some theory (or theories) of justice.

A second context is a bit more complex but no less important. The tolerance of gender inequality is closely related to notions of legitimacy and correctness. In family behaviour, inequalities between women and men (and between girls and boys), are often accepted as 'natural' or 'appropriate' (even though they are typically not explicitly discussed). Sometimes the operational decisions relating to these inequalities (e.g. providing more health care or nutritional attention to boys *vis-à-vis* girls) are undertaken and executed through the agency of women themselves. The perceived justness of such inequalities and the absence of any contrary sense of deep injustice play a major part in the operation and survival of these arrangements.[4] This is not the only field in which the survival of extraordinary inequality is based on making 'allies' out of those who have most to lose from such arrangements. It is, therefore, important to scrutinize the underlying concepts of justice and injustice, and to seek a confrontation between theory and practice.

2 CO-OPERATIVE CONFLICTS

There are many areas of social organization in which all the parties have something to gain from having a workable arrangement, but the gains that are made respectively by different parties differ greatly from one working arrangement to another. There are co-operative elements in these arrangements, but also elements of conflict in the choice of one arrangement rather than another.

This class of problem can be called 'co-operative conflicts'.[5] Such problems have been investigated in the literature of economics and game theory in different ways. For example, what J. F. Nash (1950) calls 'the bargaining problem' is a case of co-operative conflict in which each party has well-defined and well-understood interests which coincide with their objectives.

Sometimes, simplifying assumptions are made that eliminate crucial aspects of co-operative conflicts. One example is the assumption (used powerfully by Gary Becker, 1981) that the 'altruistic' head of the family acts in the joint interest of all, and everybody else in the family has exactly the same rational perception of the family's joint interest, which they all want to maximize in a rational and systematic way. This avoids the problem of

---

[4] Indeed, sometimes even social analysts tend to treat the absence of any perceived sense of unjust inequality as 'proof' that any suggestion of real conflict is mistaken—'an import of foreign ideas into the harmony of traditional rural living'. For a critique of this tradition of interpretation, see Kynch and Sen (1983) and Sen (1990c).

[5] For a characterization and analysis of 'co-operative conflicts', see Sen (1990c). This is an extension of what Nash (1950) called 'the bargaining problem'.

conflict in co-operative conflicts by making everyone pursue the same objectives, as a result of which they have no disharmony of interests, or of objectives. If women (or girls) die in much larger numbers than men (or boys), because of differential medical attention and health care, then this model requires that such differentials are what every member of the family (including the relatively more-stricken women) rationally promote and their consequences are what they jointly seek.

The existence of conflicts is, however, fully acknowledged in game-theoretic discussions of 'the bargaining problem' inside the family (see, for example, Manser and Brown (1980); Lundberg and Pollak (1994)). Different family members are seen to have partly divergent interests. It is taken for granted that every member of the family acts on the basis of promoting his or her rationally perceived individual interests, and there is no ambiguity about this. This has the effect of abstracting from the role of implicit theories of justice and of appropriateness, and instead of Beckerian 'collectivism', we have here thoroughly individualistic perception of interests and choices based on them.

There is an interesting contrast here that is worth a comment. The situation of *real* conflict between different members of the family is well caught by the game-theoretic perspective in a way that the Beckerian formulation does not. On the other hand, the socially influenced *perception* of the absence of conflict between family members may well be closer to Becker's formulation than to the standard game-theoretic one. What is needed is a combination, which acknowledges the possibility of real conflicts of interests (unlike in Becker's framework) coexisting with a socially conditioned perception of harmony (unlike in the standard game-theoretic model). Implicit theories of justice and traditional understandings of what is 'natural' and 'proper' can play a major part in making people with divergent interests feel united around shared perceptions of common objectives. Thus, despite the illumination about conflicts provided by game-theoretic models, they do tend to ignore some of the more important causal influences—related to perceptions of legitimacy—that give stability to extreme inequalities in traditional societies.[6]

Theories of justice are important in bringing out the tension between perceptions of justice and what may be required by the demands of fairness or less partial rational assessment. Practical uses of theories of justice can be particularly important in the long run, since social change is facilitated by a clearer understanding of tensions between what happens and what is acceptable. While such an impact may be indirect, and while the connections between ethical analysis (on the one hand) and social perceptions and

---

[6] In this paper I am concerned specifically with the situation in the 'Third World', but I believe that the problem of gender inequality even in the economically advanced countries of Europe and North America can be better understood by bringing in conceptions of justice and legitimacy as determinants of individual behaviour.

practical politics (on the other) may not be instantaneous, it would be a mistake to ignore the long-run practical importance of a clearer understanding of issues of justice and injustice.

3 THE CLAIMS OF UTILITARIAN JUSTICE

No ethical theory has had as much influence in the modern world as utilitarianism. It has been the dominant mode of moral reasoning over the last two centuries. We can do worse than begin with the question: Why *not* go for the utilitarian theory of justice as the basis of analysis of gender inequality? The fact that utilitarianism had a radical role in providing effective critiques of many traditional inequities (Bentham's own 1789 practical concerns were much inspired by his outrage at what he saw around him) makes it particularly appropriate to look for a positive lead from that quarter.

Unfortunately, utilitarianism provides a rather limited theory of justice for several distinct reasons. First, utilitarianism is ultimately an efficiency-oriented approach, concentrating on promoting the maximum sum total of utilities, no matter how unequally that sum total may be distributed. If equity is central to justice, utilitarianism starts off somewhere at the periphery of it.

It is, of course, possible to use utilitarianism to reject many inequalities, since inequalities are often also thoroughly inefficient. But given the lack of a basic concern with equality in the distribution of advantages, the utilitarian concentration on the promotion of utilities is not particularly oriented towards justice.

Secondly, the efficiency that utilitarianism promotes is, of course, specifically concerned only with the generation of *utilities*. Under different interpretations of utilities variously championed by different utilitarian authors, this amounts to promoting either maximal pleasures, or maximal fulfilment of felt desires, or maximal satisfaction of perceived preferences, or some other achievement in a corresponding mental metric.[7] As was discussed in the last section, one of the features of traditional inequalities is the adaptation of desires and preferences to existing inequalities viewed in terms of perceived legitimacy. This plays havoc with the informational basis of utilitarian reasoning since inequalities in achievements and freedoms (e.g., in morbidities, mortalities, extents of undernourishment, freedom to pur-

---

[7] It is sometimes thought that the 'desire-fulfilment' theory of utility is radically different from a 'mental metric' approach, since it examines the extent of fulfilment of what is desired, and the objects of desire are not themselves mental magnitudes: for this and related arguments see Griffin (1982; 1986). But the utilitarian formula requires interpersonally comparable cardinal utilities, and this demands comparisons of intensities of desires for different objects, by different people. Thus, in effect, the dependence on mental metrics is extensive also in the desire-fulfilment formulation of utilitarian calculus.

sue well-being) get concealed and muffled in the space of conditioned perceptions.

There is, in fact, some empirical evidence that the deprived groups such as oppressed women in deeply unequal societies even fail to acknowledge the facts of higher morbidity or mortality (even though these phenomena have an objective standing that goes beyond the psychological perception of these matters).[8] Basing the assessment of justice on a measuring rod that bends and twists and adapts as much as utilities do, can be formidably problematic. The difficulties are certainly big enough to discourage us from looking for a utilitarian theory of justice as an ethical arbitrator or as a conceptual frame of reference for analysing the problem of gender inequalities.

4 THE RAWLSIAN THEORY OF JUSTICE

Compared to the utilitarian approach the Rawlsian theory of 'justice as fairness' has many decisive advantages. The Rawlsian theory also has merits in terms of scope and reach over more relativist and less universalist approaches that have sometimes been proposed.[9]

The Rawlsian approach avoids the peculiar reliance on selected mental characteristics that utilitarianism recommends. It also provides a foundation based on the idea of fairness that links the demands of justice to a more general mode of reasoning.[10] The use of ideas of fairness, rationality, reasonableness, objectivity, and reflective equilibrium provides Rawls's theory of justice with a depth of political argumentation that is remarkably effective. More substantively, the concern with equity in addition to efficiency as reflected in Rawls's principles of justice puts equity at the centre of disputes about justice in a way that utilitarianism (peripherally concerned, as it is, with equity) fails to do.[11]

[8] On this see Kynch and Sen (1983). It is, of course, a different issue as to how these 'objective' matters relate to human perceptions generally (including those of professional doctors), and I am not addressing here the foundational question of objective–subjective divisions. On that issue, see Hilary Putnam (1987; 1991).

[9] Relativism raises many different types of issues. There are questions of cultural relativism, which are sometimes invoked to dispute criticisms of traditional societies. There is also the question of a separate 'feminist' approach to justice. These is, in that context, the methodological problem as to whether the advantages of men and women in a theory of justice can be judged in the 'same' standards. On these matters and also on their bearing on theories of justice, see Okin (1987; 1989), Nussbaum (1988a; 1988b) and Ruth Anna Putnam (1992).

[10] I am referring particularly to the use of 'the original position' in Rawls (1958; 1971). See also Rawls (1985; 1993). In his later presentations Rawls has integrated the reasoning based on 'the original position' with a constructivist programme inspired by Kant (1785).

[11] Equality is valued in Rawls's first principle (demanding 'equal liberty') as well as the second (of which the Difference Principle particularly brings out the concern with the worse off members of the society). The special concern with liberty, which is a part of the first principle, is also an attractive feature of justice, even though the lexicographic priority that liberty gets over other human concerns can be disputed. On this see Hart (1973).

The Difference Principle of Rawls focuses on primary goods as the basis of assessing individual advantages. Primary goods are things that every rational person is presumed to want, such as income and wealth, basic liberties, freedom of movement and choice of occupation, powers and prerogatives of office and positions of responsibility, and the social bases of self-respect. In this list there is a clear recognition of the importance of a variety of concerns that affect individual well-being and freedom and which are sometimes neglected in narrower analyses (e.g., in the concentration only on incomes in many welfare-economic analyses of inequality).

Despite these advantages there are some real problems in using the Rawlsian theory of justice as fairness for the purpose of analysing gender inequality. In fact, these problems are quite serious in many other contexts as well, and constitute, in my judgement, a general deficiency of the perspective of the Rawlsian theory of justice. Perhaps the most immediate problem relates to Rawls's use of the respective holdings of primary goods as the basis of judging individual advantage. The difficulty arises from the fact that primary goods are the *means* to the freedom to achieve, and cannot be taken as indicators of freedoms themselves.

The gap between freedoms and means to freedoms would not have been of great practical significance if the transformation possibilities of means into actual freedoms were identical for all human beings. Since these transformation possibilities vary greatly from person to person, the judgements of advantage in the space of means to freedom turn out to be quite different from assessments of the extents of freedoms themselves. The source of the problem is the pervasive diversity of human beings which make equality in one space conflict with equality in other spaces.[12] The particular issue of inter-individual variations in converting primary goods into freedoms to achieve fits into a more general problem of divergence between different spaces in which the demands of equity, efficiency, and other principles may be assessed.

One of the features of gender inequality is its association with a biological difference which has to be taken into account in understanding the demands of equity between women and men. To assume that difference away would immediately induce some systematic errors in understanding the correspondence between the space of primary goods and that of freedoms to achieve. For example, with the same income and means to buy food and medicine, a pregnant woman may be at a disadvantage *vis-à-vis* a man of the same age in having the freedom to achieve adequate nutritional well-being. The differential demands imposed by neo-natal care of children also have considerable bearing on what a woman at a particular stage of life can or cannot achieve with the same command over primary goods as a man might have at the corresponding stage in his life. These and other differ-

[12] I have discussed this issue in Sen (1980; 1990*b*; 1992*a*).

ences, in which biological factors are important (though not exclusively so), make the programme of judging equity and justice in the space of primary goods deeply defective, since equal holdings of primary goods can go with very unequal substantive freedoms.

In addition to these differences which relate specifically to biological factors, there are other systematic variations in the freedoms that women can enjoy *vis-à-vis* men with the same supply of primary goods. Social conventions and implicit acceptance of 'natural' roles have a major influence on what people can or cannot do with their lives. Since the sources of these differences may appear to be 'external' to the human beings, it is possible to expect that they can be somehow accounted *in* when constructing a suitable basket (and index) of primary goods. If this could be adequately done, problems arising from these 'external sources' would be accountable *within* Rawlsian calculus.

However, in many circumstances this may not prove to be possible. Some of the social influences appear in most complex forms and may be hard to formalize into some component of primary goods. The sources of pervasive social discouragement are often hard to trace and harder to separate out.

Perhaps more importantly, as was discussed earlier, some of the constraints that are imposed on what women are free or not free to do may closely relate to women's own perceptions of legitimacy and appropriateness. The presence of this influence plays havoc, as was discussed earlier, with the utility-based evaluation of justice. That problem has some bearing on the Rawlsian perspective as well. The behavioural constraints related to perceptions of legitimacy and correctness can strongly affect the relationship between primary goods and the freedoms that can be generated with their use. If women are restrained from using the primary goods within their command for generating appropriate capabilities, this disadvantage would not be observed in the space of primary goods. It is not clear how these constraints, many of which are implicit and socially attitudinal, can be incorporated within the framework of the 'external' category of primary goods.

I would, therefore, argue that despite major advantages in adopting the Rawlsian theory of justice in analysing gender inequality, there are also serious problems, arising particularly from variations in the correspondence between primary goods and freedoms to achieve. These problems are not specific to gender justice, but they apply with particular force in this case.

There is another problem that may be briefly mentioned here. This relates to the domain of applicability of the Rawlsian theory of justice. In the original presentation (Rawls, 1958; 1971), 'justice as fairness' did appear to be a theory with a very wide domain, applicable in many diverse social circumstances, with a universalist outlook. Without formally contradicting anything presented in that earlier version, Rawls's more recent presentations (Rawls, 1985; 1987; 1988*a*; 1988*b*; 1993) have increasingly stressed some special features of Western liberal democracies as preconditions for applying the principles of justice.

Rawls has emphasized that his 'political conception' of justice requires tolerance and acceptance of pluralism. These are certainly attractive features of social organization. If these were parts of the requirement imposed by Rawls's theory, without making it illegitimate to apply other parts of his principles of justice even when these conditions were not entirely met, the domain of his theory would not have been substantially reduced, even though its demands would have been significantly expanded. However, Rawls has sometimes asserted precisely that conditionality—making the requirements take a fairly 'all or nothing' form. This has the immediate effect of making it an illegitimate use of his theory to apply his principles of justice in circumstances where the conditions of tolerance are not met.

In the context of many 'Third World' countries in which the problems of gender inequality are particularly acute, Rawls's requirements of toleration are not at all well met. If, as a result, it becomes right to conclude (as seems to be suggested by Rawls) that his theory cannot be applied in such societies, then there is not a great deal to be said about gender inequality in those circumstances with the aid of 'justice as fairness'.

I personally would argue that Rawls over-restricts the domain of his theory, since it has usefulness beyond these limits.[13] The theory comes into its own in the fuller context of toleration that make Rawls's 'political conception' more extensively realizable, but the important questions of liberty, equity, and efficiency outlined by Rawls have substantial bearings even in those circumstances in which the demands of toleration are not universally accepted.

5 FREEDOMS, CAPABILITIES, AND JUSTICE

I have argued elsewhere in favour of judging individual advantage directly in terms of the freedom to achieve, rather than in terms of primary goods (as in Rawls, 1971), incomes (as in standard welfare-economic discussions), resources (as in Dworkin, 1981), and other proposed spaces. The 'capability perspective' involves concentration on freedoms to achieve in general and the capabilities to function in particular (especially when assessing freedoms to pursue well-being).[14] Individual achievements in living could be seen in terms of human functionings, consisting of various beings and doings, varying from such elementary matters as being adequately nourished,

[13] On related matters see Putnam (1992).
[14] On this see Sen (1980; 1985*a*; 1985*b*; 1993). For an excellent review of discussions relating to this perspective, see Crocker (1991*b*). See also Griffin and Knight (1989), Crocker (1991*a*), and Anand and Ravallion (1993).

avoiding escapable morbidity, etc., to such complex functionings as taking part in the life of the community, achieving self-respect, and so on.

An important part of our freedom to achieve consists of our capability to function. In the functioning space an achievement is an n-tuple of functionings that are realized, whereas a capability set is a collection of such n-tuples of functioning combinations. The capability set of a person represents the alternative combinations of functioning achievements from which the person can choose one combination. It is, thus, a representation of the freedom that a person enjoys in choosing one mode of living or another.[15]

When we want to examine a person's freedom to achieve in a more general context (including the achievement of social objectives), we shall have to go beyond the functioning space into the corresponding representations of broader achievements, e.g., promoting her social objectives such as reforming some feature or another of the society in which she lives. By pointing our attention towards freedoms in general, the capability approach is meant to accept the relevance of freedom over this *broader* space, even though the formal definition of capabilities may not take us beyond human functionings as such.[16]

A number of questions have been raised about the cogency, scope, and applicability of the capability approach to justice. I have dealt with some of the issues elsewhere (Sen, 1992a; 1992) and will not go into them here.[17] There are also interesting issues in the relationship between this approach and the perspective emerging from Aristotelian analysis of capability, virtues, and justice, and these have been illuminatingly discussed by Martha Nussbaum (1988a; 1988b). These issues too I shall not pursue here. Instead I shall try to comment on some particular features of this approach that may be particularly relevant in developing a capability-based theory of justice in general, and can be usefully applied specifically to analyse gender inequality.

I would argue that any theory of justice (1) identifies a space in which inter-personal comparisons are made for judging individual advantages, and (2) specifies a 'combining' procedure that translates the demands of justice to operations on the chosen space. For example, the utilitarian approach identifies the relevant space as that of individual utilities (defined as pleasures, fulfilment of desires, or some other interpretation), and picks the combining formula of simply adding up the individual utilities to arrive

---

[15] On some technical issues in evaluating freedom, see Sen (1990a; 1991a; 1992a). It is important to emphasize that the freedom to choose from alternative actions has to be seen not just in terms of permissible possibilities, but with adequate note of the psychological constraints that may make a person (e.g., a housewife in a traditional family) desist from taking steps that she could, in principle, freely take. On this and related issues, see Laden (1991).

[16] A distinction made between 'agency objectives' in general and 'well-being objectives' in particular is relevant here. The capability to function is closely related to well-being objectives but the approach (of which this outlook is a part) encourages us to look beyond this space when we are concerned with a person's 'agency freedoms' (see Sen, 1985a).

[17] See also Crocker (1991b).

at a sum total that is to be maximised. To take another example, Nozick's (1974) 'entitlement theory' specifies the space as a set of libertarian rights that individuals can have, and uses as a combining formula an equal holding of these rights. Similarly, the Rawlsian approach demands maximal equal liberty for all in the space of some specified liberties (through the 'First Principle') and supplements it by demanding a lexicographic maximin rule in the space of holdings of primary goods (included in the 'Second Principle' in the form of the 'Difference Principle').

It should be obvious that the specification of the space of functionings and capabilities in particular, and of achievements and freedoms in general, does not amount to a theory of justice. It merely identifies the field in which the 'combining' operations have to be defined. The assertiveness of the claim rests on the acceptance of the peculiar relevance of this space in judging individual advantage in formulating a theory of justice.

I have argued elsewhere that a theory of justice must include aggregative considerations as well as distributive ones.[18] It will be a mistake to see the space of functionings and capabilities as being exclusively related to specifications of the demands of equality. In assessing the justice of different distributions of individual capabilities and freedoms, it would be appropriate to be concerned both about aggregative considerations and about the extent of inequality in the distribution pattern.

It is not my purpose here to argue for a particular formula for combining the diverse considerations of equality and efficiency, and I am not about to propose a rival specification to the lexicographic maximin rule used by Rawls, or to the simple summation rule used by the utilitarians. There are good grounds for attaching importance both to overall generation of capabilities (this includes aggregative considerations in general and efficiency considerations in particular) as well as to reducing inequalities in the distribution of capabilities. Within that general agreement various formulae can be found that do not coincide with each other but which can be—and have been—defended in a reasonable way in many presentations. I have not gone beyond outlining a space and some general features of a combining formula, and this obviously falls far short of being a complete theory of justice. Such a complete theory is not what I am seeking, and more importantly for the present purpose, it is not especially needed to analyse gender inequality. The *class* of theories of justice that are consistent with these requirements is adequate for the present purpose.

6 GENDER AND JUSTICE

Earlier in this paper I have tried to outline the connection between common perceptions of legitimacy and appropriateness (shared even by women

---

[18] This is discussed particularly in Sen (1992a).

themselves) in traditional societies and the gender inequalities that are generally accepted in those societies (even by the women themselves). In that context I illustrated the inequalities with some standard indicators of minimal success in living, such as survival rates. This was just one illustration of the kind of variable in terms of which inequalities can be assessed. Being able to survive without premature mortality is, of course, a very basic capability. When a fuller accounting is done, many other capabilities would have obvious relevance, varying from the ability to avoid preventable morbidity, to be well-nourished, to be comfortable and happy, etc., on the one hand, as well as more complex freedoms to achieve, including social goals and objectives, on the other.

This way of judging individual advantage provides an immediate connection between (1) the basis of the class of theories of justice outlined in the previous section, and (2) the empirical realities in terms of which gender inequality can be effectively discussed. The main advantage in being concerned with this space rather than the space of resources, primary goods, incomes, etc., is that the perspective of freedom to achieve tells us a great deal more about the advantages that the persons actually enjoy to pursue their objectives (as opposed to the means they possess that may differentially privilege different people to promote their aims).

It has been suggested by Rawls (1988b), in a critique of my line of reasoning, that comparing people's capabilities would require the use of one universal set of 'comprehensive' objectives shared by all, and that demanding such uniformity would be a mistake. I agree that it would be a mistake to demand such uniformity, but is it really needed?

People do, of course, have different particular aims. Whether at a deep and sophisticated level a shared set of general objectives can be fruitfully assumed is an important question that has been addressed in the Aristotelian perspective by Martha Nussbaum (1988b).[19] But no matter what position we take on that particular question, it is important to recognize that inter-personal comparison of capabilities are not rendered impossible by the absence of an agreed 'comprehensive doctrine'. By looking at 'intersections' between different individual orderings, agreed judgements on capabilities can be made without invoking a single 'comprehensive' doctrine shared by all.[20] There can be incompletenesses in such orderings but that is a problem that applies to the indexing of primary goods as well.[21] The really serious cases of inequities that tend to move us towards agitating for social change would typically be captured by a *variety* of orderings, even when they would disagree with each other in many subtler issues.

The specification of the relevant space opens the way not only for the assessment of inequalities in those terms but also for understanding the

[19] See also Crocker (1991b).
[20] On this see Sen (1970; 1990b; 1992a).
[21] On that problem see Plott (1978); Gibbard (1979); Blair (1988) and Sen (1991b).

demands of efficiency in that context. This is particularly important in understanding gender inequality for two distinct reasons.

First, as was argued earlier, gender relations do involve 'co-operative conflicts'. There are benefits for all through co-operation, but the availability of many different arrangements (yielding different levels of inequality in the generated capabilities) superimpose conflicts on a general background of co-operative gains. To deny the existence of the efficiency problem would be a great mistake, and cannot serve the cause of gender equality in a practical world. Efficiency issues have to be tackled *along with* problems of inequality and injustice.

Secondly, gender inequality is made acceptable to women themselves (along with the more powerful male members of the society at large) by playing up the demands of efficiency in particular social arrangements. The relatively inferior role of women and the shockingly neglected treatment of young girls are implicitly 'justified' by alleged efficiency considerations. The alternative of chaos and gross inefficiency is frequently presented, explicitly or by implication, in discussions on this subject. That line of argument has to be critically scrutinized and challenged.

To meet that general presumption and prejudice, what is needed is a serious analysis of the feasibility of alternative arrangements that can be less iniquitous but no less efficient. To some extent such an analysis can draw on what has already been achieved in other countries. In the light of specific circumstances, more particular analysis of feasibilities may also be needed.[22] The identification of deprivation has to be linked directly to the demands of fair division.

The central issue is to confront the underlying prejudice directly and to outline the need for and scope of reducing inequalities in capabilities without accepting that this must cause great inefficiency. The implicit prejudices call for explicit scrutiny. We have to be clear on the nature of the 'theory' underlying the practice of extreme inequality, and be prepared to outline what justice may minimally demand. The advantage of a theory of justice defined in terms of the capability space is to place the debate where it securely belongs.

BIBLIOGRAPHY

ANAND, S., and RAVALLION, M. (1993). 'Human Development in Poor Countries: On the Role of Private Incomes and Public Services', *Journal of Economic Perspectives*, 7.

---

[22] One of the most important fields of investigation in this context is the role of the freedom to accept remunerative employment on the part of women. On this see Sen (1990c) and Martha Chen (1992).

BECKER, G. S. (1981). *A Treatise on the Family*. Cambridge, Mass.: Harvard University Press.

BLAIR, D. H. (1988). 'The Primary-Goods Indexation Problem in Rawls' *Theory of Justice*', *Theory and Decision*, 24.

BENTHAM, J. (1789). *An Introduction to the Principles of Morals and Legislation*. (London: Payne), republished Oxford: Clarendon Press, 1907.

BOSERUP, E. (1970). *Women's Role in Economic Development*. London: Allen and Unwin.

—— (1990). 'Economic Change and the Roles of Women', in Tinker (1990).

CHEN, L., HUQ, E., and D'SOUZA, S. (1981). 'Sex Bias in the Family Allocation of Food and Healthcare in Rural Bangladesh', *Population and Development Review*, 7.

CHEN, M. (1992). 'A Matter of Survival: Women's Right to Work in India and Bangladesh', in this volume.

COALE, A. J. (1991). 'Excess Female Mortality and the Balance of the Sexes in the Population: An Estimate of the Number of "Missing Females"', *Population and Development Review*, 17.

CROCKER, D. A. (1991*a*). 'Toward Development Ethics', *World Development*, 19.

—— (1991*b*). 'Functioning and Capability: The Foundations of Sen's Development Ethics', IDEA Montclair Workshop, mimeographed, Colorado State University.

DRÈZE, J., and SEN, A. (1989). *Hunger and Public Action*. Oxford: Clarendon Press.

DWORKIN, R. (1981). 'What is Equality? Part 1: Equality of Welfare', and 'What is Equality? Part 2: Equality of Resources', *Philosophy and Public Affairs*, 10.

GIBBARD, A. (1979). 'Disparate Goods and Rawls's Difference Principle: A Social Choice Theoretic Treatment', *Theory and Decision*, 11.

GRIFFIN, J. (1982). 'Modern Utilitarianism', *Revue Internationale de Philosophie*, 36.

—— (1986). *Well-being*. Oxford: Clarendon Press.

GRIFFIN, K., and KNIGHT, J. (eds.) (1989). 'Human Development in the 1980s and Beyond', *Journal of Development Planning*, 19 (special number).

HARRISS, B., and WATSON, E. (1987). 'The Sex Ratio in South Asia', in J. H. Momson and J. Townsend (eds.), *Geography of Gender in the Third World*. London: Butler and Tanner.

HART, H. L. A. (1973). 'Rawls on Liberty and Its Priority', *University of Chicago Law Review*, 40.

KANT, I. (1785). *Fundamental Principles of Metaphysics of Ethics*. English trans. T. K. Abbott. London: Longman, 1907.

KLASEN, S. (1994). 'Missing Women Reconsidered', *World Development*, forthcoming.

KYNCH, J., and SEN, A. K. (1983). 'Indian Women: Well-Being and Survival', *Cambridge Journal of Economics*, 7.

LADEN, T. (1991). 'Freedom, Preference and Objectivity: Women and the Capability Approach,' mimeographed, Harvard University.

LUNDBERG, S., and POLLAK, R. A. (1994). 'Noncooperative Bargaining Models of Marriage', *American Economic Review*, 84.

MANSER, M., and BROWN, M. (1980). 'Marriage and Household Decision Making: A Bargaining Analysis', *International Economic Review*, 21.

NASH, J. F. (1950). 'The Bargaining Problem', *Econometrica*, 18.

NOZICK, R. (1974). *Anarchy, State and Utopia*. Oxford: Blackwell.

NUSSBAUM, M. C. (1988a). 'Nature, Function, and Capability: Aristotle on Political Distribution', *Oxford Studies in Ancient Philosophy*, suppl. vol.

—— (1988b). 'Non-Relative Virtues: An Aristotelian Approach', *Midwest Studies in Philosophy*, 13; revised version in Nussbaum and Sen (1993).

—— and SEN, A. K. (eds.) (1993). *The Quality of Life*. Oxford: Clarendon Press.

OKIN, S. M. (1987). 'Justice and Gender', *Philosophy and Public Affairs*, 16.

—— (1989). *Justice, Gender and Family*. New York: Basic Books.

PLOTT, C. (1978). 'Rawls' Theory of Justice: An Impossibility Result', in H. Gottinger and W. Leinfellner (eds.), *Decision Theory and Social Ethics*. Dordrecht: Reidel.

PUTNAM, H. (1987). *The Many Faces of Realism*. La Salle: Open Court.

—— (1991). 'Objectivity and the Science–Ethics Distinction', in Nussbaum and Sen (1993).

PUTNAM, R. A. (1992). 'Why Not a Feminist Theory of Justice?', in this volume.

RAWLS, J. (1958). 'Justice as Fairness', *Philosophical Review*, 67.

—— (1971). *A Theory of Justice*. Cambridge, Mass.: Harvard University Press.

—— (1985). 'Justice as Fairness: Political not Metaphysical', *Philosophy and Public Affairs*, 14.

—— (1987). 'The Idea of an Overlapping Consensus', *Oxford Journal of Legal Studies*, 7.

—— (1988a). 'Priority of Right and Ideas of the Good', *Philosophy and Public Affairs*, 17.

—— (1988b). 'Reply to Sen', mimeographed, Harvard University.

—— (1993). *Political Liberalism*. New York: Columbia University Press.

—— et al. (1987). *Liberty, Equality and Law*, S. McMurrin, ed. Cambridge, and Salt Lake City: Cambridge University Press, and University of Utah Press.

SEN, A. K. (1970). *Collective Choice and Social Welfare*. San Francisco: Holden-Day. Republished Amsterdam: North-Holland, 1979.

—— (1980). 'Equality of What?', in S. McMurrin (ed.), *Tanner Lectures on Human Values*, i. Cambridge: Cambridge University Press; repr. in Sen, *Choice, Welfare and Measurement*. Oxford, and Cambridge, Mass.: Blackwell, and MIT Press (1982); and in Rawls et al. (1987).

—— (1985a). 'Well-being, Agency and Freedom: The Dewey Lectures 1984', *Journal of Philosophy*, 82.

—— (1985b). *Commodities and Capabilities*. Amsterdam: North-Holland.

—— (1989). 'Women's Survival as a Development Problem', *Bulletin of the American Academy of Arts and Sciences*, 43; shortened version in *The New York Review of Books*, Christmas, 1990.

—— (1990a). 'Welfare, Freedom and Social Choice: A Reply', *Recherches Economiques de Louvain*, 56.

—— (1990b). 'Justice: Means versus Freedoms', *Philosophy and Public Affairs*, 19.

—— (1990c). 'Gender and Cooperative Conflicts', in Tinker (1990).

—— (1991a). 'Welfare, Preference and Freedom', *Journal of Econometrics*, 50.

—— (1991b). 'On Indexing Primary Goods and Capabilities', mimeographed, Harvard University.

—— (1992a). *Inequality Reexamined*. Oxford, and Cambridge, Mass.: Clarendon Press, and Harvard University Press.

—— (1992b). 'Missing Women', *British Medical Journal*, 304.

—— (1993). 'Well-being and Capability', in Nussbaum and Sen (1993).

TINKER, I. (1990). *Persistent Inequalities*. New York: Oxford University Press.

Inequalities Between the Sexes in Different Cultural Contexts

Susan Moller Okin

Theories of justice, confronted with the challenges of feminism, postmodernism, and multiculturalism, are undergoing something of a crisis. How can they be universal, principled, founded on good reasons that all can accept, and yet take account of the many differences among persons and social groups? Feminists have been in the forefront of pointing out that large numbers of persons have typically been excluded from consideration in purportedly universalist theories. And some feminists have then gone on to point out that many feminist theories, while taking account of sexist bias or omission, have neglected racist, heterosexist, class, religious, and other biases. Yet, while to some extent acknowledging this neglect, some of us discern problems with going in the direction of formulating a theory of justice entirely by listening to every individual's or group's concrete point of view and expression of its needs. Is it possible, by taking this route, to come up with any principles at all? Is it a reliable route, given the possibility of 'false consciousness'? Doesn't stressing differences, especially cultural differences, lead to a slide towards relativism? The problem that is being grappled with is an important one. There can no longer be any doubt that many voices were not heard, while most theories of justice were being shaped. But how can all the different voices express themselves, and be heard, and still yield a coherent and workable theory of justice? This question is one to which I shall (eventually) return.

It is a daunting task for a feminist theorist accustomed to writing about justice between the sexes in the context of Western industrialized societies to venture into the subject area of women in different cultural contexts in far poorer countries. The difficulties I faced in writing this paper stemmed partly from an initially inadequate knowledge, which I have done, and am continuing to do, what I can to rectify. But they were also brought about by the current prevalence among feminists of charges of 'essentialism' or, as Ruth Anna Putnam names it in this volume, 'substitutionalism'. It is 'essentialist', some say, to talk about women, the problems of women, and especially the problems of women 'as such'.[1] White, middle- and upper-class feminists, it is alleged, have been insensitive not only to the problems

---

A shorter version of this paper has been published in *Political Theory* 22, February 1994. I am grateful to Elisabeth Hansot and Martha Nussbaum for comments on an earlier draft.

[1] 'Essentialism', employed in the context of feminist theory, seems to have two principal meanings. The other usage refers to the tendency to regard certain characteristics or capacities as 'essentially' female, in the sense that they are unalterable. Used in this second way, essentialism is very close to, if not always identical with, biological determinism.

of women of other races, cultures, and religions, but even to those of women of other classes than their own. 'Gender', therefore, is a problematic category, unless qualified by race, class, ethnicity, religion, and so on (see Childers and hooks, 1990; Harris, 1990; Minow and Spelman, 1990; Spelman, 1988). Those who are often referred to as essentialists, and whom Ruth Anna Putman, adopting the term from Benhabib (1987) but adapting it to her own purpose, calls 'substitutionalist' feminists, allegedly commit the mistake of subsuming all women under the category to which they themselves belong. They 'substitute the experience of white middle and upper class women (mainly professional women) for that of all women' (Putnam, this volume, p. 311).

If this is so—if, when writing about women, privileged women are really talking only about themselves and their own situations, there is little chance that feminists like myself will have anything of note to say about the situations of poor women in poor countries with cultures that may differ considerably from our own. However, I shall argue that the anti-essentialist critique is overblown, overvalued, and largely invalid; and I shall do this in part by drawing on the knowledge I have been acquiring about women whose life circumstances are in many respects different from those of the majority of western women. Thus, in this paper, I shall make a qualified defence of essentialism. Before doing so, however, I wish to acknowledge that at least some of the allegations of anti-essentialists are valid, when applied to some feminist theories. Feminists with such pedigrees as Harriet Taylor, Charlotte Perkins Gilman, Virginia Woolf, Simone de Beauvoir and Betty Friedan all seem to have assumed, for example, in works written from the mid-nineteenth century up to the 1960s, that the women they were liberating would have recourse to servants or (as it is so often euphemistically and impersonally put) 'household help'. With the partial exception of Woolf, who remarks briefly on the difficult lot of maids, they did not pay attention to the 'help', the vast majority of whom were also, of course, women—and, in the US context, usually black women. I think, however, that such problems are far less present in the works of most recent feminists. Few contemporary feminist theorists are neglectful of differences of class and race where these are relevant to their arguments.[2]

---

[2] Sexual orientation is another matter; it is far more difficult to refute claims that lesbian women are neglected in much feminist theory. See Rich, 1980 for one of the most trenchant critiques of earlier feminist theories from this perspective. In the context of this volume, however, the issue of sexual orientation seems less able to be grasped than other issues of difference. As the evidence and argument that follow will indicate, most women in poor countries would seem to have little or no opportunity to live as lesbians. It is therefore impossible to gauge how many might wish to, or how they would wish to do so, if they could. Traditional, including religious, taboos, added to compulsory or virtually compulsory marriage (often at a very young age) and dependency on men, seems likely to make lesbian existence far more impossible, even unthinkable, for many Third World women than it is for Western women. This is, undoubtedly, an oppressive situation, but one that I cannot discuss further here.

But the charges of 'essentialism' and 'substitutionalism' seem to grow ever louder.

What is largely missing from anti-essentialist or anti-substitutionalist writing, however, is the evidence and argument that would be required to show, first that and how the alleged failing is present in a theory. Surely here, as in other cases, it is not unreasonable to place the burden of proof on the critic. To be convincing, she needs to show that and how the alleged 'essentialist's' or 'substitutionalist's' theory omits or burdens (which latter word I take to mean 'rationalizes the disadvantages suffered by') persons other than those few the substitutionalist does take account of (since they are just like him/herself). If one is going to make a case that certain groups or categories of people are excluded from a theory, one needs both to *show* that they are and, if possible, to suggest how their inclusion would affect the theory. We know, for example, that Rawls largely ignored issues of gender in *A Theory of Justice*, not only because he does not mention sex as one of the characteristics that is unknown in the original position, but also because he fails to discuss many distributional issues of enormous concern to women—including the issue of the justice or injustice of the gender-structured family.[3] One of the problems of feminist anti-essentialism, however, is that it tends to substitute the claim 'We're all different' for both argument and evidence. One of the few critiques of feminist essentialism that I think is done with much success at all is put forward in a paper by Angela Harris, where she first shows how ignorance of the specifics of a culture mars a particular feminist analysis of a problem, and then demonstrates how, in

---

[3] Putnam charges John Rawls, in *A Theory of Justice*, with an even more extreme substitutionalism that results from concern only with persons like himself. I, among others, have criticized Rawls for virtually leaving both women and the family out of *A Theory of Justice*, and for assuming a gendered division of labour. However, I think Putnam's statement that 'the single voice which is heard in the original position is . . . the voice of a white upper or middle class adult male who is heterosexual . . . from a Christian background . . . in perfect health and not old' is quite unsubstantiated. Rawls explicitly says that the veil of ignorance is to hide, among other things, one's 'place in society, his class position or social status . . . his fortune in the distribution of natural assets and abilities, his intelligence and strength and the like . . . his conception of the good . . .' How, then, can the voice issuing forth from this position be *so* singular a voice as Putnam claims it is? Given that the parties in the original position are also 'rational' (in the economic sense) and 'mutually disinterested', we must ask why, if they were upper- or middle-class heterosexual, healthy Christians, would they be concerned with the well-being of anyone unlike themselves? Why are considerable portions of Rawls's theory focused on the situation of 'the least advantaged'? How do we explain his concern with such issues as the distributions of primary goods between classes and between the more and the less talented? How, especially, do we explain the derivation of the difference principle? And how do we explain Rawls's concern with the issue of toleration—especially religious toleration and toleration of those whom the majority find hard to tolerate? Surely the preoccupation of his theory with these issues reflects the very purpose for which he invented the veil of ignorance in the first place—so that many different points of view would be considered. As Rawls explains it, the veil exists so as to 'nullify the effects of specific contingencies which put men at odds and tempt them to exploit social and natural circumstances to their own advantage' (Rawls, 1971: 136). This interpretation of Rawls's theory as designed to take differences between persons into account, rather than to ignore them, is developed in Okin, 1989a.

some respects, black women in the USA have had a qualitatively, rather than a simply quantitatively different experience of rape than that of white women (Harris, 1990: 594, 598–601). Even here, though, I think the anti-essentialist critique is only partly convincing. For Harris is as much disturbed by white feminists saying that black women are 'just like us, only moreso' as she is by their marginalizing black women or ignoring them altogether. As I shall argue, what Harris regards as this essentialist 'insult to black women'—that the problems of women of different races and cultures are in many respects 'similar to those of white, western women but moreso'—is exactly the one I reach in this paper, when I apply some of our Western feminist ideas about justice to the situations of poor women in many poor countries.

In 'Why not a Feminist Theory of Justice?' Putnam gives as specific examples of feminist substitutionalism all the chapters of Seyla Benhabib's and Drucilla Cornell's book, *Feminism as Critique*, except the Introduction, and my *Justice, Gender, and the Family*. Before moving on to the central task of this chapter, I should like to respond, briefly, to Putnam's reading of my book. While she acknowledges that I make reference to particular problems of black women, poor women, and single mothers, she objects that 'when Okin discusses the vulnerability of women and their children, she focuses primarily on the situation of white women, and indeed of privileged white women' (Putnam, this volume, p. 313). But this is not so. In a chapter central to the book's argument I show, on the basis of empirical data, that contemporary American families of many different types are typically unjust, and that most women suffer vulnerability from the division of labour within marriage, from the choices they make about training and work in anticipation of gender-structured marriage and, often, from the breakdown of marriage. Any careful reading of it confirms that the chapter—and, indeed, the book as a whole—is decidedly *not* focused on middle- or upper-class housewives or professional women whose husbands or former husbands make a good living, as Putnam suggests.[4] Moreover, when in this

---

[4] The chapter, 'Vulnerability by Marriage', is thirty-five pages long. On all but six pages (two of which are taken up with summarizing a couple of non-feminist theories), I refer to differences amongst US women themselves and/or their socio-economic situations. In the end notes, many more such distinctions are drawn. The differences in personal characteristics of women attended to in the text include race, age, and sexual orientation. In addition to six explicit references to racial differences in the text of the chapter, much that is said about poverty and single female parenting is obviously more likely to apply to women of colour than to white women. The situational differences, also quite frequently referred to, include whether women themselves and/or their husbands or male partners are earning much or little; whether women are single, separated, divorced or married; whether or not they are mothers; whether or not they are single parents; whether they do full-time or part-time wage-work or do not work outside of the home; whether their work is professional work or not; whether they do it voluntarily or out of economic necessity; and so on. The policy recommendations made in the final chapter also confirm that the book is not a work of substitutionalist feminism. So does much of the rest of the book, especially ch. 3, where I criticize Alasdair MacIntyre's and Michael Walzer's communitarian theories on the grounds that the 'traditions' and 'shared

SUSAN MOLLER OKIN

most empirically based chapter of the book I do generalize—as one surely must in writing anything of this type—I usually use phrases such as 'most women', 'wives tend to . . .', 'in many marriages', 'often', 'typically', or 'except in rare cases', when a bald ('essentialist') generalization would be misleading. More often than not, indeed, the *exceptions* are actually those more-privileged women whose point of view Putnam claims I focus on at the expense of those of all other women.

I wish now to put anti-essentialist feminism to what I think is a reasonably tough test. In doing this, I take up the gauntlet that Elizabeth Spelman throws down in the course of the anti-essentialist argument of *Inessential Woman*. She says, referring to the body of recent research about women that has appeared in many fields:

Rather than assuming that women must have something in common as women, these researchers should help look to see whether they do . . . Rather than first finding out what is true of some women as women and then inferring that this is true of all women . . . we have to investigate different women's lives and see what they have in common *other* than being female and being called 'women.' (Spelman, 1988: 137)

Trained as a philosopher, however, she does not seem to consider it appropriate for her to take up this challenge of actually looking at some of the new empirical evidence. Having said the above, she turns directly back to discussing Plato. Trained as a political scientist, I shall attempt to look at some comparative evidence. I'll put some Western feminist ideas about justice and equality to the test by seeing how well these theories—developed in the context of women in well-off, industrialized countries—work when used to analyse the very different situations of some of the world's poorest women, living in poor countries.[5] How well do our accounts and explanations of gender inequality stand up in the face of considerable cultural and socio-economic differences?

1 DIFFERENCES AND SIMILARITIES IN GENDER OPPRESSION: POOR WOMEN IN POOR COUNTRIES

Does the assumption 'that there is a generalizable, identifiable and collectively shared experience of womanhood' (Putnam, this volume, p. 312,

meanings' they defend frequently fail to represent the needs and/or interests of many oppressed groups.

[5] I focus, though by no means exclusively, on my own recent book, for several reasons: because in Putnam's paper, she finds it such a good example of substitutionalist theories that are *not* widely applicable and cannot cope with differences; because it's one of the furthest developed attempts at a feminist theory of justice so far (though Iris Young's *Justice and the Politics of Difference* (Princeton, NJ: Princeton University Press, 1990) develops feminist ideas about justice at least as far, although along the lines of stressing difference); and because I was curious to see whether my analysis (both of theory and society)—developed in the context of the USA—was applicable to the very different situations of poor women in poor countries.

quoting Benhabib and Cornell, 1987: 13) *have* any validity, or is it indeed a substitutionalist myth, rightly challenged by Third World women and their spokesfeminists? Do the theories devised by First World feminists, particularly our critiques of non-feminist theories of justice, have anything to say, in particular, to the poorest women in poor countries, or to those policy-makers with the potential to affect their lives for better or for worse?

I shall address, in turn, four sets of issues that have been addressed both by recent feminist critics of Anglo-American theories of justice, and by those development scholars who have in recent years concerned themselves with the neglect or distortion of the situation of women in the countries they study. First, why and how has the issue of inequality between the sexes been ignored or obscured for so long, and addressed only so recently? Secondly, why is it so important that it be addressed? Thirdly, what do we find, when we subject households or families to standards of justice: when we look at the largely hidden inequalities between the sexes? And finally, what are the policy implications of these findings?

1.1. *Why Attention to Gender is Comparatively New*

In both development studies and theories of justice, the lack until quite recently of attention to gender—and in particular to systematic inequalities between the sexes—seems to be due primarily to two factors. The first is the assumption that the household (usually assumed to be male-headed) is the appropriate unit of analysis. A clear dichotomy between the public (political and economic) and the private (domestic and personal) has been taken for granted, and only the former has been regarded as the appropriate sphere for development studies and theories of justice, respectively, to attend to. In ethical and political theories, the family is often viewed as an inappropriate context for justice, since love, altruism, or shared interests are assumed to hold sway within it. Alternatively, it is sometimes assumed or argued that the family is 'naturally' a realm of hierarchy and even injustice. (For a critique of such views, see Okin, 1989*b*, ch. 2.) Occasional theorists, like Rousseau, have made *both* of these claims. In economics, development and other, households have until recently simply been taken for granted as the appropriate units of analysis, on such questions as interests or the distribution of income and wealth. And sometimes here, too, the claims involve a curious mixture of hierarchy and altruism: the household 'head'—an adult male, if one is present—is presumed to allocate resources optimally for the group as a whole (Sen, 1990*b*: 131, citing Becker, Samuelson, and critics). The public/private dichotomy and the assumption of the male-headed household have many serious implications for women, as well as for children, which will be discussed below (Dasgupta, 1993; Jaquette, 1982: 283; Okin, 1989*b*: 10–14 and 124–33; Olsen, 1983 and 1985; Pateman, 1983; Sen, 1990*b*).

The second factor contributing to the neglect of gender is the simple failure to disaggregate data or arguments by sex. In the development literature, it seems to appear simply in this form (for criticisms of this failure, see e.g. Chen, Huq, and D'Souza, 1981: 68; Jaquette, 1982: 284). In the justice literature, the neglect of women used to be obscured by the purportedly generic use of male pronouns and other referents—'mankind', and so on. Of late, the (rather more insidious) practice that I have called 'false gender neutrality' has appeared. This consists in the facially inclusive use of gender-neutral terms ('he or she', 'persons', and so on), when the point being made is simply invalid or otherwise false if one actually applies it to women. Such superficial, terminological responses to feminist challenges not only strain credulity but sometimes result in nonsense (Okin, 1989b: esp. 10–13, 45). Despite such differences, then, the effect is the same in both literatures; women have not, until recently, been taken into account, so the inequalities between the sexes have been ignored.

The public/domestic dichotomy has serious implications for women, as I shall explain further below. It not only obscures intrahousehold inequalities. It also results in the failure to count a great deal of the work done by women as work, since all that is considered 'work' is what is done, for pay, in the public sphere. All of the work women do in bearing and rearing children, cleaning and maintaining households, caring for the old and the sick, and contributing in various ways to men's work, does not count as work. This is clearly one of those instances in which the situation of poor women in poor countries is not qualitatively *different* from that of most women in rich countries, but rather 'similar but worse'. For even more, in some cases far more, of the work done by women (and often by children, too) in poor countries is rendered invisible, not counted, or subsumed under men's work. The work of subsistence farming, tending to animals, domestic crafts (especially if not for the market), and the often arduous and extremely time-consuming fetching of water and fuel, are all added to the category of unrecognized work of women.[6] Chen notes that women who do all these things 'are listed [by policy-makers] as "housewives",' even though 'their tasks are as critical to the wellbeing of their families and to national production as are the men's.' (Chen, 1983: 220; see also Dasgupta, 1993; Drèze and Sen, 1989: ch. 4; Jaquette, 1982; Sen, 1990b; Waring, 1989).

[6] This is so in spite of the fact that the detailed division of labour between the sexes varies considerably from culture to culture. As Jane Mansbridge has recently written, in a discussion of gratuitous gendering: 'Among the Aleut of North America, for example, only women are allowed to butcher animals. But among the Ingalik of North America, only men are allowed to butcher animals. Among the Suku of Africa, only the women can plant crops and only the men can make baskets. But among the Kaffa of the Circum-Mediterranean, only the men can plant crops and only the women can make baskets. . . .' (Mansbridge, forthcoming) However, the work done by women is less likely to be 'outside' work, or to be paid or valued. Her analysis is derived from data in George P. Murdoch and Caterina Provost, 'Factors in the Division of Labor by Sex: A Cross-Cultural Analysis', *Ethnology*, 12 (1973), 203–25.

1.2. Why Does It Matter?

This may seem like a silly question. Indeed, I hope it will soon be unnecessary, but it isn't, yet. I therefore argue, at the outset of *Justice, Gender, and the Family*, that the omission from theories of justice of gender, and of much of women's lives, is significant for three major reasons. Each of these reasons applies at least as much to the neglect of gender in theories of development. The first is obvious: women matter, and their well-being matters at least as much as that of men. I say 'at least as much' because the well-being of children is so intrinsically bound up with that of women, as I shall explain further below. As has been documented by many feminist scholars and organizations, women in the USA and, to different degrees, women in other industrialized countries are disproportionately represented amongst the poor, the exploited and underpaid, the assaulted, and the powerless. (See, for example, Center for American Women and Politics Fact Sheet, 1989; Estrich, 1987; Okin, 1989*b*: esp. ch. 7; Rhode, 1989 and 1991; Walby, 1986.) As scholars of development have recently been making clear, the multiple inequalities between the sexes in a number of poor countries have not only highly detrimental, but *fatal* consequences for millions of women. Amartya Sen has recently argued that—because of severe sex-based deprivations of various kinds—as many as 100 million fewer women exist in the world today, than might normally be expected on the basis of male/female mortality rates in societies less devaluing of women—not only the Western industrialized world, where women outnumber men quite significantly, but Africa, too, where the numbers are more equal. Compared with the average African sex ratio of 1.02 women to each man, Sen estimates that there are 30 million 'missing' women in India, and 38 million 'missing' in China. These statistics, Sen says, 'form something like the tip of an iceberg much of which is hard to observe' (Sen 1990*b*; see also Dasgupta, 1993; Drèze and Sen, 1989: ch. 4, Drèze and Sen, 1990: Introduction, pp. 11–14; but cf. Harriss, 1990; Wheeler and Abdullah, 1988). So here too we can reasonably say that the neglect of sex as a variable in much of the development literature until recently has obscured 'similar, but *much* worse' injustices than those that have been hidden in Anglo-American theories of justice.

The second reason I have raised (in the US context) for the necessity for feminist critiques of theories of social justice is that equality of opportunity—for women and girls, but also for increasing numbers of boys—is much affected by the failure of theories of justice to address gender inequality. This is in part due to the greater extent of economic distress in female-headed households. In the USA, nearly 25% of children are being raised in single female-headed households, which include three-fifths of all chronically poor households with children. Estimates of the proportion of households throughout the world that are headed by a single female range from one-fifth to one-third, with the percentage much higher in regions with significant male out-migration (Chen, 1983: 221; Folbre, 1992; Jaquette, 1982: 271). Many millions of children of both sexes are directly affected by the higher rate of poverty among such families.[7] Theories of justice or of economic development that fail to pay attention to gender ignore this, too.

In addition, the gendered division of labour has a serious impact on the opportunities of girls and women, compared with those of boys and men, virtually regardless of economic class.[8] The opportunities of females are significantly affected by the structures and practices of gendered family life, particularly by the fact that women are almost invariably primary caretakers, which has much impact on their availability for full-time wage-work, results in their frequently being *over*-worked, and renders them less likely than men to be considered economically valuable. This factor, too, operates 'similarly but moreso' within poor families in many poor countries. There, too, adult women suffer—often more severely—many of the same effects of the division of labour as do women in richer countries. But, in addition, their daughters are likely to be put to work for the household at a very young age, are much less likely to be educated and to attain literacy than sons of the same households and, worst of all—less valued than their brothers—they have less chance of staying alive, because they are more deprived of food or of healthcare (Dasgupta, 1993; Drèze and Sen, 1990: ch. 4; Sen, 1990; Papanek, 1990).

Thirdly, I have argued, following in the footsteps of John Stuart Mill, that the failure to address the issue of justice within households is significant because the family is the first, and arguably the most influential, school of moral development (Mill, 1869: ch. 4; Okin, 1989*b*: esp. 17–23, 185–6). It is the first environment in which we experience how persons treat each other, and in which we have the potential to learn how to be just or unjust. If children see that sex difference is the occasion for obviously differential treatment, they are surely likely to be affected in their personal and moral development. They are likely to learn injustice, by absorbing the messages, if male, that they have some kind of 'natural' enhanced entitlement and, if female, that they are *not* equals, and had better get used to

---

[7] Poverty is both a relative and an absolute term. The poorest households in poor countries are absolutely as well as relatively poor, and can be easily pushed below subsistence by any number of natural, social or personal catastrophes. Poverty in rich countries is more often relative poverty (though there is serious malnutrition currently in the USA, for example, and drug abuse, with all its related ills, including AIDS, is highly correlated with poverty). Relative poverty, though less directly life-threatening, can however be very painful, especially for children living in societies that are not only highly consumer-oriented, but in which many opportunities—for good healthcare, decent education, the development of talents, pursuit of interests, and so on—are seriously limited for those from poor families.

[8] By saying 'virtually regardless of economic class', I am not implying that their opportunities are not also differentially constrained depending on their position in the class structure. What I mean is that numerous constraints of being female in a sexist society are likely to be experienced by women of all classes.

being subordinated if not actually abused. As Hanna Papanek notes, in the context of poor countries: 'Domestic groups in which age and gender difference confer power on some over others are poor environments in which to unlearn the norms of inequality,' and 'given the persistence of gender-based inequalities in power, authority, and access to resources, one must conclude that socialization for gender inequality is by and large very successful' (Papanek, 1990: 163–5, 170). The comparison of most families in rich countries with poor families in poor countries—where distinctions between the sexes often start earlier, and are much more blatant and more harmful to girls—yields, here too, the conclusion that, in the latter case, things are not so much different as 'similar but moreso'. Many Third World families, it seems, are even worse schools of justice, because they are more extreme inculcators of the inequality of the sexes as natural and justified than their developed world equivalents. And thus there is even more need for attention to be paid to gender inequality in these contexts.

1.3. Justice in the Family

What do we find when we compare Anglo-American feminists' findings about justice within households in their societies with recent discoveries about distributions of benefits and burdens in poor households in poor countries? Again, in many respects, the injustices of gender are quite similar.

In both situations, women's access to paid work is constrained, both by discrimination and sex segregation in the workplace and by the assumption that women are 'naturally' responsible for all or most of the unpaid work of the household (Bergmann, 1986; Fuchs, 1988; Gerson, 1985; Okin, 1989b: 147–56; Pateman, 1988: ch. 5; Sanday, 1974; Sen, 1990b: esp. 128–30). In both situations, women typically work longer total hours than men:

Time-use statistics considering all work (paid and unpaid economic activity and unpaid housework) reveal that women spend more of their time working than men in all developed and developing regions except northern America and Australia, where the hours are almost equal. (United Nations Report, 1991: 81 and ch. 6 passim. See also Bergmann, 1986.)

In both situations, vastly more of women's work is not paid, and is not considered 'productive'.[9] Thus there is a wide gap between men's and

[9] See Dasgupta, 1993 on the effect of members' perceived 'usefulness' on the allocation of goods within poor families. Western as well as non-Western studies show us that women's work is already likely to be regarded as less useful—even when it is just as necessary to family well-being. So when women are really made less useful (by convention or lack of employment opportunities), this problem is compounded. Dasgupta questions simple measures of useful- ness, such as paid employment, in the case of girls (1993: 309). Where young poor women aren't entitled to parental assets, and their outside employment opportunities are severely restricted, the only significant 'employment' for them is as child-bearers and housekeepers— so marriage becomes especially valued even though its conditions may be highly oppressive.

women's recorded and perceived economic participation. The *perception* that women's work is of less worth, largely because either unpaid or poorly paid (despite the fact that in most places they do more of it, and it is crucial to the survival of household members) contributes to women's being devalued and having less power both within the family and outside of the household (Blumstein and Schwartz, 1983; Dasgupta, 1993; Drèze and Sen, 1990: ch. 4; Okin, 1989*b*: ch. 7; Sanday, 1974; Sen, 1990*b*). This in turn compounds the likelihood that the division of labour between the sexes will continue, reinforcing women's complete or partial economic dependence upon men.

Thus women often become involved in a downward spiral of socially caused and distinctly asymmetric vulnerability (Okin, 1989*b*: 138; Drèze and Sen, 1989: 56–9).[10] The devaluation of women's work, as well as their lesser physical strength and economic dependence upon men, in turn allows them to be subject to physical, sexual and/or psychological abuse by their husbands or other male partners (Gordon, 1988; United Nations Report, 1991: 19–20; Global Fund for Women Report, 1992). However, in many poor countries, as I have mentioned, this power differential extends beyond the abuse and overwork of women to deprivation in terms of the feeding, healthcare, and education of female children—and even to their being born or not. 'Of 8,000 abortions in Bombay after parents learned the sex of the foetus through amniocentesis, only one would have been a boy' (United Nations Report, 1991; see also Dasgupta, 1993; Drèze and Sen, 1989: ch. 4; Sen, 1990). In both situations, then, women's participation in work outside the household is likely to improve their status within the family. However, this is not necessarily assured. It is striking to compare Bergmann's analysis of the situation of 'drudge wives' in the USA, who work full-time for pay and who also perform virtually all of the household's unpaid labour, with Sanday's finding that, in some Third World contexts, while women who do little of the work that is considered 'productive' have low status, many who do a great deal of it become 'virtual slaves' (Bergmann, 1986: ch. 11; Sanday, 1974: 201).[11]

Thus, though most poor women in poor countries work long hours each day, they are often economically dependent on men. This, too, is 'similar to, but worse than' the situation of many women in richer countries. It results from so much of their work being unpaid work, so much of their paid work being poorly paid work, and, in some cases, from men's laying claim to the wages their wives and daughters earn. Feminist critics since Ester Boserup's pioneering work in 1970 have argued that women's econ-

---

[10] In *Justice, Gender, and the Family*, I referred to this as a cycle, rather than a downward spiral. However, Louise Tilly has recently pointed out to me that the latter term is more accurate, since a cycle ends up where it started, and what I am describing is a deteriorating condition.

[11] There is conflicting evidence on this matter. See, for example, Papanek, 1990: 166–8.

omic dependency on men has been in many cases actually exacerbated by changes that development theory saw only as progressive. All too ready to assume that women were 'housewives' and economic dependants, mainstream theorists did not notice that central elements of 'development', such as technology, geographic mobility, and the conversion from subsistence to market economies were not by any means universally beneficial, but processes that frequently benefited men while cutting women out from their traditional economic and social roles and thrusting them into the modern sector 'where they are discriminated against and exploited, often receiving cash incomes below the subsistence level . . . in turn increas[ing] female dependency' (Jaquette, 1982; see also Boserup, 1970; Tinker, 1990: ch. 1).[12] What was development for men often turned out to be regressive for women.

In both rich and poor countries, women who provide the sole economic support for their families often face particular hardship. Some, but not all, reasons for this are the same. Discrimination against women in access to jobs, pay, retention, and promotion are common to most countries, with obviously deleterious effects on female-supported families. Many such women in both rich and poor countries also suffer from severe 'time-poverty', since they are carrying the double burden of domestic and bread-winning responsibilities. However, as Chen's paper in this volume shows, the situation of some poor women in poor countries is more like that of Western women in the nineteenth century than that of contemporary Western women: even though they have no other means of support, they are actually prohibited (by religious laws or oppressive cultural norms) from engaging in paid labour. For such women, it can indeed be liberating to be helped (as they have in some cases been by outsiders like Chen) to resist the sanctions invoked against them by family elders, neighbours, or powerful social leaders. Though many forms of wage-work, especially those available to women, are hardly 'liberating', except in the most basic sense, women are surely distinctly less free if they are *not* allowed to engage in it, especially if they have no other means of support. Many employed women in Western, industrialized countries still face quite serious disapproval if they are mothers of young children or if the family's need for their wages is not perceived as significant. But at least, except in the most oppressive of families or subcultures, no one *forbids* them to work. By contrast, as Chen's paper and some of her other work make clear, the basic right to be allowed to make a much-needed living for themselves and their children is still one

---

[12] This seems similar to changes in the work and socio-economic status of women in Western Europe in the 16th to 18th centuries. The separation of much of production from the domestic sphere constructed the idea of men as breadwinners (who were therefore thought to need to be paid a wage on which a family could subsist) and the idea that women and children were dependent upon men (and could therefore be paid below-subsistence wages). In fact, many working-class women, then as now, either had no man to depend on, or one who earned insufficient to support a family.

that many women in other cultures are denied (Chen, 1983 and this volume).

Here, then, is a real difference—an oppressive situation that few Western women still face, though the practical obstacles to their being both mothers and wage-workers are still substantial. But to return to similarities: another that I discovered, while comparing some of our Western feminist ideas about justice with studies of the situations of poor women in poor countries, has to do with the dynamics of power within the family. I have applied to contemporary US families Albert Hirschman's theory of the effects of differential exit potentials on power within relationships (Okin, 1989*b*: ch. 7), and much the same point has been made by Barbara Bergmann, Victor Fuchs, and David Heer (Bergmann, 1986; Fuchs, 1988; Heer, 1963).

I have argued that while, unlike some of the social contexts within which Hirschman's theory was developed, marriage usually involves some *mutual* dependence and vulnerability; in crucial respects, gender-structured marriage involves women in a downward spiral of socially caused vulnerability that is not shared by men. As I demonstrate in some detail, the typical division of labour within marriage makes wives far more likely to be exploited both within the marital relationship itself and in the workplace (Okin, 1989*b*: ch. 7). To a great extent, and in innumerable ways, women in our society are *made* vulnerable, economically and socially, by the gendered practices of marriage. They are first set up for vulnerability during their developing years by the socially reinforced expectations that they will be the primary or sole caretakers of children, and that they need to try to attract and retain the economic support of a man, to whose work-life they will be expected to give priority. They are rendered further vulnerable by the actual division of labour within almost all current marriages. They are disadvantaged at work by the fact that wage-work is still largely structured around the assumption that 'workers' have wives at home. They are rendered far more vulnerable by becoming the primary caretakers of children or elderly parents, and their vulnerability peaks if their marriages dissolve and they become single parents. That this is socially and not naturally caused vulnerability—and that it is therefore a matter of injustice—is often overlooked, because of the unfounded assumption that women are inevitably the primary caretakers of the young, the sick, and the old.

Recent research on the differential socio-economic outcomes of divorce for men and women in the USA confirms that their exit options are, in this respect, very disparate. As Lenore Weitzman concludes, from her study of divorce in California:

For most women and children, divorce brings precipitous downward mobility—both economically and socially. The reduction in income brings residential moves and inferior housing, drastically diminished or nonexistent funds for recreation and leisure, and intense pressures due to inadequate time and money. Financial hard-

hips in turn cause social dislocation and a loss of familiar networks for emotional
support and social services, and intensify the psychological stress for women and
children alike.   (Weitzman, 1985)

Weitzman's striking finding, that in the first year after divorce the average
ex-wife's household income (adjusted for need) drops by 73% while the ex-
husband's rises by 42%, has been challenged by some critics as exaggerated. However, dubious assumptions are made by some of these critics, and
other studies conducted in a number of different states confirm the fact that
there is indeed a significant difference in the socio-economic outcome of
divorce for men and women (Bell, 1988; Glendon, 1987; Kay, 1987;
McLindon, 1987; Okin, 1989b: esp. 160–7; Okin, 1991b; Rhode, 1989;
Wishik, 1986. For critics of the 'different outcomes' view, see Duncan and
Hoffmann, 1988). There is little doubt, then, that the typical asymmetric
dependency of wives on husbands affects their potential for satisfactory
exit, and thereby influences the effectiveness of their voice within marriage.
It is highly likely that most wives, aware of their relatively dismal prospects
after divorce, take this into consideration in deciding how firm a stand to
take on, and even whether to raise, important issues that are likely to be
conflictual—including the division of paid and unpaid work within
the family. We simply cannot understand the distribution of power within
the family without taking the differential exit factor into account, and the
notion that marriage is a just relationship involving mutual vulnerability
cannot survive this analysis.

Similar analyses of the dynamics of power within the family have recently
been applied to the situation of women in poor countries by Dasgupta and
Sen (Dasgupta, 1993; Sen, 1990b). Dasgupta uses the exit theory in explaining the 'not-uncommon' desertion by men of their families during
famines: 'The man deserts [his wife] because *his* outside option in these
circumstances emerges higher in his ranking than any feasible allocation
within the household.' (1993: 329) He regards the complex theory he
employs—John Nash's game-theoretic programme, as 'needed if we are to
make any progress in what is a profoundly complex matter, the understanding of household decisions' (1993: 329).[13] But the conclusion he reaches is
very similar to mine: any factor that improves the husband's exit option or
detracts from the wife's exit option thereby gives him additional voice, or
bargaining power, in the relationship. Likewise, anything that improves the
wife's exit option—her acquisition of human or physical capital, for example—will increase her autonomy and place her in a better bargaining
position in the relationship (Dasgupta, 1993: 331–3). Thus when circumstances of severe poverty combine with a lack of paid employment opportunities for women, increasing women's dependency on men, men's power

[13] Sen (1990b) also uses the Nash model, though he does not preclude other ways of
analysing such bargaining situations.

within the family is likely to be greatly enhanced—in many cases legitimized by highly patriarchal cultural norms.

Employed in this context, the theory not only *explains* (much as does my employment of Hirschman's theory) the self-reinforcing nature of women's lack of power within the family. It also points to the *injustice* of a situation in which the assumption that women are responsible for housework and childcare, their disadvantaged position in the paid workforce, and their physical vulnerability to male violence all contribute to giving them little bargaining room when their (or their children's) interests conflict with those of the men they live with, thereby in turn worsening their position relative to that of men.

Sen's application of the Nash model to what he terms 'cooperative conflict' within households in Third World societies adds another interesting dimension to the discussion (Sen, 1990*b*: esp. 134–40). As well as using Nash's model to analyse the effect of the respective 'breakdown positions' (exit potentials) on bargaining power within households, Sen stresses the importance for outcomes, and for the strength of bargaining positions, of the *perceptions* of the involved parties—both the perceptions of their welfare or interests and the perceptions of their respective contributions. Given a highly traditional division of labour, he argues that women's perceptions of their own welfare are likely to be far less distinct from their perceptions of the interests of their families as a whole than are men's,[14] with the result that even less value will be attached to their own personal interests, within the already unequal bargaining situation. To add further to the inequality, because of the sex-based biases about what constitutes productive work, the women's perceived contributions to the household are likely to be considerably less than their actual contributions. Thus Sen concludes that the effects of the differential exit potentials of the two sexes are likely to be further compounded, in traditional families, by these two other factors. And he notes that, much as I have argued in relation to intrahousehold power in industrialized countries, a weak breakdown position can lead to an even weaker one in the future course of a woman's own life, and has repercussions from one generation to the next. On the other hand, strengthening her breakdown position can place a woman in a position to develop it even further (Sen, 1990*b*: 137–8).

The theory connecting exit potential with power within the household, then, whether in its more or its less mathematical form, seems to be at least as applicable to the situations of very poor women in poor countries as it is to relatively well-off women in rich countries.[15] Indeed, one must surely say,

[14] The evidence he cites for this point is from a study of Indian women: V. Das and R. Nicholas (1981), ' "Welfare" and "Well-Being" in South Asian Societies', ACLS-SSRC Joint Committee on South Asia (New York: Social Science Research Council).

[15] As Sen says: 'Some disadvantages of women would apply in both types of situations. For example, frequent pregnancy and persistent child rearing . . . must make the outcome of cooperative conflicts less favorable to women through worse breakdown position and a lower

in this case, too, 'similar, but *much* worse'. The distribution of power within the family is an even more crucial issue in the former situation than the latter. For the stakes are undeniably higher—no less than life or death for more than 100 million women, as has recently been shown (Drèze and Sen, 1990: ch. 4; Sen, 1990*a*).

1.4. Policy Implications

Some of the solutions to all these problems that have been suggested recently by scholars addressing the situation of poor women in poor countries, quite closely resemble solutions that have also been proposed by Western feminists primarily concentrating on their own societies. (By 'solutions to problems' I mean to refer to both what theorists and social scientists need to do, to rectify their analyses, and what policy-makers need to do, to try to solve the social problems themselves.) First, the dichotomization of public and domestic spheres must be strongly challenged, both in theory and in practice. In the context of the industrialized world, feminist theorists have argued that the myriad interconnections between life within the household and life outside of it must be recognized, and that theorists need to develop and advocate, and policy-makers to implement, programmes that will reduce the cycle of vulnerability that presently pursues women from home to work and back home again (Okin, 1989*b*: 124–33 and ch. 8; Olsen, 1983 and 1985; Pateman, 1983 and 1988). Women must be taken seriously as wage-workers, and the workplace, schools, and other relevant institutions restructured so as to recognize the fact that most workers are, at various times in their lives, also parents, and carers for the elderly and the sick. Childcare and other domestic and nurturing work must be regarded as real work, not as the private, 'natural', and politically irrelevant responsibilities of women. Social policies reflecting this need to be mandated. Some examples are childbirth and parental leaves, flexible working hours, subsidized high-quality daycare, properly enforced and adequate child-support payments for single parents.

   The public/private dichotomy needs to be challenged just as much in less developed countries, though some of the policies that are feasible in richer countries are at present economically impracticable in poorer ones. But they are resisted by those in power in both contexts, due to the persistence of beliefs that women's domestic roles and responsibilities are 'natural' and virtually unquestionable. Mary Anderson and Martha Chen, after long experience working to improve the lives of poor women in poor countries,

ability to make a perceived contribution to the economic fortunes of the family. Other disadvantages are much more specific to the nature of the community, for example, greater illiteracy and less higher education of women in most developing—and some developed—countries today, and these too would tend to make the breakdown positions worse for women.' He adds: 'The "perceived interest response" and the "perceived contribution response", can be tremendously more regressive for women in some societies.' (1990*b*: 137)

report that they have 'learned one clear lesson from the dilemmas posed by . . . basic sexism, inherent value conflicts, and cultural blind spots':

That is, when we emphasize women's equality with men, and their 'rights' to an equal share of the benefits of development, we meet continual resistance *both in our own development assistance agencies and amongst the powers that be in the recipient countries* . . . On the other hand, when we avoid value discussions and emphasize that women are economic producers in their roles both inside and outside their households, much of the resistance has faded. When we can demonstrate that development projects which take the gender factor into account are more apt to succeed in meeting their goals than are projects which ignore it, people who are committed to development are less frequently defensive. (Anderson and Chen, 1988)

As Chen writes, in the context of poor rural regions: 'so long as policy-makers make the artificial distinction between the farm and the household, between paid work and unpaid work, between productive and domestic work, women will continue to be overlooked.' (Chen, 1983: 220) Challenging the dichotomy will also point attention to the inequities that occur within households—abuse, food, healthcare. As Papanek argues, 'Given a focus on socialization for inequality, power relations within the household—as a central theme in examining the dynamics of households—deserve special attention.' (Papanek, 1990: 170)

Secondly, it follows from the above that the unit of analysis both for studies and for much policy-making must be the individual, not the (male-headed) household.[16] As feminists in industrialized countries have argued, the simultaneous assumption but neglect of all that goes on within the household obscures a great deal of inequality between the sexes, which traverses the supposed separation between public and private life. Noting that, given the greater political voice of men, public decisions affecting the poor in poor countries are often 'guided by male preferences, not [frequently conflicting] female needs', Dasgupta concludes that:

the maximization of well-being as a model for explaining household behaviour must be rejected. . . . Even though it is often difficult to design and effect it, the target of public policy should be persons, not households. . . . Governments need to be conscious of the household as a resource allocation mechanism. (Dasgupta, 1993: 336)

Given the effect of paid work on women's position and bargaining power within the family—including its greater influence in Third World countries on matters of life or death—it is clear that policy-makers should improve women's employment or self-employment opportunities. In all countries,

---

[16] This point seems to have been first explicitly made in the context of policy by George Bernard Shaw, who argued in 1928 that the state should require all adults to work and should allocate an equal portion of income to each *person*—man, women, and child (*The Intelligent Woman's Guide to Socialism and Capitalism* (1928; reprinted New Brunswick, NJ, 1984)).

the assumption that 'workers' are men (with wives at home) has obscured the need for social structures that make being a parent consistent with being a worker. And, especially since women are even more likely in poor countries than richer ones to be providing the sole or principal support for their households, as Chen points out, they require as much access as men to credit, skills training, labour markets, technologies—and, I would add, equal pay for their work (Chen, 1983: 221). Policies facilitating women's full economic participation and productivity are needed increasingly for the survival of their households, for women's overall socio-economic status, and to enhance their bargaining position within their families. As Drèze and Sen say, 'important policy implications' follow from the 'considerable evidence that greater involvement with outside work and paid employment does tend to go with less anti-female bias in intra-family distribution.' (Drèze and Sen, 1989: 58) Because of the quite pervasive unequal treatment of female children, and its tragic consequences, the need for equal treatment of women by policy-makers is in some countries far more urgent than the need of most women in richer countries—but again, the issue is not so much different as 'similar but moreso'.

Finally, I shall speculate about two different ways of thinking about justice between the sexes in cultures very different from ours. I have tried to show that, for feminists thinking about justice, Rawls's theory, if revised so as to include women, the family, and issues of gender justice, has a great deal to be said for it, and that the veil of ignorance is particularly important (Okin, 1989a, 1989b). If everyone were to speak only from his or her own point of view, it is unclear that we could come up with any principles of justice at all. But the very presence of the veil, which hides from those in the original position any particular knowledge of the personal characteristics or social position they will have in the society for which they are designing principles of justice, forces them to take into account as many voices as possible, and especially to be concerned with those of the least well-off. It enables us to reconcile the requirement that a theory of justice be universalizable with the seemingly conflicting requirement that it take account of the multiple differences among human beings.

In place of what she regards as 'substitutionalist' feminism, Putnam proposes an 'interactive' (some might call it 'dialogic') feminism: 'that we listen to the voices of women of colour and women of a different class, and that we appropriate what we hear' (Putnam, this volume, p. 315).[17] Listening and discussing have much to recommend them; they are fundamental

---

[17] As Joan Tronto has pointed out to me, Putnam's use of the word 'appropriate' is odd in this context, given that she is arguing against a kind of intellectual imperialism on the part of privileged Western feminists, and for the necessity of listening to the voices of women of colour and of different classes. What is the benefit for these women of their speaking if what they say is 'appropriated' by feminist theorists?

to democracy in the best sense of the word. And *sometimes*, when especially oppressed women are heard, their cry for justice is clear—as in the case of the women Chen both studied and helped, who were quite clear that being allowed to leave the domestic sphere in order to earn wages would improve their situations considerably. Other studies of specific groups of Third World women confirm that many who are wage labourers are well aware of the enhanced status they have thereby gained. But some whose caste status or religious rules prohibit them from working outside of their homes are divided within their own minds between accepting the prevailing devalued status of the work they do at home (even if for the market), and experiencing discontent on account of the contradiction they face between female respectability as defined in their culture and their own potential to be more highly valued and less exploited and dependent.[18]

Moreover, in some cases, women actively participate in, and appear to endorse unambivalently, practices that seem to outside critics to be highly oppressive. Must we conclude that what is not perceived as oppressive is not oppressive? Or can we reasonably conclude that we do not always find out what is just by asking persons who seem to be suffering injustices what they want? Oppressed people have often internalized their oppression so well that they *have* no sense of what they are justly entitled to as human beings. This is certainly often the case with gender inequalities, in many different cultural contexts. As Papanek writes: 'The clear perception of disadvantages . . . requires conscious rejection of the social norms and cultural ideal that perpetuate inequalities and the use of different criteria— perhaps from another actual or idealized society—in order to assess inequality as a prelude for action.' (Papanek, 1990: 164–5) And as Sen states: 'There is much evidence in history that acute inequalities often survive precisely by making allies out of the deprived. The underdog comes to accept the legitimacy of the unequal order and becomes an implicit accomplice . . . It can be a serious error to take the absence of protests and questioning of inequality as evidence of the absence of that inequality (or of the nonviability of that question).' (Sen 1990b: 126) People may be seriously deprived yet relatively cheerful—in the 'small mercies' situation, where their lack of discontent is based on the 'unquestioning acceptance of their culture's priorities and evaluations of persons' worth' (Sen, 1990b: 127–8). Thus deprivations sometimes become gagged and muffled. But it would be ethically deeply mistaken to attach a correspondingly small value to the loss of people's well-being because of their using such survival strategies.

Coming to terms with very little is no recipe for social justice. It is,

---

[18] Chen in this volume; Zarina Bhatty, 'Economic Role and Status of Women: A Case Study of Women in the Beedi Industry in Allahabad', ILO Working Paper, Geneva (quoted in Sen, 1990b); Maria Mies, *Lacemakers in Narsapur: Indian Housewives Produce for the World Market* (London: Zed Press, 1982), cf. 173–4 with 157.

I believe, quite justifiable for those not thoroughly imbued with the inegalitarian norms of a culture to come forth as constructive critics of these norms. But critics originating from outside of a culture need not be distant or detached. They are much more likely to come up with helpful and relevant criticism if they find out as much as they can about the culture and the meanings of its practices and differential allocations of resources from its members themselves. Understanding these people's own perceptions of their situations is extremely important. (For a good example of this, see Boddy, 1982.) But the aim of this endeavour, in cases where serious inequalities exist, should not be simply to understand, but rather to do so with a view to politicizing the deprived so that they can begin to ask new questions about their cultural norms, with a view to improving their situation. Given this proviso, then, *committed* outsiders may often be better analysts and critics of social injustice than those who live within the relevant culture. And what they might well do, as part of their constructive criticism, is to try to encourage those within the culture to think about some of its oppressive, or at least questionable, practices from various points of view, including that of the least advantaged. In essence, then, after engaging in dialogue in order to understand the practices as well as possible, they would encourage those within the culture to engage in Rawlsian theorizing—to try to imagine themselves in the original position, not knowing who in the social order they were to be once the veil of ignorance were lifted.

Let us think for a moment about what light this might shed on some of the most cruel or most oppressive institutions and practices that historically or currently have been used to 'brand' women—foot-binding, clitoridectomy and purdah. As Papanek shows, 'well socialized' women in cultures with such practices internalize them as necessary to successful female development. Even though, in the case of the former two practices, these women may retain vivid memories of their own intense pain, they perpetuate the cruelties, inflicting them or at least allowing them to be inflicted on their own daughters (Papanek, 1990; see also Boddy, 1982). Now clearly a theory of human flourishing, such as Nussbaum and Sen have been developing, would have no trouble delegitimizing such practices. But given the choice of a Rawlsian outlook or an 'interactive feminist' one, as defined by Putnam, I'd choose the former any day. For in the latter, speaking from their own standpoint alone, well-socialized members of the oppressed group are all too likely to rationalize the cruelties. The men, who perceive themselves as benefiting from them, speaking from their standpoint alone, are even less likely to object. But behind the veil of ignorance, is it not much more likely that both the oppressors and the oppressed would have second thoughts? What Muslim man is likely to take the chance of spending his life in seclusion and dependency, sweltering in head-to-toe solid black clothing, or being forbidden to earn a living by the rules of purdah? What pre-revolutionary Chinese man would have cast his vote for the breaking of toes and hobbling through life, if he well might be the one with the toes and the crippled life? What man would endorse gross genital mutilation, not knowing *whose* genitals? And the women in these cultures, required to think of such practices from a male as well as a female perspective, might thereby, with a little distance, gain more notion of just how, rather than perfecting femininity, they perpetuate the subordination of women to men.

Martha Nussbaum writes of what happens when outsiders, instead of trying to maintain some critical distance, turn to what amounts to the worship of difference. Citing examples of sophisticated Western scholars who, in their reverence for the integrity of cultures, defend such practices as the isolation of menstruating women, and criticize Western 'intrusions' into other cultures such as the provision of typhoid vaccine, she finds this strange and disturbing phenomenon:

Highly intelligent people, people deeply committed to the good of women and men in developing countries, people who think of themselves as progressive and feminist and anti-racist . . . taking up positions that converge with the positions of reaction, oppression, and sexism. Under the banner of their radically and politically correct 'anti-essentialism' march ancient religious taboos, the luxury of the pampered husband, ill health, ignorance, and death.   (Nussbaum, this volume, p. 66).

As Nussbaum later concludes, 'identification need not ignore concrete local differences: in fact, at its best, it demands a searching analysis of differences, in order that the general good be appropriately realized in the concrete case. But the learning about and from the other is motivated . . . by the conviction that the other is one of us.' As the work of some feminist scholars of development shows, using the concept of gender and refusing to let differences gag us or fragment our analyses does not mean that we should overgeneralize, or try to apply 'standardized' solutions to the problems of women in different circumstances. Chen argues for the value of a situation-by-situation analysis of women's roles and constraints, before plans can be made and programmes designed. And Papanek, too, shows how helping to educate women to awareness of their oppression requires quite deep and specific knowledge of the relevant culture (Chen, 1983 and this volume; Papanek, 1990).

Thus I conclude that gender itself is an extremely important category of analysis, and that we ought not to allow feminist thinking about injustice to be paralysed by differences among women. So long as we are careful, and develop our judgements in the light of empirical evidence, it is possible to generalize about many aspects of inequality between the sexes. From place to place, from class to class, from race to race, and from culture to culture, we find similarities in the specifics of these inequalities, in their causes and effects, although often not in their extent or their severity.

BIBLIOGRAPHY

ANDERSON, MARY, and CHEN, MARTHA (1988). 'Integrating WID or Restructuring Development?', Paper prepared for WID Colloquium on Gender and Development Cooperation.

BELL, ROSALYN B. (1988). 'Alimony and the Financially Dependent Spouse in Montgomery County, Maryland', *Family Law Quarterly*, 22, 3.

BENHABIB, SEYLA (1987). 'The Generalized and the Concrete Other', in Benhabib and Cornell (see below).

—— and CORNELL, DRUCILLA (1987). 'Introduction: Beyond the Politics of Gender', in *Feminism as Critique*. Minneapolis, Minn.: University of Minnesota Press.

BERGMANN, BARBARA R. (1986). *The Economic Emergence of Women*. New York: Basic Books.

BLUMSTEIN, PHILIP, and SCHWARTZ, PEPPER (1983). *American Couples*. New York: Morrow.

BODDY, JANICE (1982). 'Womb as oasis: the symbolic context of Pharaonic circumcision in rural Northern Sudan', *American Ethnologist*, 9, 682–98.

BOSERUP, ESTER (1970/1986). *Women's Role in Economic Development*. London: Allen and Unwin.

Center for American Women and Politics Fact Sheet (1989). *Women in Elective Office*.

CHEN, LINCOLN C., HUQ, EMDADUL, and D'SOUZA, STAN (1981). 'Sex Bias in the Family Allocation of Food and Health Care in Rural Bangadesh', *Population and Development Review*, 7, 55–70.

CHEN, MARTHA ALTER (1983). *A Quiet Revolution: Women in Transition in Rural Bangladesh*. Cambridge, Mass.: Schenkman Publishing Co.

—— (1993). 'A Matter of Survival: Women's Right to Employment in India and Bangladesh', this volume.

CHILDERS, MARY, and HOOKS, BELL (1990). 'A Conversation about Race and Class', in Marianne Hirsch and Evelyn Fox Keller (eds.), *Conflicts in Feminism*. New York: Routledge, Chapman and Hall.

DASGUPTA, PARTHA (1993). *An Inquiry into Well-Being and Destitution*. Oxford: Clarendon Press.

DRÈZE, JEAN, and SEN, AMARTYA (1989). *Hunger and Public Action*. Oxford: Clarendon Press.

—— ——, eds. (1990). *The Political Economy of Hunger*, Vol. I: *Entitlement and Well-Being*. Oxford: Clarendon Press.

DUNCAN SAUL, and HOFFMAN, GREG (1988). 'What *Are* the Economic Consequences of Divorce?', *Demography*, 25, 4.

ESTRICH, SUSAN (1987). *Real Rape*. Cambridge, Mass.: Harvard University Press.

FOLBRE, NANCY (1992). 'Mothers on Their Own: Policy Issues for Developing Countries', Paper prepared for The Population Council: International Center for Research on Women.

FUCHS, VICTOR (1988). *Women's Quest for Economic Equality*. Cambridge, Mass.: Harvard University Press.

GERSON, KATHLEEN (1985). *Hard Choices: How Women Decide About Work, Career, and Motherhood*. Berkeley, Calif.: University of California Press.

GLENDON, MARY ANN (1987). *Abortion and Divorce in Western Law*. Cambridge, Mass.: Harvard University Press.

Global Fund for Women Report (1992). *Ending Violence Against Women: A Resource Guide*. Menlo Park, Calif.

GORDON, LINDA (1988). *Heroes of Their Own Lives*. New York: Viking.

HARRIS, ANGELA P. (1990). 'Race and Essentialism in Feminist Legal Theory', *Stanford Law Review*, 42, 581–616.

HARRISS, BARBARA (1990). 'The Intrafamilial Distribution of Hunger in South Asia', ch. 10 of Drèze and Sen (see above).

HEER, DAVID (1963). 'The Measurement and Bases of Family Power: An Overview', *Marriage and Family Living*, 25, 2.

HOCHSCHILD, ARLIE (1989). *The Second Shift: Working Parents and the Revolution at Home*. New York: Viking.

HOOKS, BELL (1984). *Feminist Theory: From Margin to Center*. Boston: South End Press.

JAQUETTE, JANE S. (1982). 'Women and Modernization Theory: A Decade of Feminist Criticism', *World Politics*, 34, 267–84.

KAY, HERMA HILL (1987). 'Equality and Difference: A Perspective on No-fault Divorce and its Aftermath', *University of Cincinnati Law Review*, 56, 1.

McLINDON, JAMES B. (1987). 'Separate but Unequal: The Economic Disaster of Divorce for Women and Children', *Family Law Quarterly*, 21, 3.

MANSBRIDGE, JANE (1993). 'Feminism and Democratic Community', in *Democratic Community*, ed. John Chapman and Ian Shapiro. New York: New York University Press.

MILL, JOHN STUART (1869), reprinted 1988 (ed. S. Okin). *The Subjection of Women*. Indianapolis, Ind.: Hackett.

MINOW, MARTHA, and SPELMAN, ELIZABETH V. (1990). 'In Context', *Southern California Law Review*, 63, 6, 1597–1652.

OKIN, SUSAN MOLLER (1989a). 'Reason and Feeling in Thinking about Justice', *Ethics*, 99, 2, 229–49.

—— (1989b). *Justice, Gender, and the Family*. New York: Basic Books.

—— (1991). 'Economic Equality After Divorce', *Dissent*, Summer, 383–7.

OLSEN, FRANCES (1983). 'The Family and the Market: A Study of Ideology and Legal Reform', *Harvard Law Review*, 96, 7.

—— (1985). 'The Myth of State Intervention in the Family', *University of Michigan Journal of Law Reform*, 18, 4.

PAPANEK, HANNA (1990). 'To Each Less Than She Needs, From Each More Than She Can Do: Allocations, Entitlements, and Value', in Tinker (see below).

PATEMAN, CAROLE (1983). 'Feminist Critiques of the Public/Private Dichotomy', in *Public and Private in Social Life*, ed. Stanley Benn and Gerald Gaus (London: Croom Helm); also in Pateman, *The Disorder of Women* (Stanford, Calif.: Stanford University Press, 1989).

—— (1988). *The Sexual Contract*. Stanford, Calif.: Stanford University Press.

PUTNAM, RUTH ANNA (1993). 'Why not a Feminist Theory of Justice?', this volume.

RAWLS, JOHN (1971). *A Theory of Justice*. Cambridge, Mass.: Harvard University Press.

RHODE, DEBORAH (1989). *Justice and Gender*. Cambridge, Mass.: Harvard University Press.

—— (1991). 'The "No-Problem" Problem: Feminist Challenges and Cultural Change', *Yale Law Journal*, 100, 6, 1731–93.

RICH, ADRIENNE (1980). 'Compulsory Heterosexuality and Lesbian Existence', *Signs*, 5, 4.

SANDAY, PEGGY R. (1974). 'Female Status in the Public Domain', in Michelle Zimbalist Rosaldo and Louise Lamphere (eds.), *Women, Culture, and Society*. Stanford, Calif.: Stanford University Press.

SEN, AMARTYA (1990*a*). 'More than 100 Million Women Are Missing', *New York Review of Books*, 20 Dec.

—— (1990*b*). 'Gender and Co-operative Conflicts', in Tinker (see below).

SPELMAN, ELIZABETH V. (1988). *Inessential Woman: Problems of Exclusion in Feminist Thought*. Boston: Beacon Press.

TINKER, IRENE, ed. (1990). *Persistent Inequalities: Women and World Development*. New York and Oxford: Oxford University Press.

United Nations Report (1991). *The World's Women: Trends and Statistics, 1970–1990*. New York: United Nations Publication.

WALBY, SYLVIA (1986). *Patriarchy at Work: Patriarchal and Capitalist Relations in Employment*. Minneapolis, Minn.: University of Minnesota Press.

WARING, MARILYN (1989). *If Women Counted: A New Feminist Economics*. San Francisco, Calif.: Harper and Row.

WEITZMAN, LENORE J. (1985). *The Divorce Revolution: The Unexpected Social and Economic Consequences for Women and Children in America*. New York: The Free Press.

WHEELER, E. F., and ABDULLAH, M. (1988). 'Food Allocation within the Family: Response to Fluctuating Food Supply and Food Needs', in I. de Garine and G. A. Harrison, *Coping with Uncertainty in Food Supply*. Oxford: Clarendon Press.

WHITEHEAD, ANN (1990). 'Rural Women and Food Production in Sub-Saharan Africa', ch. 11 of Drèze and Sen (see above).

WISHIK, HEATHER RUTH (1986). 'Economics of Divorce: An Exploratory Study', *Family Law Quarterly*, 20, 1.

Why Not a Feminist Theory of Justice?

Ruth Anna Putnam

Why not a feminist theory of justice? How are we to hear this question? And in what sort of context does this suggestion arise? Is it as if we were in some store, shopping around for a suitable theory of justice, and someone suggested a feminist theory, as in another context someone might suggest a bottle of Pinot Noir? Or is it as if one were choosing a career and someone suggested becoming a philosopher? The latter comes closer to the right sort of tone. Choosing a career is a serious matter, much hangs on it. Choosing a career is a commitment, afterwards one is committed to behave in certain ways and not in others. Similarly choosing a theory of justice, to the realization of which one will then be committed, is a serious matter: it will shape one's subsequent conduct. Again, when one chooses a career one chooses to bring about certain things, to build a career—careers do not lie on shelves, ready-made, waiting to be bought. Similarly, choosing a theory of justice is choosing to bring about certain things; even if the perfect conception of justice already existed, one would have to work out how to apply it to the society in which one happens to live. Just as one's prior conception of a career may be modified as one prepares for and then pursues it, so one's conception of justice may be modified as it is used to combat the injustices one encounters.

One is prompted to seek a theory of justice when one's more or less inarticulate sense of justice is outraged by some feature or features of a society.[1] If the outrageous features include a large number of systematic injustices to women, then one might well suggest seeking a feminist theory of justice. Thus when Drèze and Sen point out that millions of women are 'missing' in South and West Asia, in China, and in North Africa, one is moved to agree with Susan Moller Okin that we confront 'a major "justice crisis" in contemporary society arising from issues of gender' (Drèze and Sen, 1989: 50 ff; Okin, 1989: 7). One may then seek a feminist theory of justice as a basis from which to launch one's protest against the gender injustices that explain these horrific statistics.

Suppose now that Pinot Noir has been suggested, or a career in philosophy, and the response is, 'No, that will never do'. Then one asks, 'Why not?' So, one might ask with a different emphasis, 'Why *not* a feminist

---

[1] I just said that one is prompted to seek a theory of justice because one is outraged by injustices. That suggests that the citizens of a Rawlsian well-ordered society do not seek a theory of justice; one might suppose that they take themselves to have found the perfect theory of justice already. I don't want to be committed to that view. I think of a well-ordered society as a human, worldly society, and any such society can be further improved. As our institutions become more just, we shall, I hope, become more sensitive to injustice.

theory of justice?' if someone were to reject the suggestion that a feminist theory of justice would enable us to deal with some of the glaring injustices of our society that the existing theories neglect. Obviously, a theory of justice which would establish and entrench women as first-class citizens and relegate men to second-class status would be no better than a theory which attempts to justify the oppression of women. What is wanted, as Okin notes correctly, is a humanist theory, a theory which treats all human beings as equal from the moral point of view, or at least all those human beings who are in Seyla Benhabib's phrase 'capable of speech and action' (Benhabib, 1989: 6). So, I shall understand the phrase 'feminist theory of justice' in a weaker sense. A feminist theory of justice focuses attention on those issues of justice which it claims to be (a) of particular concern to women *as women*,[2] and (b) generally ignored by major contemporary theories of justice. Okin's book *Justice, Gender, and the Family* may be regarded as a feminist theory of justice in this sense in spite of the fact that she seeks a humanist theory. Hers is an important voice that we need to hear on our way to a fully human theory of justice.

My present engagement with theories of justice is prompted by Chen's concluding remark (Chen, in this volume, p. 55) that we need a concept of justice that takes seriously the problems of women who must provide for themselves and their children but face enormous traditional barriers to gainful employment. Glover, responding to Chen, wonders whether our saying that these women suffer from injustice is just an expression of our Western bias, whether we can defend that judgement against the objections of communitarians and relativists. He concludes that more needs to be said in defence of moral objectivity (Glover, in this volume).

Chen's and Glover's remarks suggest that we have no adequate theory of justice. Against that, one may be inclined to say that the Rawlsian conception of justice as fairness is the sort of thing Chen seeks and that Rawls's theory provides an adequate account of what makes his conception objective, or at least objective enough for our purposes. What is needed is a basis on which women whose very survival is at stake can stand and demand access to gainful employment as a matter of right, not as a matter of mercy for which they would have to beg. Such a basis would also enable one to justify the intervention of various relief organizations such as BRAC in traditional village life.

Any appeal to Rawls's theory for these purposes must, however, defeat or circumvent two objections. First, as already mentioned, it has been shown, e.g., by Okin, that Rawls's theory fails to take adequate notice of the problems of women; this failure, she argues, is built deeply into the structure of the theory. While I agree with the first part of Okin's claim, I shall oppose her suggestion that women must be represented as women in the

[2] Elizabeth Spelman writes, 'I have come to think even of the phrase "as a woman" as the Trojan horse of feminist ethno-centrism' (Spelman (1988: x)).

Rawlsian original position. Secondly, Sen believes that Rawls, in his more recent writings, has restricted the applicability of his theory to societies that are already democratic in the sense that they practice tolerance of a plurality of conceptions of the good life (Sen, in this volume, pp. 265–6; see also 1989). This condition fails to be met in many of the Third World countries with which we are concerned in this volume. I am inclined to dispute this reading of Rawls's more recent papers; in any case, when we appropriate Rawls's theory for our purposes, we are not obliged to accept his restrictions. Although the priority of liberty is a key feature of Rawls's theory, and although freedom of conscience (read: tolerance for a plurality of conceptions of the good) seems to be the most important of the liberties, one can nevertheless protest against any violation of either principle even while one objects also against violations of these most fundamental requirements of justice.

My strategy will be the following. After laying out abstractly what I take to be major threats to a universalistic theory of justice (Part 1), I shall examine what I take to be the most important, most influential contemporary liberal theory—that due to John Rawls—from a feminist perspective. As I do this, benefiting from the work of leading feminists, I note also that criticisms analogous to those raised by feminists can be raised by a variety of other more or less disadvantaged groups (Part 2), and that since a concrete human being tends to belong to the intersection of various groups, no one who speaks as a member of one of these groups can quite succeed to speak for that concrete person (Part 3). The problem we face is how to preserve the universality of justice while paying heed to the multiplicity of voices of distress (Part 4). I try to find some answers to this problem, first within the framework of Rawls's 'four stage sequence' (Part 5) and then in a more general pragmatist approach (Part 6). Finally, I address Sen's concern that the scope of Rawls's conception of justice is too limited and Glover's worry that extending its scope to Third World countries may be mere Western arrogance. In the end (Part 7) I claim that we need a universalistic theory; it is implicit in my discussion that such a theory will be in some sense 'Rawlsian'.

1 THE ISSUES

Before I begin, and before I become bogged down in more or less specific details, I want to state the underlying philosophical issues in general terms. What I shall call the liberal conception of justice presents itself as universal; it is the Enlightenment successor to the conceptions of justice found in Judaism and its daughter religions, and these too present themselves as universal, as do socialist conceptions. Justice is universal in a double sense. On the one hand, justice grants rights to and imposes obligations on every human being (with appropriate caveats for natural incapacities); on the other hand, it limits the claims that any human being may press in the name of justice. Disagreements about justice tend to be disagreements about these limits. For example, if justice demands adequate nutrition for all, then those in authority have an obligation to enable healthy adults to earn that nutrition for themselves and their children (as well as to provide it to those unable to work). This obligation would not be fully discharged if the government, as in Bangladesh, sets up food-for-work sites but does not allow women to work. On the other hand, if justice does not demand adequate nutrition for all, then upper caste Hindu widows are entirely at the mercy of their male relatives; they cannot demand as a matter of right to be allowed to seek gainful employment outside the homestead.

The notion of justice at issue in this paper is political justice, and in our world that means for the most part justice within national boundaries,[3] it means, for the most part, that we as individuals are obliged to demand that our governments enact just policies and to support such policies when they are enacted. However, given that we live in societies which are far from just, many of us encounter opportunities to rectify to some small extent existing injustices or to refuse to benefit from them. When we act in this way it is justice not charity which we pursue, it is justice not charity which our beneficiaries receive. Their dignity as they demand justice is and remains intact, and justice requires that we acknowledge this. In contrast, one often, not always, begs for charity and receives it humbly or even with shame. However, justice is not confined within national boundaries, both nations and the citizens of different nations may deal with one another justly or unjustly. In particular, when natural disasters cause famines, food aid across national boundaries should not be regarded as charity but as what is owed to those stricken, by their more fortunate neighbours.

This view of the universality of justice has come under attack in recent decades. Because a conception of justice limits the claims that may be pressed, the following objection arises: how can one be bound by a conception of justice, in particular how can one's legitimate claims be limited by such a conception, if one has had no voice in formulating it? In the pursuit of universality, justice speaks with a single voice, but that voice, so the challenge maintains, is the voice of the dominant group in society. It seems inevitable that the resulting conception of justice will be biased, will fail to provide adequate grounds for the claims of the less favoured.[4] This

---

[3] Justice within national boundaries is, however, not confined to citizens. Issues of who is entitled to the full range of rights and obligations of citizenship are among the most fundamental of justice conflicts. Moreover, even non-citizens are able to press some claims in the name of justice.

[4] There is also the reverse challenge, the claim that the voice of justice is the voice of the poor and the powerless, resentment and envy masquerading as moral indignation. I don't accept that characterization of justice although I readily agree that the poor and the powerless are victims of injustice.

challenge may be understood as a challenge to *widen* the scope of justice. Thus when women in India and Bangladesh attempt to break the bounds of occupational purdah, they seek to be included among those who have the right to seek gainful employment outside the home. Similarly, the struggle against apartheid in South Africa seeks to extend various rights and privileges of citizenship to previously excluded groups. Needless to say, I support wholeheartedly these and other attempts to *widen* the scope of justice. However, and this is what I intend to show, in the writings of some feminists, attempts to widen the scope of justice have opened a line of reasoning which threatens to *fragment* justice by emphasizing the diverse particularities of those to whom justice applies.

Because a conception of justice imposes obligations, the view that justice, and in particular a liberal conception of justice, is universal, has been charged with incoherence. How can the view be binding on members of another tradition, especially if that tradition does not recognize the fundamental moral equality of human beings, or if its conception of the person is different from that which is implicit in the liberal conception of justice? I take it that this objection, unlike the earlier one, seeks to *narrow* the scope of the justice; a particular conception of justice is said to cover not all human beings but only those who belong to the tradition in which that conception originates. Thus, this objection, too, if it could be sustained, would result in a fragmentation of justice.

Both attempts to widen and attempts to narrow the scope of justice threaten fragmentation. I shall concentrate for the most part on showing how the former threat develops. I shall then suggest how one can pay attention to the claims of particular groups within our society without sacrificing universality. In conclusion, more briefly, I shall examine relativist and communitarian attempts to narrow the scope of justice.

2 RAWLS THROUGH WOMEN'S EYES

I shall begin by showing how a feminist critique of a liberal conception of justice threatens to undermine the possibility of a universal conception of justice. Although my argument is limited to a liberal conception of justice and to its liberal critics, similar arguments could be presented not only for other interpretations of liberal justice and their critics but for socialist conceptions of justice and their socialist feminist critics as well.

We must begin where we are, that is, in a world in which vast numbers of people live at the edge of starvation and/or under dictatorships of various forms.

We must begin where we are, that is, in a world in which women suffer more than men from economic deprivation and in which women are struggling to overcome the special handicaps that were traditionally imposed upon them.

We must begin where we are (or where, at any rate, this writer is), that is, in a society in which many people have become conscious of the injustices suffered by women, people of colour, the aged, children, the disabled, gays and lesbians, pregnant women, the ill, the poor; the list seems to grow each year. Of course, the categories overlap. Women, for example, are found in all of them, as are members of oppressed racial, ethnic or religious groups. The aged are often ill or disabled, and so on.

We must begin where we are, that is, two decades after the publication of John Rawls's *A Theory of Justice* (1971). One cannot, at least in the English-speaking world, think about justice without taking one's position relative to that work. I take it that the Rawlsian conception of justice as fairness articulates the liberal conception of justice, and that the liberal conception of justice is the dominant conception in post-Enlightenment industrial democracies.

We must begin where we are, that is, in the presence of a mature feminist movement.

We must begin where we are, that is, in a world in which women of colour and lower class women point out that the dominant feminist critique fails to speak to their situation, keeps them as invisible as they have always been.

I shall elaborate on these points by recalling, briefly, Rawls's theory of justice as fairness. As I go along in this exposition, I shall interject objections and concerns, many of these are feminist, all of them are particularist in the sense that they are prompted by injustices suffered by a particular group of people and do not seek to transcend that particular perspective.

I shall follow the interpretation which Rawls has given to his own work in his 1985 article 'Justice as Fairness: Political not Metaphysical'. We must distinguish between the conception of justice, which is embodied in the two, by now, famous principles of justice, and the theory, which clarifies and justifies the principles and explains how they are to be applied to the basic social and political institutions of a society.

The two principles are formulated as follows:

1. Each person has an equal right to a fully adequate scheme of equal basic rights and liberties which scheme is compatible with a similar scheme for all.

2. Social and economic inequalities are to satisfy two conditions: first, they must be attached to offices and positions open to all under conditions of fair equality of opportunity; and second, they must be to the greatest benefit of the least advantaged members of society.   (Rawls, 1985: 227)

Rawls has pointed out, and presumably does not mean to rescind this, that realization of the second part of the second principle must be consistent with a 'just savings principle', a restriction which becomes increasingly relevant to practical political and economic decisions as we become more and more aware of ecological issues (Rawls, 1971: 292).

Justice as fairness is offered 'as a political conception of justice for a democratic society, it tries to draw solely upon basic intuitive ideas that are imbedded in the political institutions of a constitutional democratic regime and the public traditions of their interpretation' (Rawls, 1985: 225). The most basic of these ideas is that of 'society as a fair system of cooperation between free and equal persons' (ibid.: 231), where 'a person is someone who can be a citizen, that is, a fully cooperating member of society over a complete life' (ibid.: 233). While this does not rule out occasional illness or accidents, for which provisions must be made, Rawls adds rather startlingly 'for our purposes here I leave aside permanent physical disabilities or mental disorders so severe as to prevent persons from being normal and *fully* cooperating members of society in the usual sense' (ibid.: 234; my italics). This is both disturbing and puzzling. A person was defined as someone capable of being a fully co-operating member of society; are we then to conclude that a permanently disabled human being is not a person, or at any rate not a citizen? If not, how fully co-operating must one be before one will be regarded as a citizen? Surely one wants to remember here that the extent to which a disabled person can participate in political and economic life depends not only on the nature of the disability but on the provisions made by the society to enable handicapped people to participate in public life. If handicapped people are not citizens before such provisions are made, how will they make their voices heard? And if they are not regarded as persons, who will even speak for them? It will not do to answer that we have spokespersons even for non-humans, e.g., for whales, for the claims made on behalf of whales are not justice claims while those made by and for handicapped people are. Of course, the text of *A Theory of Justice*, especially the interpretation of equal opportunity in the light of the difference principle, has always seemed to me to support the kind of efforts that have recently culminated in passage of the Americans with Disabilities Act (see Rawls, 1971: 17). Perhaps we are to read these discussions as a reminder that a just society attempts to enable all its citizens to participate in the 'skillful and devoted exercise of social duties [lest they] be deprived of one of the main forms of human good' (ibid.: 84).

Unfortunately, the second point in Rawls's more explicit account of what is meant by the claim that citizens of a democratic society regard themselves as free persons, increases one's disquiet. To say that citizens of a democratic society consider themselves as free is to say that they 'regard themselves as self-originating sources of valid claims' (Rawls, 1985: 242). What does this rather puzzling statement mean? It seems to mean that people recognize moral rights and duties that are not rooted in the political conception of justice. In other words, our (various) moral conceptions in so far as they are compatible with the requirements of political justice give rise to moral claims and obligations. Rawls contrasts this view of ourselves and each other as free and equal persons with that prevailing in a slave-holding society. In such a society, 'slaves are human beings who are not counted as sources of claims . . . they are not publicly recognized as persons at all. Thus, the contrast with a political conception which allows slavery makes clear why conceiving of *citizens* as free persons in virtue of their moral powers and their having a conception of the good, goes with a particular political conception of the person' (Rawls, 1985: 243; emphasis mine). This will not do. The framers of the US Constitution would have agreed wholeheartedly with Rawls that citizens are free persons in the sense explained, but they would also have maintained that only white men of a certain social standing are citizens. All other human beings (men and women of African descent, white women, men without property), they would have claimed, fail to have the moral powers to the requisite degree or lack other capacities necessary to be fully co-operating members of society. In other words, the egalitarian tendencies of justice as fairness are undermined by Rawls's use of the word 'citizen'. Monarchies, to be sure, have no citizens, they have subjects. But in many historical societies, including our own in the not too distant past, a notion of citizenship limited to *some* human beings has prevailed. These citizens conceived of themselves and each other as free and equal persons, they may even have claimed to live under a democratic regime; that was scant comfort to those who were completely or partially excluded from the rights of citizenship.

Obviously, Rawls means to say something quite different. Justice as fairness is based on the assumption of universal citizenship in a modern democracy. Only when all women and all men of whatever colour or economic status are considered to be free and equal persons does it even make sense to say, as he does in *A Theory of Justice*, that inequalities based on sex, race or other fixed natural characteristics are justified only if they are to the advantage of the less favoured, and that this is in fact 'seldom, if ever' the case (Rawls, 1971: 99). How then can we explain this careless and potentially dangerous (to anyone who is not a white middle or upper class male) substitution of the word 'citizen' for the word 'human being'? Of course, those who have always enjoyed citizen status in so-called democratic societies might well fail to remember that for most of our history neither 'human being' nor 'human being capable of speech and action' have been co-extensive with 'citizen'.

Let us complete Rawls's account of the respects in which citizens regard themselves as free persons. 'Citizens are free,' we are told, 'in that they conceive of themselves and of one another as having the moral power to have a conception of the good' (Rawls, 1985: 240) and 'as capable of taking responsibility for their ends' (ibid.: 243). Here it is worth noting that one's conception of the good will include 'a view of our relation to the world—

religious, philosophical, or moral—by reference to which the value and significance of our ends and attachments are understood' (ibid.: 234). In a democratic society citizens may change their conception of the good in these as well as in other respects without loss of any basic political or economic rights. Now it is, of course, true that over the course of the last 300 years religious toleration over a wider and wider range of faiths, and the lack of any faith, have become a common feature of democratic societies. But we must remember that toleration has grown slowly, and that a certain amount of religious and moral intolerance and even outright oppression still plays a role in our public life. One welcomes, therefore, the fact that Rawls notes that meaningful freedom of conscience requires not merely permission to worship as one pleases, if one pleases, but absence of political or economic inequalities based solely on a difference in faith (and I would add: sexual preference). One wonders, however, why Rawls devotes several sections in *A Theory of Justice* to liberty of conscience and toleration, but only one paragraph to problems of sexism and racism. To be sure, in that paragraph he points out that 'from the standpoint of persons similarly situated in an initial situation which is fair, the principles of explicit racist doctrines are not only unjust. They are irrational' (Rawls, 1971: 149). It is clear that he would say the same about sexist doctrines. Unfortunately, the irrationality of racism and sexism is far from obvious to many persons, including many Americans. Why does he not devote more space to these urgent matters? Rawls might respond by saying that further arguments for racial and sexual political and socio-economic equality are implicit in the general argument for the two principles. He may add that he chose to argue explicitly for freedom of conscience because (a) he wished to give one sustained argument under the rubric of the first principle, and (b) he chose this particular topic because freedom of conscience is built into the historical foundations of the liberal conception of justice, while opposition to the exclusion from political life of non-white males and all women is a more recent development. But is that not all the more reason to develop the liberal argument against racism and sexism? Finally, Rawls might say that the argument against racism and sexism belongs to partial compliance theory, but so does his own argument concerning conscientious objection. To be sure, conscientious objection was a burning issue during the years just prior to the publication of *A Theory of Justice*, but so were a host of issues related to overcoming the vestiges of slavery and issues raised by feminists. Once again one cannot fail to notice that in a country which does not draft women, conscientious objection to service in the armed forces is a particularly male issue (see also Okin, 1989: 95–6).

A person's conception of the good includes various attachments and loyalties to persons and groups of persons, and justice requires that one may change one's conception of the good within the limits of justice without suffering political or economic sanctions. Unfortunately, divorce (surely a change of attachment, hence a change in one's conception of the good) has often economically disastrous consequences for women and their children. Because women tend to earn less than men, because women tend to be the parent whose career is 'put on hold' while the children are young, and because of current divorce legislation, the economic situation of women tends to deteriorate drastically after divorce (Okin, 1989: ch. 7). Feminists note that Rawls and other major theories of justice fail to pay attention to this problem. Once again one cannot help being aware of the fact that one hears a male voice.

3 SUBSTITUTIONALISM

The aim of *A Theory of Justice* was to develop and justify a conception of political justice which would specify fair terms of social co-operation for free and equal persons. To do so, Rawls introduced the idea of the 'original position', i.e., of 'a point of view, removed from and not distorted by the particular features and circumstances of the all-encompassing background framework, from which a fair agreement between free and equal persons can be reached' (Rawls, 1985: 235). As is well known, the parties in the original position, whose task it is to agree on principles of justice, were to be behind a veil of ignorance, they were to be ignorant of all particulars about themselves and their society, though they were to have general knowledge. Rawls refers to the original position as 'a device of representation' (1985: 236 and elsewhere); it represents what we are to think about and what we are to leave out of consideration when we seek principles of justice to guide our political evaluation of the basic institutions of our society. Such disinterested reflection is at least one kind of political philosophizing. Thus, we may also think of the original position as the forum in which political philosophy is done, provided we do not limit access to professional philosophers.

Criticisms of Rawls's theory of justice are often formulated as criticisms of the original position.[5] Feminist critics have noted that the original position is profoundly monological and that the one voice heard is that of a man. Women, they point out, are both literally and figuratively excluded from the original position. Women are figuratively excluded because the parties are described as heads of households in order to guarantee that each care for some members of the next generation. Although women certainly care for their children as much as do men, and although we have in our society a large number of female-headed households, many of which belong

---

[5] Some critics have denied that rational choosers so situated would choose the Rawlsian principles, others have suggested modification in what is known to the parties, i.e., in what we are to consider and not consider when we think about justice. Finally, there are critics who reject the very idea of an 'original position behind a veil of ignorance'.

to the economically least advantaged group, the phrase 'head of household', these critics say, when it is not qualified, refers to a man.

What difference would it make if women were included in the original position? Okin writes: 'If Rawls were to assume throughout the construction of his theory that all human beings are participants in what goes on behind the veil of ignorance, he would have no option but to require that the family, as a major social institution affecting the life chances of individuals, be constructed in accordance with the two principles of justice' (Okin, 1989: 97). If Okin means here that the parties in the original position are to be ignorant of their sex, I am in wholehearted agreement with her. But I believe that Rawls never meant to say that the parties knew themselves to be men, i.e., he never meant to say that when we ponder questions of justice we should consider only questions of interest to men. Whether the principles of justice are to be applied to the family is, in any case, not decided in the original position itself. What counts among basic structures to which a conception of political justice is to be applied is part of the general knowledge that the parties retain even behind the veil of ignorance.[6] Rawls envisages that the principles will be applied in a four-stage sequence: the Original Position, a constitutional convention, a legislative assembly, and finally, the courts. If the principles will be applied to the family, this will happen at the second and perhaps only at the third step in the four stage sequence, i.e., during a constitutional convention and/or at the legislative stage. Finally, if as Okin's remark suggests, the principles of justice will be the same whether or not the parties in the original position know themselves to be men, or are ignorant of their sex, or include both men and women who know their sex, then I fail to understand the point of the demand that women be included in the original position.

I want to make quite clear what I am saying and what I am not saying. Of course, everyone should be included in the original position, and of course, justice should prevail in the family as well as in the larger society. But just what does Okin want when she wants the family to be constructed according to the principles of justice? How much of this constructing is to be done by legislation? Legislation, either by the state or by religious authorities with the ability to enforce their will, has always regulated marriage, remarriage, and divorce. Legislation has also regulated what happens within a marriage, sometimes to a greater and sometimes to a lesser degree, injustices may be due to such regulations as often as they are due to the lack thereof. It is precisely such regulations, when they prevent women from being equally valuable members of the family by restricting their activities to the homestead, that seem to explain the 'missing women' who are a major concern of this symposium. Thus, while it may be more or less clear to all of us what

---

[6] One might, of course, wonder whether that general knowledge is not already biased in favour of whatever groups are dominant in society or in the academy where that general knowledge is developed and disseminated.

justice in the family demands (or at least what it prohibits), I doubt that any single remedy will do the trick. When women speak out on these matters, their voices seem to be pointing in two directions, wanting marriage and the family to be both more and less private (more and less subject to legislation) than they have been. In fact, there is no ambivalence and no contradiction. Women object to the fact that their personal choices are limited by political (or religious) choices in which they did not participate, since legislators (or religious authorities) are, for the most part, male. Sometimes the remedy for this situation is to liberalize restrictive legislation, at other times it requires the introduction of protective legislation, and sometimes what is needed is not legislation but education. None of this is, I believe, contentious.

The question I wish to raise is whether women are to be represented as women, and hence men as men, or whether the original position is to be sex-blind. It is, I hope, evident that my objections below are directed only against the first alternative. I fully agree with Okin when she says that the concept of the original position in which the parties are ignorant of their sex as well as of other particulars 'is a powerful concept for challenging the gender structure' (Okin, 1989: 109).

That women are literally excluded from the original position is seen when we recall that it may be taken to represent the forum in which we engage in political reflection, in particular in reflection concerning matters of justice. When we look at the development of liberalism, in particular of the conception of justice as fairness, and at the ongoing discussion in political philosophy, the continued adjusting of the reflective equilibrium, we notice that women are under-represented in these discussions. There is, to be sure, a considerable feminist literature, but for the most part feminist voices fail to be heard and appropriated by male philosophers. Feminists have, therefore, demanded that women be included in the original position, or in the philosophical reflections which it represents. Once again, I cite Okin. 'In a *gender-structured society* there is such a thing as the distinct standpoint of women . . . The notion of the standpoint of women, while not without its own problems, suggests that a fully human moral or political theory can be developed only with the full participation of both sexes' (Okin, 1989: 106–7). Here it seems to be clear that women are to be represented as women and are to speak as women, for they are to be present in approximately equal numbers with men and in positions of comparable authority. Women so represented would insist that the principles of justice be applied to the family. For: 'the theory as it stands contains an internal paradox. Because of his assumptions about gender, [Rawls] has not applied the principles of justice to the realm of human nurturance, a realm that is essential to the achievement and maintenance of justice' (ibid.: 108). I am inclined to think that the charge of 'internal paradox' is far too strong since it depends on certain empirical developmental theories, in particular that of Chodorow (ibid.: 106, 131–2 and n. 58). These theories suggest to Okin that men and women raised in gender-structured families, hence experiencing different psychological and moral development, cannot agree on principles of justice even when they are 'behind the veil of ignorance'. The very fact that Okin and I are inclined to accept the Rawlsian principles, or something very much like them, suggests to me that empirical theories cannot be extrapolated to highly abstract theoretical settings. This is not meant to be understood as either a criticism or an endorsement of developmental psychology, feminist or otherwise; I am unqualified to deliver either.

Obviously, women should not be silenced or ignored in our *actual* philosophical reflections, nor should they be excluded from equal participation in our *actual* political lives when the principles of justice are translated into effective legislation. However, the demand that women be included in the *hypothetical* original position as women (as opposed to being included as persons-who-do-not-know-their-sex) seems to me misleading, even misguided. The demand that the parties in the original position know their sex and that both sexes be equally represented, leads, it seems to me, directly to the demand that the parties know their race, religion, sexual preference, state of health, etc. Translated into actual philosophizing and practical politics, this would mean that there would be only persons pleading for 'special interests' but no one attempting to take a more or less impersonal stance; it would mean only particularist moral and political philosophy but no universalistic views, only lobbyists but no legislators, only prosecutors and defence attorneys but no judges. In short, a small tear in the veil of ignorance would lead, I believe, to it being rent altogether. What follows is my argument for this apprehension.

The single voice which is heard in the original position is not the voice of MAN. It is the voice of a white upper or middle class adult male who is heterosexual and, if he is not a practising Christian, he comes at least from a Christian background; he is also in perfect health and not old.[7] Thus, if women are to be included in the original position, lower class men and men who are not white need also be included, as well as Jews and Pagans, gay men, old men and disabled men, and no doubt others who are so invisible that we have not yet begun to think about them. Why is it that some feminists, though not all, have failed to notice how many men are not heard? I believe that the main reason is that these feminists happen to be women for whom sexism is the dominant, often the only, form of oppression that they experience, i.e, they are white professional women. For these women, it is easy, consciously or unconsciously, to fail to notice and even to perpetuate the implicit class, race, etc. bias of the dominant theories of justice. They recognize that human experience has been identified with male experience, they do not recognize that a particular kind of male

---

[7] Here I have been guided by characterizations offered by Seyla Benhabib (1987: 81) and Audre Lorde (1984: 116).

experience, that of upper or middle class males of European descent has been substituted for male experience. As a result, when they insist on the representation of women, they fail to ask which women are to be represented. In fact, they substitute the experience of white middle and upper class women (mainly professional women) for that of all women.[8]

I do not here refer to the fact that not all women are feminists, nor to differences among feminists concerning the just society; these matters are acknowledged. I refer to the fact that some feminists substitute their own point of view for that of all women.[9] Seyla Benhabib has suggested that we must replace the 'substitutionalist universalism' that characterizes modern universalistic political theories by an 'interactive universalism'. Instead of substituting the experiences of 'white male adults who are propertied or professional' for the experiences of all human beings, interactive universalism 'acknowledges the plurality of modes of being human . . . [and] aims at developing moral attitudes and encouraging political transformations that can yield a point of view acceptable to all' (Benhabib, 1987: 81). I am suggesting that some feminist theories of justice have offered us a 'substitutionalist feminism' that needs to be replaced by an 'interactive feminism'.

How true is the charge of substitutionalism? Let us consider first, briefly, the charge of substitutionalism as raised against Rawls. I believe enough has been said to substantiate the claim that we hear the voice of an able-bodied man. Perhaps being gay or lesbian falls under one's conception of the good; still just as Okin insists that more needs to be said about the difference that divorce makes in the lives of men and women, so more needs to be said about the difference that sexual preference makes in the lives of straight and gay people. Just as failure to do the former constitutes substitutionalism, so does the latter. Those of us who are at or near retirement age are painfully aware of the fact that the parties in the Rawlsian original position will return to a life of gainful employment; they are not old and we do not know whether they gave any thought to the aged. (The just savings principle does not prescribe saving for this generation's old age, it saves for the benefit of future generations.) Finally, I suggested that we hear the voice of someone who comes from a Christian background; that is not quite accurate. We hear the voice of someone for whom tolerance, not only of religion properly so called but of a quite wide range of conceptions of a life worth living, is of the utmost importance. However, for many religious persons, including

---

[8] I borrow the language of substitution from Seyla Benhabib who recognizes the particular nature of the male voice that is heard in our supposedly universalistic theories of justice. The charge that the woman's voice we hear is also a particular kind of voice is documented by bell hooks, Audre Lorde, Elizabeth Spelman, and others.

[9] Of course, one can only speak from one's own point of view, but one can, indeed when deliberating about justice one must, attempt to discount one's personal preoccupations, and one can refrain from claiming to speak for a greater collectivity than one is capable of representing.

the Muslim women in Bangladesh and the Hindu widows in India, the problem of main concern is not whether the government will tolerate their religious practices but whether their religious practices will allow them to survive at all. As an anonymous wit has said with respect to a different country, the problem is not freedom *of* religion but freedom *from* religion. For the overwhelming majority of Christian sects, though not for all, that is simply not a problem, and it is not a problem recognized by Rawls.[10]

For the charge of 'substitutionalist feminism' I offer these pieces of evidence. First, in the introduction to *Feminism as Critique*, Benhabib and Cornell write: 'Third world women have challenged precisely the assumption that there is a generalizable, identifiable and collectively shared experience of womanhood. To be Black and to be a woman, is to be a Black woman, a woman whose identity is constituted differently from that of white women', a remark which suggests that they too are aware of the dangers of substitutionalist feminism. Unfortunately, this remark introduces the question, 'How can feminist theory base itself upon the uniqueness of the female experience without reifying thereby one single definition of femaleness as the paradigmatic one—without succumbing, that is, to an essentialist discourse on gender?' (Benhabib and Cornell, 1987: 13) None of the authors who contribute to their book ever return to the issue raised by Third World feminists, a debate internal to white feminism has been substituted for that issue.

Secondly, having mentioned that 'feminists have been criticized for developing theories of gender that do not take sufficient account of differences *among* women, especially race, class, religion, and ethnicity,' Okin writes: 'While such critiques should always inform our research and improve our arguments, it would be a mistake to allow them to detract our attention from gender itself as a factor of significance. Many injustices are experienced by women *as women*, whatever the differences among them and whatever other injustices they also suffer from' (Okin, 1989: 6–7).[11] Of course, there are injustices that are suffered by women as women: women are raped, women are battered, women are abused, medical research has focused on men to the detriment of women, etc. But when medical research

---

[10] Rawls does discuss 'intolerant sects' (1971: 35), and to what extent they are to be tolerated in the just society. He does not discuss whether a just society that tolerates such a sect has any obligations to protect the sect's members from the sect's hierarchy.

[11] Further evidence is gleaned from this: in *Sister Outsider*, Audre Lorde prints a letter which she wrote to Mary Daly. In this letter Lorde points out that in her book *Gyn/Ecology* Daly has made 'the assumption that the herstory and myth of white women is the legitimate and sole herstory and myth of all women to call upon for power and background, and that nonwhite women and our herstories are noteworthy only as decorations or examples of female victimization . . . This dismissal,' she continues, 'does not essentially differ from the specialized devaluations that make Black women prey, for instance, to the murders even now happening in your own city.' (69) This letter, though written in anger, is a plea for a feminist movement that will recognize racial and ethnic diversity as well as what women have in common; acknowledges Daly's contributions as well as noting her failings. Lorde published this originally private letter because Daly never responded to it.

does focus on women, it substitutes white women. 'Currently, only reproductive research involves women subjects in large numbers. However, the
majority, if not all, of the participants are white women . . . it results in the
development of products with little to no information on how they affect
obese women and women with high blood pressure, how they interact with
hypertension medications, or impact other cardiovascular problems which
disproportionately affect women of colour, particularly African American
women.' (Sojourner, 1991)

Another example. For Okin, rape is essentially an act of violence by a
man against a woman, it becomes an issue of political injustice only when
the courts refuse to recognize and prosecute marital rape.[12] In contrast, for
bell hooks in *Ain't I a Woman: black women and feminism*, rape of a black
woman by a white man is an act of racism as well as sexism, indeed it is a
quintessential racist act, a devaluation not simply of a woman but of black
womanhood. Of course, it is unfair to compare Okin's book and hooks's on
this issue, since their aims are quite different. Okin's book is devoted to
issues of justice, gender, and the family, while hooks describes her book
as 'an examination of the impact of sexism on the black woman during
slavery, the devaluation of black womanhood, black male sexism, racism
within the recent feminist movement, and the black woman's involvement
with feminism' (hooks, 1981: 13). Hooks's point is that we will not succeed
in eradicating sexism unless we eradicate racism and classism at the same
time. In contrast, Okin concentrates primarily on the ways in which
the gender structure of the family, and the parallel gender structure of
the employment market, make women and their children economically
vulnerable, though she recognizes that as a result of being economically
vulnerable, married or partnered women are also more or less defenceless
against physical and psychological abuse. Nevertheless, I believe that when
Okin discusses the vulnerability of women and their children, she focuses
primarily on the situation of white women, and indeed of privileged white
women.[13]

I do not mean to suggest that Okin ignores the existence of non-white, in
particular of black, women. She notices that, unlike most white women,
black women have always worked, that the educational and career choices
women make in the expectation of getting married are particularly disadvantageous to women who do not get married, in particular 'poor urban
black women, whose actual chances of marrying and being economically

---

[12] What has just been said is true as far as the book goes; however, I am sure Okin
understands that while the courts recognize and prosecute extra-marital rape, it is difficult for
rape victims to establish the fact that they have been raped. That difficulty is due to the gender
structure of our society against which Okin's argument is directed.

[13] Of course, both Okin and hooks focus on the situation of women in the United States;
they do not claim to speak for women in other countries, in particular, they do not claim to
speak for women in the developing countries. What I have to say in the next few pages is thus
only indirectly related to the topic of this conference.

supported by a man are small' (Okin, 1989: 142), that the divorce rate is much higher for black women than for whites, and that court-ordered child support is, on the average, highest for white women and least for black. But the bulk of Okin's discussion deals with women who, during their married or at least their child-rearing years, do *not* work (hence not poor black women) and with the impact of divorce on such women, with the special problems of married women raising children while attempting to have professional careers (hence not poor women), with equal parenting (which assumes the presence of the father in the home or at least his living in near proximity) and with the need for quality day-care. Only the last of these seems to me to be of equal importance to women across the socio-economic spectrum.[14] However, the need for day-care seems to be peculiar to urban societies, or perhaps only to urban societies in which the extended family has disintegrated.

Okin is surely correct in believing that for many American women the chief obstacles to economic security lie in the gender structure of the market place and the family, and that these are deeply inter-twined. In contrast for the poor women of Bangladesh and upper caste Hindu widows studied by Chen, the chief barrier is the occupational purdah imposed by their respective religions and enforced by both religious and secular authorities.

When one speaks of substitutionalism, one does not charge bad faith. No doubt Rawls is sincere in believing that his argument for the principles of justice is an argument that anyone behind the veil of ignorance would be able to accept, or to put it another way, the argument is addressed to and believed to be rationally acceptable by any reader. And in spite of the difficulties already raised and the modifications to be suggested, I find the conception of justice as fairness quite compelling; I would not devote so much attention to it were it otherwise. The medical researchers who use only white women in their research do not think that non-white women do not matter; they fail to ask the question whether there are medically significant differences between white and non-white women. Feminists whose arguments revolve primarily about the experiences and needs of women like themselves but speak about women as women, do not deny the existence of women who are more or less different from them; they fail to appreciate the magnitude and significance of the difference. I suspect that none of us can avoid substitutionalism, all of us implicitly substitute our own perspective for a more general one. Indeed, in pointing out the dangers of

[14] Day-care providers, one cannot help feeling, take the place occupied by domestics in the utopias of an earlier generation of feminists. Of course, we need quality day-care, of course, government subsidies should enable the children of poorer parents to receive the same high quality care as those of the better off, and, of course, only day-care will keep single parents off welfare. But it is hard to believe that day-care will ever become a high prestige job, or a very highly paid one, hence it is troubling that it should play such a central role in the more just future society envisaged by Okin.

substitutionalism, I speak from a perspective which magnifies the differences between women; feminists might retort that I substitute my own experiences for those of women for whom the similarities dominate. Nevertheless, recognizing the possible universality of substitutionalism, I plead nevertheless that we should attempt to overcome it.

Let us suppose then that, in the spirit of Benhabib, we try to replace substitutionalist feminism by an interactive feminism, that we listen to the voices of women of colour and women of a different class, and that we appropriate what we hear. What will we have learned? We will have learned that for women who have always had to earn a living (in the fields, in factories, in stores and offices, doing piece-work at home, or working as domestics in other women's homes), the demand that women be allowed to leave the domestic sphere is not a demand for liberation. On the other hand, we will have learned that for women who are by religious law confined to the home, being able to go out and earn a living is literally a matter of physical survival. We will have learned that the phrase 'women and minorities' denies the existence of minority women since everyone understands it as 'white women and minority men'. We will have learned to care more about women's medical needs and about safety on the streets and less about chances for tenure or making partner in a law firm. We will have learned that women worry about the safety of their sons as well as their daughters. We will come to understand that it is our responsibility as feminists, as white professional women, to learn from all these other women.

4 THE DILEMMA

Elizabeth Spelman, who suggests learning from women of colour and poor women as a strategy for overcoming feminist racism and classism, writes in her book *Inessential Woman*: 'Modern feminism is faced with a dilemma: will throwing out the bath water of white middle-class privilege involve throwing out the baby of feminism? . . . If we can't isolate gender from race or class, if we can't talk about the oppression women face as women, or about the experience of women as women, isn't feminism left without a foundation, without a specific focus?' (Spelman, 1988: 171–2).

I should like to rephrase these questions. Modern theories of justice, she should have written, are faced with a dilemma: will throwing out the bath water of white, middle-class male privilege throw out the baby of universalism? If they cannot appeal to a conception of justice which is based on the idea that all human beings capable of speech and action are *equal* from the political point of view, that what is justice for one is justice for each, and that nothing is justice unless each can come to see that it is just, then those who are excluded, exploited, or otherwise oppressed have no

Archimedean point on which to stand and from which to move the world. I am not so politically naïve as to think that mere moral appeals, even appeals to political morality, will carry the day, but I am also not so politically cynical as to think that appeals to justice carry no weight at all. We need, therefore, an adequate theory of justice.

The principles of an adequate theory of justice are principles to which the disadvantaged can refer when they demand that justice be done; they are principles which will enable us to settle divisive disputes because they are acknowledged by all parties to the dispute; they are, in short, principles to which we can all agree. The argument just reviewed began with feminists demanding that women be included in the original position, that is, that the monological reflection which leads to Rawls's principles should be replaced by a dialogue in which women are able to remind men of their particular problems. If women are not included in the reflection which leads to the adoption of principles of justice, it was suggested, the resulting principles will not enable women to press their claims, hence women will not be able to agree to these principles. But, so the argument continued, there are many kinds of women and many kinds of men whose concerns will not be expressed by white, middle-class men and women. Must we then introduce the voices of men and women who are poor, or persons of colour, or disabled, or not Christians, or old, or ill, or homosexuals? Must they all participate in the conversation which is to lead to the formulation of a conception of justice?

Rawls has introduced the notion of an overlapping consensus in order to explain how an agreement concerning justice may be reached in a liberal society in which persons embrace widely divergent comprehensive moral/religious doctrines (Rawls, 1987). That appeal to an overlapping consensus fails to respond, however, to the concerns of this paper. It is one thing to *find* that as part of one's comprehensive conception of the good one subscribes to a conception of political justice that one holds in common with other members of one's society; it is quite another thing to be *confronted* with a conception of justice that determines which of one's claims are legitimate, when one of one's claim is that one has been 'unjustly' excluded from the deliberations that led to the adoption of this conception. Thus I ask, yet again, whether the original position must include representatives of all disadvantaged groups. An affirmative answer would entail a radical reconception of the original position: the veil of ignorance would be rent. The representatives of the disadvantaged groups would know to which group they belong, though they would still be ignorant of the details of their individual lives, they would be, to use Benhabib's phrase, neither completely generalized nor fully concrete others (Benhabib, 1987).

It seems to me clear that this new kind of 'original position' will not do for three reasons. First, we shall continue to be haunted by the spectre of substitutionalism. Secondly, we shall be unable to come to an agreement on any conception of justice. Thirdly, it is impossible to perform the suggested thought experiment. Consider the first point. The argument just reviewed made us aware of the fact that when persons speak as representatives of a certain group, e.g., 'women as women', they may in fact speak only for a subset of that group, e.g., white, middle-class women. There is then no reason to think that the conception of justice to which all these 'representatives' could agree would not be again a 'substitutionalist' conception of justice. This concern may also be expressed by pointing out that there would be no guarantee that all groups that deserve to be heard would be heard. Perhaps orthodox Jewish women would be 'represented' by Jewish men speaking 'as Jews', or by women speaking 'as women'. No doubt, there are groups whom no one as yet even *mis*represents; their situation is comparable to that of homosexuals as recently as twenty years ago, that is, their voices would be inaudible. In fact, every human being belongs to more than one 'group'. One is not merely a philosopher, one is also male or female, white or a person of colour, married or single, childless or with children, hetero- or homosexual, aged or young, physically challenged or not, belonging to some faith community or other or to none, and one may or may not subscribe to unpopular political ideals. These features and yet others make one the concrete unique individual that one is, and every theory of justice, whether it claims to be universal or admits frankly that it is particularist, will substitute the experience of some more or less generalized other, for one's own concreteness. Should we then, each of us, in the name of universal moral equality, construct our very own conception of justice? Surely, this would defeat the point of a conception of justice. Unless a conception of justice is shared, or has at least the potential of being shared, by both the advantaged and the disadvantaged, the oppressor and the oppressed, it does not provide a basis from which the latter can with dignity press their claims against the former. A conception of justice tailor-made for some individual's particular circumstances cannot be such a shared conception. Yet where would one stop once one has stepped on the slippery slope and suggested looking for a feminist theory of justice and then notices that a feminist theory would be open to objections just like the objections that lead some feminists to demand that they be included in the original position?

What has just been said must not be misunderstood as a general condemnation of groups, or of persons who speak as representatives of certain groups. It is only at the first stage in Rawls's four-stage sequence, that is, when one searches for a conception of justice, that permitting some groups to be explicitly represented will open the door to total fragmentation. The lesson to be learned from the above discussion is that everyone (not merely 'heads of households') needs to be present in the original position, i.e., all of us need to reflect upon and participate in the conversation concerning

principles of justice, but not only must we make an effort to discount what
concerns each of us as a concrete individual, we must also refrain from
acting as spokespersons for some group to which we belong; the veil of
ignorance must remain whole.

I now turn to the second point. Here we ignore the worry about
substitutionalism. Everyone participates in the reflections and conversations which are to lead to the adoption of principles of justice that are to
enable us to settle our most divisive disputes. Once again, one would be
expected to ignore or discount one's particular situation, but know to which
groups one belongs and consider the kinds of claims one would wish to be
able to press as a member of one of these groups. For example, as an
American working woman one would wish to tailor the principles of justice
so that they would permit demands for equal pay for equal work, but as a
Bangladeshi woman working at a food-for-work site, one would wish to
tailor the principles so that they would permit enough food for oneself and
one's family for a day's work. As an American Jew, I would seek principles
which would permit me to obey the rules of my religion; as a Hindu widow,
I would seek principles which would enable me to transgress the rules of my
religion. In each case it would be the government that would be expected
to act as guarantor. As an American man, on the other hand, I might worry
that equal pay for equal work would lead to a lowering of my income; as a
Hindu man, I might worry that allowing Hindu women to work outside the
home would undermine my authority. In other words, the conflicts which
we hope to resolve by an appeal to mutually agreed-upon principles of
justice would be brought into the original position. Knowing to which
group (or groups) one belongs, one would be able to estimate how the
adoption of one set of principles or another would affect one's life prospects. I doubt that under such conditions one would be able to come to an
agreement on anything except the most general and vacuous principles (see
also Rawls, 1991: 141). Fragmentation may be avoided but only at the cost
of having a conception of justice that is hardly better than no conception at
all.

Finally, this is my third point, we must remember that the original
position is a hypothetical position, a device of representation. In so far as it
represents thinking of which every one of us is capable, it is obvious that no
one can think, simultaneously, or even in succession, as a woman and as a
man, as Jew and as Muslim, as one who has AIDS and as one who does not,
etc. etc. What one can do, according to Rawls, is to attempt to ignore any
considerations that depend on one's being a woman or being a man, being
a Jew or being a Muslim, etc.

I have also suggested that we may think of the original position as
representing philosophical discussions. Different persons are then quite
able to think and articulate the views from different perspectives. However,
my first point suggests that in so far as they do that, none of these persons

can claim to offer a universal conception of justice, nor can they be sure to speak for all members of the group they claim to represent; my second point suggests that any philosophical agreement achieved by persons who speak and think only from limited perspectives would be vacuous.

Once again I need to guard against being misunderstood. I do not claim that there is no place for group representation; in spite of the dangers of substitutionalism, the realities of political life are such that only organized groups of the disadvantaged can hope to be successful in the struggle for justice. Again, in spite of the dangers of substitutionalism, the complexities of philosophical, political, and moral discourse are such that we need to hear frankly particularist voices lest we ignore what William James called 'the cries of the wounded'. Indeed, I want to insist on heeding what we have learned from persons in other countries, from feminists, from persons of colour, from members of various other disadvantaged groups. Our dilemma is precisely how to preserve the universality of justice while giving due considerations to the variety of voices of distress.

5 SOME ANSWERS

What we learn from the cries of the wounded modifies what Rawls calls our 'considered judgments', and since they stand in reflective equilibrium with our conception of justice, it may be the case that our conception of justice needs to be modified as well. Thus I do not claim that principles of justice once adopted will stand in perpetuity. I do not know whether this represents a serious disagreement with Rawls. Rawls insists that when one reflects on principles of justice, one must not only discount one's particular circumstances but one must also assume that the principles one adopts are adopted once and for all (Rawls, 1971: 147, 176). He wants to rule out the possibility of saying to oneself: 'I'll try to live by these principles, but if it is either too hard or too disadvantageous, I'll reconsider.' Someone with that attitude betrays a lack of seriousness, a lack of a sense of justice; of course, I quite agree with that. My point is, rather, that what we learn from the complaints of the victims of injustice may be that our conception of justice itself needs to be modified because it fails to acknowledge injustices which we nevertheless recognize to be such. However, it may also be the case that what we learn is that our realization of our conception of justice in legislation and practice has been woefully incomplete, i.e., that our society falls very short indeed of being even 'near just'. I am inclined to think that both are the case.

Consider the first alternative. The principles of justice themselves need revision; they fail to provide a basis from which certain disadvantaged groups may press claims that we recognize to be just. To use an example of Sen's: 'a person may have more income and more nutritional intake, but less freedom to lead a well-nourished existence because of a higher meta-bolic rate, greater vulnerability to parasitic diseases, larger body size, or pregnancy' (Sen, 1989: 25). If Sen is right, Rawls's theory fails to accom-modate the claims of say, pregnant women. Yet the existence in the USA of the WIC programme (providing food supplements for pregnant and nurs-ing women) shows that we already recognize these claims to be just. On re-entering the original position, we would retain the knowledge that the principles must leave room for these kinds of claim, but we would once again not know (i.e., discount) who we are, to what group we belong. This would make it possible, once again, to reach agreement on a substantive conception of justice. I believe that this represents the sort of reflecting and revising one would in fact attempt if one were dissatisfied with the liberal conception of justice or its Rawlsian articulation, or indeed some other, e.g., a socialist conception, because it fails to be in reflective equilibrium with one's considered judgements. The revised conception would again claim to be universal, to both legitimize and limit the kinds of claims persons can press in the name of justice. One example of such a 'revision' is Rawls's own reformulation of his first principle in light of an objection offered by H. L. A. Hart (1973).[15] Another example is Sen's shift, in response to the problem mentioned above, from an index of socially pri-mary goods to an index of capabilities. This move responds to the concerns of a variety of 'less favored' groups, including pregnant women, and the women at the food-for-work sites in Bangladesh. Unlike the search for particularist theories of justice, Sen's proposal retains the universality of principles of justice while taking due account of the diversity of human beings. It is, as he says, a shift in the information available to the parties in the original position, i.e., a shift in what we are to think about when attempting to articulate our conception of justice (Sen, 1989).[16] As far as I know, Sen has never spelled out how the principles of justice would be reformulated if one substituted capabilities for primary social goods. It is not clear to me, for example, whether the Rawlsian distinction between political and civil liberties on the one hand and opportunities, income, and wealth on the other would be entirely obliterated, or to what extent some-thing like it might be retained. In particular, considering the plight of women whose religion condemns them to such economic inferiority that their very lives are at stake, one would like to know how a capabilities approach might combine the ability to practise one's religion with the ability to receive adequate medical care and nutrition, so that, for examples, the ability of mullahs and village elders to limit the mobility of women

---

[15] Rawls replaced the phrase 'the most extensive total system of equal basic liberties' by 'a fully adequate scheme of equal basic liberties'.

[16] This is not the first time Sen made this suggestion. It has been rejected by Rawls, e.g. in Rawls, 1988. This is not the place to recount or to attempt to adjudicate this dispute. I do, however, lean toward Sen's position.

would be curtailed in order to increase the ability of women (and female children) to survive.

Whether or not the principles of justice need modification or have been modified, the construction of a conception of justice is not an idle exercise, rather it is to enable us to overcome deep and pervasive conflicts within democratic culture. To do that we apply the principles of justice first to the basic institutions of our society, then in the confines of these institutions to legislation, and ultimately to individual decisions of judges and administrators. We do so either from the point of view of equal citizenship or from the point of view of a representative of a least advantaged group; here what we have learned from listening to a variety of voices is of the utmost importance. Rawls assumes that the least advantaged group is *economically* disadvantaged, anyone whose average income and wealth is equal to or less than that of an unskilled labourer, or anyone whose income and wealth is less than half of the median, belongs to it (Rawls, 1971: 98). To be sure, Rawls is aware of the fact that one may be disadvantaged in other ways. As noted above, he recognizes that inequalities may be based on such fixed natural characteristics as one's sex, race or ethnicity. If so, these inequalities determine least favoured positions and in a just society must be, and must be able to be shown to be, to the advantage of those least favoured. But, Rawls continues, 'these inequalities are seldom, if ever, to the advantage of the less favored, and therefore in a just society the smaller number of relevant positions should ordinarily suffice' (ibid.: 99). This will not do. Feminists and civil rights advocates deserve credit for pointing this out. Ours is not a just society, and there are deep political disagreements concerning both the nature of the injustices and the permissible remedies. By making explicit what he takes to be our implicit convictions about justice, Rawls hopes to provide a basis for resolving these differences at least sufficiently to continue to function as a community. But then we must ask not merely who will *remain* least favoured in a just society but who *is* least favoured now. Indeed, even when we take up the point of view of the economically least favoured, it behoves us to ask why they are in that position. It is one thing to be an unskilled labourer because one lacked, for whatever tragic personal reasons, the drive, the opportunity, or the ability to become anything else, it is another to be an unskilled labourer because the colour of one's skin barred one from acquiring skills. In the former case justice requires that the economic distance between the labourer and those in a better position be to the former's advantage, in the latter case, in addition and more importantly, racist barriers to training and education must be removed. It is one thing to be a widow who finds herself at a disadvantage in the labour market when she is forced to return to it after a lengthy voluntary absence, it is another to be a widow who is prevented by caste rules from entering the labour market. The kind of changes that Okin advocates to protect women of the former kind do not require changes in the religious convictions of anyone in the United States, the kind of changes required to rescue Metha Bai do. It is one thing to know that one's life is made difficult by institutions that one recognizes to be unjust, it is another to be required to break rules that one still accepts as proper. Of course, I am not saying that Rawls would fail to see that Metha Bai suffers an injustice that is quite distinct from that of the American widow: Metha Bai's freedom of movement is severely restricted. Even if Metha Bai were a rich widow she would still be a victim of this injustice. But that is to say that the position of Hindu women is a position of disadvantage, a position from which the institutions and laws of India need to be scrutinized.

Feminists point out that the point of view of women (all women) is the perspective of a least favoured group; hence, they argue, we must look at the basic structures from this perspective. Such scrutiny reveals unequal citizenship as well as unequal economic status and unequal bases of self-respect; none of these inequalities are to the advantage of women. Not only are women under-represented in our legislatures and the judiciary; even in situations of direct participatory democracy (town meetings, for example) studies have shown that the most authoritative participants turn out to be white, middle-class men (Young, 1989). We must note, however, that these privileged men silence, or out-talk and out-vote, not only women but people of colour, poor people, and the elderly of either sex. Political impotence, in turn, undermines self-respect, and has effects on the distribution of public moneys, thus leading to unequal access to public services. While married women whose husbands belong to the politically influential group are protected against the last mentioned effect of unequal citizenship, it is in general true that a vicious cycle keeps the poor powerless and the powerless poor.

Most women are economically disadvantaged because of complementary features of the family and the labour market. Because in the traditional family women carry the major burden of home-making and child rearing, they cannot compete in the labour market on equal terms with men who can devote themselves wholeheartedly to their work. This inequality is exacerbated when we compare single mothers with married men. Because women are shunted into less prestigious and lower paid jobs, their careers are more easily sacrificed to the needs of their children, than are those of the fathers. Although Rawls (1971) mentioned the family as one of the basic institutions of society and described how children will acquire a sense of justice through growing up in a just family, and although he recognized that the stability of the well-ordered society depends on its citizens having a sense of justice, he never discussed the applications of the two principles of justice to the family and does not confront the implications on the worlds of work and politics of a restructuring of the family (Okin, 1989: ch. 5).

If the principles of justice are applied to the family, one is forced to conclude that men and women should share equally in providing for the family's economic, physical, and emotional needs. This requires that not only in the family but also in the worlds of work and education and on every level, the distinction between women's jobs and men's jobs will have to be eradicated, on every level the issue of equal pay for equal worth will have to be raised. Everywhere and in every way barriers to women's flourishing must come down. Both women's economic well-being, and that of their children, and women's self-respect are at stake (ibid.: 1989, chs. 7 and 8). I shall not pursue this issue further, the arguments are familiar to all of us.

Most of what has just been said concerning women is easily repeated if we replace 'men' and 'women' everywhere by racial or ethnic phrases. We all know that the job of railroad porter was a 'black job', we all know that the job of grocer in certain parts of New York is now 'Korean' and used to be 'Jewish'. Medical schools were not only bastions of male privilege, they were and are bastions of white privilege as well. School administrators are predominantly male, they are also predominantly white. And in all these cases also the self-respect and the economic well-being of the less favoured and their children is diminished. Precisely because it seems that the veil of ignorance must be retained lest we lack any conception of justice at all, it is important that a large variety of relevant 'least advantaged' positions be recognized.[17] From all these positions arguments analogous to those by Okin and other feminists can be offered, from all these positions claims need to be pressed—pressed as claims of justice not as appeals to charity. It seems to me that the main result of an 'interactive universalism' would consist precisely in enhancing one's ability to recognize a multiplicity of 'least advantaged' positions and an ability to hear and heed the complaints raised from these perspectives.

6 A SECOND LOOK

For the last several pages I have assumed that a universal conception of justice is at hand to which all the less favoured groups may appeal. Doing that, I have ignored the earlier worry that the universal conception of justice is the result of reflections which substitute the experiences of a privileged group of human beings for the experiences of all of us, that it may,

[17] I owe this point to a personal communication from Robin Avery. She brought to my attention the situations of (a) homeless, intravenous drug users who need stable housing situations if they are to kick the habit, and (b) of HIV-infected persons whose symptoms do not match the criteria for AIDS established by the Centers for Disease Control and who are, therefore, not deemed disabled and denied benefits. These persons seem to be women, the poor, children, and intravenous drug users.

therefore, 'in effect burden or exclude anyone who does not share the characteristics of privileged, white, Christian, able-bodied, heterosexual, adult men' (Minow and Spelman, 1990: 1601) by whom and for whom the conception was developed. Moreover, in speaking of group perspectives, especially of the perspective of women, I have ignored the burden of the second part of my argument, namely that those perspectives may substitute the experiences of more privileged (less oppressed) members of the group for the experience of all its members. The loud trumpet of universalism and the lesser trumpets of various communalisms threaten to drown out the cries of oppressed individuals; yet these individuals need to be able to appeal to the universalism of justice, and they need to be able to join their feeble voices into one mighty cry. With these observations, I have returned to the problem raised in the beginning; however, I shall now formulate it somewhat differently. The principles of justice, whatever they may be, must be universal if they are to reflect the liberal conception of justice, for the fundamental intuition behind that conception is the moral equality of all human beings capable of speech and action. The principles must be accept-able to all as a basis from which they may press their claims and as grounds of the obligations which they assume, otherwise they fail to provide a resource for settling disputes concerning the proper allocation of burdens and benefits. The task of articulating such principles appears impossible; whatever we do, so it seems, we shall either offer principles so vague and so general that they are useless, or we shall come up with principles that ride roughshod over the legitimate interests of some. It is time to make a new beginning.

I do not consider principles of justice to be eternal truths, nor, as already indicated, do I consider it helpful to regard a conception of justice, once adopted, to be the last word. Instead, I take principles of justice to be hypotheses concerning what social arrangements will best encourage hu-man flourishing. As hypotheses based on rather extensive human experi-ence, we may think of these principles as analogous to laws of science, provided we take laws of science themselves as hypotheses that aid us in our understanding and control of nature. Thinking of science in this light we recall that the formula which we now know as the ideal gas law was some centuries ago an empirical generalization based on relatively crude obser-vations of actual gases. As better instruments were constructed, better data were obtained, and more accurate formulae were developed containing additional variables that refer to the properties of particular gases. In the nineteenth century the theory of gases as swarms of molecules was devel-oped, and in that theory Boyle's original formula reappears as the ideal gas law. We need to remember also that the better instruments which enabled scientists to discover both the more accurate empirical formulae and the molecular theory were developed with the aid of theories based on data obtained with the older, cruder instruments. In every sense, science pulls itself up by its own bootstraps.[18] At every stage of scientific progress there are laws which are taken to be universal and which are applied to particular circumstances. We do not ask how we can retain the universality of the laws while paying due attention to the particular circumstances in which we apply them. Knowing that a law was discovered in one sort of setting may cause us to be cautious when we apply it to another sort of setting, but one of the aims of scientific investigation is to discover laws that are universal, that can be applied in all circumstances to which that sort of law is relevant. Learning to be a chemist is learning both what the laws of chemistry are and how to apply them; the particular problem at hand will determine what to ignore and what to heed in a given situation and which laws are relevant to it.

Using this account of science as a model, let us consider again the problem of the fundamental principles of justice. Boyle's law of gases was based on relatively crude observations, the earliest versions of the liberal conception of justice (say the version implicit in the pre-Jacksonian understanding of the US Constitution as it was at that time) was clearly a conception by and for middle and upper class, white males. Yet that conception turned out to be broad enough so that those who subscribed to it were able to hear the demands of poor white men for the right to vote and hold public office. Once Jacksonian democracy was firmly established, the conception of justice, or at any rate the way in which it was interpreted had changed. Using the Rawlsian notion of social primary goods, we might say that participation in the political process was added under the rubric of liberty. Thus when slavery had been abolished, the enlarged conception of justice enabled the newly freed African–American men to demand the right to vote and hold public office. Women, too, began to demand all the rights and privileges of citizenship.[19] In fact, the conception of justice implicit in the institutions and practices of liberal democracies have developed over time, and will, presumably, continue to develop. Just as laws of science that hold only approximately because they are based on crude data enable us to discover laws that hold more precisely, so a conception of justice that is partial because based on substitution (crude data) enables us to advance to a more comprehensive conception. Like science, democracy must pull itself up by its own bootstraps.

Given, then, an admittedly imperfect universal conception of justice, how will it be applied to a particular social problem? Having emphasized the

[18] This description of scientific progress should be acceptable both to realists who would, however, want to add that the successive descriptions approach more and more closely to what Bernard Williams (1978) calls 'the absolute conception' of the world, and to those who reject that notion and are satisfied with a more modest understanding of scientific progress.

[19] It is worth remembering that some white women failed to acknowledge the justice of the African–Americans' demand, and some African–American men failed to acknowledge the justice of the women's demand.

diversity of human beings, one wonders whether one will be overwhelmed by details. It is not sufficient to have a universal conception of justice, it is also necessary to deal with problems of justice politically, that is, not as individual problems but as problems of a certain kind. Just as scientists learn which circumstances to heed and which to ignore, so we must learn to know when it is appropriate to think of, say, women as women, and when it is necessary to think specifically of Japanese Buddhist women, when it is important to think of the homeless as homeless and when it is necessary to think specifically of homeless persons with AIDS, etc. Political genius consists at least in part in recognizing possible alliances where none were suspected, just as scientific genius consists in recognizing a common factor in apparently disparate phenomena. Each social problem is, for some of us, our problem. Each problem is also, at least at first sight, for most of us *not* our problem. The very first task any of us face when we are the victims of injustice is to see that we are victims of *injustice* and not simply of the arbitrary cruelty of some individual, i.e., we must see that ours is a political problem, not merely a personal one. Our next task is to make others see that there is a problem. The technique called 'blaming the victim' is used to prevent us from taking that very first step, and when it fails at that, it is used to prevent others from acknowledging that our problem calls for a political solution.

In science we need to identify the laws or theory relevant to solving the problem at hand; we work with the best theory that we already have, though in the course of solving our problem we may also change the theory. Likewise, in dealing with a political problem we work with the best theory that we already have, and in the course of applying the theory to concrete problems, we learn how it must be modified. I have discussed this above; now I want to emphasize that the origin of a scientific theory does not matter, what matters is how well it fares in experimentation and application, whether experience satisfies or frustrates the expectations to which the theory gave rise. The origin of the principles of justice in a tradition dominated by white Christian bourgeois men does not matter, what matters is how well it enables the rest of us to press our claims successfully, without either stepping on each other's toes or simply changing places with our erstwhile oppressors.

The view I have attempted to sketch in this section is a version of what Richard Rorty (1991: 68) calls 'Dewey's experimentalism in moral theory', its 'whole point' is, as he writes, 'that you need to keep running back and forth between principles and the results of applying principles.'[20] Without the universality of justice there are only particular cruelties and particular pains, without attention to the particular cruelties and the particular pains, theories of justice are utopian fantasies, at best comforting, at worst causes

[20] A similar approach is found in Minow and Spelman, 1990.

of great suffering.[21] With a universal but modifiable conception of justice and attention to particulars, victims of injustice may press their claims with dignity. There is no doubt that our conception of justice has widened over the last several centuries and will continue to widen; the process of widening I have envisaged in this section will not lead to fragmentation: on the contrary, our principles have become and will continue to become more inclusive.

7 UNIVERSALISM REVISITED

I now turn to the claim that the liberal conception of justice is a conception of justice only for modern constitutional democracies. Sen (1989: 14) seems to read Rawls's insistence that justice as fairness is a political conception of justice in this way when he writes: 'The definitional exclusion contained in Rawls's "political conception" limits the scope of the concept of justice drastically and abruptly, and it would often make it hard to identify political rights and wrongs that a theory of justice *should* address.' While agreeing with Sen's sentiment, I want to dispute his reading of 'Justice as Fairness: Political not Metaphysical'.

When Rawls (1985: 224) speaks of a political conception of justice he means both that it is a conception of justice 'worked out for a specific kind of subject, namely, for political, social, and economic institutions', and that it should be 'so far as possible, independent of controversial philosophical and religious doctrines' (ibid.: 223) because 'as a practical political matter no general moral conception can provide a publicly recognized basis for a conception of justice in a modern democratic state' (ibid.: 225). According to Sen (1989: 15–16) 'on grounds of the absence of toleration a whole lot of comprehensive doctrines may be ruled out of court (indeed, in some cases none may remain), and yet there may be very perspicuous problems of justice and injustice in disputes between different sides. To be without a theory that can deal with such problems (when the different sides are intolerant), and to see the disputes as lying *outside* the purview of the so-called political conception of justice, would appear to be oddly limiting.' Sen goes on to point out that even an intolerant political party may point out the injustice of the policies of an intolerant government that fails to provide for the victims of famine, and that they may do so using Rawlsian arguments. Of course, this last point of Sen's is correct, and Rawls may well accept it.

What Rawls (1985: 225) points out repeatedly is that 'since justice as fairness is intended as a political conception of justice for a democratic society, it tries to draw solely upon basic intuitive ideas that are embedded

---

[21] I take it that both Christianity and Marxism are, or were in their origins, theories of justice.

in the political institutions of a constitutional democratic regime and the public traditions of their interpretation. Justice as fairness is political in part because it starts from within a certain political tradition.' We need not read this as claiming that justice as fairness may be used as a basis for social critique *only* of democratic societies. Indeed, who would make such a claim? Surely one cannot say from *within* the liberal tradition that its conception of justice applies only to democratic societies. From within the liberal tradition one does say that its conception of justice can be realized only under a democratic regime; from within the liberal tradition one acknowledges that the conception of justice serves as a publicly recognized regulative ideal only in democratic societies. However, these acknowledgements are in themselves criticisms of other societies; one says in effect that non-democratic societies are *eo ipso* unjust. One cannot say from within the liberal tradition that one cannot criticize non-liberal regimes precisely because universalism is built deeply within the foundations of the liberal conception of justice. Every human being capable of speech and action is entitled to live in a society which realizes the liberal conception of justice. (Contrast this with the Jewish prohibition of eating shellfish which explicitly applies only to Jews.) Again, there is nothing incoherent in demands for liberty when they are raised by revolutionaries against an intolerant regime, though such demands may strike an outsider as hypocritical if that outsider believes that the revolutionaries would establish a dictatorship.

But, perhaps, from *outside* the liberal tradition one can say that its conception of justice cannot serve as a basis of critique within a non-liberal society. Lest this claim seem immediately absurd—surely Germans could have and should have objected on liberal grounds against National Socialism—a non-liberal society must here be understood as a society without a tradition of toleration. This is the sort of objection which communitarians and moral relativists raise against any claim to universalism. With respect to the liberal political conception of justice, the claim is either that a liberal critique will be unintelligible in such a society or at the least that it will have no motivational force. This is not the place to examine the communitarian critique of Rawls or more generally the claims of moral relativism. It suffices to say that (1a) Sen is surely right in holding that the second principle of justice may serve as a basis for a critique of economic arrangements even when neither the regime nor its critics accept the first principle. Such critiques are intelligible and have motivational force, they have been known to lead to reform or revolution. (1b) When Amnesty International criticizes regimes of all stripes for human rights violations, i.e., violations of Rawls's first principle, its protests are not pointless. While Amnesty cannot take credit for any revolutions (nor would it wish to), it has been and continues to be able to save some lives. Clearly, it is able to make its objections intelligible and to find ways to give them motivational force.

(2) When Rawls (1985: 225) says that he has articulated the political conception of justice implicit in the democratic tradition, he is *not* saying that it cannot be applied to other societies; he says, rather, that whether it can be so extended is a separate question which he wants to avoid prejudging. I take it that Sen's point is that we need a political conception of justice that can be applied to all societies, and I am saying the liberal conception of justice is one such conception. I do *not* say that the liberal conception is the only such conception, nor do I say that *A Theory of Justice* or 'Justice as Fairness: Political not Metaphysical' provide the best articulation of that conception. I am saying that the liberal conception of justice is the best we have, I am also saying that we must treat it as provisional, being ever ready to deepen and broaden our understanding of it.

(3) One wonders where this position *outside* the liberal tradition is located. The communitarian and relativist critics of liberalism are in fact not products of traditional societies, they are themselves heirs of the liberal tradition. Perhaps this is why, in the end, I find it difficult to make their position intelligible, but that is the subject of another paper.

If it were the case, however, as communitarians and relativists claim, that justice judgements make sense, or have a truth value, or have motivational force only relative to 'social meanings' (Walzer, 1983), 'an adequate moral system' (Wong, 1984), or relative to an agreement (Harman, 1975), then justice would be fragmented. It would be nonsensical to judge the social meanings of one society in terms of the social meanings of another, to judge one adequate moral system from the perspective of another, or one agreement in terms of another. It would then be nonsensical or pointless or a mere expression of one's frustration to say that the practices of another society based on different 'understandings of justice and rationality' (MacIntyre, 1988) are unjust. While a particular action or even a particular practice can be judged from within the comprehensive understanding to which both agent and critic belong, and Walzer (1987) has argued that such criticism can be far-reaching, there would be no point of view from which it would make sense to judge an understanding of justice and rationality itself. But to object to the fact that, e.g., women in India receive less adequate nutritional and health care than men (Sen, 1990) is neither pointless nor nonsensical. It is, in fact, a first step toward understanding a situation which needs correcting. It would, of course, be insufferable arrogance to straight away condemn Indian fathers and husbands without understanding the complex reasons for this phenomenon; it is that complex situation which needs modifying.

Narrowing the range of applicability of the liberal conception of justice leads once again to fragmentation. The liberal conception of justice would then be reconceived as the 'Western' conception, an alternative to, say, the Indian conception (but India is, in fact, a constitutional democracy!) and so on. But why would it stop there. Surely there are significant differences in

the traditions of different European countries (e.g., Catholic versus Protestant) or of the diverse communities (Muslim, Hindu, Sikh) in India etc.
Once again, as earlier when considering a feminist theory of justice, I can
see no natural stopping point once we step on the slippery slope of demanding communally anchored theories of justice. Moreover, even internal
criticism will be called into question. Is it not always open to the guardians
of the old order to claim that their critics have stepped outside the tradition?
Women, in particular, are endangered by moves toward communal conceptions of justice since the traditions of most communities have denied
women's moral equality; so are 'minorities' (racial, ethnic, religious, etc.)
for most communal traditions refuse to grant them an equal place. I
conclude that demands for feminist theories of justice or for limiting the
range of the liberal conception of justice to the so-called 'West' (is Australia
west?) is not to the advantage of the least advantaged. Let us not open, in
the name of toleration, the doors to intolerance, but let us, in the name of
universalism, be prepared to learn from the cries of the oppressed, whoever
and wherever they are.[22]

BIBLIOGRAPHY

BENHABIB, SEYLA (1987). 'The Generalized and the Concrete Other: The Kohlberg–
Gilligan Controversy and Feminist Theory' in S. Benhabib and D. Cornell, eds.
Feminism and Critique. Minneapolis, Minn.: University of Minnesota Press.
—— (1989). 'In the Shadow of Aristotle and Hegel: Communicative Ethics and
Current Controversies in Practical Philosophy', *The Philosophical Forum*, XXI,
77–95.
BENHABIB, SEYLA and CORNELL, DRUCILLA (eds.) (1987). *Feminism and Critique*.
Minneapolis, Minn.: University of Minnesota Press.
DRÈZE, JEAN and SEN, AMARTYA (1989). *Hunger and Public Action*. Oxford:
Clarendon Press.
HARMAN, GILBERT (1975). 'Moral Relativism Defended', *Philosophical Review*, 84,
3–22.
HART, H. L. A. (1973). 'Rawls on Liberty and Its Priority', *University of Chicago
Law Review*, 90, 534–55.
HOOKS, BELL (1981). *Ain't I a Woman: black women and feminism*. Boston: South
End Press.
LORDE, AUDRE (1984). *Sister Outsider*. Freedom, Calif.: The Crossing Press.

[22] I am indebted to Robin Avery; to members of the audience when an earlier version of this
paper was read at the New School for Social Research, and above all to my colleagues Ann
Congleton, Alison McIntyre, and Ken Winkler who subjected an earlier draft to searching
criticism and helped to clarify my thinking. I am also indebted to my commentator Susan Okin
and to other members of the conference on Human Capabilities: Women, Men and Equality,
at which the penultimate version of this paper was read. None of these are responsible for the
errors which remain.

MacIntyre, Alasdair (1988). *Whose Justice? Which Rationality?* Notre Dame, Ind.: University of Notre Dame Press.

Minow, Martha and Spelman, Elizabeth V. (1990). 'In Context', *Southern California Law Review*, 63, 1597–652.

Okin, Susan, Moller (1989). *Justice, Gender and the Family*. New York: Basic Books.

Rawls, John (1971). *A Theory of Justice*. Cambridge, Mass.: Harvard University Press.

—— (1985). 'Justice as Fairness: Political not Metaphysical', *Philosophy and Public Affairs*, 14, 223–51.

—— (1987). 'The Idea of an Overlapping Consensus', *Oxford Journal of Legal Studies*, 7, 1–25.

—— (1988). 'The Priority of Right and Ideas of the Good', *Philosophy and Public Affairs*, 17, 251–76.

Rorty, Richard (1991). *Objectivity, Relativism, and Truth*. Cambridge: Cambridge University Press.

Sen, Amartya (1989). 'The Territory of Justice', Discussion Paper Number 1425, Harvard Institute of Economic Research.

—— (1990). 'More than 100 Million Women are Missing', *The New York Review of Books* 20 Dec.

Sojourner, Sabrina (1991). 'Race, Class and Reproductive Freedom', *National Now Times*, 23, 8.

Spelman, Elizabeth V. (1988). *Inessential Woman: Problems of Exclusion in Feminist Thought*. Boston: Beacon Press.

Walzer, Michael (1983). *Spheres of Justice*. New York: Basic Books.

—— (1987). *Interpretation and Social Criticism*. Cambridge, Mass.: Harvard University Press.

Williams, Bernard (1978). *Descartes: The Project of Pure Enquiry*. Harmondsworth: Penguin.

Wong, David B. (1984). *Moral Relativity*. Berkeley, Calif.: University of California Press.

Young, Iris Marion (1989). 'Polity and Group Difference: A Critique of the Ideal of Universal Citizenship', *Ethics*, 99, 250–74.

Gender, Caste, and Law

Cass R. Sunstein

The study of the law of sex discrimination requires an inquiry into law of two different kinds. The first area of law consists of legal practices that sustain and support sex discrimination. When there is sex discrimination, what contribution does law make? The second area consists of the law, constitutional or otherwise, that might operate against social practices or laws that produce sex discrimination. Suppose that we were committed to sex equality. How would we use the law to bring about this result? What form would the antidiscrimination principle take?

The questions will not receive the same answers in all nations. In developing countries, for example, the norms that produce sex discrimination are in significant part reflected in custom rather than law. Indeed, in developing countries the line between custom and law is extremely thin, even artificial. The norms that make sex discrimination possible have a large customary place in developed countries as well; but legal practices are far easier to identify and criticize as such.

Moreover, the use of law to eliminate sex discrimination creates special puzzles and confronts special obstacles in developing countries. Is there any tradition of judicial invalidation of laws that offend basic rights? Is there a tradition of judicial invalidation at all? Does some centralized authority have power to eliminate practices or law intruding on human rights? What role is reserved to courts, the Constitution, and laws purporting to protect such rights? Sometimes the answers to these questions will make it exceptionally hazardous to rely on Western-style models, which consist of judicially enforced legal rights, brought to bear on legislative and administrative practices.

Notwithstanding these difficulties, I believe that it is indeed possible to sketch the kinds of legal practices that produce sex discrimination, and also to outline the kind of antidiscrimination norm that is entailed by a commitment to sex equality. I also believe that this norm has a fair claim to universality. It is clear that there are powerful commonalities, with respect to sex discrimination, in seemingly diverse systems, and those commonalities often have a great deal to do with law. And in describing and implementing a legal norm of sex equality, other nations would do well to learn from the conceptual mistakes of American law.

In this essay I identify a legal norm for opposing sex discrimination, which I call an *anticaste principle*. I will describe the anticaste principle in some detail below, but for the moment the principle should be taken to forbid social and legal practices from turning sex, a morally irrelevant characteristic, into a systemic source of social disadvantage. A pervasive aspect of a caste system based on gender, uniting many seemingly diverse nations, is that women's sexual and reproductive capacities are turned into objects for the use and control of others.

I claim that the anticaste principle should be used as the basis for a legal assault on a number of social practices. These include above all the exclusion of women from places where political power is exercised; unequal access to education; subjection of women to public and private violence; and unequal access to nutrition and health care. The anticaste principle might well be made the basis for a movement in international human rights law, an area that is quite primitive on issues of sex equality.[1]

I do not argue that it is law that is responsible for most sex discrimination in the world, nor do I suggest that law can operate as a kind of *deus ex machina*, bringing justice where there is now oppression. But often law can accomplish a good deal. It can set forth aspirations. It can give voice and content to injuries and assaults that are indeed felt, sometimes very deeply, but that have been buried and hence rarely articulated. In this way it can energize people and make them feel that in important ways, they are not alone. It can produce real victories in the real world. Usually it cannot produce massive social change by itself; but it can bring about some improvements in people's lives.

This essay is divided into three parts. Part 1 briefly outlines the American law of sex equality. My purpose here is to describe an especially interesting body of law, and also to suggest the lessons to be learned from one nation's concrete experience with using law to address problems of sex discrimination. I draw particular attention to the crucial and troublesome issue of 'difference', an issue that has haunted the movement for sex equality through law in many nations. Women and men are 'different', it is frequently claimed, and the difference is said, quite plausibly, both to explain and to justify social and legal differences in the treatment of the sexes. I attempt to respond to the resulting conundrums.

Part 2 explains where American law has gone wrong, introduces the anticaste principle, and tries to explain why that principle is superior to plausible alternatives. In Part 2, I also discuss the idea that legal intervention is unacceptable because it involves an unacceptably paternalistic interference with women's current preferences. The point bears especially on efforts to impose international norms of human rights on diverse countries. I conclude with a brief discussion of the increasingly prominent view that the appropriate approach for law is to rely on free markets, which, it is said, will eliminate invidious sex discrimination and overcome gender caste.

Part 3 begins with some disclaimers about the limitations of law in creating and dismantling sex discrimination. It then applies the anticaste

---

[1] See, for example, the United Nations Convention on the Elimination of All Forms of Discrimination Against Women (1980), reprinted in Senate Executive Documents, 96th Cong., 2nd Sess. 9–19 (1980).

principle to a number of disputed issues of sex equality. The applications consist of no more than a brief outline. My purpose here is not to set out a full programme for legal reform, but instead to offer some notations on the role of law in creating and maintaining gender caste, and to provide a few ideas about how law might serve as a corrective.

1 AMERICAN LAW

I will introduce the matter of gender difference and law through the lens of American constitutional law. It turns out that this seemingly parochial subject offers large and very general lessons. An understanding of American law should go at least some distance toward providing an understanding of some of the problems posed by sex equality law in other nations, even those that are or seem quite different from America. After discussing the experience of one nation, I will try to develop some principles for general use.

1.1. An Example

It will be useful to begin with *Muller* v. *Oregon*,[2] one of the most important sex discrimination cases in all of American law. In the *Muller* case, the Supreme Court upheld a law limiting the number of hours that women could work per week or per day. The law did not apply to men. The law was attacked on the ground that it interfered with freedom of contract, an attack that drew strength from a previous decision in which the Court had struck down a sex-neutral maximum hour law.[3] Despite that precedent, the Court held that the sex-based maximum hour law was permissible.

The Court's reasoning was simple. According to the Court, the law was justified because of 'the difference between the sexes'. These differences included 'woman's physical structure and the performance of maternal functions'. The Court emphasized empirical work apparently showing that a reduction of the working day was necessary in light of '(a) the physical organization of women, (b) her maternal functions, (c) the rearing and education of the children, (d) the maintenance of the home.' The legally relevant differences between men and women therefore included not merely physical ones, but also a set of social roles unique to women. For the Court, a 'difference justifies a difference in legislation'; and for the Court there is an 'inherent difference' between men and women.[4]

---

[2] 208 US 412 (1908).   [3] *Lochner* v. *New York*, 198 US 45 (1905).
[4] Ibid. at 421, 420 n. 1, 422–3. Compare this description of attitudes in prerevolutionary America: 'So distinctive and so separated was the aristocracy from ordinary folk that many still thought the two groups represented two orders of being . . . Ordinary people were thought to be different physically, and because of varying diets and living conditions, no doubt in many cases they were different. People often assumed that a handsome child, though apparently a

The key question in the *Muller* case was therefore whether men and women were 'different'. If they were, they could be treated differently. If they were not, they had to be treated the same. Because men and women were obviously different, different treatment did not offend the equality principle.

For the modern observer, there are several striking features in the *Muller* opinion. The first is the Court's assumption—supported in the case by an elaborate but highly anecdotal factual brief from Louis Brandeis—that the differences between men and women are sufficiently real and sufficiently large to justify a maximum hour law targeted at women alone. Perhaps these differences do not exist in sufficient scope to justify such differences in law. This is in fact the general answer offered by current constitutional law in America. The Supreme Court says that measures of the sort upheld in *Muller* reflect 'overbroad stereotyes', and these are unacceptable under the equal protection clause of the American Constitution (see Part 1, section 1. 2. below).

Notwithstanding this change, it is striking that current sex equality law, in America and generally elsewhere, asks the same question asked in *Muller*: are men and women the same? The difference in legal outcomes stems not from a different approach to the subject, but from the fact that men and women are usually thought to be the same. Women are no longer said to be 'different', at least not very often. It is for this reason that different treatment, through law, is generally unacceptable—a point to which I will return.

We might therefore conclude that *Muller* was wrong because it treated women as different when they are really the same. (The word 'really' disguises some complex issues of fact and value.) But the problems in *Muller* go much deeper than this. The Court treated the differences between men and women as 'inherent' when in fact some of these differences were a creation of social customs, and indeed in part of the legal system itself. Of course there are physical differences between the sexes, and the law is not responsible for all of these differences. Law cannot make men into women, or vice versa, at least not in the strict biological sense.[5] But consider the rearing and education of children, or 'maternal functions', or the maintenance of the home. With respect to these, the Court attributed to 'nature' a set of tasks that are socially produced and in part a product of law.

Indeed, those tasks are in part a product of laws of the very sort at issue in *Muller*. Such laws help freeze women out of the workforce, by making women employees more costly or less remunerative to employers. This

commoner, had to be some gentleman's bastard offspring.' Gordon Wood, *The Radicalism of the American Revolution* (New York: Knopf, 1991), 27.

[5] Though this issue is more complex than it appears. See T. Laqueur, *Making Sex* (Cambridge, Mass.: Harvard University Press, 1990); J. Butler, *Gender Trouble* (New York: Routledge, 1990).

form of discrimination will of course contribute to a division between the
social roles of men and women. It will influence women to occupy the
domestic sphere and encourage men to leave that sphere.

Thus far the problem with the approach in *Muller* is that the Court saw
differences as inherent when in fact they were a product of society and law.
But a separate and perhaps even more serious problem is that the Court
treated the differences between the sexes as a sufficient *justification* for laws
disadvantaging women. Recall here the Court's claim: 'Difference justifies
a difference in legislation.' Let us suppose that men and women are different. Even if this is so, the decision to turn any difference into something
with social consequences, or into a social disadvantage, is a legal and hence
social one. That decision must be justified. By itself, the mere fact of
difference is insufficient to justify disadvantage. Even if we are dealing with
natural differences, the normative claims of nature are quite weak.[6]

The point is often overlooked. But there are innumerable differences
among human beings—height, eye colour, strength, hormones, capacity to
smell, gender—and those differences are made meaningful only through
social and legal decisions. Such decisions turn differences into advantages
and disadvantages. Sometimes, such decisions make differences into something that is interesting or even noticed. The translation of a difference into
a disadvantage requires a reason; it is not, standing alone, a reason at all.[7]
A law that would impose a minimum wage for people with blue eyes could
not plausibly be justified on the ground that such people are 'different'
(even though they are).

Perhaps more fundamentally, differences between men and women may
well be insufficient even to explain disadvantage, or to help us to understand how it came about. Sometimes lawyers, politicians, and others act as
if there is a natural or tight connection between the 'real' differences
between men and women and the different social roles of men and women.[8]

---

[6] See, for the classic discussion, John Stuart Mill, *Nature*, in J. M. Robson ed., The
Collected Works of John Stuart Mill (Toronto: University of Toronto Press, 1967): 'If the
artificial is not better than the natural, to what end are all the arts of life? To dig, to plough,
to build, to wear clothes, are direct infringements on the injunction to follow nature . . . All
praise of Civilization, or Art, or Contrivance, is so much dispraise of Nature; an admission of
imperfection, which it is man's business, and merit, to be always endeavoring to correct or
mitigate . . . In sober truth, nearly all the things which men are hanged or imprisoned for doing
to one another, are nature's every day performances . . . It remains true that nearly every
respectable attribute of humanity is the result not of instinct, but of a victory of instinct; and
that there is hardly anything valuable in the natural man except capacities—a whole world of
possibilities, all of them dependent upon eminently artificial discipline for being realized . . .
The duty of man is the same in respect to his own nature as in respect to the nature of all other
things, namely not to follow but to amend it . . . Conformity to nature, has no connection
whatever with right and wrong . . . That a thing is unnatural, in any precise meaning which can
be attached to the word, is no argument for its being blamable.'
[7] See C. MacKinnon, *Feminism Unmodified* (Cambridge, Mass.: Harvard University Press,
1987), ch. 2.
[8] See C. MacKinnon, *Sexual Harassment of Working Women* (Cambridge, Mass.: Harvard
University Press, 1979), ch. 2.

But this is at best speculative. We lack anything like a good account of how sex differences relate to social roles and of the complex causal connections between the two.

In *Muller*, the Court relied on differences to justify inequality, as if gender differences came first and inequality second. In fact the opposite may be true.[9] It is inequality, through social norms and law, that creates many of the relevant differences between the genders: the different social roles of men and women, with men being concentrated in the public sphere and women in the private sphere. It is inequality that helps make the differences into something socially and legally relevant.

I do not claim that there are no differences between men and women, either before or after society has acted. Surely there are important biological differences. What those differences *must* mean for society is not likely to be a question that any of us is in a position to answer. Nor have I shown that every social or legal difference between men and women is impermissible. But it should by now be clear that differences, even if real, do not justify laws that treat women unequally, or that turn women's differences into a social disadvantage.

1.2. Notes on American Sex Equality Law

Muller is no longer the law. Under the current understanding of the American Constitution, most legal distinctions between men and women are invalid. Indeed, many people think that there have been extraordinary advances in sex equality law in America and the West in general. It is unquestionably remarkable to find that since the 1970s, the Supreme Court has invoked the Constitution to strike down a number of laws discriminating on the basis of sex. But how much has the Court contributed to sex equality in America? What might the Court have done differently? Here we will find some surprising answers. Indeed, we will find some modest but intriguing continuity between contemporary law and *Muller*.

In this section I offer a brief survey of American law, and then say something about the consequences of the law for sex equality.

1.2.1. A brief survey A key early moment in American law came in *Bradwell* v. *Illinois*,[10] in which the Court upheld Illinois' refusal to licence a woman to practise law. The revealing and much-quoted concurring opinion by Justice Bradley reads in part as follows:

The natural and proper timidity and delicacy which belongs to the female sex evidently unfits it for many of the occupations of civil life. The constitution of the family organization, which is founded in the divine ordinance, as well as in the

---

[9] An argument of this kind is made ibid.   [10] 83 US 130 (1873).

nature of things, indicates the domestic sphere as that which properly belongs to the domain and functions of womanhood. The harmony, not to say identity, of interests and views which belong or should belong to the family institution, is repugnant to the idea of a woman adopting a distinct and independent career from that of her husband . . .

It is true that many women are unmarried and not affected by any of the duties, complications, and incapacities arising out of the married state but these are exceptions to the general rule. The paramount destiny and mission of woman are to fulfill the noble and benign offices of wife and mother. This is the law of the Creator. And the rules of civil society must be adapted to the general constitution of things, and cannot be based upon exceptional cases.

It is striking that some version of these views continues to capture the opinions of many people throughout the world and indeed in the United States itself.

The law continued in this vein for an extremely long time. It was not until 1971—nearly a century later—that sex discrimination through law came under serious constitutional challenge. In a seemingly minor case decided in that year, the Court struck down a statute giving a preference to men over women in establishing the hierarchy of persons entitled to administer the estate of a decedent who died intestate.[11] The Court said that the state must show that 'a difference in the sex of competing applicants' bears a 'rational relationship to a state objective'. It concluded that here the gender classification was 'arbitrary'.

In this case, the Court indicated that the ordinary 'rational relationship' test would continue to apply to sex discrimination. This test is extremely deferential to the legislature. Under the 'rational relationship' test, the state must not be completely arbitrary; but it may usually adopt crude devices for categorizing people. The result of the 'rational relationship' test would be that in practice, almost all sex discrimination would be upheld. But two years later, in *Frontiero* v. *Richardson*,[12] the Court indicated that legal rules discriminating on the basis of sex would henceforth be treated with great scepticism.

In the *Frontiero* case, the Court struck down a law allowing men in military service automatically to claim their spouses as dependents for purposes of receiving medical and other benefits, but requiring women to prove actual dependency. The case was important because the discriminatory law made the package of employment benefits larger for men than for women. Men automatically obtained protection of their spouses; women did not. In this way, the law was a direct successor of that in *Muller*, providing a comparatively greater incentive for men to enter the workforce. Laws of this kind make into a self-fulfilling prophecy their assumption that men are more frequently workers than women.

---

[11] *Reed* v. *Reed*, 404 US 71 (1971).   [12] 411 US 677 (1973).

Four of the nine justices in *Frontiero* wrote that sex discrimination should be treated like race discrimination. This revolutionary step would mean that courts would give so-called 'strict scrutiny' to all discrimination on the basis of sex. If 'strict scrutiny' were applied, government could rarely, if ever, draw lines between men and women. The opinion's important passages are worth quoting at length:

There can be no doubt that our Nation has had a long and unfortunate history of sex discrimination. Traditionally, such discrimination was rationalized by an attitude of romantic paternalism which, in practical effect, put women, not on a pedestal, but in a cage . . . As a result of notions such as these, our statute books gradually became laden with gross, stereotyped distictions between the sexes and, indeed, throughout much of the 19th century the position of women in our society was, in many respects, comparable to that of blacks under the pre-Civil War slave codes. Neither slaves nor women could hold office, serve on juries, or bring suit in their own names, and married women traditionally were denied the legal capacity to hold or convey property or to serve as legal guardians of their own child . . .

It is true, of course, that the position of women in America has improved markedly in recent decades. Nevertheless, it can hardly be doubted that, in part because of the high visibility of the sex characteristic, women still face pervasive, although at times more subtle, discrimination in our educational institutions, in the job market and, perhaps most conspicuously, in the political arena.

Moreover, since sex, like race and national origin, is an immutable characteristic determined solely by the accident of birth, the imposition of special disabilities upon the members of a particular sex because of their sex would seem to violate 'the basic concept of our system that legal burdens should bear some relationship to individual responsibility . . . The sex characteristic frequently bears no relation to ability to perform or contribute to society.

As noted, only four justices joined this opinion. Five of the nine justices refused to do so and hence 'strict scrutiny' has not been applied to sex discrimination. In the next key case, *Craig* v. *Boren*,[13] the Court announced that laws distinguishing between men and women would not face strict scrutiny, but nonetheless 'must serve important governmental objectives and must be substantially related to achievement of those objectives'. In principle, this standard is an intermediate one, somewhere between 'strict scrutiny' and 'rational basis' review. In practice, the standard has meant that the Court will almost always invalidate laws that contain explicit sex discrimination. This has been an extraordinary development and an enormous victory for the lawyers attempting to eliminate laws discriminating on the basis of sex.

Thus, for example, the Court has invalidated laws setting out different drinking ages for males and females;[14] providing for all-female nursing

[13] 429 US 190 (1976).   [14] Ibid.

schools;[15] making a husband the 'head and master' of property jointly owned with his wife, and thus allowing him to dispose of the property without his wife's consent;[16] requiring the consent of the mother, but not the father, for adoption of a child born out of wedlock;[17] allowing payment of social security benefits to a widow under all circumstances, but to a widower only if he can prove that he was receiving at least one-half of his support from his wife;[18] and providing that husbands, and not wives, could be required to pay alimony on divorce.[19]

In a very few cases, the Court has upheld laws discriminating explicitly on the basis of sex. When it has done so, it has invoked 'real differences' between males and females. (Recall *Muller.*) Three cases are especially important in this regard. In *Michael M.* v. *Sonoma County Superior Court,*[20] the Court upheld a law defining statutory rape as sexual intercourse with females under the age of 18 years. The Court acknowledged that the law treated males differently from females, but said that 'young men and young women are not similarly situated with respect to the problems and the risks of sexual intercourse. Only women may become pregnant, and they suffer disproportionately the profound physical, emotional, and psychological consequences of sexual activity . . . A legislature acts well within its authority when it elects to punish only the participant who, by nature, suffers few of the consequences.' Thus the Court emphasized that women were naturally deterred from engaging in sexual intercourse; that males were under no 'similar natural sanctions'; and that the discriminatory law could therefore serve the interest of equality.

In *Rostker* v. *Goldberg,*[21] the Court upheld a law requiring men, but not women, to register for the military draft. The Court reasoned that only men would be needed in combat, for which women were ineligible. 'Men and women, because of the combat restrictions on women, are simply not similarly situated for purposes of a draft or registration for a draft.' Discrimination was therefore acceptable. The combat restriction was not challenged in the case, and most people agree that the Court would have rejected any such challenge.

In *Califano* v. *Webster,*[22] the Court upheld a law giving retired female workers higher monthly old-age benefits than similarly situated retired male workers. Under the law, women could exclude more lower earning years than men, for purposes of developing the computation formula from which old-age benefits would be calculated. The Court emphasized the compensatory purposes of the law, discriminating (that is, treating differ-

---

[15] *Mississippi University for Women* v. *Hogan*, 458 US 718 (1982).
[16] *Kirchberg* v. *Feenstra*, 450 US 455 (1981).   [17] 441 US 380 (1979).
[18] *Califano* v. *Goldfarb*, 430 US 199 (1977).   [19] *Orr* v. *Orr*, 440 US 268 (1979).
[20] 450 US 464 (1981).   [21] 453 US 57 (1981).   [22] 430 US 313 (1977).

ently) not to subordinate women, but to restore them to a position of equality. It said:

Reduction of the disparity in economic condition between men and women caused by the long history of discrimination against women has been recognized as . . . an important governmental objective . . . The more favorable treatment of the female wage earner enacted here was not a result of 'archaic and overbroad generalizations' about women or of 'the role-typing society has long imposed' upon women . . . The challenged statute operates directly to compensate women for past economic discrimination.

Thus far I have discussed laws that discriminate explicitly on the basis of sex. What if a law has large discriminatory effects, but does not expressly treat women differently from men? What if a law harms women, but does not explicitly discriminate against them? In a key case, the Court concluded that such a law would be permissible so long as the law was minimally 'rational'. *Personnel Administrator* v. *Feeney*[23] involved a law providing an employment preference for veterans in state government. Because very few women were veterans, the law operated overwhelmingly to the advantage of men.

In upholding the law, the Court relied on the fact that some women were veterans, and many men were not. Since the law did not single out sex as a classifying factor, and merely had a discriminatory effect, it would be upheld unless it could be shown that it had been motivated by a discriminatory purpose. Discriminatory purpose, said the Court in the key passage, implies 'more than intent as volition or intent as awareness of consequences. It implies that the decisionmaker selected or reaffirmed a particular course of action at least in part "because of", not merely "in spite of" its adverse effects upon an identifiable group.'

In practice, this means that almost all laws that have a discriminatory effect on women will be upheld. It is exceptionally difficult to prove that a law was adopted 'because of' its adverse effects on women. It follows that employment practices that harm women—by, for example, imposing height and weight requirements, or refusing to adjust for childcare responsibilities—are fully acceptable.

This brief survey should be sufficient to provide a picture of current American law under the Constitution. Laws that discriminate explicitly on the basis of sex are seen as raising issues of sex discrimination. The governing equality principle forbids those laws in the vast majority of circumstances. A discriminatory staute is acceptable only if it responds to 'real differences' between men and women, or (what may be a subcategory of the same point) if it is plausibly compensatory for past discrimination.

[23] 442 US 256 (1977).

The category of 'real differences' is in turn read narrowly. It generally does not include differences in what we might call the social situation of men and women: the fact that women care disproportionately for children, are less likely to be wage workers, are more likely to be financially dependent on their spouses, are shorter and less heavy. Thus, for example, the fact—and it is a fact—that women are more likely to be financially dependent on men does not justify sex discrimination in the social security law. But laws that discriminate in their effects are almost always permissible.

We might describe contemporary American law most generally as a prohibition on *unreasonable sexual differentiation*. Women must be treated the same as men when they are the same as men. Since women and men generally are the same, explicitly discriminatory laws generally are invalid. Laws that are neutral, in the sense that they do not explicitly refer to sex, are acceptable, since they do not embody sexual differentiation at all.

I have emphasized the law of the American Constitution; but it is important to note that there are prohibitions on sex discrimination in ordinary, nonconstitutional law as well. The basic American civil rights law (enacted in 1964) forbids sex discrimination in employment, including hiring, firing, promotion, pay, and working conditions.[24] It is worthwhile to observe that this provision—the most important legal prohibition on sex discrimination in the United States—was added to the bill not by its supporters, but by Southern Senators hoping to defeat the bill in its entirety. The Southern Senators believed that a prohibition on sex discrimination was so clearly ridiculous that its inclusion would doom the bill as a whole. Remarkably, the authors and advocates of the bill had originally excluded sex discrimination from the set of prohibitions, and it appears that they were singularly unenthusiatic about the idea of adding sex to the list of forbidden discriminations.

Nonetheless, the bill passed with the new addition, and it has been extremely important. Going beyond the Constitution, which applies only to government and which requires explicit discrimination or discriminatory purpose, the civil rights law applies to the private sector, and it requires employers to offer persuasive justifications for all measures that have a discriminatory effect on women. Height and weight requirements will therefore be invalidated unless they can be firmly justified. This basic civil rights law has also been held to forbid sexual harassment on the job.[25]

A separate legal provision forbids discrimination by institutions receiving federal funds, including colleges and universities. American law also requires equal pay for equal work,[26] though equal is defined narrowly. Despite the urgings of some, American law does not guarantee equal pay for 'comparable work'. Discrimination on the basis of pregnancy is also banned.[27]

[24] 42 USC 2000e *et seq.*   [25] *Meritor Savings Bank* v. *Vinson*, 477 US 57 (1986).
[26] 29 USC 206(d).   [27] 42 USC 2000e(k).

1.2.2. A note on consequences Many people think that American law, thus understood, reveals a highly developed understanding of the principle of sex equality. But what has American law actually accomplished for women?

The results are ambiguous. Professional women have probably been benefited a good deal, and it is possible that in employment, there have been very general improvements.[28] No employer can reserve jobs to men, and this has in all likelihood made a major difference. The ban on sexual harassment has probably improved working conditions for thousands and perhaps millions of women. It may well have contributed to changes in male and female attitudes as well, imposing social stigma on a practice that is a continuing source of discrimination for women throughout the world.[29]

It is far from clear, however, that American women are very much closer to equality as a result of the apparently major changes in American law.[30] American women earn about 65 cents for every dollar earned by American men, and there is no evidence that antidiscrimination law has had an important effect on this disparity.[31] It is hard to connect the legal decisions to general improvements in the labour market status of women. There is no good evidence that these decisions have materially improved women's income or women's access to jobs.[32]

Several areas of special importance seem unaffected by the changes in law. For example, a serious problem for American women consists of what happens after divorce. A California study showed that men can expect their standard of living to increase by 42 per cent, whereas women can expect theirs to fall by 73 per cent.[33] This is typical of a pattern experienced internationally, in which a high financial cost is exacted from women who leave their marriages. The high costs of 'exit' have a large range of effects during marriage, with respect to the allocation of power within the marriage and with respect to the practise of physical abuse and battery. These effects are a product of family law, not of nature.

The recent change in antidiscrimination law has not remedied this situation. In some cases, it may even have made things worse. If courts cannot treat women better than men in awarding alimony, they may neglect the sacrifices women have made for men's careers, and they may devalue the domestic contributions made by women. In the area of social insurance and welfare, the legal decisions require similarly situated men and women to be treated 'the same'. But these decisions have accomplished very little in

[28] Evidence of benefits is offered in Donohue, 'Prohibiting Sex Discrimination in the Workplace: An Economic Perspective', *University of Chicago Law Review* 54 (1989), 628.

[29] C. MacKinnon, *Sexual Harassment of Working Women* (1979), is the classic discussion.

[30] See Becker, 'Prince Charming: Abstract Equality', *Supreme Court Review* (1987), 201.

[31] Becker, 'Politics, Differences and Economic Rights', *University of Chicago Legal Forum* (1989), 169, 172.

[32] See G. Rosenberg, *The Hollow Hope* (Chicago, Ill.: University of Chicago Press, 1991).

[33] See L. J. Weitzman, *The Divorce Revolution* (New York, The Free Press, 1985), 338–9.

improving women's lives. This is partly because with respect to poverty, women are simply not similarly situated to men.[34]

It is ironic but true that many of the key sex discrimination cases in America were brought by men, seeking to overturn protectionist laws that perhaps 'stigmatized' women in theory but may have benefited them in practice. If the law had sought to make a real difference, could it have done so? What would it have done?

2 THE ANTICASTE PRINCIPLE DEFINED

2.1. What's Wrong With American Law

I suggest that American equality law has gone wrong in two ways. First, it has misidentified the class of laws that raise issues of sex discrimination. Secondly, it has mischaracterized the relevant equality principle. The two points are related.

More concretely, American law sees sex discrimination always and only in laws that explicitly treat women differently from men. This understanding has caused two problems. First, a few laws that treat women differently from men are acceptable, and indeed promote the goal of equality, rightly understood. *Califano* v. *Webster* is an explicit and unusual reflection of this point. For example, the law of alimony and child custody might work in the direction of equality if it actually took sex into account. Sex-neutral rules might well harm the cause of equality. As I have noted, if courts cannot take sex into account, there is pressure for them not to take into account the disproportionate contributions of women to domestic life. The result is less money at time of divorce and less sex equality.[35]

Secondly, and more important, some laws raise issues of sex discrimination even if they do not treat women differently from men, as that concept is conventionally understood.[36] The reason is that existing social practices, and indeed men, are used as the baseline from which to decide whether women can make out a claim of inequality. In particular, women can be treated the same as men only insofar as they *are* the same as men. But sometimes women are not the same as men, and they should nonetheless be allowed to make an inequality claim.

Let me be more concrete. Suppose that the law forbids women from having an abortion, or excludes pregnancy from a disability programme. Under current American law, there is no issue of sex discrimination.[37] Men cannot get pregnant; women and men are to that extent not similarly

[34] Becker, 'Politics, Differences and Economic Rights', *supra* note 31: 176–8.

[35] The point is made nicely in Becker, *supra* note 30, and Becker, *supra* note 31.

[36] The reference to convention is necessary because by itself, the 'similarly situated' test is purely formal, and could be used to reach a very wide variety of results.

[37] See *Geduldig* v. *Aiello*, 417 US 484 (1974).

situated. A law that restricts abortion or excludes pregnancy therefore raises no equality problem. But this is an odd way to think about the equality issue. If the law takes a characteristic limited to one group of citizens, and turns that characteristic into a systemic source of social disadvantage, surely there is a problem of equality.[38] It would take only a minor extension of this point to suggest that laws that disproportionately burden women—consider a veterans' preference for employment—might well be subject to legal doubt, at least where there is no firm sex-neutral justification for such laws.

We can connect this issue to the broader failure of American law to do as much as it might have about existing inequalities. Ironically, many of those existing inequalities are a product of contemporary law—a point that applies in numerous countries other than America. Consider a few areas. The criminal justice system treats men and women differently, so that women are disproportionately subject to criminal violence. The failure to provide adequate protection against rape, sexual harassment, and other forms of sexual assault and abuse might well be seen to raise equality issues. Indeed, the fact that rape within marriage is generally not a crime, and that domestic violence is often not the object of real police attention, might well be treated as an embodiment of sex discrimination.

Or return to the fact that after divorce, women's economic welfare goes sharply down, whereas men's goes sharply up. This is not the result of nature, but instead of legal rules that assure this result. The relevant rules might well be subject to legal attack. Or consider again the veterans' preferences laws, and more important the existence of a social security system that was designed for and that benefits male breadwinners, while helping women much less because they do not follow conventional male career paths.[39]

Now we are in a position to make some general observations about the question of sex 'differences'. It is often said that women and men are different, and that the differences help to explain and to justify social and legal inequality. Indeed, differences are usually invoked as the justification for disadvantage. It is often said, for example, that women are different from men and that different treatment in social practice and in law is therefore perfectly appropriate. Here the reasoning of the old *Muller* Court continues to capture a good deal of current thinking about law, not simply in America, but throughout the world.

The claim will not do. As we have seen, the question for decision is not whether there is a difference—often there certainly is—but whether the legal and social treatment of that difference can be adequately justified. Differences need not imply inequality, and only some differences have that

---

[38] The point is further developed in Sunstein, *The Partial Constitution* (Cambridge, Mass.: Harvard University Press, 1993).

[39] See Becker, *supra* note 31: 176–8.

implication. When differences do have that implication, it is a result of legal and social practices, not the result of differences alone. Since they are legal and social, these practices might be altered even if the differences remain.

An analogy may be helpful here. The problems faced by handicapped people are not a function of handicap 'alone' (an almost impenetrable idea—what would current handicaps even mean in a different world?), but instead of the interaction between physical and mental capacities on the one hand and a set of human obstacles made by and for the able-bodied on the other. It is those obstacles, rather than the capacities taken as brute facts, that create a large part of what it means to be handicapped.

It would be implausible, for example, to defend the construction of a building with stairs, and without means of access for those in wheelchairs, on the ground that those who need wheelchairs are 'different'. The question is whether it is acceptable, or just, to construct a building that excludes people who need an unusual means of entry. That question may not be a simple one, but it cannot be answered simply by pointing to a difference. The same is true for sex.

We can go further. Differences between men and women are often said to explain sex inequality, indeed to be the origin of inequality. But as the *Muller* case reveals, it might be equally right to think that differences are an outcome of inequality, or its product.[40] Certainly some and perhaps many of the 'real differences' between men and women exist only because of sex inequality. Differences in physical strength, for example, undoubtedly have a good deal to do with differences in expectations, nutrition, and training. The nature and degree of difference between men and women is notoriously variable across time and space. The variations are sufficient to show that what we attribute to nature is often a social product.

Even differences in desires, preferences, aspirations, and values are in significant part a function of society and even law. The point suggests that it is wrong to base sex discrimination policy entirely on what women currently 'want',[41] a subject taken up below. Many of the differences that are said to justify inequality are really a product of inequality.

[40] See C. MacKinnon, *supra* note 7.
[41] M. Wollstonecraft, 'A Vindication of the Rights of Women', in C. Poston (ed.) (New York: Norton, 1975; originally published in 1792); J. S. Mill, 'The Subjection of Women', reprinted in J. S. Mill, *On Liberty and Other Essays* (J. Gray, ed., New York: Oxford University Press, 1991), 471. See also Sen, 'Rational Fools', *Philosophy and Public Affairs*, 6 (1977), 317; Nussbaum, 'Shame, Separateness, and Political Unity', in *Essays on Aristotle's Ethics* (A. Rorty ed., 1988), 395; Sunstein, 'Preferences and Politics', *Philosophy and Public Affairs*, 20 (1991), 3. Consider as well Tocqueville's observations: 'Should I call it a blessing of God, or a last malediction of his anger, this disposition of the soul that makes men insensible to extreme misery and often gives them a sort of depraved taste for the cause of their afflictions? Plunged in this abyss of wretchedness, the Negro hardly notices his ill fortune; he was reduced to slavery by violence, and the habit of servitude has given him the thoughts and ambitions of a slave; he admires his tyrants even more than he hates them and finds his joy and pride in servile imitation of his oppressors.' Alexis de Tocqueville, *Democracy in America* (New York: Arlington House, 1987), 317. On the related phenomenon of cognitive dissonance, see Leon

We can go even further. It is possible that many of the differences between men and women are noticed, or have anything like their current social meaning, only because of inequality. It is at least possible that the differences between men and women have such foundational status only because of the ways in which inequality and social practice make gender crucial. I do not claim that women are 'the same' as men, or that law should try to make them 'the same'. I claim only that the differences are noticed and have consequences in significant part because of sexual inequality.

Some people go so far as to argue that there is nothing in the brute biological facts to establish that there are just two sexes.[42] On this view, the biology of the matter could mean that there is one sex, or three, or five, or ten. As counterintuitive and even bizarre as this may seem, I think that it is not entirely implausible. The fact that men and women really are different—and this is indeed a fact—does not mean that the division of human beings into two, and only two, categories is compelled by biology. That division is social and sometimes legal.[43]

Whether or not this last point seems at all reasonable, I hope that I have said enough to suggest the enormous difficulties in the effort to approach the law of sex equality through the lens of 'differences'. It is especially odd

---

Festinger, *A Theory of Cognitive Dissonance* (Stanford, Calif.: Stanford University Press, 1957); on some of its implications for social theory, welfare, and autonomy, see Jon Elster, *Sour Grapes* (Cambridge: Cambridge University Press, 1983).

[42] See sources cited in *supra* note 5.

[43] There are important and revealing connections between discrimination on the basis of sex and discrimination on the basis of sexual orientation. I believe that the two forms of discrimination are closely related, indeed in some ways the same thing; they are both connected with maintenance of a caste system based on gender. This is not the place for a discussion of the point, but the treatment in text of the issue of 'differences' seems to raise it, and I therefore offer a few tentative speculations along these lines.

Consider the social and legal ban on same-sex marriages, a ban that can be found in one or another form in almost all nations. The ban on same-sex marriages is not thought to raise a problem of sex inequality in most legal systems. But might the legal ban (and the social taboo) not be crucially a product of a desire to maintain a system of gender hierarchy, a system that same-sex marriages tend to undermine by complicating traditional and still-influential ideas about 'natural difference' between men and women? There could well be differences here between the reasons for stigmatizing/outlawing male homosexual relations on the one hand and female homosexual relations on the other. Might not the ban on male homosexual relations be an effort to insist on and to rigidify 'natural difference', in part by ensuring firm and clear lines, defined in terms of gender, about sexual (and social) activity as opposed to sexual (and social) receptivity or passivity? Might not the ban on lesbian relations be at least in part an effort to ensure that women are sexual available to men? I speculate that considerations of this sort help to maintain the legal and social taboo on homosexuality, in a way that might well be damaging to both men and women, and to both heterosexual and homosexual alike, though of course in very different ways and to quite different degrees.

If these points seem exotic, we might think about a close analogy: legal and social bans on racial intermarriage. It is certainly not exotic to insist that such bans are typically (though not always) an effort to maintain a system of racial caste. For example, the American legal system has come to see such bans as an effort to maintain white supremacy, or racial caste, by keeping racial lines firm and distinct. This is so even though bans on racial marriage are formally equal:

to attribute social and legal practices involving gender to 'nature' or 'divinity'. (Recall Justice Bradwell.) If the law is to do something about sex inequality, it should look elsewhere.

2.2. An Alternative: The Antidiscrimination Principle as an Anticaste Principle

There are striking and significant international commonalities in sex inequality as between men and women.[44] If we take these commonalities as a whole, we might well describe them as amounting to the creation of a system of caste based on gender. That system, like so many others, is then attributed to 'nature' and 'natural differences'. A principal feature of the caste system consists in the translation of women's sexual and reproductive capacities into a source of second-class citizenship. Those capacities are often made into objects for the use and control of others.

In these circumstances, the appropriate equality principle is not an outgrowth of the question of differences, but an opposition to caste. The legal objection should be understood as an effort to eliminate, in places large and small, the caste system rooted in gender. A law is therefore objectionable on grounds of sex equality if it contributes to a caste system in this way. The controlling principle, to be vindicated through law, is not that women must be treated 'the same' as men, but that women must not be second-class citizens.

This principle might operate not only against laws, but also against social customs and practices that have law-like effects for social organization. Instead of asking, 'are women similarly situated to men, and if so have they been treated differently', we should ask, 'does the law or practice in question contribute to the maintenance of a caste based on gender?'

The concept of caste is by no means self-defining, and I will have to be a bit tentative about it here. I do not suggest that the caste-like features of all societies with sex inequality are the same. I do claim that the similarities are what make those features a reason for social and legal concern.

The motivating idea behind an anticaste principle is that without very good reasons, social and legal structures ought not to turn differences that are highly visible and irrelevant from the moral point of view into social disadvantages. They certainly should not be permitted to do so if the

---

whites and blacks are treated 'the same' by such bans. Bans on same-sex marriages might similarly seem to treat men and women 'the same', and thus to involve discrimination on the basis of sexual orientation rather than discrimination on the basis of sex. But here is my hypothesis: in terms of their purposes and effects, bans on same-sex marriage have very much the same connection to gender caste as bans on racial intermarriage have to racial caste. Related points are discussed in Law, 'Homosexuality and the Social Meaning of Gender', *Wisconsin Law Review* (1988), 187; Rich, 'Compulsory Heterosexuality and Lesbian Existence', in *Blood, Bread and Poetry* (New York: Norton, 1986), 23.

[44] See Okin, in this volume.

disadvantage is systemic. A difference is morally irrelevant if it has no relationship to individual entitlement or desert. Sex is certainly a morally irrelevant characteristic in this sense.[45] A systemic disadvantage is one that operates along standard and predictable lines in multiple important spheres of life, and that applies in realms that relate to basic participation as a citizen in a democracy. These realms include education, health care, freedom from private and public violence, wealth, political representation, and political influence. The anticaste principle suggests that with respect to basic human capabilities and functionings, one group ought not to be systematically below another.[46]

In the areas of sex discrimination, the problem is precisely this sort of systemic disadvantage. A social or biological difference has the effect of systematically subordinating the relevant group: not because of 'nature', but because of social and legal practices. It does so in multiple spheres and along multiple indices of social welfare: poverty, education, health, political power, employment, susceptibility to violence and crime, and so forth. That is the caste system to which the legal system should be attempting to respond.

The anticaste principle is grounded in a familiar conception of equality. It was set out long ago by John Stuart Mill: 'The principle which regulates the existing social relations between the two sexes—the legal subordination of one sex to the other—is wrong in itself, and now one of the chief hindrances to human improvement; and . . . it ought to be replaced by a principle of perfect equality, admitting no power or privilege on one side, nor disability on the other.'[47] As I understand it here, the anticaste principle is not 'egalitarian'. It is perfectly comfortable with significant disparities in the resources of different citizens. Its target is far more narrow: the creation of second-class citizenship, based on a highly visible and morally irrelevant characteristic. And while I cannot defend this claim here, I believe that the anticaste principle is universal in its scope.[48] It applies even in areas in which it would (for example) collide with religious convictions and firmly entrenched traditions.

[45] I realize that there are some complexities here. My claim is that social advantage or disadvantage cannot plausibly be based on the sex characteristic, even if that characteristic might sometimes be relevant to social roles.

[46] On capabilities and functionings, see Sen, in this volume; Nussbaum, in this volume. I am adding to these discussions a suggestion that in the context of gender, the problem lies in the particular fact that one group is systematically below another along the relevant dimensions, and an explanation of how this situation is produced by social practices and law.

[47] See J. S. Mill, 'The Subjection of Women', *supra* note 41. Mill's comments on his own argument remain highly relevant: 'And there are so many causes tending to make the feelings connected with this subject the most intense and deeply-rooted of all those which gather round and protect old institutions and customs, that we need not wonder to find them as yet undermined and loosed less than any of the rest by the progress of the great modern spiritual and social transition; nor suppose that the barbarisms to which men cling longest must be less barbarisms than those which they earlier shake off.'

[48] See Nussbaum, in this volume, on this point.

Of course there are difficult issues of strategy, timing, and implementation. Some legal interventions may not be fruitful; they may even be counterproductive. Some may breed confusion and resentment. Others may be unintelligible. Still others may disrupt a society's basic organizing frameworks, in a way that does great harm and little good. Outsiders (and insiders too) will often know too little, and they must be exceptionally careful about introducing legal principles that do not cohere with cultural norms. Context will therefore matter a great deal. All this is important; but it is quite a different matter from the issue of principle that I am now discussing.

2.3. Women's Preferences?

I want to deal now with an influential claim, bearing directly on the anticaste principle, about the relationship between sex discrimination and law. The claim is that in many different nations, women are frequently content with the sexual *status quo*, and that legal efforts therefore represent an unacceptable form of paternalism. If women themselves are content, on what basis can the legal system intervene? Is not legal intervention an illegitimate interference with women's right to liberty or autonomy?

These questions raise some complex issues; I deal with them briefly here.[49] The chief response is that the satisfaction of private preferences, whatever their content and origins, does not respond to a persuasive conception of liberty or autonomy. The notion of autonomy should refer instead to decisions reached with a full and vivid awareness of available opportunities, with all relevant information, or without illegitimate or excessive constraints on the process of preference formation. When there is inadequate information or opportunities, decisions and even preferences should be described as unfree or nonautonomous.

Private preferences often do adjust to limitations in current practices and opportunities. People may well adapt their conduct and even their desires to what is now available. Consider here the story of the fox and the sour grapes.[50] The fox does not want the grapes because he considers them to be sour; but his belief to this effect is based on the fact that the grapes are unavailable. It is therefore hard to justify their unavailability by reference to his preferences. Mary Wollstonecraft's *A Vindication of the Rights of Women*[51] applies this basic idea to the area of discrimination on the basis of sex. The book can well be seen as an extended discussion of the social formation of preferences and the phenomenon of the adaptation of preferences, beliefs, and desires to an unjust *status quo*. Thus Wollstonecraft

---

[49] See also Sen, in this volume; sources cited in *supra* note 41.

[50] Jon Elster, *Sour Grapes* (1983), which is an extended argument on the point; see also Sunstein, *The Partial Constitution*, ch. 6.

[51] M. Wollstonecraft, *A Vindication of the Rights of Women*, ed. C. Poston (New York: Norton, 1975) (originally published in 1792).

writes: 'I will venture to affirm, that a girl, whose spirits have not been damped by inactivity, or innocence tainted by false shame, will always be a romp, and the doll will never excite attention unless confinement allows her no alternative.'[52] Mill makes the same points in his work on sex equality.[53]

Amartya Sen offers an especially vivid real-world example from India. In 1944, the All-India Institute of Hygiene and Public Health surveyed widows and widowers about their health. About 48.5 per cent of the widowers said that they were 'ill' or in 'indifferent' health, compared to 2.5 per cent of widows so describing their condition. In fact the widows were in worse condition than the widowers.[54] In these circumstances it would seem odd to base health policy on subjectively held views about health conditions. Such an approach would ensure that existing discrimination would be severely aggravated.

When an adaptation of this sort is at work, respect for preferences is unjustified on grounds of autonomy and welfare as well. A social or legal system that has produced preferences, and done so by limiting opportunities unjustly, can hardly justify itself by reference to existing preferences.

There is suggestive evidence in the psychological literature to this effect, and the evidence bears directly on the claim that law should respect existing preferences with respect to sex discrimination. Most generally, the beliefs of both beneficiaries and victims of existing injustice are affected by efforts to reduce the cognitive dissonance produced by such injustice.[55] The strategy of blaming the victim, or assuming that an injury or an inequality was deserved or inevitable, tends to permit nonvictims or members of advantaged groups to reduce dissonance by assuming that the world is just—a pervasive, insistent, and sometimes irrationally held belief.[56]

Victims also participate in dissonance-reducing strategies, including the lowering of self-esteem to accommodate both the fact of victimization and the belief that the world is essentially just. Sometimes it appears easier to assume that one's suffering is warranted than that it has been imposed cruelly or by mere chance.[57] The phenomenon of blaming the victim also

---

[52] Ibid.

[53] See Mill, *The Subjection of Women*, supra note 41, writing against the claim that the existing desires of women are a product of consent.

[54] See Amartya Sen, *Commodities and Capabilities* (Amsterdam: North-Holland, 1985), 82.

[55] See *infra* note 56. Consider also the discussion of women's illiteracy in Bangladesh in Nussbaum, 'Aristotelian Social Democracy'. Drawing on Martha Chen, *A Quiet Revolution: Women in Transition in Rural Bangladesh* (Cambridge, Mass.: Schenkman, 1983), Nussbaum explores the fact that many women in Bangladesh did not demand or even want greater education or literacy, and indeed expressed satisfaction with their current educational status. Of course desires of this sort were a product of a lack of available opportunities and of social and cultural pressures.

[56] See M. Lerner, *The Belief in a Just World: A Fundamental Delusion* (New York: Plenum Press, 1980).

[57] Consider here the astonishing fact that after a draft lottery, those with both favourable and unfavourable results decided that the outcomes of the purely random process were

reflects the 'hindsight effect', through which people unjustifiably perceive events as more predictable than they in fact were, and therefore suggest that victims or disadvantaged groups should have been able to prevent the negative outcome. All this bears directly on sex discrimination.

Other work in this vein reveals that people who engage in cruel behaviour change their attitudes toward the objects of their cruelty and thus devalue them. Observers tend to do the same.[58] Such evidence relates to sex equality law in general.

Of course poverty itself is the most severe obstacle to the free development of preferences and beliefs. Programmes that attempt to respond to the multiple deprivations faced by poor people, of whom women are a disproportionately high number, might well be approached in this light. Indeed, poverty and similar forms of intense social disability can impair the formation of goals themselves, breeding instead a combination of frustration and resignation.[59] Severe deprivation influences and even closes off the development of desires. An important reason to respond to the deprivation is to promote freer and better processes of desire formation.

One goal of a legal system, in short, is to ensure autonomy not merely by allowing satisfaction of preferences, but also and more fundamentally in the processes of preference formation. John Stuart Mill himself was emphatic on this point, going so far as to suggest that government itself should be evaluated in large measure by its effects on the character of the citizenry.[60] The view that freedom requires an opportunity to choose among alternatives finds a natural supplement in the view that people should not face unjustifiable constraints on the free development of their preferences and beliefs.

A crucial feature of a system of caste based on gender consists of profound effects on the preferences and aspirations of women. The point is sufficient to show that existing preferences should be no obstacle, in principle, to an effort to eliminate a system of caste through law.

2.4. Markets?

With the extraordinary recent outburst of international enthusiasm for free markets, it should not be surprising to find the view that all invidious discrimination on the basis of race and sex will be eliminated by *laissez-faire*.[61] On this view, the appropriate approach for law is to eliminate

deserved. Rubin and Pepau, 'Belief in a Just World and Reaction to Another's Lot', *Journal of Social Issues*, 29 (1973), 73–93.

[58] See M. Lerner, *supra* note 56.

[59] See Eckstein, 'Rationality and Frustration in Political Behavior', in K. Monroe (ed.), *The Economic Approach to Politics* (New York: Harper Collins, 1991).

[60] See Mill, *Considerations on Representative Government* (New York: Liberal Arts Press, 1861).

[61] See, e.g., R. Epstein, *Forbidden Grounds* (Cambridge, Mass.: Harvard University Press, 1992).

constraints on market ordering, and to rely solely on property rights and freedom of contract.

In many ways, free markets are indeed an ally of sex equality. Legal barriers to female employment are a form of government intervention in the market, and they have often been an effective and severe hindrance to equality. In a free market, women will do well to the extent that they are able to carry out the relevant tasks. Frequently women do perform as well as or better than men. Once discriminatory laws are eliminated, free markets may well accomplish a great deal in breaking down gender caste.

Suppose, for example, that an employer prefers to hire only men. Suppose that he believes that women belong in the home. In the end, he should be driven out of the market. An employer who discriminates may well fail. As experience has shown in many nations, competitive pressures have worked powerfully against sex discrimination.

As a complete solution, however, free markets will be inadequate. In this section I want to outline some of the reasons.[62] There are four major problems.

The first problem is that in a market system, third parties might be able to impose costs on people who agree to treat women equally with men.[63] Customers and others sometimes withdraw patronage and services from nondiscriminatory employers. A law firm that hires female lawyers might find itself punished in the market-place. There are many parallels in developing countries, in which certain services are traditionally provided on a single-sex basis. In these circumstances, market pressures do not check discrimination, but instead guarantee that it will continue.

Secondly, sex discrimination can be perhaps an ordinary market response to generalizations or stereotypes that, although overbroad and perhaps even invidious, provide an economically rational basis for market decisions. Stereotypes and generalizations are of course a common ingredient in market decisions. There are information costs in making distinctions within categories, and sometimes people make the category do the work of a more individualized and sometimes more costly examination into the merits of the particular employee. Such categorical judgements are not only pervasive, but usually legitimate. But categorical judgements might well dis-serve the cause of equality.

In the area of sex discrimination, for example, an employer might discriminate against women not because he hates or devalues them, but because he has found from experience that women devote more time to childcare than do men, or that they are more likely to take leave for

---

[62] A more detailed discussion, with many citations, can be found in Sunstein, 'Why Markets Don't Stop Discrimination', *Social Philosophy & Policy*, 8 (1990), 22.

[63] See Akerloff, 'The Economics of the Caste System', in G. Akerloff, *An Economist's Book of Tales* (Cambridge: Cambridge University Press, 1979).

domestic duties. This form of 'statistical discrimination'[64]—judgements based on statistically reasonable stereotyping—can ensure that second-class citizenship will persist for women, even or perhaps especially in free markets.

The third problem is that women, acting rationally in response to market signals, may fail to attempt to overcome their second-class status, or fail to invest in 'human capital' (the economists' term for production of economically valued characteristics), simply because of the current social practices and the gender *status quo*. Suppose, for example, that there is current discrimination for any number of reasons—because employers prefer women, or because third parties impose pressures in discriminatory directions, or because employers engage in statistical discrimination. If so, there will be harmful effects on women's decisions about education or training, and indeed on their aspirations in general. As market participants, women might well invest less than men in training to be (say) doctors or technicians if these professions discriminate against women and thus reward their investment less than that of men.

Finally, markets will in some ways incorporate the norms and practices of men, at least if men are in a position to rule the society. Consider the many ways in which employment expectations and requirements are structured for traditional male career patterns. In these circumstances, a legal system committed to an anticaste principle might in some cases attempt to restructure market arrangements so as to put women on a plane of greater equality. This is so not by allowing women to be 'like' men, but sometimes by changing the criteria themselves, at least when those criteria do not have a firm independent justification. In American law, the prohibition on discrimination on the basis of pregnancy, and provisions for parental leave, are prominent examples.

These considerations suggest that while free markets can often help further the cause of gender equality, they are not a panacea. Supplemental legal controls are often necessary.

3 WHAT THE LAW MIGHT DO AND UNDO: DISCLAIMERS, EXAMPLES

In this section, I offer some examples of how the law might create or oppose sex equality. 3.1. is a disclaimer, outlining some of the limits of law. 3.2. briefly discusses what I see as the most fundamental issues for a legal norm of sex equality. 3.3. offers some notes on questions of sexuality and reproduction.

---

[64] See Phelps, 'The Statistical Theory of Racism and Sexism', *American Economic Review*, 62 (1972), 659.

3.1. The Limits of Law: A Cautionary Note

Western lawyers tend to think that much of the problem of sex discrimination lies in law. The distinctive history of sex inequality in the United States and elsewhere might well justify this view. When women have been subordinated, it has frequently been through law—not merely through old enactments depriving women of the power to vote, to hold property, and to enter into contracts, but also through current rules involving family law, welfare law, and the criminal justice system.[65] Moreover, many of the attitudes and customs of Western men and women have plausibly been influenced by legal practices.

But much of sex discrimination lies elsewhere than in law, and this is conspicuously so in the many nations in which the line between law and custom is elusive. Often no formal law is responsible for the sexual subordination of women. Sometimes subordination is the result of custom.[66] Sometimes subordination is produced by attitudes that are extremely deeply engrained, indeed that attribute existing norms and practices to nature or to divinity. Sometimes efforts to dislodge those attitudes will make no sense to people; sometimes such efforts will be close to unintelligible. Sometimes sexual subordination is partly the result of the physical power of men. In such cases, it is wrong to think that law, as Westerners understand that term, is an important causal agent in women's subordination.

Moreover, there are limits to what can be done through law, even with a properly defined equality principle. For example, most of the formerly communist countries had wonderful constitutions, with powerful and explicit guarantees of individual rights, including rights against sex discrimination. But these documents were worth less than the paper on which they were written. In practice, the relevant rights, including rights against sex discrimination, were not protected at all. The legal guarantees were, in James Madison's words, mere 'parchment barriers',[67] of no use against public and private power.

Currently, we can find powerful legal guarantees of sex equality in such places as Albania, Czechoslovakia, Greece, Hungary, Portugal, Romania, China, and Spain.[68] Do women have equality in all of those nations? Do they have equality in any of them? Certainly not.

---

[65] Some of this is well discussed in Becker, *supra* note 31.

[66] I will not deal here with the complex issue of what counts as law and what counts as custom. In many developing countries, the line between the two is extremely thin. I follow convention in understanding law, roughly, as the product of the will of some sovereign constituted with law-making power, and custom as norms or practices that do not have this sort of authority. The best discussion of this is H. L. A. Hart, *The Concept of Law* (Oxford: Oxford University Press, 1961).

[67] *The Federalist*, No. 37.

[68] See J. Seager and A. Olson, *Women in the World: An International Atlas* (New York: Simon & Schuster, 1986), 12.

For legal guarantees to be effective, a number of conditions must obtain. It helps to have an independent judiciary, willing and able to enforce legal rights against public and private institutions. With or without an independent judiciary, it is important to ensure that government officials are genuinely respectful of legal guarantees. It helps to have public and private lawyers who are willing to take on cases of sex discrimination.

The point helps explain an anomaly in many Western nations. In such nations, there are usually powerful guarantees of freedom from discrimination on the basis of sex. But in many Western nations, women face frequent sex discrimination. Consider, for example, the prohibition on sexual harassment, a prohibition that is frequently violated in practice. Legal rights mean little, even with an independent judiciary, if people are without real access to lawyers or others who can make credible threats against violators.

All this suggests that the law can operate against sex discrimination only if the relevant nation already has in place many of the features of a legal culture. If those features do not exist, a legal right to be free from sex discrimination can mean very little. Perhaps international law can serve as a catalyst here.

3.2. Citizenship, Education, Physical Security, Health, Others

In this section I outline the possible consequences of an anticaste principle, operating through law. I will be extremely brief and cursory; the issues deserve much more attention than I can offer here. My goal is simply to give a sense of the legal and social practices against which an anticaste principle might operate.

The first task of such an anticaste principle is to ensure nondiscrimination with respect to the most fundamental matters. Among these, citizenship belongs first. No one is a citizen unless entitled to vote and to hold political office. A system in which women may not do these things runs afoul of the equality principle.

The right to equal education is closely connected with citizenship. To exercise the functions of a citizen, women need to be educated on equal terms with men. Violations of this principle are omnipresent. In no fewer than 76 poor countries, less than half of eligible girls are even enrolled in secondary schools.[69] There is an especially large gap between men and women in terms of literacy. The gap is widening.

In Western nations, a core area for the law of sex discrimination has involved violations of the right to own property, the right to enter into contracts, and the right to sue and be sued. The last of these is often denominated 'the right to protect one's rights'. The right to litigate is an indispensable political right; it is a natural corollary of the right to vote. The

[69] See J. Seager and A. Olson, *Women in the World: An International Atlas* (New York: Simon & Schuster, 1986), 12.

rights to own property and to enter into contracts are necessary if women are to have basic civil capacity.

In many developing countries, current law continues to forbid women from owning land, and when property is held jointly, it is controlled by the husband. The law deprives women of equal rights over land in Brazil, Chile, Bolivia, South Africa, Zimbabwe, Libya, Nigeria, and Saudi Arabia. In most of these countries, women are also deprived of equal rights of inheritance.[70] An anticaste principle should be directed against these restrictions.

The connection between physical security and citizenship is perhaps indirect. But in order to be citizens, people need a degree of independence and immunity from private and public violence. Otherwise they are entirely subject to the whim of others. Protection against sex-based public and private violence is therefore a precondition for the status of citizenship. This is an important task in eliminating caste-like features of current regimes. To dismantle a caste system through law, it is generally necessary to extend government protections against violence to groups formerly oppressed in this way.

For women, the particular problem is extremely severe. In Peru, 70 per cent of all crimes reported to the police involve women being beaten by their partners.[71] In Japan, wife-beating has been the second-most frequent reason cited by women for divorce.[72] About 31 per cent of all female murder victims in America in 1988 were killed by husbands and boyfriends. Women were more than twice as likely to be killed by husbands and boyfriends than were husbands and boyfriends to be murdered by wives and girlfriends.[73] Battery of women by men is exceedingly common, with estimates ranging as high as four million women per year and including a large number of married women.[74]

An anticaste principle should be directed against this form of subjection. In some circumstances, at least, it is easy to see what form the principle would take as a matter of law. Rape within marriage should be criminalized. Sexual assault should be taken as seriously as other crimes. The failure to provide protection against violence, on the street or in the home, should be seen as a denial of equal protection of the laws. International human rights policy might well be harnessed to these ends.

Of the most fundamental legal rights entailed by the anticaste principle, equal access to adequate nutrition and medical care deserves an especially prominent place. A key element of second-class status consists of group-based subjection to inferior health. Nutrition and medical care are therefore central ingredients in the provision of sex equality. If women are deprived of adequate food and medical care, and men are not similarly deprived, the

---

[70] Ibid.   [71] International Atlas, 102.   [72] Ibid.
[73] See G. Rosenberg, *supra* note 32, 214.   [74] Ibid. 215.

anticaste principle has been violated. Any legal equality norm should be directed against this outcome.

In the same category are laws and practices that deprive women of equal employment opportunity. No law should exclude women from jobs open to men. If taken seriously, this principle would of course have large consequences in many nations.

3.3. Sexuality and Reproduction

I have said that a principal locus for sex discrimination consists of social and legal practices that turn women's sexual and reproductive capacities into objects for the control and use of third parties. If this is so, a number of issues treated as sex-neutral under American and much of Western law should be approached not through the lens of 'difference', but under the anticaste principle. Laws and norms that treat women's sexual and reproductive capacities in this way often do not run afoul of the idea that the similarly situated must be treated similarly. Often, at least, some of the relevant practices appear sex-neutral. Often men and women are not similarly situated.

There are many examples. These include access to contraception, sometimes foreclosed through law; legal restrictions on abortion; forced prostitution, which creates a kind of international traffic in women; female genital mutilation; marriage of young girls and teenagers, recognized in law and often against their will; sexual violence; sexual harassment; the making and distribution of pornography, especially that involving girls and young women; and perhaps surrogacy arrangements. In all of these areas, the principal problem is that women's sexual and reproductive capacities are made into commodities for the use and control of others.

A legal anticaste principle might well play a major role here. For example, sexual harassment could be recognized as a violation of equality under law. Forced prostitution could be forbidden. The age of marriage could be raised to 18, and the prohibition on marriages below that age could be taken seriously by the relevant officials. Access to contraception could be seen as a legal right operating as part of the principle of sex equality.[75]

I have only started to sketch these points here.[76] But the elimination

---

[75] See World Health Organization, *Reproductive Health* (Geneva, WHO, 1992): 'Without fertility regulation, women's rights are mere words. A woman who has no control over her fertility cannot complete her education, cannot maintain gainful employment . . . and has very few real choices open to her'; K. Bhate *et al.*, *In Search of Our Bodies: A Feminist Look at Women, Health and Reproduction in India* (Bombay: Skakti, 1987), 1: 'Women's oppression is intimately connected with the control of women's reproductive potential.'

[76] Some of these problems are discussed in more detail in Sunstein, 'Neutrality in Constitutional Law (With Special Reference to Pornography, Abortion, and Surrogacy)', *Columbia Law Review*, 92 (1992), 1.

of legal and social controls on women's sexuality and reproductive capacities should be a central part of the effort to combat gender caste through law.

4 CONCLUSION

Women are second-class citizens throughout the world. For all the differences among nations, there are striking commonalities as well. Much of this is a product of law. Exclusion from political participation; inequality in the ownership of land and in rights of inheritance; restrictions on contraception and abortion—all these, and many more, are legal controls. I have suggested that at a minimum, a legal norm of sex equality should counteract legal contributions to the creation and maintenance of a caste system based on gender. Even when law is not the source of caste, a legal commitment to gender equality, deployed against discriminatory social customs, could do a considerable amount of good.[77] This commitment should, I suggest, operate through the international law of human rights, as it currently does not.

It could be important to put a principle of sex equality into the laws of developed and developing countries alike, preferably in the relevant constitutions. This is only a first step. Enforcement of any legal guarantee requires the existence of something like a legal culture, with rights, citizen awareness of rights, lawyers, and access to independent tribunals. But social norms and legal practices should not be seen as altogether distinct spheres. A movement for sex equality could help energize the law; and an effort to inculcate legal principles of sex equality could have pervasive social effects as well.

[77] Subject to the qualifications involving timing and strategy, noted above.

Emotions and Women's Capabilities

Martha C. Nussbaum

> Dazed with fear, Okonkwo drew his matchet and cut him down. He was afraid of being thought weak . . .
>
> 'When did you become a shivering old women?' Okonkwo asked himself. 'You are known in all the nine villages for your valour in war. How can a man who has killed five men in battle fall to pieces because he has added a boy to their number? Okonkwo, you have become a woman indeed.'
>
> Chinua Achebe, *Things Fall Apart*

So, for fear of 'female' emotion and its weakness, Okonkwo kills his foster son Ikemefuna, whom he loves. So, for loathing of his love and the 'womanish' passivity into which it casts him, shaming him before others, he kills a piece of his own upbringing and his own character.[1]

Women are emotional, emotions female This view, familiar in Western and non-Western traditions alike, has for thousands of years been used in various ways to exclude women from full membership in the human community and to shape—often in ways detrimental to their own flourishing—the moral education of men.[2] If we are to make a convincing

I am extremely grateful to all participants in the WIDER conference for their valuable comments, and especially to Cathy Lutz, whose work I have long admired, for the quality of her commentary. Others whose comments have played a role in the rewriting of the paper are Martha Chen, Nancy Chodorow, Jonathan Glover, Christine Korsgaard, Onora O'Neill, Richard Posner, John Roemer, Cass Sunstein, and Susan Wolf.

[1] Achebe, *Things Fall Apart* (London: Heinemann, 1958, repr. Picador 1988), 25: 'His whole life was dominated by fear, the fear of failure and weakness. It was deeper and more intimate than the fear of evil and capricious gods and of magic, the fear of the forest, and the forces of nature, malevolent, red in tooth and claw. Okonkwo's fear was greater than these. It was not external but lay deep within himself. It was the fear of himself, lest he should be found to resemble his father. Even as a little boy he had resented his father's failure and weakness, and even now he still remembered how he had suffered when a playmate had told him that his father was *agbala*. That was how Okonkwo first came to know that *agbala* was not only another name for a woman, it could also mean a man who had taken no title. And so Okonkwo was ruled by one passion—to hate everything that his father Unoka had loved. One of those things was gentleness and another was idleness.'

It is a significant point in the novel that anger is perceived as manly, not womanish, and that anger frequently can be used to keep down the gentler emotions. Thus Okonkwo's cruelty and anger toward his wives and children is analysed as a direct outgrowth of his fear of weakness. I shall have more to say about this in what follows.

[2] For examples from India, and an argument that both male and female flourishing are damaged by this situation, see Roop Rekha Verma's paper in this volume, and also her 'Development and Gender-Essentialism', in Glover, Nussbaum, and Sunstein (eds.), *Women, Equality, and Reproduction* (forthcoming); for connections between Indian emotion categories and female receptivity, see Marya Simon, *The Weavers* (a cycle of poems) (forthcoming). For Chinese traditions, which depict the best man as passionless, see Lee Yearley, *Mencius and Aquinas* (Albany, NY: State University of NY Press, 1990), and for a penetrating analysis of traditional Chinese emotion categories, which links them closely to the analysis of emotion in

case for women's equality and to develop a single account of human functioning and capability for both women and men, we evidently need to come to grips with this issue and take some stand on the role of emotion in good human functioning.

1 EMOTIONS AND RATIONALITY

This project is urgent, since emotions are condemned as enemies of reason not only by many traditions but by the view of rationality that dominates our public life, the view of economic Utilitarianism. Charles Dickens already brilliantly made the point, when he imagined the following exchange between the Utilitarian pupil Bitzer and Mr Gradgrind, economist and grief-stricken father:[3]

'Bitzer,' said Mr Gradgrind, broken down, and miserably submissive to him, 'have you a heart?'

'The circulation, sir,' returned Bitzer, smiling at the oddity of the question, 'couldn't be carried on without one. No man, sir, acquainted with the facts established by Harvey relating to the circulation of the blood, can doubt that I have a heart.'

'Is it accessible,' cried Mr Gradgrind, 'to any compassionate influence?'

'It is accessible to Reason, sir,' returned the excellent young man. 'And to nothing else.'

Bitzer understands Reason to be a calculative faculty altogether distinct from the emotions, and sufficient without them to accomplish an adequate judgement. Indeed, so well has he learned his lessons in economic rationality that he does not grasp what an emotional response is. Like Okonkwo, Bitzer won't hear of softness. Unlike Okonkwo, he doesn't even seem to fear it—perhaps because he has a 'scientific' argument for his position, derived from Mr Gradgrind himself. For Utilitarianism prefers reasoning that is detached, cool, and calculative, concerned with quantitative measurement. And it has a way of erecting this preference into a norm, defining Reason and the Rational in terms of it, branding everything else as

ancient Greek Stoicism, see Lothar von Falkenhausen (forthcoming). Other valuable examples are cited in Catherine Lutz, *Unnatural Emotions: Everyday Sentiments on a Micronesian Atoll and Their Challenge to Western Theory* (Chicago, Ill.: University of Chicago Press, 1988). The Utku Eskimos studied in Jean Briggs's *Never in Anger* (Cambridge, Mass.: Harvard University Press, 1981) urge the elimination of most of the major emotions, and especially anger, for both males and females—see further below.

[3] I discuss the novel's account of imagination and emotion more fully in *Poetic Justice: The Literary Imagination in Public Life* (Boston: Beacon Press, forthcoming 1995). Ch. 2 has appeared in an earlier version in *New Literary History*, 22 (1991), 879 ff. For further discussion of *Hard Times* in connection with development economics, see M. Nussbaum and A. Sen, 'Introduction', in Nussbaum and Sen (eds.), *The Quality of Life* (Oxford: Clarendon Press, 1993). The edition of the novel I use is the Penguin edition, ed. David Craig (Harmondsworth, 1969).

mere Irrationality. Such thinking has had and is having a profound effect on our public culture, not only in economics but also in the law.

One typical contemporary example will indicate the situation. In his 1981 book *The Economics of Justice*, Richard Posner (the leading thinker of the law-and-economics movement) begins by announcing that he will begin from the assumption 'that people are rational maximizers of satisfactions'; the 'principles of economics', after all, are 'deductions from this assumption.'[4] Posner now goes to propose an extension of economic analysis to all areas of human life. He justifies this extension by appeal to a norm of rationality that is defined by contrast to emotion:

Is it plausible to suppose that people are rational only or mainly when they are transacting in markets, and not when they are engaged in other activities of life, such as marriage and litigation and crime and discrimination and concealment of personal information? Or that only the inhabitants of modern Western (or Westernized) societies are rational? If rationality is not confined to explicit market transactions but is a general and dominant characteristic of social behavior, then the conceptual apparatus constructed by generations of economists to explain market behavior can be used to explain nonmarket behavior as well . . . I happen to find implausible and counterintuitive the view that the individual's decisional processes are so rigidly compartmentalized that he will act rationally in making some trivial purchase but irrationally when deciding whether to go to law school or get married or evade income taxes or have three children rather than two or prosecute a law suit. But many readers will, I am sure, intuitively regard these choices . . . as lying within the area where decisions are emotional rather than rational.[5]

Posner's official purpose is to show respect for members of non-Western as well as Western societies (and, we later see, for women as well as men) by showing that their decision-making processes are rational. But without argument of any kind, he simply excludes emotion-based reasoning (and much else besides) from his account of the rational, which he takes over uncritically from the narrowest of economic conceptions. This entails that any decision-making process that later turns out not to conform to this narrow model must be regarded by Posner as 'irrational', therefore substandard. If women and non-Western peoples do not, after all, conform to the economic–utilitarian model—then so much the worse for them. And the book makes this consequence evident. For though often Posner manages to construe in economic terms behaviour that may seem quite non-

[4] Richard A. Posner, *The Economics of Justice* (Cambridge, Mass.: Harvard University Press, 1981), 1. I have discussed Posner's utilitarianism in two reviews of his book *Sex and Reason* (Cambridge, Mass.: Harvard University Press, 1992), in which he proposes to extend economic analysis to the sphere of human sexual relations. A short review is in *The New Republic* 20 April 1992, and a longer one, more concerned with the issues of this paper, in *The University of Chicago Law Review*, fall 1992. Posner has now significantly modified his views about the adequacy of utilitarianism as a normative theory of public reasoning, since he recognizes that it does not suffice to generate the Millean libertarian principles that he would favour.

[5] Posner, *Economics of Justice*, 1–2.

utilitarian,[6] by the end of the book he is forced to recognize many examples of decision-making that do not conform to this model—above all, the US Supreme Court's privacy jurisprudence, especially in the areas of abortion and contraception. He draws the predictable conclusion: the Supreme Court's reasoning is a 'topsy-turvy world', for which the 'rational' reader should have no respect at all.[7] The same conclusion would be drawn, evidently, about the reasoning of a woman, or a member of a non-Western society, were it to become clear to Posner that this reasoning relied on the emotions or on other non-economic processes. Elsewhere Posner refers to a mother's grief at the death of a child as an example of a 'nonrational' process.[8]

Is Posner Okonkwo? If so, then the matchet of utilitarian rationality is ready for the softness in us all: for Posner's view, repudiating emotion-based judgement as irrational and (so to speak)[9] womanish, is entirely typical in public life. Sometimes it is claimed that women, on account of their emotional 'nature', are incapable of full deliberative rationality, and should not perform various social roles in which rationality is required. To take just one example: in 1872 Myra Bradwell was denied a licence to practise law in the state of Illinois. The US Supreme Court, upholding the

[6] Here Posner follows the lead of Gary Becker, *The Economic Approach to Human Behavior* (Chicago, Ill.: University of Chicago Press, 1976), *A Treatise on the Family* (Cambridge, Mass: Harvard University Press, 1981). For criticism of Becker's models, see Sen's paper in this volume, and my discussion of it in the Introduction.

[7] Posner, *Economics of Justice*, 345. Posner's view of the privacy issue has now significantly changed. In *Sex and Reason* he argues that it is legitimate to fill gaps in the explicit provisions of the Constitution by finding a general right to privacy, and very important for courts to do so if they are to prevent arbitrary and wilful impositions of legislative power. He strongly upholds the Supreme Court's contraception rulings, supports the outcome, though not all the reasoning, in *Roe* v. *Wade*, and argues that *Bowers* v. *Hardwick* (in which the Supreme Court refused to recognize a right to privacy where consensual adult homosexual relations were concerned) was both wrongly decided and extremely ill argued. His own 'libertarian' theory of sexual legislation holds that the law may intervene in sexual matters only in order to protect the 'liberty or property' of others.

[8] Posner, *The Problems of Jurisprudence* (Cambridge, Mass.: Harvard University Press, 1990) 453, n. 40: 'And recall the nonrational component in Aristotelian deliberation. See Martha C. Nussbaum, *The Fragility of Goodness: Luck and Ethics in Greek Tragedy and Philosophy*, 307–10 (1986).' Posner's reference is to a section in my discussion of what I call 'non-scientific deliberation' in Aristotle where I argue that the emotions are, for Aristotle, an important part of *rational* deliberation: 'Far from seeing them as obstacles to good reasoning, he makes proper passivity and passional responsiveness an important and necessary part of good deliberation' (307). The central example is one of grief for a child's death, taken from Euripides' *The Trojan Woman*. Posner is so thoroughly convinced that emotions cannot be rational that he can read this discussion and summarize it as a discussion of 'non-rational' components. In more recent work, however, Posner significantly modifies this view: see especially the essay on rhetoric in *Overcoming Law* (Cambridge, Mass.: Harvard University Press, 1995).

[9] This qualification is necessary where Posner is concerned, since he has explicitly said that he thinks the association of emotion with women is misleading: females are just as rational, in the utilitarian sense, as males. But many holders of such a view do not so stipulate. And Posner himself, in *The Problems of Jurisprudence*, discusses compassion and related emotions in a chapter entitled 'Literary and Feminist Perspectives'.

denial, wrote that 'the natural and proper timidity and delicacy which belongs to the female sex evidently unfits it for many of the occupations of civil life.'[10] This Okonkwo-like line of thought[11] does not require Utilitarianism to get going, clearly; indeed I regret to say that in the Western philosophical tradition it can be traced at least as far back as Aristotle himself.[12]

Sometimes the appeal to women's emotional nature takes an apparently more positive form—though with consequences no less pernicious for women's equality. Here it is claimed that, on account of their emotional 'nature', women are in fact well equipped to perform certain valuable social functions: for example, raising children, caring for the needs of a husband. These functions are indeed important; and women's fitness for them gives them social importance. But they must be exercised in the home; and, properly exercised, they will confine women to the home for much of her life. Again, this is a very old argument in both non-Western and Western traditions of thought. It is prominent in both Hindu and Islamic traditions, and in Chinese thought as well.[13] It is at least as old, in Western philosophy, as Xenophon's *Oeconomicus*, which faithfully reflects Athenian popular thinking of the time on this issue. In modern times it is again extremely common. It is central to Rousseau's arguments for denying women the sort of education in judgement that fits males for public life.[14] It has recently played a very influential role in the social sciences in the United States—in Erik Erikson's assertions that women's 'inner space' defines for her a special field of activity, connected with nurturing and the home; in Talcott Parsons's very influential account of the family, in which the woman plays an 'expressive' (emotional, nurturing) role, the man an 'instrumental' (rational, practical, calculating) role, and in which the woman's role prevents her, in all but the most unusual cases, from holding a full-time job.[15] Advocates of women's equality have often uncritically accepted this contrast between emotion and civic rationality, arguing that women who wish to prove their fitness for citizenship must follow the Stoics

[10] *Bradwell* v. *the State*, 83 US (16 Wall.) 130 (1872). For a discussion of the case I am indebted to Susan Okin, *Women in Western Political Thought* (Princeton, NJ: Princeton University Press, 1979), 252–6. See also Cass Sunstein's paper in this volume.

[11] Sometimes we find a related position about women's anger that would not have been endorsed by Okonkwo, who thinks of anger as 'male': thus Seneca's *Medea* claims, in a way typical of the Greek tradition, that women's jealous rage is stronger than any 'violence of fire or swelling gale'. Rage, like timidity, can be thought a barrier to full civic equality—especially when it is the rage of a woman that is in question.

[12] *Politics* 1260a 12–13: women have the deliberative faculty, but it is 'lacking in authority'—apparently, *vis à vis* their 'irrational' emotions.

[13] On Islam, see Valentine Moghadam, *Modernizing Women: Gender and Social Change in the Middle East* (Boulder, Colo., and London: Lynne Rienner, 1993). On Hindu traditions, see Verma's paper in this volume; on China, see Li.

[14] On these arguments, with references to some other analyses, see my paper 'Human Capabilities' in this volume.

[15] For an excellent account of these views, see Okin, *Women*, ch. 10.

and get rid of (or at least very much curtail) the emotions, in order to be fully rational.[16]

Women in developing countries are particularly vulnerable to such 'arguments': for they are the intersection point of the traditional gender-based denigration of emotion with a colonial form of 'argument' that holds the people of developing countries to be, in general, excessively emotional and unfit for self-government. Stereotypes of the people of India, or of Africa, as 'intuitive', 'irrational', 'emotional' are too common to require illustration—and one can add that this simple portrait is all too often produced by alleged admirers of these societies as well as by detractors.[17] The intersection between the ethnic and the gender-based denigrations is sometimes made explicit, as in Havelock Ellis's striking observation that among women, 'as among children, savages, and nervous subjects', emotions are dominant over reason.[18]

Evidently if we wish to defend a universal norm of human functioning that includes women as fully equal participants, we must do what we can to answer these claims. And we must begin by scrutinizing the opposition between emotion and reason that is unreflectively assumed in them. In this chapter, then, I shall argue that this contrast, as it is frequently drawn, rests on an inadequate philosophical understanding of the emotions and their relation to belief and judgement; that a more adequate understanding shows that emotions pose no obstacle to the elaboration of a universal norm in which women are fully equal subjects.

I shall argue (1) that the strongest philosophical account of the emotions shows that they are not brutish irrational forces, but intelligent and discriminating elements of the personality, closely related to perception and judgment; (2) that other common objections that have led to the conclusion that emotions are (in a normative sense) irrational can also be effectively answered; (3) that there is no good reason to think that women, as such, are more emotional than men: such differences as do appear are best explained by appeal not to 'nature' but to socialization and ways of life; and (4) that, all this being the case, it is up to us to decide what forms of emotional life are fruitful and appropriate, within an overall picture of human functioning, and to transmit the capability for these emotions to all human beings, without regard to gender.

[16] Mary Wollstonecraft is a striking example of this line of argument; like most ethical thought in her century, hers is profoundly influenced by Stoicism. See Jane Roland Martin, *Reclaiming a Conversation* (New Haven, Conn.: Yale University Press, 1985).

[17] For criticism of some of this, where India is concerned, see M. Nussbaum and A. Sen, 'Internal Criticism and Indian Rationalist Traditions', in M. Krausz (ed.), *Relativism* (Notre Dame, Ind.: Notre Dame University Press, 1989), 299–325. And Sen, 'India and the West', *The New Republic*, June 1993. On Africa, see the excellent rebuttal of the simple view in Anthony Appiah, *In My Father's House: Africa in the Philosophy of Culture* (New York: Oxford University Press, 1992).

[18] Havelock Ellis, *Man and Woman* (Boston: Houghton Mifflin, 1929), cited in Catherine Lutz, *Unnatural Emotions*, 74.

2 OBJECTIONS TO EMOTION

In order to answer the charge that emotions are irrational, and thus inappropriate in good deliberation, I must first make them more precise. For a number of very different charges have been made against the emotions; and all of these can be, and have been, expressed using the convenient umbrella term 'irrationality'. And yet there really are several very different arguments here, and in some cases built upon incompatible views of what emotions are. So any defence must begin by disentangling them. I do not claim that this list is exhaustive; but the objections I introduce here are the ones that seem to me the most germane to a debate about women's social role.

First, then, there is the common objection that the emotions are blind forces that have nothing (or nothing much) to do with reasoning. Like gusts of wind or the swelling currents of the sea, they push the agent around, surd unthinking energies. They do not themselves embody reflection or judgement, and they are not very responsive to the judgements of reason. (This picture of emotion is sometimes expressed by describing emotions as 'animal', and elements of an animal, not fully human, nature in us. That idea is itself often closely connected to the idea that emotions are somehow 'female' and reason 'male'—presumably because the female is taken to be closer to the animal and the instinctual.) It is easy to see how this view of emotions would lead to their dismissal from the life of the citizen and the good judge. For forces of the sort described do seem to be a threat to good judgement; and their dominance in an individual would indeed seem to call into question the fitness of that individual for the functions of citizenship. It is this picture, presumably, that underlies the pejorative judgements of writers like Ellis and other anti-emotion psychologists; and indeed the view was at one time dominant in psychology, though never, I think, in philosophy.[19]

A very different argument is made in the chief anti-emotion works of the Western philosophical tradition. Variants of it can be found in Plato, Epicurus and Lucretius, the Greek and Roman Stoics, and Spinoza.[20] It appears to be common in the Chinese and the Indian philosophical traditions as well.[21] These philosophers all hold a view of emotions incompatible with the view that underlies the first objection. They hold, namely, that emotions are very closely related to (or in some cases identical with)

[19] Lutz, *Unnatural Emotions*, discusses these associations well; but she is wrong, I think, to claim that this objection to emotion is the predominant one in the history of Western philosophy, and that criticizing it entails a fundamental criticism of 'Western theory'.

[20] I discuss these views historically in *The Therapy of Desire: Theory and Practice in Hellenistic Ethics* (Princeton, NJ: Princeton University Press, 1994), and defend a related position in my own way in *Upheavals of Thought: A Theory of the Emotions*, The Gifford Lectures for 1993, delivered April–May 1993 at the University of Edinburgh and forthcoming with Cambridge University Press.

[21] On the Chinese analysis, see Yearley and von Falkenhausen; for Indian cognitive views of emotion, see Simon.

judgements. So lack of judgement is not at all their problem. The problem, however, is that the judgements are false. They are false because they ascribe a very high value to external persons and events that are not fully controlled by the person's virtue or rational will. They are acknowledgements, then, of the person's own incompleteness and vulnerability. Fear involves the thought that there are important bad things that could happen in the future and that one is not fully capable of preventing them. Grief involves the thought that someone or something extremely important has been taken from one; anger the thought that another has seriously damaged something to which one attaches great worth; pity the thought that another is suffering in a non-trivial way, through no fault of his or her own; hope involves the thought that one's own future good is in important respects not under one's own control.

In all of these cases, the emotions picture human life as something needy and incomplete, something that has hostages to fortune. Ties to children, parents, loved ones, fellow citizens, country—these are the material on which emotions work; and these ties, given the power of chance to disrupt them, make human life a vulnerable business, in which complete rational control is neither possible nor, given the value of these attachments to the attached, even (from their point of view) desirable. Thus emotions are sources of softness, holes, so to speak, in the walls of the self.[22] It is this view, it seems, that underlies Okonkwo's reaction against emotion, his view that a real man would have a hard and not a gentle self.

But according to these philosophers—and according to ordinary people who inspire and/or follow them—that picture of the world is in fact false. As Socrates already said, 'A good person cannot be harmed.' One's own virtue and thought and will are the only things of real worth; and one's virtue and thought cannot be damaged by fortune. Another way of expressing this is to say that the good person is completely self-sufficient.

This argument is sometimes connected with a relative of the first argument, through the idea of stability. A good judge, these philosophers insist, is someone stable, someone who cannot be swayed by the currents of fortune or fashion. But people in the grip of the emotions, because they place important elements of their good outside themselves, will change with the gusts of fortune, and are just as little to be relied upon as the world itself is. Now hopeful, now in tears, now serene, now plunged into violent grief, they lack the stability and solidity of the wise person, who takes a constant and calm delight in the unswerving course of his own virtue. Thus this second picture can lead to some of the same characterizations as the first, and even to some of the same associations of emotion with the female—since women, they observe, often have commitments to children and loved ones that are (for contingent social reasons, on this view) more

[22] For an analysis of Seneca's imagery for emotion, with many such examples, see Nussbaum, *Therapy*, ch. 12.

intense than those of males. But it is important to notice how different, in the two cases, the reasons for the conclusions are. On the first view, emotions are innate; on the second, they are taught with the teaching of evaluative beliefs. On the first, they can be neither educated nor entirely removed; on the second, both are possible. On the first, emotions are unstable because of their unthinking internal structure; on the second, because they are thoughts that attach importance to unstable external things.

As will become clear in what follows, I very much prefer the second objector's view to the first, in the sense that I think it is based on a far more profound and better argued view of the relationship between emotion and belief or judgement. On the other hand, it should already be plain that one might accept this analysis of the emotions and yet refuse to accept the Stoic conclusion that the emotions are (in the normative sense) irrational and wholly to be avoided when we seek to deliberate rationally. For, as one can see, that conclusion is based on a substantive and highly controversial ethical view, according to which the good person should be totally self-sufficient, and ties to loved ones, country, and other undependable items outside the self are without true worth. Okonkwo, like many males in many cultures, probably holds some such view. But one might dispute it. And then one would wish to retain the evaluative judgements contained in (or, as the Stoics think, identical with) the emotions, and to draw on them in practical reasoning, as acknowledgements of what is in truth valuable and good in a finite human life.

A third objection, while compatible with some respect for the emotions in parts of private life, assails their role in public deliberation. (It is compatible with the second objector's analysis of emotions as closely linked to judgements about the worth of external objects, and probably not compatible with the first objector's claim that they are altogether without thought.) Emotions, this objector charges, focus on the person's actual ties or attachments, especially to concrete objects or people close to the self. They consider the object not abstractly, as one among many, but as special—and special, in part at least, on account of its prominence in the agent's own life. They always stay close to home and contain, so to speak, a first-person reference. Thus, love ascribes great worth to a person who is in an intimate relationship with the agent; and its intensity usually depends on the existence of an actual connection of some sort between agent and object. Grief, again, is usually for a loss that is felt as cutting at the roots of one's own life. Fear is usually either completely self-centred or felt on behalf of friends, family, loved ones. Anger is aroused by slights or damages to something that is one's own. In all these cases, emotions seem to bind the moral imagination to items that lie close to the self and stand in a relationship to the self. They do not look at human worth or even human suffering in an even-handed way. They do not get worked up about distant lives, unseen sufferings. This, from the point of view of many moral theories—including Utilitarianism, Kantianism, and their relatives in non-Western traditions[23]—would be a good reason to reject them from a public norm of rationality, even though they might still have some value in the home. I believe that this objection, although rarely clearly distinguished from the first two, underlies quite a few arguments that connect women's emotionality with restriction to a domestic role, suggesting that exactly the abilities that make them good in that role undermine their status as citizens.

A closely related further objection is that emotions seem to be too much concerned with particulars in general, and not sufficiently with larger social units, such as classes. And this is a point that has seemed to many Marxists, and to other political thinkers as well, to make emotion-based reasoning altogether unsuitable in political reflection, and even subversive of it. (Or, in some versions, it is in a sense political, but so committed to bourgeois individualism that it is unsuited for critical political reflection.) Love, it is claimed, directs the attention to an individual, and deflects it from impartial reasoning about collective action; grief, too, is a form of personal self-indulgence. In Doris Lessing's *The Golden Notebook*[24] the heroine, a Marxist novelist, faces this objection from her political allies in the Communist Party: they claim that her emotional way of perceiving events (which they connect both with her femaleness and with her literary profession) betrays a residual attachment to the bourgeois world, and is inconsistent with her politics. On some versions of this objection, emotions may be useful enough in a private ethical domain, so long as they do not overstep their bounds. On the orthodox Marxist version, which does not recognize an ethical domain apart from the political, they are altogether without worth.

A fifth objection, finally, focuses not on the emotions as a class, but on erotic and romantic love in particular. For even some moral views that ascribe a positive role to other emotions, such as fear, pity, hope, sympathetic brotherly love, and even anger, holding that they would figure in the deliberations of an ideally rational and sympathetic judge, view romantic love with a special scepticism. Whereas other emotions need to be balanced and moderated, but will still be retained and even cultivated within social morality, this one, and the erotic desire to which it is closely linked, are seen as subversive of the public domain. A powerful version of this objection is, I believe, in Adam Smith's *The Theory of Moral Sentiments*, a work that on the whole defends emotions as essential ingredients in deliberative rationality.

Smith's objection[25] is that love seems to have about it something hidden

---

[23] On China, see Yearley, where I believe that this argument can be found alongside the second.

[24] Lessing, *The Golden Notebook* (London, New York and Toronto: Bantam, 1981).

[25] I discuss Smith and the argument in detail in 'Steerforth's Arm: Love and the Moral Point of View', in *Love's Knowledge: Essays on Philosophy and Literature* (New York: Oxford University Press, 1990).

and mysterious, something that both repels social scrutiny and impedes the lover from participation in the social world. Love is based to a great extent on a strong and not fully governable response to morally irrelevant particularities; to that extent, it cannot be explained or justified to another, cannot become a part of the giving and receiving of reasons that is the essence of public rationality. Adam Smith observes that a person who has been wronged can explain to a friend the nature of the wrong and can reasonably expect the friend both to comprehend and to share his anger. But a person who is in love cannot completely explain why it has happened in the way it has, for this person at this time. And the sentiment is one that he both cannot and would not ask a friend to share. At the same time, love asks lovers to avert their eyes from the wider world of social concern. It demands an exclusivity of vision that does not balance the claims of the loved one against other claims, and often prevents the due consideration of those other claims. In short: the world of love is a world of mystery and privacy, in which lovers neither see nor are seen with the vision characteristic of general social and political concern. It thus proves not only irrelevant in social reasoning, but powerfully subversive of it. (Once again, this objection is independent of the non-cognitive view of emotion put forward in the first objection: for Smith's view of the passions is in fact a strongly cognitive view.)

One might well wonder why this objection should be linked, as it often has been, with a denunciation of women's alleged irrationality: for surely not only women fall in love, not only women feel erotic desire. And yet, the objection is in fact in its history strongly gendered, in both non-Western and Western traditions, males being portrayed as reasonable beings who ought to be above all that, and usually are; females as dangerous seductresses, natural inhabitants of that world of passion and passivity, who lure unfortunate males to their destruction—or that of their rationality.[26]

And finally, even if we should manage to give a successful answer to all these objections, and thus to defend the claim that emotions are a valuable part of the 'capabilities' of the good person and the good citizen, we will

[26] Thus Smith speaks of a 'charm' from women that temporarily eclipses men's rational powers. Nor are women treated as moral subjects: the argument depicts them as if they lived entirely in the emotions' enclosed and irrational realm. For the American analogue, consider the passage from Thomas Jefferson that forms the epigraph to my paper 'Human Capabilities' in this volume. For Indian, Latin American, and Chinese versions, see the papers by Verma, Valdés, and Li. Rabindranath Tagore's novel *The Home and the World* (London: Penguin, 1985, first published in India, 1915–16, first English publn. Macmillan, 1919) offers a fascinating contrast on this issue. The traditionalist and hyper-patriot Sandip takes the view that women embody 'the living image of Kali, the shameless, pitiless goddess'; they are prevented from destroying men, insofar as they are, only by artificial social 'fetters'. Nikhil, the critical humanist, denies this: the fault lies in society generally, for its excessive exaltation of erotic desire: 'Man has so fanned the flame of the loves of men and women, as to make it overpass its rightful domain, and now, even in the name of humanity itself, he cannot bring it back under control. Man's worship has idolized his passion. But there must be no more human sacrifices at its shrine'.

face one further very shrewd objection, having to do with the need for emotion in public life. Suppose we grant, then, that the most perfect social thought, both private and public, uses emotions. Nonetheless, given that the production of emotionally balanced people is likely to be a taxing job, requiring a radical reordering of human development for men as well as women from infancy on up, what priority should politics give to this task? It would seem a recipe for political disaster to tell it that it must accomplish this goal before it reshapes social institutions. Politics cannot wait around until people perfect themselves inside: it must design institutions so as to bring about intelligent results, even in the absence of good judgement and response on the part of individuals. This is what economic analysis enables us to do, and this is why it is so important. So to place the accent on emotion in a project in development economics is to engage in idle Utopian thinking instead of addressing the urgent issues.[27]

Each of these objections is a profound one. To answer them all definitively would require me to elaborate and defend a full theory of the emotions. This obviously cannot be done here—all the more since that is a project I have undertaken elsewhere.[28] What I propose to do here is to sketch out plausible answers to the six objections, drawing, often, on ancient Greek and Roman philosophical traditions in which a cognitive view of emotions finds, I believe, an especially valuable defence. I am now convinced that these theories of emotion are closely related to both classical Indian and classical Chinese theories, and indeed to very many nontheoretical intuitive accounts of emotion from very many parts of the world. This is no surprise, if the view is true.[29] I hope, therefore, that I shall be forgiven for focusing on the philosophical material I know best, and simply pointing to some of the non-Western parallels.

3 ANSWERING THE OBJECTIONS

3.1. Emotions as Blind Animal Forces

The first objector insists that emotions are irrational in the normative sense, that is, bad guides to choice, because they do not partake in reason in even the broadest descriptive sense—are just blind impulses that neither contain a perception of their object nor rest on beliefs. This position is in one sense, I feel, hardly worth spending time on, since it has never been strongly

---

[27] I owe this objection to John Roemer.

[28] In *Upheavals of Thought* (forthcoming, 1996). Especially pertinent to this project are Lectures 5 and 6, dealing with compassion and its role in public life.

[29] To say that the view is true for all human beings (and in fact for higher animals as well, as I argue in *Upheavals of Thought*) is not to neglect the evident differences among societies in the particular repertory of emotions they construct and recognize. Recognition of the element of 'social construction' in emotion is, in fact, a prominent part of the theory itself.

supported by major philosophers who have done a great deal of their most serious work on the emotions—including many who for other reasons dislike the emotions intensely. And by now it has been widely discredited even where it once was popular: in cognitive psychology, for example, and in anthropology.[30] But it still has a hold on much informal thinking and talking about emotions, where the correct observation that emotions are not included in Mr Gradgrind's sense of 'reason' is all too often taken to licence the conclusion that they do not partake of any sort of reasoning or cognition.[31] Therefore it seems important to say something about what has led to the widespread conclusion that it is not a tenable view.

Western philosophers as diverse as Plato, Aristotle, the Greek and Roman Stoics and Epicureans, Spinoza, and Adam Smith[32] have agreed that it is very important to distinguish emotions such as grief, love, fear, pity, anger, and hope from bodily impulses and drives such as hunger and thirst, and this in two ways. First, emotions contain within themselves a directedness toward an object; and within the emotion the object is viewed under an intentional description. That is to say, it figures in the emotion as it appears to, is perceived by, the person who experiences the emotion. My anger is not simply an impulse, a boiling of the blood: it is directed at someone, namely, a person who is seen as having wronged me. The way I see the person is itself intrinsic to the nature of my emotion, and to its role in action. (Why would a boiling in my blood move me this way rather than that?)[33] Gratitude contains an opposed view of another person's relation to my good; distinguishing anger from gratitude requires giving an account of these opposed perceptions. Love is not, in the relevant sense, blind: it perceives its object as endowed with a special wonder and importance. Once again, this way of perceiving the object is essential to the character of the emotion. Hatred differs from love in nothing so much as the opposed character of its perceptions. Emotions do oppose one another, but not

[30] Lecture 1 of *Upheavals of Thought* is devoted to stating and answering this objection; in Lecture 2 I examine a wide range of materials in cognitive psychology and anthropology that support my reply; in Lecture 3, turning to a developmental account of emotion, I link my cognitive view with recent work in object-relations psychoanalysis. I refer the reader to this material for references to the literature. Lecture 1 will appear before the book's publication, in a volume in memory of Bimal Matilal, ed., J. N. Mohanty. For related arguments, see also my *Therapy of Desire*, ch. 10.

[31] This is strikingly true in the law, where there is a growing literature on empathy and emotion in which the defenders of emotion seem to accept the sharp distinction between emotion and reason foisted on them by emotion's attackers. See, for example, Toni Massaro, 'Empathy, Legal Storytelling, and the Rule of Law: New Words, Old Wounds', *Michigan Law Review*, 87 (1989), 2099–127; Lynne Henderson, 'Legality and Empathy', *Michigan Law Review*, 85 (1987), 1574–653. The same thing happens in actual judicial opinions: even the defenders of compassion and mercy speak of them as 'irrational'. For examples, see my 'Equity and Mercy', *Philosophy and Public Affairs* (Spring 1993). A welcome exception to the trend is M. Minow and E. Spelman, 'Passion for Justice', *Cardozo Law Review*, 10 (1988), 37–76.

[32] Since these later philosophers are deeply indebted to Stoicism, I shall in what follows be focusing on the original ancient Stoic positions.

[33] I owe this way of putting the point to Christine Korsgaard.

blindly: they differ with one another in a way to which perception is central—fear struggling with hope, anger with gratitude, love against panic.[34] Emotions, in short, whatever else they are, are at least in part, ways of perceiving. And if one does not bring in this intentional content, it is impossible to understand how they can play the role in action that they clearly do play.

Furthermore, my second point, emotions are also intimately connected with certain beliefs about their object. The philosophical tradition I have mentioned is not unanimous about the precise relation between emotion and belief: some hold that the relevant beliefs are necessary conditions for the emotion, some that they are both necessary and sufficient, some that they are constituent parts of what the emotion is, some that the emotion just is a certain sort of belief or judgement. Let us begin, therefore, with the weakest view, on which most agree: the view that emotions are so responsive to beliefs of certain sorts that they cannot come into being without them. What leads these philosophers to accept that view? Consider, again, a case of anger.[35] Anger, they argue, seems to require the belief that I, or something or someone important to me, have or has been harmed by another person's intentional action. If any significant aspect of that complex belief should cease to seem true to me—if I change my view about who has done the harm, or about whether it was intentional, or about whether what happened was in fact a harm, my anger can be expected to abate or to change its course accordingly. If, for example, I discover that B, and not A (as I had believed) is the murderer of my child, I will transfer my anger from A to B. If I believe that C has been insulting me behind my back, and then discover that no such insults in fact took place, my anger can be expected to fade. Even if some residual feeling of excitation and irritation should remain, it would not seem right to call it anger. If I am angry at D because she has forgotten my name (an example actually given by Aristotle in the *Rhetoric*), and should then become (deeply and fully) convinced that forgetting a name is not an offence at all, then, once again, I can expect my anger to abate. Anger, then, requires certain beliefs for its existence; and it can be modified, or even removed, by the modification of belief.

Much the same is argued for other major emotions, such as grief, fear, pity or compassion, love, and gratitude. Fear requires the belief that important damages may happen to me in the future, and that I am powerless to prevent them. I do not fear what I believe I control: thus, I do not fear that I will suddenly start telling lies or smashing up the room, if I believe that I am not the sort of person who is out of control with respect

---

[34] I am grateful to Cass Sunstein for valuable observations on this point.

[35] I discuss ancient Greek and Roman views of anger in *Therapy*, chs. 3, 7, 11, and 12. The most important texts are Aristotle, *Rhetoric* II. 2–3, *Nicomachean Ethics* IV. 5; the fragments of Chrysippus' *Peri Pathon*, collected in *Stoicorum Veterum Fragmenta*, ed. J. von Arnim (Stuttgart: Teubner, 1903, repr. 1979) Vol. III; Seneca, *On Anger (De Ira)* and *On Mercy (De Clementia)*; Cicero, *Tusculan Disputations* III–IV.

to these actions. Nor do I fear what I believe to be trivial: I do not go around fearing the loss of a coffee cup.[36] Again, if I become convinced that a damage is impossible, I will cease to fear it. If some residual upheaval remains, it will seem right to call it excitation or agitation, but not fear. Pity requires the belief that another person is suffering big and important things, through no fault of his or her own; it is in that way the other-directed analogue to fear.[37] And so forth. The beliefs in question may be very deeply rooted in the person's psychology; so getting rid of them cannot be expected to be, always, the job merely of a one-shot argument. Some of them may even be held beneath the level of consciousness.[38] But beliefs they are, none the less, as we can tell when we manage to bring them to the surface for inspection. And without these beliefs, no emotion can take root.

This, as I have said, is the weakest position. Most of the ancient Greek and Roman thinkers go further. The next plausible step to take is to hold that the beliefs in question are also constituent parts of the emotion, part of what identifies it, and sets it apart from other emotions. For it seems highly implausible that we can individuate and identify complex emotions such as anger, fear, and pity, simply by reference to the way they feel. To tell whether a certain pain is fear or grief, we have to inspect the beliefs that are bound up with the pain. To tell whether a certain happy, pleased feeling should be called love or gratitude—once again, we must inspect not just the tonality of the feeling, but also the beliefs that go with it. Thus most ancient Greek and Roman definitions of emotion (and many modern Western definitions as well—Spinoza is, of course, the most conspicuous here) mention beliefs as well as feelings, and mention them not just as causes, but as constituents of the complex passion.[39]

It appears to many thinkers, furthermore, that the beliefs we have mentioned are—usually, at any rate—sufficient for the emotion. That is, if I really succeed in making you believe that B has been insulting you behind your back, that will suffice to make you angry with B; I do not need, as well, to light a fire under your heart. Whatever fire there is, is fire about the insult, and is produced by awareness of the insult. If I want to make the

---

[36] The Stoic philosopher Epictetus urged the too-fearful person to do exercises in which he would begin by considering the loss of a cup, and progress, by gradual steps, to the acceptance of the possible loss of other things—his household pets, his children, his wife, his own life! In each case, he grows to regard them as trivial and dispensable.

[37] On ancient Greek analysis of pity, see my *The Fragility of Goodness: Luck and Ethics in Greek Tragedy and Philosophy* (Cambridge: Cambridge University Press, 1986) Interlude 2, and 'Tragedy and Self-Sufficiency: Plato and Aristotle on Fear and Pity', *Oxford Studies in Ancient Philosophy*, 10 (1992) and, in a shorter version, in A. Rorty (ed.), *Essays on Aristotle's Poetics* (Princeton, NJ: Princeton University Press, 1992). The later history of the debate about its role in public judgement is traced, and adjudicated, in Gifford Lectures 5 and 6.

[38] The Epicurean tradition suggests that this is especially likely to be true of beliefs about the badness of one's own death.

[39] Von Falkenhausen argues convincingly that much the same is true of the Chinese tradition; and I believe that the Indian tradition has a similar position, though perhaps intentional perception is stressed more than belief.

people of Athens furious with the Spartans, once again, all I need to do is to convince them that they have been insulted, offended, mocked, or damaged in some significant way by deliberately undertaken Spartan actions. Much of the ancient science of rhetoric rests on this observation; and modern political speech is no stranger to it either. When George Bush wanted to make the American public fear the prospect of a Dukakis presidency, he did not need to doctor their insides or inject ice water into their veins. All he needed to do was to make them believe that a Dukakis presidency would mean big and significant dangers for them that they would be powerless to control: Willie Hortons running free in the streets of every city, ready to prey on their innocent families. Okonkwo's belief that holding back from killing Ikemefuna would be evidence of womanish softness was sufficient to fill him with fear; his feeling that his own standing in the community is injured by his father's gentleness is sufficient to inspire him with rage; and so forth. This position is compatible with the view that emotions have further, non-cognitive components (such as feelings or bodily alternations): but it insists that the relevant beliefs are sufficient causes of these further components.

The greatest Stoic thinker, Chrysippus, went one step further, holding that emotions were simply identical with beliefs or judgements. His position is not a simple one to grasp, since his notion of judgement is far more dynamic than most modern notions. His idea is that to judge that p is the case, is a two-step process: one first entertains the 'appearance' of p, puts it before one's eyes, so to speak. Then one can do one of three things: one can reject it, saying that's not the way things are really. One can suspend judgement about it, neither accepting nor rejecting it. Or, finally, one can accept or assent to it, embrace it and take it into oneself as the way things are. It is his view that this activity of assenting to a certain sort of claim about the world is what having an emotional experience is. For example, grieving just is embracing the fact that (say) the most important person in my life is dead and will never return. Such activities of assenting or accepting are not calm or inert: reason itself moves (reluctantly or with alacrity, cautiously or imprudently) to embrace the relevant appearance. Nor are they without their affective side: accepting the fact that my loved one has died is itself a wrenching of my entire existence—like putting the world's knife into my own insides. Only an analysis of this sort, Chrysippus believes, can do justice to grief's discriminating power and its object-directed intentionality. Emotions are not irrational pushes and pulls, they are ways of viewing the world. They reside in the core of one's being, the part of it with which one makes sense of the world.

This is, I believe, a powerful analysis; and I have defended it at greater length elsewhere. (One might argue that this is the position that best makes sense of Okonkwo's fear: for it is portrayed as a way of seeing seated 'deep within himself', at the heart of his interpretations of the world.) One does not need to accept this view, in order to question the simple opposition between emotion and reason; any of the weaker versions of the cognitive position will do for that purpose. But it is probably the position in this family with the strongest philosophical arguments in its favour; and it certainly has had the most distinguished philosophical history, in the Western tradition, being endorsed by Chrysippus, Seneca, and, much later, Spinoza.[40]

Notice that this family of cognitive views still makes ample room for saying of some (or even of all) emotions that they are, in the normative sense, irrational. For emotions must now be assessed by assessing the relevant beliefs or judgements. These may be either true or false; and they may be either rational or irrational. (These are two independent dimensions of assessment: a belief might be false but rational, if I formed it on the basis of good evidence, and yet it happened to be wrong; it may also—and more often—be true but irrational, if I formed it hastily and uncritically, but it just happens to be the case.) But in no case will emotions be irrational in the sense of being totally cut off from cognition and judgement; and thus there is no more reason to think them unsuited for deliberation—just because they can go wrong—than there is reason to dismiss all beliefs from deliberation, just because they can go wrong.

3.2. Emotions as Acknowledgements of Neediness

We must now turn to the second objector. For in answering the first objector I have endorsed that objector's account of what emotions are, finding in them both object-directed intentionality and a close relation to beliefs. According to this objector, the emotions are linked to beliefs with a particular subject matter: beliefs that ascribe high worth or importance to things and persons outside the self. To make these judgements of worth is to acknowledge one's own neediness and lack of self-sufficiency. We can now locate the cognitive dimension of the emotions more precisely: they enable the agent to perceive a certain sort of worth or value. And (for those to whom such things do have worth) emotions are thus necessary for a full ethical vision.

But are these acknowledgements of neediness and incompleteness good? The objector states that beliefs that one has these deep needs from the world are always false: the only resources one really needs come from within oneself and one's own virtue. These false beliefs are, moreover,

[40] In the Gifford Lectures I argue that the view needs to be modified in two ways in order to be philosophically adequate: we must get rid of the claim that emotions always involve linguistically formulable *propositions*, making room both for non-linguistic emotional experiences (Lecture 4 is devoted to emotion and music) and also for experiences that are more indefinite and inchoate than the Stoic propositional analysis would allow. Even in these cases, however, emotions involve a view of the world that contains ideas of value or salience; and I argue that this is true even of the emotions of small infants and non-human animals.

socially damaging, sapping confidence and robbing action of its force and its stability. One can get rid of them: and a life without them is a more satisfactory and stable ethical life than the one in which they occur.

This means, for the Greek and Roman Stoics, radically rewriting the vision of the world and what has importance in it that their young pupils would be likely to have absorbed from their culture. For as they saw (here following Plato), most influential literature treats the events that befall finite and vulnerable people as deeply significant, and involves the audience in their good or ill fortune. It shows a hero like Achilles grieving for the death of Patroclus, rolling in the dirt and crying out, rather than recognizing that such things have no true importance.[41] What we should have, instead, are paradigms of exemplary self-sufficiency and detachment: for example, the story told by Cicero of a father who, informed of his son's death, calmly remarked, 'I was already aware that I had begotten a mortal.'[42] Socrates, in this tradition, is the exemplum par excellence, the great antidote to tragedy. Thus Epictetus writes that a person's goal should be:

To study how to remove from his own life mournings and lamentations, and such expressions as 'Alas' and 'Wretch that I am', and misfortune and ill fortune, and to learn the meaning of death, exile, prison, hemlock—so he can say in prison, 'O dear Crito, if this is what pleases the gods, so be it'—and not that other exclamation, 'Wretch that I am, an old man, it is for this that I have kept my gray hairs.' Who says this? Do you think I am talking about some insignificant lowly person? Doesn't Priam say these very things? Doesn't Oedipus? In fact, don't all kings talk like this? For what else are tragedies but the sufferings of people who have been wonderstruck by external things, displayed in the usual metre?   (*Disc.* 1.4.23–30)

This is a profound vision of the ethical life: profound, first of all, because it is based on a deep conception of what emotions are, one that I believe to be more or less correct, and one that has deep roots in the experiences of people in many different cultures. Profound, as well, because it raises deep questions about what a good human life should be, what sorts of vulnerabilities are compatible with the constancy that the ethical and political life require. These questions can hardly be resolved by a hasty dismissal of the tradition, or by charging that it is simply, here, the institutionalization of unreflective male prejudice against emotion. (Indeed, reading the Roman Stoics makes it perfectly clear that these people were concerned about the dignity of each and every human being: about the ability of females to achieve full human freedom, about the urgency of getting males to refrain from the obsessive pursuit of worldly wealth and honour that made the

---

[41] See Plato, *Republic*, 387–8; on this critique of literature, see 'Tragedy and Self-Sufficiency', and also 'Poetry and the Passions: Two Stoic Views', in J. Brunschwig and M. Nussbaum (eds.), *Passions & Perceptions* (Cambridge: Cambridge University Press, 1993).

[42] Cicero, *Tusculan Disputations* III. 30. Yearley gives closely related examples from the Mencian portrait of the sage. And Indian traditions contain similar pictures of detachment. Okonkwo seems to aim at a similar self-sufficiency.

politics of Nero's time irrational by anyone's normative standards.) And the view is profound, finally, because, like all the most searching and incisive philosophical thought, it shows its own argumentative structure to its reader, and thus shows, as well, how and where one might take issue with it. In particular, it shows both friends and opponents of the emotions that the radical anti-emotion conclusion rests on normative premises about self-sufficiency and detachment that are highly controversial. Let us at least begin to question those premises.

In my earlier chapter in this volume, I presented a sketch of the central elements in human life, claiming—plausibly, I think—that it was derived from intuitions that are both widely and deeply held across many differences of place and time. The list included both capabilities and needs, and showed how, in complicated ways, the two shape one another. What the Stoics want to do, we can now see, is to make human life anew, focusing entirely on capability and marginalizing need. In effect, they want to give the human being what, in my analysis, looks like the life of a god, rather than the life of a human being. They claim that making this change does not remove social cohesiveness and ethical virtue. But one might have some doubts about this.

Consider the emotion of compassion (pity).[43] Compassion requires, as Aristotle long ago argued, the belief that another person is suffering through no fault of his or her own. The suffering must be thought to be of serious importance. And, finally, the person who has compassion must believe that his or her own possibilities are similar to those of the person who suffers. This acknowledgement of one's own vulnerability is traditionally thought, and not implausibly, to be linked with beneficence and a generous vision of the enemy; the refusal of pity, as in Dickens's Bitzer, as in Okonkwo preparing to wield his matchet, is connected with a hard and arrogant disposition of mind.

The foundation of compassion, and its social role, is the belief that many common forms of bad luck—losses of children and other loved ones, the hardships of war, the loss of political rights, bodily illness and deficiency, the prospect of one's own death—are in fact of serious importance. In order to remove compassion from human life (and the other closely related emotions with it) the Stoics have to remove that fundamental belief. But then we must ask what reasons they give their good person to care profoundly about the bad things that happen to others; what reasons they give her to get involved, to take risks, for the sake of social justice and beneficence.

It has always been difficult for philosophies based on the idea of the self-sufficiency of virtue to explain why beneficence matters. No major thinker

---

[43] I use both words because 'pity', in recent times, has acquired connotations of condescension to the sufferer that it did not have earlier, and still does not have when used as a translation for Greek *eleos*, Latin *misericordia*, or Rousseau's *pitié*.

of this sort is willing to say that it does not matter: and yet for Socrates, for the Stoics, for Spinoza, for Kant, it seems difficult to motivate consistently, given the alleged moral irrelevance of external goods, the self-sufficiency of the virtuous will. Repudiating pity, as they all do, leaves very few motives for the acts usually prompted by pity; and if they are performed out of very different motives, say, on account of pious obedience to Zeus's will, it is not clear that their moral character is the same. This problem is especially deep for the Roman Stoics. For in order to convince any member of their society that theirs is even a plausible view, they must show that it makes room for the defence of family and country, for risk-taking acts of other-regarding virtue, and for beneficence in the distribution of material goods. Seneca repeatedly endeavours to satisfy these demands—with significantly mixed results.

The moral vision of the emotions, by contrast, beginning as it does from the idea of the vulnerability of human life and the importance of certain 'external goods', has no such problem. Here the natural response to the sight of the need of another similar to oneself is to come to the aid of that need; for one believes that the need is very important, and that the social world is inhabited by weak creatures who can survive and flourish only if they come to one another's aid. One believes that one is oneself such a creature. Rousseau shrewdly argues that the absence of this belief is what leads to much social callousness and cruelty:

Why are kings without pity for their subjects? It is because they count on never being human beings. Why are the rich so harsh to the poor? It is because they do not have fear of becoming poor. Why does a noble have such contempt for a peasant? It is because he never will be a peasant . . . It is the weakness of the human being that makes it sociable, it is our common sufferings that carry our hearts to humanity; we would owe it nothing if we were not humans. Every attachment is a sign of insufficiency . . . Thus from our weakness itself, our fragile happiness is born. (*Emile*, Bk IV, 263, 259)

Utilitarianism, we know, begins from the fact of common suffering, and is, at its best, motivated by a wish to relieve pain. This it shares, for example, with Buddhist and Hindu traditions, in which compassion for suffering is appropriately made a central source of social motivation. So it is a very serious internal criticism of utilitarianism if it can be shown that the ways of reasoning that it designates as 'rational' undermine the full acknowledgement of suffering, the growth of compassionate fellow-feeling.

In short, if we reject the Stoic tradition on the matter of self-sufficiency, we must, to be consistent, reject its arguments for the dismissal of emotion—they stand or fall together. The argument with the Stoics is not finished; and yet we have some good reasons to feel dissatisfied with their position as a basis for social morality. If, however, we should reject their claims about the worth of external goods, then we have no good reason to reject the emotions: and we must grant that they are, in many central cases, at least, both true and rational, worthy of guiding our deliberation.

And something more seems to follow. If one agrees with most of this tradition in holding that certain sorts of beliefs about the importance of externals are not only necessary, but also sufficient for emotion—and this seemed to be a very plausible position to take—then one will have to grant that if emotion is not there, that judgement is not (fully) there. This means that those who accept the judgements about the worth of externals that the Aristotle/Rousseau tradition puts forward (against the Stoics) must, to be consistent, admit emotions as essential elements in good reasoning about these matters. And this has consequences for economic reasoning. Economic accounts of human motivation as based on 'rational self-interest' have recently been criticized a good deal, both in philosophy and in economics itself, on the grounds that such accounts fail to do justice to the way in which good reasoning ascribes intrinsic worth to persons, and to the ties of sympathy and commitment that bind people to one another in defiance of self-interested calculation. A leading example of such criticism is Amartya Sen's famous paper, 'Rational Fools', which defends sympathy and commitment in a manner closely related to my argument concerning pity or compassion.[44] What reflection about the structure of the emotions suggests, however, is that one cannot fully articulate Sen's more complex normative theory of reasoning without including prominently the emotions in which parts of that reasoning are embodied. It does not seem to be a consistent position to accept an anti-Stoic account of what has worth, and yet to reject the guidance of love, grief, pity, and gratitude—since such judgements of worth seem to be sufficient for those emotions.[45]

The world from which emotions are banished is an impoverished world, in which no ultimate ends exist but states of oneself. This norm is not only a very dubious basis for an account of good reasoning, but also an empty universe that cannot sustain an agent's interests long or fulfil her search for meaning. Consider Dickens's Bitzer, with whom we began: we hardly understand how Bitzer goes on living, or what he lives for. With his 'mechanical laugh', he strikes the reader as a machine propelled from behind, rather than a human being summoned to action by some beauty or wonder before her.[46] It cannot be rational to make ourselves into such beings—even when we write economics!

[44] A. Sen, 'Rational Fools', *Philosophy and Public Affairs*, 6 (1977), 317–44, repr. in Sen, *Choice, Welfare, and Measurement* (Oxford: Blackwell, 1982), 84–106.

[45] In Gifford Lecture 6, I use this point to establish that Posner has compassion, through a reading of two of his recent judicial opinions in which the evaluations that (on this view) suffice for emotion are amply present.

[46] Okonkwo is different, because, like Mr Gradgrind, he is not consistent. The love for Ikemefuna that turns him into a 'shivering old woman' is a powerful source of motivation throughout the novel, as is his intense attachment to his own status and reputation. In fact it is the tension between these two attachments that produces the tragedy.

3.3. Emotions and Impartiality

The calculating intellect claims to be impartial and capable of strict numerical justice, while emotions, it alleges, are prejudiced, unduly partial to the close at hand. Each human being should count as one, and none as more than one, it insists. But in the emotions, the loves of family and close friends seem all-encompassing, blotting out the fair claims of the distant many. Thus the emotional reasoner, accustomed to cherishing particulars rather than to thinking of the whole world, reasons in a way that is subversive of justice.

This, however, we may doubt. The abstract vision of the calculating intellect is a blunt and relatively obtuse instrument, unless aided by the vivid and empathetic imagining of what it is really like to live a certain sort of life. The person who approaches a distant life with compassion, experiencing what it is like to live such a life, is enabled by that imaginative work to see further and deeper than a person for whom that life was just a number in a mathematical function. Here I want to turn to Dickens once more: for, in his account of the political economy lesson of the circus girl Sissy Jupe, he shows us vividly the rationality and reach of emotion-based vision, the relative coarseness of mathematical calculation.

Sissy is told by her utilitarian teacher that in 'an immense town' of a million inhabitants, only twenty-five are starved to death in the streets. The teacher M'Choakumchild asks her what she thinks about this—plainly expecting an answer expressing satisfaction that the numbers are so low. Sissy's response, however, is that 'it must be just as hard upon those who were starved, whether the others were a million, or a million million.' Again, told that in a given period of time 100,000 people took sea voyages and only 500 drowned, Sissy remarks that this low percentage is 'nothing to the relations and friends of the people who were killed.' In both of these cases, the numerical analysis comforts and distances: what a fine low percentage, says M'Choakumchild, and no action, clearly, need be taken about that. Intellect without emotions is, we might say, value-blind: it lacks the sense of the meaning and worth of persons that the judgements internal to emotions would have supplied. Sissy's emotional response, by contrast, invests the dead with the worth of humanity. Feeling what starvation is for the starving, loss for the grief-stricken, she says, quite rightly, that the low numbers don't buy off those deaths, that complacency just on account of the low number is not the right response. No such number is low enough. Because she is always aware that there is no replacing a dead human being—the central fact, we might say, around which the emotions weave their fabric—she pushes for more relief, more protection, less complacency. Dealing with numbers one can always say, 'This figure is all right'—for none of them has any intrinsic meaning. (And really, notice that 500 deaths out of 100,000 is incredibly high for ocean crossings, whether by sea or air.)

Dealing with imagined and felt human lives, one will accept no figures of starvation as all right, no statistics of passenger safety as low enough. Judge which approach would lead to a better public response to a famine at a distance, to the situation of the homeless, to product testing and safety standards.

We may add to this general argument a genetic thesis. It is, that intimate bonds of love and gratitude between a child and its parents, formed in infancy and nourished in childhood, seem to be the indispensable starting-point for an adult's ability to do good in the wider world of adult social concern. Such initial cares need further education, to be sure; but they must be there if anything good is to come of education. This point is at least as old, in the Western tradition, as Aristotle's criticism of Plato in *Politics* II, where he insists that removing the family—rather than ensuring impartial and equal concern for all citizens—will ensure that nobody cares strongly about anything. It is brilliantly developed in Dickens's chilling account of the education of the young Gradgrind children, who are taught to calculate but never encouraged to love.[47] Their minds and hearts become thoroughly listless, lacking in any motivational energy for good, and in understanding of what human good there is to be done. We see the same point in Achebe's tragic portrait of Okonkwo's son Nwoye. Deprived of love not only by his father's refusal of feeling but also by the murder of his only companion, he becomes sluggish and listless—until the other-worldly promises of Christianity give him a source of meaning beyond the life he has previously known. It is clearly the promise of Christ's inextinguishable love that effects his conversion.[48]

3.4. Emotions and Classes

As for the related objection that emotions are too much concerned with the individual, and too little with larger social units such as classes, we must grant that in fact the emotions do tend to see the world in a variegated and particularized way. In this sense, the vision of community embodied in the emotions is a liberal vision, in which each individual is seen as valuable in her own right, and as having a distinctive story of her own to tell.[49] While emotions emphasize the mutual interdependence of persons, showing the world as one in which we are all implicated in one another's good and ill,

---

[47] Their father refers to love as 'the misplaced expression'. For a more detailed account of these aspects of the novel, see chapters 2 and 3 of *Poetic Justice* (Boston: Beacon Press, 1995).

[48] And it is really too late, where the issues of this argument are concerned. For the next novel in Achebe's trilogy, *No Longer At Ease*, shows that Nwoye, now christened as Isaac, proves an inept and unperceptive father, whose rigidity causes his son Obi's disaster. Thus the tragedy of non-emotion transmits itself from generation to generation.

[49] See also Lionel Trilling, *The Liberal Imagination: Essays on Literature and Society* (New York: Charles Scribner's Sons, 1950).

they also insist on respecting the separate life of each person, and on seeing the person as a separate centre of experience—including emotional experience.

It is in this sense no accident that mass movements frequently fare badly in an emotionally rich form such as the novel: as the Communist friends of Doris Lessing's literary heroine are quick to notice, as Lukács was quick to notice when he condemned as 'petit bourgeois' the political vision of Tagore's *The Home and the World*.[50] To the extent that they neglect the separate agency of their members, their personal experiences and their qualitative differences, mass movements will be seen as obtuse, and perhaps also as repressive. Whether we are dealing with Dickens's Coketown or Tagore's West Bengal, the violence done by abstract politics to individual lives is likely to grab our sympathy.

This political attitude has its dangers; and sometimes the suspiciousness of any form of collective action that is natural to emotion-based reasoning can lead to error—as when, in *Hard Times*, Dickens seems to assume that trade union movements must be repressive and obtuse toward their members. Far more often, however, this attitude is compatible with, and actually motivates, radical socio-economic criticism—as when, in Sissy Jupe's lesson, the emotions themselves showed the real meaning of hunger and misery, directing the calculative intellect to interpret the numbers in a new and more critical spirit; as when, in Tagore's mordant portrayal of early Indian nationalism, we find Sandip and Bimala neglecting, in their abstract nationalistic zeal, the real economic misery of the poor traders who cannot earn a living unless they sell the cheaper foreign wares, whereas the compassionate particular vision of Nikhil[51] makes each human life really count for one.[52] And indeed it seems appropriate for any form of collective action to bear in mind, as an ideal, the full accountability to the needs and particular circumstances of the individual that an emotion-based form like the novel recommends, in its form as well as its content. This, after all, is what Sen's capability approach has all along recommended for development economics: the recognition that each individual has a separate life story, and that good planning should aim to understand those stories, so

---

[50] He writes that the novel is 'a petit bourgeois yarn of the shoddiest kind', and that Tagore is 'a wholly insignificant figure . . . whose creative powers do not even stretch to a decent pamphlet.' Quoted in Anita Desai's Introduction to the Penguin edition of the novel (1985), p. 7. I have discussed the related case of Henry James's *The Princess Casamassima* in 'Perception and Revolution' in *Love's Knowledge*.

[51] This is seen also in his refusal to dismiss the English governess: 'I cannot . . . look upon Miss Gilby through a mist of abstraction, just because she is English. Cannot you get over the barrier of her name after such a long acquaintance? Cannot you realize that she loves you?' This is a self-referential moment: for it is evident that the vision of the novel as a whole is this sort of particularized vision.

[52] This is complicated, since Sandip and Bimala think of themselves as very emotional creatures indeed, and in a certain sense are so. But Nikhil seems correct when he diagnoses their state as one of a self-generated overheated excitement, not an acknowledgement of a real tie to any other person or entity.

that it can make each distinct individual capable of fully human functioning. An account of class actions, without the stories of individuals, would
not show us the point and meaning of class actions, which is always the
amelioration of individual lives. Raymond Williams put this point very well,
defending traditional realist narrative and its emotional entanglements
against this political criticism:

> Moreover we should not, as socialists, make the extraordinary error of believing that
> most people only become interesting when they begin to engage with political and
> industrial actions of a previously recognized kind. That error deserved Sartre's jibe
> that for many Marxists people are born only when they first enter capitalist employ-
> ment. For if we are serious about even political life we have to enter that world in
> which people live as they can as themselves, and then necessarily live within a whole
> complex of work and love and illness and natural beauty. If we are serious socialists,
> we shall then often find within and cutting across this real substance—always, in its
> details, so surprising and often vivid—the profound social and historical conditions
> and movements which enable us to speak, with some fullness of voice, of a human
> history.[53]

So too, I think, in Lessing's and Tagore's novels: their heroine and hero,
on account of the rationality of their emotions, are able to grasp the human
significance of political movements and events in a way that their more
dogmatic associates are not.[54] So too, as well, with Sen's capability approach: precisely because it is determined to come to grips with each
persons' concrete life story, precisely for this reason it can pursue radical
goals in a truly productive way.

3.5. Love and Blindness to the General Good

This objection is closely related to our third one: but it takes a narrower
focus. Adam Smith's analysis concludes that most of the major emotions,
including anger, grief, pity, fear, and some forms of love, are all appropriate
in the good citizen and judge, and capable of taking cognizance of the good
of distant others in morally appropriate ways. To this extent he accepts the
argument I made: that emotion-based reasoning can see very well into the
good of people far away, just on account of the special vividness and worth
with which the emotions endow the objects of their imagining. Smith holds,
however, that romantic and erotic love are special exceptions to this rule,
always inappropriate when we seek to deliberate rationally and powerful
obstacles to good citizenship and judgement. He leaves little doubt in his
reader's mind that women are a primary cause of this problem: seductresses
of male rationality and far gone in irrationality themselves.

---

[53] Raymond Williams, *The Politics of Modernism* (New York: Verso, 1989), 116.
[54] As the impoverished trader Panchu says to Nikhil, 'I am afraid, sir . . . while you big folk
are doing the fighting, the police and the law vultures will merrily gather round, and the crowd
will enjoy the fun, but when it comes to getting killed, it will be the turn of only poor me!'

This is a difficult objection to answer briefly, since what we need in order to answer it properly is a comprehensive theory of the development of moral motivation in the child and the links between this motivation and erotic desires and attachments. I shall therefore confine myself to suggesting, tentatively, an answer that emerged from my analysis of Dickens's *David Copperfield*, which I read as implicitly responding to and criticizing the sort of position Smith defends.[55]

David Copperfield presents the reader with a fascinating picture of the complex interweavings between erotic desire and novel-reading, and between both and moral motivation. For David, when he retreats from the gloomy 'firmness' of the Murdstones to the room where his father has left a collection of novels, spends hours passionately 'reading for life'—and not just reading, but also enacting his favourite novel plots, some of which (the plot of *Tom Jones* for example) have a marked erotic content. He casts himself always, he tells us, in the hero's role, Murdstone in that of the villain; and it is perfectly clear, though he does not name his mother, that she plays the heroine's role. In this way, the activity of novel-reading nourishes and gives expression to his already passionate emotions for his mother, which include a perception of her as vulnerable and in need of help, a desire to come to her aid, a fierce jealousy of Murdstone. The romantic plots of the novels strengthen his fantasy life, giving new intensity to the emotions he feels for the real people, whom he now sees as the characters. Love fuels imagination, and imagination gives new strength to love.[56]

What the novel makes clear, however, is that this erotic susceptibility in David—although not altogether morally unproblematic—is not the simple obstacle to good judgement that Smith believes it to be. For it is an essential part of what has made him the generous, exuberant, merciful, gentle moral being he is. The suggestion is that people who are capable, at times, of becoming completely wrapped up in another particular individual in a way that is not based altogether on judicious moral assessment are likely, too, in social life to prove more generous, less retentive and judgemental, than people who always see things from the moral point of view. Their passionate involvement in life, furthermore, gives them more energy and exuberance in social beneficence; and since David's erotic imagination focuses from the first on images of protecting that which is weak and needy, those images, too, enter into his conduct as a social agent.

This romantic conception of citizenship needs further development and argument.[57] But I hope this suffices to indicate in what direction I believe

[55] I discuss the novel in 'Steerforth's Arm' in *Love's Knowledge*, in 'Equity and Mercy', and also in Gifford Lecture 3, my developmental account of emotion.

[56] Later on, he links this receptivity with images of gender change as, telling stories to Steerforth in the moonlight, he becomes himself a heroine, 'Daisy' and 'The Sultana Scheherezade'.

[57] I develop it, with reference to Joyce and Whitman, in Gifford Lecture 10.

we ought to move in answering this objector. Such an answer would show that a stance toward life for which women have frequently been criticized might actually be an ingredient in the best conception of citizenship.

3.6. Emotions and Institutions

But why focus so much on emotions? And why urge development economics, which has so many other urgent tasks, to take emotions so seriously? For even if emotions are essential for human flourishing and even for ideal citizenship, what we should be doing is to design things so that they will produce good results even when we don't have ideal people. This is a profound objection, and I shall not be able to give it a comprehensive answer. But four points, I believe, can be made in defence of this emphasis.

First, in any well-ordered society we do in fact need ideals of the citizen, and of rationality, in order to guide moral and civic education and norms of both family and political life. Every society does employ some such ideal. Even when we are aware that we will never succeed in producing a nation of ideal people, even when we are also determined to design institutions to protect people against the non-ideal behaviour of their fellow citizens, still, we do bring people up in one way rather than another, in accordance with a certain public conception or conceptions. If those conceptions are not adequate, they will be inadequate. For example, if we do not teach the equality of all citizens, we will by default be giving support to racism and other forms of prejudice. In this case, the ideal of rationality that I recommend, if adopted, would reshape the education of children and the structures of family relations in many ways; and I am arguing that this will have an impact on gender conceptions and gender relations in our society, even if not perfectly realized. One may note that Adam Smith did not fail to investigate the emotions just because he believed that we could not produce emotionally perfect people.[58] In fact, he devoted half of his philosophical output to this topic, probably a larger ratio than any other major philosopher in the history of the subject.

Secondly, we should recall that the overall aim of the capability approach in development economics is to secure to each and every person the necessary conditions of fully human functioning in all the major areas of human flourishing. This means that we need to understand what human flourishing requires, in order to support it more adequately. An ideal of rationality that includes emotion is a component part of an ideal of human flourishing. And so my conclusions give direct instructions to policymakers concerning what requires support. This can be expected to have an impact on the design of institutions (especially in the areas of education and

[58] For an excellent account of his view of the limitations, see R. Coase, 'Adam Smith's view of Man', *Journal of Law and Economics* 19 (1976), 529–46.

of family policy) in many ways. In other words, when we depart from classical liberalism by taking a greater interest in the good, and in self-realization, we need to do some hard close thinking about what the good requires, precisely in order to design institutions that will give people support on the way to being at least capable of flourishing.

Thirdly, although it is correct that in many areas of public life we can indeed design things institutionally in such a way as to yield the results that an 'ideal person' would have chosen, even when we don't have such 'ideal people', there are always going to be some areas of public life in which we really need the individual people to be fully rational in something like the complete way an ideal would recommend. In US political life, for example, one of these areas is the judiciary. The design of judicial institutions leaves latitude for flexibility and individual interpretive and normative reasoning. There are good reasons for leaving this latitude: for no document can contain instructions so precise and so unambiguous that it will settle every problem in advance, and even to try for this would no doubt conduce to a baneful rigidity in the law.[59] But once the latitude is there, we need judges who exemplify rationality; and so we need an adequate conception of rationality to give them guidance. In the area in question, it is especially clear that the absence of an adequate account of the relationship between emotion and reason has led to some very bad judicial reasoning in the criminal law, and in constitutional law as well. What I am saying in effect is that we can't produce an entire society of 'perfect people', but we had better do the best we can with our judges, by trying to make the conceptions of rationality involved in their education more philosophically adequate.[60]

Finally, there is a point that should already be obvious from my discussion of Adam Smith. It is some ways the deepest and most important point in favour of ideal thinking. It is that the design of public institutions itself embodies an ideal conception of rationality. Adam Smith's account of the 'judicious spectator' is not just a nice account of the way nice people think. It is a device that is central to his thinking about how social and economic institutions are well designed. The idea of what a judicious spectator will feel, think, and approve is an artificial construction by which we gain insight concerning justice, and the just structure of institutions. This point is even clearer if we consider John Rawls's *A Theory of Justice*,[61]

---

[59] Furthermore, there are general results in the theory of social choice that show systems of general rules to be insufficient to determine a rational political outcome. In particular, Allan Gibbard has shown that it is impossible to design a voting system that cannot be manipulated by strategic voting. This result has general implications for the rationality of other systems of rules. This gives us still broader reasons to hold that we need to be concerned with the full personal rationality of individual social actors, and not merely with systematic and institutional considerations.

[60] On emotion in the criminal law, see 'Equity and Mercy', and Gifford Lecture 6.

[61] Cambridge, Mass.: Harvard University Press, 1971.

since Smith tends to believe that things are in good order as they are, whereas Rawls actually puts his construction of the person to work in the design of principles and policies. Rawls makes it explicit that a conception of the person, which includes a comprehensive normative account of rationality, is basic to his argument for his conception of justice. Only when we understand what these 'ideal people' are like, what information they do and do not use, and how they reason, will we have a purchase on the proper design of institutions and the just distribution of resources. I believe that Smith and Rawls are correct: we need an ideal of reason in order to design institutions justly. But if this is so, and if, as I have argued, many conceptions of reason (including Rawls's)[62] err by their neglect of the emotions, then, in order to have just social institutions, we need to think more about emotions.

I have argued that the emotions are best understood not as blind and brutish, but as intelligent forms of evaluative perception, either identical with or very closely linked to judgements; that, while Spinoza and the Stoics are right to link emotions with beliefs about our lack of self-sufficiency, there are reasons to think such beliefs both true and politically valuable; that while emotions do begin at home, so to speak, the love and gratitude of the home is a necessary prerequisite for an adequate awareness of the needs of those at a distance; that emotions do focus on particulars rather than on classes, but that in so doing they show the point and ultimate goal of class action; that even the connection of emotions with extra-moral sexual energies can make a valuable contribution to both private and public life; that even when we know we will be dealing with imperfect people in an institutional setting, there are strong reasons for giving these features of our rationality our most serious consideration.

4 EMOTIONS AND SOCIAL CONSTRUCTION, EMOTIONS AND GENDER

It will by now be clear that my view of the emotions is closely connected to recent views (defended in anthropology above all) according to which the emotions are 'socially constructed'. What is meant by this is that there is no emotional experience without belief; beliefs, however, are learned, and learned in society. Therefore both the fact that a person has emotions (rather than living a Stoic life) and the particular repertoire of emotions she has will be best explained by examining the society in which she was raised, and asking what it has taught her to think.

My view is, as I have said, closely related to these views: and yet it is in

---

[62] For an account, and criticism, of Rawls's view of the emotions, see my 'Perceptive Equilibrium' in *Love's Knowledge*.

certain ways distinct from them also.[63] For I insist on stressing the connection between emotional experience and judgements about the importance of 'external goods'—people and things outside the person that the person him or herself does not fully control. Such judgements are likely to be found in some form in any society given the general structure of human life, its mortality, its susceptibility to illness and fatigue, its dependence on goods that are in short supply. Society may give emotions a particular focus and colouring: Roman beliefs about what the object of love is like, about what is worth getting angry about, about what is really to be feared, differ in subtle ways from Greek beliefs on similar topics—and so forth. But it would be surprising indeed if there were not a great deal of overlap among societies in the general repertory of emotions they teach. And if we add to this the picture of early infant experience that I sketched in my previous chapter, it seems likely that emotions of fear and love and gratitude and envy and anger have their roots in infancy itself, long before society has had a chance to shape the infant very much in its own image. The infant's interactions with its parents are, of course, still shaped in certain ways by societal teachings that vary from one culture to another; but I think it is still possible to develop a general account of infant experience, where emotions are concerned, that will convincingly bring together the common experience of many different cultures. This means not only that it is highly unlikely that we could ever develop a fully Stoic society, even if we wanted to do so (even the Stoics did not think this a real possibility); it means, too, that the emotional repertories of different societies will be likely to have a great deal of overlap, in such a way that it is possible for us to see ourselves in their accounts of what they fear, and cherish, and get angry about, as they themselves in ours.

What now of gender? For it is almost universally, if unclearly,[64] observed—even among philosophers who hold a cognitive view of the emotions—that women are frequently more emotional than men. How should someone with a cognitive account of emotion explain these phenomena, or purported phenomena?

My view holds that the emotions do not arise from 'nature' at all: then, a fortiori, they do not arise from some female as distinct from male nature. In fact, on the account of the emotions I have offered, there is no intrinsic reason why the emotions should be distributed along gender lines at all.

[63] For a more extended account of this, see 'Constructing Love, Desire, and Care', forthcoming in Laws and Nature: Shaping Sex, Preference, and Family (New York: Oxford University Press, 1995).

[64] As Christine Korsgaard observed in discussion, this claim is so vague as to have very little content. Does it mean that women have a larger number of types of emotion than men? A larger number of episodes of the same types? Longer, or more intense episodes? Episodes directed at a larger number of objects? That they spend a larger proportion of their time in an emotional frame of mind? That they make more of their decisions by appeal to emotion? And so forth.

And of course they are not always so distributed. In some societies, extremes of fear, anger, and grief are judged normal and socially appropriate for males as well as females.[65] In still others, emotions are judged inappropriate for both.[66] In some societies, emotions are judged appropriate for both, but different emotions in each case.[67] But to the extent that women are commonly more associated with the emotional than are men, there is within my view an explanation ready to hand.

Emotions, I have said, are acknowledgements of neediness and dependence, acknowledgements of the importance of things outside the self that the person does not control. To some extent all human beings have such attachments to undependable external things. (Even the Stoics, after the time of Zeno and Cleanthes, stopped claiming that any fully 'wise' (i.e., completely unemotional) person was really alive.) But one can see that contingent social facts about control and dependency can shape the course of these attachments. Two areas of social difference between males and females seem to be especially significant. First, in many societies, from Okonkwo's Umuofia to the contemporary US, women are more likely to be brought up to think that it is right to have strong attachments to others, and to think of their own good as a strongly relational matter; males are more likely to be urged in the direction of self-sufficiency and the curtailment of deep need.[68] This is not a universal cultural fact; and the ancient Greco-Roman world was, it seems to me, far less gender-divided than modern American society is on this question. There are emotions, furthermore, for which it is less likely to hold, even for Americans: angers, fears, and anxieties connected with status, money, and reputation are very likely to be expecially linked with the socialization of males, in US society as much as in ancient Rome and in Umuofia. But the diagnosis has some explanatory force.

A second difference, of a very different sort, takes us further. The emotions, we recall, are connected with judgements about the importance

[65] Ancient Athens and Rome—prior to philosophical intervention—seem to be such societies.

[66] See especially Jean Briggs's account of an Eskimo tribe, the Utku, who are very like Stoics in their theory and practice of emotional extirpation. Some Indian norms of detachment also apply equally to serious people of both genders.

[67] Modern America, like Okonkwo's Africa, seems to be such a case, anger being judged more appropriate for males than for females, fear and compassion and love more appropriate for females. Anne Fausto Sterling assembles an impressive amount of data showing that emotions of babies are differently labelled according to the sex the observer believes the babies to have. In one American experiment, for example, alleged girls were labelled frightened when they cried, while alleged boys (actually the very same individual infants) were labelled angry. Such labelling is a part of the process of norm-transmission that culminates in actual emotional differences.

[68] See, here, Carol Gilligan, *In a Different Voice* (Cambridge, Mass.: Harvard University Press, 1982), and Nancy Chodorow, *The Reproduction of Mothering: Psychoanalysis and the Sociology of Gender* (Berkeley, Calif.: University of California Press, 1978) on which see further below.

of external things that one does not control. Now obviously there are some important features of human life that nobody ever fully controls. One cannot make oneself immortal, one cannot will that one's children should be healthy and happy, one cannot will oneself happiness in love. But nonetheless, differences in degree of social autonomy and control between males and females do affect the extent to which the sense of powerless governs the course of one's life. The heroines of Seneca's tragedies, driven mad by emotion, are usually wives who have no avenue to happiness but through their marriage. They have neither full citizenship nor full education; they have no avenue to productive self-expression outside the home. Thus, for them, everything hangs on the fate of this one attachment; and when it collapses they are, accordingly, in a state of complete disorder, as though they had no self at all. Roman males never experienced exactly that: for they had many things to cherish, not all of them dependent on the whim of a single other person (who is not encouraged by socialization to be especially dependable).

This situation is not just history or fiction: it is a daily fact of life for women in most parts of the world. We can see it at work in the life of Saleha Begum, for whom a husband's disability—given social laws against women's work—meant hunger for herself and her family; and even more clearly in the story of Metha Bai, whose only hold on life is her father's fragile health. Such women are far more dependent on fortune than are most males in their society, in all sorts of ways: dependent even, frequently, for their daily food and medical care. What wonder, then, if they should experience more fear, more grief, and also, frequently, more anger?

These two social facts point, it seems (not incompatibly) in opposite directions. The first suggests that one might need to reform the moral education of men such as Okonkwo, in order to make them value more properly the attachments to others that are so large a part of women's lives. The second, however, suggests that there is a degree of neediness, dependency, and powerlessness that is not connected with any intrinsic good in anyone's life—and that it would be best to move women, and indeed everyone, out of this condition of extreme dependency. In both cases, what we need, clearly, in order to make further progress, is an account of the good human life and good human functioning that will tell us which attachments to externals are truly valuable and which are not. I have tried, in my first chapter, to sketch a candidate for such an account: but much more remains to be done if it is to be concrete enough to offer any real guidance, especially where the structure of family attachments is at issue.

'But women in every culture love and support their children.' Both antifeminists and certain (alleged) feminists have pointed to the universal fact of mothering as evidence that there is, after all, a separate female nature, intuitive and emotional rather than calculative and intellectual. Appeals to mothering play a large role in many types of anti-feminist and 'feminist' argument, 'explaining' why logic is not a female domain, why women's thinking is bound to be intuitive and associative rather than logical, why women are better suited for some jobs than others, etc. So any analysis that claims, as mine does, that emotions are gender-linked only for contingent social reasons needs to consider this case and take a stand on it.

I have already shown the direction in which I would search for the response, by saying that my approach combines an interest in social teaching with an interest in much earlier and less explicit learning. The emotional repertory is very largely shaped in infancy. And yet infancy is not a time in which unshaped 'nature' simply expresses itself; it is a time of complex interaction and highly charged experience. I have said that it seems plausible that this experience, though differently shaped by different societies, has certain common features, since all societies have in common certain pervasive human problems. I can now add that it seems very likely that most societies have shared certain gender-based patterns in this crucial early phase of experience, in such a way that 'mothering' is reproduced in females from generation to generation. The work of Nancy Chodorow has, I believe, convincingly established this conclusion.

Chodorow's work is convincing because she realizes that the phenomena cannot be explained simply by pointing to behavioural patterns that a child acquires during its recognizable socialization: they lie deeper, in such a way as to be part of the structure of the personality itself:

The capacities and orientations I describe must be built into personality; they are not behavioral acquisitions. Women's capacities for mothering and abilities to get gratification from it are strongly internalized and psychologically enforced, and are built developmentally into the feminine psychic structure. Women are prepared psychologically for mothering through the developmental situation in which they grow up, and in which women have mothered them. (See above, n. 68)

But to say that these orientations are built into personality is not to say that they derive from an innate 'nature': for the structure of the personality is itself formed, though at an earlier date and at a level of depth that is not readily accessible to conscious analysis.[69] By focusing on these earliest interactions and the structures of personality they transmit, Chodorow is able to explain gender-differentiation as an outgrowth of social tradition—here operating at a very deep level both to shape the personality of the mother and her care of female and male infants and then, in turn, to reproduce that gender-differentiated structure in the lives of infants who will themselves grow up to take part in gender-differentiated societies.

---

[69] Both contemporary cognitive psychology and object-relations psychoanalysis now hold that even very young infants have very rich and complex attitudes to external objects. For one gripping summary of recent research, see Daniel Stern, *Diary of a Baby* (New York: Basic Books, 1992).

Chodorow's argument is highly complex, and I hesitate to attempt, here, a summary that is bound to be but a caricature of her more subtle and finely demarcated analysis. But her central conclusion is that, very widely if not universally, mothers' interactions with female infants reproduce the maternal personality, forming people who conceive of their own maturity and adulthood as involving close ties of a nurturing sort. The mothering of male infants, by contrast, tends to produce people who conceive of maturity and independence in terms of the denial of need and dependence. Thus Chodorow agrees with the social diagnosis of the ancient Stoics, though she extends the causal analysis of these differences back into infancy in a way that they did not (though they would very likely have sympathized with the project). But her normative evaluation agrees more with my argument here than with the Stoic argument: for she argues that the degree of self-sufficiency males come to expect of themselves is in various ways crippling to them, both in their emotional lives generally and above all in their relationships with women. And women's confinement to the mothering role has, itself, adverse social consequences, affecting their self-definition and what they can bring to work, to citizenship, even to relationships with others.

The diagnosis ends with a proposal. These things will not be easy to alter, given the depth and pervasiveness of the causes, Chodorow holds. If they are to be altered, it will only be through a reformation of parenting itself. But this, she believes, is possible:

Children could be dependent from the outset on people of both genders and establish an individuated sense of self in relation to both. In this way, masculinity would not become tied to denial of dependence and devaluation of women. Feminine personality would be less preoccupied with individuation, and children would not develop fears of maternal omnipotence and expectations of women's unique self-sacrificing qualities. This would reduce men's needs to guard their masculinity and their control of social and cultural spheres which treat and define women as secondary and powerless, and would help women to develop the autonomy which too much embeddedness in relationship has often taken from them.

We live in a period when the demands of the roles defined by the sex-gender system have created widespread discomfort and resistance. Aspects of this system are in crisis internally and conflict with economic tendencies. Change will certainly occur, but the outcome is far from certain. The elimination of the present organization of parenting in favor of a system of parenting in which both men and women are responsible would be a tremendous social advance. This outcome is historically possible, but far from inevitable. Such advances do not occur simply because they are better for 'society', and certainly not simply because they are better for some (usually less powerful) people. They depend on the conscious organization and activity of all women and men who recognize that their interests lie in transforming the social organization of gender and eliminating sexual inequality. (See above, n. 68)

I wholeheartedly agree with this conclusion. I would only add that when people of this sort ask themselves where their interests lie, they should not, if they are truly rational, use a narrow economic conception of 'interests' and think of themselves simply as maximizers of their own feelings of satisfaction. The question should, instead, be considered in terms of the interest a really rational being has in leading a rich and flourishing life that would combine into a more or less coherent whole all those forms of human functioning that have intrinsic value.

5   EMOTIONS AND GENDER JUSTICE

The question of the emotions thus becomes part and parcel of the general question of human functioning and human capability. In asking what emotions it is good to have, what emotions form part of truly rational judgement, we are asking, in effect, what forms of dependence and affiliation with undependable items outside ourselves it is good for a human life to have. And this involves asking how much uncertainty and dependency a person can live with while retaining integrity and practical reason; how far trust in others is a good thing and at what point it becomes naïvety; whether, indeed, it is best to live a life of what Thrasymachus (speaking of justice) called 'a very noble kind of naïveté', or a life that consists in prudently maximizing one's own satisfactions; whether it is good to love anyone at all, given the depths of the pain that love can inflict; whether it is good to build a society on the basis of these needs, loves, and attachments, or rather on the basis of respect for the self-sufficiency of reason. In short, it is the question of the human good.

It is not surprising that there should be deep division—among human beings and indeed perhaps within each human being—over these questions. For vulnerability is indeed painful, and trust difficult to sustain in an inhospitable and uncertain universe. The anti-emotion position will keep coming back, in philosophy and in life itself, as long as there are people who cannot bear to live in a world of deep attachments, who seek another purer world. And it will remain, therefore, a topic of dispute whether the emotions, seen as acknowledgements of incompleteness, are good or not, whether their associated beliefs are true and rational or false and pernicious. It seems right to end this paper not with a dogmatic answer to that question—though my argument will have made clear where my own sympathies lie—but with an acknowledgement of its complexity. These lines of Wallace Stevens seem to me a wonderful metaphor of the emotional life, in all of its mystery, wonder, and pain:[70]

[70] Wallace Stevens, 'Anatomy of Monotony', in *Collected Poems* (London: Faber and Faber, 1923), 107.

The body walks forth naked in the sun
And, out of tenderness or grief, the sun
Gives comfort, so that other bodies come,
Twinning our phantasy and our device,
And apt in versatile motion, touch and sound
To make the body covetous in desire
Of the still finer, more implacable chords.
So be it. Yet the spaciousness and light
In which the body walks and is deceived,
Falls from that fatal and that barer sky,
And this the spirit sees and is aggrieved.

Martha C. Nussbaum:
Emotions and Women's Capabilities

Commentary by Catherine Lutz

Martha Nussbaum gives an insightful and sweeping survey of five common objections to the rationality of emotions. They are the view of emotions as animal impulses which are never deliberative; the view of emotions as signs of social vulnerability or individual incompleteness; the accusation that the emotions direct attention only to the local and encourages lack of consideration to the distant; that they blind us to the universal and abstract in favour of the individual; and finally, that romantic and erotic love in particular prevent good citizenship and an ability to detect and pursue the general good.

I think Nussbaum has precisely captured the main dilemma that swirls through much academic thinking (mainly in the West perhaps) when she begins her paper with a critique of Posner's attempt to valorize certain 'non-Western' social patterns of behaviour. He does so by asserting that the behaviour in question is rational or sensible because it conforms to market principles. Emotions and all those social categories of people associated with emotionality take a second seat here, then, as she shows. Even arguments against national self-determination have hinged on such race and gender-based arguments. The images are or were common enough: the colonial 'native' ready to run riot as the forces of rational imperial order recede, the stereotypes of native women as saddled with an unbridled sexuality or an empty, beast of burden mentality (Hammond and Jablow, 1977; Hull, Scott, and Smith, 1982). No less in the post-colonial era, however, as Nussbaum suggests (particularly in another paper with Sen (1989)), have these theories of the emotions been deployed, if with a kinder grip. So the woman outside the Euro-American world has been portrayed by bureaucratic planners (but sometimes also by Western feminists) as an irrational collaborator in her own subordination: she is ready to throw herself on her husband's funeral pyre or submit to the mutilations of cliterodectomy (Amos and Parmar, 1984; Mohanty, Russo, and Torres, 1991). Moreover, even relativism—that friendly ideology exemplified by much anthropology—finds itself seemingly required to valorize others by addressing their gender practices as rational, that is, as simple and non-emotional choices they have made to live in particular ways. I can find this strain of thought barely submerged in my own ethnography of the lives of women and men on a Micronesian atoll (Lutz, 1988).

There is a double-faced role that emotions seem to play in characterizing other people in the contemporary United States. They both humanize and devalorize, or rather they can do either, depending on context. Women are more natural, in this cultural scheme (Ortner, 1974), and this explains their emotionality (Lutz, 1990): it has to do with hormones, with maternal instincts, with menstruation. Nature has two values, however, and so too does women's emotionality. But what has this to do with development? Nussbaum suggests that it contributes to poor conceptualization of women's lives by planners, and it can also be added that the problem of women in development illuminates the more general question of deformation of thought about others in the Third World by élites in the developed world.[1]

It helps raise the issue of the continued power—in the West at least—of an evolutionist view of social change among world societies. Women's status in society has been taken traditionally as an index of evolution from what was known as barbarism to what was known as civilization. Third World women have also been attributed a special role in the 'progress of their race'. For example, Fanon (1965) describes the French colonial strategy in Algeria of encouraging women to drop their veils. The woman's veilless, rational behaviour would theoretically set the standard for and lead Algerian men into the future. These kinds of notions can still be found, albeit in altered form, in contemporary development thought in the West.

To return to Nussbaum's paper, I want to suggest several areas in which we might begin discussion of her stimulating thought. The first is with the question of the role of individualism in all of this. Nussbaum points this out in her discussion of the view of emotions as false judgements. Emotion's perceptions are false because, in her words, 'they ascribe a very high value to external persons and events that are not fully controlled by the person's virtue or rational will. They are acknowledgments, then, of the person's own incompleteness and vulnerability'. They are not, in short, so easily contained within the boundaries and language of an individual self. When the cultural logic is exposed in which most emotions are excluded from definitions of the mature, good life, we can also note that the language of choice is central to this logic. Simply put, rationality defined economistically is about making choices, and we do not choose to have emotions. Choice is what it is all about, and while it is certainly difficult to make an argument *against* the value of choice, in the West this language tends to be at least as redolent with the perfumed smells of the department store as it is with the great issues of freedom from state tyranny. Choice, access to a cornucopia of manufactured commodities, and rationality are all closely intertwined in this way of thinking. The question that is raised for

---

[1] An example is found in research on popular media representations of the 'non-Western' world (Lutz and Collins, 1993). When popular photographs were read by a sample of white middle-class Americans, differences were found in the degree of emotional attributions to the photographed person depending on his or her race. While the photographs they looked at were ones which intended to humanize the other by showing universal feelings of love between family members, smiles of greeting and so on, the people who viewed them made less emotion attribution to darker skinned people and less positive emotion attribution as well.

me is about whether individualism is not the reinforcing bars inside the concrete of this scheme of relationship between emotion, rationality, and gender. Choice is often seen as an individual matter, it being more difficult in common (US) parlance to imagine choices which emerge out of interpersonal processes. Emotions, too, are seen as individual attributes, but as theorization moves on, it appears that the inherently social qualities of the emotions have been more readily acknowledged than the social roots of intelligence. That is, one's anger is seen as a problem of social relationship such as injustice before one's IQ score is so seen. And this scheme plays into the one in which women are seen as more socially oriented, men more context independent. This latter association has been used both to argue for women's inherently more nurturant and domestic nature as well as for women's obligations to do the emotional labour (Hochschild, 1983) for the community as a whole (of mourning, loving, worrying, and so on). Even more to the point of our discussions here, this leads directly to a cultural contradiction in views of women in development. No longer in the vanguard of progress, emotional women are by definition *less* likely to be seen at the forefront of contesting social relations as they are, less able to imagine a new future, and to contribute to development. Is critical rationality denied to women in this way? How do we most effectively argue for a rationality that is socially rather than individualistically based without excluding critique?

There is a second, closely related issue raised by Nussbaum's paper, and that has to do with power and women's emotionality. The notion that emotions are a sign of vulnerability can be seen as an inscription of social relations of power into the psyches of women and men. In other words, the often unequal power of women and men and of northern and southern peoples to control their lives might be seen as reified into mental attributes. Women's emotionality is then an ideological symptom of their powerlessness, not a cause of their social position. So, too, is the putative femininity of the Third World in Western minds, as Kabbani (1986) has pointed out. We are left with difficult questions. Are the 'psychological abilities' of self-sufficiency and rationality simply the rationalizations of social relations of power? Is it possible to define, free from coercions of power, the proper role of rational emotions in life and in gender identity? There is progress, however, in recognizing that unjust social systems are reproduced in part through individual's living out emotional ideals such as that of avoiding anger at all costs and of feeling compassion exclusively for life forms defined as 'innocent'. The problem is then construable, as Arlie Hochschild has done, as that of emotional labour. We can ask what kinds of emotional and other labour needs to be done to have a just society, who ought to do that labour, and where exploitation of that labour might be occurring.

I much admire the generosity and restraint with which Nussbaum ends her paper. There she sees in the anti-emotion position a rich, valuable, and well considered view of the good life as one with less of the pain of attachment; she sees it as the search for a pure world of possibly noble self-sufficiency. It often feels different when I encounter this view, however: it feels much like a judgement of the sort that Nussbaum, I, and others have found in the cultural theories of emotion, a judgement about the irrationality, and dangerous subjectivity, natural and so less cultured, lesser life of me and my kind, or of people different in ways other than by gender. I think I see the imperial self-confidence of a person already holding most of the marbles as a source of the focus on self-sufficiency, a marginalizing of others' needs.

A final suggestion for discussion is that we move to cases. The logic that Nussbaum discusses is, I think, absolutely central to discourses of gender and race, not only in the field of development but in public arenas where matters of national and international policy are formulated. We can look at the recent example of the war in Iraq and Kuwait. In the United States, there was a massive argument mounted by the state and much of the press (and seemingly accepted by their audiences) that the war was ultimately a moral venture, the use of military might to make right a situation of injustice (the invasion of Kuwait). The pursuit of the war, however, was portrayed in completely utilitarian terms, as a rational set of plans pursued dispassionately. The (male) people who ran the war could rely on the argument that smart bombs require cool male heads (although women can serve as helpmates at lower levels). The emotional rhetoric of outrage over the plight of the incubator babies in Kuwait City was central to the initial pursuit of the war, but the emotional content of the Baghdad bomb-shelter baby pictures was portrayed in pragmatic terms: damage control, the illicit use of those images by Iraqi officials to falsely manipulate the emotions of others, etc. These matters show a complex picture, one of whose features is the exceptionalism of anger as an emotion proper for men. This exception has proved crucial time and again in preserving male and white privilege to make ultimate decisions and arguments about the justice of a situation, to set the parameters and boundaries of discussions about the ought, which is what anger is about. There is also the response of President Bush to casualty figures, a response which runs very close to the fictional example Nussbaum gives us from Dickens. Bush responded like Sissy, noting that the numbers of American casualties were low, but saying that any death was one death too many and expressing deep sympathy for the survivors. His failure to even count the Iraqi dead among those to be considered reveals a common strategy of emotional and political response, which is to invest only some problems (and not just those closest to hand, *pace* the Kuwaiti babies) with emotional value, and in this way to wage war more effectively. Staying close to the home of cases which matter to us carries the risk that Nussbaum so astutely points out—'of considering the object not abstractly, as one among many, but as special . . .' and so of being emotional, nonrational, and discountable, but it also forces us to participate in the system we analyse, to acknowledge the historicity of ideas, and to work with a system whose complexities we know best and whose ongoing operation we are in a real position to effect.

BIBLIOGRAPHY

AMOS, V., and PARMAR, P. (1984). 'Challenging Imperial Feminism', *Feminist Review*, 17, 3–19.

FANON, F. (1965). *A Dying Colonialism*. New York: Grove Press.

HAMMOND, D., and JABLOW, A. (1977). *The Myth of Africa*. New York: Library of Social Science.

HOCHSCHILD, A. (1983). *The Managed Heart: Commercialization of Human Feeling*. Berkeley: University of California Press.

HULL, G., SCOTT, P. B., and SMITH, B. (1982). *All the Women are White, All the Blacks are Men, but Some of Us are Brave: Black Women's Studies*. Old Westbury, NY: Feminist Press.

KABBANI, R. (1986). *Europe's Myths of Orient*. Bloomington, Ind.: Indiana University Press.

LUTZ, C. (1988). *Unnatural Emotions: Everyday Sentiments on a Micronesian Atoll and their Challenge to Western Theory*. Chicago, Ill.: University of Chicago Press.

—— (1990). 'Engendered Emotion: Gender, Power and the Rhetoric of Emotional Control in American Discourse', in C. Lutz and L. Abu-Lughod (eds.), *Language and the Politics of Emotion*. Cambridge: Cambridge University Press.

—— and COLLINS, J. (1993). *Reading National Geographic*. Chicago, Ill.: University of Chicago Press.

MOHANTY, C., RUSSO, A., and TORRES, L. (1991). *Third World Women and the Politics of Feminism*. Bloomington, Ind.: University of Indiana Press.

NUSSBAUM, M. C., and SEN, A., 'Internal Criticism and Indian Rationalist Traditions', in M. Krausz (ed.), *Relativism* (Notre Dame, 1989).

ORTNER, S. (1974). 'Is Female to Male as Native is to Culture?', in M. Z. Rosaldo and L. Lamphere (eds.), *Woman, Culture, and Society*. Stanford, Calif.: Stanford University Press.

A Note on the Value of Gender-Identification

Christine M. Korsgaard

In the course of this conference Susan Wolf raised the question of what role we should like to see the concept of gender playing in an ideal world, perhaps the future world. Could the fact of gender play a far more restricted role in our lives than it does now? As Cass Sunstein put it, could being male or female matter as little to a person as having blue eyes or brown ones? And if it did, would we have lost something of value? Would it be better or worse to live in a world where gender mattered little to the sense of one's identity?

Martha Chen and Margarita Valdés reminded us that such questions, almost science-fictional in their remoteness from the situation even of 'developed' nations, have little to do with the problems of women in the Third World. For these women, progress often depends on getting those in power to focus on the differences between men and women, and on drawing attention to the special features of women's lives. Ruth Anna Putnam reminded us that this is true even in our own society: medical research, for instance, in taking men's bodies to be the basic human bodies, has neglected women's health. But this of course is not because either developing or developed societies have ignored *gender*. It is because they have ignored *women*. That is another matter altogether.

Despite its remoteness, Susan's question is an important one for anyone considering the situation of women anywhere because it gives voice to a concern that so many people feel. In seeking absolute equality, are feminists seeking the elimination of differences? This is not just a worry on the part of men with vested interests. Many people of both genders feel as if their gender were a deep fact about their identities, as if being male or female were something important to them, and therefore as if feminism might be asking them to give up something important.

I do not believe that gender has to be or should be a deep fact about the identity of a human being. To see why, we need to consider what is involved in having a gender. As far as I can see, there are five aspects to gender-identity as it has traditionally been conceived. (1) One is supposed to share certain qualities or attributes with the other members, or at least most of the other members, of one's gender. (2) The members of a gender are assigned certain tasks, for which these attributes supposedly make them especially well suited. (3) The members of a gender are subject to a certain gender ideal. Gender ideals are supposed to be associated with gender-correlated attributes: a perfect woman is a woman who exhibits the special attributes of women (or at least the positive ones) to a high degree. It will follow that she is especially well suited for the tasks assigned to women. (4) Gender is supposed to be a determinant of sexual orientation, and also to define what it is that one is oriented towards. And (5) because of all these things, the members of a gender have a shared history and shared experiences, creating special bonds among them.

It all starts with the presumption of shared attributes. Many differences in physical, mental, psychological, and moral attributes have been correlated with differences in gender. Popular discussions of feminism have focused very heavily on the question whether any of these correlations actually exist, and, if they do, whether they are natural or the product of socialization. Although I think that many of the claims about natural correlations are nonsense, I also think that for most purposes it is not important to establish this point. Even if there are differences naturally correlated with gender, they are so correlated only statistically and on the average. No one can deny *or ever has denied* that there are *some* women who are physically large and strong, talented at mathematics or political leadership, hopeless at dealing with children, or tasteless in matters of appearance. No one can deny or ever has denied that there are *some* men who are sensitive to the feelings of others, naturally inclined to nurture, mechanically inept, or devoid of physical courage. The rough statistical character of the correlation of other attributes with gender holds even for the one kind of correlation that we know exists naturally, the correlation between gender and other physical differences. There are after all flat-chested women, and men with ample hips; there are women with moustaches, and men without body hair; there are very tall women and very short men. Even if there are norms of gender, there are individuals who deviate from those norms.

According to an old quip, Christianity has not been tried and found too difficult, but rather has been found too difficult and so not tried. Despite some currently popular claims about the bankruptcy of the Enlightenment, I believe that this is true of Enlightenment ideals. Communitarians, champions of the family, and the promoters of ethnic and gender-identification may suppose that they have somehow discovered that the ideal of the sovereign individual is inadequate for human flourishing. But the truth is that many of them have simply balked when they realized how different a world that respects that ideal would have to be from the one we live in now. The centrality of gender is one of the things that would have to go.

Even if members of genders do tend to be alike, there are individuals who are different. If the genders are treated differently, these individuals will be treated wrongly. By Kantian standards the argument is over: it does not matter whether these individuals are many or few. No important attributes other than the biologically definitive ones are universally shared by the members of a gender: the tasks of life therefore cannot properly be distributed along gender lines. Tasks can be distributed according to taste and ability directly; there is no need for gender membership to mediate that process. And whenever individuals deviate very far from gender norms, gender ideals become especially arbitrary and cruel. Human beings are fertile inventors of ways to hurt ourselves and each other, and gender ideals are one of our keenest instruments for the infliction of completely factitious pain. People are made to feel self-conscious, inadequate, or absolutely bad about having attributes that in themselves are innocuous or even admirable. Of course this is by no means all that is wrong with gender ideals. As they stand they contain elements that are not just difficult for some to live up to but impossible for anyone to meet. Women are supposed to have an almost magical ability to comfort the afflicted, to say the right words or make the right gesture. Men are expected to possess a high degree of completely instinctive sexual know-how. The absurd idea that people are supposed to be born knowing how to handle some of the most delicate and complex matters of human life creates a lot of unnecessary anxiety. It also stands in the way of people making the needed efforts to learn.

Shared history and the sense of a shared fate is another matter. This is the feature of gender-identification that many people find most attractive. Indeed, human beings will always both identify with and value the company of those whose lives are like their own. Perhaps the experiences of pregnancy, giving birth, and early child-care will always be a bond among women who have children, as Nancy Chodorow suggested in our discussion. But these are bonds among mothers, not among women, and not every woman is a mother. The shared history of women is largely a product of growing up under the same oppressive gender ideals, being assigned the same tasks, and having the same presumptive sexual orientation. The identification produced by this shared history will disappear to the extent that more arbitrary features of gender-identification are abolished from our lives.

I say 'to the extent' because I do not want to make assumptions about whether all of the features of gender-identification can or should be abolished. One feature of gender-identification about which I have said little so far is the familiar pair of assumptions that there is such a thing as sexual orientation towards one of the genders and that it is determined by the gender that one has. Homosexuals accept the first of these assumptions but challenge the second; theoretically it is possible to challenge them both. What would our social world look like without them? Lately we have made some progress in our treatment of homosexuals, in the sense that enlightened people are now committed to putting an end to the grosser forms of discrimination against them. But certainly their condition is still treated by society as deeply exceptional. To speak rather abstractly, our social world has mechanisms intended both to facilitate erotic life and to keep erotic forces from breaking out in the wrong place. The public culture of romance, the practices of dating, engagement, and marriage, our gender-based traditions in clothing and cosmetics, and the restrictions on who can share washrooms, public dressing rooms, and dormitory rooms are all institutions designed to handle eroticism, with the double aim of making it possible while regulating its form. And all of our institutions for handling eroticism do so on the assumption that people, or most people, are heterosexual, and that therefore that is the form of eroticism which is to be facilitated and where necessary contained. One worry that is sometimes rather apologetically voiced by heterosexual men is that if gender plays a diminished role in human life, eroticism may play a diminished role as well. It is hard to believe that there is any serious danger of that, but there is a related worry which is real. One might well wonder whether and how we can create a public culture of eroticism that depends less than the one we have now on rigid assumptions about gender itself, and perhaps also about the relationship between gender and sexual orientation. No one yet has a concrete picture of institutions which could provide erotic life with a public surface that does not depend heavily on gender, and this blank spot in the imagined scene may well induce a certain fearfulness. But after all, it is not as if our old institutions have been doing a *good* job either at curbing unwanted erotic aggression or at facilitating erotic flourishing. At present we know little about these matters. That may well be a reason for optimism.

The sense of a shared history with the members of one's gender will disappear only if and when other features of gender-identification are long gone. It is the remoteness of this prospect that makes the diminishment of gender-identification seem so science-fictional. As long as the recent history of the two genders is different, gender will of course remain an important part of our identities. And feminism itself is a central part of our own recent history. What woman, living now in the parts of the world where feminism is taking hold, could say that it is unimportant to her sense of herself that she is a woman? The adventure of making changes, breaking down barriers, being the first to penetrate various inner sancta, creates a strong bond among contemporary women. This may make it *especially* hard for us to imagine a world in which gender is not deeply constitutive of identity. But this is a fact about where we stand in history, not about our nature. There are other tasks for human beings to perform and so to share. With luck we will move on.

PART IV
WOMEN'S EQUALITY: REGIONAL PERSPECTIVES

Gender Inequality in China and Cultural Relativism

Xiaorong Li

INTRODUCTION

This paper questions the romanticized 'local cultural' notions of women's well-being and their adverse impact on women's struggle for equality as, for instance, in the People's Republic of China (PRC). It argues, on the basis of one case study, that the non-relativist notion developed in the 'capability approach' provides a promising alternative in addressing the problems raised originally by relativists.

Specifically, I will contend that the notions of gender relations and women's well-being that have been touted by some women activists, either as official spokespersons of governmental ideology or independent feminists, have limited and misguided women's cause for equality. Such misconceptions, as this paper tries to establish, have contributed to the failure to liberate women. In particular, I will examine the conceptions of women's quality of life as expressed by political ideology, traditional norms, and women's own perceptions.

Alongside these lessons I draw, I will explore an alternative notion—a Kantian-Aristotelian notion, as embodied in Nussbaum and Sen's 'capability approach' toward the value of gender equality. Such a notion provides a more plausible foundation for evaluating the well-being of women (as well as men). The 'capability approach' presents a cross-cultural notion of being human and the human good that is at the same time sensitive to cultural traditions. Thus, it embraces the hope of overcoming the pitfalls of cultural insensitivity while avoiding the mere projection of local preferences.

[1]

In this section, I will make a case against the claim by relativists that, because of differing cultural conceptions of women, family, and society, it is insensitive, if not imperialist, to criticize Chinese women's apparent lack of gender equality.[1] I make my case by demonstrating that uncritical and unreflective local traditional cultural notions of women's well-being have been detrimental to women's struggle for a better quality of life in China.

Gender inequality in the PRC is not so much ignored as misunderstood. The PRC government has, since the early years of its rule, paid much

---

[1] See E. Marks and I. de Courtivronk (eds.), *New French Feminism: An Anthology* (New York: Schocken Books, 1981), 137–40 (in which this seems to be the view).

attention, in its ideology and policy-making, to women's subordinate status. The revolution helped to raise the status of women. Legislation like the Marriage Law of the 1950s not only outlawed the most extreme forms of female subordination and repression, such as prostitution, concubinage, sale of women, and child brides, but also gave women the opportunity to make their own marital decisions. Women were no longer restricted to the home—they joined the agricultural and industrial work forces. Education, which was denied to women in traditional China, has become more accessible. And the arena of politics is no longer exclusively male.

However, gender disparity has persisted and has even increased in recent years. After the Marriage Law gave women the right to choose husbands, the traditional business of selling women for marriage is coming back. In 1990 alone, 18,692 cases were investigated by the authorities.[2] While women are said to have equal opportunity to work, many have to take lower-paid and less challenging jobs.[3] While women are said to have an equal say in politics, leadership positions are dominated by men, or given to women simply as window-dressing.[4] The nation's education system has given first priority to males, and illiterates and school dropouts have been mainly female.

Women in China have thus failed to 'hold up half the sky', as Chairman Mao promised they would do if they simply embraced a communist 'new China'. The failure cannot simply be attributed to governmental negligence and policy shortcomings. Its roots extend to conceptional manipu-

[2] Sheryl WuDunn, 'Feudal China's Evil Revived: Wives for Sale', *New York Times*, 3 August (1991). The pressure to produce male offspring has led to a startling increase in female infanticide. Newly released data from China's 1990 census support the suspicion that 5% of all infant girls are unaccounted for and infanticide is said to be largely responsible. See Nicholas Kristof, 'A Mystery From China's Census: Where Have Young Girls Gone?' *New York Times*, 17 June (1991).

[3] In 1988, women accounted for only 36.5% of China's total number of scientific and technological personnel, 37% of the teaching staff, and 48% of the accounting and statistical staff. See 'Accomplishments of 8 Million Female Cadres.' *People's Daily*, 8 March (1988), 1.

[4] In 1988, the Politburo of the CCP Central Committee had no woman full member or alternate member. There were 12 vice-ministers among the more than 200 in total. There were only 10 women provincial governors or vice-governors, compared to about 50 men at this level. See FBIS, 'CCP Official Says Policy on Women Unchanged.' OW121006, *Beijing, Xinhua*, 12 January (1988).

According to a survey of women cadres by the All-China Woman's Federation in 1987, some women complained that their applications for the Party membership were not accepted because the Party had to have nonparty member/women as representatives. The same survey also revealed that outstanding women are often passed over for men who are merely 'fairly competent.' See *Women's Work (funu gongzhuo)*, 4 (1987), 6–9.

Further criticism has been levelled at the 'quota' system used to protect women's promotion. This system was said to shield incompetent women cadres and give women positions without real power. This system thus manipulates women in order to propagate the 'equality' ideology.

lation and illusions in the areas where the following questions are relevant: 'What is women's well-being?' and 'How is well-being measured?'

One version of relativism, the 'local tradition' relativism[5] argues that notions of women's well-being (or, human good in general) should be drawn from local culture. It rejects universal notions because such notions would be culturally insensitive, neglecting historical and cultural differences.

Different cultural traditions and communities, it is said, diverge in their understanding of human values as well as women's status and roles in society. In this view, any attempt to produce a cross-cultural notion of human well-being is bound to enshrine certain understandings of the human good and to dismiss others.

This version of relativism is based on the fear that dominant social prejudices would be imposed on women by a dominant group's (stronger foreign culture, majority social members, or popular consensus) understanding of human value. Because societies are often patriarchally structured and controlled by dominant groups, cultural relativists do have a point for suspicion: the dominant understandings of human good will be likely to put females at a disadvantage.[6] This concern suggests some of the difficulties that attend any project of building a non-relativist norm of women's well-being.

But the same difficulty besets cultural relativism itself. Who should speak for 'the local tradition' in the absence of any universal normative evaluation? Should it be the local government (the state), the traditional philosophical or religious doctrines, or women's own perceptions of their interest? As the Chinese case makes clear, voices from these 'local' structures, without critical reflection, turn out to represent the patriarchal *status quo* and put females at a disadvantage.

Consider, for example, three Chinese conceptions of women's well-being that are perfectly 'local cultural'. One is the Communist Party-state's political ideology that drove the official campaigns for gender equality since the 1950s. Secondly, the ideas expressed in dominant traditional philosophy and religion, such as Confucianism and Taoism, which shaped the Chinese mentality and rituals of daily life, have also functioned as a voice of 'local culture'. Finally, the voice most frequently referred to by the relativist is that of Chinese women, expressing their desired roles in society. We shall see whether and how these three expressions reflect dominant male understandings of the role of women.

---

[5] Nussbaum has given it this name. 'Local tradition relativism' is different from metaphysical relativism, which suspects that there is any determinate way the world exists apart from the interpretive workings of the cognitive faculties of living beings. See Nussbaum, 'Human Capabilities, Female Human Beings', in this volume.

[6] Ibid.

410   XIAORONG LI

1 THE OFFICIAL VOICE

The official ideology in China has worked against the idea of women's freedom to choose and a respect for them as individuals, equal to men in dignity. It has treated gender equality as instrumental to political solidarity, and women as instruments for enhancing the national GNP. The increased role of women in workplaces outside the home is praised by the governmental All-China Women's Federation (ACWF) for its 'contribution to the building of socialist material and spiritual civilization'.[7] When the ACWF shows concern over insufficient educational training for women, it worries that 'if this situation is not remedied, the country's socialist modernization drive will be impeded'.[8] Similarly, rural women's status is studied only 'for the purpose of getting rid of this cancer [the illiteracy of rural women] in Chinese society as a burden on China's modernization'.[9] Recently, the ACWF's local divisions in Guangzhou and Shanghai have set up cosmetic surgery businesses in the accelerated national quest for profit. This has the effect of a symbolic call by authorities for women to beautify themselves in order to enhance men's strive for business profit or managerial excellence. At the same time, women are being systematically rejected for executive positions and find themselves before a growing pool of jobs in bars and hotel lobbies; working as waitresses, accompanying ladies, and prostitutes.

During the 45 years of communist rule, only when women's inferior treatment conflicted with the objectives of political campaigns did the issue of gender inequality become a policy concern. Thus, campaigns for women seemingly took place only in connection with political movements such as the Great Leap Forward movement of 1957-9, the rural 'responsibility system' reform since 1978 and the 'one-child' family planning project. Accordingly, gender equality has been largely reduced to 'labour equality' and pursued in the name of the national interest.

The recent drive for profit proceeds in the absence of equal opportunity for women to take high-skilled and highly paid positions. Profit-minded companies refuse to hire female graduates from universities because their parenting responsibilities may impede business.

The 'equality campaigns' indoctrinated women to view their roles in society in a particular way rather than helping them to cultivate their capability to reflect on and challenge the traditional patriarch *status quo*. The party line has always dominated the definition of 'women's liberation'. During the Great Leap Forward movement, 'liberation' meant enabling

[7] Shen Zhi, 'Development of Women's Studies—The Chinese Way', *Trends in Academic Circles*, 25 December (1984), 42. This article summarizes proceedings at the First National Symposium on Theoretical Studies on Women.
[8] Ibid.
[9] From a report by Zhang Hua, a lecturer in sociology from Beijing University, at the Beijing Information Exchange Meeting, March 1991.

women to perform heavy manual labour in the field—'what men can do, women can do also'. In the Great Cultural Revolution, 'liberation' meant that women should become no different from men, even wearing men's clothing and behaving in a 'unisex' manner. During the current economic reforms, official publications argue that the 'responsibility system'[10] and labour efficiency considerations justify women's return to the kitchen, resuming the role of 'a virtuous wife and good mother'. The 'new Chinese woman' is told by the authorities that she could attain 'equality' with men by turning herself into a 'man'. Male character traits are presented as the common humanity that woman, as man's equal, is to live up to. Woman's 'equal' entitlement to humanity means her entitlement to 'man-ness'. The underlying assumption is that women are degenerate exemplars of humanity (man-ness). As in other societies, such a judgement of inferiority is often used, as Nussbaum observes, 'to justify and stabilize oppression'.[11]

The Chinese woman is told that she is 'liberated', but she is discouraged from and punished for thinking independently on gender issues. Lacking opportunities for critical thinking and information, she must adhere to rigid instructions on how to be the 'equal' of men. State persecution of critical thinkers has stifled critical thinking by women (as well as by men) and helped to reinforce biases against women despite the government's vow to eradicate them.

The ideology that motivates the state-sponsored 'women's equality' campaigns has mixed instrumentalist and utilitarian ideas. These campaigns have aimed at certain utilities defined by the state's political interest, either increasing the GNP or mobilizing massive support for the party. They have made the need for gender equality *contingent* on the government's political objectives. Such an instrumental notion, however, has proved to be no guarantee of equal treatment for women. This is because, first, all tolerated campaigns and activities, including the women's movement, have to adhere to official party doctrines ('the four cardinal principles',[12] for example), which are antithetical to freedom of thought and expression, among other civil liberties. Thus, any official campaign to improve the treatment of women will not tolerate criticism of the established party line.

Secondly, the official campaigns for gender equality are defective because they are based only on the instrumental value of women's social status. Efforts to reverse the inferior social status of women will fail if women's equality and freedom of choice are not valued for their own sake. The Chinese Communist Party's repeated purges of liberal ideas since the

[10] Under the 'responsibility system', each rural family is assigned a piece of the collectively owned land and the family collects the products after paying a portion to the state. This system was part of the 1978 rural reform package.

[11] Nussbaum, 'Human Capabilities, Female Human Beings', in this volume.

[12] The principles of insisting the party's absolute leadership, proletarian dictatorship, socialism, and Marxism–Maoism.

1950s, such as the anti-rightist movement and the Cultural Revolution, have excluded any sincere promotion of such values.

The voice of the party-state, which turns out to be the voice of the dominant male, has not only misrepresented women's real interest in equality, but has also contributed to the failure of the official 'equality campaigns'. If the party-state ideology, which controls public media and the educational system, is taken to be the voice of the 'local community', then, as the above analysis shows, it could be very detrimental to women's struggle against subordination.

2 PATRIARCHAL TRADITIONS OF CHINESE THOUGHT

I have shown that the party-state ideology does not represent the 'local community' voice for Chinese women. Do the dominant philosophy and religion better represent that voice? Have they been able to offset the prejudices against women and express their real interest? There are reasons to take these thoughts as the voice of Chinese cultural tradition because they still strongly influence people's decisions in daily life, especially social attitude towards women. According to a report on the second National Symposium on Women, family (not individual human beings) is still widely regarded as the cell of society responsible for the functions of reproduction, production, consumption, providing for the old, and nursing the young. And women are regarded as the nucleus around which family responsibilities are conceived.[13]

The core of traditional thought, however, has perpetuated, through philosophy, religion, and aesthetics, a subordination of women. Confucianism, a moral philosophy dating to 400 BC, morally evaluates a person according to his or her adherence to social roles prescribed by ancient rituals that were designed for collective achievement. The goodness of a man is determined by how well he plays his set of social roles as son, husband, father, and/or public official (servant). Accordingly, a woman is judged by her performance as daughter, wife, and mother. These roles carry very specific moral codes passed on from generations' worth of ritual practice: one virtue of the wife is 'obedience' to her husband, who in return is to provide for her and protect her. The virtue of a child is filial piety to the parents, whose virtue is, in return, love and fairness. Confucian philosophers argue that when different roles are performed in accordance with traditional rituals, society as a whole will be harmonious, with each assuming his/her role and all carrying out the mandate of heaven.

The roles assigned to women, however, were inferior since they involved only domestic and thus less important activities. This inferiority was clear to Confucius, who once said, 'Women and small men are the only burden-

[13] Zhu Qing, 'Summary of the Second National Symposium on Women's Studies', *Trends in Academic Circles*, January (1987).

some people'.[14] That is to say that women do not belong to the Confucian moral category. Women are not only accorded less respect, but also, their inferior roles are said to be part of, and necessary for, the natural (heavenly) harmonious order. There is no room for women's own voice. Their mission and destiny in life (a conception of their good) has been predetermined by a male-dominated society and the theorists who justify the *status quo* social hierarchy. The long-dominant Confucian moral tradition, repeatedly enforced by rulers through laws and social customs over many generations, has been largely responsible for preventing women from identifying themselves as equally worthy human beings.

Over time, the social enforcement of Confucianism distorted its valuable points to suit political expediency. Chinese society, during its long history of male domination, carried to the extreme the Confucian view of women as subordinate to men, and failed to substantialize the equally important Confucian idea of loving, caring, responsible, and just male roles. The statute that 'Wives should be obedient to their husbands' every wish' was first stressed in the Western and Eastern Han Dynasties (206 BC–AD 220). The social institution for the absolute repression of women was completed in the Song Dynasty (906–1279). Its key moral code was the 'three obediences and four virtues'. These were: obedience to the father before marriage, to the husband after marriage, and to the son after the husband's death; and the virtues of loyalty, proper speech, modest demeanour, and diligent work. Central to this tradition were the ideas that 'men should be respectable and women humble', and that 'the lack of learning in woman is a virtue'.

Consequently, the Confucian ideals of family, society, and women's role have not significantly changed over the past 2,500 years. For example, women in today's China continue to be evaluated first and foremost by their traditionally primary roles as wives and mothers, and are expected to make sacrifices for the family. A traditionally female virtue, the idea of 'sharing', still functions as a norm for female performance of their social roles: women as wives 'share' their husbands' career achievement, fame, and success, by playing the roles of housekeepers and raising children while taking lower paid and less challenging jobs. Women are told to be satisfied by such a 'sharing'. A variant of this norm is expressed in the phrase, 'behind-the-scene greatness': women's greatness stands behind their husbands' achievements, fame, and success; each successful man has a virtuous woman supporting him. In both views, the virtue of female excellence is couched in the context of family unit. Female moral values are defined in terms of men's success.

The defect of this form of Confucianism is its collective moral evaluation, which does not embody the concept of individual worth of female social members, and respects a female only for her performance of the tradition-

---

[14] *Analects (Lun Yu)*, by Confucius, 17: 23.

ally predetermined social roles. One may point out that, in the same way, male Chinese have also been restricted by their traditional roles and prevented from developing their complete human capabilities, such as the capability to love and care for their spouse and family before and above their country, or to achieve excellence in housework. However, the rigid traditional hierarchy works mainly to the disadvantage of women. In the traditional family, a woman had no inheritance rights as a result of being perceived as not fully human; she was merely an instrument for housework and reproduction; she remained at home and was subjected to restrictive and humiliating rituals, enslaved by the father, brother(s), and husband.

Buddhism, an imported religion, is perhaps another main source of the view of women as inferior. Briefly stated, the traditional contempt for women in China is linked to the Buddhist ascetic teaching that women are the source of all evils on earth because female sexuality causes men to commit crimes. Thus, women are condemned for distracting Buddhist monks from reaching 'the other shore'—Faramita. Buddha advised his disciples, 'Women are the vicious enemy of a wise man.' One doctrine of the Buddhist Mahayana (Great Vehicle), called 'nine meditations to extinguish six desires', was adopted in order to condition monks to see rotten corpses when they looked at beautiful women. Buddhism became well-adapted and widely accepted in Chinese society for reasons that cannot be discussed here. It is clear, though, that its success strengthened the social prejudice against women.

Taoism, the rival teaching to Confucianism, may have been the only major philosophical school that worships femininity. In the Taoist bible *Dao De Jing*, Lao Tzu, the founder, built his cosmology (the 'natural' order) and ethics—the philosophy of Yin and Yang—on female virtues and characteristics traditionally attributed to women, such as gentleness, softness, humbleness, tolerance, obedience, and women's function to give birth and take 'lower positions', etc. Lao Tzu wrote:

> The Tao is an empty vessel; it is used, but never filled.
> Oh, unfathomable source of ten thousand things!
> Blunt the sharpness,
> Untangle the knot,
> Soften the glare,
> Merge with dust . . .[15]

The philosophy of Lao Tzu uses conventional female images to interpret conflicts and interactions and the cycle in nature and human life. He suggests a technique to survive natural calamities.

> The valley spirit never dies;
> It is the women, primal mother.

[15] Lao Tzu, *Dao De Jing*, ch. 4.

Her gateway is the root of heaven and earth.
It is like a veil barely seen.
Use it; it will never fail.[16]

However, Lao Tzu's Taoism hardly embodies a fair conception of femininity. Some of the female images, such as 'obedience' and 'humbleness', regarded as 'natural' by Lao Tzu, are products of certain social divisions of labour and perpetuated by social prejudices. Thus, despite his favourable view of women, Lao Tzu takes for granted the dominant social perspective of his time and views women from the conventional position of a dominant male. Unfortunately, the legacy of Lao Tzu, perhaps contrary to his intention, serves to reaffirm socially constructed gender difference as the 'natural order', providing a philosophical justification for the unjust practice.

Moreover, since his philosophy aims at revealing the skills to survive, to prevail, and to win, his praising of 'female' (Yin) virtues is a mere stratagem. Women are valued by him, but only because of their usefulness for other ends. This instrumentalist evaluation of women's status explains why Taoism did not spur the development of significant feminist philosophies, for it failed to generate a real respect for women for their own worth as equal human beings.

This unfortunately over-simplified survey of major Chinese conceptions of women and their status in family and society provides only preliminary and limited insights about their defects as a 'local traditional' voice for women. These conceptions, as I have tried to demonstrate, played a harmful role in women's struggle for equality by perpetuating the subordinating social *status quo* as 'natural' social order.

3 FALSE SELF-CONSCIOUSNESS

Who, then, should be the voice of the Chinese 'local traditional' view on female virtues or women's well-being? What about women themselves who are raised and live in the Chinese cultural context? Talking about women's own opinions, we have to be cautious. It is not always true that the victims of an unjust treatment have a clear sense of what is just. For example, according to a research from the Chinese Academy of Social Sciences, the lack of protection of women's equality is often due to the lack of demands by women themselves to exercise their rights. They tend to rely on the state and society for assigned benefits and care.[17] Does this mean that they are not equal human beings since they lack the demands for equality? Subordinated groups have often absorbed their oppression so well that they are

---

[16] Ibid., ch. 6.
[17] See proceedings of the third National Symposium on Women in 1990.

unaware of their own equal worth. Only the subordinated group's critically reflected opinions of social norms would represent its long-term real interest. An implementation or restoration of justice should make reference to such reflected views. Chinese women have not yet come to terms with such critical thinking and conscious rejection of their own subordination due to their deprivation. They are raised and conditioned to perceive the *status quo* social order as 'natural'. For example, at the peak of women's awakening in the 1980s, some activists felt the future of women lay in reinforcing traditional female virtues. They claimed that they were in favour of the moral model of 'a virtuous wife and good mother'. Some activists claimed the rediscovery of traditional roles with a sense of liberation:

> . . . women should establish their credit. They need a more complete education than men—to cultivate refinement . . . develop poise . . .—so that they can become the mistresses of society . . . When people see women, including their own wives, being polite, well-behaved, and well-dressed, they will say, this is such a civilized society, and those are such respectable women.[18]

This tendency to return to the past looking for female virtues and women's proper role in society is revealing about the formation of illusion ('false-consciousness'). First, women are still so captivated by their long-standing indoctrination by the patriarchal society. Growing up in the shadow of the Chinese sexist morality, women have, deposited within them, a 'psychological complex': the inferior mentality. They feel comfortable with the idea that women are not expected to do the same thing as men; they often resort to passive acceptance when confronted with problems. This mentality leads them to set low standards for themselves, to be easily satisfied and to be intimidated by difficulties. Their ideal in life is often to find a husband who is emotionally stronger and economically better off.[19] The way '(political) power abandons women and women distance themselves from power' is also a symptom of this 'inferior complex'. Due to social discouragement, Chinese women tend to be passive about politics and regard it as a dirty game played by men. This attitude provides evidence that women have not transcended male domination and have taken it so much for granted that they even inflict repression on themselves.[20]

Secondly, they have not had much opportunity to be exposed to, nor allowed to, hold alternative ideas of female role. In the absence of alternative conceptions, they could only react against, from an older traditional point of view, the alienated tough heroine model idolized by the communist

[18] Tang Min, 'Women's Training Must Be Improved', *Fujian Youth* (July 1985), 19.

[19] Zhang Xiping, 'Cultivation of New Women', *Youth Studies*, 9 (September 1985).

[20] Zhou Yi and Wang Jian, 'The Puzzle Why Women Avoid Political Power', *Chinese Women* (March 1991).

revolutionaries—someone who is intellectually and almost physically equal to men, and lacking entirely in feminist sensitivity and uniqueness. Such a repressive model was perpetuated through a series of Cultural Revolution model operas, ballet, movies, and stories in the late 1960s and 1970s, in which the heroines wore men's clothing, marched like men, and did battle with or against men. As the crazy years of the Cultural Revolution passed, so did the pressure women felt to become the same as the dominant males. And they are left with the traditional models.

Thirdly, I speculate that Chinese women will also have to learn how to appreciate an opportunity to reflect on their culturally immersed aspirations. It is not enough to overcome a false consciousness. In addition to fighting to remove countless socially imposed and self-imposed hurdles, they face the task of learning how to live as reflective, choosing, and equal human beings. Some successful women, for example, can't help feeling a loss even after they have found ways to realize their talents and potential capabilities. One female secretary at a provincial Party Committee said she felt a need to 'apologize' to her family. 'Along with my success in career, there appears in my heart the uneasiness—the increasing sense of guilt towards my child.'[21] This indicates an unavoidable hesitation women experience when they are confronted with the choice between tradition and modernity. But to become men's equal at the workplace and in politics, women have to go beyond the humble image that was conventionally assigned to them. As Ye Changzheng, a member of the Chengdu Municipal Political Consultative Committee, realizes when she comments on the lack of women participants in politics, they should become politically active in order 'to cultivate Chinese women's independent personality, give up the feeling of petty and low in their sub-consciousness, break the pattern of strong men and weak women, shift their focus of social role from husbands and children to their career success.'[22]

It may seem clear in the case of China, that women's unreflective opinion, as a 'local traditional' voice, has helped to perpetuate dominant establishment. A movement among women themselves to struggle against their own inferior mentality has to be the first step towards equality.

The above survey of three possible voices of the Chinese 'local tradition' lend evidence to the defect of 'local cultural' relativist approach. While the relativist legitimately fears that a cross-cultural conception of women's well-being would reinforce some dominant groups' view, the restriction to local communal tradition does not seem to help avoiding the perceived danger.

[21] 'The Other Side of Female Success', from a Chinese women's magazine (December 1988).
[22] Ye Changzheng, 'Sharing Power, Transcending Power', *Chinese Women* (March 1991).

[2]

In the place of the misleading 'local cultural' notions, as those shown in the above cases, I will, in an unfortunately brief section, adapt an alternative notion to the Chinese context, suggesting how it may provide sensible guidelines in measuring the quality of women's life in China. This is the notion that has been eloquently developed in Nussbaum's and Sen's 'capability approach'.[23] Their notion is Kantian because it stresses the value of respect and freedom of choice based on practical reasoning and critical reflections;[24] and it is Aristotelian because it is based on a notion of human flourishing. I will probe how this approach can encounter the 'local tradition' relativist's charges. Especially, I am interested in the question how the 'universal traits' of general human well-being, which the 'capability conception' claims to capture, apply to our case and how it responds to the Chinese experiences.

Nussbaum[25] argues that a cross-cultural assessment of women's well-being is feasible by applying a 'thick vague conception of the good'. She claims that this conception defines the 'shape of the human form of life' and a good human life, which 'abstract[s] from traditional gender distinctions as morally irrelevant'.[26] Starting from the intuitive idea of a human being who is 'capable and needy',[27] she argues that a life, if it is constituted by certain traits, is characteristically *human*, no matter within what culture it is lived. These traits include the fact of mortality (a fear of and an aversion to death); the bodily needs for food and drink, shelter, sex, and mobility; the capacity for pleasure and pain; the cognitive capabilities; early childhood development; practical reason; affiliation and concern for other human beings; relatedness to other species and to nature; humour and play; and separateness.[28]

---

[23] See Martha Nussbaum, 'Nature, Function, and Capability: Aristotle on Political Distribution', *Oxford Studies in Ancient Philosophy*, suppl. vol. (1988); *Love's Knowledge: Essays on Philosophy and Literature* (Oxford: NY: Oxford University Press, 1990); and other articles referred in the footnotes of this paper. Also, see Nussbaum and Sen (eds.), *The Quality of Life* (Oxford: Clarendon Press, 1993); Sen, 'Equality of What?', in Sterling McMurrin (ed.), *Tanner Lectures on Human Values*, vol. I (Salt Lake City, Utah: University of Utah Press, 1980); *Resources, Values and Development* (Oxford: Blackwell, and Cambridge, Mass.: Harvard University Press, 1984); *Commodities and Capabilities* (Amsterdam: North-Holland, 1985); 'Well-being, Agency and Freedom: The Dewey Lectures, 1984', *Journal of Philosophy*, 82; 'The Concept of Development', in Hollis Chenery and Srinivasan (eds.), *Handbook of Development Economics*, vol. 1 (Amsterdam: North-Holland, 1988); 'Gender Inequality and Theories of Justice', in this volume.

[24] The Kantianism in Nussbaum's conception has not been adequately appreciated, though she declares that 'my approach agrees with the Kantian approach far more than it disagrees, disagreeing primarily in wishing to attend more centrally to need, limitation, and vulnerability in defining the being for whom justice is being sought.' 'Human Capabilities, Female Human Beings', in this volume.

[25] I have to focus on Nussbaum's view in order not to get into a discussion of the differences between her view and that of Sen's.

[26] Nussbaum, 'Human Capabilities, Female Human Beings'.

[27] Ibid.   [28] Ibid.

Now, for Nussbaum, what human beings are, empirically speaking, regardless of their nationality, colour, gender, and religion, has an evaluative claim in a most general way on what human life *should* be lived. Hence, 'this list of capabilities is a . . . minimal conception of the good.'[29] In other words, it serves as a criterion to judge whether a creature is a human being and whether the creature's life is lived as a human life in any cultural contexts, be it Chinese, Indian, or European, for it captures 'the characteristic activities of the human being: what does the human being do, characteristically, *as such*, and not, say, as the member of a particular local community.'[30] This list hence sanctions women's entitlement to general humanity and provides a measurement of female well-being, transcending the views from local political ideology, traditional norms, or women's own opinions. To contest this point, we can run the sort of thought-experiment Nussbaum proposed: take away certain properties such as being Chinese, or being female, and we still have a human being in front of us. But take away properties on her list, especially the capability of practical reasoning to plan the future, to choose and to respond and love other humans, we no longer have a human life at all.[31]

Though these traits depict a minimal human life, they do not characterize a *good* human life. For Nussbaum, there is a higher threshold below which a life is not considered good. Nussbaum describes a *good human life* as a life in which one is able to live to the end of a complete human life as far as is possible; to have good health; to be adequately nourished; to have adequate shelter; having opportunities for sexual satisfaction; being able to move around; to avoid pain and have pleasure; to have adequate education, enabling one to use five senses and the cognitive capabilities; to care and love others; to be able to form a conception of the good and to engage in critical reflection; to affiliate, having the capability for justice and friendship; to live with concern for and in relation to animals, plants, and nature; to be able to laugh and play; to live one's own life and nobody else's, in one's own surroundings and context.[32]

In differentiating a minimal *human* life from a *good* human life, Nussbaum has introduced two thresholds, the first is 'a threshold of capability to function beneath which a life will be so impoverished that it will not be human at all', and beneath the second, 'those characteristic functions are available in such a reduced way that, though we may judge the form of life a human one, we will not think it a good human life'.[33] Accordingly, a society may have provided the conditions for a *human* life, in the minimal sense, but not the conditions for a *good* human life.

[29] Nussbaum, 'Aristotelian Social Democracy', in R. Bruce Douglass, Gerald R. Mara, and Henry Richardson (eds.), *Liberalism and the Good* (New York and London: Routledge, 1990), 224.
[30] Nussbaum, 'Human Capabilities, Female Human Beings'.
[31] Ibid.   [32] Ibid.   [33] Ibid.

It is significant to note that the first threshold, an evaluative criterion of societies or forms of life for being *human*, would fail authoritarian societies, including religious fundamentalist or communist societies. Authoritarian societies systematically deprive the conditions for certain basic capabilities to function, such as the capability to engage in practical reasoning, the need for separateness and strong separateness. And clearly, in Nussbaum's view, an impoverished society in which the state makes an escape from hunger and homelessness impossible is not a *human society*.

Nussbaum emphasizes that a life has to have *all and every* traits at the first threshold in order to be human. Accordingly, a *human* society has to create and maintain conditions that make such a human life possible. No one trait is prioritized over others. At the second threshold, the basic capabilities collectively, rather than any one or a few of them, define a *good* human life: 'a life that lacks any one of these, no matter what else it has, will fall short of a good human life'.[34] These human goods are many and each is 'distinct in quality' and of 'central importance'.[35] A trade-off of some capacities for others does not make a human life *good*.

All are of central importance and all are distinct in quality. This limits the trade-offs that it will be reasonable to make, and thus limits the applicability of quantitative cost-benefit analysis.[36]

Consequently, a society that fails to provide all the conditions for a good human life is not a good society. Nussbaum would thus reject the apologetic claim that suppressing the exercise of the capabilities of practical reason and of affiliation (required for the exercise of political/civil liberties), for instance, is justified by the achievement of the capability to have good health, adequate nutrition and shelter and so on (normally referred to as social/economic rights). Variable capabilities are 'incommensurable' for 'we cannot satisfy the need for one of them by giving a larger amount of another one'.[37]

Nussbaum's thresholds are therefore highly idealistic, judging societies against a standard that would fail many contemporary societies in a test of their being human and being good. Since each condition on Nussbaum's first list is viewed as necessary, and together as sufficient for something (a creature or a society) being counted as human, her first level threshold implies that many societies do not qualify as being human, including, for example, the famine-rampaged and severely impoverished countries, as well as authoritarian societies, such as China, where the state punishes individualism and invades the most intimate personal space. We may all agree that life in these societies is less humane. But we would hesitate to

[34] Nussbaum, 'Human Capabilities, Female Human Beings'.
[35] Nussbaum, 'Human Functioning and Social Justice: In Defense of Aristotelian Essentialism', *Political Theory* (forthcoming).
[36] Nussbaum, 'Human Capabilities, Female Human Beings'.
[37] Nussbaum, 'Human Functioning and Social Justice'.

view them as non-human societies. In the same way, we would hesitate to view a blind person (lacking the capability to perceive by sight) as not human, as Crocker points out.[38] Nor would we regard the Chinese woman, who has been raised in a way as to lose her capability for critical thinking, as not human. As Crocker proposed, for a weaker and more plausible interpretation, we may read Nussbaum's 'threshold' not as necessary and sufficient conditions but a more or less minimum for what counts as human.[39]

Note that Nussbaum's rejection of trade-offs does not imply that Chinese women, in our concern here, should choose to cultivate excellences, say, in both caring for family and flourishing in professional careers. The 'capability approach' does not require the actual exercise by each citizens of all the capabilities. Rather, it emphasizes that a good life should have the possibility (opportunity) to exercise them. Chinese women may choose to flourish in housework or child-nursing, as some have expressed such a preference. Nussbaum's theory advocates the provision of conditions for them to achieve excellence elsewhere as well, for example, in politics and higher education, if they choose to do so.

A problem might appear to lie in the possible conflict between various goods on the list. These capabilities may not be able to function simultaneously. As we have discussed early, Chinese women share the trauma facing all mothers of our time if they decide to achieve both fulfilling work and loving child-care, two intrinsically valuable human functionings. In this situation, we seem to run into a dead-end if no ranking or trade-off is permissible. Nussbaum's reply to this challenge is to point to current and remediable institutional arrangements that have forced those women who pursue both goods into unnecessary tragic conflicts. She hopes that by acting to change the social world in which we live, we can have these goods all at once.[40] Justice for women is in this way closely tied to a just society. Even under just social institutions, however, Nussbaum concedes that, given the circumstances of life, we may have to live with a tragic value-conflict.[41]

Though treating all goods as essential, Nussbaum does attribute 'a special role' to two of the capabilities, *practical reason* and *affiliation*, considering them as 'architectonic, holding the whole enterprise together and making it human'.[42] Other things equal, these two distinguish human beings from other creatures. 'What is distinctive, and distinctively valuable to us, about the human way of doing all this is that each and every one of these functions is, first of all, planned and organized by practical reason

---

[38] David Crocker, 'Functioning and Capability: The Foundations of Sen's and Nussbaum's Development Ethics, Part 2: The Capability Ethic', paper presented at the WIDER conference, August 1991.
[39] Ibid.   [40] Nussbaum, 'Aristotelian Social Democracy', 212.
[41] Ibid.   [42] Nussbaum, 'Human Capabilities'.

and, second, done with and to others.'[43] Here, the development of the capability to evaluate, choose, plan, and execute plans of life or conception of the good, and the capability to live to and with others, are said to need 'special attention' because 'none of the others will be truly human without them'.[44]

It is important to point out that this recognition of 'practical reason' as an essential character of a good human life is the key to distinguishing Nussbaum's 'capability approach' from the 'local tradition' cultural relativism. Recall that this version of relativism emerges, partially, from a fear for the danger to impose ruling ideology upon the disadvantaged female in a society tormented by gender discrimination. As I have shown, the cultural relativism's rejection of any universal or cross-cultural conception, and its proposal to assess women's conditions by 'local traditional' norms, have not been able to avoid this danger in the case of China. Instead, such an approach has contributed to, as the Chinese case demonstrates, perpetuating the *status quo*.

The capability to conduct practical reasoning, which is restricted by the Chinese political ideology as well as the Confucian moral doctrines, would provide Chinese women with the power to reflect and criticize the pervasive social norms. Their having not been portrayed as capable of practical reasoning does not imply that they cannot achieve the capability for practical reasoning. What philosophers or ethicists conceive as social norms may not correspond to, nor reflect, what people really are or have in common, especially when philosophers themselves disagree on what the norms are. As Nussbaum observes, with regard to the dispute as to whether the capability of practical reasoning is essential, 'the very act of entering a disagreement seems to be an acknowledgement of the importance of the component',[45] as long as the disagreement is based on reasonable argumentation.

In any case, traditional philosophy and cultural norms may not be the only (nor indisputable) place to search for answers to the questions as to whether Chinese women are capable of practical reasoning or whether the capability to engage in independent reflection is foreign to them. The answer should, among other things, come from ongoing free and open debates, participated not just by men.

Studies show encouraging signs. Women activists in China are beginning to develop a critical attitude toward the dominant traditional notions of women's roles. Some have been able to rise above the illusion, rejecting the precommunist model on the basis that it cannot give a fair presentation of the aspirations of contemporary women.[46] One critic sees the traditional model as detrimental to women's independence: 'Woman is not the moon.

[43] Nussbaum, 'Human Capabilities'.   [44] Ibid.   [45] Ibid.
[46] Zhu Qing, 'Summary of the Second National Symposium on Women's Studies', *Trends in Academic Circle* (January 1987).

She must rely on herself to shine . . . Hopefully each person can find her own path in life and develop her own brilliance.'[47] Luo Ping, an associate professor at the Department of Philosophy, Wuhan University, criticizes the idea of sharing husbands' fame, viewing it as an example of the feudal saying 'If a husband makes a fortune, his wife is honored' ('fugui girong').[48]

Already in 1984, Wang Youqin, a vocal student then at Beijing University, boldly suggested that women have to take the first step toward their liberation. ' "Spiritual footbinding" has deformed our soul . . . It is not high mountains and wide rivers that hinder our footsteps, but rather our own spirit.'[49] She was one of the first to raise the issue of women's internalized sense of inferiority and refer to women as victims of their own preconception. It has been proposed that:

the official propaganda on equality should not promote the model of 'virtuous wife and good mother', who prioritize family duties, nor advocate female strongman who 'shoulder both burdens' [of family and career]. What should be promoted is equality in social values, family obligations, and rights, thus to wake up women's consciousness of their status as human beings.[50]

Some critics have also expressed doubts about the view that the participation of women in work is needed for a socialist modernization. In a report on the second National Symposium on Women's Studies, some speakers were quoted saying:

To acquire genuine equality, it is far from adequate for women merely to participate in social labor and strive for political and economic emancipation; they must fight for the awakening of their self-consciousness, a complete establishment of their values, and a thorough liberation of their personality.[51]

The increasing awareness demonstrates that the capability to engage in critical thinking is not alien to Chinese women and they are able to cultivate and exercise it. The commonly held picture of obedient Chinese women, as I have shown, is rather a reflection of the dominant male viewpoint, reinforced by the actual lack of freedom of choice (for male members too) under the communist rule.

While agreeing with Nussbaum that an evaluative list of what are 'deepest and most essential in human life need presuppose no external metaphysical foundation',[52] I find her description of the 'internalist account' sometimes puzzling. For example, she writes at one place that the list of properties of

---

[47] Ting Lan, 'Woman Is Not the Moon', *Women's World* (June 1985), I.

[48] See Luo Ping's presentation at the Symposium on Chinese Women's Social Participation and Development, March 1990, Zhengzhou, China.

[49] Wang Youqin, 'Let Us Have A New Concept of Womanhood', *Chinese Women* (March 1984), 1. Ms. Wang is now an editor for the *Woman—Human* journal and a visiting scholar at Stanford University.

[50] 'About the Issues of Women's Political Participation', From the Editor, *Chinese Women* (1991).

[51] *Trends in Academic Circles* (January 1978).　　[52] Nussbaum, 'Human Capabilities'.

human beings can be obtained by 'looking at ourselves, asking what we really think about ourselves and what holds our history'.[53] I suspect that, as the Chinese experience may have taught us, in this more or less closed society with a history of Confucian practices and authoritarian rule, a quite different list of human life essentials could have been sorted out by taking an 'internal' look at its history and at what it is all about being Chinese. The question is 'who is the "we"'. As my analysis shows, a deeply rooted traditional perspective is very persistent on projecting its demands on a list of life essentials if selected in this way.

However, Nussbaum clearly states elsewhere that a notion of what human beings are should be arrived at through a critical reflection of what we are and we aspire to be, taking into consideration of all available relevant information,[54] especially when she singles out 'practical reason' as a more fundamental property of a *good* human life. A notion of what human beings are and should be, in Nussbaum's words, relies on: 'the exchange of reasons and arguments by human beings within history, in which, for reasons that are historical and human . . . we hold some things to be good and others bad, some arguments to be sound and others not sound'.[55]

The 'capability approach', in any case, does not propose to muzzle or ignore local voices, such as the three voices about women's well-being in the case of China. Rather, it wishes to retain plurality through 'plural specification' and 'local specification' of the components of human life in specific and historically rich cultures. Nussbaum's 'vague and universal form' is meant to provide 'sufficient overlap to sustain a working conversation' between different plural specifications.[56] This approach, after all, would retain 'rich and full formation' of a conception of women's well-being, to be gathered from the voices, in our case, of Chinese women and those affected, who live their life in the Chinese cultural environment. It would criticize the Chinese tradition only when this tradition (as it does) prevents women from functioning in a fully human way.

Finally, how does the 'capability approach' deal with the legitimate fear by 'local tradition' relativists that a universal conception of the human would perpetuate the established practices and norms? To conclude, I will use Nussbaum's reply[57] to this question as a suggestive motion for the development of a conception of women's well-being. Her suggestions coincide with the conclusions that could be derived from my early analysis of the Chinese case.

Her first suggestion is to consider the experiences and sense of important functions from females as well as males. This will result in new perspectives on the conception of human (and women's) good that had not emerged as

---

[53] Nussbaum, 'Human Capabilities'.

[54] For a constructive discussion of a critically reflected conception of the good, see John Rawls, *A Theory of Justice* (1971), ch. 7, esp. s. 64, 416–24.

[55] Nussbaum, 'Human Capabilities'.   [56] Ibid.   [57] Ibid.

so important when only males were reflecting. This step will offset the institutionalized projection of male preferences in local culture. The goodness of excellence in professional careers, for example, which has been excluded from the list of Confucian female virtues (their 'obedience to father, brother, and husband', for instance), may become important now, and has indeed been so regarded as the recent female reflections have shown. Secondly, Nussbaum warns that, 'one must not assume that the statements of people who have long been subordinated are reliable indicators of what is truly essential'.[58] The result of long-term subordination is evident in the case of China. What we need to do to avoid misleading by unreflective and uncritical self-expressions, Nussbaum suggests, is to provide education, raising consciousness, making sure that women have 'adequate information' about alternative ways of life, and 'real freedom to form a conception of the good without fear'.[59] To cultivate the critical reflective capability and to gain, above all, the freedom to do so, are two tasks that Chinese women have to strive to achieve. And they are beginning to recognize the importance of these tasks, as I remarked early. Thirdly, concurring with the implication of my discussion about the unreflective Chinese local traditional voices, Nussbaum advises that we must 'be skeptical of the accounts we find in local traditions'. The study on the case in China substantiates her concern that the traditional accounts often tell us characteristics of the lives of women that derive from male desires to have power over them, for example. Women are said to be less reasonable or less rational and can only take the submissive and obedient roles.

Taking caution in these areas, the 'capability approach' aspires to deal with problems raised by 'local tradition' relativism, advancing a conception of women's well-being that attends fully to the rich culture and tradition of local communities, while opening up for cross-cultural scrutiny. Such a scrutiny gives it a universal perspective and embodies the hope to divulge 'false consciousness'.

[58] Ibid.   [59] Ibid.

Inequality in Capabilities Between Men and Women in Mexico

Margarita M. Valdés

I have been asked to make some comments about the way the topics in the papers read at this conference connect with the problems faced by women in Mexico. First, I would like to say why the capabilities approach of which a lot has been heard in this conference seems to me especially adequate for assessment of the situation of women in the Third World with respect to justice, and a good basis for eventually proposing policies and strategies that could help to improve that situation. Secondly, I will refer to some peculiarities of Mexican society which make the situation of poor women in Mexico somewhat different from that of Indian women as described by Marty Chen in her paper. And finally I will refer to the problem of 'substitutionalism' and the dangers of 'cultural imperialism' and will try to say something concerning the way some feminist discussions in the First World are seen by women of the Third World.

Sen's proposal to take capabilities as that on which one should base judgements of equality or inequality, and hence of justice, seems to me extremely acute. Focusing on capabilities, more than on anything else, allows us to grasp the peculiarity of that which makes variable the quality of a human life, and reveals the true nature of some of the difficulties faced by women's development in the Third World. In my view, Sen is right to emphasize that it cannot be that all there is to justice is the maximization of utilities, nor just giving, or trying to give, people access to the same ammount of 'primary goods', 'resources', 'rights' or whatever. If people are not given positive freedom to function and thus to make an adequate use in and for their lives of all those 'goods', the mere fact of having them will not necessarily make their lives better. As Sen points out in his paper, primary goods are just '*means* to the freedom to achieve'.[1] Therefore, one of the primary concerns for the practice of justice should be that of examining how capabilities are distributed, and how they can be increased among people, and not just the question of how much of this or that people are to be given. Of course, what people are given could increase their capabilities, but the value and importance of that would be, so to say, derivative from that of the corresponding capabilities it allows them to develop.

I would like to thank Mark Platts for carefully reading my text and suggesting many ways of improving it, both stylistically and conceptually.

[1] See Amartya Sen, 'Gender Inequality and Theories of Justice', in this volume.

Now, when we look at the situation of women in Latin America,[2] we don't find that their rights are legally restricted, nor that they are legally forbidden to participate in general in the different spheres of public life, nor that they are legally prevented access to different 'resources'. However, it must be clear to anyone who examines their condition impartially that they suffer from inequality and injustice; and this is so because they lack precisely what Sen so appropriately calls 'capabilities', that is to say, the positive freedom to function in different spheres of their lives—and this to a much greater extent than the poor male population. Statistics on education and employment in Mexico reflect in a perspicuous way this lack. If we examine them, we find that although women are as numerous as men in Mexico and have the same legal rights to participate actively in education and paid employment, their actual participation in these fields is notably limited. Only 29% of the economically active population in Mexico are women[3] (but notice that only 23% of these earn a wage, the other 6% either are working in 'home-based industries' where they do not receive pay or in the informal sector where they do not have a fixed salary). As regards education, 15% of the female population is illiterate, and only 38% of those students who finish High School are female.[4] In the big cities, more than 10% of women have never attended school and only 57% have finished primary school.[5] If we consider women's levels of participation in education and employment in rural areas, they are still more discouraging.

What all this means is that although the 'primary goods' or 'resources' of education and employment are in principle open to women, the majority of them do not participate in those spheres and therefore cannot attain all those functionings that could only come about through education and employment. Again, as regards women's situation with respect to employment, statistics reveal that only 25% (approximately) of women older than 15 have paid employment,[6] that they are paid considerably less than men

---

[2] I will focus specially on the situation of women in Mexico, but I think that it can be taken as representative of the situation of other women in Latin America.

[3] See *Evaluación del Decenio de la Mujer, 1975–1985* (Mexico: Consejo Nacional de Población, 1985), 35. [4] Ibid.: 57–8.

[5] See C. Welty, 'Participación Económica Femenina y Fecundidad en el Área Metropolitana de la Ciudad de México', in Cooper, Barbieri, *et al.* (eds.), *Fuerza de Trabajo Femenina Urbana en México*, vol. 1 (Mexico: UNAM, 1989), 193.

[6] Numbers published by the Mexican Population Agency don't seem to be very reliable on this matter. So, for example, in *Resultados Principales de la Encuesta Nacional Demográfica de 1982* (Mexico: Consejo Nacional de Población (no date)), 56–8, it is held that only 15% of women older than 15 have a paid job in the country, 25% in small cities and 30% in the big cities. By contrast, in *Evaluación del Decenio de la Mujer, 1975–1985* (Mexico: Consejo Nacional de Población, 1985), 35–6, it is held that 37 out of every 100 women older than 15 were working for pay or 'had the possibility of working' in 1985. Again, in *Informe de la Delegación Mexicana Sobre la Conferencia Mundial Para el Examen y Evaluación de los Logros del Decenio de las Naciones Unidas para la Mujer: Igualdad, Desarrollo y Paz* (Mexico: Consejo Nacional de Población, 1985), 12, it is held that only 20% of the economically active population are women; compare this with what is said on the same topic in the preceding paragraph in the text.

for doing the same job, and that there is a marked division of labour according to sex.[7] Besides, given the social arrangements that women themselves seem to accept, when they work outside their homes they depend on the father's (or other male's) permission to do so, they have to give a good part or all of what they earn for family subsistence, and, except for some privileged cases,[8] they have to accept responsibility for all of the unpaid work in the household. Of course, the entire responsibility for young children falls on the mother even where she has an outside job. And as if this were not enough, in the great majority of cases, women have to fight against the system of 'social meanings and values' of the community—as described by Seyla Benhabib[9] in her paper—if they want to assume full responsibility in their jobs (women's jobs are socially considered a kind of 'second best' in relation to all kinds of 'family obligation'). What this clearly shows—without even considering the generalized feminization of poverty, to use Susan Moller Okin's expression, or the subjection of women to men in many other areas—is a dramatic inequality between men and women in Mexico.

Now, as I said before, if we analyse the situation of Mexican women using the capabilities approach proposed by Amartya Sen, the injustice to women becomes evident: women are not functioning in many character-istically human ways because of local patriarchal social structures and because of the ancestral history of subjection: these have denied them the possibility of functioning in many different areas and have therefore kept their capabilities at a very low level. The activities of the great majority of women, as in most traditional cultures, are restricted (due to a great variety of social pressures) to the domestic area, so that even if they were given a greater amount of 'pleasure', 'primary goods', 'rights' or whatever, they would still lack the positive freedom to function in many human spheres. As Amartya Sen remarks, the fact that traditional women in the Third World seem to accept the unjust social arrangement in which they live, makes any solution that might otherwise be proposed more complex. That is to say, any policy designed to improve the situation of women should take as central the fact that among the things needed by women in order to be able to function in many human ways is a change in the way they are socially perceived, both by themselves and by others.

Now, in order to complete this explanation of injustice to women in the Third World, we need an argument to show that there is no reasonable basis for denying women the positive freedom to function that men have,

[7] See María de la Luz Macías, 'División del Trabajo por Sexos y Salarios en la Industria de la Transformación en el Distrito Federal, Guadalajara y Monterrey', in Cooper, Barbieri, *et al.*, *Fuerza de Trabajo Femenina*, vol. 2.

[8] In these cases it is always another *female* member of the family or another *woman* employed as a domestic worker who does the household chores.

[9] See Seyla Benhabib, 'Cultural Complexity, Moral Interdependence and the Global Dialogical Community', in this volume.

that is to say, that no 'principle of difference' could reasonably be invoked to justify the inequality in capabilities between men and women. In this connection I see a very valuable point in Nussbaum's paper when she defends a variety of Aristotelian Essentialism for the case of human beings.[10] Her subtle and intelligent exploration of the most important aspects of the human form of life, and her consequent introduction of concrete basic functionings and capabilities for all human beings, constitute a very strong argument in favour of gender equality. Moreover, on the one hand, her 'thick vague theory of the good' has the advantage of being 'contextually sensitive' (that is, of allowing for multiple specifications depending upon the varied local conceptions), while on the other side, her argument in favour of essentialism blocks all forms of relativism that could be invoked to try to justify substantial differences in functionings and capabilities from one human being to another or from one culture to another. I therefore see Nussbaum's contribution as not only an excellent companion to Sen's proposal, but also as a necessary supplement to it.

I would like now to make some comparisons between the situation of Mexican poor women and that of poor women in India and Bangladesh as described in Martha Chen's paper.[11] From the merely legal point of view both groups of women are guaranteed the same employment opportunities as men, as well as equal pay for equal work. However, this *de jure* situation is far from being reflected in the situation *de facto*. Poor women in Mexico and in India do not have the same options as men as regards getting a paid job outside the household, and when they do get it they are paid less than men. Moreover, in both regions there is an accepted division between the private and the public spheres, an ancestral custom of dividing work according to gender, and a traditionally patriarchal family organization. However, the lack of a caste system in Mexico and the fact that there is not such a close connection between the wealth and status of households and the kind of work women are allowed to do, make things perhaps less dramatic for women in Mexico than in India. Another difference I perceive, to the advantage of Mexican women, is the 'extended' conception of the Mexican family which offers better protection for widows and single mothers and makes it easier for women who have young children to get gainful employment outside their homes; while at work in the big cities more than half of the women can leave their children with close relatives who look after them without expecting any payment.[12]

As in India, during the last two decades there has been a steadily increasing participation of poor (Mexican) women in gainful employment;[13] the

[10] See Martha C. Nussbaum, 'Human Capabilities, Female Human Beings', in this volume.
[11] See Martha Chen, 'A Matter of Survival: Women's Right to Employment in India and Bangladesh', in this volume.
[12] See Carlos Welty, 'Participación Económica Femenina', 204.
[13] See Orlandina Oliveira, 'Empleo Femenino en México en Tiempos de Recesión Económica', in Cooper, Barbieri, *et al.*, *Fuerza de Trabajo Femenina*, vol. 1, 29–66.

reasons for this are in part similar to and in part different from those which explain the phenomenon in India. First, the economic recession in the eighties in Mexico had as a consequence a general drop in salary levels, thus obliging women to join the workforce (in formal or in informal employment) in order to contribute to the family budget. Secondly, given the notable decrease of salaries in the primary sector, men tried to find better opportunities in other sectors and women came to take over some of the jobs traditionally considered as 'men jobs'. This, I am sure, is helping to abolish the traditional division of work according to gender. Finally, many foreign firms looking for a cheap labour force have invested in in-bond plants (called 'maquilas') generally located near the border with the USA and in these plants they have preferred to hire a great majority of women, both because of their greater manual ability and because of their stronger commitment to their work. So a variety of economic factors during the last twenty years have impelled Mexican women to seek work outside their homes; as in the case of Indian women, their only motivation for taking a paid job (in the great majority of cases) has been extreme neediness. But even if that is so, I see very positive features of this phenomenon. On the one hand, as Susan Moller Okin has maintained in this conference,[14] employment makes women less dependent on men, gives them a chance to improve their status within the family, and so enables them to establish a better bargaining position in their relations with men. On the other hand, the mere fact of having a job outside the home breaks the social isolation of women who have traditionally been secluded in the domestic sphere: this creates a manifold of prospects for them to function in different social spheres and to react against their subordinated situation. It should be no surprise that in the big Mexican cities many poor women workers have started participating actively not only in workers' unions, but also in social and political urban movements; for given their need for adequate urban services if they are to have outside jobs, and given their direct experience of the many deficiencies in those services in the poorer sectors of the cities, they have organized themselves and other women so as to demand urban reforms that might start to change the face of the poor sectors where they live.[15] It should also be noted that, even if on rather a small scale, the participation of women in paid employment is starting to change the cultural patriarchal patterns that have been responsible for inequalities in capabilities between men and women in Mexico and hence for the division of work according to gender, with all its consequences.[16]

[14] See Susan Moller Okin, 'Inequalities Between the Sexes in Different Cultural Contexts', in this volume.

[15] See Alejandra Massolo, 'Participación de la Mujer en la Tercera Jornada', in Cooper, Barbieri, et al., Fuerza de Trabajo Femenina, vol. 2.

[16] See, in this connection, José Manuel Valenzuela-Arce, 'La mujer Obrera: Reproducción y Cambio de Pautas Culturales', in Cooper, Barbieri, et al., Fuerza de Trabajo Femenina, vol. 2.

I would like to finish these comments by touching upon a problem which is mentioned both in Ruth Anna Putnam's and in Jonathan Glover's papers for this conference. Putnam's paper discusses the problem of 'substitutionalism' and that of Glover's mentions the danger of new forms of 'cultural imperialism'. The problem at bottom seems to me to be the same: they worry about the right that feminist thinkers in the First World have to diagnose what is going wrong for women belonging to different cultural traditions in the Third World. Given that the problems of women in the First World are not the same as those of Third World women, perhaps their respective situations are not comparable or 'commensurable'. In this connection, I would like to mention two things. First, there is my favourable surprise at seeing that many of the papers read at this conference (written by 'feminist thinkers of the First World') showed so much sensibility for the particular problems faced by the poor female population in the Third World. Secondly, if we accept something like 'the thick vague conception' of human good proposed by Martha Nussbaum, as Glover remarks, we can have good grounds for supposing that, notwithstanding the cultural peculiarities which arise from different ways of realizing the goodness of human life within distinct cultures or traditions, there is enough in common to all of us to 'sustain a general conversation', in Nussbaum's words, and thus to enable us to perceive the phenomenon of injustice to women either in our own or in other cultures.

Concerning 'substitutionalism' it seems to me that there is no such problem if the criticisms from one culture to another focus on the general human needs and capabilities; a problem could arise in cases in which, under the false presumption that some ways of realizing specific human functionings are 'better' than others, one human group tries to impose its own ways on others. That would, of course, be an act of 'cultural imperialism'. What feminist thinkers need is a great deal of imagination and sensibility so as to be able to recognize ways of realizing some given human functioning in other cultures which are different from the forms that functioning takes in their own culture. I am sure that this is not an easy matter, but it is not an impossible thing to do. We can all recognize a difference between, on the one hand, criticizing the fact that many Indian or Mexican women do not dress as First World women do and, on the other, criticizing the fact that they have less to eat than men do, or have less access than men to medical care, or are not given the same educational opportunities as men, or don't have the same employment options as men, or are not allowed the same sexual freedom as men. Of course, there are more subtle and difficult cases than those just mentioned; but they should be considered and discussed one by one—and in each case one should keep in mind that the ways people achieve some functioning can vary from culture to culture. One should not judge before trying to understand.

I have tried to show the ways in which many of the questions discussed at this conference relate to problems faced by women in Mexico. Of course, some of the topics discussed by feminist thinkers in the First World would be considered as far-fetched or even pointless by poor women in the Third World. The reason for this is not that those topics are not important in themselves; the reason, I believe, is that poor women in the Third World are under pressure to respond to more immediate and urgent matters. In even the smallest details of their everyday life they have to face explicit and manifold manifestations of injustice to them, and so are not 'capable' of seeing the deep roots of that injustice. After all, one needs to be free of those pressures if one is to have the capability of thinking clearly in this area. The time will come, let us hope, when women of the Third World will be capable, in Sen's sense, of seeing the importance of these topics.

Femininity, Equality, and Personhood

Roop Rekha Verma

Equality has been at the centre of an animated debate in feminist movements. On the question of equality the feminist movements have been divided and in the course of answering it they have developed and matured. The basic dilemma which the demand for equality between man and woman faces is that woman seems to stand as a loser in either case: with or without equality. On the one hand, it has long been obvious that woman, as a class, has remained in a state of subjugation and inferiority that cannot be allowed to continue. On the other hand it seems that with each step towards equality woman has to lose something that is distinctively hers and is as much cherished as equality itself. So, it seems that woman either has to pay too heavy a cost, the cost of diminishing her womanhood itself for equality, or has to reconcile herself to her extremely constricted existence. And the dilemma is no ordinary one. It is a paradox too. Because the search for equality is aimed at restoring to woman her possibilities and her dignity, in fact the whole world which always was as much hers as man's but remained eclipsed from her. But if this search destroys her womanhood itself then it certainly is self-defeating.

The most well-known solution to this paradox is to delete equality from the feminist agenda altogether and to argue for the recognition of the 'feminine qualities' in their own right. To examine whether this is the only way out of this paradox, it is necessary to have a closer look at the notions of femininity and equality, and to ask if there is something paradoxical in either of the two notions. The present paper takes up this task. First the conception of femininity found in the dominant Indian tradition will be described. Then, along with a brief criticism of this conception, an analysis of the notion of personhood will be taken up, to show that the traditional perspective on woman deprives her not only of many valuable roles and experiences, but of personhood too. A major contention of the paper in this context is that this perspective reduces *man's* personhood as well. It will, therefore, be argued that the 'feminist' struggle should actually be viewed as a struggle for humanity as a whole. Next, the conception of equality will be taken up in order to determine in what sense, if at all, equality between man and woman is desirable. The paper presents an androgynous concept of personhood and favours retaining equality on the feminist agenda.

1 FEMININITY

The conception of femininity and the accompanying images of womanhood found in the traditional Indian philosophies and mythologies do not form a consistent and uni-dimensional picture, and the metaphysics of these systems do not always reflect the social philosophies which were attached to them or developed in their lineage. The metaphysical categories of some Indian philosophical systems seem gender-neutral; for example, Nyāya, Vaiśeṣika, Chārvāka, Jaina, and Bauddha. The Vedāntine Brahman (Absolute) should allow no real distinctions of gender, as it allows no distinctions at all. However, there is some scope for drawing an analogy between the principle of Māyā at the cosmic level and the conception of femininity at the mundane level, as both Māyā and woman are seen as a source of ignorance and bondage. Similar connections may be worked out between the role of Prakṛti in the metaphysical dualism of Puruṣa and Prakṛti of Sāmkhya philosophy and the status of woman as conceived in the social philosophy of the later day. In Sāmkhya philosophy Prakṛti is the cause of the bondage of Puruṣa and in the social philosophy of Dharmashāstras woman's nature is to corrupt man. Both the words 'Māyā' and 'Prakṛti' are in feminine gender whereas the words 'Brahman' and 'Puruṣa' are in masculine gender. The word 'Puruṣa' ordinarily means man as distinguished from woman. But in Sāmkhya philosophy it means 'Soul' or Atman.

Although such connections as these can be worked out between various metaphysical systems and social philosophies on the gender question, there is in fact no necessary relationship between the two, and to some, the connections and the accompanying comparisons may seem highly crude. For example, in Sāmkhya philosophy, where the comparison of its metaphysical categories of Puruṣa and Prakṛti with male and female principles is most attractive, there are difficulties in treating Puruṣa simply as the male principle, because Puruṣa, which is Atman or Soul, is 'attached' to both man and woman as entities of empirical reality. So it would be more accurate to treat 'Puruṣa' as a gender-transcending category rather than as a masculine category. However, the analogies utilized to explain the relationship between Puruṣa and Prakṛti do echo the social philosophy that accords the woman the status of unavoidable evil. Similarly, Brahman encompasses everything and all the distinctions are submerged in it. Therefore it also should be conceived as a gender-transcending category.

In ancient Hindu mythology the symbolism and iconography relating to the theme of the feminine range over a wide variety of moods, powers, and roles. This mythology presents not only Sītā who is an epitome of unquestioning surrender and sacrifice, but also Saraswatī (Goddess of learning), Durgā (Goddess of protection and power), Kalī (Goddess of power), and Lakshmī (Goddess of wealth). In fact, hardly any aspect of life has escaped iconolatry in female forms. The traditional iconography of these goddesses is in harmony with the concepts they embody. Whereas the image of Saraswatī arouses feelings of peace and fulfilment, those of Durgā and Kalī arouse awe and fear. Yet we find that this variety in the mythological imagery is missing in the actual theories of femininity which display the stereotyped view of woman as essentially weak and vulnerable beings. There seems to be a separation between the metaphysical/mythological frameworks on the one hand and the social/theoretical frameworks on the other, as if they deal with entirely different worlds, having no connection, or at most having a very loose one only, with each other. The consequence is that despite very lofty conceptions of womanhood in some metaphysical frameworks and mythological constructions, when it comes to view the woman as a reality on the ordinary plane of life, the perspective becomes narrow and partial. And it has remained so even latterly, where new cultures and mythologies are fused with the ancient ones.

This narrow conception of femininity is well-known throughout the world. Its stereotype is remarkable, cutting across cultural and temporal differences. Whether it be ancient Indian texts like Rāmāyana, Mahābhārata, and Dharmashāstras or western philosophers like Aristotle, Hegel, Kant, Locke, Nietzsche, and Rousseau, they all have more or less the same conception of womanhood. They all view the 'essences' of manhood and womanhood as sharply contrasting with each other and allot entirely different roles to men and women, generally placing woman in powerless and inferior rank in the socio-political context. This conception is very familiar and needs no elaboration. One classical example of this view in Indian thought is Manusmṛti (a Dharmashāstra or law code). The views of Manusmṛti have found frequent mention by both the protagonists and the antagonists of the aforementioned conception in the oriental debates. However, Manusmṛti is not alone in advocating this notion of femininity. Many Samhitās included in the Dharmashāstras (e.g., Yāgyavalkya Samhitā, Vyās Samhitā, Vishṇu Samhitā, and Gautam Samhitā) and the epics like Rāmāyana and Mahābhārata, which have a very strong grip over the Indian masses, directly or indirectly reflect a similar view. It may be noted that 'Indian culture' should not be equated simply with 'Vedic culture' or 'Hindu culture', since it is highly plural and complex. Yet it is true that as far as the conception of femininity is concerned, it remains almost constant in the midst of this plurality. The reason is twofold. First, the culture that arose from the later Vedic literature (that is, Dharmashāstras, epics, Purāṇas, etc., which developed in the lineage of Vedic literature) has influenced the other cultures in India; and secondly, as was pointed out earlier, different cultures have themselves not much differed in their perspectives on woman. There are differences of degree and detail, but by and large the approach is the same.

To bring to the fore the degree to which the social philosophy of the most dominant cultural stream of India has gone in extending the aforementioned notion of femininity, a brief summary is presented below.

1.1. Woman as a Necessarily Weak and Dependent Being

Manusmṛti[1] and the other Dharmashāstras[2] contain several pronouncements in this regard. Woman is not allowed to do anything independently ever, not even in her own house (*Manu*, ch. 5, sl. 147, 148; ch. 9, sl. 2). She is always to be protected and subjugated (*Yāgyavalkya Samhitā*, sl. 85; *Vishṇu Samhitā*, ch. XXV). She is declared unfit for independence ever (*Manu*, ch. 9, sl. 3).

1.2. Woman Must Always Obey and be Governed

Dharmashāstras give long lists of the duties of the wives, and these mostly consist of following various types of commands and performing all the household chores (*Vishṇu S.*, ch. XXV; *Vyās S.*, sl. 19–35). *Vyās Samhitā* asks woman to be 'obedient to the dictates of her lord and to follow him like his own shadow, seek his good like a trusted friend and minister to his desires like a servant' (sl. 26–7). Many other texts say similar things. However, even blind obedience does not give her any rights or security. There are provisions for abandoning even a faithful wife (*Yāgyavalkya S.*, ch. I, sl. 76).

1.3. Woman as Only an Auxiliary to Man

All the aforementioned pronouncements point to the instrumental existence of woman. Most of her duties are towards her husband who is frequently mentioned as her lord or master. She has nothing as her own, not even her faith. She is supposed to have no independent faith or religious rites. Even her instrumentality is restricted to domesticity and sexuality. It does not extend to the emotional and intellectual plane (*Manu*, ch. 9; *Vyās S.*, sl. 19–35, *Yāgyavalkya S.*, ch. I). According to Manu, several dispositions with which a woman is endowed by God since birth include indulgence in bed and jewellery (ch. 9, sl. 17). *Vyās Samhitā* says that a woman has no separate existence from her 'lord' in matters of piety, gain, and even desires; 'the scriptures have enjoined this dependency of love' (sl. 19, 20). But no 'dependency of love' is enjoined upon men. There are innumerable

---

[1] *Manusmṛti* with the Sanskrit Commentary *Manvartha-Muktāvali* of Kullūka Bhaṭṭa; ed. J. L. Shastri (Motilal Banarasidass, 1983). All references from Manusmṛti are from this edition. It will henceforth be mentioned as 'Manu'. The translations are from the vol. 25 of *Sacred Books of the East*, ed. F. Max Müller (Motilal Banarasidass, 1985).

[2] *The Dharmashāstra*, Trans. M. N. Dutt (Cosmo, 1978). All references to Samhitās are from this text. It will henceforth be mentioned as 'Dharma'.

injunctions prohibiting women from dressing nicely, visiting people, seeing social festivities, thinking of other men, and even laughing in the absence of their men. The restrictions after a husband's death are even more severe, ranging from not mentioning any other man's name to emaciating her body (*Manu*, ch. 5, sl. 157) and even self-immolation (*Vyāsa S.*, sl. 50–1 for a Brahmin's wife only), although a man is allowed to tie the nuptial knot again after having performed the rites of his wife's death (*Manu*, ch. 5, sl. 168). Man is granted the right of punishing and 'abandoning in distant places' his wife if she has vices, where non-conformity to the husband's wishes is also counted as a vice (*Vyās S.*, sl. 49, 52–3), but the woman is asked to accept and even worship her husband even if he is guilty of 'great sin' (mahāpātakam) and is virtueless, disloyal, and wicked (*Manu*, ch. 5, sl. 154; *Vyās S.*, sl. 48).

1.4. Woman Mainly as a Means to Beget Sons

Some Dharmashāstras seem to be obsessed with the fact of woman's motherhood and regard it as immoral to waste any possibility of her conception. Thus, a father's (or brother's) failure to 'give away' his daughter (or sister) in marriage before her menstruation is equated with the 'sin' of killing the foetus (*Vyās S.*, sl. 7; *Yāgyavalkya S.*, ch. I, sl. 64), and a husband commits the same sin if he does not visit his wife in season (*Vyās S.*, sl. 46). It is enjoined that if a girl does not have anyone to 'give her away' in marriage then she should give herself away. Here the duty to get married before menstruation overrides the duty not to do anything independently. Similarly, the preference for male children is so very high that some Dharmashāstras even recommend breach of chastity in the circumstance of the husband's death (*Gautam S.*; *Yāgyavalkya S.*, ch. I, sl. 68–9). One of the many justifications for abandoning one's wife is her failure to give birth to a male child (*Yāgyavalkya S.*, ch. I, sl. 73) because it is the sons and the grandsons through whom the family is supposed to survive (*Yāgyavalkya S.*, ch. I, sl. 78).

1.5. Woman as Basically Mean and Immoral

In some parts of the Dharmashāstras and the epics, woman is conceived as essentially intemperate and immoral. There are details of her moral weaknesses which include her passion for man, her fickle-mindedness, and her natural tendency to be disloyal. These are the traits which 'God has put in the woman at the time of creation'. That is why men are advised on the one hand to guard themselves against women's charms and, on the other, to keep strict vigil on their women 'day and night', to satisfy them with tact and gifts, and to keep them busy with domestic chores (*Manu*, ch. 9, sl. 14–17).

1.6. Woman as Goddess and as an Essential Partner of Life:
Feminine Virtues Self-negating

Although by and large tradition views the woman highly negatively, it has some liberal tendencies too. In fact sometimes the woman has even been given the status of Goddess, to be respected and worshiped. Thus, as mentioned in the beginning, many cosmic powers are conceived in a feminine image and these images are worshipped. The tradition also demands the company of the wife in almost every auspicious ceremony. The place of the mother is very high. The mother and the land of one's birth are said to be superior to even heaven. Even *Manusmṛti* has that famous and oft-quoted verse that Gods reside where woman is worshipped (ch. 3, sl. 56). And the *Vyās Samhitā* says that an unmarried man is 'only half and as a half can not beget a whole' (sl. 14) and that 'a wife is weightier than the world with its virtues and wealth because with the help of no auxiliary other than a wife can he bear its burden' (sl. 15). The *Yāgyavalkya Samhitā* asks the husbands, brothers, fathers, and kinsmen to 'adore woman with ornaments, clothes and food' (ch. I, sl. 82). *Manusmṛti* also emphasizes the importance of keeping women happy with ornaments, food, etc. (ch. 3). This apparently elevated status of women is linked with the feminine virtues which, like most other cultures, are mainly self-negating: self-sacrifice, tolerance, and submission. Some self-expanding qualities are also regarded feminine, e.g., love, care, and tenderness.

This last feature exposes the inner contradiction as well as the separation between the sacred and the profane in the Indian traditional notion of femininity. As noted earlier, the splendour of feminine imagery in the religious symbolism completely vanishes at the secular level, and despite the imagery of the all powerful Kālī, Durgā, and Saraswatī, the actual law codes of the tradition present a woman as essentially weak and incapable of higher learning and responsibilities. Moreover, sometimes we find both the low and the lofty conceptions of woman simultaneously. For example, in the texts we find both pictures of woman: as essentially a self-seeker and as the epitome of love and sacrifice. However, with respect to some texts there are grounds for suspicions that (1) the injunctions to keep woman happy are really not as charitable as they seem to be without attending to the context and (2) in the injunctions to worship woman, 'worshipping' perhaps does not mean treating them with unconditional respect and as intrinsically valuable. The verses preceding and succeeding the above-quoted verse (sloka) of Manu ('Gods reside where woman is worshipped') emphasize the desirability of keeping the women-folk happy, and after these verses is the one which says that if women were not happy, they would not look attractive to their husbands and therefore would not produce children (ch. 3, sl. 61). Thus 'worshipping' here seems to mean only keeping them satisfied with respect to their basic needs, and this is a means to the ulterior aim of begetting children. Further, a woman's happiness is visualized very pettily, as confined to food, clothes, and ornaments. The vast world of knowledge, art, skills, social interaction, fun, and responsibilities is kept hidden from her.

Now, it has often been pointed out how extolling the self-negating 'virtues', and attaching them exclusively to femininity, causes women to take pride in their subjugation and to resist a change for the better. The paradox mentioned in the beginning of this paper is to a large extent due to the halo created around womanhood by the mystification of this concept. In fact mystification of any category creates such paradoxes: and it has been the most subtle and hence the most powerful instrument of preventing change towards an egalitarian society. Generation after generation, women have been moulded by the ethics of self-negation and trained to take pride in being the exclusive, or at least the best, custodians of this norm. They are thus led to think of themselves as placed on a very high pedestal from which they can hardly dare to step down, partly because of the fear of a new identity but mostly because of the fear of *stepping down* itself. Because it would, after all, mean leaving the pedestal. This has been the case in every culture but in the dominant culture of India, leaving the pedestal has been even more difficult since the pedestal has been the highest possible, that of a goddess.

Since Wollstonecraft and J. S. Mill, it has been shown that there is no ground for maintaining the correctness of the above-noted concept of femininity. An appeal to nature would not help, since as we succeed in gauging the 'nature' of women after neutralizing the effect of cultural conditioning of the tradition, we find an entirely different form of femininity emerging before us. This form is much more varied than the traditional one—much more human and much more capable of social participation and responsibility. Whatever naturalness the old notion of femininity seems to have, is due to long cultural conditioning.

However, what has not so often been noticed, or at least not underlined, is that the traditional philosophy of woman deprives her not only of many significant roles and experiences but of full personhood as well. And what is least realized is that it deprives man of the same thing too. In the division of 'essences' and roles which this philosophy propagates, both man and woman are the losers, although the levels of their losses are different. What is meant by saying that one does not have full personhood? What is personhood? The category of 'person' is generally contrasted with the category of 'thing'. But in the present context it is to be distinguished as well from living beings such as vegetation and animals. To me three things seem essential for an entity to be categorized as a person: autonomy, self-respect, and sense of fulfilment and achievement. The autonomy of a person involves freedom of choice and non-instrumentality of his[3] existence. An autonomous person has a purposive life, but the purposes of his life are shaped by his own experiences, interests, and capacities. They will not be predetermined for him either by any cosmic agency or by any other institution. Thus, the autonomy of a person entails his intrinsic worth. It is essential to point out that the autonomy of the person need not be conceived on the pattern of atomistic individualism. It would indeed involve a sort of individualism, because the grounds of a person's preferences are to be found in his own experiences and priorities. But it is recognised that his experiences do not exist in complete isolation from others and do not arise out of a vacuum. His connectedness with others and with his environment also is part of his being and shapes his perceptions and perspectives. If an individual's life conditions are such that his connectedness with others has not been accommodated in his perceptions and purposes, and the institutions of society impose their own purposes on him, his autonomy, to that extent, would be compromised. In such a case the question would arise as to whether, in the larger interest, this individual's autonomy and therefore personhood is worth leaving intact. Certainly the intrinsic worth of a person covers his relationship with the world around him and therefore his moral ideal has to integrate this 'otherness' in it. There would be alienation to the extent to which the world, the relationships which an individual lives, and the purposes he seeks are not seen by him as *his*. An individual's autonomy presupposes not his nomad-like existence but interactive harmony with the 'other' around him.

Self-respect, the second requirement of personhood, involves a sense of dignity, consciousness of autonomy, and worth. It also involves consciousness of one's capacities and rights and, more importantly, commitment to one's responsibilities. Self-respect has to be distinguished from self-aggrandizement. A self-respecting person has a sober assessment of his place in the wider context of the life and the world. Self-respect is the realization of a fine balance between one's worth on the one hand and smallness on the other. The third requirement, sense of fulfilment and achievement, is possible only for an autonomous being. It is proportionate to the awareness of one's capabilities and their realization. All these features of personhood are amenable to degrees and hence personhood itself is a matter of degree.

It is clear that in the traditional Indian view a woman is hardly a person. She has no autonomy. The conditions of her life from beginning to end leave no possibility of developing self-respect. And there is no question of a sense of achievement because she is never in a position to set her own goals or to know herself. That this view affects man's personhood also, is not as easily appreciated. In fact, the division of male and female traits and virtues affects man's autonomy too. The division artificially imposes a

[3] For the sake of simplicity expressions like 'he/she', 'his/her' are not used.

predetermined form on manhood and restricts man's creativity and sensibility to certain preconceived categories only. He has to suppress and keep under-developed his tenderness and emotions and is trained to see himself as tough and non-caring. His cultural training forces him to feel ashamed of his emotionality and feel demasculinized by his desire to tend, care, and give in. His roles in his relationships with women conceived in such a way determine that, instead of self-respect, he develops self-aggrandizement.

Thus both man and woman are dehumanized in the traditional conception and their relationships are made immoral. They live in intimacy without genuine love and care. Their best relationships are made purely utilitarian; woman lives in them for security and man for selfish needs. The relationships are not viewed as intrinsically valuable, whereas it is these relationships which, if not so viewed, nurture the best sentiments of human beings and enhance their autonomy and worth. The foundation of man–woman relationships, like some other relationships, is mutuality of love, respect, and understanding. This requires recognition of equality between the two, rather than dominance. If this condition of equality is not fulfilled, the relationships are bound to degenerate, and this brings degeneration to those who live in these relationships. This is what the traditional conception has done. Thus, the feminist demand for equality is in fact the demand for a correction in the whole outlook towards both man and woman. It is the demand for restoring personhood, not only to woman but also to man. In this sense the feminist struggle must be viewed as the struggle for the liberation of humanity on the whole.

But that women need 'equality' with men is itself being disputed among the feminists. It is maintained that man and woman are different. Their ethics are different, their epistemologies are different, and their dispositions and needs are different too. The allegation is that in aiming at equality the preference remains for masculinity, since the norms we set before us are masculine norms. Thus, in this struggle for 'equality' we are repeating the old mistake of valuing masculine dispositions as superior to the feminine dispositions and 'rushing to be born again in the masculine norm'. Surely, if this is so, the feminist movement would be both self-defeating and impossible. It is undeniable that woman is different from man, and that she can not be, and should not be, converted to manhood. But the important question is: in what respect is woman different from man? Is she different from man in her intellectual/emotional make-up or in her moral capacities and perspective? Or, is the difference mainly biological and physical? To me the latter seems to be the case and the point of saying this is only factual not evaluative. That is, the point of the equality thesis is not to rate higher those dispositions and capacities which were traditionally regarded as masculine and then to claim that women have them too. By maintaining this thesis I do not wish to say only that women are (can be) as good and great as men are but to say *also* that they are (can be) as bad and morally neutral as men.

A man is not good or bad simply because he is a man. Similarly a woman is not good or bad simply because she is a woman. Masculinity and femininity are morally neutral. In other words, morality is gender-neutral.

The respect in which woman is different from man is important, namely, that she can give birth to offspring, which a man cannot do. This is the case as far as the *natural capacities* are concerned. Thus it is motherhood which is the main differentia of womanhood. It seems that this distinction be-tween man and woman does not imply the division of dispositions, values or cognitions which either the traditions or some modern feminists have advocated. Whenever cultural conditioning is weakened, and often despite the cultural conditioning, the facts point against these divisions. If the motherhood of woman does not handicap her in any respect, it does not make her superior either. The protagonists of the 'feminine model' of ethics and education seem to assume the validity of the dichotomy between masculine and feminine dispositions and virtues. They seem to assume that autonomy, competitiveness, rationality, insensitivity, objectivity, etc., are masculine traits whereas love, affection, compassion, and care are feminine traits. Some have included even cheerfulness and gullibility as feminine qualities. To show that this division is based on facts, methods like inter-views are used. But unless the factor of cultural conditioning is taken into account, these methods will not be reliable. To take an example, love and care are supposed to be specially feminine qualities in India. This would be supported if one attends to women's responses to certain types of situations only. However, as is often pointed out in the Indian debates, very often it is the mothers and the mothers-in-law who willingly perpetuate cruelties against the daughters and the daughters-in-law. Their negligence towards female children is as 'natural' as their love and affection for the male ones. Similarly their desire to dominate when they grow older is as 'natural' as their desire to surrender in their young age. These desires or tendencies change also from context to context, from opportunity to opportunity. There is no pattern to mark 'naturally feminine' virtues.

When contrasting the 'ethic of care' and the 'ethic of justice', we need to review the concepts of 'care' and 'justice'. It is questionable whether these concepts must be defined in typically feminine and masculine dichotomous terminology. Care, as distinguished from blind love, is not entirely devoid of rationality and often needs objectivity. On the other hand justice would often require an appreciation of one's internal state, one's sense of humili-ation or violation or fear. This is needed for care as well. Thus the contrast does not seem to be so well-founded.

The call for feminine models to establish alternative systems of values and virtues does have a point; namely, to register protest against the uncritical presumption that whatever has thus far been regarded as mascu-line is alone valuable—that the traits commonly associated with maleness are the norms for all humanity. Celebration of gender is important as far as it underscores the valuable truth that many dispositions which were earlier belittled as 'merely' feminine, are in fact central to ethics and are also a source of power. However, it also seems to be an equally valuable truth that these dispositions are in fact not exclusively feminine, and that therefore they are a source of power not only for woman but for man too. In the new ethic, 'man', as conceived earlier, should not be the norm for all humanity. But neither should 'woman', as conceived earlier, be the model for all humanity. To the extent to which the early androgyny theories had in their subconscious the argument that certain qualities were superior, because they were masculine and because women could develop these qualities they were as good and powerful as men, they were not genuinely androgynous. A really androgynous theory will not have this bias for the dichotomy of male/female virtues and for the superiority of the 'male virtues'.

Now the question of equality is not fully answered by the androgyny theory of personhood alone, as long as differences like that of motherhood are recognized. The question of equality is mainly the question of equal treatment. The problem is that due to her motherhood woman needs special treatment in certain respects and this special treatment is to be given as her right without compromising her equality with man in the other respects. So the question is, how to reconcile this special treatment or 'discrimination' with the thesis of man/woman equality.

What is 'discrimination'? Discrimination, I suggest, is difference in treatment without the ground of a relevant natural or irremovable difference or of the necessity of serving the purposes for which an institution is established or a context is generated, provided the purposes of the institution or the context themselves do not seek to create or perpetuate differences. Equality is the absence of discrimination. Thus understood, equality is the antithesis of discrimination, not of difference. It is consistent with special provisions for the special needs of different categories of people, provided the categories themselves are not discriminatory. Therefore women, having the special feature of motherhood, have a right to get special facilities to help them perform their duties as mothers without affecting their rights and responsibilities elsewhere. It in no way falsifies their claim of equality with men. In fact, when a new life arrives in the family, the presence of father also is needed at home for longer periods. To perform this parental duty men also must have suitable arrangements in their jobs.

In the perspective presented above, the special needs of man and woman would often be found to be complementary, and not opposed, to one another. If this is appreciated, the necessity of retaining equality on the feminist agenda would be clear.

Recovering Igbo Traditions:
A Case for Indigenous Women's
Organizations in Development

Nkiru Nzegwu

INTRODUCTION

This paper may read to philosophers like an anthropological argument for the utilization of indigenous women's organization in development.[1] To some modernization theorists,[2] development economists, and policy-makers it would sound like nativism, a romantic re-creation of a precolonial reality that is of little relevance to Africa's postcolonial condition. But viewed critically, it is a radical critique of foundational assumptions about gender that underlie current development programmes. The sociological and philosophical elements of the critique connect at points where histori-cally constituted gender identities, social histories, and cultural norms expose the inadequacy of preconceived ideas about progress and culture that propel economic development. Though I shall argue my case through a detailed examination of Igbo women's history,[3] much of my argument has relevance to many other countries of Africa.

It is important to stress that this philosophical critique is not a point-by-point refutation of any specific development theories. Rather, it is a reading which interrogates foundational assumptions informing develop-

---

[1] If it does, we should see it as a manifestation of the depth in which eurocentric, colonial assumptions about knowledge have permeated scholarship. Received 'critical' attitudes to-wards the conceptual categories of non-Western societies today, are implicit reproductions of racist prejudices and biases in which these societies have historically been cast. Materials from 'other' cultures are exoticized as ethnographic literature, while the exotic materials of white-Western life is 'naturalized' and presented not only as normal but as theoretically unproblematic.

[2] Rostow (1960); Gino Germain, *The Sociology of Modernization: Studies on its Historical and Theoretical Aspects with Special Regard to the Latin American Case* (New Brunswick: Transaction, 1981); Josef Gugler and Williams Flanagan, *Urbanization and Social Change in West Africa* (Cambridge: Cambridge University Press, 1978).

[3] The textual sources of much of that history are the works of colonial officials like D. Amaury Talbot, *Woman's Mysteries of a Primitive People: The Ibibios of Southern Nigeria* (London: Cassell, 1915); M. M. Green (1964); Sylvia Leith-Ross (1965). Recent book length studies on women have come from the following: V. C. Uchendu, *The Igbos of Southern Nigeria* (New York: Holt, Rinehart & Winston, 1965); Ify Amadiume, *Male Daughters/Female Hus-bands* (Zed Books, 1987). Other writers whose works include a section on Igbo women are Richard Henderson, *The King in Every Man* (1972); Nina Mba, *Nigerian Women Mobilized: Women's Political Activities in Southern Nigeria 1900–1965* (1982); E. E. Evans-Pritchard, *The Position of Women in Primitive Societies and other Essays in Social Anthropology* (New York: The Free Press, 1965); P. Amaury Talbot, *The Peoples of Southern Nigeria: Ethnology*, vol. 111 (London: Frank Case, 1926).

ment wisdom. The generalist approach permits us to see how gender inequality is built into programmes. It enables us to understand the conceptual biases of the participatory-models of Non-Governmental Agencies (NGOs), and the technocratically oriented models of large development bureaucracies like the World Bank and the International Monetary Fund (IMF).

My argument proceeds in three broad moves. In the first section, I shall examine the 'status of women' in Igbo political structure to determine the reasons for the apathy of modern Igbo women to political activity. In the second section, I shall describe the internal structure of one such organization and examine how the utilization of literacy as the criterion of cultural adulthood leads to designing ineffectual programmes for women. In the last section, I examine the history of development in Nigeria and explore the positive contributions indigenous women's organization could bring to development.

1 THE STATUS OF WOMEN IN IGBO POLITICAL STRUCTURE

Colonialism in Africa was much more than a metaphor. It was an alienating historical condition that erased and silenced the voice of women. In eastern Nigeria in general, and Igboland in particular, the British policy of indirect rule resulted in the installation of a sexist administrative structure that, despite the demise of British imperial rule, has persisted to this day. Women's disadvantaged position in southern Nigeria today, and in the eastern parts of the country in particular, could directly be traced to two important features of the colonial government: its economic and social policies that effectively marginalized women; and the asymmetrical political structure that arrogated to male officials the power to make decisions for women. This structural bias robbed women of their historical powers and relegated them to the category of dependent minors. The enforced invisibility meant that women were denied education, employment, decision-making powers, and access to resources such as credit facilities and loan schemes.[4]

Prior to colonization, the political culture of the Igbos could theoretically be described as dual-sex.[5] Under this dual-symmetrical structure, women

---

[4] Since the late sixties noticeable changes have begun in the area of education. Parents are increasingly pushing for their daughters' education following the realization that women, more than men, invested more in the care of aged parents.

[5] Kamene Okonjo (1976), 45–58; also Green (1964), ch. 11. Though written with colonial objectives in mind (which accounts for its much criticized racist overtones), Green's book remains an incisive reading since she aims for a woman-centred view.

had their own Governing Councils—*Ikporo-Onitsha, Nd'inyom*—to address their specific concerns and needs as women. The councils protected women's social and economic interests, and guided the community's development. This dual-symmetrical structure accorded immense political profile to women both in communities with constitutional monarchies (on the western side and some parts of the eastern banks of the River Niger— Onitsha, Ogbaru, and Oguta), and in the non-centralized democracies of the eastern hinterland.

Although Igbo society was divided along gender lines, antagonistic gender relations were generally avoided because the indigenous political process was primarily consensus-seeking. The socio-political structure required and depended on the active participation of women in community life. Their views were deemed critical, not because they were women, but because of the special insight they brought to issues by virtue of their spiritual, market and trading duties, and their maternal roles. In precolonial times, the Obi of Onitsha governed in consultation with the Omu (female monarch), and later with *Ikporo-Onitsha* following the demise of the Omu institution.[6] In other parts of Igboland, *Nd'inyom* governed with *ezeala* (the spiritual custodians of societal norms). The maintenance of a harmonious gender relationship was critical to the well-being of Igbo society. The consequences for destabilizing the intricate gender structure could be agonizingly severe.

For instance, men who devalued women risked being 'sat on',[7] or shunned by women who invoked constitutionally validated sanctions to restore normalcy. Scholars like Green (1964), Judith Van Allen (1976), and Monday Effiong Noah (1985) have noted that these took various forms including besieging the man in his house and singing scurrilous songs that taunt his manhood, or roughing him up and/or destroying his prized possessions. It is interesting to note that other men in the village hardly ever came to the rescue or defence of one of their own. '*Nya ma!*' (It's the persons own business), they would say. '*O kotelu okwu umunwnayi!*' (The person brought the wrath of women on himself). Green gives a telling account of an incident in Agbaja, in which women exercised this disciplinary power by killing two unpenned pigs belonging to a male neighbour, which were eating their crops. Fearing a violent response from the male owner or his male friends, Green was startled by the owner's non-aggressive response. Turning to a male informant for elucidation, she was casually

---

[6] Even today, Ofala Okagbue, the Obi of Onitsha, seeks out women's stand and opinion before making policy pronouncements. This co-rulership is noted by Felicia Ekejiuba (1966: 219) with respect to Omu Okwei in Ossamala; Henderson (1972) with respect to the Omu of Onitsha, and Kamene Okonjo (1976: 47–51) with respect to the Omu of Obamkpa.

[7] For a detailed description of this mechanism, and how it works, see Judith Van Allen (1976: 59–86); also Green (1964: 174). For an account of this practice among Ibibio women see Monday Effiong Noah's description of the activities of *Iban Isong* (Ibibio women's organization) (1985: 24–31).

informed that the owner and the other men would not take action because 'it is the women who own us'.[8]

In Onitsha, the same sanctionary measure was enforced in the public refusal to accord a titled offender the customary respect due a person of his rank;[9] or refusing to have him properly buried until an apology was extracted from the family.[10] In extreme cases as occurred under the reign of Omu Nwagboka in the late 1880s,[11] women withdrew *en masse* from any activity in which inter-gender relationship was implicated; and in some parts of Igboland, women collectively moved out of their villages until their demands were met.[12] Leaving men to fend for themselves and their children, impressed viscerally upon them the worth and value of women. The social disruption that usually followed the violation of women's rights provided compelling reason for all to strive for social harmony.

Mutual gender respect thus developed, as each group had equal access to sanctionary powers and the judicial and constitutional backing to use its powers, if need be, against the other. Women who consistently and deliberately devalued the men of their marital village risked a visit from the ancestral mask of the ward. However, women's stronger group identification through their Governing Councils and their ability to work collectively in diverse associations gave them immense protection and coverage. Their networking skills enabled women to mobilize instantly across cultural, religious, and economic boundaries.[13] Since Igbo men lacked the same kind of network associations and gender identification commonly found with women, it was harder for them to enforce their decisions. Realizing that to take on one woman was to take on the whole, a situation the men were most anxious to avoid, they found it easier to lodge their complaints with the appropriate women's group rather than take action on their own.

Women's independence was fostered by cultural traditions that placed a premium on female assertiveness and collectivity, and did not define power as socially deviant. If men usually capitulated and were, or seemed politically 'helpless' before the collective strength of women, it is not because they were passive or timid. It was more that they were *accustomed* to women *being* in positions of power and influence, and had consequently developed respect for their administrative skill. The indigenous structures of govern-

[8] Green (1964: 174); also see Monday Effiong Noah's description of how men scuttle for cover when they hear of the movement of *Iban Isong* (1985: 26–7); and Leith-Ross, (1939: 97).

[9] This was done to the Owelle of Onitsha and former President of Nigeria, Dr Nnamdi Azikiwe, in 1976–7 when he fell out with Ikporo Onitsha. The 'Owelle' is the seventh in rank of the Ndichi Ume, the highest ranking chiefs of the Obi of Onitsha's cabinet.

[10] This happened to another Ndichie, Adazia Enwonwu, in 1975.

[11] This is part of Onitsha oral history which Henderson documented (1972: 376, 525).

[12] Interestingly, Saye women of Burkina Faso used this threat in 1981 to compel their men to build a dam. See Dankelma and Davidson (1988: 35–37).

[13] Mba (1982: 92).

ance publicly validated and reinforced women in ways that normalized their presence in the judicial, economic, and political spheres of life. Thus Igbo men could matter-of-factly accept the 'sitting on a man' mode of conflict-expression together with its graphic imagery of 'being sat on', because *in their communities* women adjudicated cases, established and enforced rules and regulations, worked in concert with Obi, *ndichie, and ezeala* in the administration of the community. Since women's political identity is a fact of life, and in their eyes *'nwanyibuife'* (women are of significance), there could be no shame in acknowledging and abiding by women's regulations.[14]

The theoretical significance of the social act of 'sitting on a man' is that it most forcefully revealed the existence of a society in which men lacked the sort of patriarchal authority so readily presented in ethnographic literature, and assumed by development policy planners. The political significance of that sanctionary force and one which is not adequately highlighted is that it afforded women a powerful constitutional check on male excesses in society, and assured that their views were adequately factored into policy decisions.[15] Reminders of the destabilizing effects of gender conflict were used symbolically to protect and reinforce women's power. Writing in the 1930s, Green notes that at times of natural disasters, which have had a particularly great impact on women's lives (for example, when there was a higher than normal infant mortality rate, or an increased incidence of stillbirths), 'women collectively . . . [held] . . . men and their magic responsible' and demanded propitiation.[16] This type of critical scrutiny established a framework within which men were held accountable and gender imbalances redressed.

In Igbo political tradition, representation without sanctionary powers to back it up implied non-representation, *'ewe onu okwu'* (not to have a say); its effect was social marginalization. Thus politically marginalized and reclassified as dependents under colonial rule, Igbo women, in the period between 1925 and 1935, incessantly organized protest rallies and picketed the offices and residences of colonial officials to wrest some form of representation.

[14] Barbara Rogers (1980) was undoubtedly correct when she observed that it is highly questionable that men in most precolonial cultures objectified women as passive objects (p. 29). She was also correct when she treated such theoretical intuitions as revealing more about those making the judgements (p. 33). See ch. 2.

[15] Many westerners including some feminists (Ann Ferguson, 1991) are opposed to the idea of factoring sex into gender constructions. Catherine MacKinnon has shown that what is feared is a situation in which any possible distribution of powers necessarily reproduces sexist patriarchal roles and stereotypes. Hardliners on the issue find it difficult to comprehend how sexism can be overcome if sex differences are acknowledged. Focusing intently on the oppressive experiences women have undergone because of sex recognition, they usually forget in their fear (1) that male differences are already factored into constructions of power; (2) that factoring in female differences to displace male monopoly of the conceptual realm does not imply invoking negative stereotypical images; and (3) that sexism comes about not because biological sex is recognized, but because it is dealt with *negatively*.

[16] Green (1964: 176).

In 1929 these protest movements culminated in '*Ogu Umunwanyi*' (the Women's War), in which they sought to modify the system to give them some form of representation similar to what they had in precolonial times. Appreciative of some of the benefits of colonialism such as better medical care and transportation networks, and aware of their educational handicap ('our eyes were not opened'), the women did not desire to overthrow the colonial rule as alleged.[17] Specifically, they just wanted to be consulted on the selection of Native Affairs officials, and in the formulation of policies. They wanted the prosecution of all oppressive and corrupt chiefs and court clerks, and offered to provide the necessary evidence to convict these officials. To introduce safeguards in the administrative system, they proposed that the post of warrant chiefs be limited to three years of service, and that women must be consulted in the selection of officers for those posts.[18] Most important of all, they wanted tax exemption for women.

The Women's War, which was fought to protest the imposition of taxation on women, began in Bende division of Owerri province and spread quickly throughout Owerri and Calabar provinces of eastern Nigeria. The 1929 financial crash had impacted negatively on women's produce trade, motivating them to seek assurances from the colonial government that they would not be taxed.[19] Faced with bureaucratic stonewalling, the women resolved not to pay any taxes nor have their properties assessed. So when the Warrant Chief Okugo sent an assessor to compile the figures, Nwanyeruwa Ojim refused to permit an assessment of her property. An alarm brought other women to the scene who proceeded 'to sit' on Chief Okugo and the assessor, Mark Emeruwa. Messages were sent to women in other villages who, on learning of the crisis, joined the struggle. Although Chief Okugo was deposed to placate the women, the women refused to allow the dethronment to deflect them from their larger objective.

In their confrontation with the colonial administration, the women mostly employed the conflict-resolution mechanism of 'sitting on a man' to signal their grievances. Unaccustomed to such militancy from women, the nervous colonial officials ordered in armed police and troops to 'quell' the disturbances, which had spread over an area of 6,000 square miles. Officially 50 women were killed and another 50 wounded by the time order was restored. Despite the heavy caualties on the women's side, the end of the war did not signal the end of the protest movement and women's agitation for representation.

[17] *Aba Commission of Inquiry Report* (1930: 263).

[18] Mba (1982: 87–91). The references on the women's war came from government documents such as *Aba Commission on Inquiry, Owerri Annual Report 1929 and 1930, Ogoja Annual Report 1929, Calabar Annual Report 1929 and 1930*. Miss Okezie's letter (*Aba District Office*, see Mba (1982), 1/21/30); from Nguru (*Owerri District Office*, see Mba (1982), 1/14/49); testimonies from Nwanyiezi of Ikefem (*Aba Commission of Inquiry Notes of Evidence* no. 148) Akulechula (ibid.: 175).

[19] Ibid. 90.

The profound historic importance of the 1929 Women's War consisted not simply in the courageous attempt of the women of eastern Nigeria to challenge invisibility and fight the devaluation of their personhood. It also unequivocally established that women's independence was a fact of life in precolonial times—and that these traditions could still be called upon to empower women. The fiery strong response of these women to the erosion of their rights conclusively showed not just that women *had* political roles and rights in precolonial times, but also that the political institutions through which they claimed these rights were integral parts of the political tradition in Igboland and Ibibioland. It also showed their political acumen, foresight and vision, and revealed the existence of a powerful, highly efficient political structure with networks that transcended ethnic boundaries. The women displayed an incisive grasp of the colonial agenda, an ability to perform rapid and accurate analyses of the fluid, complex situation, and a remarkable capacity for formulating and deploying appropriate strategies.

The Women's War was also important for another reason. It marked the rise of Western gender ideology, as evidenced by the non-participation in the women's action by a growing class of privileged women. Whereas in the past women had rallied in solidarity to assert their demands, the individualistic emphasis of the new ideology prevented the converts, the wives of administration officials, from participating in the political movement.[20] Their disinterest and lack of political consciousness was best explained as a rejection of Igbo gender ideology that had fostered women's independence and placed a premium on assertiveness and being outspoken. Suddenly, being assertive and having a political opinion signified the 'primitive African'; while being cultured and civilized meant being submissive and obedient. These status-conscious wives of local officials ironically modelled themselves into the non-assertive, self-effacing, passive women that Igbos had always derisively portrayed as '*mmili oyi*' (cold water, ineffectual).

As the writings of Leith-Ross and Green show, this Western gender ideology hardly made an impact in the rural areas between the 1930s and early 1950s. To a large extent, the pattern of life of the rural and urban poor continues to this day to manifest stronger identification with traditional norms and values than with Western cultural values. With the domestication of middle-class women by the 1950s, we find a two-tiered reality: an upper-crust Westernized society, overlaying and to some extent concealing indigenous social values and practices. At the upper-tier level, educated middle-class Igbo women find themselves shackled to a sexist system that

[20] Mba 83–5. Mba had given several reasons for the non-participation of middle-class women, namely pressures from husbands, non-membership in the community-based associations of the areas of protest, and adequate financial means. But these are inconclusive given that the women's action ran counter to the spirit of female consciousness in Igboland. In the rural areas, the wives and daughter of warrant chiefs and court officials led some of the revolt, so status and wealth cannot be called upon as valid explanations.

leaves them politically disadvantaged to this day.[21] In an environment where success is defined in economic terms, many women who have had to adopt a subordinate stance to their male partners do not realize that this is itself a form of oppression, regardless of the prosperity enjoyed. Meanwhile their economically disadvantaged 'uneducated' sisters retain a stronger sense of their identity, and a greater degree of control over their lives.

What development planners too often ignore in designing policies is that vestiges of this cultural consciousness still remain today, albeit in a modified form. The present ambivalence of Igbo women, especially middle-class women, to political action is symptomatic, not of tradition but of an alienation from Igbo history produced by the experience of colonialism. For the urban-poor and rural women, the primary disenchantment is with the so-called 'democratic' process of Western political tradition that had marginalized and stripped them of their female dignity. As early as 1929 women like Mary Onumaere were protesting against the rising power of men: 'we don't wish to be oppressed by out menfolk.'[22] Others like Nwato of Okpuala wondered at the internal contradictions of colonialism: 'we thought that white men came to bring peace to the land ... if this oppression continues, how are we to praise you?'[23]

Nigerian men in general benefited immensely from the inherent sexism of the system as the British officers were willing to work with them to install colonial rule, however much they despised them on racial grounds. Whereas in the past Igbo men had to share power with women, as they succeeded educationally, economically, and politically they egoistically clung to power and could not be depended upon to distribute resources equitably. The co-optation of African men into the Western gender stereotypes did incalculable damage to modern Nigerian political culture. Freed from the restraining checks and balances that had curtailed sexism, male bias was massively built into policies, programmes, and structures of the system to safeguard it for men. The results were the denial of effective representation to an inordinately large number of women; the exclusion of women's corrective influence in governance; and the creation of a politically passive female citizenry and sexist, dictatorial men.

2 WOMEN'S ORGANIZATIONS: THE IKPORO ONITSHA

In beginning with an analysis of the colonial impact on African cultural life, it might seem that I have fallen prey to what has most derisively been

[21] I have to admit that what has been described is the general trait of a class. In no way does it imply that all 'educated' or 'middle-class women' behaved in that manner. Exceptions like Miss Okezie, Margaret Ekpo, and Adora Ulasi could easily be found.

[22] Ibid. 89. From the government document (*Aba Commission of Inquiry Notes of Evidence* 10. 239, see Mba (1982), p. 89).

[23] Ibid. 92. From the government document (*Aba Commission of Inquiry Notes of Evidence* 10. 805, see Mba (1982), p. 92).

described as 'the predilection of African intellectuals', namely the urge to 'romanticize' precolonial traditions, and to unimaginatively explain away Africa's ills by blaming colonialism. It is certainly true at a superficial level that colonialism is not completely responsible for all the problems in Africa. But at a deeper level it is especially culpable, given the structures: economic, military, and bureaucratic, including gender, that it left in place.[24] Given the male bias of our colonial legacy, the female empowering institutions of Africa's indigenous cultures were devalued with no space created for the women in the new Western-derived one.

One place where this sexism is most evident in postcolonial Africa is in the field of development where projects are targeted at men and a wide disparity exists in the income-earning pattern of men over women. Barbara Rogers (1980) had argued that this income disparity derived from non-recognition of women as producers. Citing numerous examples she showed that the underpinning conceptual bias of development militated against women in the distribution of benefits through stereotypically treating them as 'dependents' of males who were treated as 'principal income generators'. By noting that women's labour was consistently taken for granted, Rogers showed the heavy labour-intensive demands made on women which far exceeded that made on men.

The linkage between women's self-worth and financial autonomy, which Ndiya[25] women made in 1946, is now being made by critics of development theories. Anticipating the adverse effects of a gender biased economy, Ndiya women had warned the British against the implementation of policies that would deprive women of their livelihood and self-worth. 'What shall we do insofar as we know that if the mill (being introduced by the British) is *owned* and *run* by men, we will be thrown out of a *job*?' (emphasis mine). They knew the effect of male monopoly of resources; they knew that if they became economically vulnerable and beholden to men their social worth and dignity would be severely undercut.

Zenebewoke Tadesse's (1990) analysis of women in African economy is important in that she identifies the positive impact of income-generating activities on women's self-confidence. To bring about the sort of structural changes she envisaged, women would have to be more intimately and more positively factored into development planning. It is not just that policies that accord with the *status quo* must be rejected since they reinforce the marginalized status of women. It is more that development planners should revise radically their approach if their projects are to be realistically adapted to the needs of the target group. When development planners assume that rural women must lack organizational skills, and conclude that they should devote their resources to funding 'awareness workshops', they illicitly trans-

---

[24] Femi Taiwo made this point in his paper on knowledge production which he presented at SUNY-Binghamton in March 1991.

[25] Ibibio women. See Mba, 107.

pose the apathy of the middle-class women on to rural women who have in fact continued to be politically active; they illegitimately suppose that lack of literacy skills is equivalent to lack of organizational skills.

Observing the politics and ideological power of literacy, Pattanayak (1991) notes that when literacy is construed as the basis of modernization: 'illiteracy is grouped with poverty, malnutrition, lack of education, and health care, while literacy is often equated with growth of productivity, child care, and the advance of civilization.'[26] Such a classification, Pattanayak suggests, 'naturalizes' literacy as the panacea for successful development even as research shows that the correlation between literacy and the adoption of improved agricultural practices is insignificant.[27] What this establishes is that literacy is not a substitute for practical skills, nor does lack of it obstruct improvement. There is no question that in today's world literacy is vital, but it must be put in a proper perspective. It does not have a propulsive force all its own to instil knowledge and experience.

Despite the lack of literacy skills, many African women are engaged in trading activities and agricultural production, and in addition possess a wide range of technical, organizational, and administrative experience gained through hands-on practical activities in numerous indigenous associations. As the Igbo Women's War showed, these experiences equip women to evaluate their economic situation and take on the challenges of mobilizing other women at the grassroot level to implement projects. But planners' devaluation of these capabilities—at the same time a devaluation of these women's personhood—has generally led to the exclusion of these valuable experiences from development programmes. Planners need to take account of the diverse character traits of different groups of women, and to be open and receptive to alternative models of experiences and organizational skills.

Therefore, guided by the belief that development assistance to grassroots women's organizations is often stalled through lack of historical knowledge, I shall follow my general account of Igbo traditions with a description of indigenous women's institutions that are deserving of development support. These associations deserve consideration for several reasons: they seek activities that have social and cultural relevance; they are advantageously positioned to channel resources to women who need more empowerment and autonomy; their existence has been obscured by hostile development policies; and their leadership is not currently in a position to articulate their demands or to argue for them in terms that officials of foreign development agencies expect and demand. My aim is not to invoke outmoded ancestral relics, but to point out enduring administrative structures that have relevance for development at the grassroot level.

---

[26] Pattanayak (1991: 105).

[27] R. Shanker, 'Literacy and Adoption of Improved Agricultural Practices', *Indian Journal of Adult Education* 40 (1979), 31–7.

I must begin by describing the organizational structure of these groups which, historically, played important social, economic, political, and spiritual roles in the community. Understanding the internal structure of an organization like *Ikporo-Onitsha*, I will show why an unswerving focus on literacy as the criterion of cultural adulthood leads to the adoption of ineffectual policies for women.

In much of former eastern Nigeria, most communities have a broad-based Women's Governing Council that has sole jurisdiction over the local affairs of women in a specific community. These councils are radically different from, and unconnected to the élitist, class-conscious, government-funded National Council of Women's Societies with its headquarters in Lagos. Membership in these indigenous Women's Councils is open to women of a specific community regardless of their educational or class background. In fact, literacy is not a prerequisite for participation. Some of the elderly women leaders of these councils never received formal education, yet their organizational skills and leadership are widely respected.

Unlike the Western-derived National Council, the indigenous Women's Councils have an effective hold over their membership. This is so because they represent the interests of women in their community of salience, which means their home of origin, and are therefore especially responsive to these women's special interests. Regardless of a woman's social status and educational accomplishments, a council's directives are binding on her and are never treated with levity.

In Onitsha for example, such a women's council is the *Ikporo-Onitsha* (Women of Onitsha). This council has represented, and still represents, the interests of Onitsha women in Onitsha. It does not matter whether a woman lives in Lagos, Kano, Enugu, or New York, her interest is represented by the Governing Council even in her absence. No decision that has an impact on the lives or status of Onitsha women can be made without the council's knowledge and consent. Historically, this organization has played important social, economic, political, and spiritual roles in the community. To cite just a few examples, it steered women through such politically turbulent times as the resistance to colonial policies in the late 1920s and early 1930s, the 1963 to 1967 Obiship constitutional crises, and the three-year dispute with the then East Central State government in late 1973 to 1976, following that goverment's usurpation of Onitsha women's traditional market rights.

Prior to 1890, the *Ikporo-Onitsha* had the Omu (or female monarch) as its leader. The Omu and her Council of *otu ogene* was the female principle in governance, and complemented the male principle that was embodied in the Obi (or male monarch) and the *ndichie*.[28] Each institution was responsible exclusively for the actions and activities of members of the respective

[28] For further descriptions of this see Richard Henderson (1972); Nina Mba (1982: 21–6); also see Okonjo (1976: 45–58).

sex; their powers and privileges complemented one another. On national matters, however,[29] the two collaborated in formulating and establishing the Onitsha nation's position. This constitutionally defined consultative process ensured that the female viewpoint was well-represented in decisions affecting the whole community. At a trade negotiation in the 1870s, in which the State of Onitsha was to decide whether to permit the establishment of a European trading firm, John Whitford reported on the participation of 'the old women who constituted the Board of Trade' (that was the Omu and her Council) in the decision-making process.[30]

Following the imposition of colonialism, the office of the Omu declined. The denial of recognition to the Omuship as the legitimate constitutional representative of women was politically damaging.[31] Worse still was the economic subjugation that followed. The trade and market portfolio of the Omu were gradually taken over by the British 'in the interest of trade'. New trading policies were promulgated[32] that tasked the women's ability to obtain operating capital, that deprived the office of the Omu of its revenue base, and in turn, stripped Onitsha women of their traditional influence over trade and market affairs. Their autonomy and powers were consequently undermined.

To survive the political erasure initiated by this economic trend, a radical transformation of the institution of the *Ikporo-Onitsha* took place. This transformation brought the organization into line with the changing reality of women's reduced economic circumstances and loss of power. To preserve the council's political role, the financially costly initiation and governance ceremonies were cut drastically. The excised constitutional powers were vested in the oldest surviving woman who, from then on, was addressed as *Onye-isi-ikporo-Onitsha* (the head of Onitsha women). Succession to this powerful office was simplified, and devolved automatically to the next oldest woman in line, once the full funeral ceremony of the predecessor was completed. Although the powers of subsequent *Onye-isi-ikporo-Onitsha* were nowhere near that of the Omu in precolonial times, the institution to this day commands immense respect and loyalty in Onitsha. The flexibility introduced by the radical restructuring gave the council new life and identity. Most importantly, its informal nature gave it a tactical advantage it never had before. This advantage was effectively deployed

[29] I take here the definition of nationhood that is built on ethnicity, in which a cultural nation is equivalent to a political nation-state. This is the case in European nationalism. See B. O. Oloruntimehin, 'African Politics and Nationalism, 1919–35', in Adu Boahen (ed.), *UNESCO General History of Africa: Africa under Colonial Domination 1880–1935*, vol. 7 (Los Angeles, Calif.: UNESCO, 1990), 565–79.

[30] Elizabeth Isichei, *Igbo Worlds: An Anthology of Oral Histories and Historical Descriptions* (Philadelphia, Pa.: Institute for the Study of Human Issues, 1978).

[31] For a more detailed account of this development see Mba (1982: 25–6, 49); Okonjo (1976: 45–58).

[32] The one-shilling produce inspection test was introduced in 1928 to regulate the quality of palm oil.

against the East Central State government between 1974 and 1976, to discredit and embarrass their own, Ukpabi Asika, who was then the Administrator. The police officers who were sent to track the activities of the women ran into an impenetrable thicket of elusiveness.

Today, the *Onye-isi-ikporo-Onitsha* rules through a Governing Council of 35 members: a general secretary, six to seven women leaders of opinion who advise on policy matters, and three representatives each from the nine founding villages of Onitsha. In keeping with the community's principle of equality, representation to *Ikporo-Onitsha* is on the basis of equal representation from villages, rather than population or numerical strength. Selection of representatives is based on such qualities as moral probity, strong character and charisma, articulate and fearless nature, and maturity in age. The representatives must have demonstrated leadership skills, and distinguished themselves in such other subsidiary associations. The stringent moral requirements for representatives are based on the idea that a strong moral centre is needed to deal with the tumultuous exigencies of political life. The age requirement of over 40 is not mandatory; it seems to have been put in place discretionarily to spare nurturing mothers the agony of juggling between activist community duties and child care.

The council conducts its affairs at two levels. The first is the intra-village level, in which representatives of the nine founding villages report and discuss the activities of their home constituency and vigorously represent their interests. Second is the Onitsha-national level. Here, the collective interests of Onitsha women prevail. By this I mean that issues are analysed from a gendered perspective in terms of their effect on Onitsha women as a whole. Strategies are then developed for their resolution. Because the Governing Council is a central unifying organization, its internal dynamics tend toward the promotion of shared communitarian values rather than divisive individualistic values. Except for caucus meetings, all meetings are held in an open public forum at *ilo mgbeleme* (the sacred assembly ground) where anyone can attend.

Ikporo-Onitsha branches are found in any town in Nigeria where there is a sizable Onitsha community. These branches are seen as 'international' affiliates and the members are referred to as 'abroad' members. Each of these branches has an ad hoc 'ambassadorial' relationship with the Governing Council in Onitsha, with which it maintains an open line of communication and to which it reports. Most of the branch membership are professional women: teachers, lawyers, doctors, engineers, retailers, and business women. Participation for abroad members is through the branch, and through village representatives when they relocate to Onitsha. Through firmly established networks and protocols, the branches are regularly kept informed of current local developments and of the official positions of the Governing Council. They receive directives from the council; and in turn send back their suggestions. Because Nigerians identify themselves primarily with their home of origin or 'ethnic or cultural nation', rather than their place of domicile or 'foreign land', they tend to be more interested in the progress and development of their cultural state than in the affairs of the place of domicile.

Like traditional Women's Council's elsewhere in Igboland, *Ikporo-Onitsha* has survived because of continuous organizational reviews, re-evaluation of policies, timely critical responses, and adaptability to changing social conditions. Its well-developed chain of command and stringent requirement of accountability have earned it immense respect and credibility. The council's success in ensuring accountability derives from its intense monitoring system. Nothing is hidden in an environment where everyone knows the business of others. The knowledge that 'everyone is their sister's keeper' means that you do only what you can publicly live with or defend. Fraud is possible, but what keeps people in check is not just the public exposure of their crimes, but the humiliating dressing-down that will be publicly meted out to them at *ilo mgbeleme*. What people dread above all is the alienating effect of ostracism which the Governing Council may pronounce on the culprit as a last resort.

Ostracism, the corrective sanction that impresses viscerally on individuals their dependency of social relations, highlights the limitations of West-ern notions of privacy and the primacy of the individual. The Onitsha position is that an individual's conceptualization of himself or herself as a person necessarily takes place within a social context. Only within a community of fellow beings can the idea of self-realization become intelligible. For realization implies interaction with others, establishing rites of engagement and interrelationship. Outside the border of a social realm, individuals, according to the Onitsha, become non-human, and if allowed to continue that sort of existence will break down and come to exemplify non-human tendencies. Ostracism—which bars a person from participation in family and community affairs—is a practical demonstra-tion of the idea that humans are social beings. Living in a society and being shunned by its members definitely accords an individual his or her space, but only by vividly demonstrating to them their implicit de-pendence on others. Since the ostracized person is, in effect, removed from the social to the natural realm, he or she enters the 'land of the living dead', to live a devastatingly solitary existence. Full restoration of social rights and obligation comes from recanting and paying the stipulated fine.

It is noteworthy that this power is also applied against men. In cases where gender equilibrum is threatened profoundly, ostracism can be trans-lated into withdrawal or disengagement of women's power from normal social interrelationship with men. This withdrawal force acts as a constitu-tional check, forcing men to confront their dependency on women. For instance, between 1977 and 1978, *Ikporo-Onitsha* led the whole community (men and women) in ostracizing the Obi of Onitsha Ofala Okagbue to protest his abdication of his constitutionally assigned obligation to fight for the traditional rights of Onitsha women. The same was done to the Owelle of Onitsha, the former first president of Nigeria, when his political position was defined as antagonistic to the stand *Ikporo-Onitsha* had taken officially on promoting women's welfare. Adazia Enwonwu, the Ndichi who openly taunted women for lacking significance, could not be buried as planned initially by his family, until a ritual rite of recantation was performed.

The fact that these female-centred Women's Councils have survived to this day is a testimony to both their adaptability and their resilience. They have responded progressively to the challenges of oppressive economic realities by establishing co-operatives to encourage women's trading activities.

The goals of these Women's Councils overlap with those of development agencies that are committed to grassroot development. First, the councils inculcate an ethics of community work in women, which in turn fosters a wide range of organizational, trading, and business skills. Because these skills and experiences are not abstractly named and theorized about, development officials routinely denigrate and dismiss them. Yet the hands-on administrative training that women leaders receive in the course of their service to multiple associations gives them an incisive encyclopaedic knowledge of their community. Their total understanding of cultural norms and market economics make them excellent candidates for the role of 'people professionals' in the sorts of programmes that require information on local social and cultural structures.[33]

Lack of this sort of cultural knowledge has hampered development efforts in Africa in many ways. Programme evaluators too often lack the skills to carry out a comprehensive analysis of the social impact of programmes, hence they tend to rely on preconceived ideas about women and about literacy rather than 'reading' the specific realities of the culture. Projects like water supply systems, food production, mechanized farming, workshops on fertilizer usage and business investment are diverted to men on the naïve assumption that men are 'naturally' disposed to leadership and mechanical skills, while women are non-mechanically inclined and 'naturally' disposed to a submissive role.

Numerous projects have failed for such reasons. Consider the case of water projects. Women, not men, are the traditional water managers in most African communities, and for that reason they possess all the relevant data. This came to light in a water-scheme project in northern Ghana

---

[33] Lawrence Salmen used the term in another context, to describe local experts who are unaffiliated to development agencies, but who provide technical advice. My use differs only in the sense that I am treating the cultural advice to agencies as technical. See Lawrence E. Salmen, *Listen to the People: Participant-Observer Evaluation of Development Projects* (New York: Oxford University Press, 1987).

funded by the Canadian International Development Agency (CIDA). Similar projects in other communities floundered, with the exception of one in which women were involved in the planning, implementation, and management of the project.[34] That the women co-ordinated project succeeded does not imply that men are irresponsible, but rather that they lacked the requisite knowledge about water resources to contribute effectively to the water-scheme project.

With this general moral knowledge in mind, and knowing that sustainability and accountability are the bane of development projects in Africa, let us now consider again the case of Nigerian development to determine what needs can be met by an organization like *Ikporo-Onitsha*.

3 DEVELOPMENT PROSPECTS: A ROLE FOR TRADITIONAL WOMEN'S ORGANIZATIONS

In postcolonial Nigeria, there have tended to be four main types of development projects. The first, and one that is generally given urgent national priority, is the heavy industrial type that seeks the transformation of the economy from agrarian to industrial. The second type targets male farmers in rural communities with the aim of improving their self-sufficiency through modern agricultural techniques and raising the productivity level of their cash crops. The third type of project focuses on social modernization in areas such as health care, literacy, water resources, and job training that strives to improve the general quality of life in the urban centres. Finally, the fourth category promotes self-help projects that are expected to have a far-reaching impact at grassroot levels.

In the first phase of postcolonial development in Nigeria between 1960 and 1973, the underlying model of development maintained that transformation from a communal to a capitalist economy was a prerequisite for modernization.[35] It was assumed that a technological focus, in such areas as iron and steel, road networks, bridge-building, dockyards, and agriculture was the only route to development. In line with Rostow's theory of modernization, the central assumption was that cultural development would automatically follow technological initiatives; and that the level of development of a society is determined by the number of intensive primary and secondary industries it possesses. So heavy capital-intensive projects were touted as a critical requirement for a sound economic base.

[34] This successful project was evaluated by a female consultant Theodora Carroll Foster. She met with stiff opposition from the male area co-ordinator who felt that the local women had nothing to contribute.
[35] This is Rostow's model (1960), in which modernization defined the point of 'take-off'. It is assumed that industrialization, education, population, and labour are the necessary factors for sustained growth.

Between 1973 and 1983, the second major phase commenced. It was marked by an emphasis on technological transfer that led to an increased presence of Nigerians in the middle and upper-middle management positions. Majority shareholdership (known as indigenization) by Nigerians was another important issue. The assumption was that local ownership of industrial projects guaranteed access to technical knowledge. As in the first phase, large-scale capital-intensive projects such as iron and steel and petrochemical industries, and tangible symbols of success such as stadia, monumental office complexes, and airports were the preferred goals in development. As oil money rolled in from petroleum sales—100 billion dollars between 1973 and 1981—the need to raise agricultural productivity declined as a national priority. Earlier initiatives in agricultural development were largely abandoned as the attention shifted to the development of a manufacturing sector based solely on the assembly of semi-finished products. Social and cultural projects such as adult literacy, rural electrification, and water schemes were also largely ignored and, when carried out, were haphazardly performed and monitored.

In both the first and second phases, indigenous culture was viewed as obsolete and not thought to have any significant initiating or critical role to play in industrialization. To all intents and purposes it was inert. This simplistic view of culture had devastating consequences for development, contributing to the failure of projects such as the iron and steel plant at Ajaokuta, the Aladja steel plant, the Lansat telecommunications system, and the three hi-tech incinerators in Lagos. The eventual realization that technological development presupposes a certain cultural and valuational environment led to a re-evaluation of development parameters. A different orientation exists today. The 1980s recession and the drastic decline of the economies of many African nations, coupled with the brutal effects of the Structural Adjustment Programmes insisted on by the World Bank and the International Monetary Fund have forced African nations to shift gears radically. A focus on grassroots development began in earnest in the early 1980s.

Today, development as practised by grassroot development programmes, is guided by the principle that the self-reliance of the rural and urban poor is critical to sustain cultural progress and development. At the initial stages, the NGOs programme representatives zealously approached their task with a paternalistic approach. Such an approach was counter-productive since it shut out local participation in the design of projects, with the result that local aspirations, values, priorities, and needs were excluded. The discovery that projects failed when they were not linked to the specific interests and needs of beneficiaries, brought about a change in the NGOs problem-solving techniques. To match projects to needs, participatory methodological models that stressed local participation in project design and implementation were adopted increasingly. However, a fundamental problem still remained with the models: their gender neutral emphasis ignored women.[36]

Since the attainment of independence three decades ago, Nigerian women have consistently been excluded from development. Initially, the standard argument was that development was gender neutral, and there was no need to target any specific group for programmes. Such arguments rang hollow as they masked the fact that the principal beneficiaries of development programmes were usually men. With the increasing presence of women in key decision-making positions in donor agencies, a gender perspective was added. Women, it was pointed out, constitute 70% of the workforce in agriculture in sub-Saharan Africa; so it makes sense to ask how they have benefited from massively funded agricultural projects.

But old perceptions and prejudices die hard. A telling case is that of the Washington-based African Development Foundation (ADF). In its first eight years of existence, from 1980 to 1988, only 17% of grants have gone to support the efforts of local women's organizations. Yet a recent research programme and grant guideline states its support for local women management systems:

The participation of women who are often the traditional water managers, in the design and implementation of water supply systems, is leading to improved maintenance and technological choices that are more adaptable to community needs and environmental demands. ('Perspectives on Self-Reliant Development', in *Research Programs and Grants of the African Development Foundation* (Washington, DC: ADF, 1989), 3–4)

In spite of such laudable statements, however, development co-ordinators and programme evaluators still make unwarranted assumptions about the capabilities of rural African women, and assume that their interests are served adequately in projects controlled by men. Given that a major aim of current development efforts is to facilitate grassroots development through linkages with 'existing traditional, local management systems',[37] it would seem imperative for development planners to get to know traditional women's organizations. If rural development projects fail or are non-sustainable, it could very well be that local resource organizations with an extensive pool of experienced and skilled people are being neglected.

The question really is: how relevant are indigenous Women's Councils such as *Ikporo-Onitsha* to such development initiatives and objectives? What mechanism, if any, does it have to enhance women's development, and how effectively could it respond to modern development issues? It is important, here, to see both sides of the 'development divide' to know what benefits the organization can bring to rural women's development and also where

---

[36] It is instructive to mention that this attitude occurs even with female programme officials. Being female does not imply that one is aware of the presence and complex nature of the gender stereotypes inherent in programmes.

[37] *ADF Guidelines* (1989), 6.

planners' expectations are unrealistic. Three unrealistic expectations of planners should be briefly mentioned.

First, the expectation that rural women in Nigeria will take advantage of available funding opportunities of NGOs and private voluntary agencies is unrealistic when these agencies fail to work with indigenous organizations that are in a uniquely strong position to disseminate information. Secondly, the expectation of programme evaluators that projects will be funded on the basis of well-written project proposals stacks the deck against these women. It is like asking the women to translate their needs and experiences into the language that programme evaluators would understand without providing them with the requisite conceptual and linguistic tools. The issue at stake is not simply one of literacy, it is one of conceptual fairness. The agency that acts this way is still treating the African poor with condescension and on its own Western basis in spite of protestations that it is interested in Africa's problem. Thirdly, Africa's declining economic situation may show that evaluators' desire for self-sufficiency as a project goal is unrealistic.

Now, let's turn to the positive contributions Women's Councils could bring to development. First, the organizations have grassroots orientation and legitimacy. They have a strong community base and community focus as well as extensive knowledge of their community's values and needs. Their traditional legitimacy gives them the ability to mobilize women effectively and to guarantee women's participation in programmes. Moreover, the councils' diverse membership means that they can tap an extensive pool of professionally skilled women (and men) for advice. 'Vertical linkages' between professionals and women implementors of projects match local skill to local need and help keep costs down. Professionals will view this service as part of their community service. It is noteworthy that *Ikporo-Onitsha*, for instance, used this strategem to obtain first-rate legal advice from a pool of prestigious lawyers for a four-year period without paying a dime.

Examination of the political structure of the Women's Council revealed the existence of a complex administrative structure with an effective monitoring system and inbuilt mechanisms to ensure accountability. As is well known, corruption and lack of accountability have been some of the problems that have consistently plagued development projects in Nigeria. These malpractices occur not because project managers are unqualified, but because they know that the punitive measures society will take would not undermine their social identity in the community of salience, once the booty is shared communally.[38]

Accountability, then, must be matched to the ethical motivations inherent in the cultural scheme. In the African setting, where the concept of

---

[38] Although I find Harman's (1986) generalizations rather sweeping at times, he identified correctly this linkage between corrupt officials and their communities as the bane of development in Nigeria. See Harman (1986).

person is tied to community validation, people will do whatever is in their power to be validated positively by their community of salience. What is significant in the account of *Ikporo-Onitsha's* sanction mechanisms is not so much the nature of the sanctions as that they are applied in ways that directly challenge the legitimacy and basis of the individual's self-identity and social validation. Such mechanisms could be used to guarantee a higher level of accountability in project implementation.

The complex, efficient administrative system of Igbo Women's Councils highlights the error in creating brand-new structures that are culturally alienated from local participants, rather than utilizing existing ones. Again, what is revealed from intimate contact with Women's Councils is not their unwavering female-focus, but the leaders' incisive grasp of complex, fluid, and shifting situations, and their ability to implement their strategies.

Admittedly, the existing Women's Councils are locally limited in scope, rather than national in their orientation. This will be a point against them among those who believe in de-emphasizing ethnicity as a focus of development. But there is no evidence that 'being national in outlook' (presumably, lacking a specific ethnic focus) is either necessary or sufficient for development. For one thing, the whole idea of national unity requires elaboration: what sort of unity do we wish to have, and what will be the role of ethnic plurality in it? This does not mean that development projects cannot have a national focus. But planners must be more reflective, seriously considering the conceptions they are using, and asking how indigenous ideas of nationhood and loyalty might be put to work at a trans-ethnic level.[39] To do this, they might do well to focus on the advantages that Women's Councils could bring to development.

Here is one concrete way to employ these councils. To initiate successful development projects in Onitsha, one needs to take advantage of cultural idiosyncrasies. Igbos are notoriously competitive. They care immensely for their natal communities of salience, and worry about how their progress measures up to that of rivals. Nothing will be achieved if one community is targeted for development without kindling the competitive spirit between communities. Therefore, one might suggest that a successful utilization of these Women's Councils in the role of intermediary organizations (and of their leaders as 'people's professionals') must also employ three close rival communities as the experimental base for testing the utility of the councils. The competing communities should be aware that the criterion for evaluation is sustainability of projects. They should be informed that communi-

---

[39] Policy makers who consider development as a vehicle for 'national unity' should bear in mind that Nigerians tend to view their place of domicile as a 'foreign land,' and are in turn viewed as 'strangers' by the indigenes. This belief has had negative implications for development projects. In the politically volatile climate of Nigeria, where appointments are made on the basis of nepotism, workers will lack committment to projects that are not located in their areas of salience.

ties that perform well will receive increased funding and resources in the future.

Regular inter-community or lateral feedback is critical in the experiment. The objective is to keep the communities abreast of one another's relative performance; but feedback also allows them to compare notes on their progress, and learn from one another's strengths and weaknesses. If the competitive spirit is removed, one has removed the driving force to sustain the project to the point of self-reliance.

Can and will this work? At this stage, it is important to insist once again that the reason one hears this quesion is because the councils remain so unfamiliar to Western eyes, and seem so odd when held up against Western ideas of organization. The request for ironclad guarantees that one hears in such questions is really a call for reassurance before a move into unfamiliar conceptual terraine. In reality, the question cannot be answered before trying. It cannot be answered by solipsistic agony and torment. Indeed, it cannot be answered by abstract reflection at all. It can be answered only through practical engagement—by actually working with the women and their organizations. And throughout the process there must be an open mind, a mind responsive to change and flexible in change, a mind capable of perceiving and adapting to each unique situation, a mind informed by historical and cultural knowledge. That is the sort of mind—and the sort of rationality—that development planning in Africa really needs.

BIBLIOGRAPHY

ARNOLD, GUY (1979). 'Development Problems and Multilateral Aid', in *Aid in Africa*. London: Kogan Page.

CHAPIN, MAC (1990). 'The Seduction of Models: Chinampa Agriculture in Mexico', *Grassroot Development*, 12, 8–17.

DANKELMA, IRENE, and DAVIDSON, JOAN (1988). *Women and Environment in the Third World: Alliance for the Future*. London: Earthscan Publications.

EKEJIUBA, FELICIA (1966). 'Omu Okwei: The Merchant Queen of Ossomari', *Nigeria*, Sept. 90, 213–20.

FERGUSON, ANN (1991). *Sexual Democracy*. Boulder, Colo.: Westview Press.

GREEN, M. M. (1964). *Ibo Village Affairs*. New York: Praeger.

HARMAN, NICHOLAS (1986). 'After the Ball: A Survey of Nigeria', *The Economist*, 3 May, 1–42.

HENDERSON, RICHARD (1972). *The King in Every Man*. New Haven, Conn.: Yale University Press.

LEITH-ROSS, SYLVIA (1965). *African Women: A Study of the Ibo of Nigeria*. London: Routledge & Kegan Paul, 1939, 2nd edn.

MACKINNON, CATHERINE (1987). 'Difference and Dominance: On Sex Discrimination', in *Feminism Unmodified*. Cambridge, Mass.: Harvard University Press, 32–45.

MBA, NINA (1982). *Nigerian Women Mobilized: Women's Political Activities in Southern Nigeria, 1990–1965.* Berkeley, Calif.: University of California Press.

NOAH, MONDAY EFFIONG (1985). 'The Role, Status and Influence of Women in Traditional Times: The Example of the Ibibio of Southeastern Nigeria', *Nigeria*, 53, 24–31.

OKONJO, KAMENE (1976). 'The Dual-Sex Political System in Operation: Igbo Women and Community Politics in Midwestern Nigeria', in Hafkin and Bay (eds.), *Women in Africa.* Stanford, Calif.: Stanford University Press, 45–58.

PATTANAYAK, D. P. (1991). 'Literacy: an Instrument of Oppression', in Olson and Torrance (eds.), *Literacy and Orality.* New York: Cambridge University Press, 105–8.

ROGERS, BARBARA (1980). *The Domestication of Women: Discrimination in Developing Societies.* London: Tavistock.

ROSTOW, WALT WHITMAN (1960). *The Stages of Economic Growth.* Cambridge: Cambridge University Press.

SALMEN, LAWRENCE (1987). *Listen to the People: Participant-Observer Evaluation of Development Projects.* New York: Oxford University Press.

TADESSE, ZENEBEWOKE (1990). 'Coping with Change: An Overview of Women and the African Economy', in *The Future For Women in Development: Voices From The South.* Ottawa: The North-South Institute, 44–62.

THUROW, LESTER C. (1983). *Dangerous Currents: The State of Economics.* New York: Random House.

VAN ALLEN, JUDITH (1976). '"Aba Riots" or Igbo "Women's War"?: Ideology, Stratification, and the Invisibility of Women', in Hafkin and Bay (eds.), *Women in Africa.* Stanford Calif.: Stanford University Press, 59–85.

INDEX OF NAMES

INDEX OF SUBJECTS

violence 65, 147, 149, 223, 333, 345, 349, 357
virtue 166, 174–6, 206–7, 367, 412–16, 425, 438–43
vulnerability 140–1, 143–5, 148–50, 152, 173, 177, 182, 277, 284, 286–9, 313, 365, 367, 377–9, 394, 396–8, 452

wage:
  discrimination 2, 33, 41–3, 452
  equal 38, 42, 240, 291, 307, 318, 323, 429
  labour 3, 48–9, 89, 99, 116, 282–91, 342–3, 427; in industrialized countries 29–31
war, Iraq/Kuwait 399
water schemes 458–61
wealth 38, 46, 50, 91, 195, 226, 264, 279, 321, 349, 377, 429
welfare 52, 156, 166, 190–1, 211, 255, 288, 343, 349, 351, 355
well-being 154–6, 158–9, 165–6, 169–70, 178, 183–4, 186, 193, 195–6, 263–4, 266, 280–1, 292, 323, 407, 409, 415, 417–19, 424–5
widowhood 13–15, 42, 48, 51, 55, 312, 321, 351, 429
wisdom 155, 177
womanhood 433–5, 439, 450, 453
Women's Governing Councils 446–7, 454–8, 461–4
Women's War 449–50, 453
World Bank 445, 460
World Food Programme (UN) 41

xenophobia 253